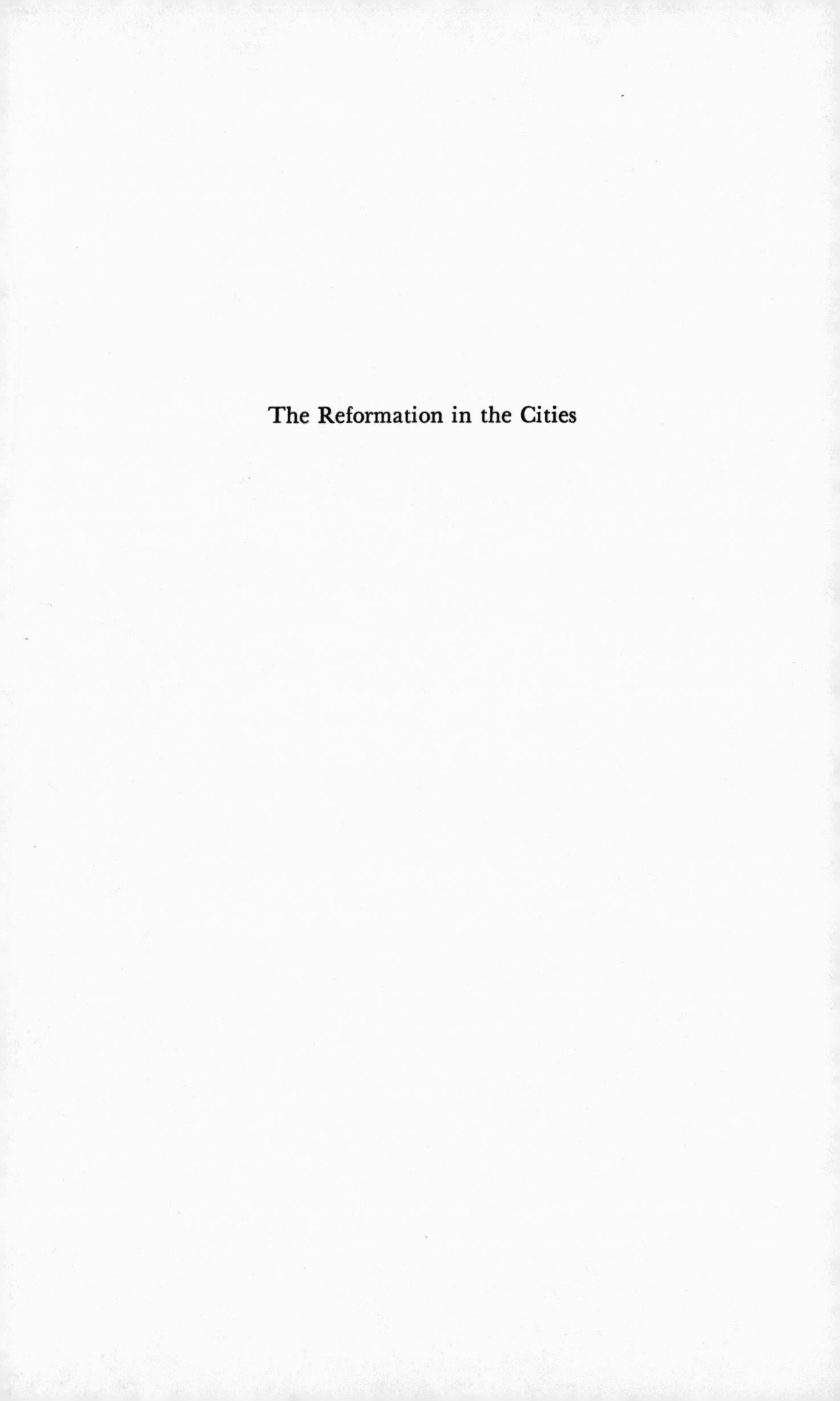

The Reformation in the Cities

The Reformation in the Cities

The Appeal of Protestantism to Sixteenth-Century Germany and Switzerland

Steven E. Ozment

New Haven and London: Yale University Press

Published with assistance from the Louis Stern Memorial Fund.

Second printing, 1980.

Library of Congress catalog card number: 75-8444
International standard book number: 0-300-01898-3 (cloth)
0-300-02496-7 (paper)

Designed by John O. C. McCrillis
and set in Baskerville type.
Printed in the United States of America by
LithoCrafters, Inc.,
Chelsea, Michigan.

Published in Great Britain, Europe, Africa, and
Asia (except Japan) by Yale University Press,
Ltd., London. Distributed in Australia and
New Zealand by Book & Film Services, Artarmon,
N.S.W., Australia; and in Japan by Harper & Row,
Publishers, Tokyo Office.

To

J. H. Hexter

Contents

Acknowledgments

This study has received generous support and assistance from many quarters. Summer stipends from the National Endowment for the Humanities and the American Council of Learned Societies made possible the gathering of primary sources and basic research. Charles Garside, Jr., encouraged the study when it was hardly more than a notion. Miriam Chrisman helped bring a first formulation to maturity and freely shared her fund of Strasbourg material. Robert Kolb and Lowell Zuck were gracious hosts during a visit to the Center for Reformation Research in Saint Louis, where I labored over the Simmler collection of sixteenth-century pamphlets. An early version of several sections of the study was debated by a remarkably confident group of scholars under the direction of Lawrence Stone in the Davis Center for Historical Studies at Princeton University. An early version of the work was also tested in discussion with a group of Dartmouth scholars organized by Fred Berthold, Jr. The manuscript was given a most careful and helpful scrutiny by William J. Bouwsma. I also received ever relevant criticism from William S. Stafford and Jane Abray, formerly my teaching assistants and now young authorities on the Reformation in Strasbourg. Finally, I must acknowledge the vigilant editing of Edward Tripp and Lynn Walterick, who have saved me from many a colloquialism and unclear statement.

Branford, Connecticut
March, 1975

S.E.O.

Abbreviations

ADB	*Allgemeine Deutsche Biographie*
ARG	*Archiv für Reformationsgeschichte*
Clemen	*Flugschriften aus den ersten Jahren der Reformation* 1–4, ed. Otto Clemen (Halle, 1906–1911)
LW	*Luther's Works,* ed. Jaroslav Pelikan et al. (St. Louis/Philadelphia, 1955)
MQR	*Mennonite Quarterly Review*
RGG	*Die Religion in Geschichte und Gegenwart* 3rd edition (Tübingen, 1957)
Richter 1	*Die evangelischen Kirchenordnungen des 16. Jahrhunderts: Urkunden und Regesten zur Geschichte des Rechts und der Verfassung der evangelischen Kirche in Deutschland* 1, ed. A. L. Richter (Leipzig, 1871)
WA	*D. Martin Luthers Werke: Kritische Gesamtausgabe* (Weimar, 1883)
WABr	*D. Martin Luthers Werke: Briefwechsel* (Weimar, 1930)
ZkathTh	*Zeitschrift für katholische Theologie*
ZKG	*Zeitschrift für Kirchengeschichte*
ZSchGes	*Zeitschrift für Schweitzerische Geschichte*

1 Introduction: Trends in Reformation Research

This is a study of changes in ideas and institutions in the sixteenth century, specifically the attraction of the Protestant Reformation during the first half of that century. In the course of the sixteenth century fifty of the sixty-five imperial cities subject to the emperor officially recognized the Reformation either permanently or periodically and either as a majority or as a minority movement. Of Germany's almost two hundred cities and towns with populations in excess of one thousand, most witnessed Protestant movements. Some of the largest—Nürnberg, Strasbourg, Lübeck, Augsburg, and Ulm, all with populations in excess of 25,000—became overwhelmingly Protestant. The Reformation won allegiance from a broad spectrum of the population, cutting across the barriers of class and education. Tens of thousands of people put aside religious values and practices sanctioned by centuries of tradition and habit. This essay tries to shed light on why so many people thought they wanted to be Protestants.

This study is also born of a desire to bring together two dominant trends in Reformation studies, one in which I was trained as a student and another to which I have become a recent convert. The first is represented by those scholars who place the Reformation in medieval perspective and concentrate on its intellectual origins in medieval philosophy, theology, and learned spirituality. The second is represented by those scholars who attempt to set the Reformation within a contemporary urban perspective, concentrating on its development within a particular city or region. The one deals with intellectual history and looks backward to the Middle Ages, the other with social history and looks forward to the development of modern institutions. The one has little interest in the social and political history of the early modern period, the other tends to lack sophistication in late medieval intellectual history. The one has mastered the thought of the Protestant reformers, but few of the events of their day. The other has only the most general grasp of the theology of Protestants and rather specializes in what was done to them by the larger events of the sixteenth century. Scholars of the first tend to be nomads, pursuing concepts and ideas through millennia. Scholars of the second tend rather to be homesteaders, squatting within limited geographical regions and historical periods and cultivating them. As even the casual eye may observe, the two approaches to the Reformation have mutually exclusive faults and mutually supportive strengths. By posing the question of the appeal of Protestant ideas to sixteenth-century society I am forcing upon this study a certain methodological collaboration. For this is a question that will not be satisfactorily answered without a direct confrontation of ideology and society. New ideologies not only reflect and justify, but also give rise to, changes in social practice. And yet, even the most radical ideas have prior points of contact and a prehistory within the societies they change. Ideas and values may have a life of their own, but they also have a definite social matrix. Diet and domicile may stratify societies, but rational creatures also retain the capacity to act, for better or for worse, beyond their material condition and past habits. I aspire in this study to relate material and spiritual, social and intellectual facts and forces, searching out their points of intersection and interaction.

The Reformation in Medieval Perspective

Three modern schools of thought have specialized in placing the Reformation in medieval perspective. The first is centered on the Catholic church historian Joseph Lortz of the University of Mainz, whose magisterial two-volume study, *The Reformation in Germany*, has gone through four editions since its publication in 1939–40.[1] Lortz shares with the distinguished Catholic historian of philosophy Etienne Gilson a view of the late Middle Ages as a period of intellectual confusion and decline. The scholastic synthesis of Thomas Aquinas is seen by Gilson to have been a unique harvest of medieval thought, after which Western intellectual achievement became progressively meager, reaching a nadir in the Protestant Reformation. For Gilson, the condemnations of Averroism in 1270 and 1277 were fateful, marking the emergence within the church of a tendency to meet opponents with the dogmatic assertions of revelation and faith rather than with reasoned argument. Such a defensive posture was promoted especially, in Gilson's view, by the Franciscans

Duns Scotus and William of Ockham. Gilson believes that their exaltation of man's will over his intellect and of God's absolute power over his biblical covenant put the rationality of faith to flight. A parallel to their work is seen in Eckhartian mysticism, in which individual experience and the hiddenness of God are stressed. This heritage is believed by Gilson to have terminated in what he calls the "speculative lassitude" and "doctrinal confusion" of the late Middle Ages and the militant fideism of the Reformation.[2]

Gilson's views have been popularized in the English-speaking world by Gordon Leff and David Knowles. Leff describes the fourteenth century as divided between the skepticism of Ockham (nominalism, the *via moderna*) and the dogmatic authoritarianism of the Augustinian Thomas Bradwardine, each in his own way rejecting the reasoned belief of the thirteenth century. Knowles maintains that after the fourteenth century men were forced to choose either a "practical skepticism" or a "blind fideism." [3] Both scholars see the foundations of ethics, metaphysics, and the priestly-sacramental system of the church shaken by a fourteenth-century restriction of the theological reach of reason and exaggeration of the degree of God's freedom over his creation. It is alleged that followers of Ockham (whom Luther called "my teacher") preferred to doubt and criticize rather than to explain their beliefs, while disciples of Bradwardine chose to assert their faith rather than understand it. Leff and Knowles, squarely within the footsteps of Gilson, view Luther and John Calvin as the final beneficiaries of these radical changes in the late Middle Ages.[4]

Sharing this assessment of the late Middle Ages, Lortz and his students have tended to make Reformation studies a science of pinpointing the breakdown of genuine Catholic teaching in late medieval humanism, Ockhamism, and popular piety—alleged seedbeds of the relativism, skepticism, and subjectivism from which the Reformation is seen to sprout. Erwin Iserloh has traced the Reformation's comparatively meager sacramental theology to the allegedly skeptical ("als ob") theology of nominalism in which Luther was trained.[5] Jared Wicks has blamed the allegedly introspective nature of Luther's doctrine of faith (characterized as a "fides certitudine meae remissionis formata"—a faith in faith) on the subjectivism of certain late medieval spiritual traditions with which Luther identified.[6] The strong apologetic undercurrent in the work of this school has been strikingly expressed in the title of Harry McSorley's 1969 study, *Luther: Right or Wrong?*, the English version of his 1967 *Luthers Lehre vom unfreien Willen.*

A second modern school specializing in setting the Reformation in medieval perspective is centered on the work of Heiko Oberman and the Institute for Late Medieval and Reformation Studies at the University of Tübingen. Oberman has opposed the image of harvest to the description of the late Middle Ages as a decline or a "waning" (Johan Huizinga). Pointing to that ecumenical group of thinkers known as nominalists or the via moderna, which he considers a "catholic via media" between the contending theological traditions which emerged in the thirteenth century, Oberman has characterized as "untenable" the views of Gilson and Lortz on the disintegration of late medieval thought. Most recently, Oberman has even cited the covenant theology of nominalism, with its peculiar divine sanction of the created, secular world, as a "modern" bridge between the sacred and the profane.[7]

Oberman stands on the shoulders of at least two generations of forerunners. In the 1920s Gerhard Ritter drew on *moderni* from Jean Gerson (d. 1429) to late fifteenth-century Heidelberg theologians to document the syncretic and constructive character of fifteenth-century thought.[8] E. A. Moody long ago cautioned moderation in the assessment of Ockham, who, he pointed out, considered himself a defender of the "old ways" against innovative Thomists and Scotists.[9] Paul Vignaux, who has defended Ockham especially against the charge of Pelagianism,[10] and Philotheus Boehner, O.F.M., who has defended him against the charges of skepticism and Erastianism,[11] have done much to make Ockham and the via moderna a part of the safe plateau of medieval thought. The Augustinian Damasus Trapp characterized the fourteenth century, when the great expansion of colleges occurred, as the most fertile intellectual period of the late Middle Ages, a time when what he calls new "historicocritical" and "logicocritical" attitudes confronted the contradictions and question-begging of the great system builders of the thirteenth century.[12] André Combes described the work of Gerson as a unique synthesis of medieval thought in its varied spiritual, scholastic, and ecclesiopolitical forms.[13] And even Gilson could single out Nicholas of Cusa as an oasis in the desert of the "journey's end." [14]

Reformation study undertaken with such a belief in the vitality of the period has tended to appreciate the common problems, if not answers, of late medieval and Reformation thought, and even to recognize a certain partnership of Protestant reformers with late medieval thinkers (primarily Franciscans and Augustinians) in attempting to resolve the crises of the late Middle Ages. The continuity of the theology of Luther, Erasmus, Balthasar Hubmaier, and Calvin with late medieval exegetical and scholastic traditions has been demonstrated,[15] as has the persistence of late medieval mysticism within the so-called Radical Reformation.[16] Efforts to broaden the approach of this second school's work are attested not only by recent collaboration with Italian Renaissance scholars,[17] but also by the Tübingen Institute's creation of an urban history section, under the direction of Ernst W. Zeeden and Hans-Christoph Rublack, which will investigate the Reformation's early development within southwestern German cities.

A final school of thought that attempts to place the Reformation in medieval perspective is a group of romantic ecumenists inspired by the Second Vatican Council and centered on the work of Hans Küng and Otto Pesch. Unlike the Lortz school, which promotes ecumenicity by trying to convince Protestants that Luther may have been wrong, this school takes the novel tack of trying to persuade Catholics that Luther and Thomas Aquinas may have been saying the same thing in different ways. For the nineteenth-century Catholic historians Heinrich Denifle and Hartmann Grisar, Luther was an ignorant and immoral heretic. With the Lortz school he became an intelligent and sincere heretic. Now, in the ecumenical scholarship of Otto Pesch, Luther is presented as not only intelligent and sincere, but also no longer properly heretical.[18] While this approach maximizes the positive continuity between the assumed best of medieval thought (Thomas Aquinas) and the Reformation, it may actually be that, rather than saying the same thing in different ways, Luther and Aquinas and the Council of Trent actually said the most different things in much the same way.

The Reformation in Urban Perspective

Whereas scholars who study the Reformation in medieval perspective argue over the nature and lineage of Protestant ideas, especially Luther's, scholars engaged in placing the Reformation in urban perspective more directly grasp the issue of the appeal of those ideas, asking who the Protestants were and why they were Protestants. This approach to the Reformation has been dominant among American scholars, whose culture may predispose them to the more practical and less philosophical issues of social and political history. It is an undertaking in which many American scholars have excelled, as is attested by brief mention of the work of Natalie Davis on Lyons, Robert Kingdon and E. William Monter on Geneva, Harold Grimm and Gerald Strauss on Nürnberg, Miriam Chrisman, James Kittelson, and Thomas Brady on Strasbourg, and Robert Walton on Zurich. But the most impressive synthesis to date has been the work of the Göttingen church historian Bernd Moeller, the first of several efforts to correlate Protestant theology and sixteenth-century society that I want to examine, with caveats, in this section. Moeller's work, especially, is a point of departure and, at several junctures, an object of criticism in this study.

Moeller, who builds on the work of Franz Lau[19] and a German sociological tradition reaching back at least as far as Otto von Gierke, sees the main appeal of the Reformation to lie in its providing a new line of defense for late medieval communal values *(Genossenschaft)* in the face of mounting centralizing tendencies *(Herrschaft)*. Moeller stresses that late medieval cities perceived themselves as sovereign sacral communities and were very jealous of their civic rights and freedoms. On the eve of the Reformation many sensed these rights and freedoms to be threatened by oligarchical tendencies within city governments and by the determination of territorial rulers to consolidate their lands. According to Moeller, the free citizen perceived that he was becoming the submissive subject of a bureaucratic state, his divine city republic something of a secular fief.[20]

Within this sociopolitical climate Protestant theology was accordingly perceived, according to Moeller, as an ally of old republican ideals. Luther's doctrine of the priesthood of all believers proved a "theological anchor" for the belief in the equality of every citizen before the law and his peers[21] and also released secular life from its medieval inferiority complex by giving lay vocations a new religious import.[22] Even more relevant to the support of besieged communal values were the theocratic visions of the Swiss reformer Ulrich Zwingli and the Strasbourg reformer Martin Bucer, which compensated for what Moeller apparently believes to have been a serious modernizing flaw in Luther's theology. Whereas Luther's doctrine of the priesthood of all believers provided a theological anchor for late medieval urban ideals, his teaching about the two kingdoms rather threatened to scuttle them. For Luther no longer believed in the coextensiveness of religious and civic communities; he made clear in the strongest terms that citizenship did not make Christians, nor city walls a church.[23] If baptism and faith alone can define Christians and the church is capable of definition as a separate *ecclesiola in ecclesia,* is not the social extension of religion endangered and the religious foundation of society threatened? Luther's doctrine of the two kingdoms, Moeller evidently suspects, harbored such a modern separation of religion and society, a foreboding of the latter's complete secular autonomy, which played into the hands of aggressive princes.[24]

Zwingli and Bucer, by contrast, are seen by Moeller to hold the line on this important point, "correcting and deepening" Luther.[25] Moeller believes that their different urban experience was the decisive factor. Unlike Luther, they were not passive subjects of a distant territorial ruler, but active members of free cities. Life in Zurich and Strasbourg, Moeller would have us believe, was conducive to a much keener sense of the unity of government and citizenry, religion and society, salvation by faith and social responsibility. Zwingli and Bucer accordingly rejected Luther's notion of a separate and invisible church of true believers (the product of the two kingdom doctrine) and reaffirmed the unity of *ecclesia* and *populus* and their singular goal of building the kingdom of God on earth. Although in this they were "more medieval than Luther" ("mehr als Luther im mittelalterlichen Denken"), their great success, which was to be continued by the Calvinists, lay in the close connection between what Moeller calls their "citified theology" ("städtisch geprägte Theologie") and late medieval *Genossenschaft* ideals.[26]

Much of Moeller's study requires further examination. It is at least arguable whether, despite certain structural differences in the respective governments, civic life in Wittenberg was in fact less "free" and "genossenschaftlich" and religious life more distant from civic destiny than in Zurich and Strasbourg.[27] It is further questionable whether Luther's differentiation of Christians and citizens and his recognition of "nonChristian" magistrates are best explained as gestures to be expected from a theologian in a small Saxon town (Wittenberg's population was about 2,500) or simply as realistic adjustments to the difficulties of surviving as a Protestant in many areas in the 1520s. Evidence here of serious differences between Luther, on the one hand, and Zwingli and Bucer, on the other, is hardly overwhelming, and it must be asked whether Moeller and others have exaggerated the intellectual disunity of Protestantism in the early years of the Reformation.[28]

However, the basic question of assessment to be raised about Moeller's study lies in the striking fact that he finally deems the Reformation most successful where it changed religious thought and practice the least. His key assumptions are that the preservation of certain medieval ethical and social ideals was the overriding concern of burghers on the eve of the Reformation and that the "more medieval" stance of Zwingli and Bucer was better adapted to this concern than Luther's more critical theology. Preoccupation with sanctification can be seen as preserving in a new mode the medieval belief in the ethical extension of religious life—a Protestant version of the *fides caritate formata,* the medieval conviction that saving faith must be ethically formed faith. Further, appreciation of the unity of religious and civic life can also be seen as preserving, again in a new mode, the strong medieval belief in the city as a unified *corpus christianum*—a Protestant version of holy community. These "more medieval" features may accordingly be seen, *mutatis mutandis,* as the positive points of contact between late medieval society and early Reformed theology and the clue to the great appeal of this theology to citizens of imperial cities. That, in a nutshell, appears to be Moeller's argument.

I believe that certain "medieval" adjustments were indeed made in later Protestantism. It may not be too much to say even that the high doctrines of individual and social sanctification in later Calvinism and Puritanism "re-Catholicized" the Reformation by reinvesting daily life with religious anxiety and making its moral quality and worldly success a sign of divine election. However, even granting a drift in this direction by certain first-generation Protestant reformers, I do not believe that preoccupation with individual and social discipline played the crucial role in the original appeal of the Reformation. If it can be shown, as I think it can, that the most important point of contact between Protestant theology and sixteenth-century society in the early years of the Reformation—the key original *Einbruchstelle*—was in fact swelling popular desire to be rid of the psychological and social burdens of late medieval religion itself, then the attractiveness of early Reformed theology may be seen to lie in its conformity with Luther's original impulse to free individual and civic life from onerous religious beliefs, practices, and institutions. The Reformation, Zwinglian and Lutheran, transvalued religious life. What made Protestant ideas initially appealing may not have been a new version of sacral community, no matter how qualified, but a certain desacralizing of late medieval religious life. What attracted may not have been a novel investment of civic life with a new religious content but its divestment of medieval religious values.

In addition to Moeller's work there are several other noteworthy recent efforts to explain the appeal of Protestant ideas, and they further orient this study. One of the most controversial is the work of the American sociologist Guy Swanson.[29] Swanson also has sought to explain susceptibility to the Protestant message in terms of political experience, although, unlike Moeller, he deals not with individual cities but with whole nations and continents. He distinguishes, with intricate subcategories, two basic types of political regime in the sixteenth century. First is the regime which autocratically identifies its own interest with the common interest and neither requires nor receives input into its decisions from groups outside the very limited inner circles of government. Swanson finds such regimes, which he describes as either "centralist" or "commensal," to exist with a religion (Catholicism) that stresses the immanence of God and the goodness of man. His explanation for this correlation appears to be that the prolonged experience of absolute political power concentrated in the hands of a few is conducive to religious belief in the compatibility of divine and human nature. Where such governments held sway, he finds that people tended to remain Catholic during the Reformation.

In contrast, Swanson distinguishes decentralized political regimes, where guilds played a major role in the decision-making process, that exist with a religion (Protestantism) that stresses the transcendence of God and man's depravity. Here, Swanson evidently believes, the perception of political power as diffused among competing special interest groups (guilds) works to diminish that belief in the sacral character of social institutions that is so congenial to Catholicism. Swanson further finds that when only partially decentralized or limited centralist regimes, in which representative bodies are given a marginal deliberative role in government policy, turned Protestant, they became Anglican or Lutheran. By contrast, the more decentralized regimes, which Swanson calls "balanced" or "heterarchic" regimes and which are characterized by their making smaller ruling groups (small councils, privy councils) fully accountable to larger representative bodies (large councils, general assemblies), rather became Zwinglian and Calvinist. In other words, Lutheranism went together with more conservative, Zwinglianism and Calvinism with less conservative, decentralized political regimes. Swanson, in contrast to Moeller, would find Luther to be "more medieval" than Zwingli in degree of social sacrality.

Historians have not taken kindly to Swanson's study and have even teamed up against him in a special symposium.[30] Most have found his sweeping classification of regimes to be faulty, even artificial, and his definition of Protestantism and Catholicism in terms of transcendence and immanence highly oversimplified. While it is no doubt true that social experience conditions religious predilection, it seems to me that Swanson's correlations, where true, also admit of a much simpler historical explanation. Swanson has elaborated a self-evident fact: regimes in which power is concentrated in the hands of a few tend, so long as they can, to restrict and even close altogether the avenues of religious and most other social change (centralist regimes remain Catholic); in contrast, regimes which are open to a diversity of self-interests and subject to regular citizen review are more susceptible to a variety of new ideas (decentralized regimes become Protestant). One would expect a higher incidence of religious and other social change to occur in areas controlled by decentralized governments which were constantly informed of and constitutionally obliged to adjust to the expressed wishes of their constituents. Government flexibility—secured by threat of force where not constitutionally guaranteed—was indeed a precondition of the Reformation's success. Rare is the city that received the Reformation by sheer government fiat or introduced it in the face of unanimous magisterial opposition. That decentralized regimes were often ripe for religious change was probably not the result of some mysterious political preconditioning for Protestant symbols and values, as Swanson would have us believe, but simply a consequence of the fact that such regimes permitted, in the normal course of their operation, a much higher degree of Protestant infiltration and influence upon government action than did closed, autocratic regimes. We know, for example, that the oligarchies of Bern and Basel held the Reformation at bay against majority sentiment for several years, whereas in Zurich a potent large council provided an organ for the citizenry to protest its religious preferences very effectively.[31] In short, whereas the form of government was without question an important factor in the ease or difficulty of the Reformation's progress, it is, I think, a doubtful explanation of its appeal.

Another arresting effort to explain the appeal of Protestant ideas is Gerald Strauss's speculation on the motives behind the embracing of Lutheran theology by the patrician magistrates of Nürnberg.[32] In March, 1525, after a rigged disputation between Lutheran and Catholic preachers, the Reformation was officially introduced into Nürnberg. Although typical religious grievances had long existed in the city—absenteeism of beneficed priests, poor performance of duty and indulgence in sexual improprieties by resident clerics, monastic abuse of the right of asylum, citation of citizens before episcopal courts—Strauss does not consider them sufficient either to explain the appeal or to necessitate the adoption of a Lutheran creed. What he does believe to have been finally decisive in bringing about that result was the close correspondence between what city officials knew from their own experience about the nature of political man and what Lutheran preachers were stressing in their theological doctrine of man, namely, that men were fallen, obstinate, and absolutely selfish creatures. The "dismal misanthrophy" of Lutheran preachers like Andreas Osiander contrasted favorably in the minds of magistrates with the less realistic "meliorism" of Catholic preachers who, unlike the Protestants, failed to appreciate the degree of individual self-abnegation necessary not only to please God, but also to run an orderly city. In short, Protestant dogma was seen to confirm political experience and to sanction desired tough measures of social control.[33]

Strauss's conclusion seems to suggest that the Reformation succeeded, as it were, by insult. Without denying the political appeal of Lutheran anthropology—Nürnberg's city fathers may even have found the correlation between their political experience and Protestant teaching flattering—the more immediate motive for turning Protestant may rather lie in Strauss's undeveloped surmise that men like the city clerk Lazarus Spengler and the Meistersinger Hans Sachs must have found in Luther's creed an end to their "quest for certainty and for the removal of doubt." [34] Contrary to modern perceptions of Catholicism and Protestantism, medieval religion left the individual believer a very anxious pilgrim, unsure, this side of eternity, whether he was worthy of divine love or divine wrath. Anxiety over this issue drove the medieval Catholic into the confessional and the sacrament of penance; claims of a "certitude of salvation" through faith inspired Protestant rejection of both. This suggests that relief from an onerous medieval religion, not a new religious burden of misanthrophy, may have been at the base of the Reformation's appeal. It is a proposition we will test further when we examine Spengler's defense of Luther's teaching.[35]

Finally, there is the work of the indefatigable Natalie Davis. No effort to set the Reformation in urban perspective builds on a more thorough grasp of a city's life than her studies of Lyons. Her test case for the appeal of Protestant ideas is the stance of the printers' journeymen in the city during the 1550s and 1560s. Why should the journeymen have been attracted to Calvinism? Davis believes that Calvinist provision for congregational participation and vernacular liturgy helped to satisfy their "appetite for belonging to and participating in a meaningful collectivity" at a time when they were bitterly alienated from their masters. Their considerable self-esteem and pride (one-half to two-thirds could read) were flattered by Protestant teaching about a priesthood of all believers and the right of every Christian to test his religion by his own study of Scripture.[36] Davis cites a similar explanation for the appeal of Calvinism to French women; it "complemented in a new sphere [the religious] the scope and independence" which French women (especially French noblewomen) had come to know in other walks of life.[37] She doubts, however, that Protestant teaching about justification by faith and Christian liberty was really comprehended or that independent searching of Scripture for religious truth was in fact very often undertaken by the laity, although she can still credit the journeymen of Lyons with forward-looking "secularistic attitudes" that distinguished between the goals of economic and of religious agitation. These attitudes even returned the journeymen to the Catholic fold when the religious benefits of an increasingly bureaucratized Calvinism began to wane and their economic self-interests were seen to be better served by alliance with the old church.[38] For Davis the connections between religious allegiance and the comprehension of religious teaching were very tenuous in Lyons; what was strong and clear to Lyons' Protestants were the indirect personal flattery and social benefits of the new religious message.

Whatever the experience of Lyons, and recognizing that there were many theologically uninformed and religiously indifferent people voluntarily and involuntarily caught up in Protestant ranks in the sixteenth century, it still remains a doubtful premise to disassociate the Reformation's theological doctrine from its social effect. While lay perception of the Reformation is not necessarily to be identified with that of the theologians, the Protestant congregations that spearheaded the Reformation did not distinguish the new religious message from its social repercussions. In the cities and towns that went over to the Reformation, Protestant theology was clearly understood by the rank and file to be the quasi-legal foundation for desired changes in religious practice and institutions. Changes in the concept, practice, and institutions of religion were seen to go hand in hand. The tedious, almost scholastic disputations that officially introduced the Reformation into cities like Zurich, Strasbourg, and Constance were not undertaken by either magistracy or citizenry in ignorance of what was at stake for the daily life of the city in the victory or defeat of a specific theological argument.[39] It is a great merit of scholarship in the tradition of Lucien Febvre that it recognizes the autonomy and social force of religion. But there is also an unfortunate tendency within this same scholarship to reduce religious perception to the level of emotion and moral sentiment ("appetite for the divine"), understating the critical nature of lay piety and the close connection of theological idea with religious practice and institutions in the late Middle Ages.[40]

Having, I hope, whetted the reader's appetite, I turn now to the constructive task, attempting first to gauge lay religious attitudes on the eve of the Reformation (chapter 2), then to convey the manifold forms of the Protestant message as originally heard by the laity (chapter 3), and finally to follow the pattern of the Reformation from inception to consolidation (chapter 4). I am fully aware that in each of these chapters I am dealing somewhat microcosmically with macrocosms. While it is true that one does not have to drink the whole ocean to know it is salty, it is necessary that evidence have sufficient scope and depth to make samplings more than suggestive. I have endeavored to provide such scope and depth by consulting every genre of pertinent literature of which I am aware and by ranging over a wide variety of Protestant centers within the empire.

2 Lay Religious Attitudes on the Eve of the Reformation

The Hazardous Enterprise of Typifying Late Medieval Religious Life

In a recent essay a prominent Protestant church historian placed late fifteenth-century Germany among the "most church minded and devout periods of the Middle Ages." [1] Those whose historical memories span centuries will know this to be also the conclusion of the eminent nineteenth-century Catholic church historian Johannes Janssen. Bernd Moeller was here siding with Janssen against the twentieth-century scholar who has done most to undo Janssen's assessment—Joseph Lortz, Catholic church historian at the University of Mainz.[2] Janssen, whose first volume of the *History of the German People Since the End of the Middle Ages* appeared in 1876, described the half century before the Reformation as one of the most spiritually sound and profound periods of German history,[3] a religious and intellectual flowering in comparison with which the Reformation was a revolution of degenerate piety. Janssen pointed to a flood of prayer books, catechisms, confessional manuals, postillen, moral tracts, religious songbooks, histories, and calendars. He cited ninety-nine different printed editions of *plenaria* in low and high German between 1470 and 1519 [4] and fourteen complete high and five complete low German Bibles printed between 1477 and 1518.[5] Janssen further found regular preaching, aiming toward conversion and penance, and full congregations. Nowhere did he find instances of what could be called easy grace.[6]

Although Janssen's greater productivity has especially associated him with the view that there was a flowering of popular piety on the eve of the Reformation, he was but one of several, and not always the most impressive, of its nineteenth-century proponents. Both before and after his work, for example, Vincenz Hasak exalted the fifteenth century as the "century of Reformation," whose "buddings and seedlings of true, unified reform" the Protestant movement of the sixteenth century savagely uprooted.[7] By "buddings and seedlings" Hasak meant primarily the multitude of religious productions which rolled from the presses between 1470 and 1520: expositions and sermons on the Lord's Prayer and the Ten Commandments; guides to the *Ars moriendi; plenaria;* expositions of the Mass; Latin and vernacular Bibles; and a variety of educational and didactic writings—all intended to guide a burgeoning lay piety.[8] Hasak concluded his largely bibliographical work with the personal declaration that after fifty years, a lifetime of diligent searching, he had found nowhere in the fifteenth century a single defense of salvation either by faith alone or by sole reliance on external works and indulgences; everywhere salvation was rather conceived as coming only by the most sincere penance, active self-improvement, and recognition of God's grace.[9]

A more nuanced, massively documented argument for a flowering of piety in pre-Reformation Germany was written a full two decades before Janssen's work appeared. This is Johannes Geffken's *Picture Catechisms of the Fifteenth Century* (1855), the first of a never completed two-part study, to which twenty-six illustrative documents—fully two-thirds of the book—were appended. Geffken, a Hamburg preacher, also spent a lifetime collecting late medieval catechetical literature to demonstrate that the fifteenth century was not characterized by ignorance of Scripture and the virtual nonexistence of vernacular Bibles, sermons, and hymns.[10] He believed Sebastian Brant correct in the opening lines of the *Ship of Fools* when he declared, "The whole land is now filled with holy Scripture!" Geffken pointed out that although sermons were conceived, written, and circulated among priests in Latin—a custom among scholastically trained clergy well into the seventeenth century—preaching quite naturally occurred in the vernacular, and regularly, and with full congregations. There was, Geffken allowed, as much preaching and church attendance then "as in our time." [11]

Geffken concentrated especially on one genre of catechetical literature—confessional manuals *(Beichtspiegel)*—which guided the daily work of the priest at that most important point of contact with his parishioners, the sacrament of penance—the confessional. Three varieties were in circulation: the learned manual for those who wished to further their theological education; the simpler manual geared to concrete practice (the most popular of which was one originally entitled *Tractatus de instructione seu directione simplicium confessorum,* by Archbishop Anthony of Florence [d. 1459], which went through seventy-two Latin and vernacular editions in the fifteenth century); and vernacular manuals and sermons on the Ten Commandments designed for popular use.[12] Geffken dwelt especially on the latter, and for a reason. In the late fourteenth and the fifteenth centuries, the Ten Commandments replaced the Seven Deadly Sins as the main guideline for oral catechesis and confession. This was an important shift which enlarged the areas of religious self-scrutiny of and by the laity. At no other time were the Ten Commandments so zealously promoted and carefully expounded. This had, in Geffken's view, important repercussions for lay piety. It complicated confession for the laity—examinations became longer and more involved—tempted confessors to be overly inquisitive in the name of God's law, and encouraged fifteenth-century preoccupation with the legal righteousness of indulgences and good works.[13] The Reformation came as a vigorous protest against all of this.

Nineteenth-century defenders of a late medieval flowering of piety have not been warmly received by modern scholars. Joseph Lortz, especially, has led a lively twentieth-century reaction against this allegedly "romantic" picture of the late Middle Ages. Far from finding a wholesome flowering of church piety, Lortz has rather found "abuse" *(Missstand)* to be the outstanding characteristic of the fifteenth century and has challenged Catholic historians to acknowledge the unpleasant truth of the church's failing.[14] Lortz sees a general predisposition to abuse anchored deep within the medieval legacy of a church that may be as readily described as secular, fiscal, and political as pastoral.[15] But its peculiar form was a centrifugal, un-Catholic "individualism" and "egoism," evidence of which Lortz finds everywhere. Councils and cardinals vied with popes, cathedral chapters with their bishops, cloisters with their abbots. Regions organized their own churches *(Landeskirchentum);* communities wanted their own religious festivals and insisted upon nominating their own clergy. Guilds demanded their own confraternities, individuals their own altars. Secular clergy, with their own possessions, special privileges, freedom from taxation, and competitive business enterprises, were ever tempted to look upon the laity in terms of profit rather than of pastoral care.[16] Creative lay movements of the period—mysticism, the Devotio moderna, and humanism—

are seen only to accelerate this "egoistic" narrowing of religious life. And within the universities an allegedly skeptical, introspective nominalism reigned supreme in theology.[17] One cannot go further from Janssen, Hasak, and Geffken than Lortz.

Modern French scholarship, moved by the aspiration to write *histoire totale,* has combined features of both evaluations of the late Middle Ages, although remaining basically in line with Lortz's negative assessment of its religious life. The most impressive of this growing genre are the recent weighty volumes of Abbé Jacques Toussaert and Etienne Delaruelle.

Toussaert, writing like Lortz in reaction to the romantic school, has found late medieval Flanders to be anything but a vibrant Christian land. Save for a religious elite, Toussaert discovers everywhere only external, formalized religiosity among laymen. The many religious habits and activities which have impressed so many earlier scholars—Johan Huizinga, for example—belie, in Toussaert's view, the presence of real religious depth.[18] People were poorly instructed in the "essentials" of religion; uninspired, moralizing sermons reduced dogma and the sacraments to bare "accessories." Doing was more encouraged than understanding, although there are few signs of a lack of trust in the church's dogmatic authority.[19] Toussaert compares the laity of Flanders to a fertile but uncultivated field, as susceptible to the free growth of religious tares as to that of religious wheat. The true believer, a member of the elite with delicate religious sensitivities, was not favored by such a system, nor was resistance offered the *chrétien-devenu-indifférent.*[20] Sincerely religious people were likely to be frustrated; the erring and uncaring free to go their own way. Toussaert leaves us with the following picture. On the one hand, people remained deeply committed to the capital religious events in their lives: baptism, the last rites, a church funeral, and burial in holy ground,[21] rituals, it may be noted, which are the least burdensome forms of religious participation. On the other hand, enthusiasm is not evident for those pillars of daily religious life, the sacraments of penance and the Eucharist. Although it was required of all adults to make confession at least once a year, especially at Easter, and some statutes recommended three to five times a year,[22] Toussaert finds that a not insignificant number of people never darkened the door of the confessional for years on end. Although everyone—even Toussaert's star example of incipient late medieval areligiosity, Philippe D'Artevelde—seems to have made deathbed confessions, Toussaert finds throughout Flanders a general disinclination toward frequent confession.[23] He surmises, I think quite rightly, that the identification and enumeration of all conscious mortal sins, required upon entrance into the confessional, may have been too difficult and unpleasant for the ordinary man. Irregularity is also found to mark lay reception of the Eucharist, despite large numbers of participants at Easter and other festive occasions, when attendance was much more diligently enforced.[24]

A study of piety in late medieval Germany has reported very similar results.[25] There, even the threat of force did not prevent many from staying away from Easter communion as well as "voluntary" communion during the year. In 1480 in the diocese of Eichstätt, fewer than one hundred persons are recorded to have received communion at times other than Easter. Absence at Easter, it is here surmised, was connected with the church's requirement of a double preliminary confession *(confessio bina),* at the beginning of Lent and once again prior to Easter. Persons who attempted to receive Easter communion after only one such confession were subject to punishment. As we shall see below, such regulations only begin to suggest the unpleasantnesses to which religiously earnest laymen could be subjected by the late medieval church.

An "external, conformist religion," not a personal, moral religion, is also the characterization of late medieval piety arrived at in Delaruelle's magisterial synthesis. Delaruelle's work is a carnival of a book, surveying more fully than any other the spectrum of late medieval lay religion both within and outside the church. We are shown the "religious theatre" with its mystery and passion plays and dances of death that made religion concrete and visual; the enormous appetite for didactic writings as the age of printing begins; the growth of confraternities, professional and parishional, which made intimacy between clergy and laity and shared religious responsibility possible, while at the same time promoting religious earnestness to the point of "pharisaism."[26] We see the formal contacts of ordinary Christians with the church at Sunday mass, during holiday processions, and at life's key stages of birth (baptism), marriage, and death. And we witness the urgent rush to pilgrimages, the cult of saints, relics, and indulgences—that *piété "visuelle",* with its manifold aberrations and intertwining of the sacred and profane:

fetishism, superstition, *gout de l'atroce* (for example, bleeding hosts), sorcery, and anti-Semitism.[27]

Delaruelle believes that people in the late Middle Ages may have been more concerned about their destinies than in earlier medieval centuries,[28] but he finds religious life within the church mechanical and even heartless, the expression of a "conception 'objectiviste' de la vie chretienne." Laymen, he concludes, joined third orders, punished themselves by fasting and flagellation, and spent great sums to endow masses, not because they felt personally called by God to do so but because they were taught and came to believe that such activities were automatically helpful to their salvation. Personal involvement, Delaruelle argues, was less important than correct ritual and association; external works were considered efficacious apart from the performer's subjective feeling—conclusions which are, to say the least, exceedingly difficult to measure.

It is within the framework of such a "religion of observances and works" that Delaruelle interprets the importance attached to (purchased) indulgences in the fifteenth century. He finds their evolution from originally hard-won rewards for going on crusades to items acquired by the only slightly onerous act of almsgiving prima facie evidence for a far-reaching "depersonalizing" or "objectifying" of religion in the later Middle Ages. And, like Lortz, he too sees a reaction setting in among the laity which "particularizes," "individualizes," and "interiorizes" religious life.[29]

Delaruelle concedes however—and it is a concession that deserves to be magnified—that beneath all this external activity a "need for security," even a certain "anguish," can be discerned.[30] Even mechanical religion was not without a certain subjectivity. A careful study of religious life in the late medieval cities of Hall and Heilbronn has found that the various religious activities were undertaken in "pitched religious excitement."[31] The many endowments of chapels, masses, and anniversaries, the numerous pilgrimages and processions, the worship of saints and relics, the purchase of indulgences, the formation of confraternities with their special indulgences and provisions to give the religious destiny of every member maximum attention both during and after life, and the foundation of preacherships were done with the sincere desire of the participants to secure their peace with God—"durch miner selen heiles willen," as the letters of endowment put it. The key question here may be not so much the degree of subjective involvement in external religious activities but the effectiveness of such activities in securing a sense of "peace with God."

Whether historians finally assess it as a wholesome flowering, an un-Catholic egoism, or the mechanical activity of secretly anguished souls, the surge in lay piety on the eve of the Reformation is manifest by every measure. Here a nod must be given the insistent scholars of the nineteenth century. However, the evidence suggests a flawed, unsatisfying piety. Here modern scholars have made their point against the nineteenth-century romantics who, with the possible exception of Geffken, tended to be more preoccupied with documenting the expressions of piety than with questioning its meaning. The problem is not, however, so clear-cut as modern scholars have assumed. Individual peculiarities aside, each finally sees a monolithic, bureaucratic church failing to satisfy interior needs, with a resulting lay reaction of individualism. For Lortz and Delaruelle, the Protestant Reformation, with its slogans of the priesthood of all [individual] believers and justification by [individual] faith alone, ran directly along these tracks. For Toussaert, that conclusion would perhaps be true for a despondent elite; in Flanders, he believes, many saw in Protestant theology no more than a convenient cover for a shallow, uncaring (external) religiosity.[32]

It may be asked whether modern scholars have in fact misread the problem of pre-Reformation piety. Abbé Toussaert, for example, believes that the basic error of the late medieval church was that of a permissive, overindulgent mother. Busy with official chores and worldly intrigues, she let laymen run free and loose as they pleased—too much freedom, not enough discipline; hence their straying. But could the problem rather have been that the late medieval church was "mothering" the laity to death with religious expectations and prescribed routines which were not modelled on a clear concept of a viable lay piety but on traditional clerical ideals? What on the surface may appear to Toussaert to have been shallow religiosity may in fact have been a piety adjusted to the needs and abilities of the laity. A striking difference between late medieval and Reformation piety, which may go far toward explaining the latter's appeal, is that, whereas the late medieval church measured lay by clerical life, the Reformation went a long way toward subjecting clerical to lay values. Protestant pastors not only entered the lay estates of citizenship, marriage, and parenthood, but also offered their congregations a spirituality constructed in conscious opposition to the imposition upon laymen of received clerical ideals.

Lortz and Delaruelle may also misread the problem of late medieval piety when they define the lay response to religious crisis as individualism and interiorizing, as if the only answer to a failing institution was to beat a retreat within. It is Catholic *parti pris* to believe that the medieval church was the only possible form of "objective" religion on the eve of the Reformation. It is further doubtful that what was personal and institutional, subjective and objective, individual and social was so disjointed in the premodern mind.[33] It is in fact a major (and apparently unconscious) contribution of Delaruelle's work to demonstrate the importance and persistence of external religious ritual and institutions *even when they failed to quiet inner anguish.* Could we not characterize mass defections from the medieval church among the religiously earnest as a search for a new objectivity—a transformation of the objective concept, practice, and institutions of religion? Could we not see as experimentation in this direction what was occurring in popular lay satellite activities such as joining confraternities and endowing preacherships, not to mention the varieties of outright heretical assembly such as the Lollards and Hussites? And was not such a transformation the stated purpose and final achievement of the Protestant Reformation? There is evidence to support the argument that the basic problem of late medieval religion was not too much freedom but too little, not too few opportunities to develop the inner life but the absence of an institutionally viable lay piety. It was surely not accidental that the popular slogans of the Reformation were "the freedom of the Christian," "certitude of salvation," and "the priesthood of all believers."

The Burden of Late Medieval Religion

Absence from confession, irregular reception of the Eucharist, mechanical performance of religious activities, drift toward religious indifference, experimentation with new religious forms by devout people—why? The answer to this question may best be found by understanding what normal religious life, from which so many were apparently straying, exacted from participating laymen. What, concretely, did the late medieval church lead people to think religion was? Apart from the deluge of Protestant pamphlets at the inception of the Reformation—which were not without certain apologetic concerns—we have for such information ready and revealing sources in the many vernacular confessional manuals and lay catechisms published in the fifteenth century.

Let us picture a child of at least seven, the earliest age at which the medieval church considered one capable of committing mortal sin,[34] who has come to church for his first confession. The priest blesses him and perhaps assists his recitation of the Lord's Prayer and Creed, and then guides his confession with questions taken from a manual specially prepared for a first or child's confession. These are random examples of the things the priest might want to know.

> Have you believed in magic? Have you loved your father and mother more than God? Have you failed to kneel on both knees or to remove your hat during communion?—These are sins against the first commandment.
>
> Have you cut wood, made bird traps, skipped mass and sermon, or danced on Sundays and holidays?—These are sins against the third commandment.
>
> Have you thrown snowballs or rocks at others? Have you had fights and hated those with whom you fought (even your brother and sister)? Have you stoned chickens and ducks? Did you kill the emperor with a double-bladed ax? [This last question is injected by the confessor to test alertness and truthfulness!]—These are sins against the fifth commandment.
>
> Have you stolen pen or paper from friends; berries, apples, nuts, and cheese from your mother? Did you steal 120 gulden from the *Rat* in Frankfurt? [Another question to test alertness.]—These are sins against the sixth commandment.
>
> Have you forgotten yourself with a common Turk?[35]—That is a sin against the seventh commandment.
>
> Have you told lies about your servants which caused them to be unjustly punished?—That is a sin against the eighth commandment.[36]

Now let us imagine an adult who has come to confession. Depending upon the penitent's sex and marital status, the following are questions he would face from a conscientious confessor. They are but a small sampling from one of the most popular vernacular confessional manuals, *The Mirror of a Sinner* (ca. 1470), which drew upon Anthony's *Tractatus*, the paradigm for fifteenth-century confessional manuals:

> Have you honored temporal rulers and lords more than God, Mary, and the sacraments? Are your prayers, alms, and religious activities done more to hide your sins and impress others than to please God? Have you loved relatives, friends, or other creatures more than God? Have you had doubts about Scripture, the sacraments, hell, the afterlife, the Last Judgment, or that God is the creator of all things? Have you befriended the excommunicated? Have you practiced or believed in magic?—These are sins against the first commandment.
>
> Have you questioned God's power and goodness when you lost a game? Have you muttered against God because of bad weather, illness, poverty, the death of a child or a friend? Have you murmured against God because the wicked prosper and the righteous perish? Have you committed perjury in a court of law? Have you sworn in the name of God or a saint that you would do something you had no intention of doing?—These are sins against the second commandment.
>
> Have you skipped mass on Sundays and holidays without a good excuse? Have you conducted business on Sundays rather than reflecting on your sins, seeking indulgence, counting your blessings, meditating on death, hell and its penalties, and heaven and its joys? Have you dressed proudly [a question especially for women], sung and danced lustily, committed adultery [a doubly deadly mortal sin on Sundays], girl-watched, or exchanged adulterous glances in church or while walking on Sundays?—These are sins against the third commandment.
>
> Have you insulted or cursed your parents, forgotten them in their old age, wished them dead? Have you insulted, cursed, or wished the clergy dead? Have you failed to offer prayers, give

alms, and endow masses for departed parents?—These are sins against the fourth commandment.

Have you at any time or in any way killed another? An adulterer out of spite and jealously? Are you a judge or witness who has condemned to death an innocent man? Are you a woman who has artificially aborted a child, or killed a newborn and unbaptised infant? Have you miscarried because of overwork, play, or sexual activity? Have you advised the death of another, or wished another dead and gone—a guildmaster, Vogt, Bürgermeister, or prelate—in the hope of gaining his position? Have you denied food to the hungry, wages to the impoverished? Have you killed another's soul by tempting him to commit a mortal sin?—These are sins against the fifth commandment.

Have you stolen a lamb, a chicken, or fruit from another's garden? Have you overploughed into another's field? Are you a wife who has enjoyed goods stolen by your husband? Do you rationalize: "finders keepers"? Have you sold watered-down wine? Mutton for castrated flesh? Dirty for clean laundry? Have you sold things for more than they are worth? Have you tried to monopolize a trade item? Have you burdened your subjects with unreasonable taxes? Have you stolen from pilgrims on their way to Rome? Robbed anyone, or directly or indirectly aided others to do so? Have you enjoyed illegally inherited goods? Have you taken a virgin's purity by force or deception? Impregnated a married woman [which makes one a debtor to the child]? Have you profited by using public funds? [Then follows a revealing list of the more serious theft of "holy things."] Have you advised that clergy be taxed without papal approval? Have you taken goods from holy places? Broken into holy places [ostensibly violating the right of asylum]? Have you appropriated ecclesiastical bequests *[legata]*?—These are sins against the sixth commandment.

Have you thought of committing adultery? Have you committed adultery? Sodomy [a sin requiring especially prompt confession and absolution]? Incest?—These are sins against the seventh commandment.[37]

As these examples make clear, confession could be a very tough inquisitorial process, and the confessor was manifestly not the penitent's friend but his judge and jury.[38] The last word of the priest was not one of absolution and consolation but the imposition of works of satisfaction. Confession was not completed upon leaving the confessional; one departed with a sentence to be served, a remedy to be applied, a task still to be fulfilled. One did not "go in peace." A Latin/German edition of the popular *Peniteas cito* (or *Penitentionarius*), nicely rhymed to aid memorization, describes the confessor with the mixed metaphor of a discerning judge who prescribes lifegiving medicine for a sinful soul:

> Utique foris iudex per personas prohibeatur
> flectere iudicium, medicus variare medelas.
> Der peichtiger als der richter soll
> mercken die sunde alsz woll
> Das er do wider ertzeney künde geben,
> das die sel müg geleben.[39]

According to a 1504 manual, the penitent must not only confess all sins committed directly by deed and indirectly by counsel or inaction, but must also narrate the exact circumstances of each transgression: with what persons and where (there is here a special concern to know if clergy and church property were involved, such being among the more important of that vast body of so-called reserved sins which only higher—episcopal or papal—authority could absolve); at what time (reflecting a special concern to know if transgressions occurred on Sundays or religious holidays, which compounded the seriousness of the sin); how often; the cause (whether it was done out of "habit, depravity, coercion, ignorance, or fear"); the manner (whether done publicly, in anger, etc.); and the result.[40] The explosive character of such extensive knowledge of the affairs of others is suggested by a special warning to priests in the *Peniteas cito* not to inform a husband of a wife's confession of infidelity.[41]

One manual cites as the characteristics of a correct confession that it be: simple (concerning only oneself, not gossip about others); humble; done with the resolve to avoid future sin; done with faith in forgiveness; often; in person (not by messenger or by letter); exact; voluntary (not done out of fear of pain); done with shame; complete;

made in seclusion with the priest (*heimlich*—although openly *[offenbarlich]* when women are the penitents); bitter; prompt (done soon after the sin); powerful and convincing; without excuses (no blaming the Devil); and executed with an attitude of submissiveness to the priest's judgment.[42] If the confession is not complete, another manual instructs, if even two or three sins are consciously withheld, then all the other confessed sins will remain unforgiven by God.[43]

As the age of printing began the impact of picture catechisms upon the popular imagination was very great. One of the most popular, specially designed and widely circulated among the laity—ten editions were printed in the fifteenth century—was a 1474 version of a fourteenth-century work entitled *The Soul's Consolation*. Each of the Ten Commandments is here driven home by an allegedly true story. The exposition of sins against the first commandment, for example, is concluded by the story of a man who loved temporal things more than God. After his death an autopsy revealed that his heart was missing from his body. His friends, knowing his character, ran to his storehouse of treasures, and there lying among them they found his bleeding heart. The moral: "Where your treasure is, there also is your heart *[sic]*." [44] Transgression of the Sabbath commandment is illustrated in this same manual by the story of a beautiful girl who loved to dance on Sundays. While sleeping off a vigorous round of Sunday dancing, she dreamed she was before a judge who ordered a hot coal placed upon her lips. Upon awakening from this nightmare she found her lips burned to a painful crisp. However, after vowing never again to dance on Sunday, she quickly recovered.[45] Just how directly the church promoted the superstitious fears of people is illustrated by the story told to instill obedience to the tenth commandment. It relates the Devil's sudden appearance in a church during Sunday service to punish a man for cruelly seducing the wife of another. (He had crawled into bed with the still sleeping woman after her husband had left before sunrise for his chores and was well into his crime before the poor woman was fully aware of the identity of her bedmate.) The perpetrator was collared by the Devil, whisked into the clouds, and abruptly dropped to his death before the stunned congregation.[46]

Other picture catechisms convey similarly dramatic messages by woodcuts depicting the suffering of sinners in purgatory and hell. In one such manual there is a picture of people in hell feeding upon their own flesh, with the caption: "The pain caused by one spark of hell-fire is greater than that caused by a thousand years of a woman's labor in childbirth." The discussion of confession in this same manual is concluded with a picture of purgatory and a commentary on its terrible pain and duration, some suffering twenty years, some one hundred, some one thousand, and some even until the Last Judgment itself.[47] Other pictures seek to shame simple people into correct behavior by depictions of the seven deadly sins in terms of well-known animal behavior (pride being portrayed by a horse, covetousness by a wolf, gluttony by a pig, anger by a lion, envy by wild dogs, lust by a rooster, and sloth by an ass).[48] The fright and shame generated by such religious "art" on the eve of the Reformation must be considered among the motives behind the liturgical simplification and iconoclasm of the early Protestant movement. Protestant attacks on these pictures and images argued that they were no longer, as traditionally claimed, "the layman's Bible," but had instead become impediments to the spiritual growth of the laity.[49]

Geffken concluded that the confessional was a veritable tyranny and found plenty of justification for Protestant criticism.[50] The abuses of the confessional were among the earliest and most prominent complaints of humanists and Protestants. Erasmus was strongly on record against them,[51] and Protestants, as we will see below, raged against the confessional as a workship for priestly mischief in which new sins and anxieties were introduced into the minds of laymen and religious energies were misdirected to ends never sanctioned by God.

Another revealing measure of the religiosity offered to laymen by the late medieval church is the popular catechism of Dietrich Coelde, the first printed German lay catechism. Coelde, a member of the Augustinian order from 1460 until 1488, at which time he became a Franciscan, had been educated at the University of Cologne. He was influenced by the catechetical writings of Jean Gerson, whose French and Latin *Opus tripartitum* some consider the first catechism, and the reform ideals of the Devotio moderna. A very popular preacher, Coelde was made *Generalprediger* for ducal Westphalia and the Rhineland region of electoral Cologne in 1492. He holds the distinction of being the "primarius catechista Germaniae" and represents the most advanced clerical thinking on lay religious practice on the eve of the Reformation.

Coelde's oft-imitated catechism, which is typical and even exemplary of the pattern of late medieval domestic catechetical literature,[52] grew initially out of his experience as a teacher of youth in the Augustinian order in Louvain. Following the example of some confessional manuals, it existed in three versions. The only copy of the first, a small catechism for simple people and children, dates from about 1470 and was dedicated to the simple people of Louvain. It was the first effort at a comprehensive popular summary for the laity of Catholic teaching on faith, the sacraments, commandments, the church, and prayer. The second version, *The Mirror of a Christian Man,* went through twenty-nine editions between 1480 and 1520. This "bestseller" incorporated the twenty-four articles and forty-eight pages of the small catechism into its fifty-three articles and one hundred pages. The final version, the great catechism known as *The Mirror of Christian Faith,* was expanded to one hundred and twenty-two articles and strictly intended for clergy and well-educated adults.[53]

What did Coelde's catechism instruct the religiously earnest layman to do? Far from espousing an externalized religiosity, it promoted the most rigorous introspection and discipline, a kind of laicized monastic routine and "worldly asceticism." The first three articles are a direct statement of the Creed, Lord's Prayer, and Ten Commandments, material all Christians were expected to commit to memory. Then follow the "Five Commandments of the Church" (article four), which state the church's basic expectations:[54] devout attendance every Sunday at mass; confession of all sins and reception of the sacrament at least once a year; fasting during the Quatember vigils, the forty days of Lent, and on the eve of the feastdays of Mary and the twelve apostles; avoidance of the excommunicated [whose names were proclaimed weekly during church services]; and seeking first spiritual cures (confession and mass) for physical illness, since the latter "generally comes from sins." Then follow prescriptions for religious security, a seemingly endless routine of self-examination and criticism. Article five brings forth "Six Prerequisites for Forgiveness of All One's Sins": do not doubt God's mercy; remember God's righteousness and severity and do not sin presuming on his mercy; do not delay conversion until the hour of death; reserve no mortal sin to oneself; hate no man, love all men; and believe correctly as a good Christian. Article six cites "Seven Things That Assure One That He Is a Friend of God in Good Standing": a feeling of oppression and sadness for having angered God by a lifetime of sinning; procurement of a good and learned father confessor so that one may always have the opportunity to confess one's sins; the devout performance of what the father confessor orders [as penance]; the resolution never again to commit a mortal sin even when worldly goods could be secured thereby; eager attendance at sermons; thorough searching of one's conscience and frequent consultation with good and learned men for spiritual guidance; and constant and sincere prayer for forgiveness of forgotten sins and preservation from unwitting sins.

Article seven presents a "Prescription for a Good Life," citing religious exercises to be done once or twice a day until they become habitual. Here especially can one see the piety of the convent being transported into the lay world. Upon awakening each morning, for example, laymen are admonished to say or think the following:

> O dear God, how I waste my precious time! How timid and slow I am! How I must burn [in purgatory] for my sloth! During the night all spiritual souls have sung God's praise [the vigils of the religious] and I have overslept! There has been great joy in heaven, and I have given it no thought. There has been great lamentation in purgatory, and I have not prayed [for those who there groan]. Many have died during the night, yet God has spared me.

"Then," continues the catechism, "you should spring from your bed, concentrate on making up for your neglect, and thank God for Christ's suffering for your sins."

Article eight sketches the attitude one should have during mass, article nine that during mealtime. Article ten directs men upon retiring to confess their failure to have been as devout, to have used their time as carefully, and to have done as many good works as they might. One should retire with a petition for Mary's intercession and with the consoling knowledge that "the departed great lords of the world who lived sinful lives now burn forevermore in hell, while you still have a way out."

Article eleven lists the five senses, article twelve the seven physical works of mercy (feeding the hungry, etc.). Article thirteen cites the seven works of spiritual mercy (counselling the simple, etc.), article fourteen the seven sacraments. Article fifteen brings forth the seven gifts of the Holy Spirit (fear of God, etc.), article sixteen the Beatitudes. Enumerated next are the "Nine Foreign Sins" (article seventeen), by which are meant sins which occur when one contributes to, overlooks, takes lightly, or silently participates in the sins of others, whether children, friends, or neighbors. Then come the "Silent Sins Which Call Out to Heaven for Revenge" (article eighteen), containing still another example of the importation of clerical values into lay religious life. Four such sins are cited: murder; withholding due wages from workers; the oppression of widows, children, and the poor; and, finally, the "sin against nature," "the sin God hates above all other sins," whether done in thought or deed, alone or with others, by men or by women—sodomy and masturbation. Several paragraphs are devoted to a most severe warning on avoiding the latter.

Article nineteen explains "Why Every Man Should Devoutly Daily Thank God"—because of the grace requisite to salvation and the promise to forgive all sins "if I in fact better myself and turn to him." Article twenty lists "Five Signs of a Good Christian": he is saddened and troubled by sins; always blames himself when God sends suffering; is true to his word and promises; takes serving God more seriously than anything else in the world; has great love for Jesus, the sacraments, and Mary; eagerly hears sermons; and loves all men.

Article twenty-one is entitled "How One Can Attain True Penance and Forgiveness of Sins" and is the background for article twenty-two, which deals with preparation for the reception of the Eucharist. It advises daily, private meditation on the "ten or twelve" most committed sins, their contrite confession, and trust in the efficacy of God's grace ("Speak, O Lord, but a word, and you make my poor soul whole"). For those who find trusting a word unconsoling, article twenty-three gives the converted sinner a somewhat more tangible and, as the title puts it, "easy way" to receive remission of purgatorial punishment, namely, by acquisition of an indulgence given for saying prayers by Saint Gregory (one) and Pope Sixtus (two), together with seven Our Fathers and an Ave Maria before the image of Christ crucified, in sincere penance and the firm resolve never to sin again.[55] The final article deals with preparation for death and instructs the dying to pray for mercy and strive for perfect penitence as they pass from this life to the next. On the deathbed one should petition God: "Take my good will for the works [I lack]"—the layman haunted to his last breath by a short supply of good works! [56]

Whether it came from the circles of the Devotio moderna or more traditional sources, humanists and Protestant reformers firmly rejected the *contemptus mundi* of late medieval piety so vividly expressed by Dietrich Coelde.[57] Protestants would disagree at practically every step with the late medieval catechism. Early Protestant catechetical literature, as we will see, is marked by a biblical simplicity that eliminates the typical cataloguing of sins, vices, and virtues, turns the catechumen away from minute self-analysis (although not withholding a good dose of the Law's terror from those whose faith may be feigned),[58] and makes the communication of religious certitude, especially at the point of death, the highest priority.[59] Simple faith in God's promise of mercy was to replace the anxious medieval quest for perfect penance. But the Reformation was neither the first nor the only solution to the burden of medieval religion which had broad institutional as well as the more individual catechetical expressions. Well before the appearance of Lutherans the reform of the old and experimentation with new religious forms was underway in cities and towns. Two of the more notable lay efforts to create the conditions for a viable lay piety concerned the restriction of traditional clerical privileges and the promotion of endowed preacherships.

Lay Restriction of Clerical Privileges

In the late Middle Ages the laity assumed increasing control over ecclesiastical institutions and responsibility for the religious and moral life of their communities.[60] This was due in large part to nonreligious factors. In Saxony, a prominent example, burghers faced new social pressures from surrounding small towns and villages brimming with fully two-thirds of the population. In the wake of significant population increases in the late fifteenth and early sixteenth centuries, there was an upsurge in the wage labor supply—the creation of poor, nonfarming, work-hungry groups who either sought employment within or undertook competitive occupations in the countryside surrounding the cities. Oversight of adjacent lands became imperative in order to monitor immigration and regulate business competition from outlying areas, a factor which finally inclined cities toward powerful territorial princes and away from local feudal magnates in the new political alliances of the sixteenth century. Cities tended to prefer the most distant overlord, powerful enough to protect them, yet far enough away to let them thrive according to their own customs, Saxon cities were careful to protect their monopolies in beer, linen manufacture, and the skilled handicraft trades, areas into which clerical enterprises were also known to venture. Defensive measures were also needed against local territorial rulers *(Landesherren),* secular and ecclesiastical, who held veto powers over many local decisions. With ever greater determination Saxon city governments, especially in the larger cities, sought to secure—normally through outright purchase—the estates of noblemen and full rights of jurisdiction *(Grundherrschaft)* over areas in and around the cities.[61]

The quality of religious and moral life was considered an essential part of the overall health and strength of a city, especially in a plague- and famine-ridden age that still believed deeply in historically displayed providential favor and disfavor. Government policing of religion and morals was not only a political act to secure civic order, but also a religious act to ensure providential blessing, to save the city from the various forms of divine wrath. Modern scholars should not underestimate the force of such sentiment in the late Middle Ages. The prohibition of dancing in pre-Reformation Zurich, for example, was phrased: "In order that the Lord God will protect us, that our crops may flourish in the fields, and that there may be good weather, dancing is forbidden." [62] Protestant preachers successfully made much of expected providential consequences when they sought magisterial support of the Reformation. Pious belief in providence was among the factors that made many rulers—Frederick the Wise is a prominent example—susceptible to Protestant arguments from Scripture.

The civic and religious communities and social and religious reform were closely related in the minds of ordinary people; what was good for the soul of the individual was also considered good for the physical well-being of the city at large.[63] In the pamphlet literature which became the popular feet of the Reformation,

Protestant reformers relayed their religious message through preexistent social criticism of Rome and local clergy, closely connecting social ills with false religious doctrine and practice.[64] In Constance, characteristically, the evolution of religious reform was seen by lay supporters not as a narrow matter of ecclesiastical discipline but as "the civil ordering of moral life on religious grounds." As Bernd Moeller has pointed out, civic control of even clerical benefices and appointments was not considered a hostile act of secularization *(Verweltlichung)* but a concerned effort to better integrate clergy into society *(Verbürgerlichung)*.[65]

Apart from the general tightening of government control within cities that is attributable to larger economic and political factors, the extension of civic control over the religious life was also carried along by the evident corruption and inefficiency of local ecclesiastical authority. On the eve of the Reformation the medieval church was failing especially on the local level. Rome's extensive ecclesiastical bureaucracy, which had been the unity of Europe during the Middle Ages, was disintegrating in many areas, hurried along by a growing regional sense of identity and administrative competence.[66] The well-entrenched benefice system of the church, the muscle of patronage, which had permitted important ecclesiastical offices to be sold to the highest bidders and residency requirements either to go unenforced or to be fulfilled by poorly qualified substitutes, revealed its deleterious effect especially on the local level.[67] Bishops were traditionally appointed from the nobility and not always known to have either a shepherd's heart or a theologian's mind. Cities were very sensitive to their lack of firsthand knowledge of and sympathy with local urban problems. On the eve of the Reformation only one Swiss bishop, Matthäus Schiner of Sitten, was of burgher origin.[68] When the first list of grievances was presented to Bishop Hugo of Constance by the reform party of Zurich, he matter-of-factly begged their understanding that "a universal error has the force of right." [69] It was not accidental that a prominent plank in early Protestant platforms was the insistence that clergy be local men married to local women, that is, those with intimate knowledge of and a personal stake in the immediate community.

Rare is the late medieval German town that did not have complaints about the maladministration, fiscality, and moral failing of clergy, although secular priests in the lower ranks were often as much victims as perpetrators of the church's policies, clearly a factor in their joining the Reformation in large numbers.[70] Among the complaints against the church and clergy in North German cities (Stralsund, Rostock, and Wismar) were the excessive number of altars and religious offices (182 altars, 204 religious offices requiring funding in Rostock); clerical freedom from taxation (clergy having "more privileges yet fewer responsibilities" than other citizens); indulgence traffic; the sterility of religious life; the excessive number and excesses of religious holidays; the selling of basic religious services (a burial, it is complained, can run to 100 marks!); and concubinage and alleged infanticide within clerical ranks.[71] As the Reformation began in Marburg the citizenry requested, among other things, that the religious pay property *(geschoss)* and wine taxes, be forbidden revenues from wills, services for the dead, and endowed anniversary masses in memory of the dead *(testament, selegerede und jargezeide),* and have their numbers reduced.[72]

The favorite revenue-gathering device of the curia in the late Middle Ages was the indulgence, and this practice, which was rapidly expanding on the eve of the Reformation, became a key burgher complaint well before Luther posted his theses.[73] City governments were not unfavorably disposed toward indulgences so long as a generous portion of the take was given over to local coffers, remaining in and serving the immediate community. However, when an indulgence was preached primarily for the benefit of distant interests—as was the case with the famous Saint Peter's indulgence protested by Luther and, strictly for political reasons, by Frederick the Wise—then citizen piety could become outraged and local resistance offered.[74]

At the base of discontent with the clergy—a point to which we will hear first generation Protestants speak at length—were the special immunities and privileges that had grown up during the Middle Ages. City governments were understandably concerned about the possible adverse effects of having large segments of their populations and great property holdings exempt from civil regulation. In Zurich in 1467, for example, religious groups held one-third of the taxable property; in Worms in 1500 one-tenth of city-dwellers were clergy.[75] Many towns considered clergy bad citizens. A popular lampoon which appeared in the early years of the Reformation in North German towns summarized a very pervasive complaint:

Priests, monks, and nuns
Are but a burden to the earth.
They have decided
That they will not become citizens.
That's why they're so greedy—
They stand firm against the city
And will swear no allegiance to it.
And we hear their fine excuses:
"It would cause us much toil and trouble
Should we pledge our troth as burghers." [76]

During the Middle Ages canon law had insisted upon and civil law had come to recognize special clerical privileges in property and person. Such recognition looked back to privileges granted the church by the Emperor Constantine and to precedents set by episcopal domination of old Roman cities in the ninth century. As holy places, churches and monasteries were considered to be rightfully due reverence and the assurance of so-called sacral peace in all their undertakings. To the popular and official mind it was inappropriate for holy persons to be burdened with such *munera sordida* as military service, compulsory labor, standing watch at city walls, and other ordinary civic obligations. Nor was it thought right that laymen should sit in judgment on those who were their shepherds and intermediaries with God. Hence, the evolution in the Middle Ages of a twofold immunity of the religious from secular jurisdiction: an *immunitas localis,* exempting ecclesiastical properties from taxes and recognizing the right of asylum in holy places, and an *immunitas personalis,* exempting clergy from the jurisdiction of civil courts.[77]

There had been classic debates over religious immunity and the scope of secular jurisdiction long before the Reformation, none so grand and ominous as Marsilius of Padua's discourse on the confrontations between Pope Boniface VIII and Philip the Fair of France and Pope John XXII and the Emperor Lewis of Bavaria. Before the Reformation there were many efforts to restrict ecclesiastical acquisition of free properties within city walls, to circumvent the threat to the normal administration of justice represented by the right of criminal asylum in churches and monasteries, and to bring the clergy under the local tax code. Such efforts were, of course, vigorously resisted by the church, often with the heavy spiritual artillery of interdict and excommunication.[78]

But lay efforts were not without success. Between the fourteenth and sixteenth centuries a significant fusion of the religious and secular spheres and leveling of clergy and laity were achieved.[79] A recent study of late medieval Augsburg has documented the successful efforts of that city to assimilate the religious into civic life, not only by government challenge of traditional clerical immunities, but also by taking the initiative from the church in the educational and cultural life of the city.[80] Zurich is another striking case in point. As early as the thirteenth century the magistracy acted to prevent ecclesiastical removal of property from the tax rolls. Cloisters were forbidden to purchase houses within the city, and children entering cloisters were not only prevented from receiving endowments from properties lying within the city limits, but were also excluded from the civil law of inheritance. A special office was created to monitor the internal administration, appointments, and business activities of area monasteries.

In the second half of the fifteenth century a steady dismantling of traditional clerical privileges began as the Zurich magistracy promoted the increasingly popular notion that the clergy should be treated "as other citizens." The religious were subjected to certain taxes; last wills and testaments were carefully regulated so that both what was left to the clergy and what was left behind by it could be controlled; and civil jurisdiction was extended over clerical crimes and disputes, not only those against the laity, but also those among the religious themselves. By the early sixteenth century the Zurich magistracy decided what matters—regardless of the parties involved—would be turned over to the ecclesiastical courts. The magistrates further placed limits on the church's use of excommunication against those negligent in the payment of ecclesiastical tithes and taxes, and intervened to tighten the lax and arbitrary marital laws of the pre-Tridentine church. In both areas the magistracy moved in directions later sanctioned by the Reformation.[81] Protestants would restrict the ban to a spiritual discipline, no longer permitting it to be used as an instrument to achieve temporal ends (such as collecting tithes); and they would prohibit clandestine marriages, making only parentally approved engagements valid,[82] and the fabrication of unbiblical impediments to marriage. It is a commentary on the coalescence of the political and religious preconditions of the Reformation that the *causa Lutheri* was the sixteenth case in which Frederick the Wise rejected religious excommunication as a misuse of spiritual power.[83]

The socializing of the clergy, the insistence that the clergy must be good citizens, is a pattern to be seen again and again in Reformation towns and cities. It is the taproot of the Protestant work ethic. Although a somewhat extreme statement, the Rostock articles on religion, which consolidated the Reformation in that city in 1534, summarized a long late medieval development of a principle that became a fundamental Protestant tenet: only those priests and monks may remain in the city who "acquire citizenship, swear allegiance, and take upon themselves the duties of citizens to pay taxes, to stand watch, and to fight to the death for the city." [84]

Lay Promotion of Preacherships

Burgher determination to integrate the religious into civic life, to make the church and clergy good citizens, was certainly motivated by the material self-interest of the community at large. However, the religious dimension should not be underestimated. Although a "more rational Bürgergeist," fed by humanist criticism, may have been operating in the background,[85] pre-Reformation anti-clericalism was not a frame of mind hostile in principle to church and religion. Scholars have observed that coexisting with such criticism were burgeoning religious publications, popular adoptions of biblical and saints' names, multiplication of confraternities, increased endowments of private masses, frequent pilgrimages to shrines, even witch-hunting.[86] Lay criticism of church and clergy is also an expression of a lively piety.

The religious dimension of the cities' self-perception has been especially highlighted in the influential study of Heinrich Schmidt (1958), which concentrates particularly on the late medieval chronicles of Augsburg, Nürnberg, and Lübeck. As revealed in their own histories, these cities saw themselves as organic parts of a cosmopolitan order of civil rights and freedoms invested with the highest religious values. The free city is seen by Schmidt to embrace a free individual, the empire the city, and the saving order of Christendom the empire.[87] The particular embodied the universal, the religious embraced the secular; sin and salvation had strong social and political connotations. "God has become a citizen of Bern," the chronicler Konrad Justinger could write self-assuredly, "and who can fight against God?" [88]

Such convictions lay behind one of the most fateful lay ventures to improve local religious life, the endowment and oversight of special preacherships *(Prädikaturen)* which in many instances were to become key bases of operation for the Protestant preachers who spearheaded the Reformation.[89] The importance of the endowed preachership is twofold. First, throughout the latter part of the fifteenth century it promoted what came to be the new (Protestant) form of worship centered on the sermon rather than the Mass. Secondly, there is a significant correlation, especially in Germany, between holders of preacherships and local Protestant leadership.[90] In Württemberg, where more than half of the towns with active preacherships (23 of 42) became Protestant,[91] the more notable preachers were Matthew Alber in Reutlingen, Johannes Brenz in Schwäbisch Hall, Johannes Oecolampadius (whose preachership was established in 1510 by his parents) and Erhard Schnepf in Weinsberg, and Johannes Mantel in Stuttgart.[92] The Franciscan preacher Johann Eberlin von Günzburg, among the most effective pamphleteers of the early Reformation, was employed after 1517 as an assistant during Lent and Advent to the preachers of Horb and Ehingen.[93] Preacherships have been described as the "infiltration route" of the Reformation into Thuringia, where practically all important reformers at sometime held such office: Wenceslaus Linck in Altenburg, Balthasar Düring in Koburg, Jacob Strauss in Eisenach, Friedrich Myconius in Gotha, Johan Grau and Wolfgang Stein in Weimar, and Martin Reinhardt and Anton Musa in Jena.[94]

In Switzerland, by contrast, there were fewer preacherships; only 16 percent of Swiss towns (14 of 87), over against 31 percent (42 of 137) in Württemberg, had them. There were none in such important places as Zurich, Schaffhausen, Baden, Solothurn, and Lucerne.[95] There is, further, more of a disproportion in Switzerland between the preachers, over half of whom either permanently or temporarily turned Protestant, and the preacherships themselves, which remained two to one a constant Catholic force. The disproportion has been related to the ability of the patrons to impose their will on the office of preacher, holding proponents of the new doctrine at bay (as in the case of Franz Kolb, whose invitation to Freiburg was blocked because of known Protestant sentiments), dismissing them outright (as happened with Tilman Limperger in the Münster in Basel), and electing known opponents of the Reformation (such as Johann Burckhardi in Bremgarten, Adam Moser in Saint Gall, and Augustin Marius at the Münster in Basel).[96]

The establishment of preacherships originated in local dissatisfaction with the irregularity and low quality of the preaching of secular clergy and the unpopularity of the supplementary efforts of mendicant preachers, who were too ready to assist.[97] The reforms of the conciliar movement following the Council of Constance (the *Reformatio Sigismundi* is a prominent example) and the increase in the number of educated and literate laymen (the fourteenth and fifteenth centuries saw a great college boom)[98] were important preconditions.[99] In the fifteenth century laymen were in a position to be more discerning and more demanding of their clergy.

Before the creation of preacherships in the fifteenth century, the primary task of regular preaching had devolved from parish priests, who theoretically always retained a special responsibility for it, to assistant priests and chaplains, whose positions, unlike those of the parish priest and the mass priest, were unendowed and looked upon by their occupants as only temporary assignments until a beneficed position could be obtained.[100] Donors preferred to invest in private masses for their own soul's salvation rather than in public sermons for their neighbors' edification.[101] And unbeneficed preachers found the performance of religious services other than preaching (that is, masses, baptisms, marriages, and burials) far more lucrative ways to spend their time. Endowed preacherships were intended to ensure regularity and to upgrade the quality of preaching by making it a vocation in its own right, and with a remuneration slightly better than that of the average burgher.[102]

In Württemberg the founders of preacherships were princes and princesses, high and low clergy, burghers of both sexes, and lay and religious corporations. Three preacherships were established by sheer government fiat (in Hall, Reutlingen, and Schorndorf).[103] Secular clergy saw in them important new endowments and ways to keep poaching mendicants at arm's length, as well as to respond to a genuine need. Since preacherships were attached to the local churches and their occupants were highly trained, ordained priests, local clergy were immediately involved. Even before the creation of preacherships, those entrusted with the responsibility for regular preaching were the subjects of close consultation between city governments and local ecclesiastical authorities, for both unpopular and popular (fanatical) preachers were proven sources of social unrest.[104] In Württemberg the rights of patronage (nomination and oversight of appointments) were always in predominantly lay or mixed hands, never in purely religious hands. Instituting a preachership was, in fact, a local cooperative venture; a decision was taken by local laity and clergy to improve a local situation, with distant episcopal authority playing a very secondary if nonetheless indispensable role.[105]

When we inquire into the motives of individual donors, it is slightly ironic to find that what proved so often to be a congenial base for Protestant operations was in fact founded by men and women who considered such an act a good work that would help to secure their salvation—an act akin to endowing a private mass.[106] A Württemberg letter of endowment states:

> Since all men who have lived and will live must appear on the Last Day before the throne of a severe Judge, there to receive the reward each has earned during his lifetime, whether good or bad, it is very necessary to prepare for that day of Last Judgment by good works of virtue.[107]

Endowment letters normally required preachers either to encourage congregations to pray for the souls of the founders or to thank the founders themselves within the body of the sermon.

The moral and educational requirements for the occupants of endowed preacherships were very high. In Switzerland the preachers were expected to be moral paragons beyond reproach ("fromm, ersam, erberlich, früntlich, priestlich"). Lengwiler finds only two out of fifty-nine Swiss preachers with blemished records (spotted by fathering illegitimate children).[108] The high educational requirements are reflected in the fact that 78 percent (46 of 59) of Swiss preachers had received university training, forty-three taking some kind of degree and fourteen holding the highest theological degree, the Doctor of Theology.[109] In Württemberg an academic degree was in fact required of all preachers,[110] a reflection perhaps of the greater opportunities for university education in Germany, which also supplied the majority of Swiss preachers. Nominations were normally sought by cities from various universities, and it became traditional for certain universities to supply the preachers for certain cities, thereby forming an alliance which could have potent ideological consequences. Although candidates theoretically could compete freely for an opening—trial sermons and interviews were held—in Württemberg preference was given to sons of resident burghers,[111] another reflection of the local needs preacherships were designed to serve.

Once elected and installed, the preacher was responsible for about one hundred sermons a year (in Saint Gall it went as high as one hundred and fifty), with an especially heavy schedule during Lent and Advent. The sermons were about three-quarters of an hour in length, clear and simple in form, following faithfully the church calendar, and stressing penance and moral betterment.[112] Because of a preacher's superior education, his (carefully enforced) exemplary life, and his frequent commerce with the laity in a predominantly nonadversary role—by way of preaching rather than within the confessional or across a Latinized Mass—he often came to exercise influence within cities beyond his immediate congregation. Herrmann writes of Thuringian preachers, later key men of the Reformation, that "they were the city's organization men, trusted advisers of government in church matters, acknowledged leaders of the masses." [113] Because the preacher, unlike the other clergy, maintained independence from the parish priest, who was still officially the local religious leader, a certain coolness and even friction could develop between the two,[114] although it was the mendicant orders that felt most threatened by the preacher's advent. However, it is still to be borne in mind that the very creation of a preachership was a sign of failure on the part of the established parish clergy fully to satisfy the religious needs of people.[115] Whatever else it may indicate, the invitation to a preacher was also a town's negative judgment upon its own religious life, an expression of self-critical piety. Preacherships are monuments to local determination to create the conditions for an institutionally viable lay piety.

Iconoclasm: The Response of Anguished Lay Piety

On the eve of the Reformation we find a piety characterized by criticism of manifest religious abuses, skepticism about long-accepted clerical privileges and revered ecclesiastical practices, and a willingness to experiment with new religious forms. The depth of this piety has been questioned in light of the apparent ease with which so many seem to have abandoned so thoroughly and violently the practices of the medieval church at the first Protestant exposé. The striking rapidity with which, in Hermann Heimpel's famous phrase, the image-makers (donors, *Bilderstifter*) became image-breakers (iconoclasts, *Bilderstürmer*)[116] has suggested that inner religious commitment could not have run very deep. We have seen Toussaert's case for pervasive religious indifference in Flanders. Similar questions have been raised about the depth of German piety by Karlheinz Blaschke, who cites a famous occurrence in Saxony of a lay procession earnestly mocking the canonization of Bishop Benno of Meissen (1066–1106).[117] Benno's canonization had been vigorously promoted by the pious Duke George, who had long wanted and, with the outbreak of the Reformation, badly needed, a regional saint. Pope Adrian VI declared Benno a saint in May 1523 and set his "raising"—the digging up with silver shovels of his bones for preservation—for June 16. Shortly thereafter a large group of laymen in Buchholtz staged a mock raising of their own. They made flags from foul rags, replaced candles with pitchforks and songbooks with chessboards, and, bearing upon a dung-wagon as the "holy relics" of the deceased bishop a horse's skull and the bones of a cow, crowded into the marketplace, there in jest to preach sermons, hawk indulgences, and praise the pope.[118] How could such basic traditional religious practices, apparently revered only a short time before, become so quickly objects of sincere and vulgar ridicule?

Bernd Moeller has sought an answer by attempting to balance the divergent views of the Catholic historians Johannes Janssen and Joseph Lortz. On the one hand, he agrees strongly with Janssen's description of the German people as deeply religious *(kirchenfromm)* on the eve of the Reformation. On the other hand, he also finds truth in Lortz's insistence that corruption and decline in church and theology were most profound. How did the two conditions so easily coexist? Moeller believes that the explanation may be that most people were simply unaware of the extent of ecclesiastical corruption, especially that in the higher church circles to which most laymen were not privy. It was accordingly the revelations of Protestant preachers that made a previously pious and trusting laity fully conscious of the sad situation churchwide and triggered the violent reactions and speedy transition by so many from the sacramental piety of the late medieval church to the unsacramental piety of the Reformation.[119]

Moeller has surely put his finger on an important point. But as crucial as the Protestant exposés were, the laity were not dependent upon them for awareness of ecclesiastical corruption. Local religious grievances abound on the eve of the Reformation and the cry reaches all the way to Rome.[120] Local reform measures restricting clerical privileges and creating preacherships attest to lay sensitivity to religious abuse and maladministration. The Protestant reformers focused and gave new theological justification to longstanding discontent, but they were not the first to apprise ordinary people of the skeletons in the closet of the late medieval church. I think Moeller would agree that the novel thing pointed out by the first generation of Protestant preachers was a much more profound matter. What separated so violently Reformation from late medieval piety was not discovery of a heretofore insufficiently known or appreciated need for religious reform but the most compelling arguments for the inadequacy of even a reformed medieval church.[121] Protestant preachers pointed out what many laymen had evidently also come to suspect—that the church and her clergy would first have to undergo a major redefinition before they could be integrated as good citizens into society. The root of the problem, I am suggesting, was not the privileges of a special clerical class or even its administrative and moral failings but the most basic beliefs and practices of the church it represented. Behind the legal battles with the church and the reform programs carried on by citizens and their governments in the late Middle Ages—and requisite to their final success—lay the need for a religious transvaluation.

From this perspective the outburst of iconoclasm at the inception of the Reformation may rather indicate the reaction of people who felt themselves fooled by something that they had not taken lightly at all but had in fact believed all too deeply and in spite of the perceived shortcomings of its representatives. It is a reaction that might have been expected from those whose piety had been sincere and "appetite for the divine" immense.

Early Protestant pamphlets speak directly to this issue, especially in the stock indulgence scene which usually culminates in the burning of the indulgence or the using of it to wipe one's rear end.

Nicholas Manuel, for example, devoted an entire act of his play *Die Totenfresser* (1523) to a discussion of the Bernese indulgence market. Seven now-knowing farmers retrospectively ponder in puzzlement how such an outrageous perversion of religion could have occurred. At least two profess never to have been taken in. One says he always thought of Christ driving out the money-changers from the temple when he watched the indulgence sellers at work, while another claims to have known all along that they were "but decoys." [122] One, however, speaks for what was surely the experience of many if not most of the pious laity who became Protestants. He recalls having been placed under the ban for insulting the pope. Fearing for his soul, he rushed to Bern to purchase an indulgence with egg money scraped together by his wife. Returning hungry and exhausted he describes how he and his wife fell upon their knees and worshipped the indulgence: "I believed I had seen very God himself." Later, "instructed by knowledgeable people and perceiving it was worthless," he became so enraged for letting himself be thus deceived that he fetched the letter of indulgence and "wiped my ass" with it. He says he is "still sick to my stomach about it." [123] A similar experience is recounted in an anonymous pamphlet of the same year which features a discussion between a father and his son. The father tells of having purchased a letter of indulgence four years earlier for six groschen, and describes vividly how efficacious he then believed it to be. He explains that people were taken in by their "deceitful" priests simply because they were so trusting: "like shepherd, like sheep." [124] The son points out that it was only with the advent of Luther and the vernacular Bible that they received both knowledge of and weaponry against such deception.[125] Together father and son burn the indulgence in the name of Johann Eck, Jerome Emser, and Thomas Murner (early Catholic apologists against the Reformation) and with the singing of a Te Deum!

The violent anticlericalism of the early period of the Reformation may be the response of those who were convinced that they had been religiously burdened in vain. Iconoclasts care. Toussaert is on the verge of discovery when he suspects iconoclasm in Flanders to be a kind of "vengeance" for the church's paraliturgical concealment of the "essentials." [126] Martin Bucer concluded in his tract on the subject that there was nothing that had "so deceived and made Christians negligent of the truly important things" as devotion to images.[127] Protestant preachers may initially have attracted audiences because they spoke to pious laymen who, like themselves, were not only aware of the failings of church and clergy, but also thoroughly persuaded that they had been doctrinally hoodwinked and religiously exploited by what was, in the end, unnecessary and untrue.

3 The Original Protestant Message

The full spectrum of sixteenth-century urban society came to embrace the Protestant message—intellectuals, artisans and workers, merchants, patricians, and magistrates. Within German and Swiss towns and cities, subjects of this study, the Reformation was in the broadest sense of the word a popular movement, by sixteenth-century standards even a democratic revolution. What did the laity perceive the Reformation to be, and why were they so attracted to it? These are questions that cannot be settled by poring over formal theological tracts and disputations, nor by enumerating so-called forerunners of the Reformation, as important as these enterprises remain. Why people became Protestants is not a problem resolved by compiling lists of longstanding social and political gravamina, or by repeating the tales of contemporary chroniclers, as revealing as both may be. Nor is it an issue set aside by identifying the vocations and inferring the economic self-interest of the first Protestant groups, as popular as such head-counts are becoming. These various approaches tell us a great deal about the preconditions of reform, which invite many reactions and admit of many solutions, but they do not explain the appeal and persistence of a particular Protestant program.

Whatever else the Reformation may be said to have done, it transformed the concept, practice, and institutions of late medieval religion in the most fundamental way. This is an important fact, and it has not been appreciated in recent efforts to explain the appeal of Protestantism. In an age when religion embraced far more than it does today, people were most sensitive to social change radiating from the religious sphere. The basic thing one needs to know in weighing the attraction of the Reformation is exactly what Protestants proposed to do to the religious life of cities and towns. How were communities to be altered, individually and socially, psychologically and institutionally, by the implementation of Protestant ideas?

The more fruitful approach to the questions I have posed may lie in the examination of those records which, so far as possible, reflect contemporary lay concerns and the Protestant message at their point of intersection. I am referring here to a variety of writings that comprise these records, among them apologetic instructions by Protestant reformers, lay defenses of the Reformation, vernacular catechetical literature, and popular plays and dramatic writings. Where such original statements, designed for the laity, were widely circulated and frequently reprinted, or where, even if short-lived, they provided a popular foundation or an official guideline for the introduction of the Reformation, they may be taken as dependable gauges of the appeal of Protestant ideas during the years of the Reformation's inception. Although produced mainly by the new Protestant preachers, these diverse writings dealt with problems immediate to the laity and in language that laymen understood. They were the new theology in applied form, and in this respect differed from the better known magisterial theological tracts. Lay perception of the Reformation cannot necessarily be identified with that of the theologians. The laity were not so ready, as the theologian Luther was known to be, to act solely on the basis of abstract doctrine, although the truth claims of the Reformation were not taken lightly. For the laity theological questions became important because they affected day-to-day practice, not because they agreed or disagreed with Paul or Augustine. Laymen were interested in the institutional consequences of theological doctrine. What they heard was not necessarily either inconsistent with or any less profound than the magisterial theological tracts, but it was a different genre of Reformation writing, in many ways a more gripping and powerful form of communication, and always one that related idea to concrete reality. The material I will examine attests the historical impact of the religious message of the Reformation. As we shall see, from Rostock in the north to Constance in the south there was unanimity both in the basic criticisms of the old religious practices and institutions and in the basic features of the new.

In this chapter I will draw on some fifty-odd examples of the above writings, taken, with few exceptions, from the years 1519–1526, the critical period of the Reformation's beginning. They represent only a sampling, but I think a revealing one when considered in light of late medieval developments (chapter 2) and the larger pattern of the Reformation's development (chapter 4). I work with the educated hunch that both expectation and final achievement measure motive. While such writings have the character of apologies and propaganda and speak to specific historical situations, they also summarize accurately the transformations in the concept, practice, and institutions of religion that occurred during the course of the Reformation. While most had individual authors, they also express viewpoints that were later embodied—to be sure in more civil form—in the catechisms and church ordinances that consolidated the final phase of the Reformation and were ratified by large majorities in the cities and towns that embraced it. The "propaganda," in other words, had institutional consequences. The revolutionary program came to rest in an established religion; the pamphlet became a church ordinance. And in their wake the religious values and habits of centuries were permanently abandoned by a very large part of Western society. If promise proved in the end somewhat to exceed achievement, it did not do so without leaving the most lasting of marks. The new Protestant institutions persisted even when they failed to achieve the reformers' expected transformation of mankind.

The Assault on the Confessional

At the turn of the twentieth century a distinguished Catholic historian wrote a short monograph on the concept and practice of penance in Germany on the eve of the Reformation. The study covered dozens of confessional manuals, catechetical writings, and deathbed instructions and did so with one purpose in mind—to refute the careless charge of Protestant historians, among them the eminent Adolf von Harnack, that only a lax half-penance, based only on fear of punishment, was expected of lay penitents by the Catholic church in the late Middle Ages.[1] Nikolaus Paulus demonstrated to the contrary that a full and sincere penance, embracing love as well as fear of God, was in fact demanded at virtually every turn. For one who knows the material it is surprising that such a debate ever occurred. But nineteenth-century Protestant historians had imbibed the reigning Ritschlian theology, which interpreted the Lutheran heritage within the categories of Kantian moral philosophy, a perspective conducive to viewing the Reformation as more of a moral shaping up than as a religiously liberating movement: Lutherans were those who gave shiftless medieval men a taste of the categorical imperative. It was a point of view that led to an inaccurate picture of both late medieval religious practice and the original Protestant message.

The first Protestants attacked the medieval church for demanding too much, not too little, from laymen and clergymen, and for making religion psychologically and socially burdensome, not for taking it too lightly. At no point did these apologists feel that they had greater justification for their criticism than at the point of the sacrament of penance and confession. Luther early laid the foundation for the Protestant assault on the confessional. By 1521 fourteen editions of his *Sermon on the Sacrament of Penance,* first published in 1519, had been printed. This tract attacked the "many books and writings" on confession and contrition which "try to frighten people into going frequently to confession." The traditional practice was criticized for demanding a contrition no man could achieve and leaving the penitent in doubt and anxious about forgiveness:

> You should not be debating . . . whether or not your contrition is sufficient. Rather you should be assured that after all your efforts your contrition is not sufficient. This is why you must cast yourself upon the grace of God, hear his sufficiently sure word in the sacrament, accept it in free and joyful faith, and never doubt that you have come to grace.[2]

In this first popular tract on the subject, Luther attempted to overturn the confessional as tribunal and the role of the priest as judge. The only requirement for absolution, he maintained, is the sincere desire to receive it and faith in God's promise to forgive those who so seek it. Although Luther would have the priest inquire if the penitent has come in such a spirit, he made clear that any penitential examination is strictly a voluntary matter between the penitent and the priest.[3]

A larger, more formal work on the subject—something of a Protestant confessional manual—appeared six months later in the spring of 1520 and quickly went through four German and six Latin editions. Here Luther dismantled piece by piece the traditional practice. So-called secret sins—(largely sexual) feelings that tantalize but never become deeds—he set aside as the invention of nosy, avaricious, and tyrannical priests.[4] He rejected the requirement to confess annually all mortal sins as an impossible demand which led only to confusion and despair. "The most mortal of all mortal sins is not to believe that one is guilty of damnable and mortal sin. . . . [before God one must simply say:] all that I am, whatever I say or do, is mortal and damnable." By so maximizing the state of sin Protestants actually sought to minimize preoccupation with sinning. Luther dismissed as "utterly useless and altogether harmful" the entire traditional catalogue of sins according to motive, theological and cardinal virtues, the five senses, the Seven Deadly Sins, the seven sacraments, the seven gifts of the Spirit, the Beatitudes, the alien sins, the twelve articles of faith, and the silent sins. Until now, he maintained, penitents leaving the confessional had rejoiced more in the liberation from the torment of how they should confess than in any absolution they had received from the priest. The tract concludes with a wholesale indictment of the traditional sacrament:

> Who can recount all the tyrannies with which the troubled consciences of confessing and penitent Christians are burdened —the deadly constitutions and customs with which they are daily harassed by silly manikins who bind and place on the shoulders of men very heavy and unbearable burdens which they themselves do not want to touch even with one finger? Thus this most salutary sacrament of penance has become nothing but sheer tyranny . . . a disease and a means to increase sins.[5]

One may add to Luther's early work the magisterial Latin tract written in 1521 by the Old Testament scholar and church historian Johannes Oecolampadius, which bore its message clearly in the title, *A Paradox: Christian Confession Is Not Onerous.* This lengthy work (117 pages) is a detailed criticism of what Oecolampadius summarized as the "destruction of minds through the tyranny of confession" *(ruina animarum ex tyrannide confessionis);* father confessors are repeatedly referred to as "psychotyranni."[6] As an antidote Oecolampadius defended three biblical forms of confession which preserved "Christian liberty" against the "innovation" of auricular confession: secretly and individually to God; publicly (congregationally) in church *(confessio ecclesiastica);* and privately to fellow Christians *(confessio fraterna; familiariter fratribus).*[7] As a rule of thumb Oecolampadius proposed: if it is not liberating, it is not Christian confession.

It was the Eisenach preacher Jacob Strauss, however, who made the confessional a special target, writing the most comprehensive popular exposés in 1522 and 1523. The first was circulated as a sermon that had allegedly been preached to "several thousand" in the vicinity of Hall and was occasioned by a general reluctance among the populace to receive the Eucharist because of the required antecedent confession of sins.[8] Strauss reported a widespread belief that to receive the sacrament without first achieving perfect inner penance and confessing every mortal sin according to the exact circumstances of each would bring eternal death. He claimed that "many thousand" could attest the fear and anxiety caused by the prospect of such confession.[9] In contradiction thereto he argued that even if such knowledge and recitation, with the resulting absolution, were possible—which he emphatically insisted they were not—then the sacrament would be received by persons purified to the point of having no need of it. To require such impossible preparation was to transform a consoling promise of forgiveness into a curse that could only drive communicants to despair and reluctance to receive the sacrament.[10] Strauss suspected the worst, that a desire to enslave the penitent to the confessor *(dienstlich knecht machen)* had always been at the base of such unrealistic requirements.[11] And he assured his reader, with a seven article elaboration, that confession presupposes only sincere faith in Christ and inspires absolute confidence about the forgiveness of sins.[12]

Strauss's second treatise is one of the great unrecognized tours de force of the early Reformation. There is hyperbole in it, but it is still a fair and powerful case, foreshadowing mature Protestant views. However the traditional sacrament of penance might be assessed—in terms of its requirements (contrite enumeration of all mortal sins according to their exact circumstances), its power of enforcement (excommunication), or its loopholes (indulgences)—Strauss submits that it is but a potent instrument of clerical self-aggrandizement and lay intimidation. It is the means by which clergy "seek to elevate the power of the pope and to reign themselves over the consciences of men, knowing, ordering, and arranging all things according to their good pleasure." [13] And its success is directly related to the degree to which it causes people to be anxious and preoccupied with their sins. In a grand summary:

> In the confessional simple folk learn things about sin and evil which have never occurred to them before, and which need not

> ever have occurred to them! The confessional is a schooling in sin. It is known and many thousand can attest how often mischievous and perverse monks out of their shameless hearts have so thoroughly and persistently questioned young girls and boys, innocent children, and simple wives about the sins of the flesh in their cursed confessional corners that more harm was there done to Christian chasteness and purity than in any whorehouse in the world. He is considered a good father confessor who can probe into every secret recess of the heart and instill into the innocent penitent every sin his flesh has not yet experienced. They want to know from virtuous wives all the circumstances of the marital duty—how their husbands do it [certain "unnatural" positions were very serious sins], how often, how much pleasure it brings, when it is done, and the like. In this way new desires and lusts are stimulated within the weak. They even teach poor wives not to submit to their husbands on certain holidays and during Lent.[14]

Strauss, a New Testament "male chauvinist," [15] considered the last a most serious source of domestic conflict, driving "thousands" of men to adultery. He noted additionally that women who could be made so submissive to priests tended always to be running to confession, "home only at mealtime." Strauss complained also about the power that mendicant confessors wielded over the judgments of kings, princes, and lords, a complaint elaborated more fully in other Protestant circles.[16]

The charge of sexual misconduct in the confessional, especially by mendicant confessors, lent itself to deadly humorous Protestant satire. In a pamphlet of 1521, which dealt primarily with the problems mendicants created for conscientious parish priests, the author, Johannes Römer, a chaplain in Worms, includes a scene in which a monk confesses the wife of a rich Junker. Warmly received by the patently lecherous monk, the woman is interrogated about her dress and soon brought to the admission that she primps in order to be sexually attractive to men. (The monk encourages her to tell all by knowingly agreeing that she has the "power to make many penises rise.") After granting her absolution and promising a monthly prayer *(ein drissigsten)* for one gulden, the monk orders her to return frequently to the monastery as a fraternal lay sister. As it turns out—this satire cuts both ways—she is as interested in the mendicant confessor as he in her. On returning home she enthusiastically tells her profiteering husband (who thinks a drissigsten for one gulden was an unheard-of bargain) that their pastor is no match for the monk: "Oh what a fine man he is. . . . How he can probe into every place! He has certainly absolved me as no pastor ever did!"[17]

Strauss's complaints against the confessional also reverberated through an equally severe Swiss tract. In response to a request from Casper von Stainnau in Solothurn for a report on lay religion in his region, Heinrich Scharpf of Klingnau sent along a popular tract by one Otto Karg entitled *A Great Grim Chain by Which the Hearts of Christians Have Been Shackled* (1524). The confessional turns out to be the most devilish link in this great chain. It is an alleged source of heresy, superstition, despair of conscience, opposition to religious tithes, monastic indolence, new sins among the young, the embarrassment of women, and the impoverishment of widows.[18]

Ultimately, Strauss declared the traditional sacrament of penance not only no sacrament but not even a command of Christ; Christ came to set free the hearts and make peaceful the consciences of men, whereas the confessional encourages preoccupation with sin and even anxiety over sins that are not sins at all.[19] Christians who wish to confess are directed by Strauss simply to do so and receive forgiveness from one another.[20] "Let the Antichrist with all his antichristians, his priests and monks, yes, let the Devil, hell itself, and all creatures say, sing, scream, thunder, hail, sleet, and threaten you as they will, you have nothing to be afraid of."[21] Laymen are finally instructed to inform their priests of the state of their souls and receive from them, not a judicial examination, but a sure confirmation of their own independent judgment. There could hardly be a more striking statement of the revolution from the traditional practice:

> When you have in faith acknowledged and confessed all your sins to God . . . then have no doubt that you are set free by God from all your sins, and go and say to your priest: "My lord, I know by the grace of God that I am now guilty of no mortal sin and therefore have no need of confession. Assure me of this in Christian love as my priest." Then tell the priest that you desire to receive the holy sacrament with other Christian people.[22]

Such confidence informed Protestant attitudes toward death and the dying, traditionally the most important sphere of operation for the confessor. Traditional deathbed practice had sought to bring the dying to perfect penance at all costs. Catholic sick and dying were instructed to deny themselves and rely absolutely on Christ's sacrifice. The logic behind such reliance was simple. One now faced God's terrible judgment and it was too late for further good works; one had no other recourse than to throw oneself on God's grace as sincerely as possible and beg, "Take Christ's merit for that which I should have done." [23] By contrast, Protestant consolation of the sick and dying dwelt nonchalantly on the "green pastures." Supremely confident of salvation by faith in Christ—a lifetime, not a deathbed attitude—Protestants endeavored to neuter the fear and anxiety of the dying to the point of making death almost unreal. Catholics, at the point of death, appear to be the strongest proponents of salvation by grace alone, while Protestants could rather look like the children of Prometheus.

Since death was the greatest of faith's temptations, as tradition had taught, Protestants, beginning with Luther's 1519 sermon on the subject, directed the mind of the dying solely to life, grace, and heaven.[24] The pastor was not to concentrate on divine wrath and hell or urge penitent remembrance of past misdeeds. Catholic deathbed practice was severely criticized for demanding an eleventh hour perfect penance, thus making its reliance on grace something of a shot in the dark. In a *Sterbeschrift* of 1522 the Ulm Lutheran Johann Diepold scolded, "Oh you monks, priests, and nuns, how well you console the dying by making them fearful and doubtful!" [25] The Protestant alternative was illustrated by the advice Urbanus Rhegius gave in his *Remedy for Both the Healthy and the Sick at the Hour of Death* (1529). He tells the fretful dying:

> Your Christian baptism is a covenant, a gracious transaction, in which you and God agree that you will have a good conscience eternally because of the forgiveness of sins through the resurrection of Christ. . . . As little as Christ can be damned can you be damned, so long as you hold fast to him in true faith. As sin, death, and hell cannot harm your Lord, so it cannot harm you. For you are in Christ and Christ is in you and you cannot be damned.[26]

Andreas Osiander later argued that a Christian's anxiety and temptation on the deathbed, while really experienced, were only the "unreal" emotions of his nature as a sinner, in truth quite harmless before the unexperienced but sure reality to which his faith directed him.[27]

Such efforts to suppress fear of death and the afterlife came in reaction to what Protestants felt was the exploitation of such emotion in traditional confessional practice—what Pamphilus Gengenbach and Nicholas Manuel would characterize with the savage phrase "Totenfresserei." [28] If Protestants contributed, as I think they did, to a Western reluctance to be realistic about death (Protestants believed that death *was* unreal for true faith), they were motivated by a desire to make the hour of death less traumatic than it traditionally had been. Protestant deathbed practice was thus consistent with the assault on the confessional in its desire to ameliorate what was believed to be an undue burdening of religious life.

The Promises of Protestant Preachers

Escape from Episcopal Bureaucracy

Many a Protestant pamphlet lamented the power of bishops and episcopal bureaucracy over the lower clergy and the laity, none more forcefully than Sebastian Meyer's response to Hugo of Landenberg, the bishop of Constance. As the Reformation became a dominant force in Zurich, Hugo, who held jurisdiction over 2,000 pastorates and more than 15,000 religious, issued on May 2, 1522, the first of several pastoral entreaties. In the preceding months prominent Zurich citizens had eaten sausages in defiance of the Lenten fast, and Zwingli, without magisterial restraint, had promoted clerical marriage (he was at the time secretly married and his wife pregnant) and the subjection of traditional religious practices to the test of Scripture. The bishop's letter warned the faithful against Zwinglian tenets and admonished obedience to the church. It was to be read throughout the diocese of Constance, which embraced the cities of Ulm, Esslingen, Ravensburg, Ueberlingen, Lindau, Schaffhausen, Zurich, and Lucerne.

Meyer, a Basel-trained Doctor of Scripture and *Lesemeister* of the Franciscan order in Bern (since October 1521), wrote a popular refutation of the bishop's letter. With his friend, the parish priest Berchtold Haller, Meyer had been preaching Protestant doctrine in Bern; he probably absorbed Protestant tenets during an earlier stay in Strasbourg. Meyer first asked Zwingli to publish his tract covertly in Zurich (despite broad popular support Bern was not to be officially on record for the Reformation until 1528) but Zwingli's printer, Christopher Froschauer, was at the time preoccupied with the publication of Leo Jud's translation of Erasmus's paraphrases of the New Testament.

Meyer eventually found a publisher in Sigmund Grimm, who published the work pseudonymously in Augsburg in late 1522.[29] The tract is among the most biting documents of the early Swiss Reformation, and strongly influenced the conversion of Nicholas Manuel, who later presided over the Reformation in Bern. While Meyer leaves not a phrase unturned in the bishop's letter, he strikes especially at the ways in which a swollen clerical bureaucracy made life difficult and expensive for both the laity and the lower clergy, and from which only a major transformation of religious life provided an escape. He cites sixteen different episcopal functionaries, pretentious papal titles ("pontifex maximus") and customs (bearing the pope on a raised chair, kissing his feet) contrived to inspire awe, and a multitude of religious orders and ceremonies;[30] the final object of all of these, he maintains, is the lay conscience and pocketbook. He attacks the inflation of religious orders:

> Everyone wants to become a priest, monk, nun, Beghard, or Beguine and live a quiet, full, noble, and blessed life, sure of heaven. To this end the religious lay aside all their worldly goods. And what happens? We have eternal strife over worldly goods! Secular and regular clergy hate each other as no other people on earth. There is a multitude of sects and orders. There are those who wear only white, others only black, still others half white and half black; one group of these wears white on the inside and black on the outside, the other black on the inside and white on the outside. Then there are those who wear all blue and others who wear all gray, and among them there are more than six sects. Some wear two, some only one, and some no points at all on their hoods. Some are with and some without scapulars, waistbands, cords, and ropes. Some go barefoot, some

> wear low-cut, some wooden, some high, and some pointed shoes. Some have large tonsures, some small, some are completely shorn. Some go with and some go without a cape. There are a multitude of hand-carried crucifixes—single and double models, painted red, white, black, blue, and even multicolored. Innumerable distinguishing saints, rules, statutes, prayers, and songs are claimed. Some eat no meat, some no bones, some no eggs, some no peelings—all as if mortal sins were there involved. Each has its reformed and unreformed factions. The one order wants to have nothing to do with money (although it has plenty of it), the other ponders day and night nothing else than how to get it. Each order wants to excel the other, and they insult one another . . . like guttersnipes. . . . Dear layman, it is all done with one purpose in mind and that is your pocketbook, which lets them have full gullets and live indulgent lives. They exist by the founding and confirmation of the pope and they help him make off with your goods. It is to that end that they receive from him special papal bulls, indulgences, and saints chosen from their midst.[31]

Meyer strongly protests the reading of the bishop's letter during Sunday and holiday services. Pastors and congregations, he groans, are already overwhelmed to the detriment of their religious education by set announcements, to which now must be added a letter three times as long as any prescribed reading from the gospel. Already there must be endured announcements of coming holy days; the passing and transfer of the rights of the recently deceased; the departed for whom masses will be said; the tax for building the mother church in Constance and Chur; the first, second, and third warnings to those guilty of crimes punishable by excommunication; the declaration of persons now placed under the ban; the proclamation of those released from the ban; the first, second, and third reprimands for violations of marriage; the urging of area peasants to make the required offerings, to pay the tithe, to hear mass on Sundays and holidays, and not to go elsewhere to make their confessions; a list of pregnant women [they were to receive special prayers, a reflection of the high infant and maternal mortality rate]; citation of faithful stewards; and censure of the public faults of the five senses which occur while resting, moving, standing, lying down, sitting, tumbling, running, sleeping, waking up, dreaming, and dancing vigorously! Is it any wonder, Meyer concludes, that among a hundred mature men hardly one is found who can recite the Ten Commandments, the Creed, and the Lord's Prayer? [32]

Meyer also devotes a statistical section to the bishop's strictures against clerical marriage and the burdens they imposed upon priests. Members of the lower clergy joined the Reformation in large numbers, and Meyer illuminates the reason. It is alleged that some 1,500 children were born annually to priests in the diocese of Constance, for each of which the bishop received a cradle fee of four gulden (Meyer accuses the bishop of having raised the fee to five gulden in the wake of Zwingli's preaching)—a yearly take of 6,000 (or 7,500) gulden. Required additionally are concubinage fees and special payments to legitimate the children born of such unions. "There are hardly two pimps in the whole bishopric who take in so much money." Meyer climaxes his exposé with an example of the absurdity to which the situation leads. He tells of a schoolmaster who left his wife to become a priest, only to find that he could not live in continence and so procured a concubine. His wife, discovering this arrangement, returned to her husband and soon took the place of the concubine. When the church learned of the situation, the priest was ordered to separate from his wife or forfeit his benefice. Choosing the former course of action, he returned to his concubine, paid the fine for concubinage, and continued in his benefice. Perhaps with this cowardly example in mind, Meyer adds a cynical parting shot, which will be echoed dramatically in the early work of Nicholas Manuel. Apart from the high financial stakes in the bishop's position, Meyer charges that the prohibition of clerical marriage is supported by many priests because it permits them to have a variety of women: "It would be too hard for them to live contentedly with one legitimate spouse." [33]

The intensity of the clergy's resentment of arbitary episcopal intrusion into their domestic life can be seen in Römer's *Dialogue,* which is devoted to the plight of parish priests. His drama peaks with a confrontation between a protagonist priest and a greedy curate who refuses to permit absolution of the priest's sin of concubinage without prior payment of ten gulden or a silver cup (which a monastic informant has told the curate the priest possesses). The priest protests, "Who punishes the Fiscal because the children of his housekeeper live in his house?" When the argument reaches the point at which the curate demands twenty gulden or the priest's arrest, the priest declares:

> I'll give you not one pfennig. I am returning home, and if any of your men tries to stop me, I'll crack his skull open. If you send me another foolish citation, I'll ignore it. I'll have my Junker [a Lutheran lay protector] drown your messenger in his fishpond. Either you treat me right or be prepared for a fight! [34]

The protest of Römer's priest is one that Meyer might also have made directly against bishop Hugo, for the bishop of Constance was at the time himself living in concubinage with the widow of a former Bürgermeister.

The modern authority on Swiss clergy on the eve of the Reformation, Oskar Vasella, has accused Meyer of some exaggeration, but still leaves him a powerful case. Clerical marriage would have been a great financial loss to the bishop of Constance. According to canon law, clergy were punishable by fine for five sexual crimes: simple concubinage *(stuprum voluntarium),* rape *(stuprum violentum),* fornication, adultery, and incest. The basic concubinage fee was one and one-half to two gulden a year, with the relationship permitted to continue as the fee was paid. When a priest who lived in concubinage contracted another relationship (adultery or incest), additional fees were involved for absolution. Conscientiously confessed clerical philandering could be very expensive, and there is much evidence of such conduct among priests, bringing them into conflict with the laity and causing many even to carry weapons for their own protection.[35] Legitimation of children born in concubinage normally cost one gulden. Bishops, however, also held a "right of spoils" over the children of priests, which could also be purchased at a negotiated price. Understandably, priests did not take kindly to the prospect of the bishop becoming their heir through their children.[36]

Conflicts of conscience occurred not only over reporting and paying the fines for sexual misconduct but also over obeying suspensions meted out for failure to do so. Suspended priests continued their religious services. To clerical conflicts of conscience were added the frustration of laymen who were also subject to the church's marital laws. The generality of these laws led to many contested engagements (the problem of so-called clandestine marriages) and the regular injection of spiritual judgment and punishment into the domestic sphere. There is evidence of lay disenchantment to the point of refusing to receive the sacrament.[37] It was not accidental that the right and even duty of clerical marriage was accompanied in the Swiss Reformation by an end to the sacramental status of marriage and the rewriting of marriage laws.[38] Although no simple correlations have been found between clergy who became Protestant and "good" sexual conduct—Zwingli's example would suggest rather the opposite tendency—or between lay anti-clericalism and the sexual misconduct of clergy, evidence indicates that many individual priests joined the Reformation to escape the ecclesiastical regulations and penalties that encumbered their domestic life.[39] Zurich proponents of new marriage laws found a ready clerical and lay audience.

Meyer saw in the Reformation the promise of a religion "according to the simple doctrine of Saint Paul." [40] Try as the bishop of Constance might to defend present practices by appeals to councils, tradition, and the "thousand church laws, exceeding in size six Bibles, exclusive of the glosses," [41] the medieval church still "maintained Christians in bondage" and left both the laity and the clergy "angry, uncertain, and anxious." [42] The reform party was opposed, Meyer argued, because it had questioned such traditional authorities, "apprised Christian people of their freedom, and removed from their consciences such intolerable burdens." [43] And why did not all people rush immediately to such freedom? Meyer blames sheer self-interest. Many, he explains, advocate the removal of traditional tyrannies until they see that such also involves the loss of their traditional privileges. Bishops want to remove the pope's yoke, but not their own on others. Priests and monks like the idea of being free from vows until they learn from Scripture that they too are hypocrites who "deceive, oppress, and suck poor people dry." And nobles and rich citizens are ready to honor the gospel until they realize that it will bring an end to the revenues they derive from illegal taxes and tithes.[44]

A New Social Ethic

First generation Protestant clergy interpreted their ministry as an activity, not a passive sacramental state, and attached great importance to the approval of an immediate community of believers. To burghers who had fought to curtail clerical privileges and immunities it was an appealing prospect: clergy were to be quite secondary to the performance of their duty. Correspondingly, secular vocations too came to be measured in terms of service to the community at large. Valuewise, Protestants stratified society in the pragmatic and ethical terms of who best could serve his fellowman. Effectiveness of service to one's neighbor, not a set social or political status, was to be the measure of value and importance within society. In one sense this was a point of view compatible with a certain social conservatism; a change in vocation and wealth was not necessarily required in order to "rise" in society. Yet it was an argument that flattered the social ideals and aspirations of men and women who needed a change for the better. In the terms of Luther's famous treatise, being a "lord over all" was not incompatible with being a "servant to all." It was a vision that held out something for everybody. Improvement without upheaval was a concept of reform that could be as effectively promoted before magistrates as among burghers and peasants.

An early popular example of the new social ethic is a pseudonymous pamphlet, ascribed by some to the many-sided reformer of Saint Gall, Joachim Vadian, entitled *On the Old and the New God, Faith, and Doctrine* (1521). It went through eleven editions between 1521 and 1526 and was translated into Latin (1522), English (1522), East Frisian (1525), low German (1529), Flemish (1529), and Danish (1535).[45] The tract is divided into two parts. The first is a self-serving history of the church from the creation to the present, among the first examples of this genre. The author intends to demonstrate that the Protestant movement, under attack for dividing families and society, is in truth the recovered form of the old, original Christian religion.[46] The second part of the tract elaborates this primitive religion in twenty catechetical articles.

The tract skillfully summarizes the Lutheran *solae*—salvation by faith alone in Christ alone as revealed in Scripture alone—turning each against a religion of ceremonies and tradition.[47] But its peculiar distinction lies in an earnest effort to tie together the revived old religion and a present ethical renewal of society. The author makes several elaborations on this theme, employing somewhat puerile logic. In support of universal distribution of vernacular Bibles (article 13), the reading, understanding, and social performance of the gospel are interwoven thus:

> All should diligently learn to read and write so that each may read the Bible frequently, especially the gospel portion, both for himself and to his children, and especially on holidays. For the gospel has such power that the more deeply one reads it, the more one comes to understand God. And the more one understands God, the stronger becomes one's faith. And the stronger one's faith in God, the more one is moved to love his neighbor and heavenly values. Also the Bible is the greatest consolation on earth in time of adversity.[48]

It is in terms of the individual and social benefits of the old religion that preachers are praised as earth's greatest treasure, and with the aid of an organic metaphor that must surely have given the author's readers pause:

> When the preacher gives his congregation pure and wholesome grain, those gathered around the table eat pure and wholesome bread [the true Word of God]. As this bread is digested and absorbed into the body, the blood becomes pure and natural. Good blood creates a good temperament, a good temperament constant health, constant health good works, and good works praise and honor. . . . The understanding that comes from true preaching brings peace to a conscience burdened with questions and doubts. A sure and knowing conscience stands by God and Scripture as on solid rock, and can withstand any temptation. The constancy of a healthy conscience shapes and forms every worldly activity, and is the source of good works pleasing to God.[49]

The promised ethical fruits of the Protestant movement were especially the topic of the first tract of the Strasbourg reformer Martin Bucer, written in 1523. A new pastor's complaint about the absence in both church and state of a sense of vocational responsibility and community service, the tract's very title was an exhortation: *One Should Not Live for Oneself Alone But for Others, and How to Go About It.* Bucer wrote the tract as the result of a vocational shift of his own, from Dominican monk to Protestant agitator in Strasbourg. He had been a member of the Dominican order since 1506. However, after meeting Luther during the Heidelberg disputation of 1518, he moved steadily into the Protestant camp. On April 29, 1521, while a chaplain at the court of Friedrich von der Pfalz, he received, as he had formally requested, release from his monastic vows. Within a short time, while serving as a secular priest in Landstuhl, he illegally married Elisabeth Silbereisen. Bucer had just entered a new position in Weissenburg in the fall of 1523 when notice was received of his excommunication by the bishop of Speyer—the last in the chain of events that brought him finally to Strasbourg in May 1523, a haven that he assumed to be safe because his father was a citizen there. Bucer associated himself with the Protestant preachers of the city, holding lectures in the home of Matthew Zell, the leader of the Protestant party since 1521. The episcopal authorities sought Bucer's removal from the city on grounds of his recent banishment from the priesthood. But Bucer successfully pled his case and secured in June, 1523 the right to remain. By August he was preaching regularly from Zell's pulpit, and in the same month Strasbourg Protestants received conditional permission from a sympathetic government to "read and preach" openly.

One Should Not Live for Oneself Alone was written after these events and in direct response to the wishes of Bucer's admiring supporters for a full statement of what the new faith meant.[50] In it Bucer held out as the promise of the Reformation the emergence of a profoundly ethical society. Mixing traditional (mainly Thomist) and Lutheran concepts, Bucer sketches the original order of creation, depicting it as the arrangement of all things in such a way that each mutually serves the other as an instrument of divine goodness; in the beginning there was universal benevolence among all creatures. Although this order was destroyed by the Fall, in Bucer's hopeful estimation it is capable of restoration.[51] He accordingly declares that vocation to be the best which best promotes the recovery of this lost original state. Since the clergy by definition practice benevolence and guide men to higher spiritual ends, the Christian ministry is exalted as being theoretically worthy of such honor. But worldly government, which is mandated to promote the common good by maintaining law and order, may likewise partake of the honor, for, Bucer taught, worthy rulers, like the clergy, must deny themselves and look first to the general welfare of their subjects. Bucer draws from government's mandate in Romans 13 the obligation to rule the world according to "divine law." [52] He describes "heathen imperial law" and other positive laws as insufficient to fulfill the divine mandate of worldly government and promote the restoration of man's original end.[53] (Such laws did not at this time recognize Protestant beliefs and practices.) Bucer does not mean to suggest, however, that the Strasbourg magistracy should simply replace present laws with some prophetic vision or the Sermon on the Mount, although some scholars might lead one to that conclusion. His "theocratic" impulses, like Zwingli's, are rather designed to secure free concourse for Protestant doctrine and practice with the most potent arguments at hand.[54]

Having praised ministers and magistrates, Bucer proceeds to scold both for unprecedented corruption, accusing them of indulging their own self-interests and ignoring the common good.[55] The apostles of Christ he proclaims "apostles of Antichrist" and God's secular vicars—imperial law was foremost in Bucer's mind—"lions, bears, and wolves." [56] Bucer draws the most dire eschatological conclusion from their failing: as surely as spiritual and temporal welfare follow the faithful administration of these offices, so surely will spiritual and temporal ruin follow their godless maladministration.[57]

In a striking section that exploited burgher anti-clerical and anti-mercantile sentiment Bucer scolds parents for wanting their children to enter the monkhood or priesthood at a time when these had become the most dangerous (to the soul) and godless of vocations, or for wanting to send them to eternal death by rearing them to be merchants who, against God's command and Christian order, live without working and off the sweat of others—like the clergy! Presently, Bucer concludes, the "most Christian stations and occupations," those which do their neighbors the most good and cause the least harm, are not the priesthood and politics but "farming, raising cattle, and the handicraft trades." He urges parents to direct their children into these "more Christian" endeavors.[58] Certainly such sentiments made no small contribution to the fact that the large gardener's guild, which in many ways reflected the plight of the urban poor, was prominent among the groups that embraced Bucer and initially championed his tenure as pastor in Strasbourg.[59]

Bucer did not end on a negative note. Borrowing heavily from Luther's *Freedom of a Christian,* he extolls the power of the new faith to restore men to their original end. He assures his new congregation that simple faith and trust in Christ mean freedom from the selfishness that prevents men from loving their neighbors as themselves, and he foresees the faithful becoming as selfless in their service to one another as Christ had been in his self-sacrifice for all men.[60] Whereas the religious anxiety created by the medieval church had frustrated such good works, the new faith, he writes, conveys a certitude and security that make selfless action possible.[61] It is, Bucer concludes, as much the nature of faithful Christians to do good works and serve their neighbors selflessly as it is for birds to fly, fish to swim, and men to speak.[62]

This was Luther's message, but heavily weighted toward the promised ethical fruits of the psychological liberation of salvation by faith. Luther too had recently praised the ethical benefits of the new theology, for example, in his exposition of the *Magnificat* (1521) for Crown Prince John Frederick, wherein the Virgin Mary, no longer the *mater misericordiae* but now a Protestant model of faith, was made to draw from her marvelous pregnancy not a sense of superiority over the common lot, but the resolve to be an even better housekeeper than she was before! [63] As Protestants won a popular audience and began to make their bid for political support, the promised ethical consequences of the Reformation became increasingly prominent. In an age when only a small number of townsmen could realistically expect to better their position vocationally and economically, Protestants cast social mobility and rank in ethical terms. In Bucer's vision the new certitude of faith offered a renewed sense of vocational importance and responsibility to citizens, from the highest magistrate to the poorest burgher: Protestants would make the best citizens!

A similar message was disseminated among common folk in the town of Kitzingen in the anonymous *Sermon Against Idolatry by the Peasant Who Can Neither Read Nor Write* (1524). The author, Diepold Peringer (or Beringer), was accepted by Kitzingen authorities as an inspired peasant preacher. He was in fact a defrocked priest who had been a controversial popular preacher in the vicinity of Nürnberg and is thought to have participated in the Peasants' Revolt.[64] The sermon, one of several preached by Peringer in Kitzingen, is a believable account of the problems encountered by Protestant preachers in dealing with simple people. The tract presents itself as a faithful recording of a sermon preached to peasants by one who felt empowered to do so by his faith ("all the faithful are a kingly priesthood") rather than by any university training.[65] The peasants depicted in the tract have the greatest difficulty setting aside certain superstitious practices which impede their service to their neighbors. The message to them, while a bit folksier, is exactly the same as that to their more sophisticated urban counterparts, many of whom were simply displaced farmers in pursuit of urban trades. The sermon may well have circulated effectively among the latter.

The tract is a sustained censure of peasants for being such dupes, especially in their naive belief in the power of saints. After having had the gospel preached among them for two years, they still do not look simply to Christ and Scripture for their needs, but continue to parade the cross and pray to saints Marx, Leonard, and Wolfgang (apparently local saints), as if such devices would insure good weather and full harvests.[66] The author explains, "in language peasants understand," that saints are nothing but "decoy birds of the shorn people." Clergy use saints to attract simple folk into the "thornbushes," that is, the various shrines and cloisters, pilgrimages (the popular Saint James pilgrimage is mentioned), and ceremonies of the Roman church—arduous dead ends to temporal and eternal salvation.[67] The constructive alternative that emerges from the fire of Peringer's criticism eloquently states the new ethic of service to one's neighbor:

> Christ is as gracious a God to you in the fields as he is in the church. If you want to find him, go over to your neighbor's house where small children lie sick and hungry, and give them what you would otherwise uselessly squander or sacrifice to some idol [an image of Christ, Mary, or some saint], while running hither and yon. There you will not only find Christ and do what he has commanded you, but you will have done it even unto him.[68]

Farel's Sommaire

Early Protestants did not confine their work to ad hoc pamphlets and sermons. They also placed in the hands of the laity detailed guides, doctrine by doctrine and practice by practice, to reformed religion. The most important early example of such catechetical works in Guillaume Farel's *Summary and Brief Description of All that Is*

Necessary for Every Christian to Have Confidence in God and Help His Neighbor.

Farel has understandably stood in John Calvin's long shadow in the history of the Reformation in Geneva. This has had the unfortunate consequence of also obscuring his earlier, pre-Geneva work among the first generation of Protestant reformers, in particular that with Johannes Oecolampadius in Basel in the early 1520s. Farel holds the distinction of having written what was not only the first French Protestant catechism but also the first comprehensive Protestant instruction in the faith for a popular lay audience, the Basel edition of his forty-two-article *Summary* of 1525. A work of marked simplicity, it was republished five times in the sixteenth century (1529, 1534, 1538, 1542, and 1552) and reportedly revered by the Protestant laity almost as a symbolic writing.[69]

In 1516 Farel had joined the indigenous French reform party led by Jacques Lefèvre d'Étaples and centered in the court of the bishop of Meaux. As Calvin would later, Farel early became convinced that Lefèvre's circle would never achieve the full reform he desired, and in 1521 he aligned himself with the Lutheran movement.[70] In this capacity he engaged in several minor yet revealing literary projects in Basel prior to the writing of the *Summary.* He translated into French a catechetical work—*La Summe de l'escripture saincte*—by the rector of the school of the Brethren of the Common Life in Utrecht, Hinne Rode, in 1523. In early 1524 he issued a copy of a Parisian condemnation of the reform party of Meaux with his own scornful commentary. In August of the same year he published a no-longer-extant pocketbook exposition of the Lord's Prayer and the Creed for laymen. At about the same time he apparently drafted a baptismal liturgy, parallel to Oecolampadius's *Form und Gestalt* (1525) and an anticipation of his own later *Manière et fasson* (1533).[71]

In addition to these works, which may be considered preparatory to the *Summary,* Farel also posted for debate at the University of Basel in February, 1524, thirteen theses which he described in his preface to the reader as "propositions on which depend the whole of Christian liberty and which shatter the tyranny of human traditions." Like other early formulations of Protestant teaching, Farel's theses attacked religious practices and laws which lacked a foundation in Scripture, and they endeavored to redirect religious energy, now refocused by the new concept of faith, toward serving the neighbor and the community at large.[72] The success of the theses made Farel an important and respected figure among Protestants in Basel and elsewhere in the rapidly growing Protestant world. The thirteen propositions—a kind of abbreviated, academic *Summary*—encapsulate the Protestant position thus:

1. Christ has prescribed a definite rule of life to which one may neither add nor subtract.
2. Only those things ordained by God are to be practiced by the faithful. It is impious to add one's own or to live under precepts other than those given by Christ; and among the latter is the ordinance permitting those who cannot live continently to marry.
3. It is contrary to the light of the gospel to observe the Jewish customs of diversity in vestments, foods, and ceremonies.
4. Lengthy [endowed] prayers, which are not conformed to the rule of Christ, are instituted and recited with peril; it would be better to distribute the endowments for such prayers to the poor.
5. The most pressing need for priests is to apply themselves to the Word of God and seek nothing beyond it.
6. One should not rashly transform the precepts of Christ into [mere] counsels and his counsels into [strict] precepts, for such is the work of the Devil.
7. He defeats the gospel who renders it uncertain, and he despises Christ who does not sincerely teach the gospel, fearing God more than man.
8. He who hopes to save himself and be justified by his own efforts and not by faith, thinking he can raise himself to the level of God by his own free will, is blinded by impiety.
9. What is required above all is what the Holy Spirit inspires; the sacrifices of Christians must be offered only to God.
10. Those who are in good health and whose energy is not consumed by the service of the Word of God must, according to the teaching of the Apostle, work with their hands.
11. Christians must abstain not only from pagan bacchanals but also from Jewish hypocrisy in fasting and other practices which are not commanded by the Spirit; it is necessary above all that Christians not fall into idolatry.

12. What resembles Jewish traditions and obligations and tramples Christian liberty under foot must be suppressed by Christians.
13. We must take care that Christ, by whose power alone all things are governed, appear radiant among us. We are confident that this will happen if in all things we are conformed to the evangelical rule, and if all dissension . . . is suppressed by the peace of God . . . which dwells in our hearts.[73]

What is here said formally and in minuscule was vividly elaborated for a popular audience in the *Summary*. As one would expect in an instructional work, Farel devotes some time to abstract definitions (God, man, Jesus Christ, and so on), following in every case the biblical record. But the practical application of the new theology is his overriding concern, and the implications of the Protestant message for daily life surge steadily to the fore. Farel turns Reformation faith against Catholic teaching about such basic and, for his audience, immediate religious concerns as merit, the church, the power of the keys, the Mass, almsgiving (to the religious), the worship of saints, and annual confession. He employs no involved theological arguments, only matter-of-fact statements about motive and consequence patently designed to secure the popular mind.

The key to the new Protestant way of life is the new concept of faith with its almost brash security and certitude. Farel presents the following summary:

> Faith is a grand and singular gift of God, which makes us sons of God. It is an affection, an experience, and a true knowledge that God our father is good, perfect, powerful, and wise, and that he in his self-love has chosen us to be his sons, saving and redeeming us by our saviour Jesus. Faith does not doubt the holy promises of God . . . but, strengthened and confirmed by the word of him who cannot deceive, it judges and holds firm to what God has said against every human judgment, experience, and understanding. Assured by immutable truth and illumined by perfect clarity, it no longer fears anything.[74]

Before such faith "merit is a word full of arrogance, repugnant to God and Scripture, fabricated by a spirit of pride and error in order to reduce to nothing the grace of our Lord." The church becomes a "congregation of believers who by their faith are one body with Jesus Christ"—not "a diversity of hierarchies, laws, ordinances, and orders created by men." And the "keys to the kingdom of heaven"? They are "the knowledge of God, the Word of God, the holy gospel, and the care of souls, which only God and no man can give and entrust to another. . . . To him who truly believes heaven is open." [75]

The Mass takes an especially hard beating in the *Summary*. Farel does not dwell on the stock theological criticism that it diminishes Christ's historical sacrifice, although that is made clear,[76] but rather stresses what would be more immediate to a simple parishioner. He points out that whereas the true church is a union of believers, no one of whom is any higher than the other, the performance of the Mass is designed to reinforce the maximum difference between priest and people. "They say even that the priest [who resacrifices Christ] has more authority than all the angels, the Virgin Mary, and all the saints who dwell with Christ. And still they are bold to touch what he touches [the Eucharistic bread], although not to drink what he drinks [the denied Eucharistic cup]!" Farel further accuses the Mass of exploiting the poor, the old, and the orphaned, since endowed masses provide the "church of the pope" an occasion to heap up worldly goods for itself. "He [the priest] who must stand before the poor people of Jesus exhibits himself in rich habits and the most varied attire, having borrowed as much from infidels and pagans as from the ceremonies of the Jews." [77] Finally, Farel makes much of the fact that the Mass is in Latin:

> When Christian people come to the table of our Lord they should first read in a language understood by all some portion of holy Scripture. . . . But in the Mass all is chanted and performed in a language ordinary people cannot understand. Those who come to the Lord's table should also be incited to help the living poor, who are known to be in need and unable to earn a living. But in the Mass one is rather incited to give to those who have already departed the world, in the words of the priest, to help the dead pass through "purgatory," which is nothing but an invention of the devil and his ministers against holy Scripture.[78]

As for almsgiving, Farel acknowledges the obligation to aid the needy and handicapped—particularly those who are of the faith—

but not to subsidize "able-bodied priests, monks, and nuns" who have devised special rules and statutes to permit themselves to live at ease and off others in seclusion from the cares of the world. "To give to such as these is not almsgiving but rather their trip to the gallows, a sword for their execution, nourishment of their wickedness and state of perdition." [79] (While such exposés were very effective in winning popular support, it should be noted that they soon created problems for the young Protestant churches, whose leaders, having so scotched the traditional fund-raising devices of the medieval church, found themselves going hat in hand to established political power, with all the fateful consequences such subservience held.)

Farel criticizes the worship of saints as an idolatrous distraction from faith and the Word of God, and sees primarily monetary motives (solicitude of new endowments) behind the practice.[80] Annual confession he condemns as a "damnable institution," a practice established against faith and Scripture, asking of men the impossible and afflicting them with vain terror of conscience and uncertainty about God's grace. He exhorts, "Christians, leave the cruel tyranny of those who have placed unbearable burdens on your backs while lifting not a finger in your behalf, and come to him who has taken and bears our burdens upon his shoulders." [81] As for the satisfaction required of penitent Christians, Farel instructs the faithful not to look for it in the penalties imposed by priests in the confessional but in the simple faith and love of one's neighbor which thanksgiving to God for a gratuitous salvation produces.[82] Faith in "Dieu tresbon et tresmisericordieux pere" is the only security in the face of death. In the final article of the *Summary,* "The Day of Judgment," Farel, anticipating fateful developments in later Calvinism, cites again this simple faith and service to one's neighbor as the singular way the faithful may signal their "election":

> Let us look at how the elect, when the occasion calls for it and our Lord works in them, show that they are the children of God. It is done by that hypocrisy, that "papelardise," that mishmash of distinctions in days, meats, clothing, and places? But there one finds no sign of that hope in God which gathers the hearts of the elect and causes them to love, honor, and place their trust in God. Such hope is rather declared by a true love of one's neighbor.[83]

Farel devotes several articles to a mirror of the good pastor, who is made to contrast sharply with the priests of Rome. In imitation of Christ, he is said to serve rather than to be served by his congregation, edifying, instructing, and exemplifying in his person the pure and simple word of God.[84] His authority extends no farther than God's word, and he expects and deserves respect and obedience only so far as he manifestly agrees with Scripture.[85] While he is to be permitted no riches, the good pastor should not be left indigent, lacking the basic comforts required by his office and forced to "moonlight" for his modest livelihood; as Farel puts it, the people owe him "une moyenne suffisance pour vivre." [86]

Farel draws an interesting parallel between Rome's exclusion of its clergy from civil jurisdiction and its refusal to permit the clergy to marry. In both cases God-given ordinances and institutions—temporal government and the estate of marriage—are seen to be spurned and individuals tyrannized. He muses sarcastically, but also tellingly, of the new Protestant values, "But if one examines closely those to whom holy matrimony is forbidden, he may well conclude that it is to the honor of marriage. For I am not sure that I should give the name men to those who so deny everything human." [87]

The year 1525 was the year of the great peasants' uprising and a time when Anabaptist separatist notions were beginning to penetrate the cities; thus Farel's views in the *Summary* on the temporal sword were especially important. His catechism did not disappoint rulers worried about citizen revolt or apathy. Romans 13 is cited no less than six times in as many pages, as it is made clear that kings, princes, and rulers are God's special agents of temporal justice and bodily redemption, and are due unconditional obedience so long as their laws do not conflict with God's commandments.[88] This article on the temporal sword suggests the influence of Luther's *Freedom of a Christian* and tracts on temporal authority. Farel distinguishes the believer's movement according to the life of his soul and spirit, where there is equality in faith and deliverance from sin, death, and suffering, and according to the life of his body, where social differences still persist and one group is subject to another. Reminiscent of Luther's tracts on temporal authority, especially those addressed in 1524 to the rebelling peasants, is Farel's insistence that Christian freedom not be taken in a carnal sense, as releasing men from their legal subjection to lords and rulers. Farel also wrote the article on the temporal sword on the defensive against Catholic allegations that Protestant ideas were anarchy's midwife, as the following endorsement of temporal power and the social status quo makes clear:

> He who resists the power of the sword resists the ordinance of God. Faith and renewal of life do not challenge this subjection, and still less does the believer's baptism. Alas, I must still emphasize that those who were serfs and in physical bondage before their baptism are not by their baptism set free [from their lords], as the pope has written [against us]. For by the confession and promise to keep the law of our Lord which is made in his baptism, the serf also promises to serve his temporal lord as before—and in complete fidelity, not just in appearance, and even if his lord is an infidel.[89]

Farel also argues, ostensibly against incipient Anabaptist teaching, that Christians should not be led to believe that they may not serve in the government, have their own servants, or administer the sword of justice. Scripture, he maintains, mandates all these things as forms of service to one's neighbor.[90]

As events forced their hand and passive acceptance of higher authority threatened their survival (as was the case especially after the Diet of Augsburg in 1530), Protestants, including Luther, endorsed active political resistance to imperial (papal) forces in the name of self-defense.[91] In the beginning, however, their concern was to reassure local and territorial rulers—initially even the emperor himself[92]—that religious reformation was no political revolution against established authority. There was to be social improvement without social upheaval. The promise of Protestant preachers was the promise of a society no longer burdened psychologically or socially by religion, a community in which religious energies and endowments directly served the common good.

Lay Defenses of the Reformation

Lazarus Spengler

Lazarus Spengler became court clerk in Nürnberg in 1496 and by 1507 had advanced to the office of town clerk *(Ratsschreiber)*, an important bureaucratic post in the sixteenth century. Because of the frequent rotation of Bürgermeister and council members and the latter's preoccupation with their own as well as the city's business interests, the city clerk came to represent continuity in government; mindful of past policy, he was a trusted adviser on present policy.[93] Spengler also moved early in reform-minded cultural and religious circles. He was a close friend of the Nürnberg humanists Albrecht Dürer and Willibald Pirckheimer, and a member of the lay-religious *Sodalitas Staupitziana*, named after Luther's spiritual mentor Johannes von Staupitz, who, together with the Lutheran preacher Wenceslaus Linck, preached to the group during the years of the Reformation's theological genesis. Both affiliations prepared Spengler for Luther's ideas. Nürnberg humanists greeted the indulgence controversy of 1517 as something of a repetition of the still simmering Reuchlin affair and were thus very sympathetic to Luther. Through his position as city clerk Spengler was also privy to the city's challenge of the episcopal courts and efforts to curb the clerical abuse of the right of asylum—important political pre-conditions of the Reformation in Nürnberg. In 1514 the city had purchased from the bishop of Bamberg full rights of patronage over two parish churches and had also undertaken a strict supervision of local monasteries; these were movements into the ecclesiastical sphere which created tension with the bishop.[94]

By 1519, after Luther had burned his bridges to the old church in the Leipzig debate with Johann Eck, it was no longer possible to straddle the Luther question. Spengler's defense of Luther's teaching in 1519 was a testimony to this year of individual decision. Published in Augsburg by Sylvan Ottmar (who also published a second, enlarged edition in 1520), it was immediately embraced and circulated by Luther. It appeared in the first collection of Luther's German writings, which was assembled in Basel and published in May, 1520, as a popular instruction in true Christian doctrine. Spengler's *Defense* formed the nineteenth and concluding selection in the collection, and bore the description, "a beautiful, true, and gallant confirmation of M. Luther's teaching."[95] As a layman's reading of Luther's message for laymen, it is a revealing commentary on lay perception of the Reformation at its inception.

Spengler first insists in the *Defense* that Luther's doctrine and preaching are "conformed to Christ, evangelical teaching, and Christian laws." Here he meets head-on what was to be the most basic criticism of the Reformation, soon to be spread abroad in anti-Lutheran pamphlets and especially to haunt Luther's mind after the Diet of Worms: the accusation that Luther errantly and most arrogantly pitted lone individual judgment against centuries of unanimous ecclesiastical tradition. Spengler's answer became a model for subsequent Lutheran apologists. He protests to the contrary that no such clear and unanimously accepted body of truth has ever existed in the church, that the meaning of Scripture has always been disputed, and that past theologians were no more immune to error than Luther.[96]

Spengler's second point is a personal testimony to what he himself found most appealing in Luther's teaching. He describes Lutheran doctrine as "conformed to what one would expect of a Christian way of life *[Christliche Ordnung]* and to reason." Never, he confesses, has he found ideas that have so gripped his mind; and he reports the concurrence of "many high and learned persons, laymen and clergy alike," who have relayed to him their gratitude to God for letting them live long enough to hear Luther and his teaching. The evangelical simplicity and reasonableness of Luther's theology stands in starkest contrast to the practices of the medieval church: the numerous pointless ceremonies; the use of the confessional to create new scruples and anxiety in the hearts of the faithful; the financial abuses and false religious security of indulgences; laws which burden souls with such trivial matters as fasting on Fridays; and the excommunication of innocent and guilty alike for even minor offenses, local examples of which Spengler has in mind. Over against "those who have preached dreams to us" and promoted their doctrine more by threat of force than by Scripture and honest reasoning, Spengler presents Luther's way as the most welcome liberation:

> To my mind, and as I think any rational man will easily see, Luther has removed such scruples and errors with sound Christian evidence of holy, divine Scripture; and for this we owe him well-earned praise and thanks.[97]

Such is the basic message of Spengler's 1519 *Defense.* He returned to it again later in the *Defense*, avowing that no well-meaning person who had heard Luther's preaching could honestly say that he had not experienced forthwith "release from many troublesome errors and scruples that have plagued his conscience." He accuses the priests of Rome, by contrast, of having transformed the mild yoke of the gospel into a terrible burden, multiplying sins and promising through indulgences a peace which is no peace, creating more anxiety than consolation and more despair than confidence, and turning men to God in fear and trembling rather than in love and trust.[98]

What Luther represented to a pious layman like Spengler was the achievement of inner freedom and release. The possibility of that achievement was to be a universal religious attraction of the Reformation to both learned and illiterate laymen alike. The laity did not receive the original Protestant message so much as a denial of the possibility of salvation by good works and religious ceremonies but as the removal of the *necessity* of salvation by good works and religious ceremonies.

This latter point was especially prominent in a second tract Spengler wrote in Luther's defense, entitled *The Main Doctrines by Which Christendom Has Until Now Been Deceived.* It was published in Wittenberg in 1522 and circulated under the name of Nicholas von Amsdorf, one of Luther's closest and most loyal associates. Amsdorf introduced and concluded the tract, which he tells the reader was written by a "knowing layman" *(eyn verstendiger Ley),* who for his own safety must remain anonymous.[99] Amsdorf, ever wordy, prefaced the tract with his own litany of burdensome doctrines: denial of marriage to priests; prohibition of foods to the laity; charging fees for absolution; making clerical concubinage a greater sin than clerical whoring; and punishing the laity more severely for breaking a fast or taking the Eucharistic cup than for adultery.[100]

The Main Doctrines (which Spengler dedicated to Frederick the Wise) explicates four interrelated doctrines by which Christendom had allegedly been led astray. The first is the belief in free will—that men can do good works and initiate their own salvation.[101] On this premise, Spengler argues, is built the second false doctrine—that salvation is to be sought by good works, especially by such apparent good works as "going on pilgrimages, securing indulgences, building churches, endowing cloisters, masses, anniversaries and like ceremonies, making great offerings, decorating churches, and fasting." All of these, Spengler protests, distract from the works that are "truly good and useful" to one's neighbor and that flow from faith and trust in

God.[102] He adds the third misleading doctrine: the authority of tradition, which he considers to be the masquerading of human commands as divine commands. Spengler accuses church teaching of having made the abuse of a religious holiday or the breaking of a fast a more serious moral matter than adultery, blasphemy, and harming one's neighbor.[103] He draws from these three doctrines a practical conclusion: when men are taught the power of free will and the necessity of good works, and the latter are defined arbitrarily by human tradition, such teaching contrives to alarm the consciences of men so that they will see no way to salvation except the payment of money, the performance of apparent good works, and the purchase of indulgences:

> Is not the entire Roman church so shot through with money traps that one can find no escape? Christian hearts are there so terrified by alleged mortal sins, the threat of the ban, requirements of "Christian obedience," and the like that in fear of conscience they seek to free themselves by money, external works, and special gifts *[iarmerckten]*, forgetful of the refuge, consolation, and blessing of Christ where indulgence is found.[104]

Spengler suggests the following criteria for distinguishing God's commands from those of men. The former always teach one to trust only in Christ, to stop worrying about oneself, and to be concerned only for one's neighbor;[105] the latter, by contrast, always turn one to external works, self-seeking, fear of (eternal) pain, and hope for a future reward.[106]

The final false doctrine explicated in the tract concerns the traditional division of the gospel into "counsels" (for the clergy) and "precepts" (for the laity)—an expression of the medieval distinction of the clerical and lay estates and belief in the religious superiority of the former.[107] Spengler accuses this distinction of subjecting laymen to clerical canons if they aspire to be perfect Christians in this life. "All are encouraged to attain the highest perfection as if no one can be pious or blessed unless he is a member of the religious." [108] He discerns also an imposition of clerical values upon laymen in the church's regulation of their clothing, food, songs, and reading. Against all such impositions he advises:

> Believe in Christ and do for your neighbor as you believe Christ

has done for you. That is the singular way to become pious and blessed; there is no other.[109]

Jörg Vögeli

Before its chief theological architect, Ambrosius Blarer, was actively on the scene, the work of reform in Constance had been effectively promoted by three local preachers: Jacob Windner, Johannes Wanner, and Bartholomäus Metzler. The defense of their work, in particular that of Metzler, became the topic of a major tract, dated February 20, 1524, by the city clerk of Constance, Jörg Vögeli. Vögeli began as a minor civil servant in Constance in 1503 and progressed through a variety of bureaucratic posts before becoming city clerk in 1524.[110] His defense of the preacher Metzler —"a defense by a lay burgher"—was preceded by several letters in support of Luther.[111] It was written in reply to thirty-three articles against Metzler issued by the office of the bishop of Constance. These articles were based on critical reports received by the bishop from members of Metzler's own congregation. They thus represent both an official and a popular reading—or misreading, as Vögeli will sometime argue—of original Protestant teaching in the city.

Vögeli treats the articles against Metzler thematically in seven groups. The first are those which accused Metzler of having excited citizens to civil disobedience, the nonpayment of tithes, and the removal of treasures and decorations from city churches. Vögeli denies the first two accusations outright, but concedes that Metzler had sanctioned a certain proper neglect of church treasures and decorations by urging the faithful to look first to the "upkeep and decoration" of the "living temple" which is their neighbor rather than to furnishings for the church.[112] Here again we see the strong emphasis on ethics and deemphasis of social upheaval that was typical of the early Protestant self-portrayal.

A second group of articles accuse Metzler of opposing clerical vows and civic oaths and denying the obligation to fulfill the last wishes of the dying. Vögeli admits that Metzler had opposed celibacy (Metzler was to marry in 1525). According to Vögeli, however, Metzler questioned civil oaths only in the sense that God rather than man must be obeyed should the two ever come into conflict; and even then disobedience to an earthly sovereign was to be only passive in form. Vögeli praises Metzler for his public opposition to the practice of deathbed endowments of masses made in fear by the dying, who superstitiously hope thereby to move more rapidly through purgatory. Metzler rather taught that masses and sacraments served only the living and present recipients and did the dead no good.[113]

The third complaint against Metzler was that he had rejected traditional practices and ceremonies like the canonical hours, alms, anniversaries, candles, masses, bells, and vigils for the dead. Vögeli points out that Metzler here opposed making formal ceremonies out of what should rather be individual habits of piety, especially when the impression existed that participation in such ceremonies brought divine favor and nonparticipation divine disfavor.[114] He elaborates sarcastically:

> My brother, how much divine favor can you expect to gain from mumbling the canonical hours, endowing great benefices and churches, ringing many bells—why does one not beat as many drums?—or by smearing the forehead with oil, which is called confirmation, and other such human inventions, when [according to 1 Cor. 13] speaking with all tongues, chastizing the body even unto death, giving away all earthly goods, and having faith strong enough to remove mountains cannot make one pleasing to God in terms of the sure faith and love of God and man which are required? [115]

For Metzler and his defender Vögeli, what has no basis in Scripture may be ignored in good conscience, indeed, for the sake of a good conscience. The following list of items is presented by Vögeli as falling within this category, and it demonstrates once again the degree to which the Reformation transformed at the popular level the most routine religious concepts and practices of the medieval church, with an eye to maximum simplification and even a certain desacralizing of religious life. According to the Protestant preachers of Constance, Christians can and should dispense with the "pope's Mass"; invocation of the saints; the "scarecrow of purgatory"; the sacrament of extreme unction; the sacrament of holy orders; the blessing of monks, nuns, and their orders; the consecration of churches, cemeteries, chalices, clothes, crucifixes, lights, salt, and water; special altar cloths; special vestments for priests celebrating Mass; the practice of fasts, feasts, "and numerous like superstitions, of which a special abomination is the baptism of bells by suffragan bishops, which makes a mockery of true baptism."[116] A close and contemporaneous parallel to Vögeli's list of dispensable practices and ceremonies appeared in a treatise by the Strasbourg reformer Wolfgang Capito, written on the occasion of the split between Luther and Andreas Karlstadt over the role of externals in the religious life. Capito sanctioned no iconoclasm, but he was as forthright as Vögeli and Metzler in citing practices that reformed Christians must henceforth put aside. Again one is struck by the consistency of early Protestant complaints:

> Since we are saved by grace and not by works, and since the papal church has pursued salvation by many physical exercises, it follows that the papal church and all its contrived practices are against Christ and disinherited by God, according to Matthew 15—I mean such things as the Mass; singing, reading, and piping the canonical hours; the consecration of priests, churches, salt, and other things; praying for departed souls and seeking aid from departed saints; revering images; going to confession; performing works of satisfaction for sin; distinguishing times, foods, and places; and other things I could mention.[117]

The fourth group of articles answered by Vögeli in Metzler's defense concerned the latter's opposition to the sacrament of holy orders and promotion of clerical marriage. Vögeli, a master of the Protestant arguments on this issue, suggests that Metzler had in fact failed to go far enough in exposing the practice of consecrated celibacy, which Vögeli characterizes as exceeding in perversity anything done by the Sodomites.[118] A related group of articles criticized Metzler for ascribing the power of the keys to heaven as much to every Christian as to the pope, cardinals, and other bishops and prelates. Vögeli retorts that Metzler did believe that the power of binding and loosing belonged to the church, but to the "universal Christian church" *(die Christliche kirche in gmain),* not the church as narrowly conceived in Rome. The priesthood, Metzler taught, was not a special dignity, superior in spiritual power to the state of ordinary Christians; it was but an "administrative office" through which priests prayed for, preached to, taught, and punished their parishioners.[119] Priestly power is a matter of "knowing Scripture in the Spirit," not the gift of a special sacrament of holy orders.[120] Vögeli adopts a striking analogy to drive home his point both to his addressee, Dr. Johann Schlupff, a pastor in Ueberlingen who had initiated the process against Metzler, and to the ordinary citizen of Constance: as all citizens of a free city, by virtue of their citizenship, may be said to be the Bürgermeister, each theoretically capable of filling this office when called upon to do so, so all who believe in Christ, by virtue of their baptism and faith, are inwardly priests and may fulfill the office of the priesthood outwardly if called upon to do so.[121]

The sixth group of articles accused Metzler of denying all but three sacraments: baptism, marriage, and the Eucharist. Vögeli protests that Metzler was not so unaware of Scripture as to make marriage a sacrament, and he reiterates the Protestant conviction that only two signs of God's promise of grace and forgiveness can be documented in Scripture, baptism and the Eucharist.[122]

Finally, the bishop's articles had censured Metzler for opposing the worship of Mary and the saints, complaining that Metzler had even compared the Virgin to ordinary wives and washerwomen. Vögeli defends Metzler's respect for Mary and the saints, but points out that Metzler rightly did not—any more than did the Virgin herself—look upon Mary as a Diana who required special prayers and divine honors.[123] Belief in saintly intercession to supplement Christ's mediation between God and man is characterized by Vögeli as "beneath child's talk." [124]

Vögeli's defense of Metzler went far toward spelling out the peculiar institutional consequences of Protestant theology. Vögeli saw the Reformation as driving burdensome superstitions of the old church not only out of the mind's eye, but also off the streets and byways of Constance.

Opposition to alleged "childish superstition" and religious practices that distract from useful service to one's neighbor is also the theme of a contrived contemporaneous *Letter of a Young Student in Wittenberg to His Parents in Swabia Written in Defense of Lutheran Doctrine* (1523). The Reformation's division of families provides the background for this anonymous pamphlet. The author is depicted as a student smitten by Lutheranism and recently transferred from the University of Leipzig to the University of Wittenberg. His pious Catholic parents, fearing for his spiritual and physical safety in the citadel of Lutheranism, have written begging him to leave at once.

His mother has even sent along a little wax lamb as a protective charm. The student's reply is an effort to enlighten his parents in the more advanced religious thinking of the Reformation.

Like his modern counterpart, he does not go about his task with an abundance of tact and charm. Fasting, pilgrimages, confession, festivals, vigils, praying the rosary, endowing masses and churches he bluntly dismisses as inventions of greedy clergy and false ways to heaven. The parents are informed that the only God-pleasing work one can do is to trust God and help one's neighbor. Nonmeritorious ethical acts are set in the place of special religious good works. "A truly faithful man does every good work, not for God's benefit or to be saved, but for the good of his Christian neighbor, out of true brotherly love." God is said to be most pleased by normal vocational activity; farming, or any other physical labor, and raising a family are presented as being a thousand times more pleasing to God than seventy ascetic years in a cloister as a monk or nun.[125] Along these lines the cult of the saints is opposed; God rather wants men to devote themselves to the "saints" who live in their midst—their poor, sick, and persecuted fellowmen.[126] The pamphlet concludes with the student declaring the father's defense of the old church to be undocumented in Scripture—a conclusion, the father is assured, based on a careful study of his letter by several learned Wittenberg theologians. To his mother the student politely explains that he must return the protective charm, and he begs her to stop trusting in such fantasy, magic, heresy, ghosts of the Devil, and superstition *(fantasey, zauwberey, ketzerey, Teüffels gespennszt, Aberglawben)*.[127]

In these few examples the Protestant message is presented by and to the laity as inner freedom from religious superstition and its many anxieties and as a new ethic of social service. The Reformation appears as an enlightenment. The special religious works and ceremonies of the medieval church are criticized as psychologically burdensome and socially useless in contrast to Reformation sponsorship of natural and useful service to one's neighbor through ordinary lay vocations. The reader senses a pervasive forswearing of earnest involvement in that which is abstract and artificial. Jacob Schenk, a Lutheran layman in Stauffenberg, put it very bluntly. Writing to his sister-in-law in defense of his wife's conversion to Lutheranism he complained that the traditional Mass "made monkeys" out of the laity. The congregation rises and sits, speaks and gestures, in imitation of the priest without fully understanding what is meant. "So we are made to act like monkeys; for what a monkey sees he also does." [128]

The Clergy As Citizens

Protestants broke down the medieval distinction between clergy and laity not only by permitting the clergy to enter the estate of marriage, but also by having them assume many of the duties of citizenship. The Protestant "priesthood of all believers," which enhanced the importance of secular life and vocations, also had a reverse effect. If it "sanctified" the laity, it also worked to "secularize" the clergy. If lay Christians were now to be a "priesthood," clerics were expected to enter certain estates of the laity.

Early Protestant sentiment on this score was especially strong. Urbanus Rhegius extrapolated from the priesthood of all believers that clergy should have no special "power, laws, possessions, honor, or glory." [129] The priesthood of all believers, which allowed only one egalitarian religious association (the local church), also inspired Protestant attacks on confraternities. In Protestant eyes, confraternities were only lay efforts to imitate clergy, to create separate and allegedly superior religious groups. In a brisk popular pamphlet Jacob Strauss posed the "true confraternity" of the church against "contrived" lay-religious confraternities thus:

> Christ wants a community based on faith and every good work. The contrived confraternities have special services in which only chosen members may participate.
>
> Christ requires no money for entrance into the community of the saints, only faith, hope, and love. Confraternities admit no one without dues or payments.
>
> Christ wants men to give what they do not need for their own upkeep to the needy poor who cannot fend for themselves. Confraternities ignore the poor and endow unnecessary worship services.
>
> Christ wants the hungry fed. Confraternities squander enough on the Founder's Day celebrations alone to support many poor workers and their families for a week.

> Christ wants us to avoid drunkenness and gluttony. On Founder's Day confraternity members, stuffed and inebriated, can be seen singing, dancing, and jumping in the air.
>
> Christ wants the naked clothed. Confraternities clothe idols and poles with silver and gold.
>
> Christ wants the poor housed. Confraternities buy up houses to rent for their own profit.
>
> Christ wants us to lend and share with the poor without expectation of repayment. Confraternities ignore the poor and lend only to the rich at great profit.
>
> Christ wants all Christians to have hearts aglow with faith. Confraternities burn long thick candles in broad daylight, as if they were trying to consume the heavenly lights of God and the saints.[130]

Nicolaus Reneyssen lumped together in un-Christian exclusiveness and divisiveness "sects, mobs, religious orders, and confraternities." [131] The extreme of Protestant sensitivity to the traditional distinction between clergy and laity may be seen in Philip Melhofer's sixty-page line-by-line exposé of the canon of the Mass as an essay on lay inferiority.[132]

Protestant ministers accordingly renounced traditional clerical privileges and immunities and assumed many of the normal responsibilities of citizenship. In doing so they formed a late stage in a lay movement which well antedated the Reformation. Although the clergy were never to be citizens as other citizens were citizens—they were, for example, excluded from holding public office[133]—they did pledge allegiance to their cities, pay certain taxes, and become completely subject to the civil law code. This was true even when, as in the case of Luther in Wittenberg, Zwingli in Zurich, and Calvin in Geneva (until late in his life), citizenship was not formally acquired.[134] The new social position and basic obligations of clergy as citizens were recognized even when formal legal status was not conferred. Exclusion from public office and like measures which kept clergy a group apart were considered by neither side to be an unfair truncating of the new position of clergy. It was a situation in which good fences made good neighbors. Having won independence from episcopal sees, city councils were not ready to encourage Protestant "papacies" to take their place. And Protestant reformers did not want their open courtship and dependence upon politicians to be stretched to the point of placing themselves in the position of having to obey man rather than God.

Although the citizenship of Protestant ministers may be said to reflect rather than to have created the signs of the time, the Protestant clergy also became citizens by their own important theological sanctions. Their praise of civic life and virtues and clerical subjection thereto was frequent and fateful. Strasbourg is an outstanding case in point. In August, 1524, the government of Strasbourg moved to take over the appointment of parish priests and to subject each to an oath of allegiance to the city. By the end of the year forty-five clerics had acquired citizenship; on January 16, 1525, all resident clerics were ordered to assume the responsibilities of citizenship.[135] This action was supported both before and after the fact by the Protestant reformers of Strasbourg, and by none more strongly than an important recent convert, Wolfgang Capito, provost of the chapter of Saint Thomas. Capito, a skilled Hebraist and holder of doctorates in canon law and theology, had long been close to Erasmus and Ulrich von Hutten. From 1519 to 1522 he served as cathedral preacher and troubleshooter for Luther's foe in the indulgence controversy, Archbishop Albrecht of Mainz.[136]

As provost of Saint Thomas, Capito was something of a prize catch for the Protestants when he joined their cause in 1523. He purchased citizenship on July 9, 1523, and thereafter wrote two defenses of clerical citizenship, one more personal and preceding the government order (October/November, 1523), a second more general and in support of government action (December, 1524). In both tracts the assumption of the responsibilities of citizenship by the clergy was treated as a patent duty, demanded by conscience, and one that Capito claimed to have long urged upon his disinclined fellow priests. He described it as an "honorable" *(erbarkeit)* and "reasonable" *(billigkeit)* thing to do. "With door and nail the city encloses and protects us, and we enjoy all its privileges. Why should we want therefore to escape its obligations?"[137] Clerical freedom from the responsibilities of citizenship is characterized as living off the sweat of others, burdening rather than serving the community. Work is a mode of brotherly love, chides Capito; the clergy especially should know that Christians are servants of others, not lords to be waited on hand and foot.[138] Priestly freedom from civic obligations is "against God, against the love of one's neighbor, against all sense of fair play, against human nature and reason, and detrimental to the community at large." [139]

Capito marshalled evidence from Scripture and local history. Clerical citizenship, he wrote, is part of what the Bible means in Romans 13 and 1 Peter 2 when it enjoins Christians to be subject to the governing authorities.[140] That surely endeared Strasbourg Protestants to the magistracy! Capito also called attention to past precedents of clerical citizenship in Strasbourg—isolated cases undertaken on a formal quid pro quo basis—which he felt to have diminished the novelty of his action.[141] He saw no insult to ecclesiastical authority in the practice, as opponents argued; just because the pope, bishops, and priests ceased being "treated as gods," he wrote, it did not forbode the end of peace, Christian obedience, heaven and earth.[142] And against those who accused him of breaking his priestly oath to give up the things of the world when he became a citizen, he bluntly protested that God surely obliged no man *not* to love his neighbor and dismissed any oath that so inclined as "in error, unjust, dishonest, and nonbinding." [143]

In 1524 the later Nürnberg reformer (after 1525) and recently resigned Augustinian monk, Wenceslaus Linck, spoke to the issue of clerical citizenship in a tract entitled *Whether Clergy Are Also Obligated to Pay Taxes and Rents and Bear Other Common Burdens.* Linck lumped together clergy and nobility as those who plotted to withhold from Caesar (Matthew 22) his just due by putting all financial burdens on "citizens, farmers, and the common man *[burger pawen und gemeyen man],* who [unlike them] must pay taxes, rents, tribute, tithes, etc." [144] Those who most burden others are described as being the least burdened members of society. Clergy are accused of promoting the illusion of separateness and special "spiritual right" by use of great titles and ceremonial pomp; claiming "all kinds of exemptions and privileges from heaven" they make themselves "sacred cows." [145]

Against clerical claims to special privilege Linck turned the Lutheran doctrine of the two kingdoms, which stressed the equal responsibility of all men to two interrelated spheres of life. The laity are praised as presently excelling the clergy in both; they are the better citizens of the world and the better members of the church.[146]

Worldly government is given higher marks for its support of the legitimate ends of spiritual power than the latter is given for promoting the God-given rights of secular power. Linck concluded that a basic decision was at hand: "Either this gospel [Romans 13] is to be suppressed, or all the exemptions of their [the clergy's] spiritless law must fall away." [147] The Nürnberg magistracy, renowned for running one of the tightest Protestant ships of state, did not choose to suppress the gospel.

Linck was not the only regular cleric to defend clerical citizenship while in flight from his religious vows. Ambrosius Blarer, the reformer of Constance, is another important example, especially since his early views on this matter became a guideline for the later dissolution of monasteries in Constance. Blarer had left a Benedictine monastery in Alpirsbach in July, 1522, and shortly thereafter addressed the magistracy of Constance in defense of his action. He was a member of a powerful patrician family and even petitioned to be heard by the council "as a kinsman and a fellow citizen." [148] Blarer characterized the setting aside of monastic vows as a matter of conscience and God's honor and traced his own decision to Luther's writings. "The works of this man," he confessed, "have advanced and secured my understanding of Holy Scripture more than all the books I have read from my youth up." Far from having bad ethical consequences, encouraging iconoclasm, or exciting revolution, as critics charged, "by no other doctrine are men's hearts so deeply stilled and satisfied in God." [149]

Blarer cast his complaints against monasteries in terms of suggested reforms. If there are to be monasteries they should have no laws that are not based on clear biblical commands, nor should souls in monasteries be burdened by sins that are not sins before God (here Blarer had especially in mind individual cases "reserved" to abbots). Inexperienced youths should be made fully aware of what they can expect if they enter a monastery. Andreas Karlstadt, the author of the first Protestant tract against monastic vows (1521), had complained that "celibacy very often destroys boys." [150] Blarer's conclusion was no less severe and surely caught the ear of many a patrician parent like his own with a son or daughter in the cloister: "I have learned very well, more from others than from myself, what anxious insecurity and spiritual death *[sorgklich gefärlichkeit und seelmord]* are brought about by lightly taken vows and eternal pledges." [151]

Blarer's tract is but a mild criticism when compared to the vow-by-vow description of the decision of the prior and members of Saint Anne's convent in Augsburg to laicize themselves. The vow of poverty, they professed, led them to live off the sweat of others, contrary to the command of Saint Paul. "We should not sit around idly, waiting for baked doves to fly into our mouths. Work, yes, work is what men must do, each according to his ability, in service to his fellowman. Idleness is forbidden; there is nothing Christian in contemplation." [152] As for the vow of obedience, they shamefully confessed themselves obedient only to their prior, not, as Romans 13 instructed, to worldly government. They described themselves as being in truth "the least obedient of people," and praised the laity for their faithful subjection to God's hierarchies of obedience—man and wife, parents and children, lords and subjects—as instructed by the Bible. The group also denied that enforced chastity was superior to the estate of marriage and renounced this vow as "unjust and against God" for all except those very few to whom God grants this special gift.[153] A touching, if perhaps exaggerated, summary drew the conclusion: "Who has lived less according to Christ's order than we? Ours is no 'order'; we have rather lived in a 'disorder' *[unordnung]!*" [154] Clergy were subjected to the work ethic, and no human activity was to be more pleasing to God than the physical, secular labor of the laity.

Of such praise of the lay estate was Protestant popularity made. The Protestant movement was an unprecedented religious flattering of secular life. It is not without insight that contemporary Protestants, among them the late Karl Barth, have spied in the Reformation's attack on clerical vows the seeds of what they critically call "culture Protestantism"—a modern Protestant infatuation with the secular world to the point of uncritically accepting it. Before his death Barth even entertained the notion that Protestants might save themselves from such secular absorption by reconsidering the Reformation's negative judgment on monastic life! [155] But the sixteenth-century destruction, in concept and in practice, of the distinction between clergy and laity was both too thorough and too culturally absorbed to permit easy Protestant reversion to so medieval a practice.

Driving the Message Home: Popular Writers and Humorists

Few movements have been assisted by a more able group of popular writers than the Protestant Reformation. It not only had a new medium (printing) and a new message, it also had supporters who knew how to communicate with laymen in the most effective way. Among the very best were Johann Eberlin von Günzburg, Pamphilus Gengenbach, and Nicholas Manuel,[156] each of whom had a secure place in history before he lifted his pen in support of the Reformation during the last years of his life.

Eberlin (d. 1533) was a Franciscan preacher in Basel, Freiburg, Tübingen, and Ulm. He broke with his order and joined the Reformation in 1521, having been intellectually converted by Luther's Reformation treatises of 1520, especially the *Address to the Christian Nobility of the German Nation.* Thereafter Eberlin traveled throughout Germany and Switzerland, pausing now and then in Basel, Leipzig, Wittenberg (where he spent the year 1522 with Luther and Melanchthon), and Ulm, finally settling in 1525 in Wertheim am Main, where he organized the Reformation for Count Georg II and wrote the earliest Wertheim church ordinance. Like the *Address to the Christian Nobility* which appears most directly to have inspired it, Eberlin's *Fifteen Confederates* (1521) contains much late medieval reform sentiment. But also like the *Address to the Christian Nobility* it is well in transition from traditional reform sentiment to the revolutionary changes of the Reformation.[157] The *Fifteen Confederates* is in fact the most ambitious early statement of a Protestant religious and social program, a veritable Protestant "Utopia" set forth at the inception of the Reformation. Luther and Zwingli may well have read it with a feeling of inferiority.

Gengenbach (d. 1525) was an established Basel publisher and noted author of popular moral and satirical writings. He holds the distinction of being the earliest dramatic poet of the sixteenth century in the German language. Nourished by the reform tradition of Geiler von Kaisersberg, Jacob Wimpfeling, Sebastian Brant, Erasmus, and his future Catholic foe Thomas Murner, Gengenbach was influenced to join the Protestant movement by Eberlin. A zealous convert—he did not hesitate to put even Luther in his place[158]—Gengenbach came to see the Reformation as the fulfilment of late medieval prophecies of reform. His *Novella* (1523), a popular response to Murner's magisterial indictment of Protestants, was considered by contemporaries to be one of the most humorous Reformation satires.

Manuel (d. 1530) was a painter of high talent, known especially for his great *Dance of Death* in the Dominican cloister in Bern. He served in the Bernese large council from 1512 to 1528 and was the provincial governor of Erlach (after 1523), where he promoted the Reformation. He had a hand in convening the disputation of 1528, which brought Bern officially into the Protestant fold, and during the remaining two years of his life he oversaw the Bernese Reformation as a member of the small council, representing the city and the Protestant cause in more than thirty diets and conferences. Like Gengenbach, who greatly influenced his late-blooming career as a writer, Manuel was a very practical, nontheoretical lay author. Like Eberlin he participated directly in every stage of the Reformation's progression, from pamphlet propaganda to popular movement to institutionalized religion. His first *Fastnachtsspiel, Those Who Feed Upon the Dead: Concerning the Pope and His Priesthood,* was performed during Lent, 1523, in the Kreuzgasse in Bern.[159]

The Protestant "Utopia" of Eberlin von Günzburg

The *Fifteen Confederates* is a collection of fifteen pamphlets that appeared in Basel individually and in rapid succession during and after the imperial diet in Worms where Luther took his famous stand in April, 1521. The first is unique both as a statement on the intellectual forces for reform within the empire as the Reformation began and as a comprehensive program of action urged upon the emperor. Two (articles 6 and 14) are lightly annotated translations of selections from Erasmus's *Praise of Folly,* while another (8) explains why Erasmus is now translated into German and Luther and von Hutten have written in the vernacular: namely, to open the eyes of the common man. Other articles can be classified around certain themes relevant to our study. Several (3, 4, 9, and 12) concern the burden of monastic life for the individuals within and for society at large outside monasteries—a favorite target of Eberlin as well. An important group (2, 5, 7, 13, and 15) addresses individual issues of local parish reform. And two (10 and 11) attempt to bring everything together in a visionary reform program, many features of which came to be reality in the Protestant world by 1530.

The first of the confederate papers, addressed to the presiding emperor, Charles V, as the Diet of Worms (1521) opened, submitted an impressive list of reformers, humanists, and schoolmasters, led by Luther and von Hutten, who are said to be working for "pure and evangelical teaching in the schools and pulpits" of the empire.[160] Charles's tutor, Adrian of Utrecht (elected Pope Adrian VI in the following year), and his Franciscan confessor, Galpion, are accused of having turned the emperor against his "two best friends in the empire," Luther and von Hutten.[161] The mendicants and non-resident benefice collectors (the "courtiers") are presented as the true enemies of the empire. Eberlin estimates that the four mendicant orders take yearly from Germany one million gulden, while the pope takes 300,000 gulden in direct payments, in addition to which are the incalculable sums paid by individuals to Rome for special exemptions and by German monasteries and parish churches in income to courtiers. Luther and his friends are the only ones who, for God and country, have stood firm against them.[162]

Eberlin's reform proposals to Charles were directed at breaking completely papal and mendicant power within Germany. He urged the emperor to undertake the following measures: (1) close supervision of mendicants and courtiers; (2) ineligibility of bishops as electoral princes (which would affect the archbishoprics of Trier, Mainz, and Cologne); (3) removal of cardinals in Germany; (4) the teaching of three languages (Greek and Hebrew in addition to Latin) in German schools; (5) "evangelical clarity" in German pulpits; (6) prohibition of the purchase of the pallium (the episcopal seal of authority) from Rome, the payment of annates to Rome, the selling of indulgences, and the formation of new mendicant groups; (7) a moratorium on admission into mendicant orders (to be allowed to die out with their present members); (8) an end to excommunication of laymen solely on grounds of alleged guilt (that is, without evidence of a specific public crime); (9) limitation of priests to one benefice, in which each must be resident; (10) preaching by all priests and bishops; (11) prohibition of any monastic vow before the age of thirty; (12) permission for all who wish to leave monasteries; (13) prohibition of benefices to courtiers; (14) an end to dispensations from Rome (all such religious matters henceforth to be confined to territorial bishops); (15) strict regulation of possessions taken into cloisters; (16) limits on the number of priests who may dwell within a city; (17) prohibition of endowments of perpetual *(ewige)* anniversaries or benefices without imperial permission; (18) subjugation of all monks and nuns to their territorial bishops; and (19) permission for clerical marriage.[163]

The ex-Franciscan Eberlin examined monastic life in four pamphlets. One, reminiscent of Blarer's defense of his departure from a Benedictine monastery, apprised parents of the perils faced by women in convents: *A Warning to All Christians to Have Mercy on Cloistered Women (Send Not Your Daughter Into a Convent Until You Have Read This Little Book).* Monasteries are depicted as presenting more obstacles to Christian life than the world does. Wealthy fathers are urged to marry their daughters to day-laborers rather than send them into convents—the odds being that greater happiness would come from the former mismatch than from the latter, since God gives to so few the power to fulfill celibate vows.[164] In addition, Eberlin alleges that cloistered women are more heavily burdened with religious works than cloistered men and are even forced to be their servants:

> It is certainly a thing to pity that nunneries are so afflicted with unreasonable statutes made by foolish, ignorant, and inexperienced monks. The poor girls are forced to work as long as the boys or longer at singing, fasting, reading, meditating, and like pitiable things. Nuns must fast often while monks eat boiled or fried meat, which the nuns must prepare but cannot enjoy. Cloistered women are forbidden even to see their parents, while monks may pursue their every interest.[165]

Eberlin would transform nunneries into preparatory schools for marriage, teaching girls Christian discipline and housekeeping.[166]

A second pamphlet, *Concerning the Long and Grievous Cry That Religious Monks, Priests, and Nuns Call the Canonical Hours,* compared singing the canonical hours with farming, housekeeping, and other physical labor—"the ways the pious laity pray"—very much to the detriment of the former.[167] Two subsequent pamphlets lobbied for the dissolution of monasteries as an act of charity for thousands who suffer under "burdensome, un-Christian, and inhumane rules"—a state, Eberlin assures his readers, that is worse than Turkish servitude.[168] Eberlin reckons that there are 24,000 persons in orders in Germany and 400,000 throughout Europe. He cites specifically the Carthusians, Benedictines, Bernardians (Cistercians), Praemonstratensians, Regulars (*canonici regulares,* canons who shared a common life but without formal monastic vows), and the Wilhelmites (a hermit congregation founded in the mid-twelfth century).[169] All are found wanting when measured by the *Testament* and other writings of Saint Francis, whom Eberlin finds to have bound his followers (and apparently all other true mendicants) to working with their hands, receiving only subsistence nourishment (never money or gold) for their labors, and remaining few in number in a nonconventual, simple life-style.[170] Monastic orders are further criticized for opposition to such notable reformers as John Hus, Jerome of Prague, Jean Gerson [who burned Hus and Jerome], John of Wesel, Johannes Reuchlin, Erasmus, and Luther.[171] "Hail, bad weather, and pestilence" are seen as God's revenge for the cloistered, and those who set them free are promised a far greater indulgence than could ever be gained by going to Rome or on a pilgrimage to the shrine of Saint James. "He who sets the cloistered free redeems a sinful soul as surely as one who, for God's sake, takes a common whore in marriage." [172]

Eberlin discusses three areas of local parish reform: mandatory lay fasting, the need for good preaching, and traditional ceremonies and practices that allegedly exploit the fears and superstitions of simple folk. In protesting mandatory fasting he rejects the modelling of lay piety on monastic piety. In pre-Reformation Germany there were as many as 161 days of fasting (65) or abstinence (96)—over one-third of the year—when pious Christians were expected to abstain from one or more types of food, basically cheese, fat, eggs, meat, milk, and/or flour.[173] Eberlin accuses the fasting laws of creating 100,000 mortal sins annually.[174] "Who would think that such a heavy yoke would be laid upon hard-working laymen by the mild and merciful mother of Christendom, a yoke which disturbs the consciences of good Christians who out of physical need must break this tyrannical law?" [175] Eberlin agrees with the medieval church that it is a "deadly" matter: "unrest in conscience, vexation among the simple, backbiting among the malicious—these are the creations of such unreasonable commands" when they are taken seriously.[176] He recounts the praiseworthy origin of fasting among early Christians as a witness to their faith while surrounded by the heathen, and condemns contemporary fasting laws as contrary to the letter and spirit of the New Testament. New Testament Christians are permitted, as they please, to subject their body to the spirit by fasting; but "no layman, young or old, rich or poor, healthy or sick, is bound on pain of mortal sin to fast during Lent." [177]

Eberlin illustrates the basic Protestant appeal to politicians when he presents true preaching as the way to a self-disciplined people. "The best and most effective way to promote Christian living among ordinary Christian people is not by many statutes and laws, stiff punishments, or hated imprisonment, but by the sincere proclamation of God's word by those appointed to do it. . . . If you had such preachers you would in a few years have well-trained Christian people." [178] Magistrates are encouraged to let no "old custom, traditional mendicant privilege, or papal bull" deter them from a forceful reform of preaching.[179] Eberlin would have them quite simply take the matter of religion entirely into their own hands. Like other Protestant apologists, Eberlin lapses into somewhat crude threats and promises. "Why are there war, hail, famine, and other plagues in the land? Because God's word is poorly preached or ignored in the churches. . . . If you want to please God, lay aside your sins, attain indulgence, do great good for an entire land or city, be God's friend now and in eternity, then promote good preaching." [180]

Protestants believed that nothing so exploited lay fears and superstition as that body of belief and religious practice which related to the dead. Gengenbach and Manuel summarized it with a phrase that must surely have embodied the most profound contemporary animosities: *Totenfresserei*—"feeding upon the dead." Eberlin characterizes the traditional death masses, processions, vigils, and memorial services as mainly occasions for priests to prey upon the deeply pious but highly gullible reverence of the German people for their dead.

> Superstition and naiveté are so obvious among simple, trusting people, and have been carefully observed by priests. The priest is such a sly and clever fellow. He projects such apostolic authority in the confessional and from the pulpit and has so many stories and explanations about everything that pertains to the dead. Simple, naive people are no match for him, and he

> easily moves them to establish perpetual masses and anniversaries and to increase weekly and monthly vespers, vigils, and masses for departed souls.[181]

Eberlin protests the costly vigils, decorated coffins, candles, mourners, masses, anniversaries, and perpetual masses as but a worldly show for the living which is of no use to the dead; he begs the common man to "wise up." [182]

A devotee of specificity and detail, Eberlin furnished in two later pamphlets comprehensive summaries of the allegedly false doctrines and burdensome practices which daily plagued local parish life. He cites myriad false teachings: the distinction between precepts (which bind the laity) and counsels (which the clergy, allegedly going a higher way, also undertake to follow); the power ascribed to indulgences; the belief that men can by their own power turn to God; that there are completely sinless works; that men can of themselves make good for their sins; that man has a free will and can choose either evil or good; that human nature is beautiful and noble; that extreme unction, confirmation, priestly ordination, and marriage are sacraments; that the reprobate are true members of the church while on earth; that priests are not subjected by God to laymen (that is, to civil rulers and laws) in temporal matters; that monastic life is a surer way to salvation than married life; that the Mass is a sacrifice; that faith alone is not the beginning of salvation; that God rewards one's works and not one's faith; that mendicant begging is meritorious of salvation; that brotherly love and physical need are not excuses for breaking papal, episcopal, or monastic laws; that unconscious, secret sins must be confessed; that a penance must be performed after confession; that inadvertent transgression of a command of the church or a rule of a monastic order is a mortal sin; that preaching should be sprinkled with the teaching of Aristotle, Duns Scotus, Thomas Aquinas, Alexander of Hales, William of Ockham, Gabriel Biel, Albertus Magnus, canon law, and "other such human statements"; that it is better to give an altar pfennig to a priest than directly to the poor; and that it is better to give alms to mendicants than to anonymous beggars.[183] "Our clergy," Eberlin summarizes,

> make heavy the light law of Christ against his command. They entangle our consciences in hellish scruples by subjecting us to

> so many papal laws and human traditions, so many censures under threat of the ban, irregularity, or interdict, and so many ordinances on fasting, celebrating, eating, drinking—from all of which Christ has set us free. They lay on us so many contrived and foolish rules for confessing, when the Christian church asks of us only a sincere and trusting acknowledgment of our sin to the priest without any special anxious enumeration. They subject us to manifold penances which God has not commanded. . . . They burden us with the great deception of indulgence—letters of indulgence and the reservation and dispensation of so many types and cases of conscience—and the theft of our benefices and endowed preachers by honorless, soulless, deceitful, fat, and lazy people known as courtiers, who come and go daily. These are the things that daily vex the consciences and plague the possessions of German people.[184]

The long success of such false teaching and tyrannical practice is ascribed by Eberlin to lay preoccupation with earning a living and naive trust in the clergy who in truth have conspired day and night to deceive them.[185] As the best present defense against such teaching and practice laymen are advised to buy or beg a Bible and to read it, and if unable to read to hire a poor student to read it to them.[186]

The *Fifteen Confederates* culminates in two pamphlets which purport to be statutes adopted in the fictional land of Wolfaria—"the land where all fares well"—to regulate religious and social life. Within a tradition of late medieval reform sentiment they summarize an original Protestant vision of what society should be. Eberlin does not, to be sure, speak for all Protestants, and in some areas he is manifestly more timid than later Protestants will be. Even so, one can already detect some of the reasons for which Protestant reformers would soon be typed by certain critics (and not always unfairly) as simply "new papists." Still, the Wolfaria statutes accurately gauge the religiously revolutionary character of Protestant doctrines and are, overall, prophetic of some basic institutional consequences of the Protestant movement. The following measures are said to have been adopted in Wolfaria to direct the religious life.[187]

> *Religious holidays.* Only nineteen religious holidays, exclusive of Sundays, together with the feastdays of the patron saints of

individual churches, are to be observed. [This is a grand total of twenty. Since there were, exclusive of Sundays, thirty-two mandatory and eighteen optional religious holidays in pre-Reformation Germany,[188] this is a reduction in the number of traditional holidays by more than one-third.]

Fast days. "All who can" are to fast the three days before Easter and on the eve of all other holidays, exclusive of Sundays. In these periods one shall receive only two meals a day (at 10:00 A.M. and 5:00 P.M.) and abstain from fish, meat, and imported wine. "Those who wish" may fast the full forty days of Lent, but no one is to be forced to do so. Fasting may not be imposed upon the laity as a penance, and efforts to create additional fast days will be met with a stiff penalty.

Conduct on holidays. The morning is to be devoted to common singing (without benefit of organs and pipes), the mass, and preaching. After lunch one may visit with friends or go walking. Young people may play skittles, prisoner's base, shoot darts, or perform (tasteful) plays. Girls may sing and throw balls. No dancing is allowed on Sundays and holidays, although it is permitted on other days. ("That is why we have so few holidays—so that everybody will really observe them!") Playing cards, dice, and chess are permitted, but with no bets over one pfennig. At 3:00 P.M. all are expected to return to church for Scripture reading, a sermon, and hymn singing. In the evening all are to come once again into church to pray for the dead and thereafter to visit the graves of parents and relatives. After sermon each should lay on the altar what he can for the poor, or leave a note telling what the poor can expect to receive at his house. And under stiff penalty the canonical hours are forbidden to be sung throughout the land.

Clergy. There are to be two priests for each parish. Each is to be a local man and, if he is married, as he should be, his wife should be a local woman. [The purpose here is both to reduce the number of clergy and to have clergy in office who are knowledgeable of and sympathetic with the area of their benefices and are eager to live there.]

For every twenty priests there is to be one bishop as overseer who meets with them monthly to counsel and instruct them in God's law. The priest's salary is to be 200 gulden a year. The bishop is to receive 15 gulden less than the other priests. There is to be a stiff penalty for giving priests special gifts in exchange for their services.

Each priest is to have one deacon who functions as sexton and receives an annual salary of 100 gulden.

There are to be no more ordained priests. When a priest or deacon dies or leaves the parish, the local congregation is not to look to the bishop for a consecrated priest, but is to meet with the clergy and choose another whom the authorities *[vogt* and *gericht],* together with the bishop, will then install *[intronisieren]* in his office. [The basic concern here is to preserve the local community's right to choose clergy who it feels best serve its needs. The procedure parallels that of the late medieval preacherships and effectively ends papal and episcopal reservation or control over local clerical offices.[189]]

Priests may remarry upon the death of their wives.

Priests are to receive no tithes.

Priests are to be respectably dressed, like other citizens.

Priests are not to be tonsured.

Priests are to have no privileges denied to other citizens ["kein friheit für andere burger haben"], although one should still honor them as "Obern."

Local government *[vogt* and *radt]* shall have power over the clergy as over all other people and shall not be hindered in judging and punishing priests who betray their trust as they judge and punish other public criminals.

He who wishes to leave the clergy may be laicized; if later he wishes to return to the clergy, he may do so.

The clergy are permitted to practice all honorable trades and occupations save those of merchant, magistrate *[vogt],* landlord *[wirt],* and council member *[ratsherr].*

Priests are to study, pray, and keep their houses in order.

No one is permitted to enter the clergy who is under thirty years of age.

Clergy may buy land and build on it as other people do.

Monks. Magistrates are to force monks and nuns to dress like others, especially when they are outside the monastery.

All cloister dwellers must be at least thirty years of age,[190] and no more than ten may dwell in any one cloister. Those who wish may leave monasteries.

Monasteries shall be nothing more than schools for the young, where boys and girls are taught Christian commandments and discipline.

Only two monasteries and two nunneries may exist in the same city or region. All others are to be dissolved and made over into hospices for the poor, for retired city servants and their children, and for pilgrims.

All endowments beyond what is needed to support the four regional cloisters and those converted into hospices shall be put into a common chest.

Mendicants. Under penalty of death all mendicant orders are dissolved. Their cloisters are to be given to the city and rented as common dwellings to homeless citizens. Those dispossessed who wish to remain monks and nuns may do so within the privacy of their own homes, without special clothing, activity, or regrouping.

Confession. It is desired that all will seek at least once each year the counsel or special instruction of their priest or chaplain. An instruction to do so shall be publicly proclaimed once each year in the marketplace, although no one is obliged to confess his secrets to the priest unless he wishes to do so. One is free to seek the counsel of the priest on doctrine or for conscience's sake as often as one wishes.

Marriage. For the sake of voluntary chasteness, girls should be married at fifteen, boys at eighteen, and widows and widowers remarried within ten weeks of their spouses' death.

For the sake of order and unity sexual impotence is declared grounds for divorce and remarriage, and no shame shall be attached to it.

The secretly married ["on gezeügnüss und rat erberer leüt"] shall be drowned. [This was not only an effective cure for clandestine marriages, but also the kind of strong-arm approach to problems that would cause zealous Protestant reformers to be condemned as "new papists."]

There are to be no exclusions from marriage because of blood relationship beyond those prescribed by the law of Moses.

Marriage shall not be observed as a holy sacrament.

Prostitutes and houses of prostitution are forbidden.

Neither confirmation, extreme unction, nor ordination shall be observed as a true sacrament.

In church men and boys will sit together in separation from women and girls.

Mass. Mass is to be read only on holidays and in the presence of the assembled community and with common prayer. [The many lucrative private masses are thereby ended.]

Church cemetery. Cemeteries shall not be located beside monasteries, but only beside the parish church. Each cemetery is to have a chapel where prayers can be said for the dead.

On the dying. It is not necessary that a priest be present with the dying save at the latter's express desire for special counsel or consolation. The present custom of deathbed confessions may be forgone,[191] although one may wish to acknowledge his public guilt and seek forgiveness from those he has wronged. The priest or deacon shall administer the Eucharist to the sick, and their neighbors shall comfort them with prayers and words of Scripture.

On wills. Every adult shall write a will. Nothing may be left to a public institution serving the common interest—schools, churches, and hospices—without the knowledge and permission of the magistrate. This lest they become too rich and occasion tumult.

On the dead. The dead are to be accompanied prayerfully by friends and neighbors to the cemetery. Their names are to be announced on Sunday and prayers offered for them. Mourning clothes shall not be worn longer than one week. Thereafter nothing special is to be done for the dead apart from alms and prayers in their memory. [This in opposition to what Protestants considered to be the Totenfresserei of endowed weekly, monthly, and anniversary prayers and masses.] "On every holiday in every sermon the people shall be admonished that one dies gladly *[gern stärb]* and that those who refuse to die willingly when their time comes shall not be buried with other Christians." [Here "terror tactics" appear to be used to take the terror—and, to Protestants, subsequent superstitious practices—out of death.]

Sacraments. Bread and wine are to be given to all in the Eucharist and, save for public sinners, without prevenient confession. Five sacraments are to be observed: baptism, Eucharist, absolution, prayer, and "diligent observance of God's word." Children are to be baptised as infants.

Common ordinance for the multitude of old monks. The clergy are to be gradually reduced in number by a ten-year moratorium on new clerics. After ten years' time no clergy shall be permitted save the two parish priests; all others will at that time be laicized. There is, however, to be no delay in suppressing mendicants.

Old or sick clergy are to enter hospices. Noble nuns are to be gathered in cloisters of fifty each, where they will live as free women until either death or marriage occurs.

Supervised "unregularized" publicly supported *collegia* are to be established in each bishopric for men and women.

Village priests. There is to be one pastor for every five hundred adults. Villages are to pool their numbers to form a parish church. Each village shall have its own chapel and attendant sacristan or deacon.

On prayer. All prayers save the Lord's Prayer are forbidden as a capital offense. Only common Christian doctrines *[gemeinen glouben leren]* are permitted, and only the Apostle's Creed may be sung in church. Henceforth one shall put away "all the religious song books *[psalterlin]*, special prayers *[kron gebät]*, rosary prayers, the *Hortulus animae*, the *Paradisus animae*, and like prayer books, and all the breviaries of the priests." [192]

On images of saints. No metal or carved (wooden) image is permitted in the church. Only plain, unostentatious painted pictures of saints about whom one can read in the Bible may appear on the walls.

Churches. Churches are to be built wide and strong and without extravagance ["sundere kostlicheit"]. They are to contain no precious stones nor any silver or gold save for the Eucharistic cup and straw. They are to have no liturgical vessels beyond what is necessary for two priests. A common tablecloth is to be used for the altar, although its color may be altered. Within churches one may read, sing, and teach only what is written in the books of the Bible. Nuns and other women are forbidden to sing or read publicly in church.

Pilgrimages.[193] Pilgrimages with mendicants to shrines are forbidden. Other pilgrimages may be undertaken, but only with written permission from the pastor and the magistrate, for which the rich must pay ten gulden and the poor perform ten days' labor.

On the Roman Chair. No German shall henceforth go to Rome either on business *[uss nutz]* or out of devotion. The bishop of Rome shall no longer be recognized or addressed as "Ober." There shall be annual meetings of the German bishops, who shall henceforth run the churches. The meetings shall occur in a different bishopric each year, and the resident bishop shall be the presiding authority. The bishop shall be the highest authority within each bishopric.

On schools. No scholastic doctor shall ever again be read save as an object of ridicule. All clerical laws and decretals are to be publicly burned. The only philosophy to be studied is that of Didymus Faventinus.[194] Latin, Greek, and Hebrew shall be taught in all schools.

Wolfaria's new temporal order envisioned an amicable hierarchical government extending from mayors of tiny agricultural villages to the king. Each village is to be ruled by a mayor, every two hundred village farms by a magistrate, who oversees the mayors. Ten such magisterial districts form a city, which a count rules; fewer than ten make a fort, which is governed by a baron. Ten cities make a dukedom or princedom, under the rule of a duke or prince, and the king, who is chosen from among the dukes and princes, is set over them. Every level of government is devoted to the common good, and each is to be mindful of the peculiar laws of the other. Higher authority is pledged to act only with the aid and counsel of lower in matters affecting both. The income and courts of all governing officials shall be modest. And no office is to be hereditary, although the children and relatives of officeholders may succeed them "if elected by all subjects." The particular social ordinances, in summary, are the following.[195]

Marriage, drinking, swearing, and gossiping. Public adulterers are to be executed, chronic drunks drowned, nonjudicial and blasphemous swearing punished by beating, and gossipers to receive public reprimands.

Gaming. All gaming is to be conducted in public. Adults are permitted limited gambling. Youth, however, are forbidden to play cards or dice for money, although they may for brief periods play chess for eggs.

Dancing. Mixed public dancing is permitted for three hours one afternoon a week. Married men and women may dance only with their spouses or relatives, and propriety in dress, motion, and song are to be observed.

Entrance into marriage. As already stated in the religious ordinances, there are to be no impediments to marriage beyond those cited in the law of Moses. The clergy must either have legitimate wives or live alone [that is, concubinage is prohibited].

Local government. Every city is to have a thirty-member council, with the count acting as mayor. Forts are to have a fifteen-member council, with the baron as mayor.

Merchants and trade. Merchants and trade are to be carefully regulated. All profiteering and monopolistic trade are abolished. No more than three trading companies are permitted to be in one place. Local products are to be protected by bans on imported wine, cloth, and produce. [A closed economy seems here to be advocated, and reflects a local orientation and isolationism that are tendencies of the ordinances as a whole.]

Food, drink, and the necessities of life. All varieties of food and drink are permitted to all persons at all times, save fastdays, and the clergy may not deny them to the laity. Wild game and fish are free, and wood may, as needed, be cut by all.

Begging. No beggars are permitted in the land. The poor are to receive church offerings and what is not given directly to them shall go into a contingency common chest. The poor are to be the special responsibility of the magistracy, not the clergy, since the clergy have exploited them for so long. Those on the public dole must wear identifying badges.

Trades. No "useless" trades are to be permitted. Needed trades shall not be allowed to suffer because there are more masters than apprentices in them. No labor for one's daily bread shall be held more honorable than farming and blacksmithing.

War. No war is to be undertaken without consultation among the princes of the land. Farmers and clergy are to be nonparticipants in fighting, although a priest shall accompany each magistrate and pray for a gracious peace should the magistrate fall in battle. No wars shall be waged for territorial gain, nor shall scorched earth policies be employed.

Castles. Castles are to be reserved for nobility. While present ones are to remain unmolested and maintained, no building of new castles is permitted.

Houses and buildings. Workers in the same trade are to live on the same street. Simplicity is to be the rule in all houses and buildings save public places such as the town hall, store, bathhouse, school, and inns, which are permitted decorations beyond the ordinary *[ubermässig kostlich]*.

Bathhouses. Bathhouses are to be segregated by sex.

Beards. All men are to wear long beards. Men with smooth faces like women shall be held an outrage. All men shall wear short, unkempt hair.

Children. All boys and girls are to attend a publicly supported school from ages three to eight. They are to be taught the Christian law from the gospel and Saint Paul, as well as Latin and German, and a little Greek and Hebrew. At age eight a decision shall be made by the community to send each child into a trade or further study.

Law and provincial law. All citizens are expected to know thoroughly local customs and laws. All old imperial and clerical laws *[alte kaiserliche und pfaffen recht]* are abolished. Lawyers are also henceforth abolished. Those who cannot speak in their own defense are to seek the assistance of their neighbor.

The ban. No one is to be placed under the ban simply on suspicion of guilt. Only for constant public transgression of God's law may the priest excommunicate anyone.

Indulgences. Any proclamation or reading of an indulgence shall be publicly punished. Service to one's neighbor shall be held a great indulgence.[196]

Coinage. Coins shall be uniform throughout the kingdom.

Clergy. No priest may hold political office.[197]

Disloyalty. Breaking promises, not returning borrowed items, ignoring one's neighbor in time of need, loaning alms, and failure to repay debts when they are due require retribution or public punishment.

Thieves. Thieves shall wear chains on both feet and work for a year as common servants of the city.

Murder. Those who murder shall be murdered. Highway robbers shall be made menial servants of the city for life.

Ostentatious living. No one is permitted to live beyond his means. Ostentatious living shall be swiftly controlled, lest resentment erupt among the poor.

Servants. Servants are to be given no wine unless they are at least thirty years of age. They are to be neither cursed nor beaten by their masters, nor are they to curse or beat their masters. If dissatisfied they may resign their positions. They are to receive no payments in advance. They are to be paid in cash. Masters are to support sick servants gratis for two months.

Clothes. There is to be moderation, conformity, and propriety in dress, although women may decorate themselves *aber doch erlich.*

Pastime. A half day shall be given over each month to planned public amusement, during which time children are to be taught games and skills (measuring, arithmetic, the stars), the use of money, and basic medical remedies.

Physical punishment. There are to be no physical punishments beyond those listed in the law of Moses.

Pilgrims. Pilgrims are to be treated civilly and aided.

Laziness. Stiff penalties are to be meted out for laziness. Everyone must engage in useful work.

A general rule on religion. "All who henceforth give money for masses, confessions, and burials, praise the canonical hours, or give alms to mendicants shall do public penance. He who honors a priest more highly than a magistrate or council member shall be publically punished. He who insults a priest, however, shall be punished as if he had insulted a magistrate." [198]

Jews and heathens. Jews and heathens in the cities are to be given friendly treatment ["früntlich halten wie unsere burger"], but may not receive civic honors, participate in government, or be permitted to insult the city's law and religion.

Heretics. No one who observes the common understanding of the gospel shall be adjudged a heretic. Scholars, clergy, the people *[landtleüt],* and rulers shall together decide on matters of evangelical doctrine and law.

Common chest. Every citizen who is worth a hundred gulden or more shall give one heller each week to the common chest. Those with less income are not obliged to do so.

What the temporal ordinances of Wolfaria suggest is an economic and political system protective to the fullest of local autonomy and business interests, while nonetheless acknowledging larger political alliances and responsibilities. In many of the civil ordinances—for example, those on marriage, the ban, indulgences, begging, schools, laws, the clergy, and heresy—the social impact of the Protestant gospel can be seen. Parallels may even be drawn between the removal of papal and episcopal religious burdens and opposition to imperial and papal laws and policies detrimental to the local economy and politics. But one should not go in search of a necessary correlation, giving weight to the former only as it subserved the latter. Guarding local autonomy and business interests against imperial and papal predators hardly required a Protestant religion in the late Middle Ages, as the examples of France and the Italian city-states attest. Providing such protection was a natural course for all save the most obtuse governments.

Wolfaria's religious ordinances, on the other hand, make clear that there were many social benefits in the religious revolution quite apart from its indirect assistance to territorial and local governments. Although the state of Saxony and the cities of Zurich and Geneva surely would not have succeeded so well without the Reformation, it accompanied rather than caused the larger social and political movements of its day.[199] People did not then, as they do not now, readily respond to great distant events that left their daily lives untouched; they reacted to what was felt immediately. And where people most felt the originality and impact of the Reformation was in the psychological and social consequences of its revolutionary religious practices and institutions, which made lasting, tangible changes in the way they conceived and lived their lives locally from day to day.

The Exorcist: Thomas Murner and Pamphilus Gengenbach

Protestants did not work for the religious restructuring of society without strong Catholic resistance. Probably the most formidable of early Catholic pamphleteers against the Reformation was the internationally famous satirist, the Franciscan Thomas Murner. In December, 1522, Murner published a large (4,800 verses) and devastating satire of Protestant pamphleteers and their works (including Eberlin and his *Fifteen Confederates*) entitled *The Great Lutheran Fool.* The chief character, the fool, is a sickly Lutheran who represents not Luther but Lutheranism as presented by Protestant apologists and interpreted by Murner as a great bodily affliction. The story develops around Murner's ultimately successful efforts to exorcise the demons that have made the fool ill. Eberlin's fifteen confederates appear as the nucleus of a "revolutionary army" rumbling in the fool's belly, which Murner finds and exorcises. Michael Stiefel [the name means "boot"], an Esslinger Augustinian who had satirized Murner as a cat—*murmawen* [which rhymes with "meowing"] is one of the popular terms born of the exchange—appears as a demon ejected by Murner from the fool's boot.[200] The Lutheran peasant Karsthans, the subject of an anonymous Protestant satire also critical of Murner in 1521,[201] is cast out by Murner from deep within the fool's large intestine with the aid of a powerful laxative.

By the end of the drama the fool has been greatly weakened by the ordeal of exorcism and lies spent upon his deathbed. Even in this depleted state, however, he intensely desires a Beguine. The disappointed Murner finally places at his disposal a seventy-eight-year-old "virgin" Beguine. The fool, protesting that there is no such thing, manages to resist her and to die as Murner's great friend, receiving from Murner himself the last rites with full honors.[202] The old Beguine represented "pretending virtue," the final form in which Lutheranism assailed the fool. Like an old Beguine, Murner was saying, Lutheranism, ever feigning purity, accuses all others of unrighteousness and brings conflict into every house it enters.

Earlier in the drama a more direct characterization of the affliction of Lutheranism was presented in a debate between Murner and Luther. Murner, the exorcist, is promised Luther's daughter [Luther was unmarried in 1522] if he will convert to Lutheranism. Propositioned, Murner asks to know exactly what it means to be a Lutheran, to which request Murner's Luther replies with the equivalent of a detailed Catholic perception of the Reformation in 1522. Even allowing for the understandable parti pris and exaggeration, the issues set forth by Murner's Luther are not so inconsistent with those that we have seen Luther's Lutherans espouse. To be a Lutheran, Murner's Luther explains, is to hate and ridicule the pope, his bishops, and clergy, and to accept no papal authority, no prescribed fasting, confession, or prayer. It means to direct toward the emperor the same rebellious attitude as one directs toward the pope, obeying neither him nor his allies. Lutheranism means complete freedom from authority. "Christian faith frees us from all earthly authority. Before there ever was an emperor, king, or prince, we were all born free in our baptism." [203] Lutheranism means further denying the sacrifice of the Mass and the sacraments of confession, confirmation, extreme unction, and marriage. It is the destruction of monasteries and churches, iconoclasm, persecution of monks and nuns, and universal conflict. It is the confidence that only Lutherans know the truth and all others teach lies. And, Murner's Luther concludes, it is membership in a secret *Bundschuh* devoted to revolution against all clergy: "To turn the world upside down—that is to bring the gospel into its own!"[204] Later in the play, as Murner stands by, Luther dies, steadfastly refusing to the end confession and the last rites of the church. An accompanying woodcut depicts the reformer's dead body passing into a toilet.[205]

Murner's *Great Lutheran Fool* is not easily excelled in the annals of religious satire, but Pamphilus Gengenbach went a long way toward topping it. His response was entitled simply *Novella* (1523) and featured two main characters, a gout-stricken parish priest who accuses the Reformation of every ill and his sacristan who is sure that Luther can do no wrong. The pastor aspires to march to Wittenberg and smite Luther hip and thigh in debate. The sacristan reminds him that Luther has already put many learned men to shame: "Up against him you would be as a child!" Among the aids the pastor says he would use to overwhelm Luther are the works of Thomas Murner. And thus the reader is alerted to a refutation.

The pastor recalls a deceased member of his congregation, a foolish peasant named Karsthans, who greatly disrupted the parish and died firm in Lutheran convictions. The pastor hopes that he is now in hell where he belongs. The sacristan, remembering Karsthans as a pious man, hopes that he is rather in heaven, receiving the reward he deserves. While en route one day to mass, the pastor is met by the spirit of a dead man, who tells how he now suffers great pain in purgatory because of "certain attachments" during his lifetime. Disappearing, the spirit promises to return the following week. The pastor is convinced that he has confronted the shade of the heretical Karsthans, and so informs the sacristan and others, who initially suspect that the pastor has seen an apparition inspired by the Devil.[206]

But the spirit, true to his word, does return. The pastor and his friends make repeated but unsuccessful efforts to learn his exact identity. Advice is sought from a Dominican theologian who suggests that the famous exorcist Thomas Murner be summoned to interrogate the uncommunicative spirit.[207] And the spirit himself now begins to insist upon Murner. A meeting is arranged, but the famous Murner proves no more successful than the others in bringing the spirit to self-revelation. (The sacristan, relishing the inefficacy of *murmawen*, advises the puzzled Murner to try a "swift kick in the ass.") Finally the spirit relents. He is not, as some have suspected, the peasant Karsthans, but Murner's dead friend, yes, the great Lutheran fool, whom Murner had exorcised and honorably buried. He explains that he now suffers in purgatory because of his deathbed lust for the Beguine. A special penance has been imposed upon him: he must search out and devour a true fool to replace Karsthans, whom Murner had exorcised from his large intestine with a special laxative. Murner, stunned and struggling, is thereupon swallowed whole by the spirit![208] The moral of the play: the Reformation survives and overwhelms the best that the medieval church and religion can send against it, even the great exorcist Thomas Murner.

Nicholas Manuel's Totenfresser

In late 1521 Gengenbach had published a dramatic poem entitled *Die Totenfresser.* It was very short and featured only seven "devourers of the dead": the pope, a bishop, a priest, a Cistercian, a mendicant, a nun, and a priest's concubine—the "chosen children and best friends the Devil has on earth."[209] Gengenbach paraded out five characters to speak against them: the souls of the dead, whose fortunes were squandered on commemorative masses;[210] beggars, who had lost their grubstake to mendicants; a poor parish priest who hungered with his flock; a nobleman who saw his investment in masses for his dead parents to be a denial of the living poor; and the ever present and always exploited peasant.

Gengenbach's little work was the model for the masterful six-act drama of the same name by Nicholas Manuel, which was performed on the Kreuzgasse in Bern during Lent in 1523. The theme is the same—the heavy investment of the Roman church in death—but those who now feed upon the dead have increased from seven to sixteen. Manuel's play is also more subtle. It is both an exposé of clerical ranks and a prophecy of their impending doom. The characters not only admit ulterior motives but do so while recognizing the handwriting on the wall. The play exposes the jig as being up. As a performed popular play, *Die Totenfresser* illustrates, even better than the vernacular pamphlets that were read to the nonliterate laity, how these laymen came to have as profound a grasp of the issues of the Reformation as any Protestant don. Even the modern scholar comes away with the feeling that it has all here been said, and with unique forcefulness.

The first act, our major concern, is a series of soliloquies, held in the presence of a corpse, by each of the Totenfresser, while the saints Peter and Paul watch in puzzlement in the background. The audience is warmed to the theme by the opening dialogue between a priest and a sacristan. The former praises death as a great windfall: "the more the better / Would that there were ten corpses . . . !" The sacristan agrees: "I like dead people better than fighting and screwing / They are our food and pay." Praying for them is "more fun than baptising children!" [211] So begins the play.

The first to speak at length is the pope, who explains to his followers that the key to everything is indeed his power to bind and loose, to entangle the gospel in papal laws.

> Be quiet about the gospel
> And preach only papal law.
> We will then be lords and the laity servants
> Who bear the burdens we lay upon them.
> All is lost however
> If the gospel gets out
> And things are measured by it.
> For it teaches none to give and sacrifice to us—
> Only that we should live simple, impoverished lives.

The pope promises to keep suspicious and critical laymen in line with the ban: "I sic the Devil on them / When they speak a word against us!" (Later in the play, when the apostle Peter feels that he must disclaim the pope as his heir, a courtier warns him to watch his tongue lest he be placed under the ban. The audience is thus treated to the prospect of Peter excommunicating Peter! [212]) The pope's soliloquy peaks in a eulogy to the dead. In a few short verses it summarizes the popular origins of the Reformation:

> Church offerings, weekly, monthly, and annual masses for the dead
> Bring us more than enough.

Pity the hardship it inflicts upon the children of the givers!
But if we will now just take care
We can remain free and secure
In no way bound to any layman
Neither by tolls, taxes, or other burdens.
We owe only holy water, salt, and three hazel nuts!
—On earth none have it better than us.
Indulgences lend a hand
By making men fearful of penance.
We also put a lot of stock in purgatory
(Although Scripture doesn't have much to say about it).
The reason is that we must use every chance
To scare the hell out of common folk.
For that is what keeps the cover on our deception.
So if you want to continue
In your comfort and mischief
I will help you with my laws
So that no one dare oppose you.
You may steal and strike whom you please
And no layman will dare lay a hand on you—
So long as we keep up our pretences!
So let us plague and punish the world
For wine, grain, meat, and cash
And be thankful to the dead
Who make it possible for us to fleece the living.[213]

The pope is followed by a cardinal ("I owe the dead / The power and honor of my red cap / Which lets me take in 20,000 gulden a year").[214] Next comes a bishop, who explains how papal law permits him to be both shepherd and wolf to his flock and shepherd and pimp *(hirt* and *hurenwirt)* to his priests. He can both grant indulgences (shepherd) and impose the ban (wolf) on his congregation. And he holds effective control over priests thanks to the papal law against clerical marriage. Priests unable to "contain" pay concubinage and cradle fees as high as 1,500 gulden a year. He warns, however, "Should priests ever come by legal wives / We would lose the fat in our sausage." [215]

A diocesan prior follows to urge the pope never to slacken preaching, singing, and protesting his power over heaven and hell.

"That's what keeps the poor fools, the laity, under control." [216] A cathedral dean enters with a mercenary attack on the gospel; he prefers instead old wives' tales, Thomas Murner's *Gauchmatt* [a moral satire written in 1519], Aesop's *Fables*, and papal law. "Of what use can the gospel possibly be? / It's completely against us priests." [217]

The next speakers are a priest and a priest's concubine. It is to be noted that the closer the character is to ordinary people, the more strongly his speech conveys a sense of impending doom. The priest warns that the laity are wise to the clergy and know how to use the vernacular Bibles that now fill the land. He finds his scholastic training no match for laymen who know the Bible, and sees the power of the ban as the church's last line of defense.[218] The concubine, one of two speakers depicted as actually suffering within the system (see also the young monk's lament below), has come to make a complaint. During the past ten years she and her husband have paid fifty gulden in concubinage and cradle fees to the bishop. A prostitute in Strasbourg before her illegal union with the priest, she laments that living with a priest has only brought her a more greedy pimp! "O dear God, may I live to see the day / When this bishop is no longer my keeper / That's my only wish." [219] Although the fact has gone unappreciated by scholars, the Reformation was no small boon to hundreds of women who, in its wake, made the transition from priest's whore to honorable wife.

A chaplain follows. He too is worried about laymen who are reading and turning the gospel against priests. But his special fear is that the clergy will be forced into marriage (as Saint Paul teaches they should be):

> It is better that we are free
> To carry on our mischief
> And vary at will our mistress.
> As soon as we are bothered
> By our housekeeper's age or shape
> Or displeased by her private parts
> We now can send her packing.
> But we would lose this freedom for life
> Were we forced to choose one wife.
> And we would also then be obligated.[220]

An abbot enters, fretful because common folk have stopped buying indulgences, refuse to give alms, no longer fear the ban, and cannot be persuaded to endow masses and anniversaries for the dead. Scripture has made them more "uppity" than ever before. They come flashing sticks and New Testaments, demanding alms for themselves, attacking human traditions with chapter and verse, and protesting that cloisters have no justification in Scripture.[221]

An abbey prior is alarmed because people no longer fear even hell and purgatory.[222] They believe nothing, he says, that is not immediately supported by Scripture, and when indulgences are offered them or the ban threatened they reply with vulgar mockery, "I wipe my ass with your Roman indulgence and ban!"[223] A steward follows alarmed over the impending economic consequences. Already he knows twelve priests who are forced to live on only 5,000 gold crowns a year![224]

The next speaker is a young monk, who, like the priest's concubine, finds himself unpleasantly trapped within the system. He has made vows he cannot keep. If he stays he will become the "Devil's martyr"; if he flees he fears he will be hunted down and punished.[225] A nun follows, almost as unhappy. She confesses to having a guilty conscience about the easy alms, indulgences, and endowments that come the way of nunneries that do nothing for mankind but are very profitable to the pope.[226]

Humor returns to the play with the entrance of an old Beguine. An old whore who entered the Beguinage only after her "teats began to hang down like an empty sack on the end of a stick," she is delighted to find that cloistered life not only permits her to continue her old profession, but has also taught her new tricks, like how to gossip and fleece the sick. "I've learned all the prayers and blessings / In which sick people place their trust."[227] Her male counterpart, a *Nollbruder,* has fled the world for the easy cloistered life. He is now anguished because farmers and artisans scold him, an able-bodied man, for forsaking his family and worldly responsibilities. He confesses to living in constant fear that he will be forced to do honest work again.[228]

No less apprehensive is the final speaker in Manuel's play, a nomadic mendicant. He, too, is accosted by farmers who demand to know why he does not stay put and work. Having done nothing but beg for fifteen years—the only craft he has mastered—he fears complete destitution if forced into civilian life.[229]

Conclusion

For those who look to modern sectarians, German Lutherans, and Dutch Calvinists to define their Protestantism, "Protestant humorists" may appear to be a contradiction in terms. But as Gengenbach and Manuel make clear, the original Protestant movement succeeded by humor as well as by dour exposé. In pleading their case for the new piety, Protestants ridiculed traditional religion in the most outrageous way, and Western religion has not recovered from that ridicule. They were not only new believers but also irreverent "secular" men of their age, above what they considered to be the superstition of traditional religion. They lobbied in the name of man as well as in the name of God for an end to what they believed to be the pain that religion caused both the laity and the lower clergy, priests' wives, and cloistered men and women. Whatever else Protestantism was later to become as it readjusted to religious tradition and social expectation, it is not too much to call the early Protestant movement the first Western enlightenment.

The original Protestant message may still strike the modern reader as an inconsistent combination of religious radicalism and social conservatism—so many religious concepts, values, practices, and institutions shaken at their foundations, yet seemingly so few questions raised about basic social attitudes and political structures. Baptism into the new religious freedom goes hand in hand with persistence in an old social bondage—or so it seems. There is the grandiose promise to renew society without really changing it, to improve without upsetting it. Upward mobility seems strictly a moral matter involving increased sacrifices rather than new material acquisitions; Protestants would have people "rise" while staying in the same place. Established political power is scorned for failure to live up to its high mandate and forewarned not to ask of men what God has forbidden, but no political system is directly challenged, nor are new ones proposed. Popes and bishops in disagreement with Scripture forfeit respect and obedience forthwith, but short of a direct challenge to the Ten Commandments, rulers can expect enthusiastic allegiance from Protestants. Laymen may become priests and, in time of need, rulers even bishops, but there is no serious thought that the people may be king. It seems indeed to have been a very one-sided fight against medieval church and religion.

In the late Middle Ages, however, a fight against medieval church and religion was not so narrowly "religious" as it might appear to a modern reader. As we will see below, many communities believed the Reformation to be an aid not only to long-term providential blessing but also to a certain democratizing of local government. A new flexibility and acceptance of a broadened base for the processes of decision making were required for many local governments to adapt, against their initial inclination, to the religious preferences of a majority of their citizenry. If, in Germany, Protestantism aided the territorial consolidation of the princes, it also supported the most basic local concerns and self-interests, as Eberlin von Günzburg already makes so clear. In many instances cities and territories found direct economic and political benefits in breaking with the ecclesio-commercial complex that had long served the distant interests of Rome and certain banking houses far better than those of local communities. Reformers found fertile soil for their ideas in urban anticlerical and antimonopolistic mercantile *(Fuggerei)* sentiment.

Beyond the new religious perspective that it gave the individual on his own life, Protestant doctrine provided the sturdy tools requisite for a de jure dismantling of the old ecclesiastical system and the world that it had for so long controlled. As we will see below, it was especially the Scripture test of Protestants that provided magistrates and city councils a quasi-legal basis for expelling the old church. Recent efforts to isolate the theological from the religious and political in the age of Reformation, as if they were worlds apart, distort the nature of change in this period.[230] Whether they cast it in positive slogans like "the priesthood of all believers" and "the freedom of a Christian" or in hostile caricatures of the medieval church like *Die Totenfresser,* Protestants proposed a revolution in religious concept, practice, and institutions.[231] Even in its most modest form the Reformation called for, and in most Protestant areas permanently achieved, an end to mandatory fasting; auricular confession; the worship of saints, relics, and images; indulgences; pilgrimages and shrines; vigils; weekly, monthly, and annual masses for the dead; the belief in purgatory; Latin worship services; the sacrifice of the Mass; numerous religious ceremonies, festivals, and holidays; the canonical hours; monasteries and mendicant orders;

the sacraments of marriage, extreme unction, confirmation, holy orders, and penance; clerical celibacy; clerical immunity from civil taxation and criminal jurisdiction; nonresident benefices; excommunication and interdict; canon law; episcopal and papal authority; and the traditional scholastic education of the clergy.

In most regions the foundations for Protestant criticism had been laid by lay movements in the late Middle Ages, although perhaps in a more negative than positive way. Still, first generation Protestants proposed an unprecedented simplification of religious life and enhancement of secular life. Late medieval developments were a threshold as well as a foothold. Protestants broke fundamentally with the subordination of nature to grace, secular to religious pursuits, and temporal to spiritual ends that had characterized the majority medieval tradition. The new priesthood of all believers ended clerical claims to spiritual superiority; in their education, marriage and family life, and new "civilian" status, Protestant clergy were to take flesh and dwell among the people. Salvation was presented as a matter of simple but sure trust in God's promises as set forth clearly in the Bible, not an uncertain and arduous pilgrimage of good works and ceremonies as prescribed by the bishop of Rome. Vocational good works were no longer to be the necessary treadmill of individual salvation, but simply opportunities to serve one's neighbor in thanksgiving to God for a gratuitous and settled salvation. Christians were no longer to be confused and anxious pilgrims, but those with sure knowledge of the homeland. Social service was to build on rather than toward the certitude of salvation; ethical activity was to flow from rather than toward religious security. One's work was to have a religious foundation, but a strictly ethical edifice. It no longer secured or forfeited salvation but was simply the opportunity to benefit, in the most natural way, one's fellowman.

The first generation of Protestants saw themselves as removing from men and women the burden of achieving a perfection they believed them not only incapable of reaching but never intended to reach. Viewed in historical context, theirs was a religious message that made life less religious than it had previously been. If one were to seek an original theological insight at base, it might be found in Luther's denial of divinity to man either as an original endowment of the soul or as an infused supernatural grace.[232] Neither individuals nor cities were permitted a sacral character; a special divine *Seelengrund* was denied societies as well as souls. The laity were not to be subjected to clerical values; the clergy rather became citizens. Special religious good works were not to be required of laymen; normal vocational activity was the way the laity pleased God.

Protestants promoted a certitude of salvation and secular preoccupation unknown to either biblical or medieval man. The Reformation was much more than a return to biblical religion, and one must wear exceptionally thick confessional glasses to find "Pauline Christianity" a satisfying characterization of it. Nor was it simply an overhauling of medieval religion; only the most selective reader will conclude the Reformation to have been "more medieval than modern." Although one can find first generation Protestant reformers who look like new papists, the original impulse of the Reformation was not toward the theocracies, blue laws, and puritanism popularly associated with later Protestantism. The Reformation did not set out to regulate and sanctify society so much as to make society's sacred institutions and religious doctrines social. Protestants embraced and enhanced secular life only after making it clear that, as pleasing to God as secular vocations were, they contributed not one whit to any man's salvation.

The minds of generations of scholars have been set in the concrete of Max Weber's definition of Protestantism as an "infinitely burdensome and earnestly enforced" regulation of the whole of life.[233] That was neither the intention nor the perception of the original Protestant movement. Calvinism as defined by Weber is a religion in which ethical activity becomes an outlet for religious anxiety, good works signs of election, disciplined action the proof of faith.[234] It was just such a religion that the Protestant movement of the 1520s set out to overcome. Whatever else Protestantism may have become in later Calvinism and Puritanism,* it began as an

* Calvinists and Puritans appear to have expected the individual to believe that everything was already settled, and for the good (predestination), yet still live as if everything depended upon his own disciplined action (the high doctrine of individual and social sanctification). The practical result of this doctrinal combination may have had far more in common with the anxious, introspective piety of the late Middle Ages than with the simple faith and ethical purpose of the original Protestants. This of course is not to deny that the institutional consequences of Calvinism and Puritanism remained very different from those of Catholicism.

uncompromising rejection of the acquisitive religious motive and the religious anxiety that propelled it. That was the object of the assault on the confessional and the alleged Totenfresserei of the medieval church. Individual freedom and humble self-confidence were the watchwords of the first Protestants. The religious lethargy that so shocked Luther during the Saxon visitations of 1528 may have been less an aberration of original Protestantism than the later fearful trek of John Bunyan's *Pilgrim's Progress*. In a certain sense what laymen perceived in the original Protestant message was less a religion than the lack thereof.[235]

4 The Pattern of Reformation

A Magistrate's Reform?

Late medieval cities and towns had a great deal to gain from making their clergy better citizens. One might expect that townsmen and magistrates everywhere formed common fronts, working together as cohesive units for political sovereignty and religious reform against territorial bishops and regional lords. Scholars, however, have found a very different situation. The basic conflict on which the Reformation thrived is seen to be one *within* the cities themselves, in an opposition between lower and middle strata burghers and increasingly plutocratic and oligarchical local governments.[1] Protestant pamphlets in the early years of the Reformation praise individual preachers and laymen learned in Scripture as the leaders of the new movement. Magistrates and politicians are depicted as initially either in opposition to it or at best contributing passively by inaction. They are never seen, as a group, initiating or propelling the reform.[2] Many scholars have accordingly concluded that the Reformation was basically a "people's movement," in a restrictive class sense, against city hall, championed by lower and middle strata burghers intent on making not only their clergy but especially their local government a good citizen.

A seminal statement of this view is Franz Lau's highly influential article, "The Peasants' War and the Alleged End of the Lutheran Reformation as a Spontaneous People's Movement."[3] Lau challenged the thesis, championed especially by older Marxist historians, that Luther's conservative stand during the Peasants' Revolt of 1525 transformed the Reformation from a spontaneous popular movement of townsmen into a coerced reform by minority power groups working through the magistrate and city councils—an *Obrigkeits-* or *Ratsreformation* imposed by force from above and motivated by greed (for the spoils of dissolved monasteries and confiscated religious property). Lau tested this thesis against the pattern of the Reformation in North German cities during and after the Peasants' Revolt, from 1524 to 1532, taking as his key test cases Magdeburg,

Braunschweig, Göttingen, Hamburg, Lübeck, Rostock, Hannover, and Halberstadt. Despite local peculiarities, he found a common pattern of a burgher movement "von unten her" in the face of stubborn opposition from all representatives of established power and wealth—aristocracy, nobility, and city government. He further argued, contrary to the impression left by influential older studies like Schultze's *Stadtgemeinde und Reformation* (1918), that late medieval city councils were not democratically elected spokesmen for unified societies, not the so-called *genossenschaftlichen Organe* that they were so often pictured as being. They were rather basically patrician in composition and firmly aloof from a citizenry that had everywhere to organize and fight for fundamental rights through guild, parish, or residential representatives. City governments tended to be independent arbiters of the law, serving the vested interests of a small ruling class and certain business monopolies. Lau felt that the Reformation only aggravated a preexistent internal tension between government and citizenry. He concluded that it was neither an indigenous community spirit *(genossenschaftlichen Motive)* nor social adjustments made in the wake of the Peasants' Revolt, but a tenacious absolutism in city government itself (a *Ratsabsolutismus*), antedating and even being opposed by the Reformation, that promoted the development of the state church *(Obrigkeitskirche)* associated with the later years of the Reformation.

Lau's argument is supported by Johannes Schildhauer's contemporaneous work (1959), which follows closely the social, political, and religious movements in Stralsund, Rostock, and Wismar during the Reformation. Schildhauer fully documented the oligarchical nature of government, the lower and middle class origins of Protestant reformers and their early supporters, and the formation of representative citizen groups of forty (Wismar), forty-eight (Stralsund) and sixty-four (Rostock) to "speak in the name of the entire citizenry" for internal political and religious reforms. When the Reformation was consolidated in Rostock in 1534, it brought not only an end to the privileges of the clergy but also government agreement to reduce its own numbers by about one-third, to submit to a detailed yearly accounting, and to bring all internal and foreign policy decisions before the committee of sixty-four.[4] There was a broadening—one may even say a democratizing—of city government among power groups, not, however, an internal political revolt.

What Lau and Schildhauer have argued for North German cities, Bernd Moeller and others have maintained for imperial cities generally: princes, magistrates, and city councils, which were finally to gain so much in power and prestige from the Reformation, were invariably the last and least eager to embrace it.[5] Even Nürnberg, long cited as an example of a "magistrate's reform," is now considered to fit this pattern.[6]

There is certainly no contesting the fact that Protestant preachers, either indigenous Catholic converts or imported "missionaries" from Protestant centers, provided the spark for the Reformation in cities and towns. Although there was from the start no want of individual patrician and magisterial supporters, especially when one looks to the ranks of humanists, a broad spectrum of lower and middle strata burghers appears to have been the majority group within the first Protestant congregations. From the beginning the movement drew a representative cross-section of the urban population. But in the early phase of the Reformation the first Protestants were to be found among the more ideologically and socially mobile, either by reason of social grievance (as with the lower clergy and workers), ambition (as among certain guilds and the new rich), or ideals (as witnessed by university students and various humanistically educated patricians).

Parish priests, in whose ranks both literacy and religious sincerity could be found, were understandably early supporters. Preyed upon by the higher clergy and the mendicant orders, they were likely candidates; and as the clergy closest to the people they were also a dangerous group to lose in large numbers.[7] In a popular pamphlet of 1521 dramatizing their plight, Johannes Römer cited among the enemies of the lower clergy courtiers who stole their benefices, mendicants who reduced their fees by poaching among their parishioners (that is, by hearing confessions, preaching, and conducting burials), Jews who kept both the clergy and parishioners in debt, and popes and bishops who employed some nine legal devices (mostly set fees and fines) to fleece them.[8] The rank and file of first generation Protestant clergy, like medieval lower clergy, came largely from families of craftsmen and artisans *(Handwerkerfamilien)*.[9] Beyond the ranks of lower Catholic clergy, they were recruited from among schoolteachers, sextons, clerks, typesetters, printers, and clothmakers.[10]

In Saxony, humanists—ideologically mobile—formed the first

identifiable group of Luther's supporters, and miners—a rising working class—the first specific social group that could be called a Lutheran majority.[11] Joachim Slüter's first congregation in Rostock consisted of master artisans, journeymen, and harbor workers; wealthy merchants, the Hanse, and the University faculty joined the higher clergy in firm opposition.[12] We have seen that members of the gardener's guild were prominent within Martin Bucer's first congregation. Of the 2,247 Genevan refugees who listed their professions between 1555 and 1560, two-thirds were textile workers, craftsmen, metal workers, and goldsmiths.[13] In Lyons, where Protestants remained a minority, supporters of the Reformation appear to have come especially from a literate, rising new elite.[14]

Hard-core charter members of the Protestant movement, as these examples suggest, tended not to be the fixed elite of their areas, although individual patricians and rich merchants can be found at the very start. The ideological and social mobility of majority groups of Protestants was not, however, that of a revolutionary mob. Although the Reformation triggered revolts against external episcopal and eventually imperial authority once it became a unified, city-wide movement, internally there was normally a gradual period of nonrevolutionary development. This often involved riots or the threat thereof, and it could force a broadening of the base of power within a city as magistrates and councils adjusted to the wishes of new Protestant majorities. It could even tip the balance of power in favor of one or another established faction within city government, appearing most often to enhance the power of the guilds at the expense of the more aristocratic elements. But the Reformation did not require an internal political revolution.[15] The first Protestant groups did not succeed by violent political revolt but by winning established political support. Luther spoke for every major reformer and most Protestant congregations when he praised the politically nonrevolutionary character of the Reformation as a providential sign of its truthfulness.[16]

Why were magistrates and city councils, even within sympathetic governments, always more the brakes than the motor of reform? [17] It is important that government "conservatism" be kept in proper perspective. In distinguishing the various moments of the Reformation's development within a city—from (1) evangelical preaching to

(2) the formation of a (militant) popular following to (3) the grudging support and final sanction by government—two things should be borne in mind about the last. First, official approval came last not only in the order of progression but also in the sense of being the decisive, final step in the Protestant movement. Reformers fully recognized the necessity of winning magisterial sanction; it was from the start an accepted, expected part of their program, something they undertook not only coercively by whipping up a popular "army," but also by direct appeal, rational argument, and compromise. The first generation of Protestant reformers were nothing if not shrewd tacticians, careful to pace their reforms, and quick to distinguish between those areas which required a discreet retreat or an all-or-nothing fight.

In the second place, government sanction of the Reformation came last in what was for the sixteenth century an orderly and natural pattern of change. Magistrates' well-documented fear of citizen disorder and anarchy expressed not only conservative self-interest but also the understanding of their official mandate. Civil peace through law and order was, in the divine economy, government's reason for existing. Even changes backed by strong majority sentiment required gradual implementation, observing certain proprieties of law and order city-wide and empire-wide. Assurances were required that Protestant "freedom," often in the face of what appeared to be strong evidence to the contrary, was indeed religious and not the dissolution of basic social bonds. Margrave Casimir of Brandenburg-Ansbach-Kulmbach, for example, had Protestant preachers in his lands clarify from their pulpits that the new "freedom of a Christian" was no challenge to established political authority.[18] There was strong preference among governments for introducing the Reformation officially as a *fait accompli,* by way of rigged disputations, veritable charades tacitly agreed to in advance, as happened in Nürnberg,[19] Zurich,[20] and Constance.[21] It was only natural for city fathers to temporize and dawdle until both the necessity and a consensus for broad institutional change were nearly absolute and the conditions most favorable. Sympathetic magistrates advised reformers to pursue such a course of action.[22] If it is a misconception to assume that burghers and their governments internally promoted the Reformation stride for stride, it is an even greater misconception to expect that sixteenth-century governments would initiate rather than consolidate massive religious change within their cities.

From the start Protestant preachers were not isolated from the inner circles of political power. We know Spalatin's important mediatory role between Luther and Frederick the Wise[23] and the close relationship Philip of Hesse maintained with Melanchthon, Bucer, and Zwingli. When the University of Marburg was founded in 1527 Melanchthon, who had catechized Philip in the new faith, was among the first to whom he offered a chair; and Zwingli and Bucer were reformers with whom Philip felt at ease discussing power politics.[24] There are many examples of sympathy and support among Bürgermeister, council members, and key city bureaucrats. In Constance the patrician reformers Ambrosius Blarer and Johannes Zwick had close relatives at the pinnacles of power. Zwick's brother Konrad was elected to the small council in 1525; Blarer's father had been Bürgermeister and his uncle, Thomas Blarer, joined the small council in 1524. Blarer was also a close friend of the powerful city clerk Jörg Vögeli, a serious student of Luther and the Bible as early as 1519 and Luther's public defender against charges of heresy in 1523.[25] In Nürnberg the city clerk Lazarus Spengler wrote the first lay defense of the new theology (1519). He was even included, along with his fellow citizen and humanist Willibald Pirckheimer, in the papal bull which condemned Luther in 1521.[26] In Rostock the advent of the learned syndic Johann Oldendorp, an articulate and enthusiastic Lutheran who served from 1526 to 1533, was a decisive turning point in the reform of the city. Not only were there *Martinianer* in the city councils, but the dukes of Mecklenburg, Rostock's territorial rulers, took a *sic et non* stance toward Protestants. Albrecht VII remained Catholic, his wife was reportedly "gut martnichs," and he helped the Reformation by inaction. The Worms decree against Luther went unpublished in Mecklenburg as it did in the Saxony of Frederick the Wise. Duke Heinrich appointed the future Protestant leader Slüter to the Peterskirche in 1523, and his son's tutor was educated in Wittenberg.[27]

The Bürgermeister of Strasbourg and Ulm also gave Protestants important growing room in the early years. Jacob Sturm, who assumed office in 1524, and less well-known council members were sympathetic to the Strasbourg reformers from the start, and after the city officially embraced the Reformation the Strasbourg magistracy could act with greater decisiveness against its radical critics than did the reformers themselves, largely because Anabaptist and Spiritualist teaching threatened the civil order it was mandated to uphold as well as the new religious truth it was then committed to support.[28] Bernhard Besserer, Ulm's Bürgermeister through the period of the Reformation, came to be better known for moderating the zeal of Ulm's Lutheran reformers.[29] In Augsburg, where the great merchant-bankers remained loyal Catholics, the Bürgermeister Ulrich Rehlinger was among the earliest supporters of the Reformation. Only one councilman, Ulrich Arzt, the brother-in-law of Jacob Fugger the Rich, appears from the start to have been an outspoken opponent of basic Protestant reforms. Even the powerful jurist and city clerk (from 1497 to 1534) Conrad Peutinger, while never a Protestant, supported such basic reforms of the new theology as clerical marriage, the Eucharist cup for the laity, and liturgical use of the vernacular—practices that Protestants had got away with in Augsburg years before the Reformation was officially sanctioned. The Augsburg magistracy was of course guided by decisions that affected the larger political welfare of the city. Magisterial support of the Reformation was conditioned by imperial pressures to remain Catholic and by the important human factor that many officials had sons and daughters, or relatives with sons and daughters, in church offices and convents.[30] Such were among the considerations that dictated a cautious advance even when Protestant conviction ran very high.

Powerful Protestant groups in imperial cities put the diplomatic skills of their governments to a test during the 1520s. On the one hand, city councils were very conscious of their *machtpolitisch* dependence and legal obligations to the emperor, who pressured them from above to remain Catholic at all costs; on the other, they felt the pinch of their obligations to a citizenry that was pressing for Lutheran or Zwinglian reforms from below. It was a situation conducive to a defensive, hedging posture. Some cities, like Nürnberg and Strasbourg, were to perform virtuoso balancing acts.[31]

The dilemma of the government in Ulm is revealing and representative. By the end of 1523 the Ulm magistracy was convinced that Lutheran ideas were too entrenched *im gemeinen man* to be forcibly suppressed. The response was a policy of cautious compromise and delay. Preachers in both camps were instructed, in accordance with the Reichsregiment's mandate of February, 1523, to confine their sermons to a simple exposition of Scripture, avoiding disputed doctrinal points. The people were admonished to remember their oaths of obedience, and the government for its part protested ignorance and neutrality on all doctrinal issues. Palliative measures were passed—for example, a common chest ordinance in 1528 for which Protestant preachers had pushed. This policy of neutrality ("Neutralitätspolitik," as Naujoks calls it) manifestly displeased both the imperial Reichsregiment and the Protestant congregations, although reformers like Luther and Zwingli fully recognized the dilemma of sympathetic magistrates and tried to cooperate. The policy continued in Ulm as elsewhere until 1530 when the Diet of Augsburg finally forced a clear-cut decision upon imperial cities. On November 3, 1530, eighty-seven percent of the citizenry of Ulm voted against the Diet's order of a full reversion to the Catholic status quo ante and chose to embrace the Reformation.[32] The onesidedness of the vote in Ulm was reflected in other cities caught up in the "voting wave" that swept Germany following the Diet.[33] Such heavy votes in favor of the Reformation suggest the power of popular sentiment that governments had been trying to harness. It is revealing of government habit that even after the official decision in favor of the Reformation, Ulm rushed to underwrite neither the Augsburg Confession of the Lutherans nor the *Confessio Tetrapolitana* of the Zwinglian cities. It sided with a middle group of cities that hoped both to retain their important imperial bridges and to accede to the religious preferences of the majority of their citizens without hoisting an international Protestant banner.[34]

Rare indeed is the example of rapid and unqualified institutional change within a Reformation city. New religious ordinances evolved slowly and piecemeal. It was not unusual for the Mass, the centerpiece in the Protestant attack on Catholic practices, to continue to be celebrated for five years or more after the Protestant movement became dominant. In Wittenberg celebration of Mass persisted until 1525; it was not abolished in Strasbourg until 1529,[35] although its performance was restricted to the chapter churches in the spring of 1525. The slow pace of its removal in Zurich fractured the reform party irreconcilably.[36] In Nürnberg the Reformation had an evolutionary span of thirteen years (from 1520 to 1533), in

Osnabrück over twenty (from 1521 to 1542), with city councils warming to practically all the religious reforms but few of the sociopolitical demands of Lutheran workers.[37]

The constructive phase of the Reformation in Constance extended from 1520, when the free flow of Lutheran writings was permitted, until the issuance of the *Zuchtordnung* of 1531.[38] In 1524 episcopal jurisdiction over the clergy was challenged, and in 1525 the marriage of the Protestant preachers Windner and Metzler was defended by the magistracy. In the wake of the unrest created by the Peasants' Revolt, clerical privileges were restricted; with the exception of the bishop, suffragan bishop, and the functionaries in the cathedral chapter, all clergymen were required to swear an oath of allegiance to the city (127 secular and 89 regular clergymen so swore) and to contribute either in person, through surrogates, or by monetary payments to the upkeep of the city walls—all normal obligations of citizenship. The year 1527 saw the issuance of a new marriage ordinance, the subjection of the clergy to taxation, the abolition of Catholic preaching—and the exodus of the remaining Catholic clergy. Between 1527 and 1529 there was a gradual ending of the Mass and removal of images from churches, and the number of religious holidays was pruned to twenty-four. It is a telling commentary on both the magisterial hand in religious reform and the transformation of the Reformation into an established religion that the great *Zuchtordnung* of 1531, the capstone of the reform, is still criticized today as too legalistic a document to claim as its inspiration Luther's doctrine of justification by faith.[39]

Far to the north in Rostock the Reformation was similarly dragged out. Slüter began preaching Protestant doctrine in 1525, and a sympathetic government met strong Catholic criticism with a reprimand and counsel of tolerance. In 1528 Slüter married publicly. While this was done with official disapproval—no member of government was in attendance—there was, nevertheless, no official interference or censure of this important symbolic act. Students in the University, a Catholic bastion to the end, sent two kegs of wine, which were, however, confiscated en route! A Protestant order of worship was approved in December, 1530, although traditional ceremonies were also permitted to continue. In April, 1531, Franciscans and Dominicans were ordered to wear civilian clothes on city streets; in September the Protestant order of worship was installed in the main city church. The year 1532 brought permission to sell meat on traditional fast days, a law against attending mass in surrounding village churches, and the first official sanction of clerical marriage. In 1534 a comprehensive religious ordinance consolidated the reform, with even the University faculty giving in.[40] Though such gradual and piecemeal change may seem to have moved at a snail's pace, it made it possible for the Reformation to change habits invested with centuries of value without social upheaval. All things considered, it was a magistrate's type of reform—not because reform was forced upon the populace from above by the magistrate's sword, but because reform was made to percolate peacefully through the citizenry to the top from below.

Once the decision for the Reformation was official and the law of the land, the governments of Protestant cities acted decisively to ensure moderation on the part of the Protestant preachers, who often wanted to carry reform much farther than either government or citizenry were prepared to go. Success spoiled many a Protestant freedom fighter.

Martin Bucer, who would win the reputation for being the most tolerant of the Protestant reformers, considered it evidence of the corruption of secular government that it not only neglected to enforce but could even ridicule such "divine laws" as the death penalty for adultery, the abolition of prostitution, and corporal punishment for those who hindered the preaching of God's word.[41] Bucer's social vision for Strasbourg was never realized to his satisfaction. When Strasbourg's ecclesiastical ordinance was written in 1534, the government, suspecting a new papacy to be in the making, firmly rejected Bucer's proposal to place control over the religious and moral life of the city in the hands of the new church.[42] The Ulm reformer Konrad Sam also had designs that would have given sole initiative for moral discipline to the Protestant clergy, a move that the magistracy resisted as stoutly in Ulm as the Genevan councils would later do in the celebrated expulsion of John Calvin from Geneva after his ambitious power play in 1537. Concern was expressed by the Ulm magistracy, as in Strasbourg and also later by the Genevan councils, that the Reformation not become the occasion for the creation of a new papacy. On this point Naujoks has found the magistrates of Ulm, whose attitude he characterizes as "Erasmian," to have been more perceptive of majority burgher sentiment than were the victorious Protestant preachers.[43]

What can we conclude? It is possible to distinguish three agents and levels of the Reformation within the cities, each making an important contribution to the final shape of reform. Preachers and laymen learned in Scripture provided the initial stimulus; ideologically and socially mobile burghers, primarily from the (larger) lower and middle strata, created a driving wedge of popular support; and government consolidated and moderated the new institutional changes. Depending upon the point at which one examines the process, it is possible to identify the Reformation as a preacher's, a people's, or a magistrate's reform. Viewed fully, however, the Reformation was a movement that embraced and required for its completion all three moments. It was not completed with the first sermon polemics and nuclear congregations. The process of gaining government sanction was an integral part of the development pattern and of the final content of the Reformation; magisterial consolidation is an essential part of the definition of the Reformation. From this larger perspective it is an oversimplification to play a people's reform off against a reactionary magistracy, making a patrician city hall the key adversary of the reformers and their first congregations. To the extent that governments prevented Protestant preachers from erecting new papacies and enforced a certain moderation and simplicity in religious life, they may even be seen to have been more in accord with the original impulse of the Reformation to simplify religious and enhance secular life than many a zealous Protestant cleric. We must deal with sixteenth-century magistrates not only in terms of their Machiavellian uses of religion, but also with an eye to their conscientious monitoring of the clerical abuses of religion.

The Tactics of Reform

Divine and Human Righteousness

With the demise of episcopal authority, canon law, and the traditional means of religious support, Protestants early became dependent upon political bureaucracies to ensure beneficed parishes and new schools and to rewrite and enforce new *Zucht* ordinances.[44] Having known the persecution of the righteous at first hand,

Protestants believed as firmly as any medieval pope that a religiously "neutral" magistrate was a dangerous magistrate. Not only German Lutherans were ready to let the willing rulers become "emergency bishops." Short of organization, wedged between Catholic critics and radicals from their own ranks, and viewing with increasing alarm the reception of the Reformation by many as justification for gross religious indiscipline, majority Protestants demanded strong and decisive secular policing of the religious life. The winning and "grooming" of magistrates became a high priority. Biblical examples like King Jehoshaphat, who became great by supporting true religion, were paraded before magistrates, and the recalcitrant threatened with the most forceful prophecies of providential vengeance.[45] But charm and flattery were also lavishly applied.[46]

An initial problem for Protestants, as great for Zwinglians as for Lutherans, was a clarification of the role civic righteousness should play within a religion based on salvation by faith alone. In the beginning Protestants were handicapped in approaching magistrates by the very spectre of indiscipline they themselves would come so to fear. Catholic critics magnified this point on every occasion, accusing Protestants of undermining the social bonds as well as rending the religious fabric of society, and we have seen how eager Protestant apologists were to turn aside such allegations. As we have also seen, however, even strong allies like Pamphilus Gengenbach and Sebastian Meyer initially had questions about the ethical consequences of Protestantism. A copy of Gengenbach's *Ein klägliches Gespräch* (1522), which criticized Luther for hotheadedness and condemned appeals to his teaching for a justification of ethical indifference, was sent by a concerned Hans von der Planitz, electoral counsellor of Saxony at the Nürnberg Reichsregiment, to Frederick the Wise.[47] Having identified Christian righteousness with faith in Christ and stripped good works of any possible saving significance, what interest could Protestants have in penultimate civic activities? Could men content with an inner divine righteousness of faith concern themselves with the external secular affairs of the world? Might such men, in the name of inner righteousness, become too aggressive? Was evangelical law to replace secular law? Did Protestants even need magistrates? These were questions Protestants were forced to answer when they set out to win magistrates. It is not accidental that both Zwingli and Melanchthon addressed major tracts to politicians, who had no doubts about their own permanency, on the relation of divine and human righteousness.

Zwingli's important treatise *On Divine and Human Righteousness* (June 24, 1523), which fell between the two Zurich disputations that introduced the Swiss Reformation (January and October, 1523), is usually treated as a rebuttal of Anabaptist denial of the necessity of a secular state and magistracy among true Christians.[48] Although Anabaptist separatism is one side of the matter, the radicals of Zurich, like those to the north, only focused a problem intrinsic to Protestant theology, and one which would have required a response even without the so-called left wing of the Reformation. Zwingli reassured any who might have had the slightest suspicion that the new religion might lead to the demise of the magistracy. He maintained that God demanded of men a twofold righteousness—one "divine" and affecting inner attitudes toward God and man, another "human" and affecting external behavior toward God and man. Ideally, men should obey the Ten Commandments not only in their external conduct but also in their internal desire.[49] It is because the latter ability has been eradicated by the Fall that men must now be saved "inwardly" by faith alone, appealing to Christ for a divine righteousness that they will always lack on earth. Fallen men may go through the external motions, but they do not love God and their neighbor inwardly as they ought.[50] This is also, Zwingli went on to explain, the reason why external obedience to law, even if hypocritically practiced, must be enforced by secular magistrates. For although external righteousness, in comparison with inner divine righteousness, is "poor and defective" and "hardly a righteousness at all," its lapse would unleash the bestiality in fallen men and plunge society into anarchy.[51] Accordingly, after the Fall and at God's express command (Romans 13, 1 Peter 2:13), it is the office of magistrate which maintains the minimal standards of humanity and human community. In what must be one of the most curious compliments ever paid magistrates and politicians, Zwingli likened the task of the magistracy to that of a father who takes care that his misled daughter does not become a prostitute.[52]

Civic righteousness is thus most important; it may not save one, but the civically unrighteous sin against God's law and may expect his wrath.[53] In terms reminiscent of Marsilius of Padua, Zwingli also made it clear that coercive power and jurisdiction belonged only in the sphere of secular magistracy and human righteousness, denying such jurisdiction to "so-called spiritual power" and criticizing clerical exemptions from civil law as disobedience and sin against God.[54] (Catholics claiming immunity from secular courts and taxation were hardly in a position to accuse Protestants of civic neglect!) Zwingli's tract left no doubts that obedience to magistrates and promotion of civic righteousness were fundamental matters of Scripture and conscience for Protestant Christians: "He who resists magistracy resists God." [55]

When Philip Melanchthon sent his promised summary of Reformation teaching to Landgrave Philip of Hesse, in June, 1524, he too concentrated on the relation between divine righteousness *(religio, iustitia evangelica, iustitia christiana)* and human righteousness *(iustitia politica, iustitia humana)*. Philip of Hesse was assured that only "pseudolutherani" (Andress Karlstadt and Thomas Müntzer were apparently meant) excite rebellion against established authority in the name of the new religion.[56] "Inner peace" *(tranquillitas in corde et securitas)* is presented as the very defining feature of Protestant faith and "evangelical righteousness"; and "human or political righteousness," the province of the ruler, is exalted as its essential "pedagogue." [57] Men cannot be true Christians (Protestants) unless they are first men.[58] By 1525, after a sad experience with "sectarians" and the peasants, both Melanchthon and Luther were aglow with praise for the magisterial sword and secular (Roman) law as the only bar to a relapse into barbarism. Melanchthon, to Luther's discomfort, had earlier entertained the possibility of a society governed by a noncoercive evangelical law.[59] He now came to praise Roman law—the instrument by which territorial princes and their urban allies were consolidating their power over the German countryside—as not only the more effective way to govern a land, but also, because of its great scope and attention to detail, the most equitable *(aequissimum)* of human laws.[60] Melanchthon's success in convincing Philip of Hesse of the basic partnership between Protestants and magistrates, between evangelical and political righteousness, may be only too apparent in Philip's installation of the Protestant Adam Krafft of Fulda as court preacher in Marburg in August, 1525. According to the words of installation:

> He shall be our preacher, obligated by his office to stand in God's place and proclaim clearly and purely to us and all men

> the word of God and the holy gospel. This he shall do according to true Christian understanding on the basis of Scripture and with an eye to planting every good among us. He shall also be prepared to travel hither and yon and visit other pastors and otherwise let himself be sent and employed as we desire and command. And he shall do with God's grace all that is expected of a pious Christian preacher obligated by Scripture and his office.[61]

Such were the first theological embracings of magistracy. Luther would make it clear that Protestant Christians could be crack soldiers and even hangmen, and he depicted Protestant preachers as the very pillars of secular society.[62] Zwingli died a soldier, sword in hand. And John Calvin would leave in the *Institutes* a paean to civil office as "the most sacred and by far the most honorable of all callings in the whole life of mortal men." [63]

Scholars have found theocratic visions in Zwingli's treatise *On Divine and Human Righteousness* and in Bucer's contemporaneous tract *One Should Not Live for Oneself Alone* (August, 1523), which they believe to be quite alien to Luther and to foreshadow a subsequent divergence between the Reformed and Lutheran Protestant traditions.[64] The argument, briefly, is that Zwingli and Bucer, like Calvin later, more closely integrated religion and society and were determined to transform the latter by the former, subjecting rulers to Scripture's guidance and the standards of divine righteousness; Luther and his followers, by contrast, tended rather to drive religion and society apart, embracing the secular world much as they found it. The modern form of this argument has its roots in the work of Ernst Troeltsch.[65] Zwingli's and Bucer's comments in these early works on the role of government are not, however, so far from the views expressed in Luther's contemporaneous treatise *On Temporal Authority: To What Extent It Should Be Obeyed* (written in December, 1522 and published in March, 1523), a key document in Moeller's case against Luther as one who drove a wedge between religious and civic communities.[66] The different situations in which the three reformers wrote may better explain the different emphases that scholars have detected than does speculation on Old Testament theocratic notions or so-called citified theologies operating in the back of Zwingli's and Bucer's minds. Luther wrote from a defensive position over against both the emperor and certain hostile territorial rulers. Not surprisingly, he stressed the primary responsibility of temporal authority to punish manifest evil and protect the righteous (Lutherans), while strictly defining the limits of its power over the souls of Christians. Zwingli and Bucer, however, wrote from a favorable, offensive position, supported by strong and sympathetic city governments. Not surprisingly, they broadened to the fullest the perimeters of magisterial responsibility for the religious life. In both cases, however, "tyrants" were opposed with the best arguments at hand, and the strongest possible case made for government protection of evangelical doctrine and practice. There should be no doubt that in 1523 Luther, no less than Bucer and Zwingli, would have been pleased to have a truly Christian magistracy and to dwell in a uniformly Christian society.

When Luther's treatise *On Temporal Authority* is read less as an abstract theological document and more as the response to a concrete historical crisis, his stance is hardly as extreme as scholars have maintained. In the treatise a narrow, punitive function of government is stressed and the theoretical independence of "true Christians" from such government, on the ground that truly righteous men need no coercive oversight, is declared—a statement which, taken abstractly, might seem to smack even of Anabaptist separatism. Luther did not, as he makes clear in the treatise, seriously believe that such "true Christians" existed this side of eternity, but he was writing in keen awareness of the present persecution of Lutherans by papal, imperial, and territorial authorities. At the very outset of the treatise he remarks that the times have changed since he wrote the *Address to the Christian Nobility of the German Nation* (1520) urging Christian rulers, in the name of reform, to extend their power into the spiritual realm. Faced now with coercive government action against righteous Lutherans, he finds he must rather point out the limits of temporal authority.[67] In 1523 Luther was not dealing with the amenable city fathers of Zurich and Strasbourg, but with those he himself describes as "tyrants" who burn his books, order the confiscation of New Testaments, and are intent on having his head.[68] At this time in Zurich, by contrast, Zwingli was enjoying the "charade" of the first Zurich Disputation.[69] And in late 1523 Capito wrote that Strasbourg was a place where Protestants could preach "freely, unmolested, and without fear" *(unverholen/frey/on sorg)*.[70] Such could not be said so confidently of much of Saxony.

Such sobering experiences, as well as sound theological considerations, lay behind Luther's differentiation of Christians and citizens and his failure to insist upon strictly "Christian" magistrates.[71] In 1523 Luther was prepared to settle for princes who would simply fulfill their fundamental mandate to punish the wicked and protect the righteous. Even then, however, he went on to insist not only that Christians, for the sake of their neighbors, should be active in the work of government, but even that the temporal sword and authority "belong more appropriately to Christians than to any other men on earth." [72] Later, when magistrates were friendlier and sheer survival less an issue, Luther too broadened magisterial responsibility and appreciated its constructive role in religious life,[73] although always carefully qualifying government participation in the affairs of the church as the duty of a "Christian brother" and not the expression of a right intrinsic to the magisterial office itself; princes promoted religion as "members" and "friends" of the church ("Mitchristen, mitpriester, mitgeystlich, mitmechtig in allen dingen"), not as independent worldly powers.[74] That was an important theological argument, intended to safeguard the vocational integrity of clergy at their point of closest cooperation with government. It may be argued that the distinction was in fact more theoretical than practical once the Reformation was politicized. But the ability of Protestants so to distinguish the civil and religious spheres—and no Protestant reformer failed to do so[75]—proved as important to Bucer, Zwingli, and Calvin in their respective situations as it did to the Wittenberg reformers in the early years of the Reformation. Both Lutheran and Reformed Protestants maintained a basic separation of church and state within the basic unity of religion and society.[76] Luther's insistence on the uniqueness of Christian righteousness was no more a disjunction of religion and society than Bucer's and Zwingli's subjection of rulers to evangelical norms was an identification of Christian and civic righteousness. Scholars have greatly exaggerated their differences.

A final word in Luther's defense may be borrowed from Zwingli, and from a time when they were in conflict over the interpretation of Christ's presence in the Eucharist (May, 1528). Zwingli scholars have praised their man at Luther's expense by citing a statement by

Zwingli, ostensibly in criticism of Luther, that the kingdom of Christ is not only inward but "also external." [77] The statement occurs in a letter from Zwingli to Ambrosius Blarer, who had written to ask whether magistrates may order things which offend the consciences of weak Christians, or should in such cases rather remain aloof from external religious regulations, permitting each to follow his own opinion (as Romans 14:5 seemed to suggest). Zwingli answered that the latter course of action, implying magisterial neutrality in external religious matters, was a "semierror" derived from a well known paradoxical statement by Luther that the kingdom of Christ was "not external." [78] Zwingli assured Blarer that Christ mandated the external regulation of religious life: "Christ wanted and so ordered that we observe a certain way of life also in external things; it is not true that his kingdom is not also external." [79] Hence, it is both fitting and necessary for magistrates to order religious life with the consent of the church.[80]

In conclusion Zwingli pointed out that Luther himself was hardly opposed to such regulation, despite his earlier "paradox." He advised Blarer to look more at what Luther did than at what he said; Luther presently advised Saxon rulers to impose Lutheran views of the Eucharist, which offended not a few consciences, and to suppress the true views of Zwinglians! While their differences on the Eucharist remained very real, Zwingli assured Blarer that he and Luther were fully agreed with Saint Paul on the propriety and even necessity of magisterial regulation of external religious life.[81] For Luther, too, the kingdom of Christ was "also external."

Pacing the Reform

The Reformation did not succeed by flattery alone. Protestant success in winning magisterial support required willingness to pace the reform in accordance with the political realities of the day. A paradigm of the expectation and tactics of magistrates and reformers alike is the development of the Reformation in Wittenberg during the critical years 1521 and 1522.

There is no small irony in the fact that Luther's protector, Elector Frederick the Wise of Saxony, was a paragon of medieval religious piety. Perhaps at the time Europe's greatest image-maker, he unwittingly created its greatest image-breaker. An old Catholic dog, Frederick was still to learn a new trick or two from his famous university professor whom he first saw at his trial in Worms and with whom he reportedly never spoke a word.

As a young man Frederick had gone on pilgrimages, at one time spending five days in Jerusalem in 1493. He made lavish outlays (an estimated 200,000 gulden) for the rebuilding of Castle Church in Wittenberg and its adjacent monastery and commissioned paintings for both by Albrecht Dürer and Lucas Cranach. He supported the work of Mutian (who acquired Greek texts for the University library) and other humanists of the region. During his reign the number of religious offices in the monastery in Wittenberg increased fourfold (from twenty to eighty). In the year in which Luther wrote the treatise *The Freedom of a Christian* (1520) almost 10,000 private masses were celebrated by eighty-three resident clerics.[82] Nothing so attests to Frederick's medieval piety, however, as his famous relic collection. Frederick was obsessed with relics, and with the assistance of Pope Julius II he made extensive arrangements for their location and collection throughout Europe and the Near East. The relics were arranged in receptacles of crystal, pearl, or ivory, and consisted mostly of small pieces of bodies, bones, and clothes connected with especially important events in the life of the church. There were some large entries: for example, four whole skeletons from the society of Saint Ursula and the complete corpse of an innocent child killed by King Herod. Among the Old Testament relics were a piece of the burning bush and some soot from the fiery furnace. In the New Testament collection there was something from virtually every significant person and event in the life of Jesus: Mary's milk, a piece of the tree under which she first nursed the infant Jesus, a strand of her hair, pieces of her clothes, girdle, and veil; a piece of Jesus' crib, straw from the stable of his birth, some of the gold and myrrh brought to him by the three kings. At the time Luther wrote the treatise on the *Freedom of a Christian* Frederick's collection exceeded 19,000 pieces.[83]

After the imperial election of Charles V, in which Frederick, himself a short-term but quite unrealistic candidate, had played a key role, pressure mounted to put an end to the Lutheran movement in Saxony. Since 1518, when the official process against Luther began, Frederick was keenly aware of Luther's popularity (as was also Luther himself[84]) and insisted that no action be taken against him without an imperial hearing of his case. Frederick was legally entitled to make this request and, in light of Luther's strength, he was under political pressure to do so. Although there are signs that Frederick may have been personally attracted to the young theologian who spoke so eloquently of duty and conscience, and even to the gospel he preached, it is probable that Frederick's religious concessions to the Reformation, like his protection of Luther, were grudging, simply the price he knew he must pay for law and order in his realm.[85] Be that as it may, after the Diet of Worms (April–May, 1521), Frederick managed to prevent the publication and enforcement of the imperial edict against Luther in Saxony, and he became to all intents and purposes the Reformation's protector.

The religious revolution began in Wittenberg in earnest in the fall of 1521 while Luther, ostensibly for his own safety, was sequestered in Wartburg Castle. Already in Erfurt and Gotha there had been Protestant violence against priests. While expressing concern over the effect it would have on the Reformation, Luther interpreted such rowdyism by young artisans and students as a sign that people would no longer tolerate the civic irresponsibility (especially tax exemptions) of the clergy, nor permit themselves to be burdened further by them.[86] Through territorial representatives in and around Wittenberg, Frederick was fully informed of the Protestant innovations, their perpetrators, their theological arguments, and the reaction of both laymen and clergymen. Spurred by an intemperate Augustinian monk, Gabriel Zwilling, and with only passive resistance from the city council, Protestants turned the sacrament of the Mass into a battleground. Protestants gave the laity of Wittenberg the Eucharistic cup, treated the Mass as a memorial to Christ's historical sacrifice (not a present resacrificing to be adored and worshipped), and proposed the abolition of all private masses in the city.[87] Seven members of the University, speaking for the Protestants, wrote Frederick in defense of the changes and pointed out his duty, as a Christian magistrate "in the time of the gospel's reappearance," to support evangelical truth.[88] Frederick also heard at this time from the Catholic opposition (some of whom had lost their jobs during the recent reform of the University curriculum by Luther and Melanchthon), which strongly protested the innovations in the city's religious life.

Frederick replied to the Protestants on October 25, 1521, through Christian Beyer, the counsellor through whom he dealt with the

University. He expressed his sincere desire to be a Christian prince—that, he says, is why he founded the University in the first place—but he also made clear his equally strong concern to avoid "division, tumult, and trouble" *(zwispeldigkeit, auffrur und beschwerung)*. Fearing haste in such important matters, he insisted upon broader support in the city for the desired changes, pointedly informing the Protestants that if, as they argued, such changes were manifest gospel truth, it should not be hard to muster manifest majority support. Ever practical, Frederick also wanted to know what was to be done with the endowments that had long been given in good faith for commemorative masses, if private masses were now to be abolished. Conceding the theologians' prowess in matters of religious truth, he reiterated once again his intention to see the matter handled "so that there will result no division, tumult, and trouble." [89] The basic magisterial position was subsequently reinforced, in the wake of religious violence, by instructions to repay with physical punishment those who attempted to force religious change.[90]

The University did not respond to Frederick until December 12, 1521. Just as Frederick felt he could not bend on the fundamental mandate of his office—the preservation of law and order—the Protestant reformers of Wittenberg expressed their inability to relinquish fundamental points of the doctrine they were obligated to uphold. They protested that, in matters of religion, God rather than man must be obeyed and that, although a minority, they nonetheless spoke for the truth in rejecting the abuse of the Mass. They despaired of the broad agreement Frederick desired, seeing too many persons presently blinded in the matter of the Mass by tradition. As for the disposition of endowments for abolished private masses, the Protestants believed that inasmuch as the monastery had been founded for truth and not for error, such endowments could legitimately be shifted to serve the purposes of Christian education. Finally, they informed Frederick that the defense of error in the face of clear biblical truth was the true source of "tumult," and made clear their conviction that such was not too high a price to pay for truth.[91] The Catholic opposition also responded at this time to Frederick's standpat policy, defending anew the persistence of traditional practices, and purring the Elector's line against the Protestants: "No establishment can be maintained without obedience and order." [92]

Wittenberg Protestants had been in constant correspondence with Luther, who had returned to Wittenberg clandestinely and against Frederick's clear order shortly before their reply of December 12.[93] They doubtless believed their strong stand to be an expression of their leader's set policy. Earlier, incensed by Frederick's cutting short a disputation on celibacy and confession, Luther had scolded Melanchthon and the Wittenberg reform party for not being aggressive enough with the electoral court. "I ask you all from now on to anticipate the court's suggestions instead of meekly following them. . . . Not one half would have been accomplished had I obeyed the court's every counsel!" [94] When Scripture was absolutely clear on a capital point of doctrine that was at stake, then it was necessary to bristle and make an all-or-nothing stand—that was Luther's basic position. He himself had followed it to the letter very recently after learning that Spalatin and Frederick had, in the name of public peace, impeded the publication of his attack on the planned sale of a new indulgence in Halle by Albrecht of Mainz. Here was a capital point of doctrine on which Scripture was clear and which the Reformation forfeited at its peril. An enraged Luther wrote to Spalatin from the Wartburg on November 11, 1521:

> I will not accept your statement that the Sovereign will allow nothing to be written against Mainz or anything else that could disturb the public peace. I would rather lose you, the Sovereign himself, and the whole world . . . . Your idea about not disturbing the public peace is beautiful, but will you allow the eternal peace of God to be disturbed by the wicked and sacrilegious actions of that son of perdition [Albrecht]? Not so Spalatin! Not so Elector! [95]

"It is a smaller sin to hiss at an impious preacher [Albrecht] than to accept his doctrine," Luther assured Frederick; and he later informed Albrecht, "If your idol [the new indulgence] is not taken down, my duty toward divine doctrine and Christian salvation is a necessary . . . reason to attack Your Electoral Grace." [96]

Although the Mass was the focal point, Protestants in Wittenberg were moving on other fronts. In December proposals had been forwarded by the city council to Frederick for consideration as interim directives from the reform party until a firm religious order for the city, satisfactory to all official sides, was established. These articles, without the Elector's prior approval, were to develop into a formal but short-lived religious ordinance for the city in the following month. They were:

1. Free preaching of God's word.
2. An end to prescribed (endowed) masses, since many priests must say five, six, seven, or more masses daily, and none can do it with devotion, desire, love, joy, or a good conscience.
3. Abolition of all requiem, burial, anniversary, confraternal, marriage, and votive masses, since the Mass benefits only those who are physically present to receive it.
4. Extension of the Eucharistic cup to laymen.
5. Closing of taverns in which illegal drunkenness occurs.
6. The shutting down of whorehouses, "of which there are many in the city," and punishment of their proprietors, whoever they may be.[97]

Whereas the city council was responding to mounting internal pressures for reform, Frederick, who held the right to veto its decisions, was especially sensitive to the wishes of the emperor. The greater the distance of rulers from the reform party the greater appears their reluctance to effectuate radical changes in religious practices and institutions. Frederick returned an answer to the Protestant party on December 19, demanding that the "improper [Protestant] performance of the Mass" be stopped[98] but restating his original position in a more positive form: "The issue [must] be dealt with in a Christian and reasonable way, by disputation, writing, lecturing, preaching, and the like [that is, by actions short of actual changes in religious practice]."[99] Protestants were free to dispute, write, lecture, and preach against the Mass, but they could not in fact remove the traditional practice. Both the Elector and the Protestants might interpret that to be more than half a loaf.

On January 20, 1522, the Reichsregiment in Nürnberg ordered Frederick to stop Protestant innovations in the Mass, the flight of monks and nuns from their cloisters, and the marriage of priests in electoral Saxony.[100] This may have added to Frederick's now determined reiteration on February 13 that "disputation, writing, and preaching" were the permitted ways to reform, not formal "innovations" *(Newerung)* and tumult.[101] Gabriel Zwilling was soon dismissed from Wittenberg, and Karlstadt, despite his objections, silenced.[102]

Luther, on the point of publicly returning to Wittenberg, knew the imperial pressures on Frederick to suppress the Reformation. Despite his occasional bravado on the eve of his return,[103] Luther must have charmed Frederick with a letter he wrote on February 22. The Elector had recently and quite reluctantly begun boxing up his beloved relics in response to Wittenberg's changing religious values. Luther, long a critic of Frederick's relic collection, presented himself as Frederick's "new relic."

> Grace and joy from God the Father on the acquisition of a new relic! . . . For many years Your Grace has been acquiring relics in every land, but God has now heard Your Grace's request and has sent . . . without cost or effort a whole cross, together with nails, spears, and scourges! [104]

Luther was not to go the way of Zwilling and Karlstadt. He found reason to question Karlstadt's biblical arguments for abolishing the free celibate vows of monks (Luther capitulated here theologically and personally more slowly than his colleagues) and even saw room in Scripture for compromise on the disputed issue of communion in both kinds. Christians, he argued, were free to do as well as not to do in certain nonessential areas—and especially when the fate of the Reformation was at stake.[105] In March, 1522, having returned to the city after his long exile, Luther mounted the pulpit to direct the following course of religious change:

> The Mass is an evil thing, and God is displeased with it. . . . It must be abolished. . . . I wish private masses were abolished everywhere and only the ordinary evangelical Mass retained. Yet Christian love should not employ harshness here nor force the matter. However, it should be preached and taught with tongue and pen that to hold mass in such a manner is sinful, yet no one should be dragged away from it by the hair. . . . We must first win the hearts of the people. . . . In short, *I will preach it, teach it, write it, but I will constrain no man by force,* for faith must come freely without compulsion.[106]

Thus did Luther sanction, *expressis verbis,* the formula of concord prescribed by Frederick. The Protestants had won the right to muster popular support by disputation, writing, lecturing, and preaching. A delay in the official abolition of the Mass was for them, as it was also for Frederick, an issue more of tactics than of fundamental principle. Both sides saved face. To a certain extent the compromise smacked of that charade character of later disputations that introduced the Reformation into major Protestant cities.[107] But it was at heart a tactical pacing of reform without which the Reformation would hardly have succeeded so well as it did. The Mass was officially abolished in Wittenberg in early 1525; it had already been removed in principle in 1522. As for Frederick, he continued to stall the emperor's envoys and did not fall from papal and imperial grace until late 1523. The papal legate Aleander called for his excommunication in November of that year and in early 1524 Charles V cancelled plans for his sister Katherine's marriage to Frederick's son, Crown Prince John Frederick. Archduke Ferdinand reportedly remarked that he would prefer to see his sister drowned than enter Saxony.[108] Before he died in his bed on May 5, 1525, Frederick received the sacrament *sub utraque specie,* with cup as well as bread. Whether or not it was done from the heart, this was an overt acknowledgment both that a revolution in religious belief and practice had occurred in Saxony and that it had occurred peacefully.

The Scripture Principle

At the conclusion of the first Zurich Disputation (January 29, 1523) the Bürgermeister and councils of Zurich made the declaration that, inasmuch as Zwingli had not been refuted "by means of the Scriptures," he would continue to preach as before and all secular clergy in and around Zurich would henceforth "undertake and preach nothing except what they can defend by the gospels and other right divine Scriptures." [109] The Disputation, which officially introduced the Reformation into Zurich, had itself been conducted on this deceptively revolutionary principle. It tested the scriptural basis of traditional doctrines and practices as detailed in advance by Zwingli's sixty-seven-article assessment, from the perspective of Scripture alone, of traditional assumptions about the pope, the Mass, intercession of saints, good works, merit, clerical property, mandatory fasting, holidays and pilgrimages, clerical dress, monastic orders, religious "sects" and confraternities, the ban, the divine rights of magistrates, prayer, confession, purgatory, and the priesthood.[110] To make Scripture the only court of appeal, excluding the authority of church history and tradition, was to make the outcome something of a foregone conclusion, as all parties to the Disputation, especially the bishop's protesting spokesman, Johann Faber, knew full well in advance.[111]

What was established in the Zurich Disputation was the quasi-legal guideline of the new Protestant "ecclesiopolitical complex." Religious authority was henceforth based on Scripture alone. Religious truth was determined by Protestant ministers in dialogue with their magistrates: the ministers interpreted Scripture, and the magistrates sat in judgment on their interpretations. That was the procedure by which the Reformation won its official way. Although reformers described Scripture as "self-interpreting" *(interpres sui ipsius)*[112] and would deny by this device that magistrates really sat as judges over it, in actual fact it was magisterial sanction of Protestant interpretations of Scripture that institutionalized the Reformation. When Martin Bucer submitted a formal twelve-article summary of Protestant teaching to the Strasbourg magistracy in October /November, 1523, he listed belief in the Bible as the "singular norm, rule, and guideline" in religious matters as "the first and main article of the new theology," the common basis of the work of all the German reformers (Luther, Melanchthon, Karlstadt, and Zwingli).[113] Capito even believed the Protestant Scripture principle to be in conformity with the Nürnberg Reichsregiment's mandate of February, 1523, confining all parties to a simple exposition of Scripture. Actually the mandate, as Catholics correctly argued, recommended Scripture "according to the interpretation of writings accepted and approved by the Christian church." [114] Once firmly established, the Scripture principle seemed a boon to reformers of every stripe. It was magisterial acceptance of it that emboldened Thomas Müntzer to preach his famous *Sermon Before the Princes* in the deluded hope of winning the Saxon sword for his version of religious reform and that gave German peasants the equally deluded hope of reordering society.[115]

The Scripture principle was as great a bonanza for magistrates as for Protestant reformers. Martin Bucer, whose reputation as the most moderate of Protestant reformers deserves reconsideration, may have gone further than others in making this clear. Bucer came to Strasbourg an excommunicated and married priest, subject to both episcopal and imperial punishment.[116] As a part of his defense against episcopal efforts to remove him from the city, he delivered behind closed doors a special statement to the Strasbourg magistracy on June 17 or 19, 1523. That the magistracy ruled in favor of this renegade priest and ignored episcopal and imperial pressures to reject him is commentary enough on its disposition toward the Reformation at this date. If Bucer's statement contributed little to the magistrates' growing Protestant resolve, it certainly reminded them in new terms of the benefits involved in becoming Protestant. Bucer's statement is a striking demonstration that the Bible could be as effective a means for city councils to "bell" their bishops and clergy as it was for Protestant reformers to obtain new religious and domestic freedoms. Under attack by his bishop, Bucer appealed directly from spiritual to secular authority, making Scripture alone, as interpreted by himself and judged by Strasbourg's magistrates, the arbiter of the matter. The validity of his priesthood and his marriage as a priest were issues to be decided by himself in consultation with magistrates as they together read the Bible. Bucer demonstrated his confidence in this approach by twice offering to submit to death by stoning if his teaching and actions proved to be without clear foundation in Scripture.[117]

The bishop had pointedly reminded the Strasbourg magistracy that the imperial mandate of March 6, 1523, instructed that married priests leaving their orders forfeited both their benefices and all freedoms pertaining to the religious life. It was in answer to this threat that Bucer drove home to the magistracy the benefits of the Reformation. Echoing Capito's defenses of clerical citizenship, he protested:

> I wish to have no freedoms beyond those of other Christians and laymen. I fully recognize the authority of the magistracy over myself as over any layman and wish to give it every possible obedience, whether it pertain to honor, body, or goods, as I and every man am obligated by divine law [Romans 13] to do. I desire to be punished when I deserve it. I ask only that I be permitted to do what God has given me the right to do, and

> which none [but he] can deny, to earn my living by serving my neighbor [as a priest]. Good, divine preaching cannot be harmed by my marriage, regardless of what any law says. Saint Paul wanted even bishops, or preachers in high positions of leadership, to have honorable wives. Also I desire no special benefice.[118]

Bucer approached the council members as a magistracy ordained by God and obligated *(schuldig)* to protect those whose teaching agreed with Scripture. He concluded by saying that he and his wife submitted the judgment of their religious doctrine and their marriage to the council, not only as to their "lords" *(herren)*, but also as to their "kinsmen" *(vetter)*.[119] This was not only an expression of belief in the intimate unity of religion and society, but also a benediction upon a new spiritual authority.

In the Reformation's transition from popular movement to official religion, the Scripture principle nowhere served magisterial usurpation of episcopal authority more directly than in Constance. In November, 1523, the popular Protestant preacher Bartholomaeus Metzler was under attack by the resident bishop, Hugo.[120] Metzler offered to submit to an examination on the basis of Scripture, recanting whatever was there found wanting. With the first Zurich Disputation fresh in mind, the failing bishop was not disposed to enter again into a disputation whose ground rule was Scripture alone. The magistracy of Constance, convinced that arbitrary treatment of Metzler would bring revolt, was not ready to permit his suppression without a hearing. Appealing to the Nürnberg mandate of February, 1523, they protested that Scripture must be the test of preaching and "specially appointed learned theologians" (the phrasing was that of the mandate) must be consulted in cases of alleged heresy. The bishop was accordingly informed that "neither the vicar [Johann Faber] nor his superiors [Hugo] had the power of judgment" in the matter and that no action would be taken against Metzler until there was a hearing on the basis of Scripture.[121] The quarrel with the bishop, who received support from Archduke Ferdinand (who was, however, too distracted by the advancing Turks to seriously threaten Swiss Protestants), peaked in February, 1524, with the issuance by the magistracy of an *Instruction to All Preachers on How the Gospel of Christ Is to Be Preached and Taught in*

Constance, a document that has been characterized as the official foundation of the Reformation in Constance.[122] According to the *Instruction,* the clergy were henceforth to preach only the gospel

> according to true Christian understanding, without any admixture of human traditions that have no basis in the holy biblical Scriptures . . . and especially to omit all fables, useless little things, and matters of dispute which Christians can just as well do without, together with whatever might lead them into error or turn them against their magistrates, preaching only what truly serves the honor of God and quiets consciences, building up the love of God and one's fellowmen.[123]

This blunt document was written with the recent examples of Zurich and Strasbourg fresh in mind. It was also informed by the newly converted Protestant reformer Ambrosius Blarer, who wrote another of those remarkable tracts whose message is communicated already in its title: *Their [the Clergy's] Power Is Hated and Their Craft Mocked, Their Lies Exposed and Their Show Ended—Right Is As God Makes It.* Addressed to a magistracy containing his own kin, the tract urges that the clergy's traditional distinction between "spiritual" and "worldly" and "lay" and their claims to be "heads of the church" and "vicars of God" be ignored, since, "according to Scripture, we are all equal in Christ." Inasmuch as the clergy have "burdened consciences" and taken God's word captive "all their temporal rights, jurisdiction, covenants, and treaties should be terminated and the honor of God and his holy word observed and maintained in the place of any human obedience, power, or agreement [involving the clergy]." [124] "We, the sheep," Blarer declares, "have the right to judge the doctrine and preaching of our shepherds"; no priest, council, or pope is above the test of Scripture.[125]

Between the issuance of the *Instruction* and the cessation, for centuries, in May, 1527, of Catholic preaching in Constance, the magistrates of Constance, backed by Protestant preachers, implemented the Scripture test. When Protestant preachers married in 1525, the objections of the bishop were turned aside with appeals to Scripture.[126] In June, 1526, all preachers were invited to submit to an examination of their preaching. A year later, in May, 1527, the invitation became a requirement, the bishop's protest being met with the declaration that magistrates had biblical authority to test preachers. Blarer and the Protestants looked on such testing as a "brotherly discussion" between magistracy and clergy—also the characterization of Bucer and Luther—undertaken for the sake of every citizen's salvation and the city's peace and unity.[127]

Wherever the Reformation succeeded officially, the test of Scripture was its quasi-legal justification. Once subjected to this test the traditional concept, practices, and institutions of religion became vulnerable to Protestant and magisterial assault. How deeply the Scripture principle sank in may be indicated by the protest of Protestant princes against the second Diet of Speyer (1529), which suspended the concessions made to Protestants by the first Diet of Speyer (1526) and attempted to return religious practice to the Catholic status quo ante. The *Protestation,* which gave Protestants their name, was signed by John of Saxony, George of Brandenburg, Ernst of Lunenburg, Philip of Hesse, and Wolfgang of Anhalt. It demanded from the emperor that either a future council of the church on the divided issues be held or a clear refutation of Protestant teaching "on the basis of Scripture" made. It pleaded for understanding, saying in effect, "You have your version of the Mass in your territories; try to appreciate how important it is for us to have the version we believe true in ours." [128] And it defended further resistance with repeated appeals to "Scripture," "the soul's salvation," "conscience," "truth," and "God's honor":

> These are, as your dear majesty and those who are on the other side know, matters that touch upon the honor of God and the salvation and blessedness of us all. We are obligated by God's command and our conscience to protect them above all else. Our Lord and God, the highest king and lord of lords, has bound us in our baptism and through his holy divine word to see to them.[129]

No less striking is the Augsburg magistracy's declaration in February, 1537, to the emperor that it has abolished the Mass and traditional religious practices and subjected the city's clergy to "civil law and duties *[bürgerlichen Pflichten und Recht]* like other obedient and pious citizens." [130] Faced with internal riots, which they traced to the temporal possessions, immunities ("die berümpten Freyhaiten"), concubinage and whoring of their clergy,[131] and convinced that the pope lacked the will ("kein Lust") to call a council to settle the religious issues, the magistrates felt it necessary that they take matters firmly in hand. They were, however, in a touchy position because Augsburg clergy had accused the city of transgressing imperially guaranteed rights and privileges. The Augsburg magistracy answered this accusation by informing the emperor that the clergy's unworthy "doctrine and life" were sufficient grounds to remove their vaunted privileges.[132] Explaining that neither traditional religious practices nor the privileges of clergy have any basis in Scripture, they protested that they had acted "according to holy divine biblical Scripture": "At the peril of our soul's salvation and blessedness it is laid upon us, the magistracy, to remove completely and in no way to promote or tolerate whatever holy Scripture shows us to be against or offensive to God and his holy word." [133]

The Scripture test nicely served the political and social ends of magistrates and Protestant reformers alike. But beyond the tactics of reform, the new role of magistracy as spiritual authority was also a political expression of Protestant belief in a priesthood of all believers and devotion to a new social ethic. The original Protestant message had envisioned a society led by a laity learned in Scripture. The princes of Saxony and the magistrates of Augsburg came to see themselves in such a role.

I think that there was an intrinsic evangelical appeal to magistrates at this point and would not conclude that they were simply overawed by a so-called Protestant "myth of spiritual duty." [134] The theological lesson may finally have been lost on many magistrates, which is understandable. And few were to go as far as the Bucers and the Calvins wanted them to go, which is probably fortunate. But the ideal of a religiously enlightened political bureaucracy, committed to the highest religious and ethical values, is also a basic heritage of the Reformation.

From Pamphlet to Catechism and Church Ordinance: The Reformers as New Papists

The Reformation began with such high hopes—the end of religious tyranny, the transformation of society by a benevolent priesthood of confident believers, even the mass conversion of the Jews.[135] What began in the heady name of freedom soon came face to face with the sober demand for discipline, not only from magistrates but also from Protestant reformers. Whether they had misunderstood the high expectations of the reformers or were just not up to them, Protestant congregations in the late 1520s and 1530s were to encounter the end of a leash. Protestant leaders now undertook the extremely awkward task of making religious discipline and enforced orthodoxy prominent in a religion that had succeeded primarily in the name of freedom from religious tyranny.

Luther's scolding of Saxon Christians in the wake of the Visitation of 1527–28 approached morbidity. He was stunned to find the common man unable to recite the most basic Christian doctrine (the Creed, Lord's Prayer, and the Ten Commandments) and pastors ill-prepared and negligent of their duties. "I would never have believed that you were such ignorant people if I did not see it every day." Reminding them of "how much freedom the gospel has given you, so that now you are not obliged to observe innumerable holy days and are free to pursue your work," he announced the institution of mandatory catechism classes to overcome the ignorance created by the apparent abuse of the new religious freedom.[136] In the *Large Catechism* (1529) pastorates are seen as "declining and going to ruin," the world as being "now more wicked than it has ever been: there is no government, no obedience, no fidelity, no faith; only presumptuous, ungovernable people, whom no teaching or reproof can help." Pastors, having been released from the "burdensome babbling" of the medieval priesthood, are accused of neglecting religious education altogether, as if the new faith meant no further need of catechism. "Such security or presumption" is a "false security" and a "poisonous contagion." [137] In the *Small Catechism* (1529) the same complaint is turned against rank and file Christians; all, Luther laments in the preface, have mastered the fine art of abusing the new evangelical freedom, as if the Reformation meant a suspension of religious activity altogether.[138]

Luther prescribes a tight regimen to ameliorate the situation. Fathers are to question their children and servants daily on the catechism, seeing that children develop the habit of saying the Ten Commandments, the Creed, and the Lord's Prayer upon rising, during meals, and at bedtime—"and unless they repeat them they should be given neither food nor drink." [139] The tribunal of confession and the episcopal bureaucracy, primary objectives in the Reformation's original assault on traditional religious practice, seem now to reappear in new forms within the very homes of Protestants.

Parents are urged to become "bishops" within their households. "A person who wants to be a good citizen owes it to his family to urge them to learn . . . the catechism, and if they will not, they should be given no bread to eat." [140] Luther appears even to revert to previously criticized sermonic methods to keep people in line. In his sermons on the catechism he skirts the edges of the crude superstition of late medieval manuals like *The Soul's Consolation.*[141] He tells, for example, the story of a man who always cursed in the name of a hundred thousand devils when he became distressed. One day he fell into a river and, proceeding so to curse, drowned. "Had he been accustomed to call upon the Lord," Luther admonishes, "he would have been saved." [142]

Luther could now, on occasion, even give the impression that discipline and obedience were the way to salvation. Commenting on the commandment to honor one's parents, he writes:

> If you honor and serve them, you have this promise that God will give you a long life. That is, I [God] will give you a wife or a husband, and I will supply you with food, house, and home; you will be a fine citizen; here, in time, you shall have a sufficient life and hereafter, in eternity, an eternal life. Ah, should I not then be obedient? Especially since God promises eternal life and besides a long life here! [143]

One may even see subtle shades of later Calvinism as Luther, with distinctions that survive among the laity only in theory, describes good works as "signs" which assure one that he is forgiven:

> Let each one look to his neighbor, if he has been offended by him, and forgive him from the heart; then he will be certain that his sin too has been forgiven. Not that you are forgiven on account of your forgiveness, but freely, without your forgiveness, your sins are forgiven. He [God], however, enjoins it upon you as a sign, that you may be assured that, if you forgive, you will be forgiven.[144]

Caspar Hedio's *Magistrate's Sermon* of January, 1534, the critical year of the Reformation's consolidation in Strasbourg, is another striking example of the transformation of Protestantism from revolutionary movement into established religion. His sermon bore the subtitle, *What the Magistracy Should Ask of God for Itself and What Citizens*

Should Ask of God for Their Magistrates in These Difficult and Dangerous Times. For Hedio and the Strasbourg reform party, the "difficulty and danger of the times" lay in the spectre of a magistracy become religiously indifferent, permitting laissez faire religion to reign in a Strasbourg presently filled with what Hedio summarizes as "blasphemy, heresy, and Epicurians." His lamentation over the situation is that of many another Protestant freedom fighter on the brink of becoming a new papist:

> Many have thrown off the papacy and slipped out from under its heavy human yoke. But they do not now want to take up the gospel and place themselves under the light yoke of Christ. Many no longer go to papist confession, but they also do not go to Christian confession. One no longer prays, fasts, or gives alms as was done under the papacy. But one also does not do as one should in a true Christendom. One no longer hears mass, but then one also does not hear the gospel. Before there were many holidays, but now one doesn't even observe Sunday. With what terrible laziness the priests, monks, and nuns used to devour the income and goods of the church. All they did was eat, drink, and frolic about in the most offensive ways. But now it is the workers and the youth who run wild, and many have no respect for God, worship, good works, or any honorable thing. The same is true for the peasantry on the land.[145]

Hedio urged the council members not to heed the enemies of Christ's cross who characterize all "judgment, zeal, and earnestness" in religion as "a new papacy," wishing to permit every man to live and believe as he pleases.[146] The Strasbourg reformers were willing to risk characterization as new papists for the order they desired

The Württemberg reformer Johannes Brenz recognized the new situation Protestants faced. In the preface to his widely influential ordinance for Brandenburg/Nürnberg (1533) he is visibly aware of the difficulty, if not contradiction, involved in mandating a religion that had succeeded in the name of freedom:

> A church order is here conceived and brought together not in the belief that by the observance of such prescribed works men repent their sins and earn God's grace, for only Christ can redeem man's sin, and he has already earned God's grace for us.

> Rather this church order is prescribed in the belief that a true and orderly discipline of the congregation of the church provides both the occasion and the motivation to attend the preaching of God's word more diligently and to receive the sacrament more earnestly.[147]

Protestant church ordinances and catechisms of the late 1520s and 1530s saw to a disciplining of religious life. Doctrinal purity was maintained by regular examinations of clergy and visitations of the schools.[148] Abbreviated workday sermons of one-half to one hour's duration and regular catechetical sessions were established for the edification of laymen and magistrates.[149] Public immorality was sternly policed and the spiritual ban enforced against what the popular Wittenberg catechist Johannes Bugenhagen characterized as "public adulterers, whores, troublemakers, drunks, and blasphemers." [150] Protestant preachers were fond of reminding laymen and magistrates that adulterers were stoned in the Bible.[151]

But if certain features of the new papist were already visible in the childhood of the Reformation (as, for example, within Eberlin's ordinances for Wolfaria), the child can also be seen to be father of the man in the Reformation's maturity. Luther's *Small Catechism* is a case in point.[152] Even as a document designed to discipline religious life, the *Small Catechism* remains a study in religious freedom and simplicity, and especially when compared with its late medieval counterpart, Dietrich Coelde's *Catechism for Simple People.* There are but nine articles in Luther's "Catechism or Christian Discipline." The first states the Ten Commandments, introducing a perfunctory gloss on each with the recurring formula: "We should fear God (because of his threat to those who transgress his law) and love him (because of his promise of grace and every good thing to those who keep his law)." Then follows the Creed, which is briefly expounded in three parts according to creation (God the Father), salvation (Christ the Son), and sanctification (the Holy Spirit and the church). A statement of the Lord's Prayer appears as the third traditional catechetical piece.

Articles four to six take up the sacraments, reduced in number to three: baptism, confession, and the Eucharist. Article five—"How Simple People Should Be Taught to Confess"—sets forth the Protestant alternative to the medieval practice. Protestants did not consider confession to the priest a sacrament proper, but rather an ecclesiastical ordinance, a voluntary matter advised in place of the traditional requirement of annual auricular confession of all mortal sins. It came normally to be transacted by congregational recitation of a formalized confession of sin. Luther points out that while one should forthrightly acknowledge guilt to God for every sin, as these are quickly discovered in the mirror of the Ten Commandments, one need bring before the priest only those individual sins which have proved to be particularly distressing. The priest who hears such a voluntary confession is instructed to respond: "As you believe, so it will happen. I, by the command of our Lord Jesus Christ, forgive you your sin in the name of the Father, the Son, and the Holy Spirit. Amen. Go in peace." Here the penitent, not the priest, holds the initiative. There is no judicial interrogation, no cataloguing of sins, and no imposed works of penance. It is an irony still to be appreciated by many scholars that by so maximizing sinfulness (before God every man is guilty of every conceivable sin) Protestants tried to minimize its psychological burden (no man is required to ponder and recite his every actual sin).

Article seven of Luther's catechism instructs the father of the house in morning and evening prayers, directing him to repeat with his household the Creed and Lord's Prayer upon rising and retiring. An additional short prayer, which can also be said, is provided. Article eight brings forth brief, rhymed blessings for before and after meals. The final article, a didactic description of the daily responsibilities of what Luther calls the "holy orders and stations in life" *(heilige orden und stende)*, strikingly illustrates the breakdown of the distinction between clergy and laity by the new Protestant doctrine of the priesthood of all believers. Luther's holy orders and stations are not special religious bodies but the following groups: bishops, pastors, and preachers (here magistrates are dealt with!); husbands, wives, and parents; children; servants, maids, day-laborers, workers; masters and mistresses of households; youth; widows; and the community as a whole *(Gemeine)*. Their religious duties are not modeled on clerical ideals but are tailored to the particular profession involved; each is instructed, in fear and love of God, to be the best of whatever he or she is.[153]

It is a testimony both to the ideological continuity and the success of the original Protestant message that the goals of the revolutionary pamphlets of the first days of the Reformation remain prominent in the mandated catechisms and church ordinances of the new "established" religion. Ordinances against public immorality, for example, also put an end to the domestic irritations and litigation of clerical concubinage and the clandestine marriages of laymen. Members of the clergy now publicly displayed honorable wives and young people struck binding engagements only with the "favor, knowledge, and permission" of parental and magisterial authority.[154] It was in an article "On What Is and What Is Not a Command" that the Basel confession of faith (1534) explained how the city had preserved Christian freedom since 1529 by "uncommanding" auricular confession, Lenten and other fasting, traditional religious holidays, clerical celibacy, and the worship of saints and images.[155] Citing opposition to "superstition" and "self-indulgence" (*Ueppigkeit*) as well as the preservation of Christian freedom,[156] Protestant church ordinances reduced the number of required religious holidays—thirty-three in pre-Reformation Germany—by at least one-third.[157] The new common chest ordinances were enforced in the name of religious enlightenment and a new social ethic. "Previously," wrote Bugenhagen, reciting a litany of grievances we have seen many times in earlier tracts,

> one freely gave much grain, beer, and other gifts to the monks for their vigils, anniversaries, masses, and screeching [chanted prayers] at weddings, funerals, the baptism of children, and on the holidays of the apostles, Mary, and others. One gave without measure for images, tablets, bells, organs, and tapers for use in church and at home, not to mention the outlay for perpetual benefices and memorials, confraternities, letters of indulgence, holy pilgrimages, and other such things for which the rich had much money to spend but to which the poor wives, who had to nourish themselves by spinning, also gladly gave.[158]

It was in opposition to "childishness" that Brenz's church ordinances simplified and desacralized the burial ceremony. The Hall ordinance of 1526 discarded vigils and masses for the dead, previously assumed to aid the passage through purgatory. The dead were now to be reverently accompanied to the graveyard and their deaths proclaimed on Sundays. Such remembrances were to be expressions of friendship and consolation, and also a preparation by the living for their own deaths.[159] But never again were the practices that Protestants characterized as "feeding upon the dead" to be taken up. The Brandenburg/Nürnberg ordinance ordered the cessation "once and for all" of such "unnecessary and childish [burial] practices" as "Saint John's blessing, consecrated candles, palm branches, torches, baked goods, salt, and water, cross processions, and the graveside celebration of the sacrament of the Eucharist." [160]

It was avowed opposition to "superstition" that moved Bugenhagen to devote twenty pages of his influential Braunschweig ordinance to the topic of "consecration" *(Vom Weyhen)*. Employing arguments that must have seemed irreligious to many sixteenth-century people, Bugenhagen pronounced in this context not only an end to holy water, fire, torches, candles, and fruit, but also to fasting, the withholding of the Eucharistic cup from the laity, and priestly celibacy. He explained that superstitious belief in the existence of intrinsically religious objects (holy water, etc.) and offices (the priesthood) was what lay behind the abuses and burdens of the old church:

> There we see that they [the medieval clergy and their followers] clung not to God with their hearts and faith but rather to their cowls, foods, holy water, holy torches, holy candles, letters of indulgence, "golden" [i.e. special, festive] prayers, "golden" fasting on Fridays, confraternities, Saint James' pilgrimage, the rosary, special observances, special rules, and special dress, none of which God has commanded.[161]

Such belief only reinforces superstitious practices that distract people from the grace of Christ and true Christian prayer:

> The more holy water we have, the more poltergeister and people who fight thunder with torches and candles, or practice magic in bed with candles or in the cellar among the beer kegs, without knowing that it is all fabricated against the grace of our Lord Jesus Christ, who alone takes away our sin, and against Christian prayer by which we should call out through Christ to our loving Father in all our needs, whether of body or of soul. Water, fire, and candle are no help to us.[162]

Freedom fighters and new papists stumble over one another in Protestant church ordinances and catechisms. Luther instructs parents to train their children in the Ten Commandments "by means of warning, terror, restraint, and punishment," but then concludes that the proper approach is "to form their habits by kindness and pleasant methods; what we force into them only with rods and blows produces bad results." [163] In the Hannover church order of 1536, Urbanus Rhegius went out of his way to emphasize that although "for the sake of order, instruction, and discipline" priestly vestments, the Eucharistic chalice, altar candles, crucifix, "proper images," the baptismal font, and singing were to be retained in the worship service, all were embraced "only in the freedom of the Spirit." [164]

Especially when they took up the topic of religious punishment and the ban did Protestants seem to remember the original experience and try carefully to choose their terms, insisting that it was, for all the force it gave them, an instrument of last resort and strictly confined to the purpose of spiritual betterment (not a weapon for temporal gain as Roman excommunication and interdict had been).[165] Bugenhagen permitted normal association with banned people "as citizens" but not "as Christians," a distinction which may have lost some of its meaning in practice.[166] Brenz explained Protestant preoccupation with the Ten Commandments as a *Zucht-mayster* to Christ in terms of the need to avoid falling victim again to sins that are not really sins, "lest people be plagued again with false, fabricated sins like eating meat on Friday, cutting wood on holidays, touching the Eucharistic cup, and other such foolishness." [167] The final goal, he assures the reader, is not to terrorize but to create "peace, inner calm, and a quiet life" *(frid, rwe und ein stilles leben),* "a good manner of living" *(ein gutte gewonheyt).*[168] Bugenhagen defended the necessity of "right ceremonies" with a similar argument: "It is general knowledge that the common man and Christian hearts reached the point that they could no longer endure the many unnecessary and un-Christian ceremonies, the godless mercenary activity and preaching of lies in the churches." [169] Protestant "order" existed to preserve the liberated from a reimposition of the burdens of what was unnecessary and untrue.

Bugenhagen exhibits the sensitivity of Protestants to mandating their religion and appearing to be new papists when he explains the now "expected" confession of sins prior to the reception of the Eucharist.[170] In their assault on the confessional, earlier Protestants had scolded the medieval church for scaring people away from religion with its required confession to the priest.[171] Bugenhagen devotes one hundred of his two hundred and fifty pages largely to showing how the required Protestant confession is different from and not a reversion to the medieval practice. He reasons that people cannot be allowed to go to the sacrament "as a sow goes to the trough." Order requires an antecedent preparatory confession, which may be private (but if so *doch frey!*) or communal. If private it should not be undertaken "in secret fear and trembling"; "one simply tells his preacher or a knowing Christian brother what distresses him most." [172] Communal (congregational) confession is, however, the better course, and Bugenhagen appends a model of such confession, which may be recited with a minimum of individual anguish.[173]

A final example of the persistence of the original Protestant message within the established religion is the case of the *Handbook of the Evangelical Burgher.* Its author was the Cologne printer Arnd von Aich,[174] a layman learned in Scripture, who composed his *Handbook* in conscious opposition to Dietrich Coelde's *Mirror of a Christian Man,* the supreme late medieval lay catechism.[175] The *Handbook* was twice published, strangely enough, in Catholic Cologne (the "German Rome"), the first edition appearing perhaps shortly before or after Von Aich's death (ca. 1530), the second in 1541 at the hand of his printer son-in-law, Laurentius von der Müllen. The latter, forced to leave Cologne in 1543 after publishing a work by Martin Bucer, was followed to Bonn by another Protestant outcast, a priest named Johannes Meynertzhagen who had been dismissed for participation in a celebration of the Mass in which the laity received the Eucharistic cup. In 1544 von der Müllen and Meynertzhagen collaborated in the republication of Von Aich's *Handbook.* In the hope of gaining wider currency for the work, they printed the 1544 Bonn edition under Meynertzhagen's name. He was a favorite of the recently converted (and soon to be excommunicated) Cologne archbishop and elector Hermann von Wied and the powerful reformers Martin Bucer and Philip Melanchthon; he had also added to the Bonn edition expositions of the Creed, the Decalogue, and

Lord's Prayer, thereby earning a little recognition. After its publication a vigilant Cologne cathedral chapter and the emperor himself called for the suppression of this "most pernicious book." The Bonn edition was subsequently twice published in Nürnberg (first edition in 1555).[176] This religious handbook by and for laymen, written in opposition to the most popular late medieval counterpart, was embraced, embellished, and circulated by Protestant clergy in the 1540s and 1550s. Thus it has a certain distinction among mature Protestant catechetical literature.

The work contains one hundred and twenty-five articles (from "Faith" to "Heaven"), tripling in size Coelde's work—prima facie evidence that it is a child of the consolidation phase of the Reformation. But Von Aich was true to his prefatory declaration to write strictly "as a poor layman and evangelical burgher" for laymen and without fancy words. He even saw the work as a possible text for children in German schools. But, although he refrained from "all the glosses that have caused so much error in the Christian community or church,"[177] his hand was not stayed from filling the work with glosses of his own, which he no doubt considered essential and nonerroneous.

The *Handbook*'s unity lies in its criticism of special "religious" good works—so prominent in Coelde's catechism—and of that body of doctrine and practice which Protestants believed exploited the laity's fear of death in light of the authority of Scripture and the new ethic of social service. In an article "On Good and Fruitful Works" Von Aich summarized the way the "Evangelical burgher" should conceive and live his life:

> Those only are the good works commanded by God which are done in faith and out of love and not for the sake of salvation or temporal gain, but only to the praise and honor of God and for the purpose of doing some good for one's neighbor. . . . We Christians should remember the young man who asked Christ what should be done as good works so that eternal life might be inherited [Matt. 19:16]. We do not find that the Lord said: "Go forth and buy many masses, say many long prayers, go on a pilgrimage, endow churches, altars, towers, bells, expensive paintings, burn many candles." He also did not say: "Have no wife, remain a virgin, do not eat this or that food, fast and

> celebrate on this or that day, confess to a priest the secrets of your heart, go into a cloister, wear a cowl and the clothes of pharisees, or be buried in a gray cowl, and various similar works so highly valued by men today." Rather Christ said: "You know the commandment well," and told him the commandment to love his neighbor: "If you will inherit eternal life, keep the commandment and love your neighbor as yourself." And when the youth thought that he had already done that, the Lord said to him: "If you will be perfect (for one thing still remains for you to do), go and sell what you have and give it to the poor." He did not say: "Go and give what you have to the learned theologians, the religious, the monasteries, the high cathedral chapters, abbots, priests, monks, and nuns so that they will pray and perform works of reconciliation for you." No, he rather said: "Give to the poor who need such help, and take up the cross and follow me." Now that is for sure the true work, if done out of faith and love, that brings us to eternal life.[178]

Within this vein of ethical idealism runs a certain simplicity and tolerance within the new ordered and disciplined religious life as conceived by the *Handbook.* The article "On Fraternal Punishment and the Ban" urges "two or three warnings" before the exclusion of public sinners—defined as those who flagrantly transgress one of the Ten Commandments—from the sacrament. "Do not judge, damn, shame, and treat them tyrannically as heretics, applying the ban and tossing them out of the church for small temporal gain, as we daily see [in the use of excommunication and interdict by the Roman church]." [179]

The articles on confession and penance, which mandate a daily inner confession to God, stress the voluntary character of any counsel, help, or consolation sought from a priest and carefully avoid juridical penances: true penance is "to stop sinning and eat one's bread in the sweat of one's brow," [180] which appears to mean "straighten up and get back to work!" Von Aich's article on the sufficiency of the Lord's Prayer explains, "If special long prayers were the more pleasing to God, then the Jacobites, Thomists, Franciscans, Benedictines, and other religious would have an advantage over other Christians." [181] Although the admonition would be heeded by few as the polemics of the confessional age began—Anabaptism was in fact becoming a capital crime in the empire about the time Von Aich wrote (1529)—an article appears on the parable of the tares to admonish toleration of Jews, heathen, and heretics. It is stated that "magistrates do not have the power to kill or coerce them," and the ban and patience, not the magistrate's sword, are recommended as weapons against heretics.[182] It was a sermon that Sebastian Castellio, who also knew full well its bona fide Protestant lineage, would soon preach to John Calvin in the wake of the execution of Michael Servetus for blasphemy against the Trinity.[183]

The special concern of the *Handbook* was to secure the laity from the old Totenfresserei. In an article entitled "On Altar Priests," Von Aich blisters traditional practices in the name of the new Protestant work ethic:

> Judas, the man who sold God *[der Gottes verkauffer]*, has left behind many of his brothers under a holy guise. . . . These are the altar priests who can do nothing but read vigils, masses, commendations, and requiems for the dead, supporting themselves by services for the dead, while living the most useless and idle lives, and protesting that it would be sinful for them to earn their living by manual labor. They consider their long prayers and chants to be great works. But Saint Paul has neither taught this nor himself set such an example. Although he taught the gospel and preached diligently, he did not consider this to be his "work" (as one nowadays does), and sat around idle when he was done with it. He rather labored physically day and night and won his bread with his own hands so that no one would be burdened by his idleness—although, as an evangelical preacher, it would have been right for the community [of faith] to have housed and fed him. But he did not want to give our altar priests an excuse for their lives, selling masses and long prayers for a living. He rather commanded: "He who does not work shall not eat." 2 Thess. 3.[184]

Von Aich devoted the very next article to the subject "All Men Should Work," and among them "especially the faithful." He criticized, however, compulsive accumulation of fortunes and the belief by many who so labored that the purchase of "many masses and good works [indulgences are meant]" could save them. Such labor, says Von Aich, brings only a temporal reward.[185]

The *Handbook* also turned the Scripture principle against belief in purgatory, "which was not discovered until six hundred years after the birth of Christ." Such belief is said to have spawned a multitude of financed practices which distort and burden religious life: "indulgences, funeral masses, vigils, commendations, weekly, monthly, and anniversary masses, prayers, offerings, pilgrimages, alms, candle-burning, bell-ringing, incense, reading the *Miserere* and the *De profundis,* sprinkling holy water on graves, and the like." [186] Attesting a degree of Protestant desacralization is an article entitled, "One Should Not Believe in Any Spirits of the Dead," in which Von Aich elaborates at length that "Christians are to let their dead rest in the Lord." [187]

Conclusion

Scratch a "new papist" and one may find an old "freedom fighter." The original Protestant vision was of a society of religiously enlightened laymen who were no longer burdened by traditional religious superstition and tyranny. That vision was still bright in major consolidation tracts of the 1530s and 1540s. *Zucht* and *Ordnung* became prominent in this period, but in order to secure and subserve, not to submerge, the new freedom. It can certainly be argued that Protestant catechisms and church ordinances, where fully enforced, tended finally to secure religious freedom by ending it. Nonetheless, these same consolidation tracts of the Reformation challenge influential modern assessments of the Protestant movement. Even in these tracts the new work ethic does not appear as an answer to religious anxiety, and still less as a sanction of compulsive labor and thrift. If such traits are Protestant, as scholarship in the tradition of Max Weber has argued, then they are born of a still later Protestantism. The work ethic of first generation Protestants remained what it was at the Reformation's inception: an insistence that people, especially the clergy and the powerful institutions they represented, be useful servants within and not burdens upon their communities. That aim was the point of the struggle against the Totenfresser and it was the inspiration behind the new social ethic extrapolated from the priesthood of all believers.

Nor does the new Scripture principle appear in the first decades of the Reformation as a "paper pope," only another version of the medieval habit of "objectifying" religious authority, as scholars in the tradition of Ernst Troeltsch have argued. For sixteenth-century men the Scripture principle was the "modern" revolutionary tool by which magistrates, citizens, and Protestant reformers together legally dismantled practices and institutions sanctioned by centuries of tradition. In the sixteenth century the appeal to an interiorized religious authority beyond Scripture and tradition was not modern; it was simply the surest way to isolate oneself from the agents of change and reform.

What made people Protestants was not great distant political events any more than great distant theological doctrines, but rather the palpable institutional consequences of the Protestant program of reform. Protestant ideas revolutionized religious practice at local levels, simplifying religious life and enhancing secular life. With its vernacular Bibles and bold religious certitude the Reformation was, in its time, a lay enlightenment. To interpret it primarily through the continuing intolerance (Luther's late tracts against Jews, Calvin's execution of Servetus), social conservatism (disassociation from the demands of rebellious peasants), and superstition (belief in heretics and witches) of its age is to adopt a moralizing perspective that obscures its historical purpose and achievement and leaves only the basest motives to explain its wide and persisting appeal.

If in their practice zealous Protestant reformers tended to forget their original purpose as the Reformation succeeded, they nonetheless left the clearest reminders for the laity in the catechisms and church ordinances that they wrote. The literature of discipline remained a literature of freedom. If Protestant reformers made laymen bold to resist old superstitions and tyranny, they also gave them the wherewithal to reject in time persisting and new forms of superstition and tyranny. The understandable failure of Protestants ever fully to harmonize the new evangelical orthodoxy—which remained to many nothing more than an effort to create a new papacy—with the new evangelical freedom contributed much, in my opinion, to the development of that rational and moral approach to religion which, in the name of individual religious freedom—and perhaps also with greater fidelity to the original impulse of the

Reformation than much second and third generation Protestantism —played such a prominent role in the intellectual transition from medieval to modern times. Scratch a modern "freedom fighter" and one may find historical continuity with old Protestant "papists."

In answering the question why every city and town that had the opportunity to become Protestant in the sixteenth century did not do so, several factors must be weighed. One must inquire into the depth of grievances and the preconditions of reform. As late medieval and Tridentine reforms attest, to a degree clerical immunities could be curtailed, the burdening of lower by higher clergy controlled, and preaching and pastoral care improved without becoming Protestant. One must also ask whether there were popular preachers to "enlighten" and arouse, nuclear congregations to press, and sufficient government toleration to prevent a political snipping of the movement in its bud. If determined governments could for long periods thwart even majority sentiment in favor of the Reformation, they certainly had little difficulty circumscribing minority Protestant movements.

Finally, one must reckon with the force of tradition and habit. Many sixteenth-century people patently preferred their confessor judgmental, their ritual elaborate, their saints approachable, their indulgences plentiful, and their lives weighed *sub specie aeternitatis* on the basis of their good works. Even in the densest Protestant areas many found it difficult to surrender without further ado the values and practices of a lifetime even when convinced that they were wrong. There are examples of Protestant ordinances prohibiting nostalgic laymen from sneaking out of the cities to attend mass in surrounding village churches. No change is more difficult and fateful than ideological change.

Notes

Chapter 1

1 On the views of Lortz and their influence, see Steven Ozment, ed., *The Reformation in Medieval Perspective* (Chicago, 1971), pp. 3–11.

2 *History of Christian Philosophy in the Middle Ages* (New York, 1955), pp. 438, 464–65, 470, 498, 528; and *Reason and Revelation in the Middle Ages* (New York, 1938), p. 93. Present debates and research in late medieval religious and ecclesiastical history are summarized by Francis Rapp, *L'église et la vie religieuse en occident à la fin du moyen âge* (Paris, 1971), pp. 251–366.

3 Leff, "The Fourteenth Century and the Decline of Scholasticism," *Past and Present* 9 (1956): 30–39; 37; *Paris and Oxford Universities in the Thirteenth and Fourteenth Centuries* (New York, 1968), pp. 240–55; *Heresy in the Later Middle Ages* (Manchester, 1967), 1:307. Knowles, "A Characteristic of the Mental Climate of the Fourteenth Century," in *Melanges offerts à Etienne Gilson* (Toronto/Paris, 1959), pp. 315–25; 323; *The Evolution of Medieval Thought* (New York, 1962), pp. 311–42. The *Dictionnaire de theologie catholique* (Paris, 1941), 14:1709–11, treats the fourteenth century under the heading "La decadence." While accepting the "decline" thesis, Martin Grabmann urged a more nuanced interpretation of the late Middle Ages, with appreciation for the variety of its intellectual and spiritual movements and progress in the natural sciences (especially among Franciscans). *Mittelalterliches Geistesleben* (Munich, 1936), p. 585. John W. Baldwin's recent book, however, can still maintain that "thirteenth century optimism dissolved into the despair of the late Middle Ages." *The Scholastic Culture of the Middle Ages 1000–1300* (Lexington, Mass., 1971), p. 97.

4 Leff: "The different doctrines of the Reformation, whether of Luther or of Calvin, contained an important element of the outlook generated in the disputes of the early fourteenth century. They made the divorce which began then between theology and philosophy complete." *Past and Present* (1956), p. 39. Knowles: "Between them, Ockham and Bradwardine shattered to bits the mighty scholastic synthesis. If the seeds of Lutheranism can be found in certain aspects of Ockhamism, those of Calvinism began to germinate in the fiercely orthodox Bradwardine." "A Characteristic of the Mental Climate of the Fourteenth Century," p. 323.

5 *Gnade und Eucharistie in der philosophischen Theologie des Wilhelm von Ockham: Ihre Bedeutung für die Ursachen der Reformation* (Wiesbaden, 1956).

6 *Man Yearning for Grace: Luther's Early Spiritual Teaching* (Washington, 1968).

7 *The Harvest of Medieval Theology: Gabriel Biel and Late Medieval Nominalism* (Cambridge, Mass., 1963), pp. 5–6, 420–25; *The Forerunners of the Reformation: The Shape of Late Medieval Thought* (New York, 1966), pp. 37–43; "The Shape of Late Medieval Thought: The Birthpangs of the Modern Era," *ARG* 64 (1973): 13–33. One should also consult the work of E. J. Dempsey Douglass, *Justification in Late Medieval Preaching: A Study of John Geiler of Keisersberg* (Leiden, 1966); David C. Steinmetz, *Misericordia Dei: The Theology of Johannes von Staupitz in Its Late Medieval Setting* (Leiden, 1968); and especially the work of William J. Courtenay, who may have the last word on the nature of late medieval nominalism: "Nominalism and Late Medieval Religion" in *The Pursuit of Holiness in Late Medieval and Renaissance Religion: Papers from the University of Michigan Conference,* ed. Charles Trinkaus and Heiko Oberman (Leiden, 1974), pp. 26–58, with references to Courtenay's numerous articles on the subject.

8 *Marsilius von Inghen und die okkamistische Schule in Deutschland* (Heidelberg, 1921); *Via Antiqua und Via Moderna auf den deutschen Universitäten des xv. Jahrhunderts* (Heidelberg, 1922/Darmstadt, 1963). These are volumes one and two respectively of Ritter's three-volume *Studien zur Spätscholastik* (1921–27). See also Ritter's "Romantic and Revolutionary Elements in German Theology on the Eve of the Reformation," in *The Reformation in Medieval Perspective,* pp. 15–49.

9 *The Logic of William of Ockham* (New York, 1935), p. 7; "Ockham and Aegridius of Rome," *Franciscan Studies* 9 (1949): 417–42, which praises Ockham's lucidity vis-à-vis late thirteenth-century theology.

10 *Justification et prédestination au XIVe siècle* (Paris, 1934), pp. 126–30, 178, 187; *Nominalisme au XIVe siècle* (Montreal, 1948), p. 11.

11 *Collected Articles on Ockham* (St. Bonaventure, New York, 1958); "Der Stand der Ockham-Forschung," *Franciscan Studies* 34 (1952): 12–37.

12 "Augustinian Theology of the Fourteenth Century: Notes on Editions, Marginalia, Opinions and Book-Lore," *Augustiniana* 6 (1956): 146–274. On the fourteenth-century college boom, see A. L. Gabriel, "The College System in the Fourteenth Century Universities," in *The Forward Movement of the Fourteenth Century,* ed. F. L. Utley (Columbus, 1961), pp. 79–124.

13 *Essai sur la critique de Ruysbroeck par Gerson* 3/1 (Paris, 1959), p. 223.

14 *History of Christian Philosophy,* p. 534.

15 James S. Preus, *From Shadow to Promise: Old Testament Interpretation from*

Augustine to the Young Luther (Cambridge, Mass., 1969); Scott H. Hendrix, *Ecclesia in Via: Ecclesiological Developments in the Medieval Psalms Exegesis and the Dictata Super Psalterium of Martin Luther* (Leiden, 1974); John B. Payne, *Erasmus: His Theology of the Sacraments* (Richmond, Va., 1970); David C. Steinmetz, "Scholasticism and Radical Reform: Nominalist Motifs in the Theology of Balthasar Hubmaier," *MQR* 45 (1971): 123–43; Heiko Oberman, "The 'Extra' Dimension in the Theology of Calvin," *Journal of Ecclesiastical History* 21 (1970): 43–64; Edward D. Willis, *Calvin's Catholic Christology* (Leiden, 1966).

16 Steven Ozment, *Mysticism and Dissent: Religious Ideology and Social Protest in the Sixteenth Century* (New Haven, 1973); "Mysticism, Nominalism, and Dissent," in *The Pursuit of Holiness*, pp. 67–92.

17 See *The Pursuit of Holiness,* coedited by Charles Trinkaus, president of the American Renaissance Society, and Oberman.

18 According to Pesch, Luther writes "existential," Thomas "sapiential" theology, a difference more in method and approach than in substance. *Die Theologie der Rechtfertigung bei Martin Luther und Thomas von Aquin* (Mainz, 1967), pp. 919, 941, 950. Cf. Stephan Pfürtner, *Luther and Aquinas on Salvation* (New York, 1964) and Hans Küng, *Rechtfertigung: Die Lehre Karl Barths und eine katholische Besinnung* (Einsiedeln, 1957).

19 See pp. 121–23 below.

20 *Reichsstadt und Reformation* (Gütersloh, 1962), pp. 15–18. A somewhat expanded version of the original German has been translated into French, *Villes d'Empire et reformation* (Geneva, 1966). The French edition has in turn served as the basis for a recent English translation, *Imperial Cities and the Reformation: Three Essays* (Philadelphia, 1972). An older but still respected description of this conflict between the city republic and the territorial state on which Moeller bases so much is Fritz Rörig, *The Medieval Town* (Berkeley, 1971; original German, 1932), chapters 8–9. Basil Hall has summarized some recent research on major Reformation cities, sharing many of Moeller's views. "The Reformation City," *Bulletin of the John Rylands Library* (1971): 103–148.

21 ". . . eine ganz neue und vertiefte Begründung ihrer Existenz, indem das Grundgesetz der Genossenschaft, die prinzipielle Gleichheit und Gleichberechtigung der Genossen, theologisch verankert wird." *Reichsstadt und Reformation,* p. 35.

22 Ibid., p. 36.

23 "Es besteht also eine deutliche Kluft zwischen der spätmittelalterlichen Stadt und Luther. Man kann sich das deutlich machen zum Beispiel an seinem Brief an die Christen in der Reichsstadt Worms von 1523, in dem er die Adressaten anredet als das kleine Häuflein

wahrer Gläubiger unter den Lauen und Ungläubigen. *In der Konsequenz musste Luthers Anschauung die alte Stadtgemeinde zersprengen.*" Ibid., p. 37.

24 The Lutheran reformer of Nürnberg, Wenceslaus Linck, employs the doctrine of the two kingdoms rather to demonstrate the indivisible unity of religion and society, and especially to force clerical assumption of civil responsibilities. See pp. 87–88 below. James M. Stayer even identifies Luther with the "apoliticism" of Anabaptists. *Anabaptists and the Sword* (Lawrence, Kansas, 1972), p. 33.

25 "Der eigentliche Kernpunkt der Wandlungen Zwinglis und Bucers ist, die immer deutlichere Zusammenschau von Kirchengemeinde und Stadtgemeinde. Gerade an dieser Stelle aber war uns Luthers Lehre als im tiefsten stadtfremd erschienen; die konsequente Begründung des Kirchenbegriffs von der Rechtfertigung allein aus Gnade und Glauben sprengt die mittelalterliche Einheit der Stadt. Hier wird Luther durch Zwingli und Bucer korrigiert. Sie denken beide viel mehr als Luther von der Gesamtheit, nicht von einzelnen her. So gelingt ihnen zwar durch die stärkere Betonung des Gemeinschafts- und Organismus-gedankens im Staats- und Kirchenbegriff eine Vertiefung der Position Luthers: Das städtische Denken verschafft ihnen Zugang zu bestimmten Elementen der urchristlichen Botschaft, und auf sie berufen sie sich mit Recht." *Reichsstadt und Reformation,* p. 54. Cf. ibid., p. 52.

26 "Der Sieg der 'reformierten' Reformation in den oberdeutschen Reichsstädten erklärt sich entscheidend aus der Begegnung der eigentümlich 'städtisch' geprägten Theologie Zwinglis und Bucers mit dem Oberdeutschland in besonderem Mass lebendigen genossenschaftlichen Geist." Ibid., p. 67. Moeller is at pains to insist that although Zwingli and Bucer were here "more medieval" than Luther, they advanced well beyond customary medieval theocratic notions. While it spoke to the same medieval ideal and even had certain external parallels with it, Zwingli's and Bucer's understanding of the city was not the medieval concept of "sacral community," since, Moeller argues, they conceived the religious nature of the city to lie, not in some intrinsic institutional sacredness, but in the simple fact that the Word of God was there preached, heard, and obeyed. Ibid., p. 55. That is a pretty lame argument if it intends to continue a distinction from Luther, and Moeller appears to have dropped it in a later work. Commenting on Capito's defense of clerical citizenship, Moeller describes the change wrought in Strasbourg's self-perception by the Reformation: "Freilich geschah das um den Preis, dass das geistliche Selbstverständnis der Stadt sich veränderte. Sie war nur noch

Bürgergemeinde vor Gott, 'Kirchengemeinde;' sie hatte aufgehört, 'Sakralgemeinschaft' zu sein." "Kleriker als Bürger," in *Festschrift für Hermann Heimpel zu 70. Geburtstag* [Göttingen, 1972], 2:217. The Strasbourg reformers appear to have become good Lutherans.

27 According to Edith Eschenhagen, Wittenberg's was a "kleinbürgerliche Verfassung." The greater part of the *Rat* was skilled artisans, and the guilds had a constitutionally guaranteed place in government. It was a representative form of government and, if one leaves the veto power of the Elector aside, democratic: the *Rat*'s membership and power was given from below, from the citizenry, and subject to yearly elections, regular accountings, and passive citizen approval. Although the Elector held rights of taxation, board for his army, and fealty from the citizenry—which he regularly exercised—Eschenhagen describes the relation between Elector and *Rat* as "mehr Koordinations- als Subordinations-verhältnis." "Beiträge zur Sozial- und Wirtschaftsgeschichte der Stadt Wittenberg in der Reformationszeit," *Luther-Jahrbuch* 9 (1927): 9–118; 52, 55. For Luther's view on the religious responsibilities of the Elector and *Rat*, see my discussion of his activities during the Wittenberg movement of 1521–22, pp. 140–45 below.

28 See pp. 135–38, 215*n*71 below.

29 *Religion and Regime: A Sociological Account of the Reformation* (Ann Arbor, 1967).

30 *Journal of Interdisciplinary History* 1 (1970/71): 380, with contributions by Natalie Davis, Theodor Brodek, and H. G. Koenigsberger, and a rejoinder by Swanson. John T. Flint has defended Swanson against the historians: "A Handbook for Historical Sociologists," *Comparative Studies in Society and History* 10 (1968): 492–509.

31 Leonhard von Muralt, "Stadtgemeinde und Reformation in der Schweiz," *ZSchGes* 10 (1930): 349–84, especially 367–74.

32 "Protestant Dogma and City Government: The Case of Nuremberg," *Past and Present* 36 (1967): 38–58. The article enlarges on chapter 4 of Strauss's *Nuremberg in the Sixteenth Century* (New York, 1966).

33 Strauss, "Protestant Dogma," especially pp. 45, 51, 57.

34 Strauss, *Nuremberg in the Sixteenth Century*, p. 170.

35 See pp. 74–79 below.

36 "Strikes and Salvation at Lyons," *ARG* 56 (1965): 48–64; 50, 52.

37 "City Women and Religious Change in Sixteenth-Century France," in *A Sampler of Women's Studies*, ed. Dorothy G. McGuigan (Ann Arbor, 1973), pp. 18–45; 28. Other recent studies on this issue are Nancy L. Roelker, "The Appeal of Calvinism to French Noblewomen in the 16th Century," *Journal of Interdisciplinary History* 2 (1972): 391–418, and Miriam U. Chrisman, "Women and the Reformation in Strasbourg

1490–1530," *ARG* 63 (1972): 143–68. It is curious that not one of these studies has given even the slightest attention to that one group of women who clearly profited more from the Reformation than any other, namely, the hundreds of women living in concubinage with priests who were to make the transition from being a priest's whore to a legal, honorable wife. For a striking testimony to the burden of being a priest's concubine, see the *pfaffenmätz's* touching speech in Nicholas Manuel's *Die Totenfresser* (1523), p. 114 below.

38 *ARG* 56 (1965): 54.

39 See pp. 145–51 below.

40 See Febvre's classic essay, "Une question mal posée: les origines de la Reforme Francais," in *Au coeur religieux du XVIe siècle* (Paris, 1957), pp. 1–70, originally published in the *Revue historique* 161 (1929). It is available in English translation, *A New Kind of History From the Writings of Lucien Febvre,* ed. Peter Burke (New York, 1973), pp. 44–107.

Chapter 2

1 Bernd Moeller, "Piety in Germany Around 1500," in *The Reformation in Medieval Perspective,* p. 51.

2 Cf. the discussion in "Probleme des kirchlichen Lebens in Deutschland vor der Reformation," in H. Jedin et al., *Probleme der Kirchenspaltung im 16. Jahrhundert* (Regensburg, 1970), pp. 11–32.

3 "Geistige Arbeit und Energie auf dem festen Boden christlichen Glaubens und kirchlicher Weltanschauung war der stärkste und eigenthümlichste Charakterzug des Zeitalters . . . Es war eines der gedankenreichsten und fruchtbarsten Zeitalter deutscher Geschichte." *Geschichte des deutschen Volkes seit dem Ausgang des Mittelalters I: Die allegemeinen Zustände des deutschen Volkes beim Ausgang des Mittelalters,* 9th ed. (Freiburg i.B., 1883), p. 7. (Hereafter cited as Janssen.)

4 Ibid., p. 49. These are glossed vernacular translations of liturgical readings for Sundays, holidays, and saints' days, which were destined for the homes of the laity. There were in truth well over one hundred editions. See *RGG* 5:417.

5 Janssen, p. 51. Franz Falk in fact lists over two hundred complete Bibles in Latin, German, Italian, French, Czech, and Russian published between 1450 and 1520. *Die Bibel am Ausgange des Mittelalters: ihre Kenntnis und ihre Verbreitung* (Köln, 1905), pp. 90–97.

6 Janssen, pp. 29, 39.

7 *Dr. M. Luther und die religiöse Literatur seiner Zeit bis 1520* (1881/Niewkoop, 1967), pp. 20–22, 249.

8 Ibid., p. 204. Cf. also Hasak, *Der christliche Glaube des deutschen Volkes beim Schlusse des Mittelalters . . . 1470–1520* (Regensburg, 1868).

9 Hasak, *Dr. M. Luther und die religiöse Literatur,* p. 240.

10 *Bilderkatechismus des fünfzehnten Jahrhunderts* (Leipzig, 1855), p. 4. (Hereafter cited as Geffken.)

11 Ibid., pp. 9, 14. In such activities Geffken saw late medieval piety abuilding toward the Reformation. It is within this tradition that E. G. Léonard describes the Reformation as "not a revolt against Catholic piety but its aboutissement, sa floraison." *Histoire générale du protestantisme* 1 (Paris, 1961), p. 10. Geffken also reminds us that the beginning of the age of printing was still an *oral* age; tracts did not presuppose universal literacy but were published as much to be read publicly as privately. The propaganda media of this still oral age were so various and effective that the unlettered could receive a grasp of the basic issues of the Reformation no less profound than that of many a university scholar. On propagandizing the nonliterate through readings and songs in the later stages of the French Reformation, see Natalie Davis, "The Protestant Printing Workers of Lyons in 1551," in G. Berthaud et al., *Aspects de la propagande religieuse* (Geneva, 1957), pp. 247–57; 256. The critical theological perception of illiterate laity, attained by way of "talk" and pilgrimages, is pointed out by Margaret Aston, *The Fifteenth Century* (New York, 1970), pp. 93, 120.

12 Geffken, p. 29.

13 Ibid., pp. vii, 21, 104.

14 "Man kann aber nicht sagen, dass er die Zeit ebenso stark kennzeiche, wie das, was in allgemeinsten Sinn 'Missstand' zu nennen ist." "Zur Problematik der kirchlichen Missstände im Spät-Mittelalter," *Trierer Theologische Zeitschrift* 58 (1949): 1–26, 212–27, 257–79, 347–57; p. 9.

15 "Ineinander von kirchlich und weltlich, von kirchlich und wirtschaftlich, von kirchlich und politisch." Ibid., p. 15; cf. p. 274.

16 Ibid., pp. 17, 257, 275. "Besitz, Recht auf Zinsforderung, Gewerbebetrieb und Steuerfreiheit hatten den Geistlichen von der zivilen Seite her so stark, ja so wesensmässig zum natürlichen Gegenpart, ja Gegner des Laienvolkes gemacht, dass hier dauernd die Versuchung lauerte, den Laien nicht als Objekt der Seelsorge, sondern des Erwerbs zu betrachten."

17 Ibid., pp. 212, 347.

18 "On est entraîné dans un courant d'habitudes religieuses; on vit dans une société de baptisés que ne tourmente aucun problème apologétique, que n'excite aucune inquiétude religieuse pure; on tient plus au rite qu'à la richesse qu'il apporte ou provogue." *Le sentiment religieux en Flandre à la fin du Moyen-Age* (Paris, 1963), p. 223. (Hereafter cited as Toussaert.)

19 Ibid., pp. 67, 79, 492. Pervasive belief in the church's doctrinal authority is stressed by Moeller, "Piety in Germany."

20 Toussaert, pp. 341, 490, 595.

21 "Pour rien au monde, l'homme de Flandre ne voudrait négliger les démarches capitales pour assurer son salut: le baptême, les deniers sacrements et les funérailles ecclesiastiques. Autrement dit, aux graves moments de l'engagement chrétien par le Foi et la fixation de son sort éternel, les attitudes sont, par habitude et par désir vehement, chrétiennes et religieuses." Ibid., p. 489.

22 Etienne Delaruelle et al., *L'Église au temps du Grand Schisme et de la crise conciliaire (1378–1449)* (Paris, 1964), p. 656. (Hereafter cited as Delaruelle.) In contrast to Toussaert, Delaruelle describes the late Middle Ages as a time favorable to the sacrament of penance, associating its popularity with obsession with sin and fear of Last Judgment. Toussaert would agree when the sincerely religious—his elite—and deathbed confessions are brought to mind.

23 "Le confessionnal n'existe pas en tant que moyen de sanctification et de rédemption utilisé fréquemment; il n'existe absolument pas comme moyen de formation individuelle des consciences." Toussaert, p. 122.

24 Ibid., pp. 116–21, 203.

25 L. A. Veit, *Volksfrommes Brauchtum und Kirche im deutschen Mittelalter* (Freiburg i.B., 1936), pp. 88–90.

26 Delaruelle, pp. 615, 660, 666, 677, 689, 692, 703.

27 Ibid., pp. 738, 790, 821.

28 Ibid., p. 761.

29 Ibid., pp. 873–75, 877. Gerson, whom he describes as "le pasteur indulgent," is cited as a premier example.

30 Ibid., p. 875.

31 Gertrud Rüchlin-Teuscher, *Religiöses Volksleben des ausgehenden Mittelalters in den Reichsstädten Hall und Heilbronn* (Berlin, 1933), pp. 67, 163.

32 *Le sentiment religieux en Flandre,* pp. 88, 605. Toussaert (showing his colors) asks how a country like Flanders could be taken by heresy: "Est-ce si vrai qu'on recherche une vie religieuse plus authentique? N'est-on pas, au contraire, heureux de trouver une formule religieuse nouvelle sans obligation tangible, sans pratique extérieure et contrôlable, sans autorité, sans hiérarchie? La thèse Lutherienne de la justification par la foi, on l'adopte pour la dénaturer. Tout ce qui est 'oeuvres': c'est de la blague! Tout ce qui est du passé, églises, crucifix même, au feu!"

33 Such a distinction was critically developed in the sixteenth century by an ineffective minority group of dissenters, as I have shown in my *Mysticism and Dissent.* But that was far more a novelty than the norm.

34 Geffken, p. 25; Delaruelle, p. 656, where regular (annual) confession of all mortal sins is said to become a formal requirement between the

ages of twelve and fourteen. More generally on the topic: Peter Browe, "Die Pflichtbeichte im Mittelalter," *Zeitschrift für katholische Theologie* 57 (1933): 335–83; Henry C. Lea, *A History of Auricular Confession and Indulgences in the Latin Church* 1–3 (Philadelphia, 1896).

35 I interpret this to mean association with heretics or the excommunicated, not illicit sexual activity. Children are here being warned against spiritual "adultery" against the church.

36 From Johannes Wolff, *Beichtbüchlein* (1478), in *Drei Beichtbüchlein nach den Zehn Geboten aus der Frühzeit der Buchdruckerkunst,* ed. Franz Falk (Münster i.W., 1907), pp. 17–20. There was a certain training in the knowledge of sin through the confessional. Lists of sins and so-called *Beichttafeln,* which could be hung on the wall, were provided to laymen. Geffken includes examples in his collection.

37 *Der Spiegel des Sünders* (Augsburg, ca. 1417) in Geffken, Appendix, p. 52. There were four printed editions of this work in the fifteenth century, all appearing in Augsburg.

38 Geffken, pp. 24, 28. It is a telling commentary on the degree to which even reform-minded ecclesiastics were losing touch with lay reality in the fifteenth century that Jean Gerson looked upon the sacrament of penance and the confessional as the "primary means by which the parish priest can come to know those committed to his care." Louis B. Pascoe, S. J., *Jean Gerson: Principles of Church Reform* (Leiden, 1973), p. 154. Gerson's magisterial *Opusculum tripartitum de preceptis decalogi, de confessione et de arte moriendi* was translated into German as *Der drieckecht Spiegel* by Geiler von Kaisersberg and published in Strasbourg in 1510, influential to the very eve of the Reformation. The German text is excerpted in Geffken, Appendix, p. 29 and following.

39 In Geffken, Appendix, pp. 192–95. There are eleven editions of this popular confessional guide. It is strongly contritionist (". . . omnia peccata plangat contritio pura / Mit warer rew soltu klagen alle die sünde in deinen tagen") and summarizes the work of the conscientious confessor thus:

> Wer seynen syn und fleisz wollgeben
> Allezeit zu tugentlichenn leben,
> Der muesz zuvor on gutte haben,
> Almussen geben, toden begraben,
> Straffen, ratten, kneyen, wachen,
> Fasten, petten, andacht machen,
> Leren, lernen, waynen, wallen,
> das ist got ein woll gevallen.

It also bears a nice summary of the full penitential jargon (p. 195).

40 *Beichtbüchlein* (Augsburg, 1504) in *Drei Beichtbüchlein,* ed. Falk, pp. 84–85.

41 Geffken, Appendix, p. 192.

42 From a Heidelberg *Tractat von den zehen Geboten* in Geffken, Appendix, p. 19.

43 From a *Heidelberger Bildenhandschrift* in Geffken, Appendix, pp. 9–10.

44 *[Aus einem] Beichtspiegel von 1474 [oder vielmehr aus einem älterem Werke] Der Seele trost* in Geffken, Appendix, p. 100.

45 Ibid., p. 101.

46 Ibid., p. 106.

47 *Heidelberger Bildenhandschrift* in Geffken, Appendix, pp. 8, 16.

48 Franz Falk, "Der Unterricht des Volkes in den katechetischen Hauptstücken am Ende des Mittelalters," *Historische-politische Blätter für das Katholische Deutschland* 108 (1891): 553–60, 682–94; 109 (1892): 81–96, 721–31; 83.

49 [Martin Bucer], *Das einigerlei Bild bei den Gotglaübigen an orten da sie verehrt nit mögen geduldet werden* ([Strasbourg], 1530), pp. A 4 a, B 1 b.

50 "Durch die Beichte wurde eine wahre Tyrannei ausgeübt." Geffken, p. 24. There are, however, examples of far less demanding treatment of penitents in Geffken's collection. One, Rus's *Hauptstücke,* admonished trust in Jesus' promise of forgiveness rather than in purchased masses and the work of the priest; it found its way into Flacius's *Catalogus testium veritatis,* there enshrined forevermore as a forerunner of the Reformation. Geffken, Appendix, p. 163. Apart from Geffken, on scholarly Latin guides and scholastic discussion of penitential practice see Oberman, *The Harvest of Medieval Theology* p. 146, and Thomas N. Tentler, "The Summa for Confessors as an Instrument of Social Control," in *The Pursuit of Holiness,* pp. 103–25. Tentler's book-length study of late medieval confessional manuals is soon to appear from Princeton University Press, *Discipline and Consolation: Sacramental Confession on the Eve of the Reformation.* It is the peculiar strength of Geffken's vernacular collection to show the form these more sophisticated theories took when applied in direct practice. The further one moves from the balanced scholastic tract, and the closer one gets to the short vernacular *Beichtspiegel* for ordinary people, the more legalistic, fiscalized, and psychologically burdensome penitential practice appears.

51 Letter to Louvain theologians (July 14, 1522) in *Opus Epistolarum Des. Erasmi Roterodami,* ed. P. S. Allen V (Oxford, 1922), pp. 91–92; *Exomologesis sive modus confitendi,* in *Desiderii Erasmi Roterodami opera omnia* (Leiden 1704; Hildesheim, 1962) 5: 145–70.

52 Cf. J. M. Reu, *Dr. M. Luther's Small Catechism: A History of Its Origin, Its Distribution, and Its Use* (Chicago, 1929), pp. 1–6.

53 Albert Groeteken, "Der älteste gedruckte deutsche Katechismus und die niederdeutschen Volksbücher des seligen Dietrich Kolde von Münster," *Franziskanische Studien* 37 (1955): 53–74, 189–217, 388–410; 54–61, 190, 295. See also Groeteken, *Dietrich Kolde von Münster* (Kevelaer, 1945); Clemen Drees, ed., *Der Christenspiegel des Dietrich Kolde von Münster* (Werl/Westf., 1954).

54 Delaruelle cites other examples of these basic requirements as if they were the church's full expectations of the "good Christian." *L'Église au temps du Grand Schisme,* p. 728. They are in truth but the point of departure for religiously earnest laymen. In my opinion, neither Lortz nor Delaruelle appreciates the degree to which the late medieval church itself, through its "clericalized" concept of the good Christian, promoted an introspective conscience and that religious individualism both see as a (largely unCatholic) reaction to the medieval church. In fact, one does not have to look beyond the concept of lay piety promoted by the late medieval church to find its source. What Delaruelle says about confraternal piety can, I think, be largely extended to the piety offered laity by the late medieval church: "il est notamment caractéristique que la spiritualité proposée à ces laics soit toujours celle des moines, qui gardent sur le plan ascétique et mystique une sorte de monopole: la perfection consiste à se flageller, à assiter à des offices, à chanter des cantiques au cours de paraliturgies. Les confréries n'ont pas su trouver la spiritualité nécessaire au laic; sur ce point leur contribution à la vie spirituelle de l'époque fut inférieure à celle des humanistes" (p. 688; cf. p. 701).

55 On this genre of indulgence in late medieval sermon literature, see G. R. Owst, *Preaching in Medieval England* (Cambridge, 1926), pp. 101–10, 357 (appendix 3).

56 In *Franciscan Studies* 37 (1955): 62–74, ed. A. Groteken. On the last article see pp. 55–56 below.

57 See R. R. Post, *The Modern Devotion: Confrontation with Reformation and Humanism* (Leiden, 1968), p. 653. The popular belief that Thomas à Kempis's *Imitation of Christ,* the expression par excellence of the piety of the *Devotio moderna,* promoted a "subjective" spirituality hostile to "objective" church piety and thereby foreshadowing the Reformation, is, I think, quite mistaken. The *Imitation of Christ* was intended for the cloistered (Kempis was an Augustinian) but became widely adopted by pious laymen who wanted to pursue monastic values while remaining laymen. Like Coelde's catechism it is only a transferral of ascetic piety into the secular world and represents no break with or serious threat to traditional lay piety. If anything, it may be said to exaggerate traditional lay piety.

58 See, for example, Philip Melanchthon's commentary on the Ten Commandments (1523) and Valentin Ickelsamer's catechetical dialogue (1525) in Ferdinand Cohrs, *Die Evangelischen Katechismusversuche vor Luthers Enchiridion* 1 (Berlin, 1900), pp. 83, 136.

59 See pp. 55–56 below.

60 See Alfred Schultze, *Stadtgemeinde und Reformation* (Tübingen, 1918); Willy Andreas, "Die Kulturbedeutung der deutschen Reichsstadt zu Ausgang des Mittelalters," *Deutsche Vierteljahrsschrift für Literaturwissenschaft und Geistesgeschichte* 6 (1928): 62–113, especially p. 79; and von Muralt, "Stadtgemeinde und Reformation," pp. 352–55.

61 Karlheinz Blaschke, *Sachsen im Zeitalter der Reformation* (Gütersloh, 1970), pp. 34, 49–55, 72. Cf. also Eschenhagen, "Beiträge zur Sozial- und Wirtschaftsgeschichte der Stadt Wittenberg," who deduces Luther's social and economic conservatism from Wittenberg's social and economic history at the time of the Reformation.

62 "Und damit Gott der Herr uns behüt, die Frücht so uff dem Feld sin, und gut Wetter geb, so sol niemans tanzen." Cited by Hans Morf, "Obrigkeit und Kirche in Zürich bis zu Beginn der Reformation," *Zwingliana* 13 (1970): 164–203; 182.

63 "Es steht also in der Reichsstadt nicht politische und kirchliche Gemeinde, sondern die auch kirchlich handelnde politische Gemeinde und der Pfarrer einander gegenüber." Gerhard Pfeiffer, "Das Verhältnis von politischer und kirchlicher Gemeinde in den deutschen Reichsstädten," in *Staat und Kirche im Wandel der Jahrhunderte,* ed. W. P. Fuchs (Stuttgart, 1966), p. 81. Cf. H. W. Krumwiede, "Die Reformation in Niedersachsen: Politische, soziale und kirchlichtheologische Aspekte," *Jahrbuch der Gesellschaft für niedersächsische Kirchengeschichte* 65 (1967): 7–26; 16; and Heinrich Schmidt, *Die deutschen Städtechroniken als Spiegel des bürgerlichen Selbstverständnisses im Spätmittelalter* (Göttingen, 1958), p. 92.

64 Suzanne Ritter, *Die kirchenkritische Tendenz in den deutschsprachigen Flugschriften der frühen Reformationszeit* (Tübingen, 1970), pp. 4, 80, 113.

65 Hermann Buck und Ekkehart Fabian, *Konstanzer Reformationsgeschichte in ihren Grundzügen 1. Teil: 1519–1531* (Tübingen, 1965), p. 148; Moeller, "Kleriker als Bürger," p. 198.

66 See the succinct statement by H. G. Koenigsberger, "The Unity of the Church and the Reformation," *Journal of Interdisciplinary History* 1 (1970/71): 407–17.

67 Oskar Vasella, "Die Ursachen der Reformation in der deutschen Schweiz," *ZSchGes* 27 (1947): 401–24, 409; Joseph Lortz, *Die Reformation in Deutschland* 1 (Freiburg, 1962), p. 77; Schultze, *Stadtgemeinde und Reformation.*

68 Vasella, "Die Ursachen der Reformation," pp. 402–04.

69 S. M. Jackson, ed., *The Latin Works and Correspondence of Huldrich Zwingli,* (New York, 1912), 1:215.

70 Vasella, "Die Ursachen der Reformation," p. 420. See p. 123 below.

71 Johannes Schildhauer, *Soziale, politische und religiöse Auseinandersetzungen in den Hansestädten Stralsund, Rostock und Wismar im ersten Drittel des 16. Jahrhunderts* (Weimar, 1959), pp. 69–76. (Hereafter cited as Schildhauer.)

72 Günther Franz, ed., *Urkundliche Quellen zur hessischen Reformationsgeschichte II: 1525–47,* (Marburg, 1954), pp. 10–11.

73 "Die Kurie erhob unter keinem anderen Titel öfter Geld, als unter dem des Ablasses. Daher erregten alle ihre anderen Einnahmequellen weit weniger Anstoss." Anton Störmann, *Die städtischen Gravamina gegen den Klerus am Ausgange des Mittelalters und in der Reformationszeit* (Münster i. W., 1912), p. 12.

74 Ibid., p. 13. Wilhelm Borth, *Die Luthersache (Causa Lutheri) 1517–24: Die Anfänge der Reformation als Frage von Politik und Recht* (Lübeck/Hamburg, 1970), pp. 16–29, especially p. 20.

75 Moeller, "Kleriker als Bürger," pp. 199–200.

76 Cited by Schildhauer, p. 80.

77 Konrad Hofmann, *Die engere Immunität im deutschen Bischofsstädten im Mittelalter* (Paderborn, 1915), pp. 14, 29. Cf. the privileges attached to the original charter of the order of Cluny—an interesting commentary on the evolving clerical mystique. Joan Evans, *Monastic Life at Cluny 910–1157* (London, 1931), pp. 12–13.

78 Toussaert finds popular support for the right of asylum as a "bottle of ink" for light-fingered gentry and various nonviolent criminal elements, and as a handy refuge during wars and plagues. The threat of interdict and excommunication in defense of the right of asylum could inspire as much fear as its threat to the civil administration of justice. Toussaert gives some interesting examples. *Le sentiment religieux en Flandre,* pp. 297, 306.

79 Hofmann, *Die engere Immunität,* p. 151.

80 Rolf Kiessling, *Bürgerliche Gesellschaft und Kirche in Augsburg im Spätmittelalter: Ein Beitrag zur Strukturanalyse der oberdeutschen Reichsstadt* (Augsburg, 1971). In Hall by the time of the Reformation the city had acquired full rights of patronage over fourteen benefices, the preachership and two pastoral appointees, and penetrated the cultural and educational sphere as well. A similar development can be traced in Heilbronn. "Siegreich dringt das Bürgertum der beiden Städte in die Hierarchie der Kirche ein und gewinnt bedeutenden Einfluss auf das kirchliche Aemterwesen und die Verwaltung der Güter." Rücklin-Teuscher, *Religiöses Volksleben,* pp. 21, 163. Hubert Jedin has pointed

out how local reform efforts, guided by popular preachers, humanists, and members of the *Devotio moderna,* filled the void left by papal and episcopal leadership on the eve of the Reformation and became seedbeds of Lutheranism. *History of the Council of Trent* (St. Louis, 1957), 1:152, 164.

81 Morf, "Obrigkeit und Kirche," pp. 164–79, 194–98. It is Morf's thesis that the relation between the church and the magistracy during the Reformation, far from being an innovation or compromise by Zwingli, was in fact already prescribed by developments in the late Middle Ages. His work supports the interpretation of Robert Walton against John Yoder. Walton, *Zwingli's Theocracy* (Toronto, 1967); "Was There a Turning Point of the Zwinglian Reformation?," *MQR* 42 (1968): 45–56. Yoder, "The Turning Point in the Zwinglian Reformation," *MQR* 32 (1958): 128–40; "The Evolution of the Zwinglian Reformation," *MQR* 43 (1969): 95–112.

82 See pp. 157, 224–25 below.

83 Borth, *Die Luthersache,* p. 12, n. 10.

84 Schildhauer, p. 133.

85 See Kiessling, *Bürgerliche Gesellschaft und Kirche in Augsburg,* p. 306.

86 Ibid., p. 359; Moeller, "Piety in Germany."

87 *Die deutschen Städtechronisten als Spiegel des bürgerlichen Selbstverständmisses im Spätmittelalter* (Göttingen, 1958), pp. 71, 83, 106. Schmidt opposes the arguments of Willy Andreas, who depicts imperial cities as no less "particularistic" and "egoistic" than territorial states (p. 34). Cf. Andreas, "Die Kulturbedeutung der deutschen Reichsstadt," pp. 55–56.

88 Cited in Schmidt, *Die deutschen Städtechronisten*, p. 87.

89 "Man könnte fast sagen, dass ohne die Prädikaturen der Siegeslauf der Reformation in den Reichsstädten sich kaum vollzogen hätte. Das Wirken bedeutsamer Prädikanten . . . war Voraussetzung für das Durchdringen der Reformation." Pfeiffer, "Das Verhältnis von Politischer und Kirchlicher Gemeinde," p. 87; Vasella, "Die Ursachen der Reformation," p. 413.

90 There is still work to be done on preacherships. The following discussion is based on exemplary studies of Württemberg, Ernestine Thuringia, and Switzerland: Julius Rauscher, "Die Prädikaturen in Württemberg vor der Reformation. Ein Beitrag zur Predigt- und Pfründengeschichte am Ausgang des Mittelalters," *Württembergische Jahrbücher für Statistik und Landeskunde* (Stuttgart, 1909), pp. 152–211 (hereafter cited as Rauscher); Rudolf Herrmann, "Die Prediger im ausgehenden Mittelalter und ihre Bedeutung für die Einführung der Reformation im Ernestinischen Thüringen," *Beiträge zur Thüringischen*

Kirchengeschichte 1 (1929): 20–68 (hereafter cited as Herrmann); and E. Lengwiler, *Die vorreformatorischen Prädikaturen der deutschen Schweiz von ihrer Entstehung bis 1530* (Freiburg, 1955) (hereafter cited as Lengwiler).

91 This is my calculation from Rauscher's data, Appendix 2, p. 197.

92 Rauscher, p. 152.

93 Ibid., p. 168.

94 ". . . das Einfallstor für das Eindringen reformatorisch gesinnter Männer in den Bereiches kirchlichen Aemterwesens." Herrmann, pp. 63–65.

95 Lengwiler, pp. 20–22.

96 Ibid., pp. 77–78. Lengwiler, a student of Vasella, corrects those who have overly "Protestantized" the Swiss preacherships. While he has put Swiss preacherships in a more balanced perspective, he has not addressed the issue of whether the activities of the preachers were conducive to Protestant sentiments even though in their patrons' eyes the preacherships were bulwarks of the old church. I think the disproportion between the religious alignment of preachers (over half of whom became Protestants) and that of the preacherships (two-thirds of which remained Catholic) suggests that they may well have been.

97 "Einem Bedürfnis nach besserer Predigt sind sie entsprungen"; ". . . ein Zeugnis für die Unfähigkeit der schon funktionierenden Weltgeistlichkeit." Rauscher, pp. 155, 158.

98 See Gabriel, "The College System in the Fourteenth Century Universities," p. 82.

99 Lengwiler, p. 26. The strong hostility of the German clergy to Rome following the failure of the Council of Basel is documented by Joachim W. Stieber, "Pope Eugenius IV and the Council of Basel" (Ph.D. diss., Yale University, 1974), pp. 370–74. Many German clerics, like the Carthusian Vincent of Aggsbach, henceforth saw the papacy as the main opponent of reform. Even before the collapse of the conciliar movement with the publication of the papal bull *Execrabilis*, many German clerics were open to innovative local solutions. Preacherships were one such solution. See also Bruno Gebhardt, *Die Gravamina der deutschen Nation gegen den romischen Hof* (Breslau, 1895).

100 Herrmann, pp. 27–40.

101 Herrmann finds in letters endowing preacherships evidence for what he considers to be a widening ethical concern. A preachership was a good work for the community as a whole, serving the living *Gemeinde*, whereas an endowed private mass was a ceremony only for the departed soul of the founder (p. 40).

102 According to Rauscher, p. 175.

103 Ibid., p. 157.

104 Herrmann, p. 43.

105 Rauscher, pp. 178–80; Herrmann, p. 46: "Es war in ausgehenden Mittelalter durchaus so, dass nicht mehr der Bischof und seine Beamten der entscheidende Faktor bei der Stellbesetzung war, sondern die geistlichen Personen und Körperschaften und die weltlichen Patrone, denen das Nominations- und Präsentationsrecht und die Einsetzung in den Genuss der Pfründe zustand. Die Wirklichkeit war ganz anders, als die kirchenrechtliche Theorie."

106 Some early preacherships in fact evolved from endowed masses which stipulated that regular preaching occur with the celebration of the Mass. Rauscher, p. 156.

107 Cited by Rauscher, p. 156.

108 Lengwiler, p. 52. Like his teacher, Vasella, Lengwiler plays down allegations of widespread clerical corruption on the eve of the Reformation. But he does find the preachers' moral lives superior to those of other clergymen.

109 Lengwiler, p. 51.

110 Rauscher, pp. 161–65.

111 Ibid., p. 167.

112 Ibid., pp. 168–72; Lengwiler, p. 32.

113 Herrmann, p. 64.

114 Rauscher describes their relation in Württemberg as "kein offizielles, aber immerhin ein neutral-höfliches" (p. 181). Their mutual dependence was in fact so great that the very scheduling of religious activities would have collapsed into chaos had they been openly hostile.

115 "Die Entstehungsgeschichte der Prädikaturen hat ja gezeigt, dass neben den Bettelmönchen die Pfarrer und ihre Helfer es waren, gegen die sich die ganze Einrichtung kehrte: sie kam einen Unfähigkeitszeugnis für diese gleich." Rauscher, p. 180.

116 "Das Wesen des deutschen Spätmittelalters," in *Der Mensch in seiner Gegenwart* (Göttingen, 1957), pp. 109–35; 134.

117 Blaschke, *Sachsen im Zeitalter der Reformation*, p. 116. For parallels among fifteenth-century Hussites, see R. R. Betts, "The Place of the Czech Reform Movement in the History of Europe," *The Slavonic Review* 25 (1936/47): 373–90; 377.

118 *Von der rechten Erhebung Bennonis ein Sendbrief* (Wittenberg, 1524), ed. Alfred Götze, in Clemen 1:204. Luther also pamphleteered against the "Erhebung Bennonis." *WA* 15:553. Another example is an anonymous pamphlet mocking the journey of Cardinal Campeggio and his retinue to the Nürnberg Reichstag in 1524. The Cardinal is described by two peasants as a "strange animal" and the symbols, titles, and ceremonies of his office scathingly ridiculed. *Ein Frag und Antwort von zweien Brüdern,*

was für ein seltsames Tier zu Nürnberg gewesen im Reichstag nächst vergangen, geschickt von Rom zu beschauen das deutsch Land (Nürnberg, 1524), ed. Otto Clemen, in Clemen 1:170–84.

119 Moeller, "Probleme des Kirchlichen Lebens," p. 26.

120 See Gerald Strauss, *Manifestations of Discontent in Germany on the Eve of the Reformation* (Bloomington, Ind., 1971).

121 Luther would insist in 1531 that even if Rome had observed her religion with the rigor and discipline of the hermits, Jerome, Augustine, Gregory, Bernard, Francis, and Dominic, her "false doctrine" would still have necessitated the Reformation. *Lectures on Galatians* (pub. 1535), *WA* 40:687 (*LW* 26:459). Lucien Febvre, the most forceful foe of the abuse theory of the Reformation's origin, has argued a similar point for the origin of the French Reformation: "Reformez le clergé, la religion sera sauvée, c'est l'aveuglement du professionnel." *Une question mal posée,* p. 41. Moeller finally relates Luther's success to the fact that many simply felt he had better answers to their religious problems than did the medieval church. "Probleme des kirchlichen Lebens," p. 30.

122 *Niklaus Manuels Spiel evangelischer Freiheit. Die Totenfresser. Vom Papst und seiner Priesterschaft 1523*, ed. Ferdinand Vetter (Leipzig, 1923), pp. 54, 57. See p. 67 below.

123 Ibid., p. 53: "Ich wond, ich hette Gott selber gesehen—Biss dass ich vernam, es sölte nüt / Des war ich bericht durch witzig lüt / Do ward ich ganz von zorn entrüst / Und han den ars an brief gewüst / Nachpur Rufli, ich muss dir's klagen / Es lit mir noch in minen magen!" There is a similar "recognition" scene in a pamphlet ascribed to Eberlin von Günzburg. A pilgrim farmer tells of a "gnad brieff" he has purchased which will let him go immediately into heaven when he dies. A Protestant artisan explains to him that one can no more enter heaven with an indulgence than a cow *[sic]* can pass through the eye of a needle. *Eyn gesprech zwyschen vyer Personen / wie si ein gezengk haben von der walfart ym Grimetal, was fur unradt odder büberey, der auss entstandenn sey. Hantwerckszman. Pawer. Pfaff. Munch. Eyn trew Christlich vermanung, on alle Hantwercks leute vor mueszigang sich zcu heutten* (Erfurt, 1523 or 1524), ed. Otto Clemen, in Clemen 1:137–67; 144. See p. 115 below. Cf. also *Ein Frag und Antwort von zweien Brüdern,* p. 181, where spotting the "triegerey" of indulgences is easier done than overcoming belief in masses.

124 "Ja, so solten sie es nit thun, die sacerdotes. Wen sie uns nit guts vor predigenn, so können wir die seligkeit nit wissen, den du weist: wie der hirt ist, also sein auch die schaffe." *Ein Dialogus oder Gespräch zwischen einem Vater und Sohn die Lehre Martini Luthers und sonst andere Sachen des*

christlichen Glaubens belangend (Erfurt, 1523), ed. Otto Clemen, in Clemen 1:23–50; 35.

125 Ibid., p. 45.

126 "L'iconoclastie in XVIe siècle pourrait bien avoir été, en certains cas, une vengeance de la psychologie collective contre des excentricités qui refoulaient cet 'essential', dans l'oubli, l'ignorance ou des travestissements." *Le sentiment religieux en Flandre,* p. 83.

127 "Nun so man sein bildnuss an hiltzen/steynenen/silberen / güldinen creutzen lang anschawt / und sich meynt gleich andechtig zusein / richt man anders nüt auss / dann das man sich selbs betreugt / und fälschlich mit nüt trostet / dadurch man zu allem gutten desto farlessiger wurdt." *Das einigerlei Bild,* p. B 1 a.

Chapter 3

1 Nikolaus Paulus, "Die Reue in den deutschen Beichtschriften des ausgehenden mittelalters," *ZkathTh* 28 (1904): 1–36; "Die Reue in den deutschen Erbauungsschriften des ausgehenden Mittelalters," ibid., pp. 449–85; "Die Reue in den deutschen Sterbebüchlein des ausgehenden Mittelalters," ibid., pp. 682–98.

2 *Eyn Sermon von dem Sacrament der pusz, LW* 35:9–22; 15 (*WA* 2:714–23).

3 *LW* 35:18. Johannes Bugenhagen, Lutheran pastor and catechist in Wittenberg, summarized the original Protestant position thus: every Christian *must* confess *to God* that he is a sinner, but confession of sins to men, whether priests or fellow lay Christians, is a completely free matter. "Beycht aber die man den lewtten thut / weyl gott sy nicht gebotten hatt / soll gantz frey sein / ob man beychten will / und wenn / und wie offt / und wölchem man will / es sey ainem priester oder layen . . . zu hören von seynem brüder ain trostlich gottes wort / der vergebung der sünden auss dem hayligen Evangelio." *Ain Sendtbrieff herrn Joh. Bugenhagen Pomern / Pfarrern zu Wittemberg / über ain frag vom Sacrament. Item ain underricht von der Beycht und Christlicher Absolution* (Wittenberg, 1525), p. A 3 b. One can also see in this tract the evaporation of the sacrament of penance into the Protestant sermon. "Absolution sprechen / ist nichts anders / denn das Evangelion verkündigen. Denn Evangelion ist anders nichts denn ain gütten botschafft / das all sünd werden vergeben durch Christum. Glaub ich der Absolution / so habe ich vergebung der sünden / und bin ewig sälig." (Ibid., p. A 4 a.) Bugenhagen later (1531) made private or communal (congregational) confession a necessary preparation for sacramental communion. See p. 160 below.

4 *Confitendi ratio, LW* 39:27–47; 32 (*WA* 6:157–69).

5 *LW* 39:35–37, 45. Luther cited the marital laws of the church as an especially telling example. One guilty of incest—by reason of sexual relations with his wife's sister, his mother-in-law, or one related by a close degree of consanguinity—is punished by being deprived of the right to receive the "marital duty" from his wife, although he still must continue to live with her as before. Luther likens such a penance to throwing wood on a fire and commanding it not to burn. It is a penance designed to promote failure and further guilt.

6 *Quod non sit onerosa christianis confessio, paradoxon* (Basel, 1521), pp. B 1 a, B 4 a.

7 Ibid., pp. E 3 b, L 1 a–L 3 b.

8 "Sie . . . zu aim hellischen strick der gewissen unerleidlich aufgelegt haben / damit das der arm Christenmensch nitt meer mit begirigen freyen hertzen zu dem frölichen tisch unsers herren sich möcht vertreuen / und den leib unsers gotes und sein hailiges blut zu sicherer hailwertigkait empfahen." *Ain trostliche verstendige leer über das wort sancti Pauli Der mensch soll sich selbs probieren / und also von dem brot essen / und von dem kelch trincken. Gepredigет zu Hall im Intal* (n.p., 1522), p. A 3 a. On Strauss, see Joachim Rogge, *Der Beitrag des Predigers Jacob Strauss zur frühen Reformationsgeschichte* (Berlin, 1957).

9 *Ain trostliche verstendige leer,* pp. A 4 a-b, B 3 b.

10 Ibid., pp. A 4 b, B 1 a.

11 "Sy [priests] söllen dir auch weder tag noch nacht kain ruw lassen / biss sy dem seel / leib / und gut under iren tyrannischen gewalt bringen." Ibid., p. B 2 a.

12 Ibid., p. C 1 b.

13 *Ein neüw wunderbarlich Beychtbeüchlin / in dem die warhafftig Gerecht beycht und bussfertigkeit Christlichen gelert und angezwygt wirt* (Augsburg, 1523), p. B 1 b.

14 Ibid., p. B 2 a. Humiliation of betrothed women in the confessional is also among the special complaints of a popular early pamphlet ascribed to Hanns Schwalb, *Beclagung eines Leyens genant Hanns Schwalb über vil miszbrauchs christenlichs lebens, und darinn begriffen kürtzlich von Johannes Hussen* (Augsburg, 1521), ed. Wilhelm Lucke, in Clemen 1:348–60; 349. Cf. Delaruelle, p. 739.

15 As 1 Cor. 7:4 teaches him, "Das weyb ist jres liebs nit mechtig / sonder der man." *Ein neüw Beychtbeüchlin,* p. B 2 b. He ignores, however, the second half of the verse: "Likewise the husband does not rule over his own body, but the wife does."

16 Ibid., pp. B 2 b, B 3 a. Cf. Eberlin von Günzburg, p. 92 below.

17 *Ein schöner Dialogus von den vier gröszten Beschwernissen eines jeglichen Pfarrers* ([Schlettstadt], 1521), ed. Wilhelm Lucke, in Clemen 3:29–110; 81.

18 *Ain grüme / grosse ketten / darzu die hert gefäncknuss / über die kinder Gottes auffgericht* (n.p., 1524), p. A 4 a. "Summa summarum . . . nichts guts / in confession / besonder alles unglück on endt / spot / schand / missglauben in got / und vertrawen in menschliche werck / und hoffnung auff die creaturen etc." Ibid., p. B 1 b; cf. p. B 1 a.

19 "Christus in dem glauben macht frölich und frey des sünders hertz. Die beycht betriebt und unrewigt das hertz / als in der warhait sich befindet / ye mer man beycht, ye mer man beychten muss. Christus zaygt sich selbs an ain warhafftigen sichern lebendigen weg. In der Beycht leeret man sünd fürchten da kaine ist / und so man lenger fragt / und in sünden umbgryppelt / ye schwerlicher und geferlicher man von dem rechten weg veriret." *Ein neüw Beychtbeüchlin,* p. C 2 a-b. Matthew Zell remembered with pain the abuses of the confessional he witnessed in the office of Penitentiarius in Strasbourg, citing particularly the penance and fines imposed on women who miscarry. "Wir wissen das in der hymlichen beicht / so vil unzelicher gefäncknuss gewesen seind / so mitt den vorbehaltenen fällen / durch weliche man umb liederliche ding / ja umb ding so nit sünd seien / zum dickeren mal die armen leüt umbher getriben hat wie ein garnwind. . . . Ich habs erfaren in meinen ampt (wann ich auch meins genedigen herr von Strassburg Penitentiarius bitzhär gewesen) und den elenden jamer an den armen leüten / mit schmertzen gesehen / die man als vil als umb nichts häryn gen Strassburg zu mir getriben hat / etwan so eim armen wiblin misslungen ist an der geburt / oder sunst / schickt mans erst umbhär vil zu büssen / dz sye sich ab dem / das jr nie sünd gewesen ist / und grossz leyd geschehen ist / erst veriamern muss und umbs gelt darzu kummen. Und ist das aller böst / es gadt nur uber das arm völckly / die grossen hanssen (ich mein räuber / dieb wucherer / simonyer / und frundenfresser / und dergleichen) nennt man gnad iunckhern / hoch und würdigen herren." *Christliche Verantwortung über Artickel in vom Bischofflichen Fiscal dasselbs entgegen gesetzt und in rechten übergeben* (Strasbourg, 1523), p. v2r-v. Cited by William S. Stafford, "Domesticating the Clergy: The Inception of the Reformation in Strasbourg" (Ph.D. diss., Yale University, 1974).

20 *Ein neüw Beychtbeüchlin,* p. D 1 b.

21 Ibid., p. D 2 a.

22 Ibid., pp. D 3 b–D 4 a.

23 In refutation of Harnack's romantic view of Luther as the first to direct the dying to trust in Christ, Paulus cited fifteen examples of deathbed reliance on grace. ("Die Reue in den deutschen Sterbebüchlein.") In each, however, reliance on Christ and grace is still very much within the traditional framework of what the Reformation

called "works-righteousness." When one is faced with imminent death and God's wrath, perfect inner penance and the appeal to God's mercy in Christ is the only "good work" one can yet perform. The following from a 1510 *Spiel vom sterbenden Menschen* is typical. The dying man says:

> O starker Gott und himmlischer Vater mein,
> Für das streng urteil deiner gerechtigkeit
> Setz deines sohnes tod mit seiner barmherzigkeit.
> *Nimm sein verdienst für das mein, das ich solt haben tan;*
> O Herr, ohn das bedürft ich nit für dich zu gericht stan.
> Den tod und leiden deines eingebornen sohn ansich,
> Ich setz das zwischen deinen zorn und zwischen mich,
> Dass es sei ein mittler zwischen dein und mein.
> Herr Jesu Christ, mein seel empfiel ich in die hände dein.

Cited by Paulus, "Die Reue," p. 695.

24 Luther and sixteenth-century Lutherans are discussed by Luise Klein, "Die Bereitung zum Sterben: Studien zu den frühen reformatorischen Sterbebüchern" (Diss., Göttingen, 1958), who also appends the most comprehensive bibliography of Protestant *Sterbebücher* und *Sterbeliteratur* in the sixteenth century.

25 Cited in ibid., p. 60.

26 *Seelen Ertzney für die gesunden und krancken / jnn tods nöten* (Wittenberg, 1542), pp. A 8 a, B 7 a.

27 Klein, "Die Bereitung zum Sterben," pp. 77–78.

28 See p. 111.

29 *Ernstliche Ermahnung Hugo von Landenbergs, Bischofs zu Konstanz, zu Frieden und christlicher Einigkeit, mit schöner Auslegung und Erklärung, [samt:] Summarium der schädlichen tödlichen Gifte, so in diesem Mandat inbegriffen* [Augsburg, 1522/23], ed. Karl Schottenloher, in Clemen 4. The original is described as "Gedruckt zu Hohensteyn durch Hanns Fürwitzig." Augsburg was Meyer's first retreat after dismissal from Bern in October, 1524. *ADB* 21:613.

30 The offices are: Pfarrer, Caplän, monks; Dominus penitentiarius, Decani, Camerarii, Commissarii; Offizial, Vicari in spiritualibus; Cantzler, Rät, Doctores canonum, notarii, Copisten, Plundermann [!], and Insigler. *Ernstliche Ermahnung,* p. 294. "Es ist leider wahr: Diese Tyrannen haben die Kirche ihrem Stifter Christus mit Satzungen und Zeremonien abwendig gemacht. Sie füllen ihre Säckel und verheissen allen denen den Himmel, die an ihre Erdichtungen glauben, und also bringen sie Judaismum und gentilismum, durch Christum und Apostlen hingelegt und uszgerüt, widerumb uff, also das wir Jüdischer

yetz denn Juden synd, mit kilchen satzungen, gewonheitten und tusentterley Ceremonien, auch Heydnischer denn heyden, mit titlen und namen als pontifex maximus, dryen Keyser kronen, tragen in einer boren u. triumphen, mit bildern zueren, füszküssen und tusentterley pfaffen, secten, örden und vestalischen junckfrawen, wie die Heyden in Clöster zwingen u." Ibid., p. 299.

31 Ibid., pp. 310–11. In an exposé of pilgrim shrines, Eberlin von Günzburg told of a Dominican plot to create their own Saint Francis. The plan grew out of what was originally a ruse to combat Franciscan promotion of the immaculate conception of the Virgin. Bernese Dominicans, according to Eberlin, convinced a poor tailor's apprentice, who was swifter of scissor than of mind, that he had seen the Virgin and received from her the firm assurance that she had not been immaculately conceived. Recognizing the possibility of making their monastery a lucrative pilgrim shrine, they drugged and stigmatized the simpleminded tailor. Upon awakening he was convinced by the monks that, like Saint Francis, he had received his wounds from Christ. When he proved convincing to the people in the area, the monks plotted with their prior to poison him on the belief that after his death the pope would surely proclaim him a saint. The plot, according to Eberlin, failed and the monks were exposed. *Eyn gesprech zwischen vyer Personen,* in Clemen 1:144. Eberlin here apparently reports his own version of the Hans Jetzer affair, which saw a drawn out legal process in Bern from 1506–09. See *RGG* 3:663.

32 *Ernstliche Ermahnung,* p. 329. That Meyer did not exaggerate the time devoted in worship services to set announcements, see Veit, *Volksfrommes Brauchtum,* p. 87.

33 *Ernstliche Ermahnung,* p. 305.

34 *Ein schöner Dialogus,* pp. 87–89.

35 Oskar Vasella, *Reform und Reformation in der Schweiz: Zur Würdigung der Anfänge der Glaubenskrise* (Münster in Westfalen, 1958), pp. 28–34, 36, 62. In an interesting effort to put the lie to Janssen's optimistic views, Paul Tschackert calculated from the record of fines for sexual misconduct in the archbishopric of Mainz between 1519 and 1521 that clergy were, proportionately, seventy-two times more sexually immoral than laity. "Die Rechnungsbücher des erzbischöflich mainzischen Kommissars Johann Bruns aus den Jahren 1519–1531," *ZKG* 21 (1901): 330–79; 342. Although, as Vasella points out, Tschackert's data base was too small for his sweeping conclusions (*Reform und Reformation in der Schweiz,* p. 9), he does successfully document the not surprising conclusion that threats to episcopal authority were far more seriously taken than the sexual immorality of priests, the latter easily tolerated so long as the fines were duly paid.

36 Ibid., pp. 32–33.

37 Ibid., pp. 21, 42, 46–48.

38 Cf. Walter Köhler, *Zürcher Ehegericht und Genfer Konsistorium* 1 (Leipzig, 1932).

39 Vasella, *Reform und Reformation in der Schweiz,* pp. 49–51, 53–54. He summarizes: "Das Problem besass ja auch einen eminent wirtschaftlich-sozialen Aspekt. Durch die Freigabe der Priesterehe fielen für den Geistlichen ansehnliche Strafgelder weg, seine materielle Lage wurde insofern erheblich erleichtert, namentlich aber die soziale Stellung der Kinder auf eine legale Grundlage gestellt. Das waren offenkundige Vorteile, deren Wirkung an der stark verbreiteten Missstimmung wohl ermessen werden konnte. Man versteht daher die so eindrucksvolle Stimmungsmache mittels der Flugschriften in den städtischen Gemeinden wie in den Dörfern der bäuerlichen Landschaft." Ibid., p. 61. For the theological and religious side see my "Marriage and the Ministry in the Protestant Churches," *Concilium* 8: *Celibacy of the Catholic Priest* (1972), pp. 39–56.

40 *Ernstliche Ermahnung,* p. 303.

41 Ibid., p. 307. Meyer expressed admiration for the examples of independence from Rome in the Eastern churches ("Galatia"), where priests still married, and in France, where the Pragmatic Sanction of Bourges (1438) and the recent Concordat of Bologna (1516) limited papal revenues and circumscribed papal power of ecclesiastical appointment. Ibid., p. 308.

42 "Also setzen sie unser seelenheyl uff ein solch unsicher, ungwisz, zenckisch, hederisch ding, so uns Christus das uff ein sichers gesetzt . . . und das arme Christenvolk wird mit Zweifel und Zank gequält." Ibid., pp. 300–01.

43 "Vor allem aber sind wir ihnen Ketzer, weil wir die Schriften der Päpste nicht höher schätzen als das Evangelium, während wir sehen, dass diese Erlasse an tausend Stellen geirrt haben und wieder ausser Kraft gesetzt worden sind." Ibid., p. 320. "Denn wir wysen das volck zu Christenlicher fryheit und jre conscientzen von sölchen unerträglichen burdinen entladen." Ibid., p. 325.

44 Ibid., p. 303.

45 Judas Nazarei, *Vom alten und neuen Gott, Glauben und Lehre,* ed. Eduard Kück (Halle, 1896), in *Neudrucke deutschen Literaturwerke des XVI. und XVII. Jahrhunderts* 142/143, pp. vi–xi. On the question of Vadian's authorship, see the negative conclusion of T. Schiess, "Hat Vadian deutsche Flugschriften verfasst?" in *Festgabe für Hermann Escher* (Zürich, 1927), pp. 66–97.

46 *Vom alten und neuen Gott,* pp. 4–53.

47 See Ibid., articles 2–4, 6, and 10.

48 Ibid., p. 58.

49 Ibid., pp. 62–63.

50 *Martin Bucers Deutsche Schriften* 1: *Frühschriften 1520–24,* ed. Robert Stupperich (Gütersloh, 1960) 1:16, 31. Zell's self-defense appeared a few months earlier. See Miriam Chrisman, *Strasbourg and the Reform* (New Haven, 1967), p. 101.

51 *Das ym selbs niemant, sonder andern leben soll, und wie der mensch dahyn kummen mög* in *Martin Bucers Deutsche Schriften* 1:50.32–51.7.

52 Ibid., pp. 55.1-7, 11. "Wiewol aber weltlicher oberkeit dyenst, die sye der gemeyn schuldig ist, nit in dem stot, das sye das göttlich wort und gesatz predigen, yedoch gebürt yn nach göttlichem gesatz zu regieren und irs vermögen zu uffgang göttlichs worts helffen. Dann so kein gewalt ist on von gott und der gewalt, der allenthalben ist, ist von gott geordnet [Romans 13], so folget ye gewisslich, das er nach göttlicher ordnung und willen gebraucht werden soll. also das ir dyenst endtlich die wolfart deren, über die der gewalt ist, also schaffe, das dadurch das lob gottes auffgang. . . . Diss kan aber nun nit geschehen, das die underthon nutzlich regiert wurden zu worem lob des obersten künigs, wo nit die weltlich oberkeit noch göttlichem gesatz regieret und zu haltung desselbigen gerichtet ist." Ibid., pp. 55.22–56.4.

53 Ibid., pp. 56–57.

54 See pp. 135–38, 215–16*n*71 below.

55 *Das ym selbs,* pp. 57.25.

56 Ibid., pp. 57.34–58.4.

57 "Dann wie in beydem geistlichem und weltlichem uns aller nutz und wolfart zustot, wann die uns fürstehn, sollen ires ampts getreülich warten, also folget sonder zweifel unser gäntzlich verderben, so solche das ir suchen und desshalb uns uff ire und nit gottes gehorsam zyehen." Ibid., pp. 58.21-25; cf. p. 59.20.

58 Ibid., pp. 58.31–59.7. In Eberlin von Günzburg's pamphlet against pilgrimages, the Protestant artisan recommends to a converted monk, who has pledged henceforth "to earn my bread with my hands," that he should try such quickly mastered and honorable trades as "stonemason, carpenter, mailman, thatcher, and miner." *Eyn gesprech zwyschen vyer Personen* (1523/24), in Clemen 1:162.

59 See Chrisman, *Strasbourg and the Reform,* p. 113.

60 *Das ym selbs,* p. 63.22.

61 "Der glaub in uns uffricht das gäntzlich vertrawen in Christum, widerbringt und stellet er uns auch in die rechte und göttliche ordnung, in die wir geschaffen seind. Die wir auch durch solchs vertrawen erlangen und entpfahen sein geist, der uns sichert, das wir gottes kinder seind. Daruss volget, das wir im gern in aller lieb thot

gegen unsern nechsten, das er am höchsten von den seinen fordert, dyenen und wilfaren." Ibid., p. 63.1.

62 Ibid., p. 66.9-17.

63 *WA* 7:575.

64 That the author (or recorded speaker) was no *idiota* is evident from his momentary lapsing into criticism of Augustine, Jerome, Bernard, Nicholas of Lyra, Duns Scotus, Thomas Aquinas, and Albertus Magnus, and his brief resort—with apologies—to a bit of Latin, Hebrew, and Greek to explain the meaning of prayer. *Eyn Sermon von der Abgötterey / durch den Pawern / der weder schreyben noch lesen kan / geprediget zu Kitzing im Franckenland auff unsers herren Fromleychnams tag* (n. p., 1524), p. C 2 b.

65 On Peringer see *C. G. Jöchers Allegemeinem Gelehrten-Lexicon* 5(Leipzig, 1784), p. 1902; Dieter Demandt and Hans-Christoph Rublack, *Stadt und Kirche in Kitzingen* (Stuttgart, 1978), pp. 58–59.

66 *Eyn Sermon von der Abgötterey,* p. A 3 a. Peringer reassures them: "We have no need to fear Christ, as if he were a stern judge; he is a good and merciful father to whom alone we should call out." Ibid., p. C 2 a.

67 Ibid., p. A 4 a-b. Among other things attacked are mandatory fasting and the prohibition of marriages between people of a certain blood relationship. There is also criticism of those who make "idols" out of their children by overdressing them—a problem Peringer says is greater in other, richer towns. Ibid., p. B 1 a-b. The latter may be a bit of country criticism of city life.

68 Ibid., pp. A 4 b, B 2 a.

69 *Le Sommaire de Guillaume Farel reimprimé d'après l'edition de l'an 1534,* ed. J.-G. Baum (Geneva, 1867), pp. iii–xiv. *Guillaume Farel: 1489–1565,* ed. the Comité Farel (Neuchâtel/Paris, 1930), p. 39. Cf. F. J. Schiffmann, "Die erste Ausgabe von Farels Sommaire," *Jahrbuch für Schweizerische Geschichte* (1881): 87–102; Nathaniel Weiss, *Guillaume Farel. Ses premiers trauvaux 1521–24* (Paris, 1919).

70 *Guillaume Farel: 1489–1565,* p. 108.

71 Ibid., pp. 37–39.

72 The occasion of their issuance may be a commentary on Farel's well-sung fiery temperament. The Basel magistracy had authorized Oecolampadius to respond to Catholic critics who accused the reformers of scorning the doctors of the church, good works, saints, and tradition. Opposition between the two religious groups was at this time also heightened by the magistracy's dismissal, in accordance with standing law, of a married priest. Farel seized the occasion to post his theses, which he proposed be publicly debated on February 23 in the great hall of the university. The debate, which reportedly reduced the

Catholic opposition to silence, actually occurred on March 3, with Oecolampadius translating Farel's Latin and French into German before the assembled crowd. Erasmus, long settled in Basel, was highly irritated by Farel's aggressive evangelizing. Cf. Johan Huizinga, *Erasmus and the Age of Reformation* (New York, 1957), p. 167.

73 In *Guillaume Farel: 1489–1565*, pp. 122–23.

74 *Sommaire,* ch. 11, p. 22. The full title of the first edition was: *Summaire et briefve declaration d'aulcuns lieux fort necessaires a ung chascun chrestien pour mettre sa confiance en dieu et ayder son prochain. Jacques chap. I. En mansuetude et doulceur recepvez la parolle de dieu laquell est puissante de saulver noz ames* (Basel, 1525). A copy was found in the British Museum in 1928 and published in a tiny photo-reprint edition by Arthur Piaget, *Guillaume Farel: Sommaire et briefve déclaration: Facsimile de l'edition originale publie sous le patronage de la société des textes français modernes* (Paris, 1935). My references are to the Baum edition of the 1534 reprint of this original text.

75 *Sommaire,* ch. 12, p. 23; ch. 16, p. 31; ch. 17, p. 33.

76 Ibid., ch. 19, p. 39.

77 Ibid., ch. 19, pp. 36–37.

78 Ibid., ch. 19, p. 39. Farel also criticizes the withholding of vernacular Scriptures from simple people, ch. 35, p. 88; and he insists upon the training of children in Latin, Greek, and Hebrew, ch. 39, p. 110.

79 Ibid., ch. 25, p. 55.

80 Ibid., ch. 27, pp. 57–62.

81 "Pourtant Chrestiens retirez vous de la cruelle tyrannie de celuy qui a mis sur voz dos & espaules charges importables, ou il ne les touche a tout ung doigt. Venez a celuy qui a prins nostre charge & la mis sur ses espaules & porte. Fiez vous & vous asseurez en luy, & venez a luy seul & a nul autre: non pas aux prebstres ne au Pape: & il vous donnera repos & paix en voz consciences, portantz sa charge legiere." Ibid., ch. 29, pp. 70–71.

82 Ibid., ch. 31, pp. 77–78.

83 Ibid., ch. 42, pp. 122–23.

84 Ibid., ch. 34, p. 85; ch. 35, p. 86.

85 Ibid., ch. 36, p. 92.

86 Ibid., ch. 36, p. 93.

87 "En la saincte puissance du glaive, laquelle par prebstrise a este mise si bas quelle na peu faire son office, estant en subiection de ceulz qui devoient estre subiectz au glaive, pour ung peu de rasure ou dhuyle, tenant soubz les piedz ceste saincte & tres necessaire puissance. Pareillement le sainct & digne estat de mariage: lequel dignement a este institue sus tous par nostre Seigneur avant le peche de lhomme, honnore par la presence de nostre sauveur [at the wedding feast in

Cana]. . . . Pourtant si tu lieve tes yeulx regardant ceulx a qui le sainct mariage est deffendu, il est bien a lhonneur du mariage. Car ilz sont telz que ie ne scay si ie les doys appeller hommes, qui nont rien humain." Ibid., ch. 38, p. 100.

88 Ibid., ch. 37, p. 95.

89 Ibid., ch. 37, p. 97.

90 Ibid., ch. 37, p. 97.

91 See *Das Widerstandsrecht als Problem der deutschen Protestanten 1523–1546*, ed. Heinz Scheible (Gütersloh, 1969), a collection of twenty-three key texts. See especially Luther's theses of April, 1539, which permitted German princes and German people to resist the pope and emperor for the sake of both tables of the law. Ibid., pp. 94–98. Earlier movement in this direction is already present in the "Warning to His Dear German People" (1530), following the Diet of Augsburg, where Luther pledged to hold his pen if war came and not to intervene with a counsel of Christian passivity as he had done earlier in the Peasants' Revolt. *LW* 47:18 (*WA* 30/3:276–320). Not only does Luther here sanction active armed resistance, but he is also, interestingly, at great pains in doing so to distinguish his position from the earlier views of Thomas Müntzer: "He is an insurrectionist who refuses to submit to government and laws, who attacks and fights against them, and attempts to overthrow them with a view to making himself ruler and establishing the law, as Müntzer did. . . . Self-defense against the bloodhounds [the pope and the emperor] cannot be rebellious." *LW* 47:20; see also p. 14. In 1528 Philip of Hesse was absolutely clear in his mind about the right to resist the emperor for the sake of both tables of the law. *Das Widerstandsrecht*, pp. 43–47. The most mature statement of Lutheran resistance theory, which antedated and apparently influenced Beza's and later Calvinist views on the right of lower magistrates to resist tyrants, is the Magdeburg *Bekentnis, Unterricht und Vermanung der Pfarrherrn und Prediger der Christlichen Kirchen zu Magdeburgh* (1550). See the recent discussion by O. K. Olson, "Theology of Revolution: Magdeburg, 1550–51," *Sixteenth Century Journal* 3 (1972): 56–72.

92 See Eberlin's *Fifteen Confederates*, p. 92 below.

93 See Friedrich Roth, *Augsburgs Reformationsgeschichte 1517–1530* (Munich, 1901), p. 89.

94 Hans von Schubert, *Lazarus Spengler und die Reformation in Nürnberg* (Leipzig, 1934), pp. 158, 175; Strauss, *Nuremberg in the Sixteenth Century*, p. 154.

95 Von Schubert gives the historical details, pp. 189–96.

96 *Schutzred und christliche Antwort ains erbaren Liebhabers göttlicher Warhait der*

heiligen Geschrifft auff etlicher Widersprechen, warumb Doctor Martini Luthers Leer nitt samen unchristenlich verworffen, sonder mer als christenlich gehalten werden soll, in Theodor Pressel, *Lazarus Spengler nach gleichzeitigen Quellen* (Elbersfeld, 1862), pp. 16–26; 17–19.

97 Ibid., p. 21.

98 "Zum vierten wird mir kein Verständiger mit Wahrheit nimmer widersprechen mögen, dass er bei ihm selbst, wo er anders Luthers und seiner Nachfolger Predig und Unterweisung gehört hat und die Wahrheit bekennen will, viel zweifliger Irrsal und Scrupel verwickelter Conscienz entledigt ist. Denn haben nit unser Prediger Lehren und Anzeigung den grossen Theil dahin gelendt, uns viel Sünden, auch durch den Ablass Frieden und Ruh, da keine ist, zu machen und dadurch unsern Conscienzen so mancherlei enger Netz und Strick zu legen, dass nit wol möglich denen zu entfliehen. Dadurch ist der Mensch mehr geängstigt dann getröstet, mehr in Verzweiflung dann in Erquickung, mehr in übermässige Forcht dann Lieb und Vertrauen zu Gott geführt und geursacht, da doch das Joch und der Weg zu der Seligkeit nach Anzeigung des heiligen Evangelii ganz süss und heilsam und mehr durch ein ordenlich recht gegründet Vertrauen zu Gott, dann diese Gaukelpredigen zu erlangen ist . . ." Ibid., p. 22. Spengler's other points are not so striking and more attest his admiration for Luther than elucidate further features of Luther's appeal to the laity. He argues that Luther seeks Christ rather than his own gain in all that he does; that his timely appearance, as a veritable Daniel from among the people, is providential; and that he conducts himself always in the most fair and reasonable way, speaking openly, always on the basis of Scripture, and in the willingness to recant if proven wrong. Ibid., pp. 22, 24.

99 Nicholas von Amsdorf [Lazarus Spengler], *Die Hauptartickel durch welche gemeyne Christenheyt bysshere verfuret worden ist. Daneben auch grund unnd antzeygen eyns gantzen rechten Christenlichen Wesens* (Wittenberg, 1522), p. A 2 a. Hans Stille confirms Spengler's authorship and attributes his anonymity to the fact that the Nürnberg Rat was not yet publicly on record for the Reformation. "Nikolaus von Amsdorf: Sein Leben bis zu seiner Einweihung als Bishof in Naumburg (1483–1542)" (Diss., Leipzig, 1937), p. 45. Nürnberg's imperial politics is also to be borne in mind when accounting for Spengler's anonymity.

100 *Die Hauptartickel,* pp. A 4 a–B 1 a. There is the general accusation that the medieval church has "bound and burdened consciences by sins that are not sins." Ibid., p. A 4 b. Cf. Robert Kolb, "Parents Should Explain the Sermon: Nikolaus von Amsdorf on the Role of the Christian Parent," *The Lutheran Quarterly* 25 (1973): 231–40.

101 *Die Hauptartickel,* pp. C 2 b–D 1 b.

102 Ibid., pp. D 2 b–E 2 b. In his summary of Reformation doctrine for Anna, duchess of Stetin, Johannes Bugenhagen made much of the fact that the "tandtwerck" and "erdichte gute werck" which presently filled the world were of no use to one's neighbor and hence not the fruit of true faith. Lutheran faith is rather said to give birth to works needed by and useful to men, not to special "religious" good works. *Ain Christlicher Sendprieff / an fraw Anna / geborne hertzogin von Stetin in Pomern. Summa der Seligkeit auss der hailigen schrifft* (Wittenberg, 1525), p. A 3 a.

103 *Die Hauptartickel*, p. E 4 a. This is no exaggeration. In the archbishopric of Mainz, laymen were fined 300 solidi for adultery, 600 for breaking a fast. Clergy were fined sixteen times as much for burying the excommunicated as for visiting a bordello. Tschackert, "Die Rechnungsbücher," p. 344.

104 "Ist doch die gantz Romisch kirchen mitt gellt stricken der massen belegt worden / das eynem menschen nit müglich gewest / den zuempfliehen / Do hat man die Christenlichen hertzen / durch die schrecken eyngefurter todsund / des bans / Christenlicher gehorsam und der gleychen also erschreckt / das yederman zuwercken und iarmerckten / und also auss forcht unterstanden hatt / von solchen fangknussen zuerledigen / niemand hatt seyn zuflucht / trost unnd seligung uff Christum gestellt / dann da ist ablass." *Die Hauptartickel*, p. E 4 a.

105 "Alleyn ynn Christum zu glauben / und yhme alleyn zuvertrawen / und dem nehsten umb Christus willen (der dyr alle wolthat umb sonst mittheylt) auch umb sonst alles güttes zuertzeygen." Ibid., p. F 2 a.

106 "Alleyn auff eusserliche werck und dahyn gericht / sich selbs zu suchen / forchten die peyn / oder verhoffen und gewartten kunfftiger belonung." Ibid., p. F 2 a.

107 Ibid., p. F 3 a.

108 "So ist yederman geloffen volkomen zu werden / biss das sie dohynn komen seyn / als ob niemant from unnd selig werden kant / er sey dann ynn yhrem stand der geystlichkeit." Ibid., p. F 3 a-b.

109 Ibid., p. F 4 a.

110 See A. Vögeli, ed., *Jörg Vögeli. Schriften zur Reformation in Konstanz 1519–1538* (Tübingen, 1972), p. 40.

111 Edited in ibid., pp. 471–77.

112 *Schirmred ains layeschen Burgers zu Constanz / wid' den Pfarrer von Ueberlingen der one Grund der Schrifft etlich Constanzisch Prediger / und in dem / ire Zuhörere / offenlich gscholtten hat* ([Basel], 1525), p. B 1 a-b. The *Schirmred* is now available in A. Vögeli's edition, pp. 478–518.

113 Ibid., p. B 1 b.

114 Ibid., pp. B 2 b–C 2 b.

115 Ibid., p. C 3 a.
116 Ibid., p. D 1 a-b.
117 Wolfgang Capito, *Was man halten / und Antwurtten soll / von der spaltung zwischen M. Luther unnd Andres Carolstadt* (n. p., 1525), p. B 2 a.
118 *Schirmred*, p. D 1 b.
119 Ibid., pp. D 4 a–E 3 a.
120 Ibid., p. E 2 b.
121 Ibid., p. E 3 b.
122 Ibid., p. E 4 b.
123 Ibid., p H 2 b.
124 Ibid., p. J 2 a.
125 *Ein Sendbrief von einem jungen Studenten zu Wittenberg an seine Eltern im Schwabenland von wegen der Lutherischen Lehre zugeschrieben* (Augsburg, 1523), ed. Otto Clemen, in Clemen 1:7–20; 12–14.
126 Ibid., p. 15.
127 Ibid., p. 16.
128 *Sendtbrieff an seyne Geschwyhen* (n.p., 1524), p. B 2 a-b.
129 *Ain schöne underweysung wie und wir in Christo alle gebrüder und schwester seyen / dabei angezaigt nicht allain die weltlichen / wie sy es nennen / sonder auch die gaistlichen zustraffen / wa sy anders in den leibe dessen haubt Christus ist wöllen sein* (n.p., 1524), p. D 1 a; cf. p. B 4 a. Complains Rhegius: "sy wöllen auch nit schwester und brüder mit uns sonder besser dann wir sein / und sagent sy haben gewalt uns zustraffen / und wir sy nit / und sagen auch Got hab inen gewalt geborn zuherschen über allen gewalt der weltlichen oberkayt / wölches alles erdichte menschen gesatz seind." Ibid., p. A 2 b.
130 *Underricht wartzu die Bruderschafften nütz seyen / wie man sy bissher gehalten hat / und nu fürohin halten sol* (n.p., 1522), p. 3 a-b.
131 *Ein Sermon von Bruderschaften gepredigt durch Nicolaus Reneyssen von Bensshеym an der Bergkstrassen* (n.p., 1526), p. C 1 b. A confraternity is "ettliche personen / die sich also verbrüderen / zusammen sich verpflichten und verloben / jren eygnen nutz und wolfart suchen / und dar neben alle andere auch frumme Christen menschen aussschliessen / die sich nitt darein erkauffen." Ibid., p. A 4 a. A Christian brotherhood, by contrast, "gar nitt gestellt ist uff eyn versammlung ettlicher sunderlicher personen / die in einem jar / ein mal zwey- / drey / oder vier zusammen kommen und sunst nichts anderst thun / dan Vigilien und Messen für die todten singen unn lesen / on gottes befelch." Ibid., p. B 2 b. Their rejection is uncompromising: "Jederman soll wissen . . . das dise gegenwertige / und alle andern selbss erdichte Brüderschafften (sie seyen gleich von Bapst oder Bischoffen bestätigt / und mit all jrem ablass begabt) gantz nichts

helffen werden / noch etwas ussrichten für gott / wie schön und hüpsch / wie gutt und nutz sie auch immer scheynen." Ibid., p. B 3 a.

132 Melhofer shows how, at every turn, "er [the canon of the Mass] pfaffen und Buren als wyt hat von einander gescheyden als hymel unnd erd." *Offenbarung der aller heimlichisten heymlicheit / der yezigen Baals priester / durch wölche die welt lange zyt geblendt und das lyden Christi jhämerlich geschmecht worden ist / genannt Canon oder die Styllmess. 2 Timoth. 3. Ir thorheit wirdt yederman offenbar werden* (n.p., 1525), p. O 1 b.

133 Moeller stresses this point. He sees the long-term significance of the Protestant break with the medieval concept of clergy more in Protestant entrance into secular education, marriage, and family life than in the assumption of specific civic rights and duties. "Kleriker als Bürger," pp. 223–24. See also Moeller's "Pfarrer als Bürger," *Göttinger Universitätsreden* 56 (1971): 5–26.

134 Although Zurich clergy were not legally obliged formally to become citizens, Zwingli stressed their obligation to pay all taxes and rents: "Zöll und gleit und stür und schoss schuldig." Cited by Moeller, "Kleriker als Bürger," p. 218. Walton sees parallels with Marsilius of Padua and William of Ockham in Zwingli's curtailment of traditional clerical privileges and immunities and restriction of priests to purely religious responsibilities. *Zwingli's Theocracy,* p. 116. On Calvin and Genevan clergy, see W. Fred Graham, *The Constructive Revolutionary: John Calvin and His Socio-Economic Impact* (Richmond, Va., 1971), p. 159. Government sensitivity to political power of clergy can be seen in the qualifications placed on Protestant use of the ban as a spiritual discipline. When legalized in Strasbourg in 1534, it was placed in the hands of the magistracy and several elders who were as much civil as ecclesiastical agents. When Calvin's Consistory got the power of excommunication in 1541 it was in highly qualified form and accompanied by the clearest clerical disavowal of claims to civil jurisdiction. François Wendel, *Calvin: The Origins and Development of His Religious Thought* (New York, 1963), pp. 60, 73–75.

135 Chrisman, *Strasbourg and the Reform,* p. 115; Moeller, "Kleriker als Bürger," pp. 212, 219.

136 Paul Kalkoff, *W. Capito im Dienste Erzbischof Albrechts von Mainz* (Berlin, 1907). Luther corresponded with Capito in his capacity as Albrecht's representative after Capito intervened to suppress Luther's criticism of a new indulgence issued by Albrecht in Halle in September, 1521. This blistering letter was one of Luther's earliest attacks on what to him were the milquetoast reforms of humanism. *LW* 48:374–76 (*WABr* 2:430–34). Cf. p. 142 below. Capito was to hear its message again in Strasbourg from Matthew Zell, who was influential in his final

conversion to the Protestant movement in 1523. Capito reports on this at length in his first defense of clerical citizenship, *An den hochwirdigen fürsten und Herren Wilhelmen Bischoffen zu Strassburg / und Lantgraven zu Elsas. Entschuldigung D. Wolffgangs Fa. Capito. Zaigt an ursach Warumb er Burger worden. Gepredigt. Und ein offenliche Disputation beger habe. 1523.* [delivered in Oct./Nov., 1523; published in Augsburg, 1524]. Cf. Chrisman, *Strasbourg and the Reform,* p. 109.

137 *An den hochwirdigen fürsten,* p. BB 1 a-b; cf. preface, pp. DD 2 b, EE 3 b, EE 4 b.

138 *Das die Pfaffhait schuldig sey Burgerlichen Ayd zuthün. On verletzung jrer Eeren* ([Strasbourg], 1525), p. A 3 b. This is one of the most prominent criticisms of the popular *Beclagung eines Leyens genant Hanns Schwalb* (1521) in Clemen 1:352: "Unser pastores haben grosse güetter, ein Jar fünff hundertt guldin ein zu kommen Unnd samlen grosse kesten vol korn habern und Allerlay trayd Und sy thun kain arbait darumb, Sy leeren nicht, Sy predigen nicht, Sy haltten unutz korschuler, die die kirch vol blern und schreyen und wissen nicht, was sy singen, schlecht, das man das gethön hört und waiszt doch nicht, was dar in begriffen ist. Allso gewinne unser pfaffen ire güetter sonder arbait."

139 "Wider gott / wider die lieb des nächstens wider alle billichait ist / und aller natur und aller vernunfft entgegen / ja auch zu beschwerd der gemayn." *Das die Pfaffhait schuldig sey,* p. A 7 a.

140 Ibid., p. A 2 a-b. Already in the first defense Capito twice insisted that restriction of all sides to the exposition of Scripture, following the directive of the Nürnberg Reichsregiment of February 9, 1523, would settle the matter quickly. *An den hochwirdigen fürsten,* pp. HH 5 b, GG 4 a. The directive of the Reichsregiment read in part: ". . . das auch ein jeder churfurst, furst und andere stende des reichs in seiner oberkeit verfugen soll, damit mitler zeit nichts anders dan das heilig evangelium nach auslegung der schrieften von der cristlichen kirchen approbirt und angenommen, gepredigt, das auch weiter nichts neus gedruckt oder feilgehabt werde, es sei dan zuvor durch gelerte person, so darzu sonderlich verordent werden sollen, besichtiget und zugelassen etc." *Deutsche Reichstagsakten J.R.* 3 (Gotha, 1901): 746. On appeals to this mandate by both sides, see p. 146 below.

141 *An den hochwirdigen fürsten,* p. BB 1 b. Cf. Moeller, "Kleriker als Bürger," p. 208; Chrisman, *Strasbourg and the Reform,* p. 34.

142 *An den hochwirdigen fürsten,* pp. BB 2 b, GG 2 a.

143 *Das die Pfaffhait schuldig sey,* pp. A 5 b–A 6 a.

144 *Ob die Geystlichen auch schuldig sein Zinsze geschoss, etc. zugeben und andere gemeyne bürde mit zutragen. Ein Sermon auffs Evangelion Mat. 22. Ob sich getzymme Keyser Zinss geben* (Aldenburg, 1524), p. A 3 a.

145 Ibid., pp. A 3 b, A 4 a.

146 "Offtmals [auch] mer glaubens / liebe und ware geystligkeit / bey den Welltlichen layen funden wirt / Dann bey dehn so sich Geystlich nennen / dero gantz leben und geystligkeit nichts ist dann lauter ausserlich spiegelfechten und togkenspielen mit cerimonien." Ibid., p. B 1 b.

147 Ibid., p. B 3 a.

148 *Warhafft verantwortung Ambrosij Blaurer, an aynen ersamen / weysen Rat zu Costentz, anzaygend / warub er auss dem kloster gewichen, und mit was geding er / sich widerumb, hynein begeben wol / Von Luterischer maysterloszkait / Erger dich nit ab meiner that / Die christlich grund und ursach hat.* ([Augsburg], 1523), p. A 3 b.

149 Ibid., pp. A 2 b–A 3 d, B 2 a, C 1 a, C 2 b, C 4 a-b, D 1 a.

150 *De coelibatu, monachatu et viduitate* (Wittenberg, 1521), p. D 3 b.

151 *Warhafft verantwortung,* pp. E 1 b–E 3 a.

152 *Grund und Ursach auss Göttlichem Rechten / Warumb Prior und Convent in Sant. Annen Closter zu Augsburg ihren Standt verandert haben 1526* (Kempten, 1611), pp. C 3 a, C 2 b, E 3 b. The group is also highly critical of religious acquisitiveness and the selling of religious services. Ibid., pp. A 3 a–A 4 a.

153 Ibid., pp. B 4 b, D 2 a.

154 Ibid., p. E 3 b.

155 See François Biot, *The Rise of Protestant Monasticism* (Baltimore, 1963), pp. 144–51.

156 In addition to Gengenbach and Manuel, other notable Swiss pamphleteers, especially Hans Füssli and Utz Eckstein, are discussed by Frida Humbel, *Ulrich Zwingli und seine Reformation im Spiegel der gleichzeitigen, schweizerischen volkstümlichen Literatur* (Leipzig, 1912). See also Wilhelm Lucke, "Deutsche Flugschriften aus den ersten Jahren der Reformation," *Deutsche Geschichtsblätter* 9 (1908): 183–205. A representative collection of important primary sources of this genre appears in the Reformation Reihe of the series *Deutsche Literatur. Sammlung literarischer Kunst- und Kulturdenkmäler in Entwicklungsreihen,* of which the following are especially to be mentioned: *Die Sturmtruppen der Reformation: Ausgewählte Flugschriften der Jahre 1520–25,* ed. A. E. Berger (Leipzig, 1931); *Die Schaubühne im Dienste der Reformation* 1–2, ed. A. E. Berger (Leipzig, 1935–36); and *Lied-, Spruch- und Fabeldichtung im Dienste der Reformation,* ed. G. Pfannmüller and A. E. Berger (Leipzig, 1938). Among the handiest aids to Reformation pamphlets is Arnold Kuczynski, *Thesaurus libellorum historiam Reformationis illustrantium: Verzeichnis einer Sammlung von nahezu 3000 Flugschriften Luthers und seiner Zeitgenossen* (1870–74; Nieuwkoop, 1969).

157 I wonder if Heinz Scheible, who flatly declares the *Fifteen Confederates*

to be a typical, pre-Reformation late medieval reform program, has carefully read this collection of pamphlets. "Reform, Reformation, Revolution: Grundsätze zur Beurteilung der Flugschriften," *ARG* 65 (1974): 108–34; 115, 132. On Eberlin cf. *ADB* 5:575; *RGG* 2:297.

158 Gengenbach is the presumed author of an anonymous pamphlet in which Luther's *nydisch* manner and lack of Christian charity toward his opponents are severely censured. *Ein klägliches Gespräch von einem Abt, Curtisanen und dem Teufel wider den frommen Papst Hadrian* (Basel, 1522), ed. Arthur Richel, in Clemen 3:1–25. There is the still more interesting criticism here of appeals to Luther's doctrine in excuse of religious apathy. In this early period, Gengenbach seems genuinely concerned. After Luther's teaching, he asks, who will now do the seven works of mercy? People who before gave little will now give nothing to priests and the poor. Those who never fasted rightly will now give up fasting altogether. And those who prayed little before now quote Luther as saying that three or four "Our Fathers" is prayer enough. Ibid., pp. 20–22. Luther's hostility to Pope Adrian VI, whom Gengenbach admired as a reform pope, may have inspired much of this early suspicion. In 1523, Gengenbach, sensitive to heightened confessional bickering, published in Basel a work ascribed to Sebastian Meyer which was critical of both "papists" and Lutherans for failing to attain the high ethical ideals of the *Canonisten* and *Evangelisten*. *Ein kurzer Begriff von Hans Knüchel* (Basel, 1523), ed. Alfred Götze, in Clemen 1:227–46; 237. A layman of impeccable life and knowledgeable of Scripture, Hans Knüchel, is set against both sides as the kind of cleric towns should have. He is especially fond of the gospel of James' insistence that there is no true faith without good works. Gengenbach saw the Reformation as a return to simple biblical piety, an uncomplicated faith and service to one's neighbor. He dated the fall of the medieval church with the infamous Pope Sabinianus (604–06)—successor to Gregory the Great and reportedly so evil that he charged the poor for grain during a famine. Gengenbach accuses him of being the first to turn the church's treasure, which was intended to be given to the poor, inward into itself. *Der ewangelisch Burger* (1523), in *Pamphilus Gengenbach*, ed. Karl Goedeke (Hannover, 1856), pp. 192–213; 205. Some of the criticism of Luther in these works may also be attributed to "horn-tooting" for indigenous Swiss reform. None is inconsistent, however, with the lay perception of the Reformation's promise of a new social ethic. A society led by exemplary laymen, learned in Scripture, was an ideal of the original Protestant message that would survive the clerical bureaucratizing of the Reformation.

159 *ADB* 20:275. On the long confusion over dating the play (1522 rather

than 1523), see Ferdinand Vetter's discussion in his edition, *Niklaus Manuels Spiel evangelischer Freiheit. Die Totenfresser. "Vom Papst und seiner Priesterschaft" 1523* (Leipzig, 1923), p. 24. On Manuel's political career, see Jean-Paul Tardent, *Nikolaus Manuel als Staatsmann* (Bern, 1967).

160 In addition to Luther and Von Hutten, Eberlin cites Reuchlin, Erasmus, Jacob Wimpfeling (Schlettstadt, soon, however, to lead the Counter Reformation in the city), Geiler von Kaisersberg (Strasbourg), Ulrich Kraft (Ulm), Oecolampadius (Basel and Augsburg); among "vile frommen schulmeister," Crato von Uttenheim (Kraft Hoffmann) (Schlettstadt); Johann Sapidus (Witz) (Schlettstadt and Strasbourg); Michael Hilsbach (Hagenau); Georg Simler (Pforzheim); Nicholas Gerbellius (Pforzheim and Strasbourg); Johannes Brassicanus (Kol) (Tübingen); Jacob Heinrichmann (Tübingen); Giles Krautwasser (Stuttgart); Johannes Schmidlin (Fabricius) (Memmingen i.a.); Johannes Cochlaeus (Nürnberg, later Luther's great enemy); and Wilhelm Nesen (Frankfurt). *Ein klägliche Klag an den christlichen Römischen kaiser Carolum, von wegen Doctor Luthers und Ulrich von Hutten. Auch von wegen der Curtisanen und bättel münch. Das kaiserlich Maiestat sich nit lass sollich leüt verfüren,* in *Johann Eberlin von Günzburg, Ausgewählte Schriften* 1, ed. Ludwig Enders, *Flugschriften aus der Reformationszeit* 11 (Halle, 1896), p. 7. (Hereafter cited as Enders.)

161 It is suggested that Luther, Erasmus, or Karlstadt would make better father-confessors for the emperor! Ibid., pp. 5–6, 12.

162 Ibid., p. 9.

163 Ibid., pp. 12–13.

164 *Ein vermanung aller christen das sie sich erbarmen uber die klosterfrawen. (Thu kein Tochter in ein kloster, du lässest dann diss büchlein vor.),* Enders, pp. 25–27.

165 Ibid., p. 32.

166 Ibid., p. 30.

167 "Halt nit dar für das du ein besser wärck thüest, so du bi den tag ziten bist, dann so du din acker feiest oder matten meiest. . . . Es ist ein grosse hoffart das solich münch und pfaffen fürgeben, ir gots dienst si verdienstlicher dann andere frommer laien gebät, eben als ob nit husshalten und tagwerck der laien als wol gots dienst si und meer dan das schrien und brummen der tempel knecht das got nie gebotten hat, aber ihenes ist gebotten." *Von dem langen verdrüssigen geschrei, das die geistlichen Münch, Pfaffen und Nunnen die siben tag zeit heissen,* Enders, pp. 40–41.

168 *An alle christenliche oberkeit in wältlichem und geistlichem stand Teütscher nation, ein kläglich ernstlich klag aller gotsförchtigen Münch Nunnen und pfaffen, dz man inen zu hilff kumm do mit si von iren endt christischen bi woneren erlöst werden,* Enders, p. 90.

169 Ibid., p. 101.

170 Ibid., p. 97. Already in 1229 in the bull *Quo elongati* Pope Gregory IX had declared Francis' *Testament* an invalid authority for the Franciscan Order. Pope John XXII completed this "neutralization" of original Franciscanism, especially with the bull *Cum inter nonnullos* (1323).

171 Ibid., p. 99.

172 Ibid., p. 104. Eberlin's final tract on mendicants called for immediate suppression of monasteries. *Ein früntliche antwort aller gotsförchtigen, erberen, verstendigen in Teütschem land uff die jämerliche klag der ordens leüt an sie gethon,* Enders, pp. 134–41.

173 Veit, *Volksfrommes Brauchtum,* p. 118. According to Veit, this is the origin of the custom of exchanging painted eggs at Easter.

174 *Vom fasten der xl. tag vor Osteren und andern, wie do mit so jämerlich wirt beschwärt das Christenlich volck,* Enders, p. 20.

175 Ibid., p. 17.

176 Ibid., p. 19.

177 Ibid., pp. 19–21.

178 *Ein Vermanung zu aller oberkeit Teütscher Nation, das si den Predig stul oder Cantzel reformieren,* Enders, pp. 46, 51.

179 "Keren eüch an kein alt gwonheit, an kein ordens friheit, an kein bäpstlich bull, förchten got meer dan die menschen." Ibid., p. 52.

180 Ibid., pp. 51–52.

181 *Dz lob der pfarrer. Von der unützen kosten der gelegt wirt von den gemeinen unverstendigen volck uff mäss lasen, volgungen, begrebnüss, sibend, drisigst, iartag etc. Und vom lob der Pfarrer und irer nötigen Caplon,* Enders, p. 72.

182 Ibid., p. 71.

183 *Allen und ietlichen christgeloübigen menschen ein heilsame warnung das si sich hüten vor nüwen schedlichen leren,* Enders, pp. 166–69. In the midst of all these reform proposals Eberlin defends purgatory: "Welcher sagt, das kein fägfeur sy, der irret." This patently inconsistent defense of purgatory has been lamely explained by Bernhard Riggenbach as a sign of the independence of Eberlin's criticism of the medieval church, Luther having already rejected purgatory at this time. Riggenbach also points out Eberlin's classification of purgatory as an *adiaphoron* in 1522. *Johann Eberlin von Günzburg und sein Reformprogram* (Tübingen, 1874/Nieuwkoop, 1967), p. 47. By 1523 consistency appears to have caught up with Eberlin. In the *Gesprech zwischen vyer Personen* (1523/24) the pilgrim farmer tells the Protestant artisan that his priest lays great weight on anniversary masses as an absolute necessity for transit through purgatory. The artisan assures him that purgatory has no foundation in Scripture and that he should save his money. In Clemen 1:149. Already in the *Fifteen Confederates* Eberlin rejects private masses for the dead.

184 *Ein zuversichtig ermanung an die redlichen, erberen starcken und christlichen herren obern und underthon gemainer Eidgnosschafft (genant Schwitzer) das si trewlich helffen handthaben Ewangelische leer und frumme christen,* Enders, pp. 146–47.

185 "Ob dann schon vil volck solichen leren anhangt und angehangen ist, ist kein wunder, dann münch und pfaffen haben mit sorg und angst tag und nacht gedacht, wie sie unss betriegen möchten, die weil wir sorg und angst gehabt haben umb unsere libs narung für unss, unser kind und gsind, und auch das wir unss nit hetten versähen, das unsere seel sorger und helgen frässer under eim gutem schein ein soliche seel mörderi unss zu gericht hetten. Aber got si gelobt, das wor liecht kumpt wider an tag." *Allen und ietlichen christgeloübigen menschen,* Enders, p. 170.

186 "Kanstu nit selbs läsen, bestel ein armen schuler, der lisst dir umb ein stück brot als vil du ein tag bedarfft. Hastu kein buch, bist zu arm, bättel ein buch, es ist dir eerlicher ein ewangeli bätlen dann ein stuck brot. Bit andre umb gotswillen das sie dir im ewangeli läsen." Ibid., p. 165.

187 *New statuten die Psitacus gebracht hat uss dem land Wolfaria welche beträffendt reformierung geistlichen stand,* Enders, pp. 108–19. Cf. S. G. Bell, "Johann Eberlin von Günzburg's Wolfaria—The First Protestant Utopia," *Church History* 36 (1967):122–39.

188 The required holidays were the *festa Christi* (Easter [3], Ascension [2], Christmas [3]); the *festa Mariae* (4); the days of the Apostles (12); the days of Saint Martin, John the Baptist, saints Michael, Stephen, and Laurence, and Pentacost (3). Veit, *Volksfrommes Brauchtum,* p. 93.

189 See pp. 38–42 above.

190 Karlstadt's contemporaneous treatise proposed sixty years of age—the time when sexual desire and titillation were supposed to have subsided. Luther, the following year, proposed sixty years for women and "seventy or eighty" for men! See my "Marriage and the Ministry in the Protestant Churches," pp. 41–43.

191 See pp. 55–56, 80.

192 *New Statuten,* Enders, p. 117. The *Hortulus animae*—as presumably also the *Paradisus animae*—was a very popular prayer book based on priests' breviaries. There were editions in 1509, 1512, 1518, and 1520. See Hasak, *Dr. M. Luther und die religiöse Literatur seiner Zeit,* p. 228. Here the Reformation attacks popular piety in one of its most tangible forms. Cf. Ferdinand Cohrs, *Hortulus animae evangelisch* (1520) (1849).

193 Eberlin is the assumed author of an anonymous pamphlet attack on a popular pilgrimage to Grimmental, which drew 44,000 pilgrims in 1502. The city's chapel contained a miraculous portrait of a weeping

Mary. That it was still a going enterprise is indicated by the fact that Luther too singled out this pilgrimage for criticism in the *Address to the Christian Nobility* (1520), a work that greatly influenced Eberlin's conversion to the Reformation. Eberlin has an artisan expose the weeping Mary to a pilgrim farmer as a hoax accomplished by pouring water through a needle hole in the eye. *Eyn gesprech zwyschen vyer Personen,* in Clemen 1:143.

194 This is a pseudonym used by Philip Melanchthon in his 1521 anti-scholastic tract: *Didymi Faventi adversus Thomam Placentinum Oratio pro Martino Luthero Theologo, Corpus Reformatorum* 1:303.

195 *Ein new ordnung weltlich standts das Psitacus anzeigt hat in Wolfaria beschriben,* Enders, pp. 122–31.

196 "Das soll grosser ablass sein, guts thun sim nächsten menschen und verzihen dem sind." Ibid., p. 128.

197 "Kain pfaff soll zu radt gon, weder der fürsten noch der stet noch der vogtein." Ibid.

198 Ibid., p. 130.

199 Blaschke comments on the Reformation's sanction of secular confiscation and administration of ecclesiastical goods, something long sought by Saxon Landesherren: "Vor allem hat der protestantische Fürstenstaat der Reformationszeit eine vorher noch nicht dagewesene Machtfülle in sich vereinen können, weil er nun zugleich eine landeskirchliche Einheit darstellte und weil der Fürst nun zusätzlich zu seiner weltlichen Herrschaft eine oberste geistliche Stellung erlangt hatte, was in jener religiös bewegten Zeit von nicht zu unterschätzender Bedeutung war." *Sachsen im Zeitalter der Reformation,* p. 121; also, pp. 17–18, 27. Writes E. William Monter of Geneva: "If it seems reasonable to assert that the merchant notables who led the revolutionary independence movement and transformed so many of Geneva's civic institutions acted in most political and administrative questions independently of Calvin's influence (at least until 1555), it is on the other hand impossible to believe that Geneva could have preserved her precarious political independence without a Calvin. . . . The Calvinist ethic reinforced the communal ethic." *Studies in Genevan Government (1536–1605)* (Geneva, 1964), p. 120. On Zurich, see Walter Jacob, *Politische Führungsschicht und Reformation: Untersuchungen zur Reformation in Zurich 1519–1528* (Zurich, 1969), pp. 1–2.

200 *Von dem grossen Lutherischen Narren*, ed. Paul Merker, in *Thomas Murners Deutsche Schriften mit den Holzschnitten der Erstdrucke*, ed. Franz Schultz et al. (Strasbourg, 1918) 9:122, 192. On the feud with Stiefel, see Clemen 3:269, n. 2. Murner assumed the form of a cat in the woodcuts that accompanied the original edition.

201 *Karsthans* (1521), ed. H. Burckhardt, in Clemen 4:1–134. Rudolf Raillard argues, contrary to Burckhardt, that Vadian could not have been the author. *Pamphilus Gengenbach und die Reformation* (Zurich, 1936), p. 110.

202 *Von dem grossen Lutherischen Narren,* p. 274.

203 Ibid., p. 242.

204 Ibid., p. 244.

205 Ibid., p. 267.

206 *Novella,* in Goedeke, *Pamphilus Gengenbach,* pp. 262–91, 273–76.

207 Ibid., p. 278.

208 Ibid., p. 287.

209 *Die Todtenfresser* in Goedeke, *Pamphilus Gengenbach,* pp. 153–59.

210 "O got wir waren auch so blind / Und stifften iarzyt mit vil mässen / Thetten der armen gantz vergessen." Ibid., p. 157.

211 *Niklaus Manuels Spiel evangelischer Freiheit: Die Totenfresser. "Vom Papst und seiner Priesterschaft" 1523,* ed. Ferdinand Vetter (Leipzig, 1923), p. 5.

212 Ibid., p. 68.

213 Ibid., pp. 7–9. Elsewhere in the play, the pope is accused of having made "heaven, hell, marriage, oaths, sin, virtue, and every liberty" a matter of money (p. 38). He is even blamed for the contemporary loss of the island of Rhodes to the Turks (the island was beseiged in July, 1522, and fell in December) because he was too busy killing Christians for profit in France, Venice, Ferrara, Urbino, Placentia, and Parma (p. 44).

214 Ibid., pp. 9–10.

215 Ibid., pp. 11–12. See Meyer's *Ernstliche Ermahnung.* Gengenbach's bishop says: "Weren nit todten unds fägfür / So weren ietz die byschoff thür / Hetten nit so vil land und leüt / Als sy dann hand zu diser zeyt / Und müst ir hoff gsind übel essen / Die sunst all gnug von todten fressen." *Die Todtenfresser,* in Goedeke, *Pamphilus Gengenbach,* p. 154.

216 Manuel, *Totenfresser,* pp. 12–13.

217 Ibid., pp. 13–14.

218 Ibid., pp. 14–15.

219 Ibid., pp. 16–17.

220 Ibid., pp. 17–18.

221 Ibid., pp. 18–20.

222 "Ich sag an der canzlen von der hell / und von dem feufür was ich well – Es ist vergeben, sy gend nüt drumm." Ibid., p. 20.

223 Ibid.

224 Ibid., pp. 21–22.

225 Ibid., pp. 22–23.

226 Ibid., pp. 23–25.

227 Ibid., pp. 25–26.

228 Ibid., pp. 26–28.

229 Ibid., p. 28.

230 See Hans J. Hillerbrand, *Christendom Divided: The Protestant Reformation* (New York, 1971), pp. 283–88. Hillerbrand has reproduced much of this work unchanged in *The World of the Reformation* (New York, 1973), explaining that he found himself "unable to improve on my own earlier formulations" (p. ix). Whatever else might be said about such a practice, it certainly tends to take the suspense out of his future publications.

231 See Robert M. Kingdon, "Was the Protestant Reformation a Revolution? The Case of Geneva," in *Transition and Revolution: Problems and Issues of European Renaissance and Reformation History,* ed. Robert M. Kingdon (Minneapolis, 1974), pp. 53–108.

232 See my *Homo Spiritualis* (Leiden, 1969).

233 The Reformation "meant the repudiation of a control over everyday life which was very lax, at that time scarcely perceptible in practice, and hardly more than formal, in favor of a regulation of the whole of conduct which, penetrating to all departments of private and public life, was infinitely burdensome and earnestly enforced." *The Protestant Ethic and the Spirit of Capitalism,* trans. Talcott Parsons (New York, 1958), p. 36.

234 See ibid., pp. 98–128.

235 H.-W. Krumwiede writes of the Reformation's appeal in Saxony: "Die Gewissensnot Luthers war nicht sein privates Problem gewesen. Die Menschen am Ausgang des Mittelalters fühlten sich durch die Fülle kirchlicher Verordnungen, deren Befolgung keine Lösung ihrer Lebensfragen bedeutete, bedrängt. So gab Luther eine Antwort auf die religiöse Not seiner Zeit, als er zur Freiheit des Glaubens fand, zur 'mündigkeit' des Glaubenden, der nicht mehr der Mittlerschaft der Muttergottes, der Heiligen, der Priester bedurfte, sondern nur des eines Mittlers Jesu Christi." "Die Reformation in Niedersachsen. Politische, soziale und kirchlich-theologische Aspekte," *Jahrbuch der Gesellschaft für niedersächsische Kirchengeschichte* 65 (1967): 7–26. Von Muralt summarizes the Reformation's appeal to workers in Zurich: "Diese Botschaft und diese Kritik brachte dem gemeinen Manne im Volke, ganz besonders dem tätigen Handwerker, eine ungeheure Befreiung doppelter Art: Einmal von der innern Angst und Not vor dem Tage des Gerichts, dem erfolglosen Rechnen mit 'guten Werken' auf der einen, den Sünden auf der andern Seite, und zweitens eine Befreiung von nie endenden äussern materiellen Verpflichtungen der Kirche gegenüber von all den Diensten an Zeit, Messebesuch,

Wallfahrten, und an Geld, Jahrzeiten, Stiftungen, Vergabungen u.s.w." "Stadtgemeinde und Reformation," p. 361. When Genevans voted in the Reformation on May 21, 1536 they ratified their "wish to live in the holy evangelical law and Word of God . . . [and] to renounce all masses and other ceremonies and papal abuses, statues and idols, and all to which these things pertain." In Kingdon, *Transition and Revolution,* p. 97. A yoke was thought removed, not assumed, as Calvin and Farel were to learn by exile in 1538.

There is, I think, an important lesson to be learned from the experience of Lyons in the 1560s where, as Natalie Davis has shown, Protestant workers reverted back to Catholicism when the city's Calvinism became bureaucratized, meddlesome, and disadvantageous to their economic prosperity—that is, when the reformed began to act like the medieval church ("Strikes and Salvation at Lyons"). And, as the case of Augsburg during the Interim attests, gross material could finally override even the strongest spiritual sentiments.

Chapter 4

1 This is considered true whether the government was patrician or guild-dominated, since guildmasters elected to city councils soon viewed themselves as close *Kollegen im Amt* with their patrician colleagues and restricted the self-interests served by government. Eberhard Naujoks, *Obrigkeitsgedanke, Zunftverfassung und Reformation: Studien zur Verfassungsgeschichte von Ulm, Esslingen und Schwäbisch Gmünd* (Stuttgart, 1958), p. 14. Cf. Heide Stratenwerth, *Die Reformation in der Stadt Osnabrück* (Wiesbaden, 1971), pp. 38–42.

2 Ritter, *Die kirchenkritische Tendenz in deutschsprachigen Flugschriften,* pp. 332, 337, 360.

3 "Der Bauernkrieg und das angebliche Ende der lutherischen Reformation als spontaner Volksbewegung," *Luther Jahrbuch* 26 (1959): 109–34. Although Marxist views on the Reformation are increasingly sophisticated, a common ideological framework remains. The Reformation is seen as the first phase of a successful middle class revolt against old feudal structures. The Peasants' Revolt of 1525 was an abortive effort to bring the lower classes into it. The proletariat were resisted then (as now) by the rising middle class, and the revolution of the working class, which is the more profound social force in the dialectic of history, still continues. See the collection *Reformation oder frühbürgerliche Revolution,* ed. R. Wohlfeil (Munich, 1972).

4 Schildhauer, pp. 26–40, 93–98, 123, 133.

5 Moeller, *Reichsstadt und Reformation,* p. 26; Chrisman, *Strasbourg and the Reform,* p. 197; Blaschke, *Sachsen im Zeitalter der Reformation,* p. 118; Ritter, *Die kirchenkritische Tendenz in deutschsprachigen Flugschriften,* p. 329.

6 Magistracy "mostly followed slowly and with pensive hesitation the wishes of the community conveyed to it by the theologians." Gottfried Seebass, "The Reformation in Nürnberg," in *The Social History of the Reformation,* ed. L. P. Buck and J. W. Zophy (Columbus, 1972), pp. 17–40; 24, 30. Harold Grimm has some perceptive sketches of the points of contact and the shared interests and ideals of Lutheran reformers and German townsmen. "The Relations of Luther and Melanchthon With the Townsmen," in *Luther und Melanchthon. Internationaler Kongress für Lutherforschung: Münster 1960,* ed. V. Vajta (Philadelphia, 1961), pp. 32–48; "The Reformation and the Urban Social Classes in Germany," in *Luther, Erasmus and the Reformation,* ed. John C. Olin (New York, 1969), pp. 75–86.

7 Heinrich Werner, "Der niedere Klerus am Ausgang des Mittelalters," *Deutsche Geschichtsblätter* 8 (1907): 201–225; Vasella, "Die Ursachen der Reformation," pp. 409, 420. Werner refers to lower clergy as a "proletariat" and points up fifteenth century lay support of their

plight (e.g., the *Reformatio Sigismundi*). Vasella would find that an extreme characterization for Switzerland, although he documents a "pervasive burdening" of lower clergy.

8 According to Römer, popes and bishops exploit lower clergy by "comment" (or commendation, the papal right to "occupy" vacant clerical posts); "absent" (a fee for a parish post run by a representative); "Kathedraticum" (an annual fee paid "to honor the papal chair"); "subsidium caritativum" (the tax on children born in concubinage); "bischoffs gewalt" (episcopal favors); "indult" (pardon from punishment); "milchzins" (episcopal tax for concubinage); "schetzung fertonen" (unclear); and "indultum testandi" (a fee for disposing last wills and testaments so as to make the children of priests legal heirs). *Ein Schöner Dialogus,* in Clemen 3:85. Cf. Meyer, *Ernstliche Ermahnung.*

9 Bernhard Klaus, "Soziale Herkunft und theologische Bildung lutherischer Pfarrer der reformatorische Frühzeit," *ZKG* 80 (1969): 22–49; Suzanne K. Boles, "The Economic Position of Lutheran Pastors in Ernestine Thuringia 1521–1555," *ARG* 63 (1972): 94–125; 124, n. 101. In Wismar the Protestant preacher Never was the son of a master carpenter; Slüter was the son of a ferryman, and the Lübeck reformer Valentin Korte the son of a barber. Schildhauer, pp. 93–98.

10 Paul Drews, *Der evangelische Geistliche in der deutschen Vergangenheit* (Jena, 1905), p. 16; Wilhelm Pauck, *The Heritage of the Reformation* (n.p., 1961), p. 139. Cf. August Franzen, *Zölibat und Priesterehe in der Auseinandersetzung der Reformationszeit und der katholischen Reform des 16. Jahrhunderts* (Münster, 1969), p. 30.

11 Bernd Moeller, "Die deutschen Humanisten und die Anfänge der Reformation," *ZKG* 70 (1959): 46–61; Blaschke, *Sachsen im Zeitalter der Reformation,* p. 118.

12 Schildhauer, p. 113.

13 Graham, *The Constructive Revolutionary,* p. 107.

14 Protestants came especially from the "newer or more skilled occupations, occupations where the literacy rate was higher . . . At the top of urban society, it is the new elite rather than the more established elite that tends to produce Protestants." Natalie Davis, "The Rites of Violence: Religious Riot in Sixteenth-Century France," *Past and Present* 59 (1973): 51–91; 80–81; see also "Strikes and Salvation at Lyons," p. 54. Norman Birnbaum writes of Zurich: "The Reformation in Zurich entailed an alliance of a new mercantile and productive elite with a large group of lesser artisans, against the patricians (mercenaries and rentiers) and certain artisans, very possibly concentrated in the more traditional sectors of the economy." "The

Zwinglian Reformation in Zurich," *Past and Present* 15 (1959): 27–47; 39. Birnbaum, however, underestimates the degree to which the Zurich Reformation was supported by established (patrician) power. See note 15 below.

15 See Robert Walton (via Hans Morf and Walter Jacob), "The Institutionalization of the Reformation at Zurich," *Zwingliana* 13 (1972): 497–515; 507, n. 35, convincingly against Birnbaum, "Zwinglian Reformation." Von Muralt discusses the changes in the oligarchical constitutions of Basel and Bern with the success of the Reformation. In Basel and Bern, as in Zurich, the Reformation weakened aristocratic elements and strengthened the power of guilds. "Stadtgemeinde und Reformation," pp. 374–76. Such changes hardly had the force of an internal political revolt; they were rather a broadening of the Reformation's original base of support to embrace established power groups.

16 Karl Holl, "Luther und das landesherrliche Kirchenregiment," in *Gesammelte Aufsätze zur Kirchengeschichte* 1: *Luther* (Tübingen, 1923) pp. 353–54.

17 "Auf die Breite gesehen . . . sind die Magistrate alles andere als Motoren der Reformation gewesen. Viel eher waren sie Hemmschuhe." Moeller, *Reichsstadt und Reformation,* p. 26, in full agreement with Lau.

18 Gottfried G. Krodel, "State and Church in Brandenburg-Ansbach-Kulmbach: 1524–26," *Studies in Medieval and Renaissance History* 5 (1968): 164–66.

19 Strauss, "Protestant Dogma and City Government," p. 41; Seebass, "The Reformation in Nürnberg," p. 29.

20 Bernd Moeller, "Zwinglis Disputationen: Studien zu den Anfängen der Kirchenbildung und des Synodalwesens im Protestantismus," *Zeitschrift der Savigny-Stiftung für Rechtsgeschichte* 56 (1970): 275–324; 304: "Im Januar 1523 wurde in Zürich etwas wie eine 'Erfindung' gemacht."

21 Buck/Fabian, *Konstanzer Reformationsgeschichte,* p. 76.

22 See my discussion of the Reformation's development in Wittenberg, pp. 138–45 below.

23 See Irmgard Höss, "Georg Spalatins Bedeutung für die Reformation und die Organization der lutherischen Landeskirche," *ARG* 42 (1951): 101–35, especially 119, 127.

24 Rene Hauswirth, *Landgraf Philipp von Hessen und Zwingli* (Tübingen, 1968); Hans J. Hillerbrand, "Religion and Politics in the German Reformation: The Case of Philipp of Hesse," *The Journal of Medieval and Renaissance Studies* 3 (1973): 1–15.

25 Buck/Fabian, *Konstanzer Reformationsgeschichte,* pp. 43, 51–60. See p. 79 above.
26 Strauss, *Nuremberg in the Sixteenth Century,* p. 163.
27 Axel Vorberg, *Die Einführung der Reformation in Rostock* (Halle, 1897), pp. 28, 33; Schildhauer, p. 113.
28 Cf. Chrisman, *Strasbourg and the Reform,* p. 197.
29 See Max Ernst, "Bernhard Besserer: Bürgermeister in Ulm (1471–1542)," *Zeitschrift für Württemberg Landesgeschichte* 5 (1941): 88–113; Ozment, *Mysticism and Dissent,* p. 165. Other examples of pro-Reformation Bürgermeister are cited by Pfeiffer, "Das Verhältnis von politischer und Kirchlicher Gemeinde," pp. 87–88.
30 Roth, *Augsburgs Reformationsgeschichte,* p. 91; Heinrich Lutz, *Conrad Peutinger: Beiträge zu einer politischen Biographie* (Augsburg, n.d.), pp. 186–97.
31 See Hans Baron, "Religion and Politics in the German Imperial Cities During the Reformation," *English Historical Review* 52 (1937): 405–27, 614–33. Baron focuses on Nürnberg, Strasbourg, and Augsburg.
32 Naujoks, *Obrigkeitsgedanke,* pp. 57, 67–70.
33 Pfeiffer, "Das Verhältnis von politischer und kirchlicher Gemeinde," p. 90. Such votes also went against the Reformation, as in Bofingen.
34 Naujoks, *Obrigkeitsgedanke,* p. 72.
35 See E. G. Schwiebert, *Luther and His Times* (St. Louis, 1950), p. 668; Chrisman, *Strasbourg and the Reform,* p. 155.
36 Cf. the debate between John Yoder and Robert Walton, p. 180*n*81.
37 Seebass, "The Reformation in Nürnberg"; Stratenwerth, *Die Reformation in der Stadt Osnabrück,* pp. 44, 74, 167.
38 Buck/Fabian, *Konstanzer Reformationsgeschichte,* p. 60, in opposition to Bernd Moeller's chronology of the Reformation's development, *Johannes Zwick und die Reformation in Konstanz* (Gütersloh, 1961). Whereas Moeller sees an initial destructive phase (1525–26) followed by a constructive phase commencing with Zwick's arrival in 1526, Buck/Fabian rather see the destructive phase running from 1524/25–1529/30, with a concurrent constructive phase running from 1520 (or at least 1524) to the religious ordinance of 1531. Moeller is also criticized for describing the Reformation in Constance as a "patrician's Reformation," whereas it received balanced support from both patricians and guilds.
39 Buck/Fabian, *Konstanzer Reformationsgeschichte,* pp. 110–11, 139–42, 148–54; Moeller, *Johannes Zwick,* p. 96.
40 Vorberg, *Die Einführung der Reformation in Rostock,* pp. 130–55.
41 *Das ym selb,* p. 57.14.
42 Chrisman, *Strasbourg and the Reform,* pp. 222–24.

43 Naujoks, *Obrigkeitsgedanke,* pp. 77, 81–85. In Nürnberg, Protestant clergy never had an independent right to exercise the ban. Seebass, "The Reformation in Nürnberg," p. 31. On Calvin and Geneva, see p. 130 above.

44 On Saxony, see Karl Holl, "Luther und das landesherrliche Kirchenregiment," pp. 361–69; Krumwiede, "Die Reformation in Niedersachsen," pp. 12–13.

45 Melanchthon admonished Philip of Hesse: "Dei donum pax est, et eximium quidem nec poterit conservari, si in opprimendo Evangelio principes deum a se alienarint. . . . Commendo itaque religionis causam conscientiae tuae cuius si rationem habueris, mavoles Josaphat imitari quam Pharaonem." *Epitome renovatae ecclesiasticae doctrinae ad illustrissimum principem Hessorum* (June, 1524), in *Melanchthons Werke in Auswahl,* ed. Robert Stupperich (Gütersloh, 1951), 1:188.12. In an early tract against revolution, Zwingli pointedly reminded rulers of the "revolution" with which God repaid those who did not heed his word: "Ir wüssend wol, dass der hand gottes niemants entfliehen kan, auch das er nit verschlaafft . . . Also ist er waarlich uff der ban, sicht man an sinem wort. Wenn er das sendet, sol bessrung volgen, oder aber die straaff ist an der tür." *Welche ursach gebind ze ufruren etc.* (1523) in *H. Zwinglis sämtliche Werke,* ed. E. Egli and G. Finsler (Leipzig, 1916), 3:427.15-19. Zwingli also elaborated on providential vengeance in the prefatorial dedication of his *De vera et falsa religione commentarius* (1525) to Francis I, king of France (*H. Zwinglis sämtliche Werke* 3:631), and in 1530 dedicated a lengthy tract on the topic *De providentia Dei* to Philip of Hesse. In *H. Zuinglii opera* (Zurich, 1841), 4:79–144. The Osnabrück reformer Dietrich Buthmann answered magisterial prohibition of Protestant preaching with a declaration that magistrates who opposed God's word lost the right to demand obedience from their subjects. Stratenwerth, *Die Reformation in der Stadt Osnabrück,* p. 77. On Osiander's wielding the stick of providence against magistrates see Seebass, "The Reformation in Nürnberg," p. 28.

46 None laid it on thicker than the Strasbourg reformer Caspar Hedio in his *Magistrates' Sermon* of 1534 as he plied hesitant council members with Pericles and Cicero. "We read of Pericles the Athenian that when he went into the council chamber and put on his robes he thought all the time about those over whom he ruled, remembering that they were Athenian citizens, free and Greek. So should you [the Strasbourg magistracy] now ponder that those over whom you rule are citizens of Strasbourg, which shall be a city of God. Remember that they too are free men, for Christ has freed them from their sins, and they should live a new life as citizens of heaven. Remove false teaching from their

midst, guide them with true doctrine and every good order and policing. Care for them, work for them, turn to them your every energy, for it is to you and to them a matter of eternal life." *Radts Predigt. Wie die Oberkeit für sich selbst / und die Underthonen für yre Oberkeiten in diser geverlichen sorglichen Zeit zu bitten haben* (Strasbourg, 1534), p. B 1 b. According to Cicero: "As the magistrates of a city, so the city itself." Ibid., p. C 3 a. I discuss Hedio's important work below, pp. 153–55.

47 In Clemen 3:4–5; see p. 200*n*158 above.

48 See the editor's introduction, *Von göttlicher und menschlicher Grechtigkeit, wie die zemen sehind und standind* (preached on June 24, 1523, published July 30, 1523) in *Zwingli: Hauptschriften,* ed. Fritz Blanke et al., vol. 7: *Zwingli, der Staatsmann,* ed. R. Pfister (Zurich, 1952).

49 "Ein Teil der Gsatzten sehend allein den inneren Menschen an, als wie man Got, wie man den Nächsten sölle lieb haben. Und dise Gsatzt mag nieman erfüllen; also ist ouch nieman grecht denn der einig Got, und der, so durch Gnad, dero Pfand Christus ist, grecht würdt gemachet durch den Glouben. Der ander Teil der Gesatzten sehen allein den usseren Menschen an, und derohalb mag einer usserlich fromm und grecht sin, und ist innerhalb nüt des minder unfromm und vor Got verdampt. Bispil: 'Du solt nicht stelen' ist ein Gbott zu dem usserlichen Leben und Frommkeit. 'Du solt eins andren Gut nit begeren' ist ein Gbott zu der innerlichen götlichen Grechtigkeit; und reichend bede uff ein Ding, das ist: wider die Nam. So nun einer nit stilt, ist er fromm vor den Mentschen (verstand hiebi aller Laster, die man offenlich vor den Mentschen verurteilt); er ist aber bi Got ein Schelm, denn er hat die Begird und Anfechtung zu frömbdem Gut vilicht grösser dann einer, der gestolen hat." Ibid., p. 52.

50 As Luther later put it: "In that I do not kill, commit adultery, or steal . . . I do it not willingly or for love of virtue, but I fear the prison, the sword, and the hangman." *Lectures on Galatians* (1535) *WA* 40:479 (*LW* 26:308).

51 "Denn sölte uns die arm Grechtigkeit erst ouch entgon, wie uns die götlich entgangen ist, so wäre mentschlich Geselschafft nüt anderst dann ein Leben der unvernünfftigen Thieren: Welcher stercker, dem wäger. Darumb sind die Richter und Obren Diener Gottes; si sind der Schulmeister, und wer irer Grechtikeit nit gehorsam ist, der tut ouch wider Got." *Von göttlicher und menschlicher Grechtigkeit,* p. 56. One may compare Luther: "As it is the function and honor of the office of preaching to make sinners saints, and dead men live, and damned men saved, and the devil's children God's children; so it is the function and the honor of worldly government to make men out of wild beasts, and to prevent men from becoming wild beasts." *A Sermon on Keeping*

Children in School (1530), *Works of Martin Luther,* ed. and trans. T. E. Schmauk et al. (Philadelphia, 1931), 4:159 (*WA* 30/2: 517–88).

52 "Glich wie ein Vatter siner verfürten Dochter wert, dass si nit gar gemein werd, also wert die Oberkeit an der Statt Gottes, dass unser Leben nit gar ein vihische Unvernunfft werde." *Von göttlicher und menschlicher Grechtigkeit,* p. 63.

53 "Und ist dennocht der Mensch vor Got nit grecht, so er glich nüt wider si tut; so er aber wider die thut, so versündet er sich wider Got und den Menschen." Ibid., p. 70.

54 Ibid., pp. 70–71, 73, 95.

55 Ibid., pp. 74, 84, 88.

56 *Epitome,* p. 188.2.

57 Ibid., pp. 182.29, 183.12, 184.6-15, 185.2-12.

58 One may compare Luther: "Theologians and jurists must continue together or all will surely go to ruin. When theologians disappear, God's Word also disappears and there remain nothing but heathen, nay nothing but devils. When jurists disappear, then the law disappears and peace with it, and there remains nothing but robbery, murder, crime, and violence, nay, nothing but wild beasts." *Sermon on Keeping Children in School,* p. 173.

59 See Luther's letter to Melanchthon of July 13, 1521, *LW* 48:258–60 (*WABr* 2:356–59).

60 See Guido Kisch, *Melanchthons Rechts- und Soziallehre* (Berlin, 1967), pp. 114, 120–23.

61 *Urkundliche Quellen zur hessischen Reformationsgeschichte* 2:9–10. Philip's Lutheranism is attested in his letters to Nicholas Ferber, prior of the Marburg Franciscans, in early 1525. The first defended salvation by faith alone, Christ's sufficiency as mediator between God and man (against worship of Mary as a mediator), and the priesthood of all believers. A second letter, about half of which was drafted by Johannes à Campis, a Marburg pastor, presented a detailed defense of Protestant teaching on the Mass, good works, the office of the pope, the relation of faith and reason, fasting, celibacy, and human traditions. A marginal comment in Philip's hand appears at the conclusion: "Wiltu aber der schrift nit glauben, so glaubstu keinen nit, der von den todten ufsteht." Ibid., pp. 1–6. See Otto Clemen, "Zu Landgraf Philipps reformatorischen Anfängen," *Zeitschrift der Vereins für hessische Geschichte und Landeskunde* N.F. 34 (1910): 109–14 (a bibliographical aid to the question); Alton O. Hancock, "Philipp of Hesse's View of the Relationship of Prince and Church," *Church History* 35 (1966): 157–69.

62 *Whether Soldiers, Too, Can Be Saved* (1526), *Works of Martin Luther* 5:35–36

(*WA* 19:623–62). *On Temporal Authority: To What Extent It Should Be Obeyed* (1523), *LW* 45:95 (*WA* 11:245–80). "A preacher confirms and strengthens and helps to maintain government, and temporal peace of all kinds. He checks the rebellious; teaches obedience, morals, discipline and respect; instructs fathers, mothers, and children and servants in their duties; in a word, he is the teacher of all secular offices and ranks." *Sermon on Keeping Children in School,* p. 148.

63 *Institutes of the Christian Religion,* ed. John T. McNeill, trans. Ford L. Battles (Philadelphia, 1960), Bk. 4, ch. 20, sect. 5, p. 1490.

64 Walton, *Zwingli's Theocracy,* p. 169; *Martin Bucers Deutsche Schriften* 1:37, n. 16.

65 See *The Social Teaching of the Christian Churches,* trans. Olive Wyon (New York, 1960), 2:494. The most recent version of the Troeltsch thesis is the study of Stayer, who finds Luther to have much in common with apolitical Anabaptism. *Anabaptists and the Sword,* p. 33.

66 See p. 7 above.

67 *On Temporal Authority, LW* 45:83.

68 Ibid., p. 112.

69 See pp. 145–46, 210*n*20 below.

70 *An den hochwirdigen fürsten,* p. HH 1 b.

71 I am not convinced that there is an important difference between Luther and Zwingli on the issue of "Christian" magistrates, as some Zwingli scholars maintain. See especially Arthur Rich, "Zwingli als sozial-politischer Denker," *Zwingliana* 13 (1969): 67–89; 83. Both Luther and Zwingli wanted magistrates to be guided by the Bible as well as by their reason and common sense. When Zwingli subjected magistrates to the *schnur Christi,* he did not mean that they were to make the Sermon on the Mount the city charter. He meant only that they must punish overt evil and protect righteous Christians (as the Protestants of course defined the latter). "All menschen sind schuldig dem gbott gottes nachzekummen. Aber so wir dem nit nachkummend, mag uns der oberer [the magistrate] nit straffen, bis das wir offenlich darwider thund. Byspil: So du eins andren eegmahel imm hertzen begerest, mag dich der obrer darumb nit straffen. So du aber im sinen eegmahel geschwechet hast mit der that, mag er dich straffen. Also fart er [the magistrate] denn by der schnur Christi hin, so er din ussgebrochne that strafft. Also verstond wir hie 'by der schnur Christi hin': dem götlichen weg nach. Denn fart der aber nit by der schnur Christi hin, so er den sündenden nit strafft sunder uffnet, und den unschädlichen beschwärt. Als so man die unnützen büch, die müssigen pfaffen und münch und nonnen schirmt by irem mütwillen, hüren und bretspil, gyt, hochmüt und pracht. Und das sy missbruchend, das

verordnend sy nit den armen, sunder, so man davon ordenlich redt, so straffend sy den, der inredt. Das ist usserthalb der schnur Christi hingevaren." Art. 42 of *Usslegen und gründ der schlussreden oder Articklen,* in *H. Zwinglis sämtliche Werke* 2 (1908): 343.7-21. Later, Zwingli characterized a "pagan" magistrate with a pious heart as "Christian" and impious "Christian" magistrates as worse than pagans. Letter to Ambrosius Blarer (May 4, 1528) in *H. Zwinglis sämtliche Werke* 9 (1925): 459.4. What Zwingli has foremost in mind when he defines a "Christian" ruler is not some specifically Christian social program, but simply a ruler who does not hesitate to punish the wicked and protect the righteous as his basic divine mandate prescribes. "Christian" rulers are especially those who give the Reformation free concourse. There is no advance beyond Luther in any of this. When Zwingli goes on to say that a tyrant who rules *untrülich und usser der schnur Christi* may be deposed *mit got*—assuming the failure of established civil procedures (removal by the electoral process) and passive Christian resistance—he appears to mean no more than that a unanimous and spontaneous revolt against a tyrant is an expression of providence (it occurs *mit got*). *Usslegen und gründ,* pp. 344.17–346.10. Luther too taught that God rewarded tyranny with revolt and anarchy. I fail to see in any of this grounds for Rich's arguments.

72 *On Temporal Authority, LW* 45:100.

73 See Paul Althaus, *The Ethics of Martin Luther,* trans. R. C. Schultz (Philadelphia, 1972), pp. 48–54, 112; and Walther von Loewenich, "Luthers Stellung zur Obrigkeit," in *Staat und Kirche im Wandel der Jahrhunderte,* pp. 53–67; 60. Both argue against Johannes Heckel, *Lex Charitatis* (1953), who ascribes to Luther only a limited (Augustinian) appreciation of temporal government as a negative, punitive agency. See also Heinrich Bornkamm, *Luthers Lehre von den zwei Reichen im Zusammenhang seiner Theologie* (Gütersloh, 1960), p. 10. For those who wish to wander with a sense of direction through the "Irrgarten" of the doctrine of the two kingdoms, the secondary literature is helpfully brought together by H.-W. Krumwiede, *Zur Entstehung des landesherrlichen Kirchenregiments in Kursachsen und Braunschweig-Wolfenbüttel* (Göttingen, 1967).

74 See Holl, "Luther und das landesherrliche Kirchenregiment," pp. 333–35, 349, 355–57. Holl also discusses the princes' somewhat different, and self-serving, assessment of their powers during the Visitation of 1527–28. Ibid., p. 372. Irmgard Höss and H.-W. Krumwiede have a modern quarrel going over the later issue. Höss agrees basically with Holl that the princes went far beyond Luther's sanitized definition of their role in the electoral *Instruction* of June 16,

1527. Krumwiede rather sees continuity between the views of Luther and Melanchthon and the electoral *Instruction.* Höss, "The Lutheran Church of the Reformation: Problems of Its Formation and Organization in the Middle and North German Territories," in *The Social History of the Reformation,* pp. 317–39; 322. Krumwiede, *Zur Entstehung des landesherrlichen Kirchenregiments,* p. 261.

75 For Calvin's views, see the *Institutes* Bk. 4, ch. 20, sects. 1-4, p. 1485. Like Zwingli's *Von göttlicher und menschlicher Gerechtigkeit* and his article "De magistratu" in the *De vera et falsa religione commentarius,* Calvin here opposes Anabaptist separatist ideas, and with arguments that I cannot distinguish from Luther's views. But cf. Erik Wolf, "Theologie und Sozialordnung bei Calvin," *ARG* 42 (1951): 11–31; 15, 18, 27.

76 See Kisch's prolonged argument against Hans Weber and Hans Baron, who see in Melanchthon and Lutheranism a purely secular state and political ethic. Kisch rather argues: "Melanchthons Nachdenken über Rechtswesen und Staatsordnung ausmündet in eine religiös (theologisch) gefärbte Ethisierung des Rechts. Sie ist ihm trotz Trennung der geistlichen und weltlichen Bereiche Fundament und Ideal eines christlich orientierten Staatswesens mit göttlicher Legitimation." *Melanchthons Rechts- und Soziallehre,* p. 100.

77 See Rich, "Zwingli als sozialpolitischer Denker," pp. 71–72; cf. Walton, *Zwingli's Theocracy,* p. 169.

78 *H. Zwinglis sämtliche Werke* 9:452.15, 454.22.

79 "Vult ergo Christus, etiam in externis modum teneri, eumque imperat; non est igitur eius regnum non etiam externum." Ibid., p. 454.16.

80 Ibid., p. 455.24.

81 Ibid., pp. 460.3, 461.2. On Melanchthon's placement of outward ecclesiastical ceremonies under the province of the magistrate, see his *Themata ad sextam feriam discutienda* in *Melanchthons Werke in Auswahl* 1:169 (thesis 28).

82 Julius Köstlin, *Friedrich der Weise und die Schlosskirche zu Wittenberg* (Wittenberg, 1892), pp. 13–26, 95.

83 Ibid., p. 17.

84 Writes Luther to Melanchthon after the Diet of Worms (May 26, 1521): "If the pope will now take steps against all who think as I do, then Germany will not be without uproar . . . God is arousing the spirits of many, especially the hearts of the common people. It does not seem to me likely that this affair can be checked with force; if the pope begins to put it down, it will become ten times bigger. Germany has very many Karsthansen [peasant supporters of Luther]." *LW* 48:233 (*WABr* 2:347–49).

85 See Theodor Kolde, *Friedrich der Weise und die Anfänge der Reformation* (Erlangen, 1881), p. 37. Paul Kirn, who would concur, nevertheless quotes Spalatin that Frederick was slowly and carefully attracted to Luther and his gospel: "Da das Evangelion war wiederum angangen, kam s.kf.g. je länger je mehr näher und bass daran, wie wol säuberlich und mit Mussen. Wär ihm aber je gewisslich leid gwest, dass das Evangelion hätt wieder unterdrückt oder unserm lieben Vater, dem Doktor Martinus Luther, einigs Leid hätt widerfahren sollen." *Friedrich der Weise und die Kirche: Seine Kirchenpolitik vor und nach Luthers Hervortreten im Jahre 1517* (Leipzig/Berlin, 1926), p. 165. Köstlin even speculates that Frederick was gripped by the "truth claim" of Luther's gospel, "der tiefe, innerste Eindruck von Wahrheit, den er aus Luthers Predigt empfangen hatte." *Friedrich der Weise,* p. 51; cf. p. 101. Karlheinz Blaschke, who would not agree with Köstlin, has the most recent contribution to the issue, "Kürfürst Friedrich der Weise von Sachsen und die Luthersache," in *Der Reichstag zu Worms von 1521: Reichspolitik und Luthersache,* ed. Fritz Reuter (Worms, 1971), pp. 316–35, especially p. 322.

86 *LW* 48:214 (May 8, 1521) (*WABr* 2:331–32); *LW* 48:223–25 (May 14, 1521) (*WABr* 2:337–38).

87 See the report of the territorial chancellor Gregor Brück in *Die Wittenberger Bewegung 1521 und 1522: Die Vorgänge in und um Wittenberg während Luthers Wartburgaufenthalt. Briefe, Akten u. dgl. und Personalien,* ed. Nikolaus Müller (Leipzig, 1911), Nos. 5 and 10, pp. 19–20, 28–29.

88 In ibid., No. 16, pp. 35–40.

89 "So ist seiner Churfurstl. gnaden Begere. das jr sampt den andern glidern der universitet unnd capittel Alsso jn die Sache sehet, das nichts furgenomen. noch understanden werde. daraus zwispeldigkait, Auffrur und beschwerung erfolgen mocht. Sondern die Sache wol bedencken unnd uff die wege unnd mittel helffen richten. das sie der hailigen cristlichen kirchen zu gutem geraichen und auffrur und beschwerung verhut werde." Ibid., No. 20, p. 52.

90 University students and townsmen interrupted mass and forced priests from the altar with knives. Ibid., Nos. 32–33, 53, pp. 73–75, 118.

91 Ibid., No. 43, pp. 84–90.

92 They were most concerned, in the wake of the havoc being wreaked by the Protestant Scripture principle, to establish the authority of church and tradition over against Scripture alone. They quote Pope Gregory I (590–604) that councils are to be believed as much as the four gospels and the ever serviceable statement by Augustine that he would not have believed the gospel had he not first believed the church. Ibid., No. 51, pp. 107–15; 108, 110. See p. 220*n*112 below.

93 *LW* 48:352 (Dec. 5, 1521) (*WABr* 2:409). Luther took responsibility for such acts of disobedience, even signing documents to exonerate Frederick before imperial authorities. See his letters to Frederick of March 5 and 7 (or 8), 1522. *LW* 48:391–97 (*WABr* 2:454–62).

94 *LW* 48:263 (July 13, 1521) (*WABr* 2:356–59). Kurt Aland traces Luther's heavy "political correspondence" in "Martin Luther als Staatsbürger" in *Kirchengeschichtliche Entwürfe* (Gütersloh, 1960), pp. 420–50. Harold Grimm documents Luther's positive social activism in "Luther's Contribution to Sixteenth Century Organization of Poor Relief," *ARG* 61 (1970): 222–33. Both document a high degree of civil service on Luther's part.

95 *LW* 48:326 (Nov. 11, 1521) (*WABr* 2:402).

96 *LW* 48:327; *LW* 48:342 (Dec. 1, 1521) (*WABr* 2:406–08).

97 *Die Wittenberger Bewegung,* No. 68, pp. 161–62. The Wittenberg religious ordinance is the focal point of James S. Preus's recent study, *Carlstadt's Ordinationes and Luther's Liberty: A Study of the Wittenberg Movement 1521–1522* (Cambridge, Mass., 1974).

98 Frederick had received especially critical reports of Karlstadt's performance. Karlstadt was said to dispense the sacrament in both kinds, to all, even the unconfessed, and even to those who came from festive eating and drinking; twice he reportedly dropped the host only to pick it up and serve it anyway. *Die Wittenberger Bewegung,* Nos. 57 and 61. Karlstadt's planned wedding, invitations to which he sent to the Wittenberg magistracy and to Frederick (Ibid., Nos. 65 and 66, pp. 145–47), also caused some alarm.

99 "Derhalben wellest von unsert wegen geneiglich begeren, das sie sich von ungebreuchlicher einfhurung der Messen enthalten, auch den yrn zutun nit gestaten und es bey den alten gebrauch wolten bleiben lassen . . . Unnd die sache in weyter und mer bedencken nemen. Auch davon disputiren, schreyben, lessen und predigen. und solchs alles mit einer cristlichen und vernunftigen mass furnemen und hendeln." Ibid., No. 56, p. 124.

100 On the imperial pressures on Frederick see J. Volk, *Die Kirchenpolitik des 2. Nürnberger Reichsregiments von seinen ersten Anfängen an bis zu seiner Verlegung nach Esslingen 1521–24* (Leipzig, 1910); Borth, *Die Luthersache.* Primary sources are handy in *Königliche sächsische Kommission für Geschichte. Nr. 3: Planitz. Des kursächsischen Rates Hans von der Planitz, Berichte aus dem Reichsregiment in Nürnberg 1521–23,* ed. Hans Virck (Leipzig, 1899).

101 ". . . Das sie kein Newerung solten furnemen, sonnder davon disputirn, schreiben unnd predigen, bis so lanng anndere euch auch anhengig weren worden." *Die Wittenberger Bewegung,* No. 92, p. 190.

102 Ibid., No. 99, pp. 206–08; No. 97, p. 205; No. 83, p. 181.

103 There is the famous outrageous statement to Frederick: "I have no intention of asking Your Electoral Grace for protection. Indeed I think I shall protect Your Electoral Grace more than you are able to protect me. . . . He who believes the most can protect the most." *LW* 48:391 (March 5, 1522) (*WABr* 2:454–57).

104 *LW* 48:378 (Feb. 22, 1522) (*WABr* 2:488).

105 *LW* 48:278 (Aug. 1, 1521) (*WABr* 2:370–72); *LW* 48:294 (Aug. 15, 1521) (*WABr* 2:279–81); *LW* 48:311 (Sept. 9, 1521) (*WABr* 2:390).

106 *LW* 51:75–77 (*WA* 10/3:14–20).

107 See p. 125 above.

108 Kirn, *Friedrich der Weise und die Kirche,* pp. 132–46, 149.

109 *Acts of the First Zurich Disputation* (January, 1523), in *Ulrich Zwingli 1484–1531: Selected Works,* ed. Samuel M. Jackson (Philadelphia, 1972), p. 93 (*H. Zwinglis sämtliche Werke* 1 [1905]: 472–569).

110 Ibid., p. 111. See also Zwingli's *Defense Called Archeteles* in *The Latin Works and Correspondence of Huldreich Zwingli,* ed. Samuel M. Jackson (New York, 1912), 1:204 (*H. Zwinglis sämtliche Werke* 1:249–327).

111 Moeller points out that Zwingli followed the precedent and example of the Leipzig debate (1519), where Luther argued his case on the grounds of Scripture alone, rejecting traditional and conciliar authorities. "Zwingli's Disputationen," pp. 311–13.

112 Luther: "per se certissima, facillima, apertissima, sui ipsius interpres, omnium omnia probans iudicans et illuminans." *WA* 7:97.20. Bucer, *Dass D. Luthers und seiner nachfolger leer . . . christlich und gerecht ist* (Oct./Nov., 1523), in *Martin Bucers Deutsche Schriften* 1:312.22. Bucer here interprets in a benign way Augustine's famous dictum "Ego vero evangelio non crederem, nisi me catholicae ecclesiae commoveret auctoritas"—which Bucer has in the form "Evangelio non crederem, nisi crederem ecclesiae"—an important Catholic counter to the Protestant Scripture principle. Bucer argues that this statement exalts neither pope, cardinals, nor councils over Scripture. Ibid., p. 315.5. See also Bucer's magisterial *Summary* . . . in *Martin Bucer's Deutsche Schriften* 1:83.26.

113 *Dass D. Luthers und seiner nachfolger leer,* p. 316.16. "Nach fleissiger besichtigung und examinierung der lere und bücher M. Luthers und aller, so ietz etwas namens in teutschen landen haben, als sye die selbige new genante ler in schrifften und predigen treiben solten, findet sichs, das sy alle, Luther und die gleicher leer anhengig sein und sy treiben, furnemlich und zum höchsten doruff tringen, das die gotlich schrifft, so man die bibel heist, solle allen andern schrifften, satzungen und gewohnheyten so weyt furzogen werden und höher gehalten, so weyt got den menschen furzuziehen ist und höher zu halten." Ibid., p. 310.5.

114 See p. 198*n*140 above.

115 See my *Mysticism and Dissent,* p. 61, and the conclusion to the petition of the Memmingen peasants to their magistrates in *Quellen zur Geschichte des Bauernkrieges,* ed. Günther Franz (Darmstadt, 1963), p. 170.

116 See p. 64 above.

117 *Verantwortung ahn M.h. uff Episcopi Schreiben seiner persohn halben ahn ein Rath 1523* (June 17/19, 1523), in *Martin Bucers Deutsche Schriften* 1:295.7, 300.30.

118 Ibid., p. 297.25. Bucer points to precedents in Nürnberg and Worms "und vil anderer Christlicher Stett und herschafften," where honorably married priests and monks have been welcomed in place of the "adultery and whoring" of the religious. Ibid., p. 297.13.

119 Ibid., p. 301.5, .20. In a larger *Verantwortung M. Butzers,* also appearing in 1523, Bucer put the matter so to the magistracy: "Entweder ich predig das gottswort oder nit. Predig ich es nit, so versteinig mich [!], so kummst du mein ab. Predig ich es aber, so bist du [the magistracy] schuldig, mir darzu zu helffen." In *Martin Bucers Deutsche Schriften* 1:176.10.

120 See p. 79 above.

121 Buck/Fabian, *Konstanzer Reformationsgeschichte,* pp. 76–79, 82.

122 "Anfang und Grundlage aller Konstanzer Reformationsordnungen war also die vom Rat damals angeordnete evangelische Predigt deren Ueberprüfung auf ihre Schriftgemässheit der Rat öffentlichen Lehrdisputationen vorbehielt." Ibid., p. 148.

123 Cited in ibid., p. 95. Margrave Casimir of Brandenburg had a similar rationale behind his confinement of preachers to the Old and New Testaments: "damit das gemayn Christlich volck nit in ergernuss und irrung gefürt werde . . . niemant in jren predigen sonderlich zuschmähen / oder in andere wege zengkisch / ergerlich / oder auffrürisch zupredigen. . . . So ist seiner fürstlichen gnaden gnedigs pitt und begeren / dass aller seiner F.G. underthanen und verwanten / gaistlichs und weltlichs standts gedult haben / und nichts newes fürnemen / biss seiner F.G. ferner bedacht / gemüt / und maynung erfordert würde." *Handlung und beschluss / des Hochgepornen Fürsten Casimir / Marggraff zu Brandenburg zc̈. mit sampt seinen gaistlichen Prelaten / und hochgelerten / das Gotsswort betreffent* ([Nürnberg], Oct., 1524),

124 *Ir gwalt ist veracht / ir kunst wirt verlacht / des liegens nit gacht / gschwecht ist ir bracht / Recht ist wiess Gott macht* ([Augsburg], 1524).

125 Ibid., pp. A 4 b, B 1 a. Compare Capito's similar statement that Christians are "rational" as well as obedient sheep, who harken to the voice of the eternal shepherd in their prelates: "Wir sollen gelassene underthanen und als schaff sein / es ist war / Aber vernünftige

schaff / des ewigen hirtens / des stymm wir underthenigklich anbetten in unsern prelaten / wo sye sein wort anders in iren mundt nemen. Sunst halten wir sye als andere herren / und nit hirten." *An den hochwirdigen fürsten,* p. HH 4 b.

126 Buck/Fabian, *Konstanzer Reformationsgeschichte,* p. 71.

127 Ibid., p. 104.

128 *Der deuchleüchtigisten / hochgepornen Fursten und Herren. . . . endtliche Protestation auf dem Reichstage zu Speyr* (n.p., 1529), pp. B 1 b, B 2 a-B 3 a. An edited text is available in *Deutsche Reichtagsakten J.R.* 6 (1935), pp. 1191–1206.

129 Ibid., p. A 3 b.

130 *Ausschreiben an die Römisch Kaiserlich und Künigkliche maiestaten / unsere allergnedigste Herren / auch dess hailigen Römischen Reichs Churfürsten / Fürsten / Graven / Herren / Frey. und Reichstett / von Burgermaister unnd Ratgeben des hailigen Reichsstatt Augspurg / Abtuung der Päpstlichen Mess / unnd annderer ergerlichen Ceremonien und Missbreüch belangende* (Augsburg, 1537), p. C 3 a-b.

131 Ibid., pp. C 2 b–C 3 a. Clergy are accused of acting therein against God's word, the soul's salvation, and "civil frid, nutz, und wolfart."

132 "Die Freyhaiten / den Gaistlichen verlihnn / allain für die Warhait und Gotseligkait / unnd denen nit zuwider / Abbruch / oder Schmelerung / von Rechts wegen. . . . Darumb so mögen die genannten unsere Gaistliche / mit kainem grund sagen / oder darthun / das wir jnen jre Kaiserliche und Künigkliche Freyhait benummen / oder Entzogen / Sonnder / Sy haben Sich selbs / mit Leren und Leben . . . erzaigt / das sy vermöge der Recht und aller Billichkeit sollicher Freyhait nit mer Fähig . . . gewest. Das auch zu disem jren ungaistlichen leben / Sunder allen Zweifel / kain Christenlicher Kaiser / Sy zubefreyen / oder zuprivilegieren ye gedacht." Ibid., p. D 4 a.

133 Ibid., pp. A 3 a, B 3 a.

134 See James Kittelson, "Wolfgang Capito, the Council, and Reform Strasbourg," *ARG* 63 (1972): 126–40.

135 In 1523 Luther blamed the failure of the Jews to convert to Christianity on the false theology that had ruled Christendom for so long. See the discussion and pamphlets in Clemen 1:373.

136 *Sermons on the Catechism* (Nov.–Dec., 1528) *LW* 51:135–93, 135–37 (*WA* 30/1:57–121).

137 *Dr. Martin Luther's Large Catechism* (1529), trans. J. L. Lenker (Minneapolis, 1935), pp. 35, 39, 49, 56. (*WA* 30/1:129–233).

138 "Hilff lieber Gott, wie manchen iamer hab ich gesehen, das der gemeine man doch so gar nichts weis von der Christlichen lere,

sonderlich auff den dörffern, und leider viel Pfarherr fast ungeschichkt und untüchtig sind zu leren, Und sollen doch alle Christen heissen, getaufft sein und der heiligen Sacrament geniessen, können widder Vater unser noch den Glauben odder Zehen gebot, leben dahin wie das liebe vihe und unvernünfftige sewe, Und nu das Evangelion komen ist, dennoch fein gelernt haben aller freiheit meisterlich zu missebrauchen." *Luthers Kleiner Katechismus: Der deutsche Text in seiner geschichtliche Entwicklung,* ed. J. Meyer (Bonn, 1912), p. 4.11. Luther also complains that with the passing of the "tyranny of the pope" people no longer think they need receive the sacrament at all. Ibid., p. 71. It is probably a reflection as much of his raging quarrel with Zwingli, whom he suspected to be spiritualizing the Eucharist out of significance, as of his desire to discipline Saxon religious life that Luther counsels reception of the sacrament one to four times a year. It is to be noted that Luther protests that his "hard line"—the exclusion from the sacrament of all who refused to learn the catechism—is not really religious "coercion" but simply an obvious prerequisite for the Reformation's survival: just as one must know and obey the laws of the city in which one dwells lest chaos ensue, so must one respect what is considered right and wrong within the community of faith to which one belongs. Ibid., pp. 5.32, 6.4.

139 *Large Catechism,* p. 42.

140 *Sermons on the Catechism,* p. 137.

141 See p. 27 above.

142 *Sermons on the Catechism,* p. 143.

143 Ibid., p. 147.

144 Ibid., p. 178. Commentary on "Forgive us our debts as we forgive our debtors."

145 *Radts Predigt,* pp. C 4 b–D 1 a.

146 "Das sind die feynd des creützes Christi / die das jr suchen / die lassen iederman machen wie er will / Sagen von grosser senftmütigkeit und frintlichkeit / die man im predigen brauchen solle / was gericht / eyfer / ernst in sich hat / ist jnen ein new Bapstum. So man die Oberkeit jrs ampts ermanet / ist es von arm Gottes auff den fleischlichen arm gefallen. Der glaub solle frey sein das ist / es sol jeder thun und leben / wie es jm gefellet." Ibid., pp. B 4 b–C 1 a.

147 *Kirchen Ordnung. In meiner genedigen Herrn der Margraven zu Brandenburg* (Nürnberg, 1533), p. A 3 a. Brenz's order is printed in Richter 1:176–211.

148 See, for example, the *Ordnung so ein Ersame Statt Basel den ersten tag Aprilis in jrer Statt und Landschafft fürohyn zuhalten erkant* (1529) in Richter 1:120–27; 121. Bugenhagen established an office of superintendent to

oversee clergy, exercise the ban, and biannually visit the schools. He also restricted the number of preachers in Braunschweig to fifteen, about two per church, although the possibility for expansion was left open. The *Superattendant* received 100 gulden and a dwelling; his assistant 50 gulden (60 if married) and a dwelling; and preachers at the city's seven churches 35 gulden (45 if married) and a dwelling. *Der Erbarn Stadt Braunschwyg Christenliche Ordenung / zu dienst dem heiligen Evangelio / Christlicher lieb / zucht / fride und eynigkeit / Auch darunter vil Christlicher lere für die Bürger* (Nürnberg, 1531), pp. D 7 b–E 1 b. This is the high German version of the original low German (1528); excerpts from the latter appear in Richter 1:106–120. It is among the most important documents of the German Reformation, since Bugenhagen's was the hand behind the church ordinances of Hamburg (1529), Lübeck (1531), Pommern (1534), Denmark (1537), Holstein (1542), Braunschweig-Wolfen-büttel (1543), and Hildesheim (1544). *RGG* 1:1504. On the office of superintendent, see also Urbanus Rhegius' *Kirchen Ordnung der Stadt Hannofer* (Magdeburg, 1536), in Richter 1:274.

149 Basel established a daily *Frübet* (en route to work); a daily one-half hour morning sermon for *Rat* and *Gerichtsherren* in the Münster; and a mid-afternoon Scripture reading of approximately one hour's duration. Basel (1529), in Richter 1:125. Bugenhagen had services begin at 4:00 A.M. on Sundays and holidays, allowances being made for darkness at this hour in autumn. On workdays there was a one-half hour sermon at 7:00 and 8:00 A.M., alternating the seven churches. Afternoon sermons were held by the superintendent on Tuesdays and Thursdays and by his assistant on Mondays, Wednesdays, and Fridays (the latter day being optional). Braunschweig/Nürnberg (1531), p. E 2 a, E 7 b. Rhegius established a three-quarter hour sermon (in place of the traditional daily mass) "zur erbawung, ermanung und trost der zuhörer" and regular times for catechism. Hannover (1536), in Richter 1:274. See also the Strasbourg regulations for worship and catechism in Richter 1:236–38.

150 Braunschweig/Nürnberg (1531), p. F 3 a.

151 Brenz, Brandenbrug/Nürnberg (1533), pp. B 3 a–B 4 a; Bucer, p. 130 above; Eberlin, p. 104 above. Cf. also Basel (1529), in Richter 1:127.

152 Luther's was not the first of this Protestant genre. For Protestant catechisms antedating Luther's, see Ferdinand Cohrs, *Die Evangelischen Katechismusversuche* 1–3 (Berlin, 1900–1901); E. W. Kohls, *Evangelische Katechismen der Reformationszeit vor Luthers Kleinem Katechismus* (Gütersloh, 1971); and Reu, *Dr. M. Luther's Small Catechism.*

153 *Luthers Kleiner Katechismus,* pp. 5.32, 6.4.

154 On the benefits to women of clerical marriage, see 172*n*37 above.

Protestants also established vernacular schools for girls. Bugenhagen directed two hours a day on the catechism, memorizing Scripture, and reading Bible stories before "housework learning." Vernacular literacy in the catechism and Bible was designed to make women "useful, skillful, happy, friendly, God-fearing, obedient, unsuperstitious, and not obstinate." Braunschweig/Nürnberg (1531), p. D 3 a-b. As for clandestine marriages, the Zurich ordinance is exemplary: no binding engagements may be undertaken "ohne gunst / wüssen / und willen vatter / müter / vögten / oder deren / denen die kind kond zu versprechen." *Ordnung / ansehen und erkanntnus eines Ersamen Radts der Statt Zürich / wie hinfür über Eelich sachenn gericht / dessglychenn / Eebruch / Hury / Kupplery / unnd uneeliche bywonung gestrafft sol werden* (Zurich, 1526), p. A 4 b. Parents were urged, however, not to force their children into unwanted marriages. Basel (1529), in Richter 1:125. See also Brenz's *Kirchenordnung für die Stadt Hall und das hallische Land* (1526), in Richter 1:40–49; 47.

155 *Bekanthnus unsers heiligen Christlichen gloubens / wie es die Kilch zu Basel haltet* (Basel, 1534). See also Johann Toltz, *Handbüchlein für junge Christen* (1526), in Cohrs, *Die evangelischen Katechismusversuche* 1:246, 254, and the *Wittenberg Kinderbuchlein* (1526), with articles on the ban, auricular confession, sacrament of penance, purgatory, prayers and masses for the dead, and communion with cup. In Cohrs 1:156. Brenz's article on Christian freedom stresses religious, not political, liberties, and Bugenhagen makes it clear that Protestant freedom from past idolatry does not make Protestants *Bildstürmer.* Brandenburg/Nürnberg (1533), p. H 2 a; Braunschweig/Nürnberg (1531), p. P 5 b.

156 See Bucer's short-lived (because Ulm soon became Lutheran, embracing the *Confessio Augustana,* rather than Zwinglian and the *Confessio Tetrapolitana*) *Ordnung die ain Ersamer Rath der Statt Ulm in abstellung hergeprachter etlicher misspreuch* (1531), in Richter 1:157–59.

157 The Zurich ordinance prescribed seventeen holidays (reading "allerheiligen zwölfbotten tag" as one day's celebration for all twelve apostles). *Ordnung der Fyrtagen* (Zurich, 1526). Rhegius also prescribed seventeen in the Hannover ordinance, describing the reduction as a return to the prevailing custom prior to the Fourth Lateran Council (1215). Hannover (1536), in Richter 1:275. Brenz cited twenty-two holidays. Brandenburg/Nürnberg (1533), p. O 4 b f. The Basel 1529 ordinance appears to have gone the farthest in reduction of holidays. Arguing that every day is a holiday for Christians—i.e. a day of special virtue and thanksgiving to God,—it required as observed holidays only those relating to Christmas, Easter, Ascension, and

Pentacost, making the traditional holidays in honor of Mary, the twelve apostles, John the Baptist, and the church's martyrs days to be calendared and piously remembered, but not officially celebrated. In Richter 1:126. On required and optional religious holidays prior to the Reformation see p. 98 above.

158 Braunschweig/Nürnberg (1531), pp. P 6 b–P 7 a.

159 Hall (1526), in Richter 1:48.

160 Brandenburg/Nürnberg (1533), p. O 4 b.

161 Braunschweig/Nürnberg (1531), p. F 6 b.

162 "Ja ye mehr wir weyhewasser hetten / ye mehr auch poltergeister / oder das man mit liechten und Kreuttern dem donner were / und zaubere mit kreuttern im bette / und im keller bey dem pier / one das solches alles ertichtet ist / wider die gnad unsers herren Jesu Christi / der nimpt allein die sund wegk / und wider das Christlich gepet / damit wir sollen anrüffen / durch Christum / unsern lieben Vatter / in allen unsern nöten / leybs und der seelen. Das hilfft in den sachen / und kein wasser / feur / kraut." Ibid., p. G 1 a-b; cf. p. G 7 a.

163 *Dr. Martin Luther's Large Catechism,* pp. 55, 58.

164 Hannover (1536), in Richter 1:275.

165 See Brenz, Hall (1526), pp. 45–46; Basel (1534); Hannover (1536), p. 275. Martin Brecht maintains that Brenz later dropped his caution about religious coercion, so prominent in the 1526 Hall ordinance, and in ordinances of 1535 and 1559 commanded Protestants to do what was "free." According to Brecht, Brenz ended up one of the strongest *obrigkeitlich* reformers, going well beyond Luther in integrating church and state and exalting the responsibilities of Landesherren in religion. *Die frühe Theologie des Johannes Brenz* (Tübingen, 1966), pp. 57, 62, 280, 285.

166 Braunschweig/Nürnberg (1531), p. F 3 a.

167 Brandenburg/Nürnberg (1533), p. C 2 a.

168 Ibid., p. D 1 b.

169 Braunschweig/Nürnberg (1531), p. A 4 b.

170 No one may receive the sacrament unless he has first given "an account and report of his faith" to the appointed preachers. Ibid., p. F 1 a.

171 See p. 50 above.

172 Braunschweig/Nürnberg (1531), p. K 7 a.

173 "Das ist die recht Beycht / die wir auch von den unsern in die gemein als sonderlich / mit ernst bekennen sollen / als die leut thetten / die zu Johannes Tauff kamen / die bekenten in die gemein ire sünde." Ibid., pp. K 7 a, P 1 a.

174 On Von Aich, see Josef Benzing, *Die Buchdrucker des 16. und 17.*

Jahrhunderts im deutschen Sprachgebiet (Wiesbaden, 1963), p. 222; and "Die Drucke der Lupuspresse zu Köln (Arnd und Joh. von Aich)," *Archiv für Geschichte des Buchwesens* (1958), 1:365–70.

175 "Wer beide Büchlein gelesen hat, erkennt sofort, dass Coeldes Buch dem Arnd von Aich . . . nicht mehr als die Anregung zur Verabfassung des Buches und dessen Bezeichnung als 'Handbüchlein' gegeben hat;" Von Aich's is "ein buch . . . das im bewusstem Gegensatz zu Coeldes *Christenspiegel* ein ganz evangelisches Werk ist." J. M. Reu, *Quellen zur Geschichte des Katechismus-Unterrichts.* I. Teil, III. Band: *Ost-, Nord- und Westdeutsche Katechismen.* 1. Abt: *Historisch-bibliographische Einleitung.* 2. Hälfte, 3. Lieferung (Gütersloh, 1935), pp. 1272–73. The description of the editions of Von Aich's work in the *Bulletin of the Library of the Foundation for Reformation Research*, vol. 6, nos. 3 & 4 (Sept., Dec., 1971), pp. 18 (no. 14), 20 (no. 67), and 30 (no. 225) gives the misleading impression that Von Aich's *Handbook* is but a revision of Coelde's.

176 Reu, I, III: 1. 2. 3, pp. 1270–78.

177 *Des evangelischen Bürgers Handbüchlein. Welchs durch klare sprüch des Newen Testaments ein recht Christlich leben und alles was den Menschen von nöten ist zu wissen anzeygt. An viel orten gemehret, corrigirt und gebessert* (Nürnberg, 1555), in J. M. Reu, *Quellen zur Geschichte des Katechismus-Unterrichts* I. Teil, III. Band: 2. Abt., 3. Teil (Gütersloh, 1924), pp. 1498–1500. This is a reprint of the Von der Müllen/Meynertzhagen Bonn edition of 1544. Meynertzhagen's additions are segregated from Von Aich's original, to which I have confined myself.

178 Ibid., pp. 1525–26.

179 Ibid., p. 1510.

180 Ibid., pp. 1519, 1535.

181 Ibid., p. 1521.

182 Ibid., p. 1572. "Alle Oberkeyt soll sich wissen zurichten, niemand urtheylen noch tödten im unglauben denn die zeyt, so Gott die verstockten hertzen erleuchten will, ist niemand kündig, und nicht mit gewalt die Seelen also in die helle stossen." Ibid., p. 1571.

183 See my *Mysticism and Dissent,* p. 171.

184 *Des evangelischen Bürgers Handbüchlein,* p. 1522. See also Von Aich's article, "On False Preachers, Prophets, Hypocrites, and All Other Forms of Deceivers," ibid., pp. 1047–51.

185 Ibid., p. 1555.

186 Ibid., p. 1574.

187 Ibid., p. 1568. Von Aich, reflecting early Protestant criticism of Catholic deathbed practice, expected Christians to approach the hour of death with "great joy and desire." "Denn sie wissen das der todt

sein krafft und herrligkeit verloren hat durch den todt Christi, und das die glaubigen nicht gericht werden, sondern mit Gott ewiglich leben." Ibid., p. 1572. Cf. pp. 55–56 above. Another late catechetical testimony to Protestant release from the fear and uncertainty of the medieval viator is the following prayer prescribed to the father of the house in a Strasbourg lay catechism. Note that election and salvation are perceived as already settled matters. "Ich sage dir danck von hertzen / das du mich on verdienst / durch lauter gnad angenommen / zubereytet / und zum erbtheyl der heyligen geschickt gmacht hast / Dann du hast mich erloset auss gewalt der finsternüss / und in das reich der lieb deins suns Jesu Christi versetzt / inn welchem ich schon füle die erlösung / durch sein blüt / das ist verzeihung meiner sund / unnd ein auffgeende gerechtigkeyt / die alleyn auss deiner barmhertzigkeit und reichthumb deiner gnaden herkompt." *Eyns Christlichen Hauszvatters mit seinem Gesind tägliche Uebung* (Strasbourg, 1537), p. vi.

Index

APR 1990

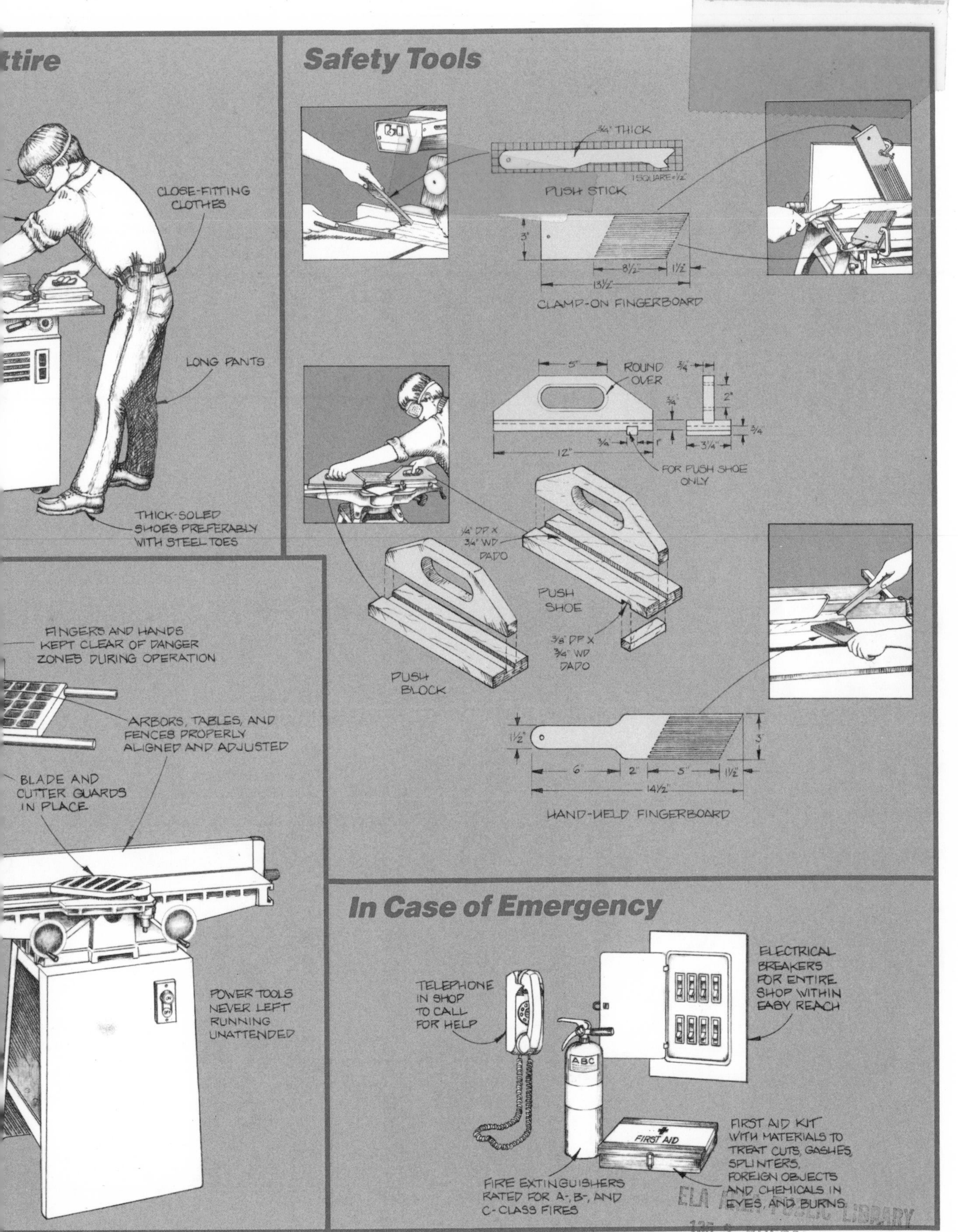
ttire
CLOSE-FITTING CLOTHES
LONG PANTS
THICK-SOLED SHOES PREFERABLY WITH STEEL TOES
Safety Tools
3/4" THICK
1 SQUARE = 1/2"
PUSH STICK
3"
8 1/2"
1 1/2
13 1/2"
CLAMP-ON FINGERBOARD
5"
ROUND OVER
3/4"
2"
3/4
3 1/4"
1"
12"
FOR PUSH SHOE ONLY
1/4" DP X 3/4" WD DADO
PUSH SHOE
3/8" DP X 3/4" WD DADO
PUSH BLOCK
1 1/2"
3"
6"
2"
5"
14 1/2"
HAND-HELD FINGERBOARD
FINGERS AND HANDS KEPT CLEAR OF DANGER ZONES DURING OPERATION
ARBORS, TABLES, AND FENCES PROPERLY ALIGNED AND ADJUSTED
BLADE AND CUTTER GUARDS IN PLACE
POWER TOOLS NEVER LEFT RUNNING UNATTENDED
In Case of Emergency
TELEPHONE IN SHOP TO CALL FOR HELP
ELECTRICAL BREAKERS FOR ENTIRE SHOP WITHIN EASY REACH
ABC
FIRST AID
FIRST AID KIT WITH MATERIALS TO TREAT CUTS, GASHES, SPLINTERS, FOREIGN OBJECTS AND CHEMICALS IN EYES, AND BURNS.
FIRE EXTINGUISHERS RATED FOR A-, B-, AND C- CLASS FIRES

·BUILD·IT·BETTER·YOURSELF·
WOODWORKING PROJECTS

Outdoor Furniture

Collected and Written
by Nick Engler

Rodale Press
Emmaus, Pennsylvania

The author and editors who compiled this book have tried to make all the contents as accurate and as correct as possible. Plans, illustrations, photographs, and text have all been carefully checked and cross-checked. However, due to the variability of local conditions, construction materials, personal skill, and so on, neither the author nor Rodale Press assumes any responsibility for any injuries suffered, or for damages or other losses incurred that result from the material presented herein. All instructions and plans should be carefully studied and clearly understood before beginning construction.

Printed in the United States of America on recycled paper containing a high percentage of de-inked fiber.

Series Editor: William H. Hylton
Managing Editor/Author: Nick Engler
Copy Editor: Kate Armpriester
Technical Editor: Larry McClung
Graphic Designer: Linda Watts
Graphic Artist: Linda Ball
Draftpersons: Mary Jane Favorite
Chris Walendzak
Alfred Owens
Photography: Karen Callahan
Illustrations by O'Neil & Associates, Dayton, Ohio
Produced by Bookworks, Inc., West Milton, Ohio

Library of Congress Cataloging-in-Publication Data

Engler, Nick.
Outdoor furniture.

(Build-it-better-yourself woodworking projects)
1. Outdoor furniture. I. Title. II. Series.
TT197.5.09E64 1988 684.1'8 88-11384
ISBN 0-87857-788-2

2 4 6 8 10 9 7 5 3 hardcover

Contents

An Introduction to Outdoor Furniture

If you've ever made a picnic table or a planter, you know that the art of making "outdoor" furniture is unique, different from any other type of woodworking. The methods and techniques are a careful blend of cabinetry and carpentry — a finished outdoor furniture project looks like a piece of furniture, but it's built like a house.

The reason for this, of course, is the weather. Out of doors, your project has to survive extreme changes in temperature and humidity. When building outdoor furniture, you have to plan ahead for the distortion and decay that happens when wood gets hot, cold, or wet. And — this is just as important — you have to provide a way for the wood to shed the rain and dry quickly to prevent as much of that distortion and decay as possible.

Outdoor Furniture Joinery

Water tends to collect wherever two pieces of wood join together. Consequently, outdoor furniture has as few joints as possible, and those joints are usually very simple — butt joints, lap joints, maybe an open mortise and tenon. This *decreases* the surface area of any board that is in direct contact with other boards. In other types of woodworking, the purpose of joinery is to *increase* the board-to-board surface area, so that you get a stronger glue bond.

Outdoor furniture joints are also cut with a good deal more "slop" than what you may consider acceptable. A good outdoor lap joint should have 1/16"-1/8" of slop to allow the wood to swell in wet weather, and to let it dry out when the rain stops. Again, this is in direct contrast to other forms of woodworking, where a sloppy joint will be a weak joint because the glue won't bond properly to all the surfaces.

One reason that you can safely use sparse, sloppy joinery in outdoor furniture is that the parts are rarely glued together. Out in the weather, wood expands and contracts enough to break even "waterproof" glue bonds. Only small parts that barely swell and shrink, such as screw plugs and dowels, can be successfully glued in place. Larger parts must be held together with hardware — nails, screws, and bolts. As in carpentry, it is the hardware, rather than the joinery, that holds the finished project together.

Another reason is that the joinery does not contribute much to the overall strength of the project. Strength is provided by *design* — two adjoining parts are often braced with a third part. Again, this is similar to carpentry, where a builder always tries to "complete the triangle" to make the structure stronger and more rigid. If the parts properly brace each other, a sloppy joint won't wobble or work itself loose.

When it comes right down to it, the joinery in outdoor furniture has little to do with holding the project together. The joints simply make the pieces fit in such a way that they won't collect water. Hardware and design do the actual "joining."

Outdoor Furniture Materials

While it's important to keep the wood in an outdoor furniture project as dry as possible, water is not the enemy. Wet wood is just as strong as dry. But wood that gets wet and *stays wet* becomes a fertile breeding ground for bacteria. The bacteria digest the wood fibers, reducing them to dust. This is what causes the wood to decay and rot.

If you can prevent the bacteria from growing, you can keep the wood strong — even though it stays soaked. Certain types of wood resist bacterial growth, and will last longer out in the weather than other varieties. In order to make your outdoor furniture projects last, it's important to *pick the right wood.* No matter how carefully you make the joints, the areas where the parts touch will tend to collect water.

Absolutely the best woods to use are the tropical varieties, in particular *teak* and *mahogany.* These woods are saturated with natural oils that either repel the water or make the wood fibers inhospitable to bacteria. These oils are part of the tree's natural defense against the moist, humid environment of the tropical rain forests.

Unfortunately, because teak and mahogany have to be imported, they are expensive. There are several domestic varieties that are almost as rot-resistant as the tropical woods and are somewhat less expensive. These are *redwood, cypress,* and all types of *cedar.*

Of these, the best is *Atlantic white cedar* (sometimes called "juniper"). White cedar becomes even more rot-resistant *after* it's cut and cured. In the early 1800's, shingle-makers along the east coast "mined" fallen cedar trunks from swamps and bogs. They found that the dead trees made better quality, longer-lasting shingles even though they had been buried in mud for scores of years. White cedar is also one of the few woods that is resistant to the ravages of salt water. It's a bit hard to find — particularly in the West — but if you live on a coast, it may be worth the search.

The least expensive alternative for most of us is *pressure-treated lumber.* This is domestic pine that has been poisoned with various preservative chemicals, so that bacteria won't grow in it. To make sure that the wood is poisoned all the way through, it's placed in a "retort" or pressure chamber. All of the air is pumped out, taking with it most of the moisture in the wood. Then the retort is flooded with preservative and pressurized to at least 175 pounds per square inch. This drives the chemicals deep into the wood.

When purchasing pressure-treated lumber, there are two things to look for. First of all, some pressure-treated lumber is more rot-resistant than others. Treating mills work with different solutions of preservatives, and consequently some wood retains more preservatives than others. The American Wood Preservers Bureau (AWPB) has a rating system for the degree of "retention," and most mills stamp this rating onto their lumber. A rating of LP-2 indicates low retention; this wood should *not* be used in direct contact with the ground or water. For wood that sits on or in the ground, you need a rating of LP-22 or better. (See Figure 1.) For most outdoor furniture projects, LP-2 lumber is adequate. However, if the project will rest on the ground or in an extremely wet location, use LP-22.

Secondly, pay attention to what *species* of wood you're buying. This, too, should be stamped on the lumber. Not all woods are well-suited for pressure-treating. Southern yellow pine, red pine, and ponderosa pine all retain preservatives well. Douglas fir, spruce, white pine, and most domestic hardwoods do not. Don't be fooled by lumber that's labeled "southern pine." This is not southern yellow pine; it's just another name for white pine.

Once you've chosen a rot-resistant wood to build your outdoor furniture project, you'll then need to select rust-resistant hardware. Not only does water create a fertile environment for bacteria; it also promotes the corrosion of many metals. Common nails and untreated hardware

1/*Look for the AWBP stamp on pressure-treated lumber. A rating of LP-22 or higher means the wood can be used in direct contact with the ground.*

2/*Common nails and hardware corrode in the out of doors, staining your project. Use galvanized or plated hardware instead.*

will rust quickly, staining the wood with long, dark streaks. Eventually, the nails and hardware will disintegrate. (See Figure 2.) Look for nails and hardware that have been "galvanized." This means that the metal has either been dipped or plated with a zinc alloy to resist corrosion. Most common screws are made from zinc chromate, a material that won't rust when exposed to *fresh* water. However, if the project will be used near salt water, purchase brass or stainless steel screws.

A Few Tips for Making and Finishing Outdoor Furniture

As you build outdoor furniture, here are a few general tips to help make the work a little easier and the finished project last a little longer:

- When you place boards side by side, as on a table top, leave ⅛"-¼" space between each board to allow the wood room to swell and shrink. Wood will expand up to ¼" *across the grain* for every 12" of width. Expansion with the grain is negligible.
- If you attach the board with nails, drive each nail at a slight angle. Vary this angle back and forth with every nail. This "hooks" the parts together.
- Whenever possible, try to orient a board so that the "bark side" faces *up* in the completed project. (See Figure 3.) This helps the lumber shed water.

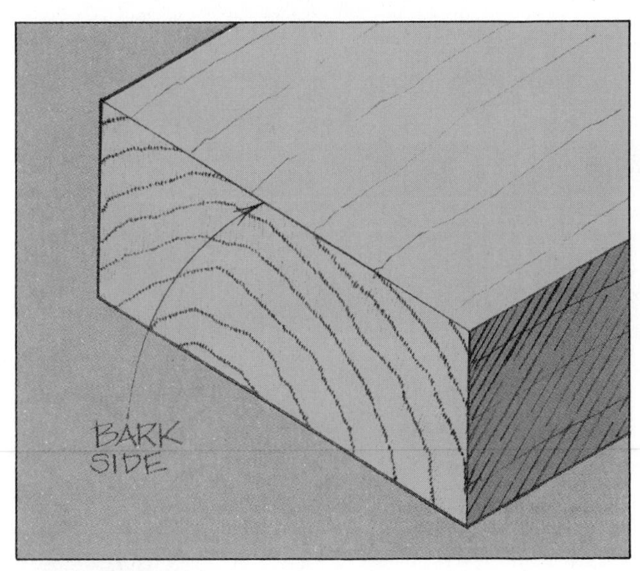

3*/Assemble projects so the boards are "bark side" up, wherever possible. This helps shed water and prevents cupping. To decide which side of a board is the bark side, look at the end grain.*

- If at all possible, never attach a board with the end grain facing up, exposed to the rain. Cap it, turn it on a lathe, or cut it at an angle to help the end of the board shed water.
- Seal the bottom ends of legs with melted paraffin wax or spar varnish to keep them from soaking up water.
- On those few occasions where you need to glue a small piece in place, use waterproof epoxy or resorcinol glue. Epoxy usually dries clear, and resorcinol cures to a dark brown.
- If you intend to apply a preservative stain or paint to the project, apply the first coat *before* you assemble the parts. This ensures that *all* the surfaces will be coated.
- You can paint or stain pressure-treated lumber, but it's wise to wait a month or so and give the wood a chance to dry out. There's no need to keep it in your shop while it dries; the lumber will dry well enough for painting out in the sun.
- Avoid finishing outdoor furniture with polyurethane. Most brands of poly-U dry too hard to expand and contract with the wood when it's placed out of doors. After a year or so, the finish will peel off. Use spar varnish or a 1:1 mixture of spar varnish and tung oil instead.
- If you plan to finish your outdoor furniture project, cedar and cypress accept finishes better than other species. Redwood, white pine, and sugar pine are also good choices for finishing. Western yellow pine and hemlock are okay if the surface is prepared and primed properly. Southern yellow pine, fir, and larch are not good choices. They may cause the paint to peel and crack after relatively short exposure to the weather.
- The denser a wood is, the harder it is for that wood to accept a finish. For that reason, avoid wood with wide bands of dense "summerwood" (summer growth). These are the dark lines in the annual rings. If the summerwood is present in narrow stripes, with wide bands of lighter "springwood" (spring growth) in between, then you can be relatively sure the wood will take a finish well.
- Quartersawn and rift-sawn boards take a finish much better than plain-sawn. However, few lumberyards carry quartersawn or rift-sawn stock anymore. When you do find it, it's very expensive. To make the finish last longer on plain-sawn boards, turn the bark side up or out, where it will be exposed to the weather. The finish adheres better to the bark side of plain-sawn boards than it does to the pith side.

Round Picnic Table and Benches

Round picnic tables are so much more conducive to good conversation than ordinary picnic tables. Each person sitting at the round table has an unobstructed view of everyone else. Consequently, no one feels left out or ignored. Unfortunately, most round picnic tables have a drawback that sometimes disturbs the conversation. Usually, each bench seats *two* people. If someone wants to sit down or get up, at least one other person has to move.

This particular table and bench set solves that problem. Each person has a bench all to himself. There's no need to beg anyone else's pardon if you need to get up for a moment. And there are *eight* seats, so there should be no lack of seating, even for large gatherings.

TABLE
EXPLODED VIEW

BENCH
EXPLODED VIEW

FINISHED DIMENSIONS

PARTS

Picnic Table

	Part	Dimensions
A.	Middle top planks (2)	1½" x 5½" x 45¾"
B.	Next-to-middle top planks (2)	1½" x 5½" x 44¾"
C.	Next-to-end top planks (2)	1½" x 5½" x 40"
D.	End top planks (2)	1½" x 5½" x 30½"
E.	Aprons (2)	1½" x 2½" x 41¾"
F.	Legs (4)	1½" x 3½" x 44¼"
G.	Stretcher	1½" x 3½" x 18⅛"
H.	Braces (4)	1½" x 2⅜" x 12½"

	Part	Dimensions
A.	Front seat planks (8)	1½" x 5½" x 17⅛"
B.	Middle seat planks (8)	1½" x 5½" x 21¼"
C.	Back seat planks (8)	1½" x 5½" x 21¼"
D.	Seat braces (16)	1½" x 1½" x 14½"
E.	Legs (32)	1½" x 3½" x 21 11/16"
F.	Stretcher dowels (16)	1" dia. x 12½"

HARDWARE

Picnic Table

⅜" x 3½" Carriage bolts, washers, and nuts (8)
⅜" x 4" Lag screws and washers (4)
#14 x 2½" Flathead wood screws (16)
10d Decking nails (1 lb.)

Benches (8)

#14 x 2½" Flathead wood screws (64)
#10 x 1¼" Flathead wood screws (32)
10d Decking nails (1½ lbs.)
8d Finishing nails (32)

1 **Cut the parts to size.**

To make the picnic table with all eight benches, you'll need to purchase ten 2 x 6s, 8′ long, twelve 2 x 4s, 8′ long, and six 1″-diameter dowels, 4′ long. Be very picky when you select the wood. You're going to be sitting and eating on those boards. You want them to be fairly clear and free from defects.

Rip and cut all the parts to the sizes shown in the Materials List, with the exception of the bench legs. Cut these parts at least 22⅝″ long or longer. This extra stock will give you room to make all three miter cuts that have to be made on this one part.

You'll find that this project goes faster if you work on both the table and the benches at the same time for the first few steps. However, to avoid getting the parts mixed up, start making neat stacks of cut stock, so you know which board belongs to which piece of furniture. To help you decide which part to pick up next, we'll keep the instructions for the table and benches carefully separated. They will be labeled *Table* or *Benches.* Read each step through before proceeding with the work, so that you're sure what part or assembly you should be working on.

2 **Miter or chamfer the ends of the legs, aprons, and table braces.**

Table: Miter the ends of the legs and table braces at 45°, as shown in the working drawings. Also, cut off the lower corners of the aprons. This will keep you from bumping your legs against sharp corners.

Benches: Miter the ends of the legs. The upper ends must be cut twice, forming an arrowhead-like point. To help speed this step, attach a stop block to your table saw or radial arm saw. (See Figure 1.) Use this block to automatically position the stock for each miter cut.

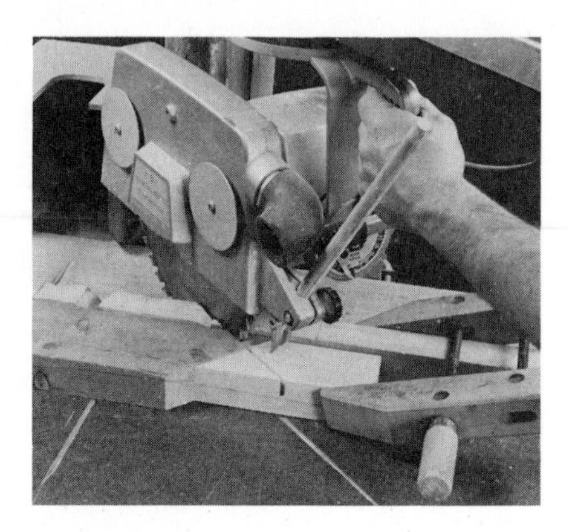

1/*Miter-cut the upper ends of the bench legs twice, to form a point. A stop block helps you position the stock on the saw with no need to measure over and over again.*

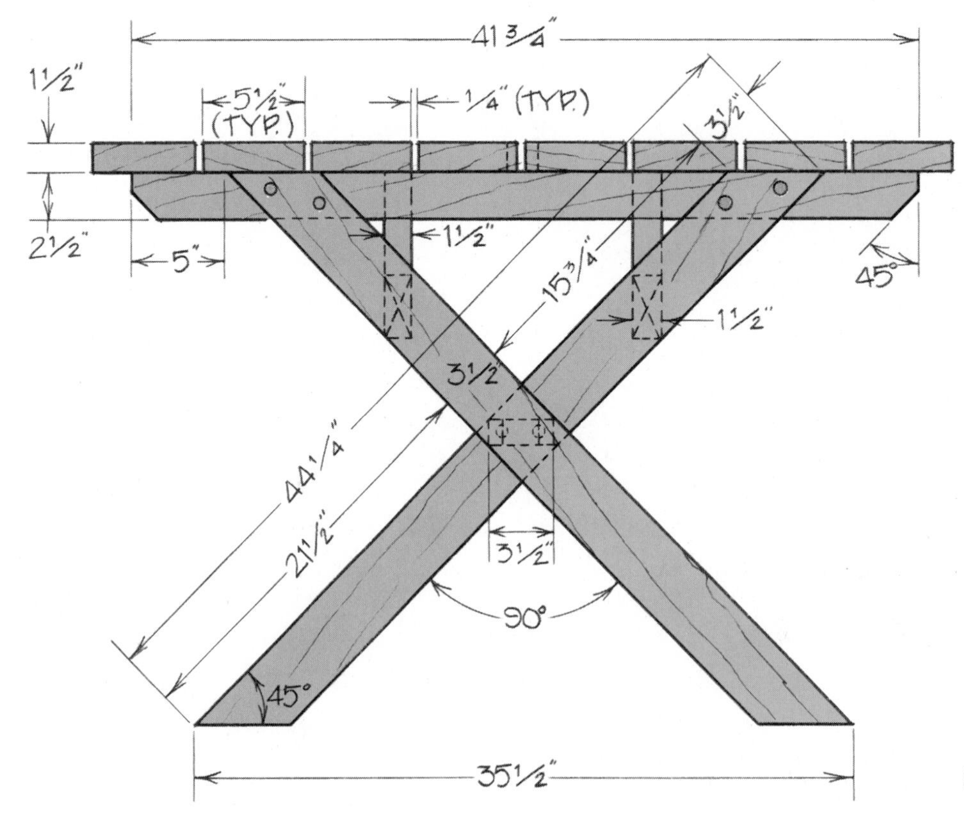

TABLE SIDE VIEW

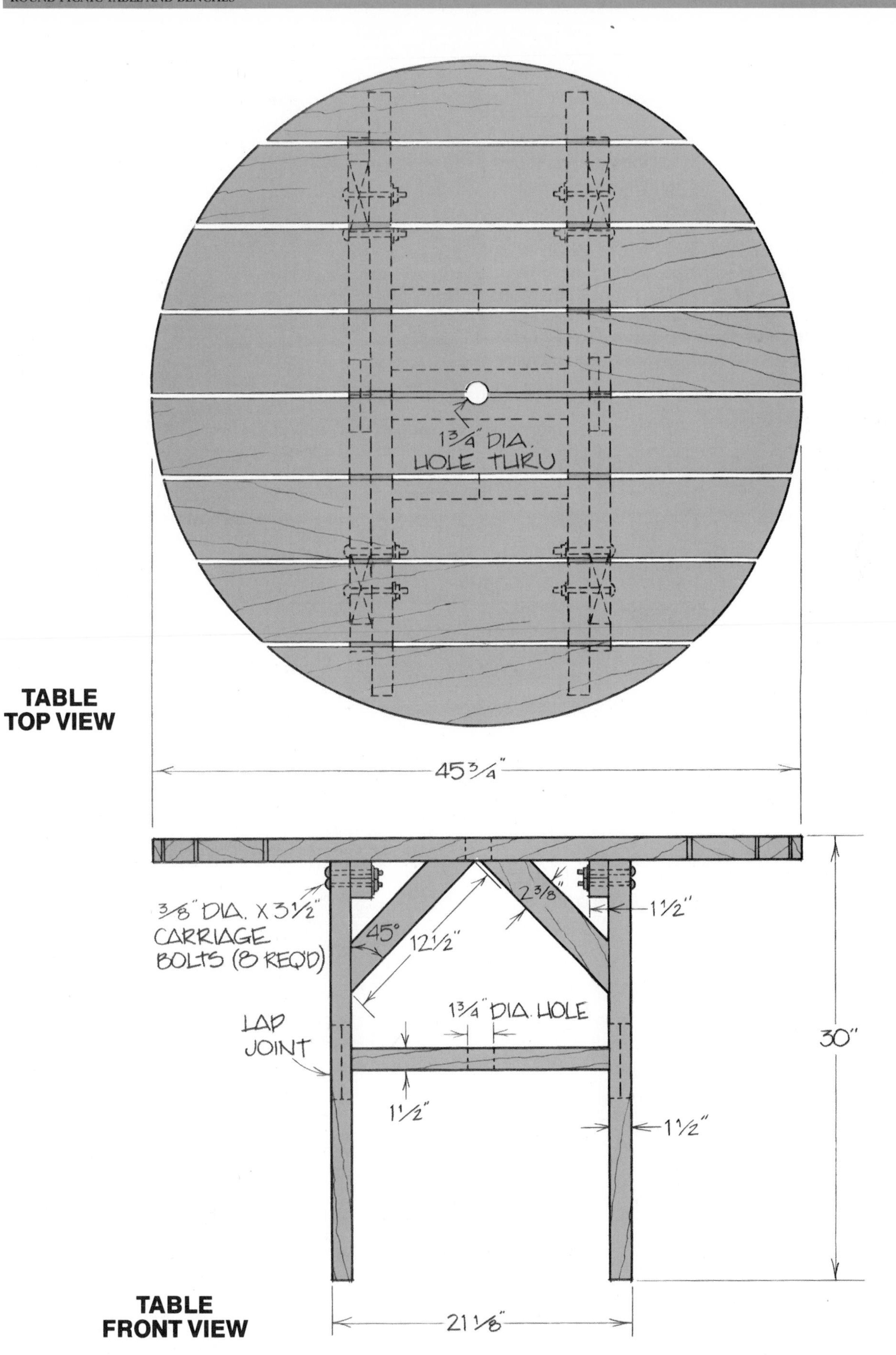

TABLE TOP VIEW

TABLE FRONT VIEW

3 Cut the lap joints in the legs.

Table: Mount a dado cutter on your table saw or radial arm saw. Adjust the height of the cutter to cut ¾″ deep, halfway through a 2 x 4. Mark the lap joints, as shown on the working drawings, then cut them with the dado. Because of the width of the lap, you'll have to make several passes over the cutter to remove the waste.

Benches: Make the lap joints in the bench legs in much the same manner as you made them in the table legs. However, the bench legs are short enough that you can easily set up a stop block to automatically position the stock before you run it over the cutter. (See Figure 2.) This will save you the trouble of measuring and marking all 32 bench legs.

2/*Cut the lap joints in the table legs and the bench legs with a dado cutter. Make each lap joint in several passes, cutting away a little more waste with each pass.*

TRY THIS! If you make the lap joints on your radial arm saw, cut the stock by pushing the motor and cutter *away* from you. If you pull it towards you, the dado cutter will tend to climb the stock.

Note: At this point in the project, it makes more sense to work on the table until you get it completely assembled, then go back and do the benches. So the next few steps pertain to the table only, and the steps following those will pertain to the benches. We won't combine instructions for both pieces in the same step again until we near the end of the project.

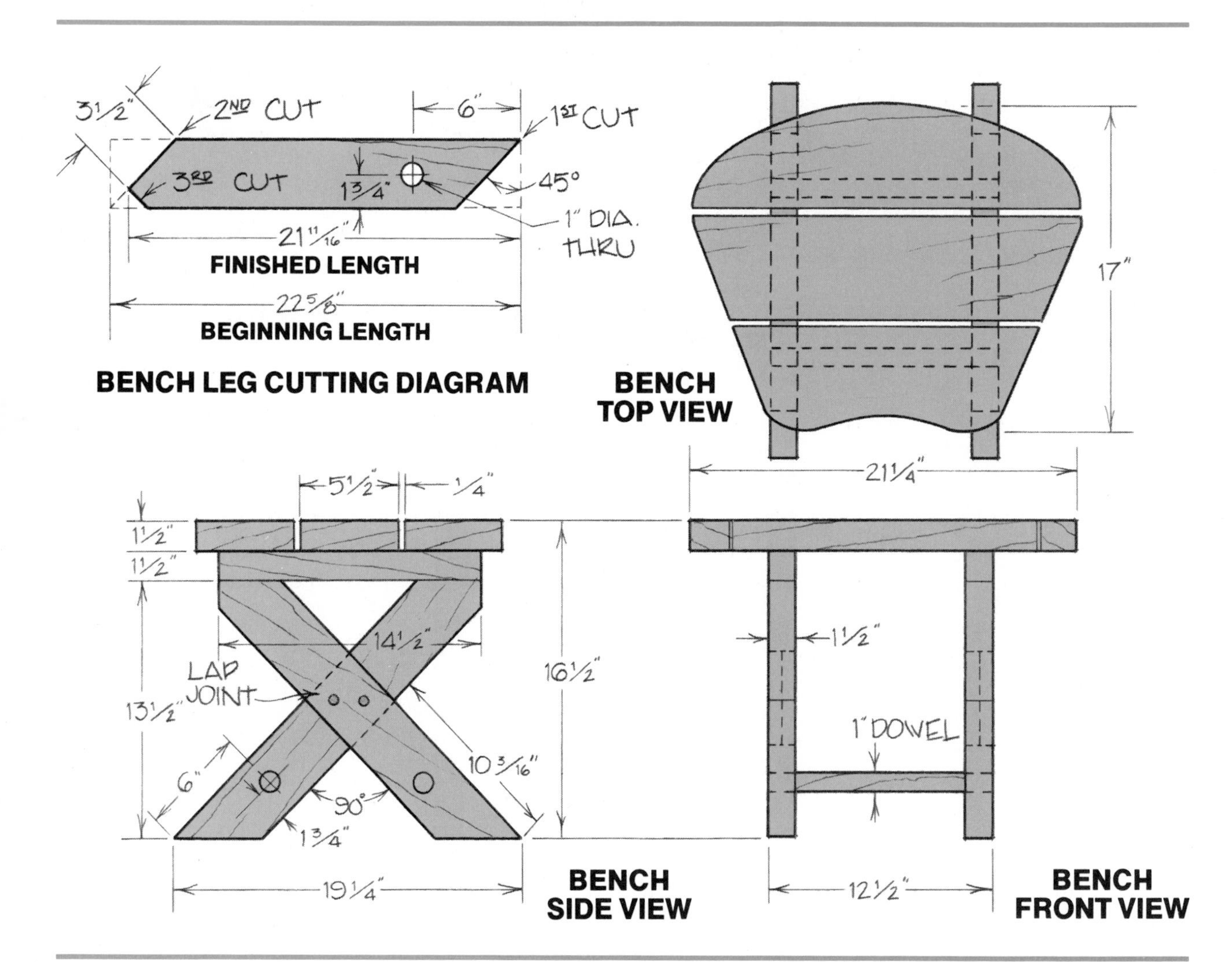

4 Cut a hole for an umbrella in the top table planks and the table stretcher.

Clamp the two tabletop middle planks together with a ¼″ spacer in between. With a holesaw, drill a 1¾″-diameter hole between the two planks, equidistant from both ends. (See Figure 3.) Also, drill a hole in the center of the stretcher. Later on, after you've assembled the table, you can use these holes to mount a large umbrella in the table.

3/Clamp the two middle tabletop planks together and cut a 1¾″ hole between them with a holesaw. After you mount the planks on the table, you can use them to hold an umbrella.

5 Sand the table parts.

Sand all the parts of the table to remove any rough spots on the wood. If you plan to paint or stain the completed project, now would be a good time to apply the first coat.

6 Assemble the table frame.

Put the table legs together to form two Xs, or "sawbucks." Clamp the upper ends of the legs to the aprons, where shown in the working drawings. Drill ⅜″-diameter holes through the legs and aprons and bolt them together.

Carefully position one end of the stretcher so that it's centered in the lap joint on one of the leg-apron assemblies where the legs cross. Temporarily nail the legs to the stretcher. Don't drive the nails home, so that you can pull them out easily. Have a helper stand up both leg-apron assemblies on a flat surface, and nail the unattached assembly to the other end of the stretcher.

Remove the nails one by one and replace them with lag screws. Drill pilot holes for the screws, then drive the screws through the lap joints and into the stretcher. These lag screws serve double duty. Not only do they attach the legs to the stretcher, they secure the legs to each other.

7 Attach the table top.

Measure the aprons to find the exact middle of each board. Also, measure all the table top planks to find the middle of each board. Starting at the middle of the aprons with the middle top planks, tack the table top in place. Use a scrap of ¼″-thick stock to space the planks evenly. Make sure the boards are centered on the aprons so that the marks you made at the middle of each board all line up. If the boards aren't properly placed, you won't have enough stock on one side of your table to cut a perfect circle. When you're certain that all the planks are properly positioned, drive the nails home.

TRY THIS! Use spiral decking nails to attach the planks to the frame. These are designed so that they won't pull loose.

8 **Saw the shape of the table top.**

Tack a small scrap of wood over the umbrella hole in the middle of the tabletop. Put a nail in the scrap, centered over the hole. Use the nail as the pivot for a string compass, and mark a circle with a radius of 22⅞″ on the top planks. (See Figure 4.) Cut this circle with a sabre saw. After you've sawn the circle, remove the scrap that you nailed to the table top. Sand away the saw marks with a belt sander.

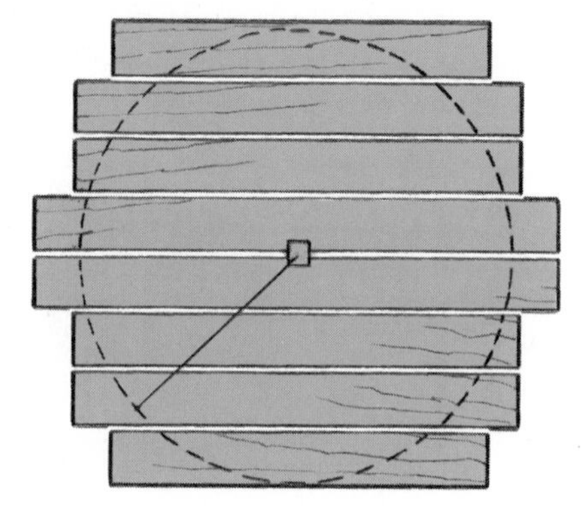

4/Nail the table top planks to the table frame, then mark the round shape with a string compass.

> TRY THIS! If you're making this project from pressure-treated lumber, take it easy when you cut the top with a sabre saw. This sort of lumber is wetter than most, so the saw blade binds, heats up, and snaps easily. Let the blade cool down every few minutes.

9 **Brace the legs to the table top.**

Tack the table braces in place underneath the table. These braces should run between the legs and the next-to-middle top planks. After the braces are positioned properly, remove the nails one by one and replace them with 2½″ long wood screws. (See Figure 5.)

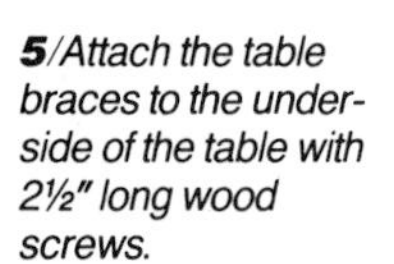

5/Attach the table braces to the underside of the table with 2½″ long wood screws.

10 **Drill holes for the stretchers in the bench legs.**

Drill a 1″-diameter hole in each bench leg, near the bottom. These holes must be placed exactly the same on all 32 legs. To position the holes easily, without a lot of measuring, make a simple jig that will hold the legs in the same place on your drill press, every time you drill a hole. (See Figure 6.)

6/So that you drill the stretcher holes in exactly the same place on every leg, make a simple jig to automatically position the stock on your drill press.

11

Sand the bench parts. Sand all the parts of the bench, just as you did the table parts. Once again, if you plan to paint or stain the completed project, now would be a good time to apply the first coat.

12

Assemble the bench frames. Put the bench legs together to form sawbucks, in the same manner that you put the table legs together. Drive 1¼″-long wood screws through the lap joints, so that the legs won't come apart. Attach the seat braces to the tops of the legs with 2½″-long screws. Arrange the leg-brace assemblies in pairs, and insert stretcher dowels in the holes in the legs. Arrange the parts so that the ends of the dowels are flush with the outside surfaces of the legs. Secure the stretchers in the legs by driving finishing nails through the legs and into the dowels.

13

Saw the shapes of the seat planks and attach them to the frames. There are two ways to saw the shapes of the seats, depending on what tools you intend to use. If you're using a sabre saw, simply nail the planks to the frames, trace the seat pattern onto the planks, and cut out the shape with the saw. This is virtually the same method you used to make the tabletop.

However, if you have a band saw, the technique is a little different and a little easier. Temporarily tack the seat planks to just *one* bench frame, centering the planks on the frame. The seat planks must be spaced ¼″ apart, just as the tabletop planks were spaced. Enlarge the seat pattern, and trace it onto the tops of the planks. Then remove the planks and cut out the shapes on a band saw.

Use this first set of shaped seat planks as templates to mark the others. Saw the remaining planks and sand the edges to remove the saw marks. Then nail the planks to the seats with decking nails.

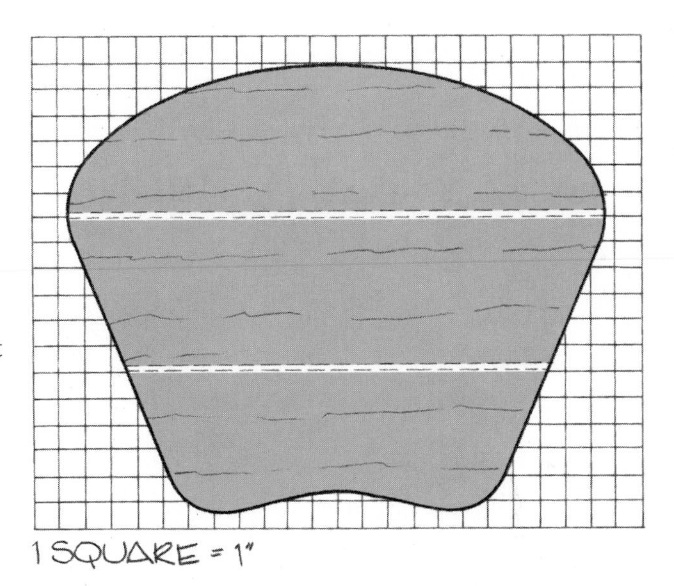

BENCH SEAT PATTERN

14

Round all the corners and apply a finish. *Table and Benches:* Round all the hard corners and edges on both the table and the benches. Pay particular attention to the tabletop and the seats. The edges of these planks should be very smooth to the touch. You'll find that a Surform® tool or a small block plane helps speed this chore.

After all the corners of the table and the benches have been rounded, apply a finish if you have decided the project needs one. Because of all the surfaces and tight crevices in the table and the benches, you'll find it much easier to use a paint sprayer to coat the completed outdoor dining set.

Sunlover's Chaise Lounge

For some people, the summer just wouldn't seem right without an outdoor chaise lounge. There's no better way to read a book or soak up the rays — or both — than lounging around on a chaise. This chaise has all the requirements to help make yours a good summer. It has wheels, so that you can easily move the piece to the sunniest spot in the yard. The back adjusts to 20°, 40°, or 60°, so you can catch those rays just right. It also lays flat, so that you can roll over and take a snooze on your stomach.

For additional comfort, this chaise is built to the same dimension as a standard-sized 23″ x 72″ cushion for outdoor furniture. These cushions are available from most mail-order department stores, such as Sears or Penney's. Purchase the color and pattern that suits you, and lay the cushion on top of the slats.

FINISHED DIMENSIONS

PARTS

	Part	Dimensions
A.	Sides (2)	1½″ x 3½″ x 68″
B.	End	1½″ x 3½″ x 21½″
C.	Brace	1½″ x 3½″ x 23″
D.	Long legs (2)	1½″ x 3½″ x 14½″
E.	Short legs (2)	1½″ x 3½″ x 13″
F.	Long stretchers (2)	1½″ x 1½″ x 57″
G.	Short stretchers (2)	1½″ x 1½″ x 23″
H.	Back supports (2)	1½″ x 2¾″ x 30⅛″
J.	Back stretcher	1½″ x 2¾″ x 18⅜″
K.	Back braces (2)	1½″ x 2¾″ x 14¼″
L.	Back adjusting rod	1″ dia. x 21⅜″
M.	Axle	1″ dia. x 30″
N.	Wheels (2)	7″ dia. x 1½″
P.	Axle pegs (2)	⅜″ dia. x 2½″
Q.	Slats (11)	¾″ x 5½″ x 21½″
R.	Narrow seat slat	¾″ x 2″ x 21½″
S.	Narrow back slat	¾″ x 3½″ x 21½″

EXPLODED VIEW

HARDWARE

⅜″ x 3½″ Carriage bolts with washers (4)
⅜″ Stop nuts (4)
#14 x 2″ Flathead wood screws (8)
#14 x 3″ Flathead wood screws (20)
1″ Flat washers (4)
12d Nails (4)
8d Finishing nails (½ lb.)

1 Cut all the parts to size.

To make this chaise lounge, you'll need four 2 x 4s, 8′ long; one 2 x 8, 8′ long, three 1 x 6s, 12′ long; and two 1″ dowels, 4′ long. Most of the frame parts can be cut from the 2 x 4s. Cut the wheel stock and the parts for the back frame assembly (supports, stretcher, and braces) from the 2 x 8. Cut the axle 1″-2″ longer than shown, so that you can trim it to fit when the time comes. Don't cut the slats yet; wait until after you've assembled the frame.

Important note: Ordinary construction or "dimension" lumber is not milled to exacting specifications, and often times parts have to be custom fitted, no matter what it says in the Materials List. This is the reason we've asked you to hold off on cutting the slats.

2 Cut the long rabbets in the sides and end.

Cut a rabbet ¾″ deep and ¾″ wide along the inside top edges of the sides and the end. Cut this joint on your table saw, making two passes over the blade. Adjust the blade and the rip fence, and make the first cut in the face of the stock. (See Figure 1.) Turn the board on its edge, and make the second cut. (See Figure 2.)

When cutting a rabbet in this manner, be careful of two things. First of all, use push sticks and featherboards to help keep your hands clear of the saw blade. This is especially important, since you have to remove the saw guard to make these cuts. Secondly, set up your saw so that you can make the second pass without leaving the waste in between the saw and the fence. If you make this mistake, the waste will kick back.

1/Make the rabbets in the sides and end in two cuts. First, cut the face of the stock...

2/Then cut the edge. On the second cut, be careful not to leave the waste in between the saw blade and the rip fence. If you do, it will kick back.

3 Cut the frame joinery in the legs, sides, and back supports.

Mount a dado cutter on your table saw or radial arm saw and adjust the height to cut halfway through the thickness of a standard 2 x 4, or ¾″ deep. Carefully mark the dadoes and end rabbets in the legs, sides, and back supports. Cut each joint, making several passes over the cutter to remove all the waste. Remember that the sides should be *mirror images* of each other.

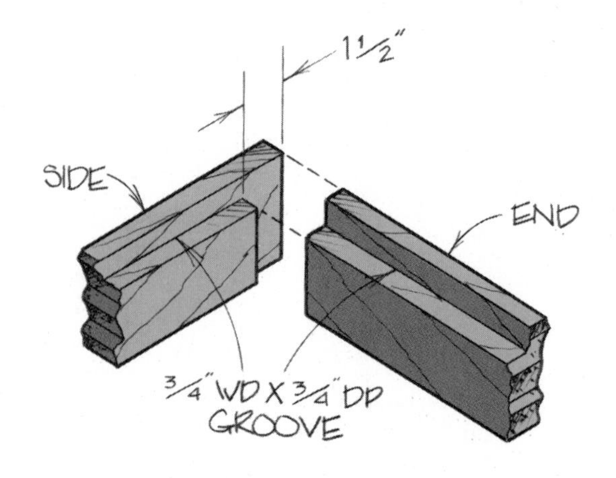

FRAME JOINERY

4 **Make the back stop notches in the sides.**

This chaise is designed so that you can adjust the back to four different positions. To do this, the back adjusting rod can be moved to one of four different stops or notches cut in each side. (See Figure 3.) To make these notches, first lay them out on the sides. Then drill a series of 1″-diameter holes, ¾″ deep, to rough out each notch. (See Figure 4.) Clean up the edges of the notches with a chisel. (See Figure 5.)

As shown in the working drawings, the notches are 1″ wide. Since most commercially milled 1″-diameter dowels are actually a little less than 1″ in diameter, the back adjusting rod should fit in each notch with a little slop. At least, that's the theory. In building the chaise, we found that the practice was another matter. Most of the notches needed to be enlarged slightly.

Note, too, that the end notches are curved slightly. When the back adjusting rod fits into these notches, the back lays flat. Because the back braces and the rod are folded up into the back frame, the path of the rod as it drops into place is a large arc. This arc is so large that you can cut the end notches straight, if you want to. Then, after assembling the back frame, you'll probably have to chisel some extra stock off the sides of these notches so the rod doesn't bind.

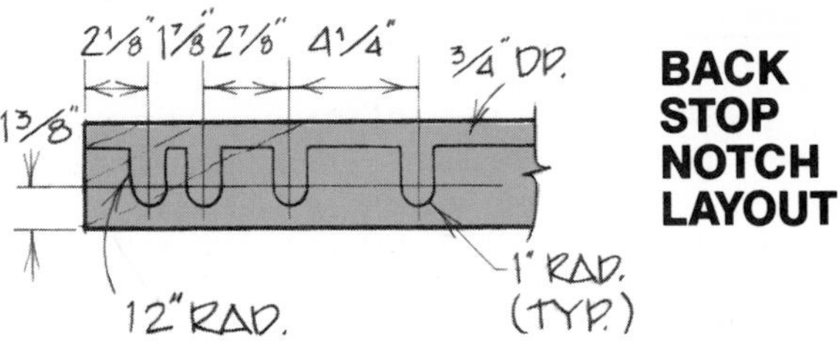

BACK STOP NOTCH LAYOUT

4*/To make each notch, drill a series of 1″ holes, ¾″ deep...*

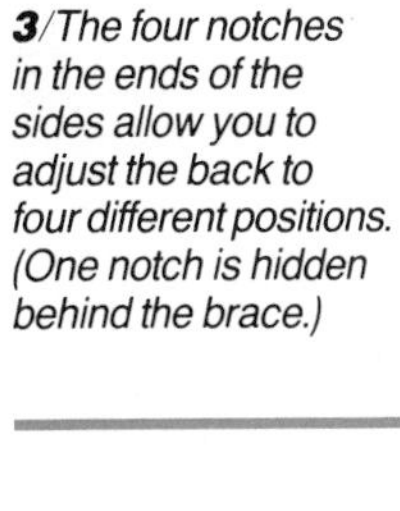

3*/The four notches in the ends of the sides allow you to adjust the back to four different positions. (One notch is hidden behind the brace.)*

5*/Then clean up the edges of the notch with a chisel.*

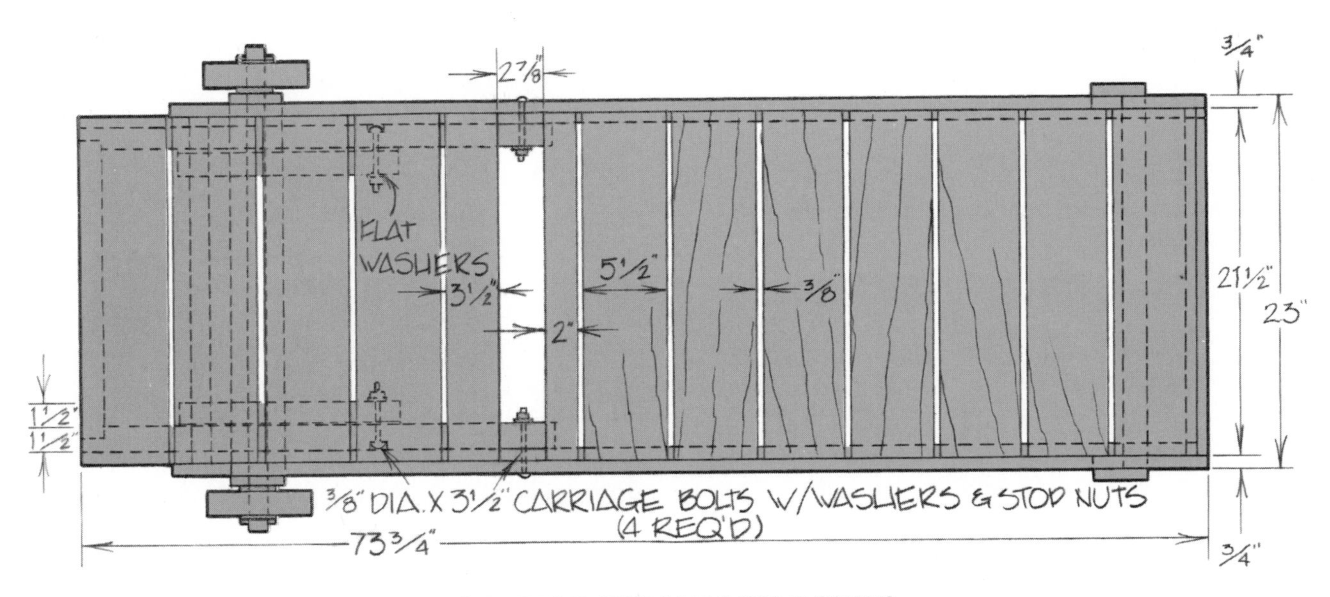

TOP VIEW (WITH BACK DOWN)

5 Cut the shapes of the back supports and back braces.

Using a band saw or a sabre saw, round both ends of the back braces, and the lower ends of the back supports. Sand away any saw marks.

Lay out the notches in the back supports for the back adjusting rod. *Don't* make these notches straight. The arc is sufficiently small so that the adjusting rod won't just bind up when you try to swing it into the notches. It won't fit into straight notches at all. Mark the arcs, using the location of the bolt holes (where you will attach the back braces to the supports) as a pivot. Drill 1″-diameter holes through the boards to make the base of these notches, then remove the rest of the waste from the notches with a band saw or sabre saw.

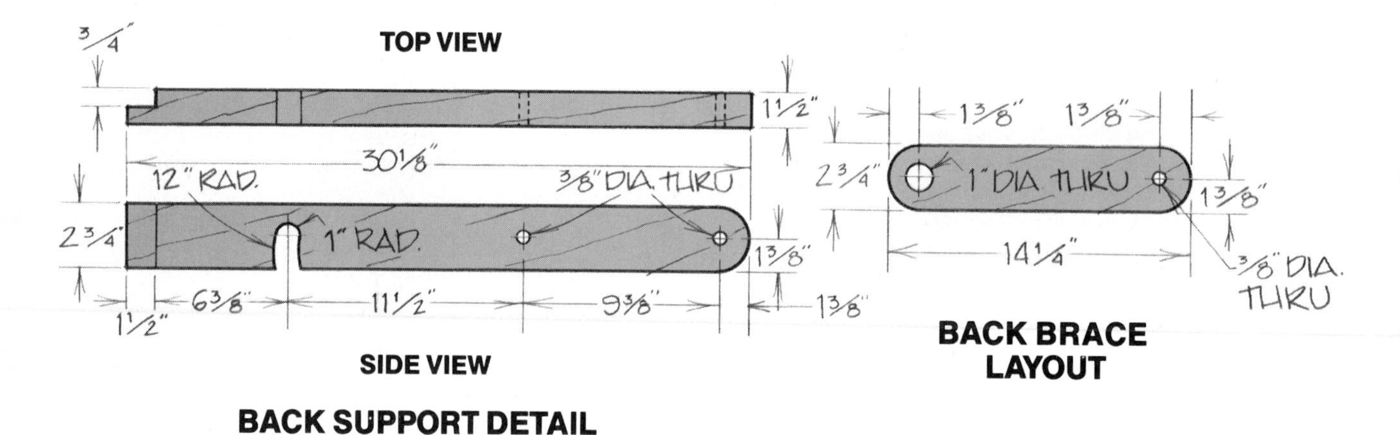

6 Drill the holes needed in the sides, back supports, back braces, and short legs.

Drill 1″-diameter holes through the back braces and short legs, where shown in the working drawings, for the back adjusting rod and the axle. Drill 3/8″-diameter holes through the sides, back supports, and back braces for the pivot bolts.

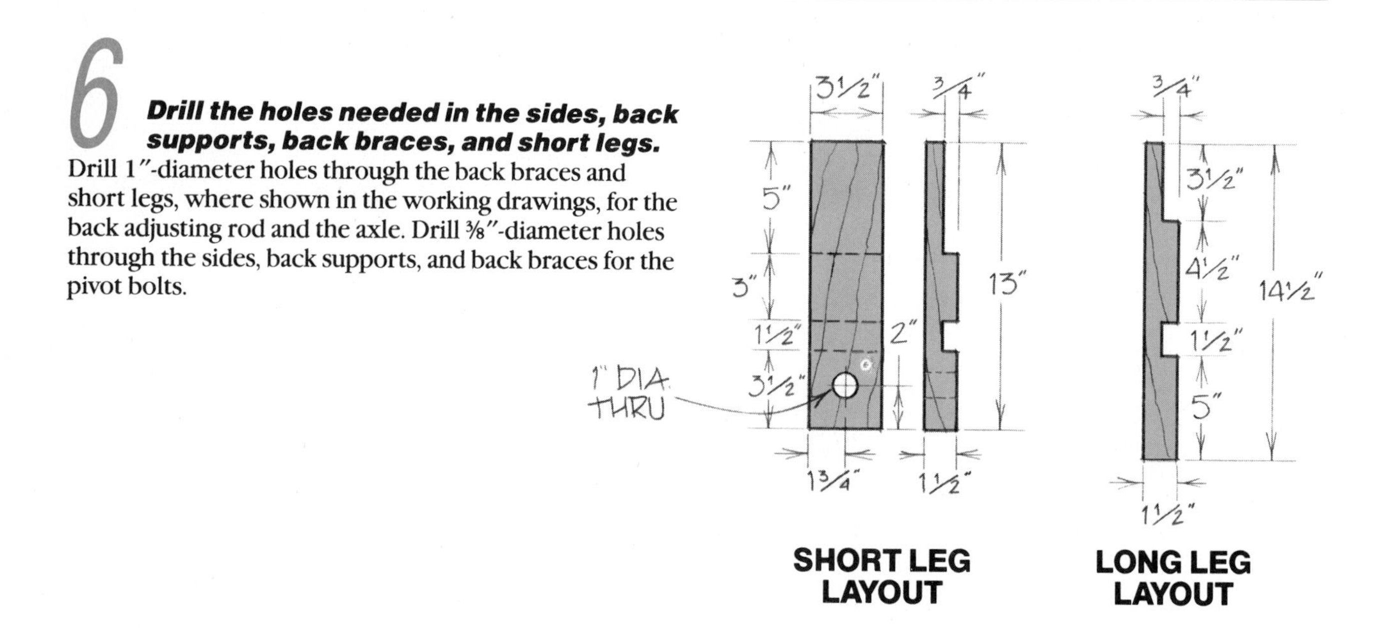

7 Finish sand the frame parts.

Sand all the surfaces of all the parts you've made for the frame, smoothing the wood and removing any irregularities. If you plan to paint or stain the chaise, now would be a good time to apply the first coat.

8 Assemble the chaise frame.

Nail the short stretchers to the long stretchers, making a rectangular frame. Attach the sides to the end with 3″-long wood screws. Then clamp the legs and the brace in place, joining the stretcher frame and the side-end assembly. When you're satisfied that all the parts are properly positioned and square to each other, secure the legs and the brace with screws. Use 2″-long wood screws wherever you're joining long grain to long grain, such as the leg-to-side joints, and 3″ long screws wherever you're joining long grain to end grain, such as the leg-to-brace and leg-to-stretcher joints.

9 Assemble the back frame.

Join the back supports to the back stretcher with 3″-long wood screws. Put the back adjusting rod through the 1″-diameter holes in the back braces and carefully position the braces along the rod. The braces should be 2¼″ from the ends of the rod. Keep the braces in place by driving a finishing nail through the end of each brace and into the rod.

Bolt the back frame to the chaise frame, and secure the bolts with stop nuts. The special nuts will keep the bolts from coming loose when you adjust the position of the back. Tighten the nuts so that the joints just begin to bind.

WARNING! The nuts and bolts that hold the back to the chaise *must* be tight enough so that if you adjust the position of the backrest and let go before you have the back brace in place, the backrest will not fall down. They shouldn't be so tight that they prevent you from moving the backrest, but they should be tight enough so that the parts bind slightly. This will prevent you from accidentally mashing your fingers. The tightness of these nuts and bolts may have to be readjusted periodically.

Bolt the brace-rod assembly to the back frame in the same manner that you attached the back frame to the chaise frame. Check the action of the back, and make sure that the adjusting rod fits easily into all the stop notches. If it binds at any position, remove some stock from the sides of the appropriate notches with a rasp or a chisel.

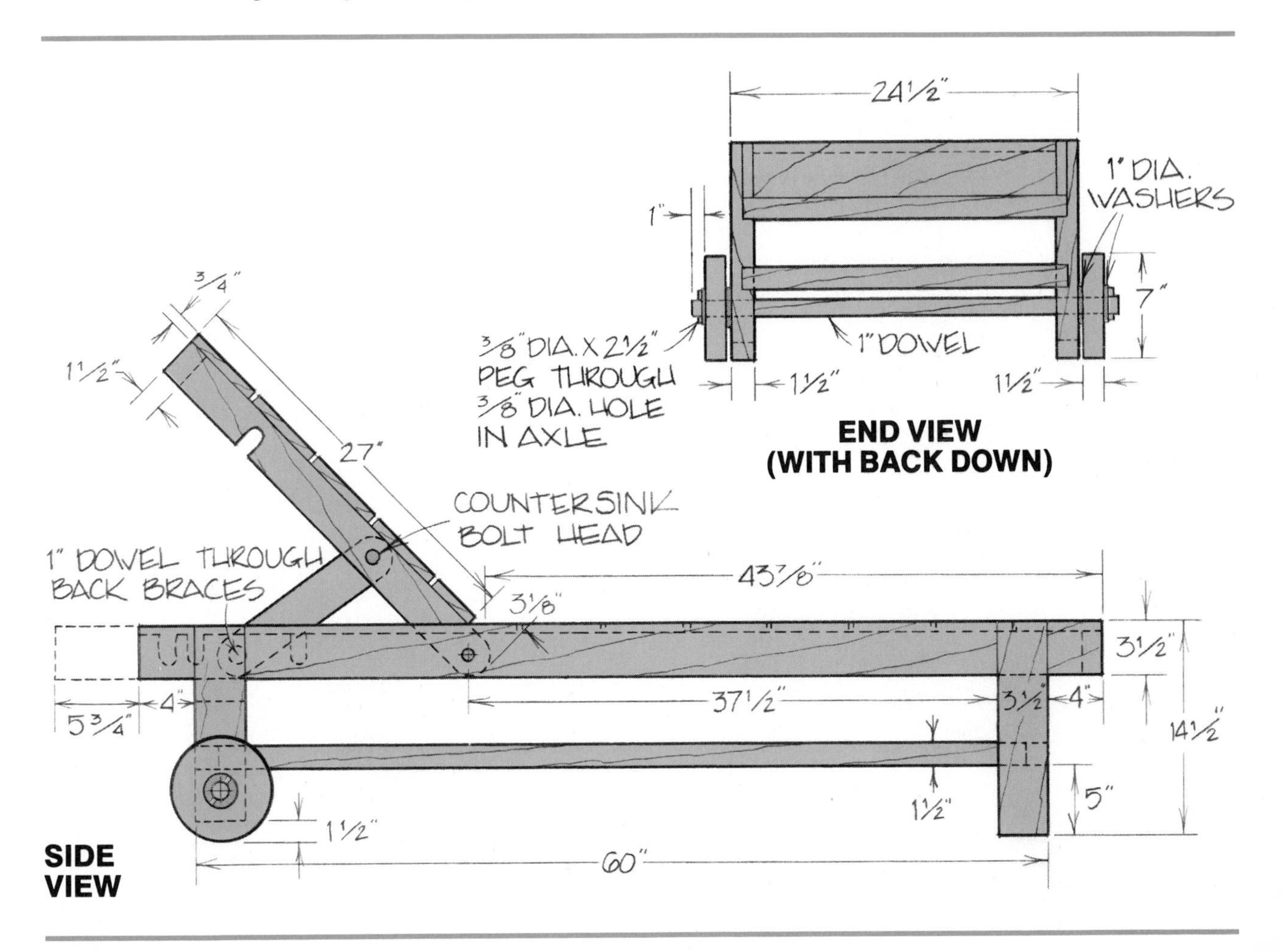

10 Attach the slats to the frame.

Measure the distance between the sides and across the back supports, all along the length of the frame. Don't be alarmed if the distance varies as much as ¼" in spots. This is a common problem when you build with dimension lumber, no matter how carefully you pick your stock. Construction grade lumber is often very wet (as much as 30% moisture content), and the wood constantly changes shape as the water evaporates in your shop.

Cut the slats to fit the frame, and tack them in place with finishing nails. Nail the back slats to the back supports, but be careful *not* to nail them to the sides. *Don't* drive the nails home just yet. First, check the action of the back to be sure the slats don't interfere. Also, check that the spacing of the slats is even and adjust their positions, if needed. When you're satisfied that everything fits and works as it should, drive the nails home and set them slightly below the surface.

11 Attach the wheels to the chaise.

Cut out the wheels with a band saw or sabre saw, and drill 1"-diameter holes through the middle. Insert the axle through the axle holes in the short legs. Place 1"-diameter washers on either end of the axle, then the wheels, then another set of washers. (These washers prevent the wooden wheels from rubbing against the pegs and legs.)

Mark the outside edge of the outside washers, on either end of the axle. Measure 1" out from these marks to mark the trimmed length of the axle. Disassemble the washers, wheels, and axle from the chaise, and trim the axle to length. Drill the ends for ⅜"-diameter pegs. (These peg holes should be 1/16" beyond the marks for the outside edge of the washers. This will give the wheels a little play on the axles, but not too much.)

Apply a little paste wax to the inside of the holes in the wheels to help them turn smoothly. Then reassemble the axle, wheels, and washers. Glue the pegs in their holes with waterproof glue to keep the wheels on the axle.

12 Sand and finish the chaise.

Sand the completed chaise lounge, rounding any hard edges. Pay particular attention to the slats — you want these to be as smooth as possible when you rest on them. Once the chaise is as smooth as you want it, apply another coat of finish, if you've decided to do so. Avoid finishes that build up on the surface of the wood, such as spar varnish. These will interfere with the action of the back.

Avoiding Splinters

Splinters are the bane of outdoor furniture projects. Outdoor furniture is more likely to throw splinters than any other type of woodworking project because it's left out in the weather where new checks and splits — the defects in wood that throw splinters — develop constantly. You cannot absolutely "splinter-proof" your outdoor furniture. However, you can decrease the risk of splinters by following a few simple guidelines:

- *Use a good grade of lumber.* Choose stock that is relatively free from defects — cracks, case hardening, loose knots, any irregularity where water can soak into the interior of the wood.
- *Sand the end grain smooth.* Next to defects, a board is most likely to throw splinters from a cut end. Sand the end grain that will be exposed on the finished project perfectly smooth. Water will run off sanded end grain, since it cannot cling in the saw marks. There is less swelling at the cut ends, and fewer checks and splits develop.
- *"Break" or round over all hard corners and edges.* After you've completed the project, round the corners with a rasp, block plane, or sandpaper. Rounding the corners helps the water to run off and helps absorb impacts so that the wood is less likely to chip or split.
- *Store your outdoor furniture in an outdoor environment.* Store outdoor furniture on a covered patio, in your garage, or in a storage barn. If you bring it inside your home, the extreme change in temperature and humidity will distort the wood and cause it to check and split.

Knock-Down Planter

The wedged mortise and tenon was a favorite device of many country cabinetmakers. There was little chance that furniture made with these joints would fall apart. If the piece seemed a little wobbly, you just knocked the wedges in a little tighter to "snug up" the parts.

The wedges in this country-style planter serve a dual purpose. They keep the planter strong and sturdy, even though the wood will constantly shrink and swell out in the summer weather. They also allow you to take the planter apart for easy storage during the winter months. Just remove the wedges and pull the mortises and tenons apart!

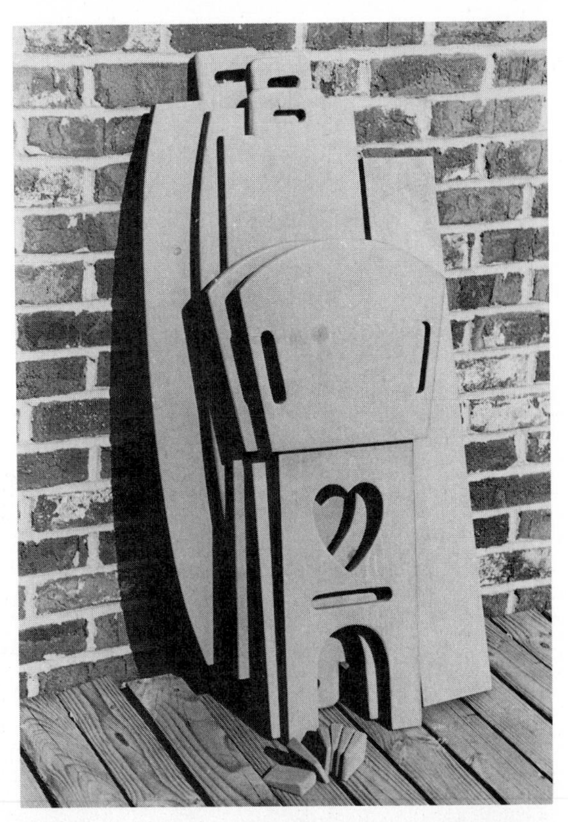

Materials List

FINISHED DIMENSIONS

A.	Ends (2)	¾″ x 11¼″ x 13″
B.	Sides (2)	¾″ x 11¼″ x 36″
C.	Legs (2)	¾″ x 8½″ x 18″
D.	Shelf	¾″ x 8½″ x 34½″
E.	Bottom	¾″ x 5½″ x 30⅞″
F.	Wedges (6)	⅞″ x 1¾″ x 2½″

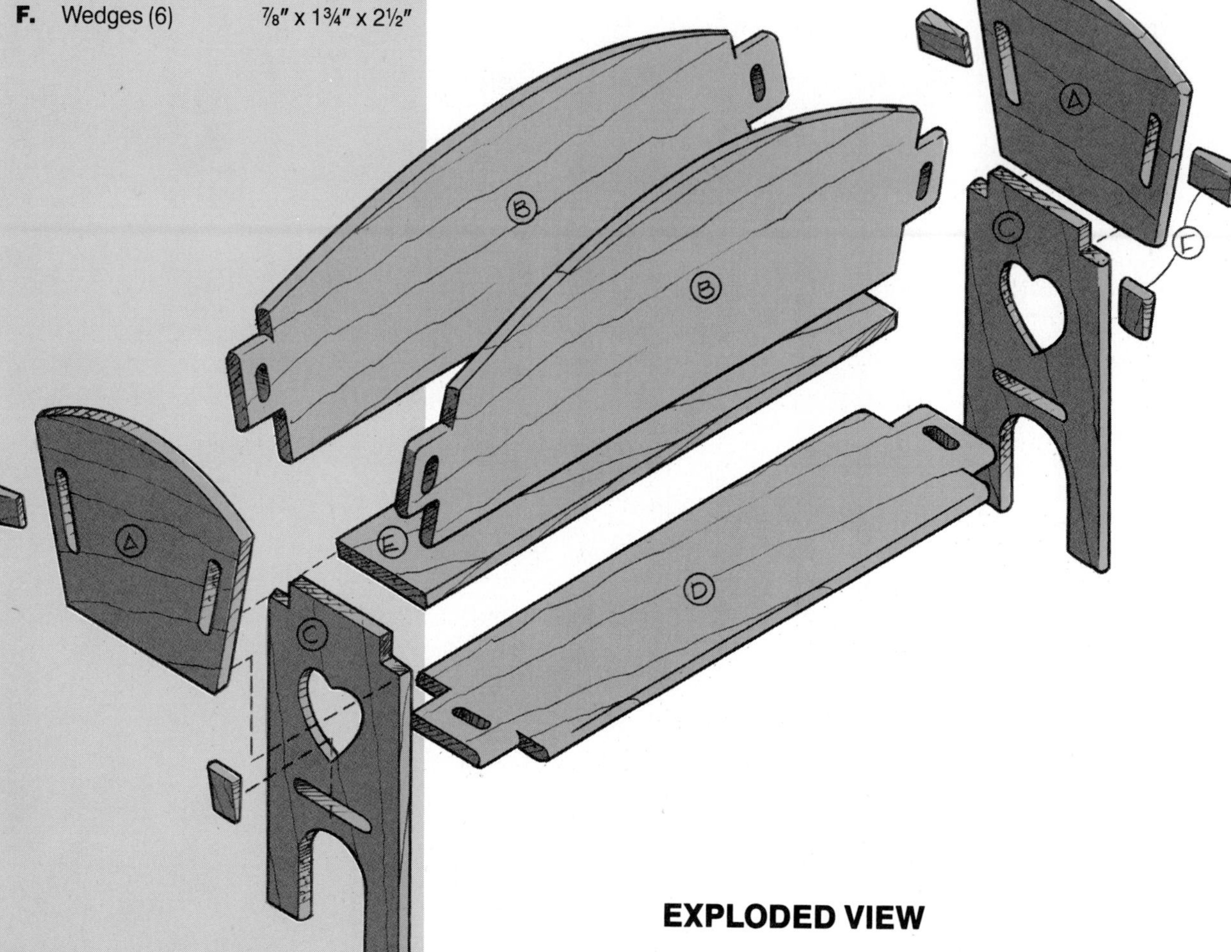

EXPLODED VIEW

HARDWARE

#10 x 1¼″ Flathead wood screws

1

Cut all pieces to size. Rip and cut all the parts to the sizes shown in the Materials List. You may wish to wait before cutting stock for the wedges; these small parts can be cut from the scraps you'll generate when you cut the other parts to shape.

2

Cut the shape of the pieces. Enlarge the patterns and trace them on the various parts that need to be shaped — ends, legs, and sides. Also, lay out the tenons on the sides and shelf. Cut the tenons and curved shapes with a band saw or sabre saw.

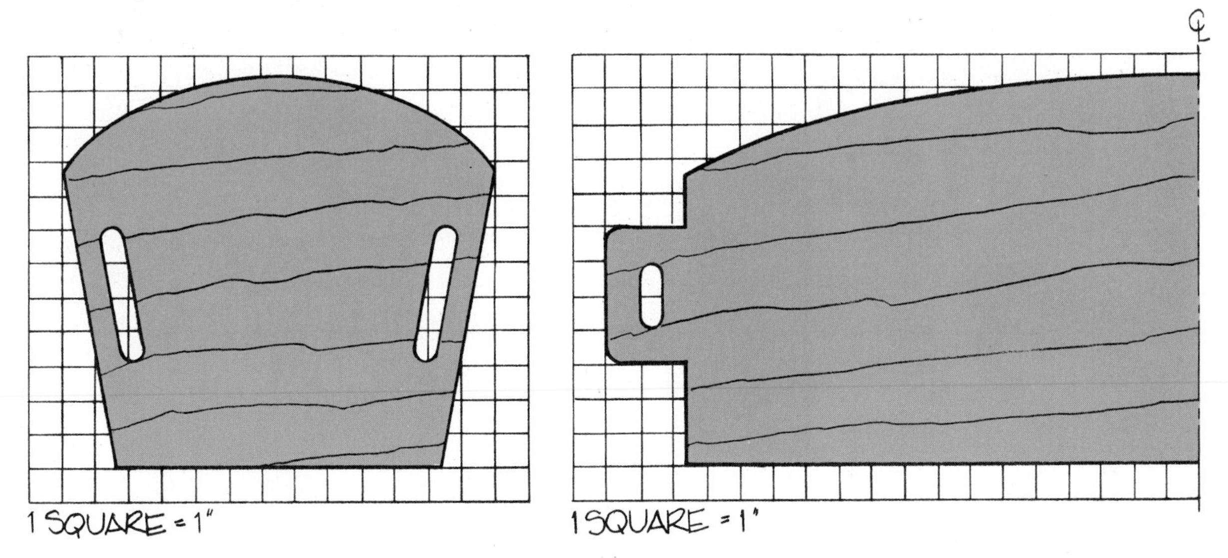

SIDE PATTERNS

3

Cut out the hearts in the legs. To cut out the hearts in the legs, make a "piercing cut." First, drill a ½" diameter hole *inside* the heart, in the waste. Insert the blade of a sabre saw in this hole, then cut up to the pattern line. (See Figure 1.) Follow the pattern line with the saw, staying to the *inside* of the line.

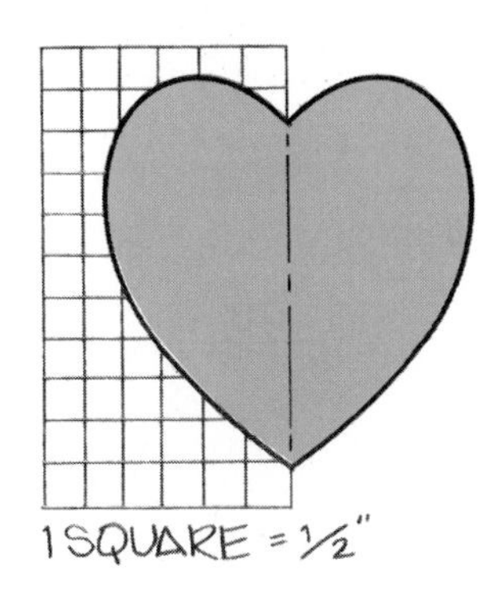

HEART PATTERN

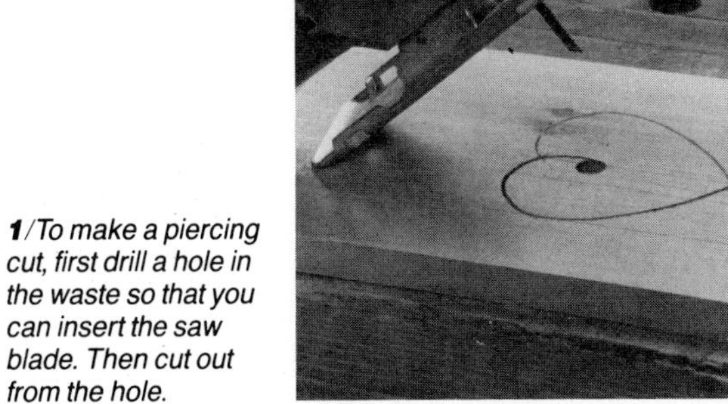

1/*To make a piercing cut, first drill a hole in the waste so that you can insert the saw blade. Then cut out from the hole.*

4 Make the mortises and wedge-slots.

Carefully lay out the position of the mortises and the wedge slots on the various parts. Note that the wedge slots are positioned so that the *inside* edge of the wedge slot will be 1/16″ inside the *outside* surface of the leg or end when the two pieces are assembled.

Drill ¾″ diameter holes at either end of each mortise or wedge-slot. Then remove the waste between the holes with a sabre saw. (See Figure 2.) Clean up the inside edges of the mortises and slots with a rasp.

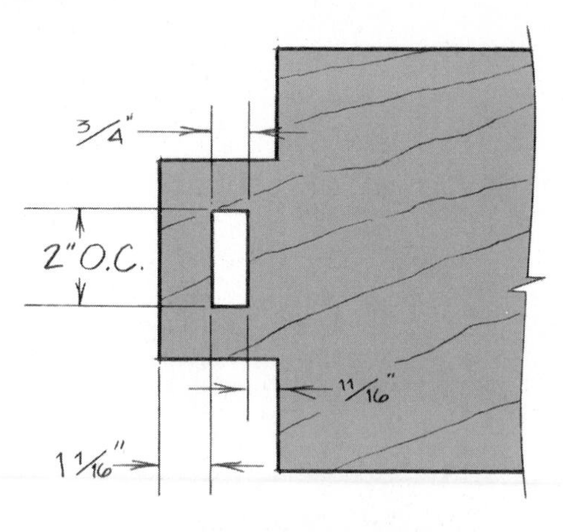

TONGUE LAYOUT

2/When making a mortise, first drill ¾″ diameter holes at either end. Then cut out the waste between the holes.

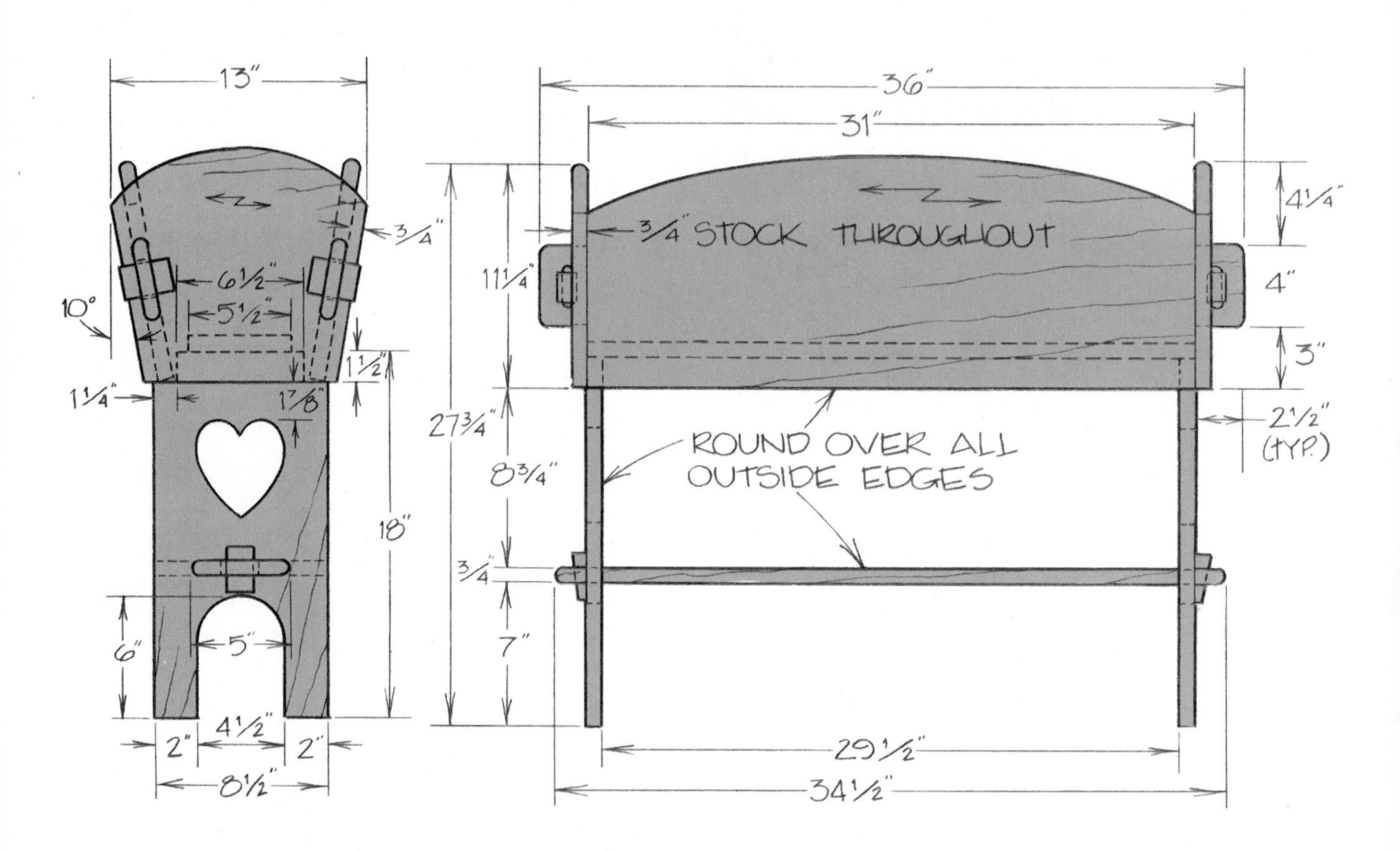

END VIEW **FRONT VIEW**

5 Fit the tenons to the mortises. With a rasp or chisel, round the edges of the tenons to fit the mortises. (See Figure 3.) You may also wish to enlarge the mortises somewhat with a rasp. The fit should be fairly loose, with about 1/16" of "slop."

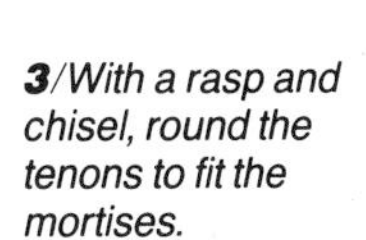

3/With a rasp and chisel, round the tenons to fit the mortises.

6 Make the wedges. On a band saw, carefully taper the wedges as shown in the working drawings. Use a push stick to keep your hands clear of the blade. (See Figure 4.)

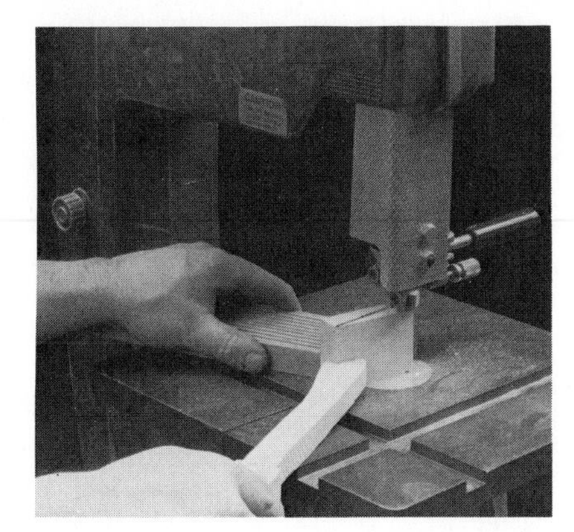

4/When cutting the taper in the wedges, use a push stick to keep your hands clear of the band saw blade.

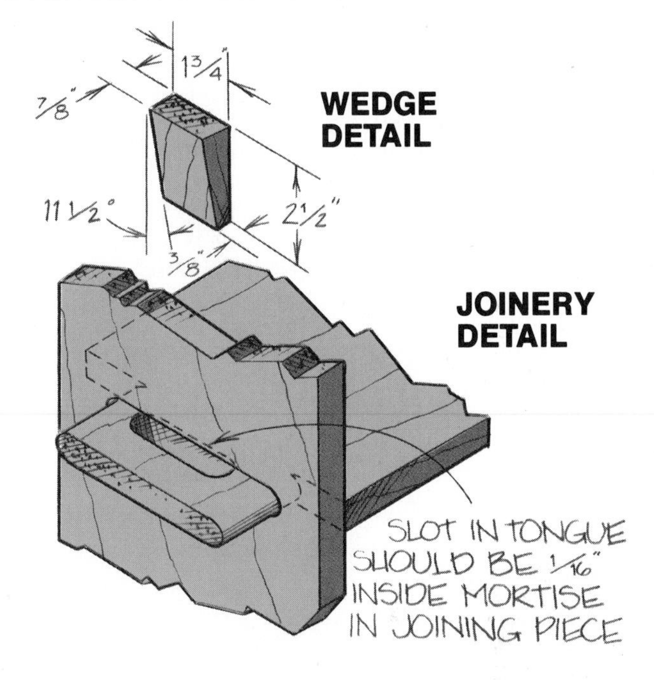

7 Attach the ends and the legs. Carefully center the legs on the inside surfaces of the ends, and clamp the two parts together. Test assemble the sides to the ends, to make sure that the sides don't hit the legs. When you're certain that all the parts will fit together properly, attach the legs to the ends with screws.

8 Sand and assemble all the parts. With a rasp and sandpaper, round over all the edges of all parts, *except* those edges where two parts butt against one another. Insert the tenons into the mortises and wedge them in place; then rest the bottom on the tops of the legs, between the two ends.

9 Finish the planter. Although it's not necessary, this planter looks great with a "milk paint" finish — the milk paint enhances the "country" design. To make an outdoor milk paint, thin exterior latex 1:1 with water. Disassemble the planter; paint the latex on; then wipe the wood down with a damp rag before the paint dries.

Contoured Porch Swing

Have you ever wondered why the gentle motion of rocking or swinging is so relaxing? There are several fascinating theories. Some psychologists say that it awakens pleasant childhood memories of being held and rocked by a parent. Others think that the memories go beyond childhood; that the motion reminds us of being held safe and warm in our mother's womb, rocked by her movements. And still others believe that the regular, repetitive motions are a means of mild self-hypnosis, whereby we lull ourselves into a calmer state of mind.

Whatever the reasons, swinging *is* relaxing. This particular porch swing is more relaxing than most because it's contoured to fit your body. The frame parts hold the slats in a gentle, comfortable curve. There are no hard flat surfaces or sharp angles to disturb your reverie.

Materials List

FINISHED DIMENSIONS

PARTS

	Part	Dimensions
A.	Seat frame (3)	1½″ x 5⅝″ x 23½″
B.	Back frame (3)	1½″ x 6¼″ x 25¼″
C.	Armrests (2)	1½″ x 4¼″ x 22″
D.	Arm supports (2)	1½″ x 4¼″ x 10½″
E.	Long slats (19)	¾″ x 1½″ x 60″
F.	Short slats (3)	¾″ x 1½″ x 58″

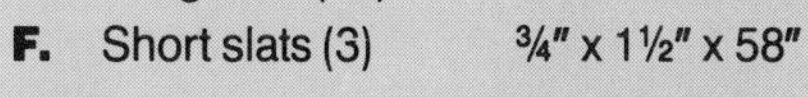

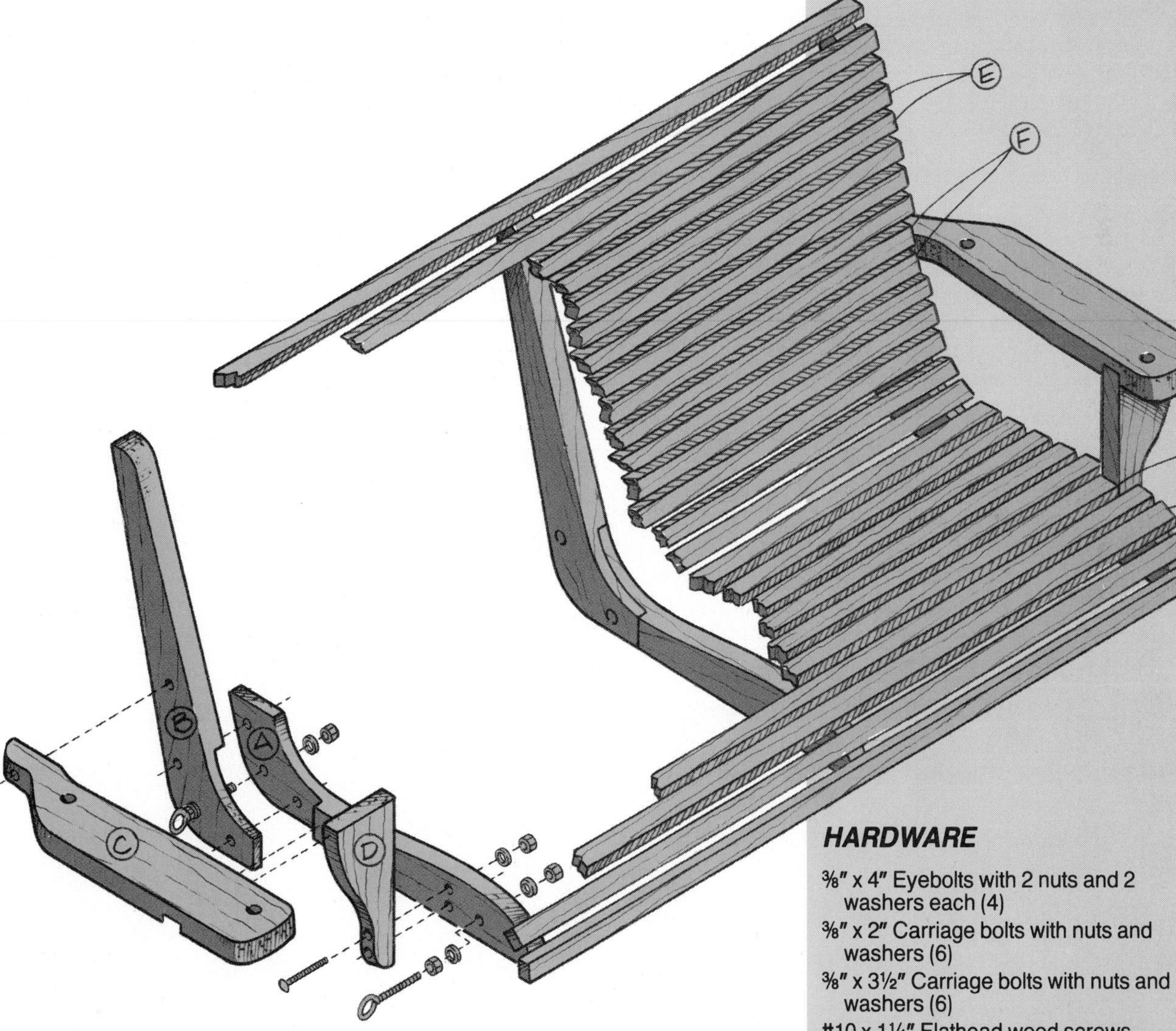

EXPLODED VIEW

HARDWARE

⅜″ x 4″ Eyebolts with 2 nuts and 2 washers each (4)
⅜″ x 2″ Carriage bolts with nuts and washers (6)
⅜″ x 3½″ Carriage bolts with nuts and washers (6)
#10 x 1¼″ Flathead wood screws (6 dozen)
#14 x 3″ Flathead wood screws (4)
Porch swing chain set, with 5′ leaders
2″ S-hooks (6)
⅜″ Screw hooks (2)

1 Cut the frame parts to size. Cut the seat and back frame parts from 2 x 8 stock. Don't contour them at this time, just cut them to length and miter one end at 80°. Also, cut the armrest and arm support parts to length from 2 x 6 stock.

2 Cut the lap joints that join the seat and back frames. Lap the mitered ends so that they form an inside angle of 100°, and their outside edges are flush. Mark the pieces where they cross to guide you when you cut the lap joints. Cut rabbets in the ends, ¾"-deep and 7¼"-wide. Using a dado cutter mounted on your table saw, make each lap in several passes. Remember, these joints must be cut at the same angle as the mitered ends — set your miter gauge at 80°. (See Figure 1.)

1/Using a dado cutter, cut lap joints into the mitered ends of the frame parts.

3 Cut the dadoes in the armrests. While you have the dado cutter set up, cut ¾"-deep, 1½"-wide dadoes in the underside of the armrests. These dadoes will hold the arm supports.

4 Cut the shapes of the frame parts. Temporarily attach the seat and back frame parts with nails. Enlarge the patterns for these parts and trace them on the stock. Then cut the contours with a band saw or sabre saw. (See Figure 2.) While you're at it, cut the shapes of the armrests and arm supports. Remember that the two armrests should be mirror images of each other. Sand all parts to remove the saw marks.

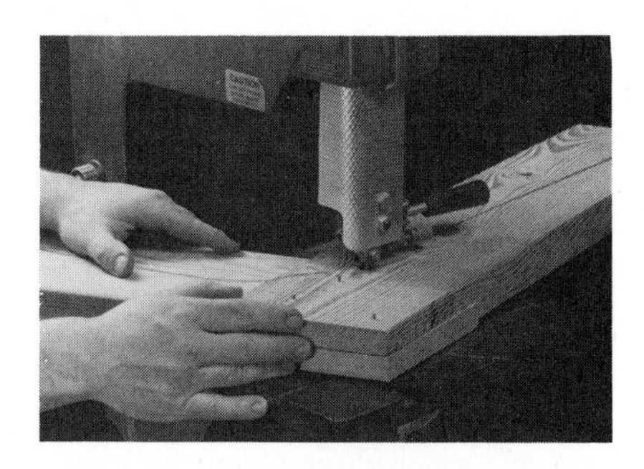

2/With the seat and back parts temporarily nailed together, cut the contours with a band saw or sabre saw.

TRY THIS! Use a disc sander to sand the convex curves on the porch swing frame parts... and a drum sander to sand the concave curves. This makes short work of the sanding chores.

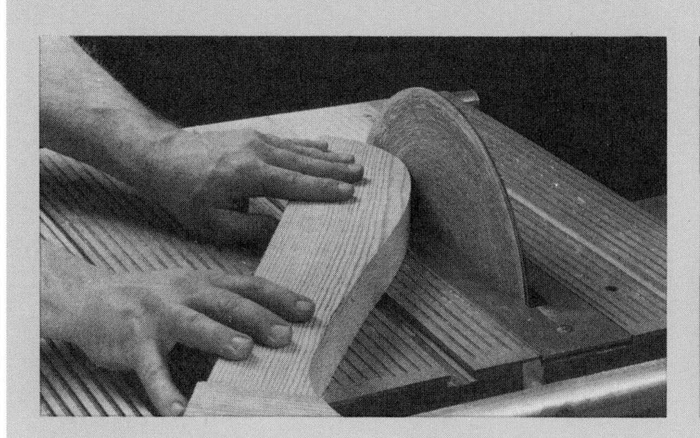

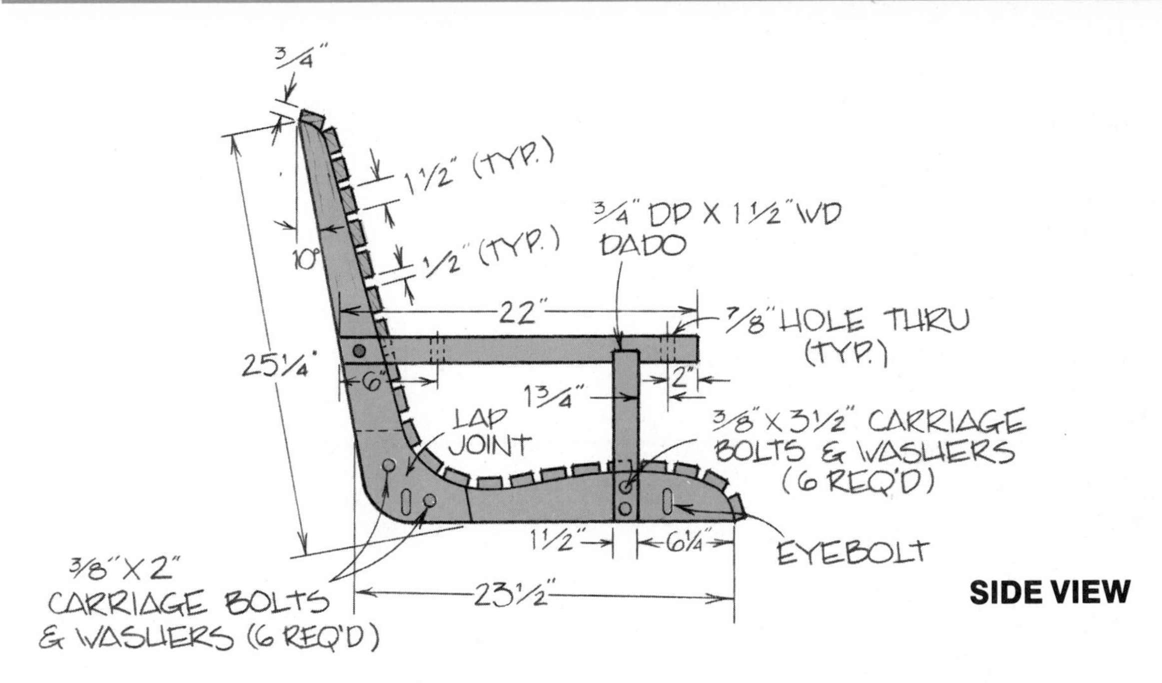

SIDE VIEW

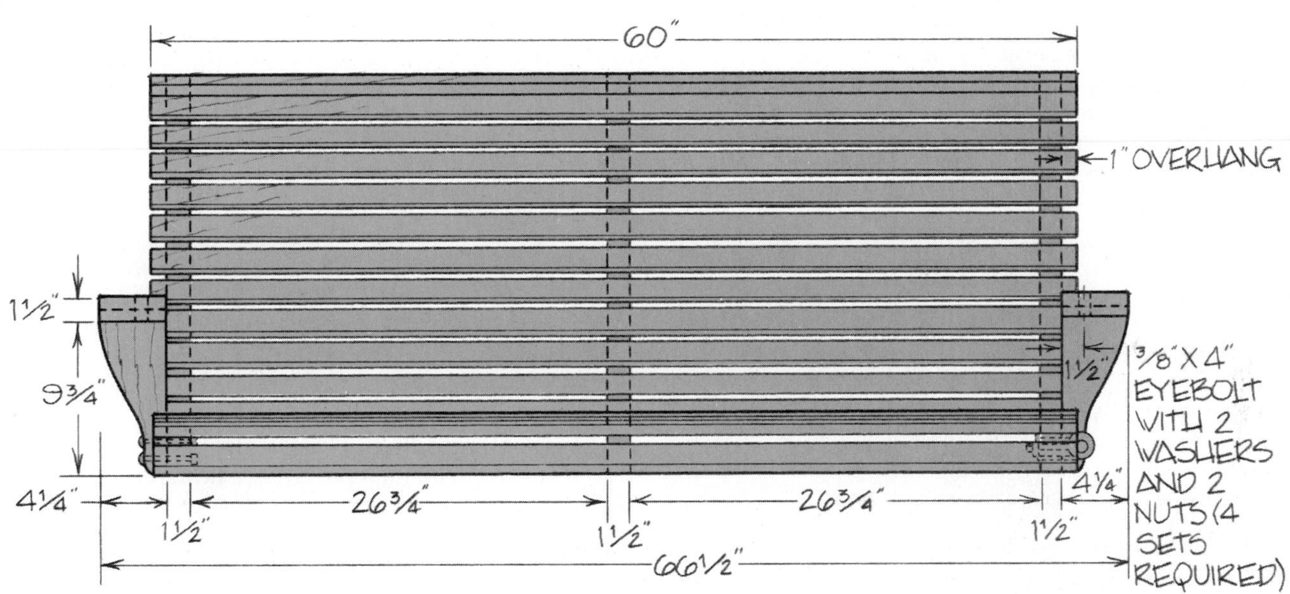

FRONT VIEW

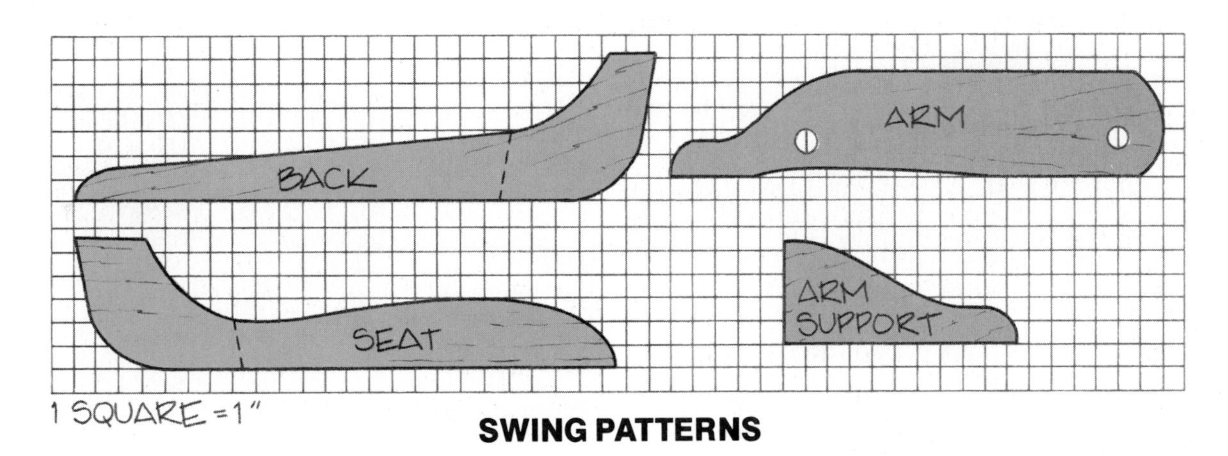

SWING PATTERNS

5 Bolt and screw the frame parts together.

While the seat and back frame parts are still nailed together, drill ⅜″ bolt holes, as shown in the *Side View.* Also, drill the holes for the eyebolts at this time, even though you won't mount the eyebolts until later on. Bolt the parts together with 2″-long carriage bolts and remove the nails.

Drill the chain holes in the armrests, then screw the armrests to the arm supports with 3″-long screws. Once again, remember that these assemblies should be mirror images of each other. Position the arm assemblies on the frame assemblies; then drill bolt holes where shown in the drawings. Bolt the assemblies together with 3½″-long carriage bolts.

TRY THIS! When you install each bolt, put a flat washer over the threaded end, then a lock washer, and finally a nut. The *lock washer* will keep the nut from working loose.

6 Cut the slats and attach them to the frame.

Rip the slats from ¾″-thick stock, and joint the edges to remove the saw marks. To help position the slats on the frame, make a paper "story tape". Cut a strip of paper 1″ wide and 48″ long and coat the back with spray adhesive or rubber cement. Apply this tape to the contour of the frame, then trim it to the exact length of the contour. Remove the tape and measure its length. Divide the length into twenty-two 1½″-wide sections, with equal spaces between each section. (The spaces should be *approximately* ½″ wide.) Stick the story tape to each of the frame assemblies and use it to mark the location of the slats. (See Figure 3.)

Once the assemblies are marked, temporarily nail the slats to them. Don't hammer the nails all the way home, so that you can easily remove them later on. Start by attaching a middle slat, somewhere in the curve between the seat and the back. Next, attach the two end slats. Finally, fill in with the rest. Use short slats where the arm assemblies bolt to the frame. (See Figure 4.)

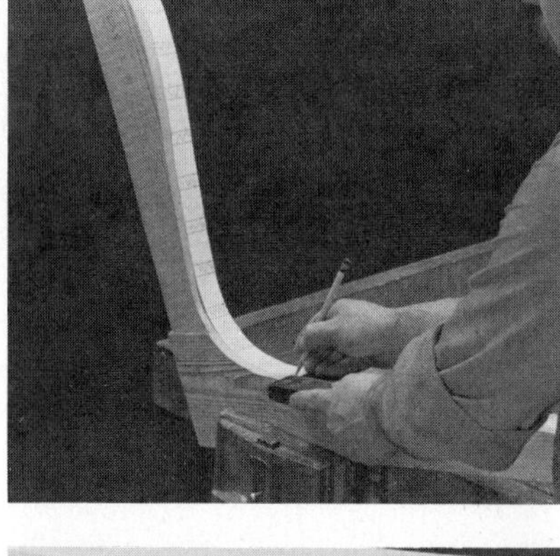

3/Make a paper story tape to help mark the position of the slats on the frame assemblies. Stick this tape to the wood with spray adhesive or rubber cement.

TRY THIS! Use *finishing* nails when temporarily attaching parts, prior to bolting or screwing them together. Finishing nails leave smaller holes, and they aren't as likely to split the wood.

Once you have nailed the slats to the frame, and you're satisfied with their position, remove the nails and replace them with screws. Countersink *and* counterbore these screws, then cover the heads with wooden plugs. (See Figure 5.) Also, cover the heads of the screws in the arm assemblies. Cement the plugs in place with waterproof glue.

4/Use short slats where the arm assemblies bolt to the frame.

5/Cover the heads of the screws with wooden plugs. Cut these plugs from scrap wood, and cement them in place with waterproof glue.

7 Finish sand the completed swing.

Round over the hard corners of the armrests and any other sharp edges that might rub you the wrong way when you sit on the swing. Sand the wooden plugs flush with the surface of the slats.

8 Mount the swing.

Attach eyebolts to the frame where shown in the *Side View* and *Front View*. Thread the leaders of the porch swing chains through the holes in the armrests, and attach them to the eyebolts with S-hooks. Mount screw hooks to the underside of a porch joist or tree limb, and attach the other ends of the chain to these hooks.

Option: If you don't have a porch or a tree from which to hang the porch swing, make a simple frame from 2 x 4's and 2 x 6's, as we show here. Position the frame in your yard, and stake it down with #4 rebar so that it won't blow over.

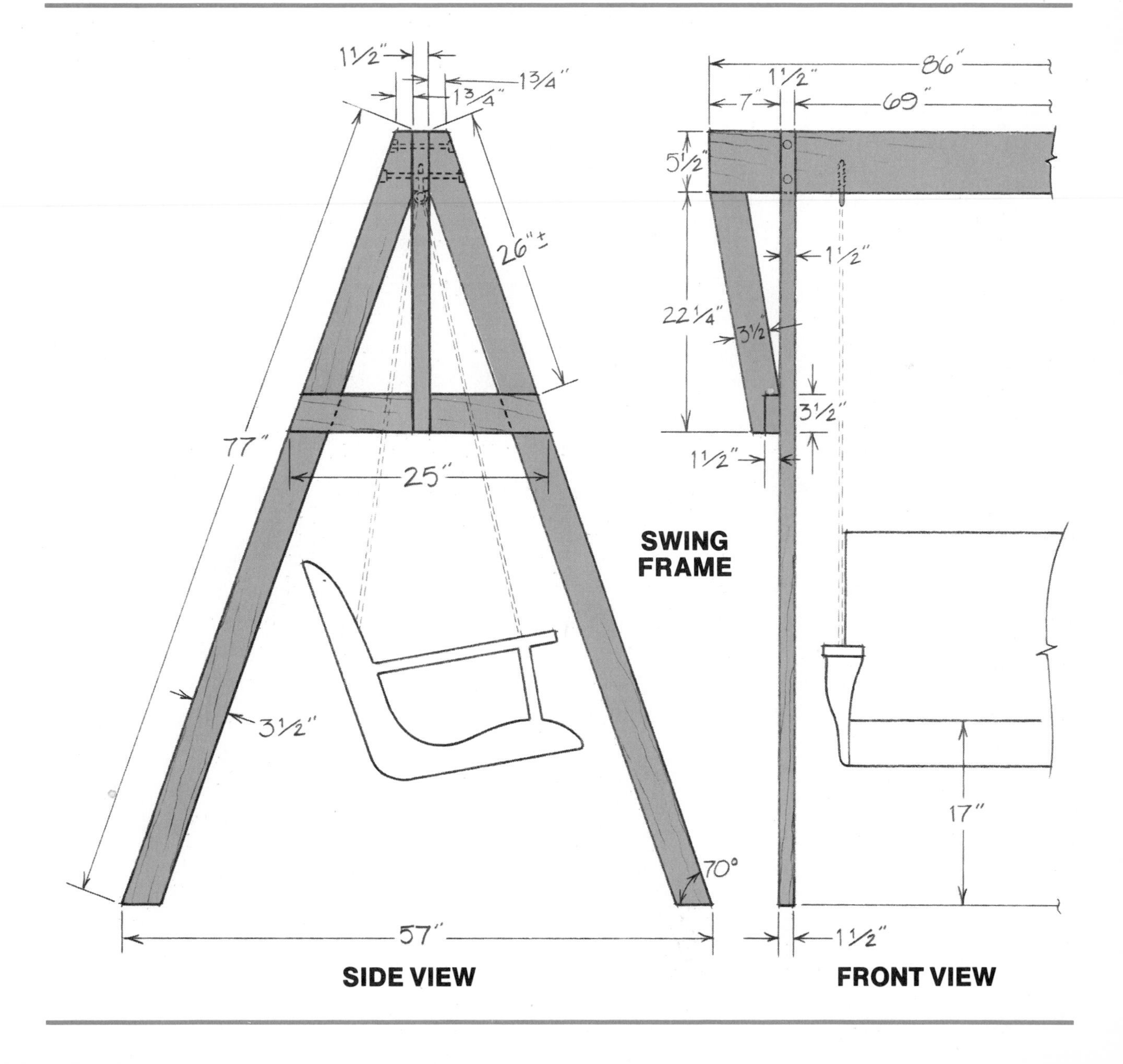

Backyard Cart

No matter what the area of your home, if you spend any time there at all, you need a workstation to make it truly livable. In a kitchen, you need countertops. A workshop requires a workbench; a bedroom, a dresser. Even in the backyard, it helps to have a good cart.

This backyard cart is designed to serve many different functions. Standing next to a barbecue grill, it becomes an outdoor kitchen. In the garden, it's a potting table. If you're in the midst of an outdoor building project, it's a portable workbench. Not only does it offer a big work surface, there are drawers and shelves for storage. And it can be rolled around like a wheelbarrow to wherever it's needed.

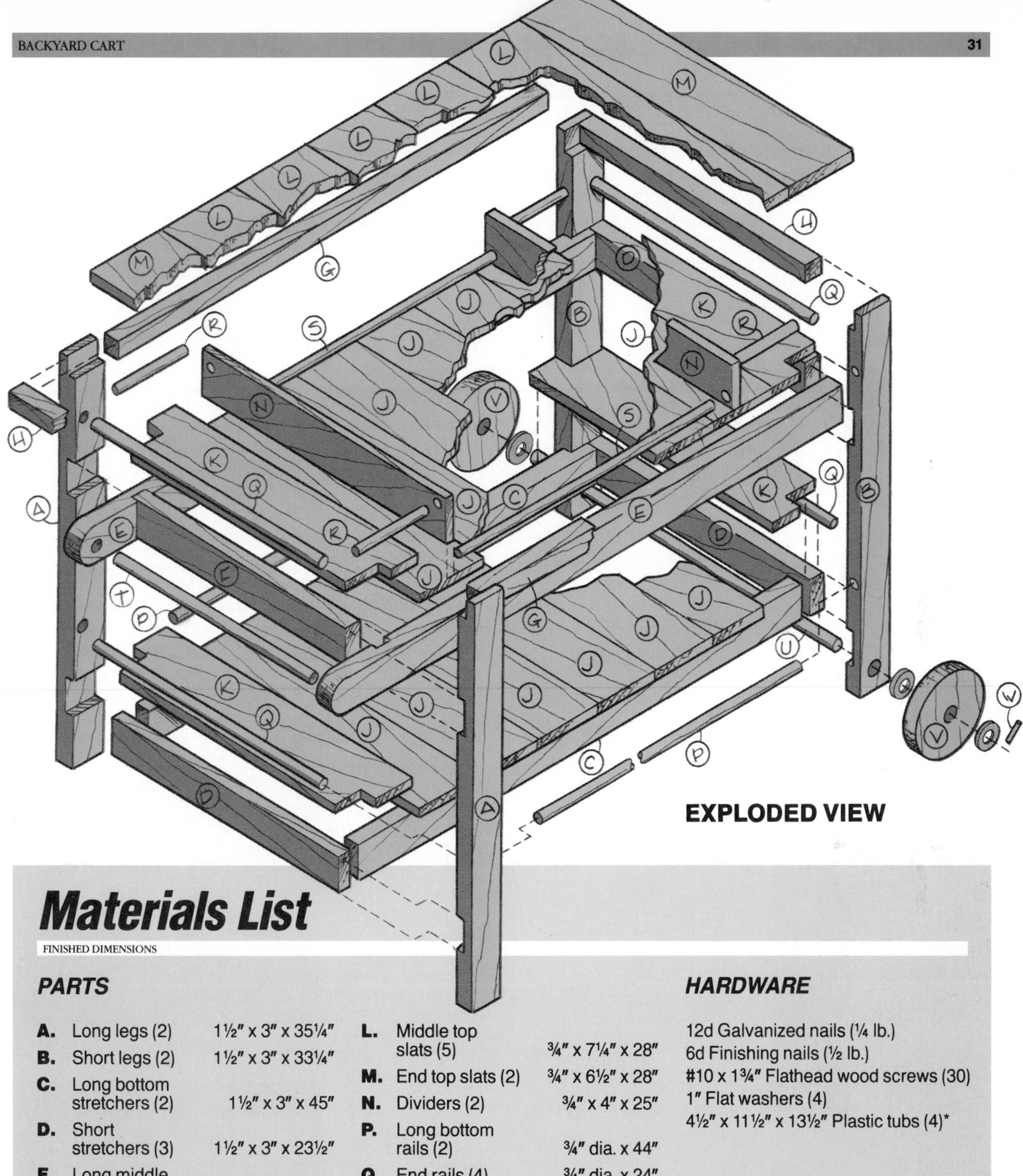

Materials List

FINISHED DIMENSIONS

PARTS

	Part	Dimensions
A.	Long legs (2)	1½″ x 3″ x 35¼″
B.	Short legs (2)	1½″ x 3″ x 33¼″
C.	Long bottom stretchers (2)	1½″ x 3″ x 45″
D.	Short stretchers (3)	1½″ x 3″ x 23½″
E.	Long middle stretchers (2)	1½″ x 3″ x 52½″
F.	Shortest stretcher	1½″ x 3″ x 22″
G.	Long aprons (2)	1½″ x 1½″ x 45″
H.	Short aprons (2)	1½″ x 1½″ x 23½″
J.	Middle shelf slats (10)	¾″ x 7¼″ x 25″
K.	End shelf slats (4)	¾″ x 5½″ x 25″
L.	Middle top slats (5)	¾″ x 7¼″ x 28″
M.	End top slats (2)	¾″ x 6½″ x 28″
N.	Dividers (2)	¾″ x 4″ x 25″
P.	Long bottom rails (2)	¾″ dia. x 44″
Q.	End rails (4)	¾″ dia. x 24″
R.	Short middle rails (4)	¾″ dia. x 6⅞″
S.	Long middle rails (2)	¾″ dia. x 30¼″
T.	Handle	1″ dia. x 22½″
U.	Axle	1″ dia. x 30½″
V.	Wheels (2)	7″ dia. x 1½″
W.	Pegs (2)	⅜″ dia. x 2″

HARDWARE

12d Galvanized nails (¼ lb.)
6d Finishing nails (½ lb.)
#10 x 1¾″ Flathead wood screws (30)
1″ Flat washers (4)
4½″ x 11½″ x 13½″ Plastic tubs (4)*

*If this size tub is not available, you may have to buy something similar and adjust the height of the middle shelf and the position of the dividers to fit.

1 Cut all the parts to size. Choose good, clear lumber for the legs, stretchers, and aprons. Purchase lumber one or two notches above the normal construction grade. Also, look for lumber that has been properly kiln-dried, so it won't warp or twist. You'll find it isn't all that expensive when all you need are small amounts.

Cut all the parts to the sizes shown in the Materials List, and joint the boards where you've ripped them to remove the saw marks. Don't rip the end slats to width just yet. The true measurements of dimension lumber vary somewhat from board to board, and these parts will have to be custom fitted after you nail down the other slats.

---

2 Fashion the legs and stretchers. Carefully mark the dadoes and rabbets on the legs. To get all four legs exactly the same, line them up side by side on your workbench and mark across them. (See Figure 1.) Also, mark the dadoes on the long middle stretchers.

Mount a dado cutter on your table saw or radial arm saw, and adjust it to cut a ¾″-deep dado. Cut each dado or rabbet joint in several passes. (See Figure 2.) If you use a radial arm saw, cut by pushing the blade *away* from you. If you cut with the normal sawing motion, pulling the blade toward you, the cutter will tend to "climb" the stock.

Drill 1″-diameter holes for the axle in the short legs. (You can get by with 1″-diameter axle holes, even though you're using 1″-diameter dowels for the axles, because most large dowels shrink somewhat after they're milled. You'll find that, on the average, store-bought 1″-diameter hardwood dowels are actually closer to 15/16″ in diameter.) Also drill 1″-diameter *stopped* holes in the long middle stretchers for the handle, and ¾″-diameter stopped holes in all the legs to hold the rails.

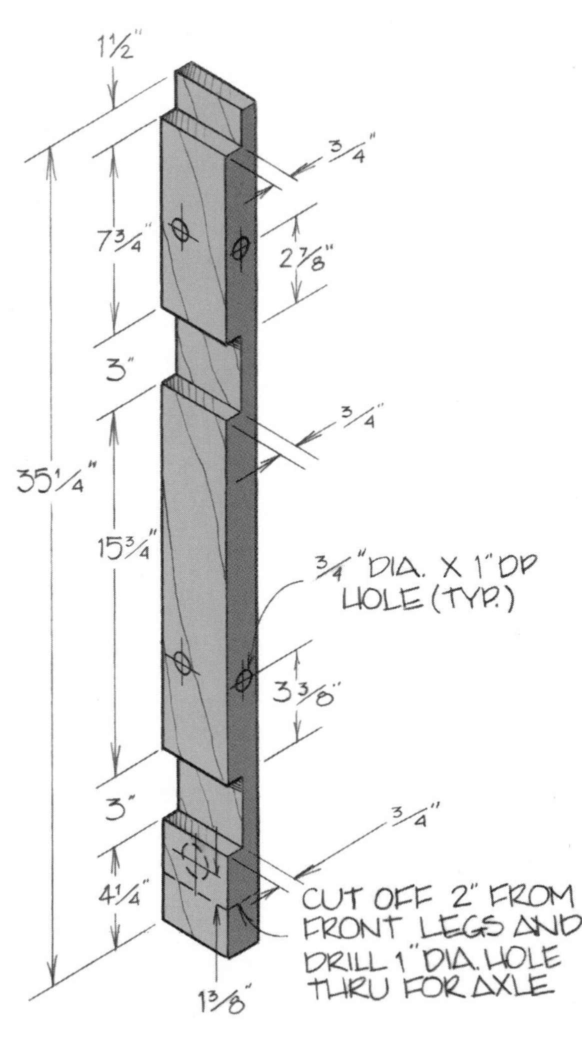

LEG LAYOUT

1/To position the dadoes and rabbets precisely the same on all four legs, line the legs up side by side and mark them all at the same time.

2/Cut the dadoes and rabbets with a dado cutter. Each joint will require several passes over the cutter.

3 **_Sand the parts._** Sand and smooth the surfaces of the parts you have made. Do not round the edges just yet. Do that later, after you have assembled the project.

4 **_Assemble the apron and stretcher frames._** Nail the bottom stretcher frame, middle stretcher frame, and apron frame together with 12d nails. Be sure to insert the handle in between the long middle stretchers *before* you nail the middle frame together.

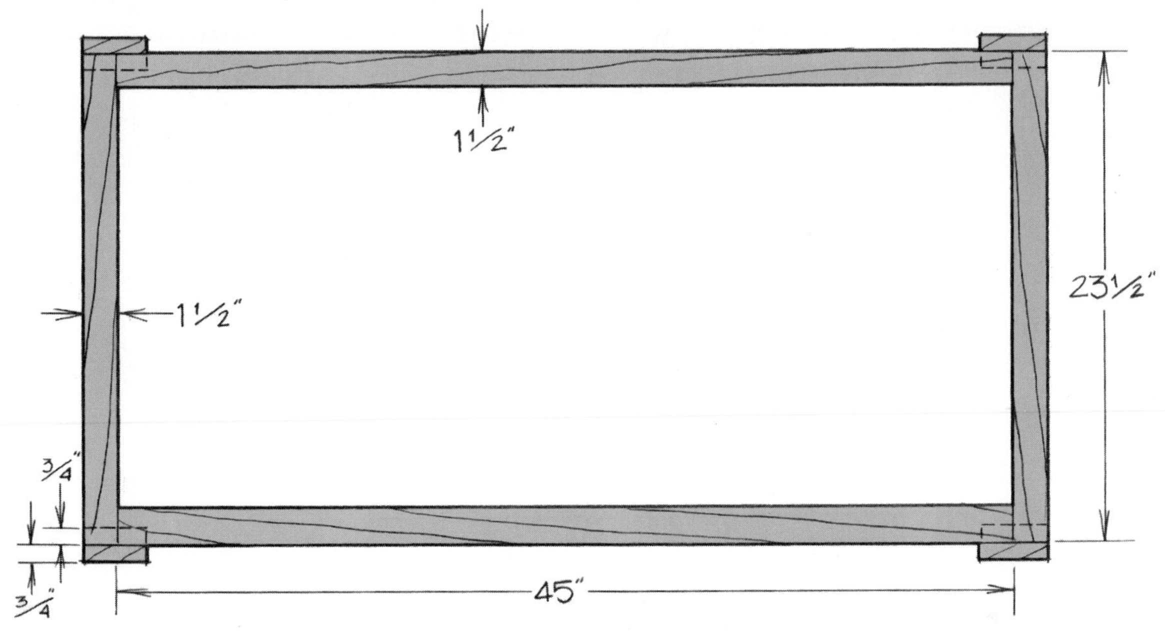

BOTTOM AND TOP FRAME JOINERY

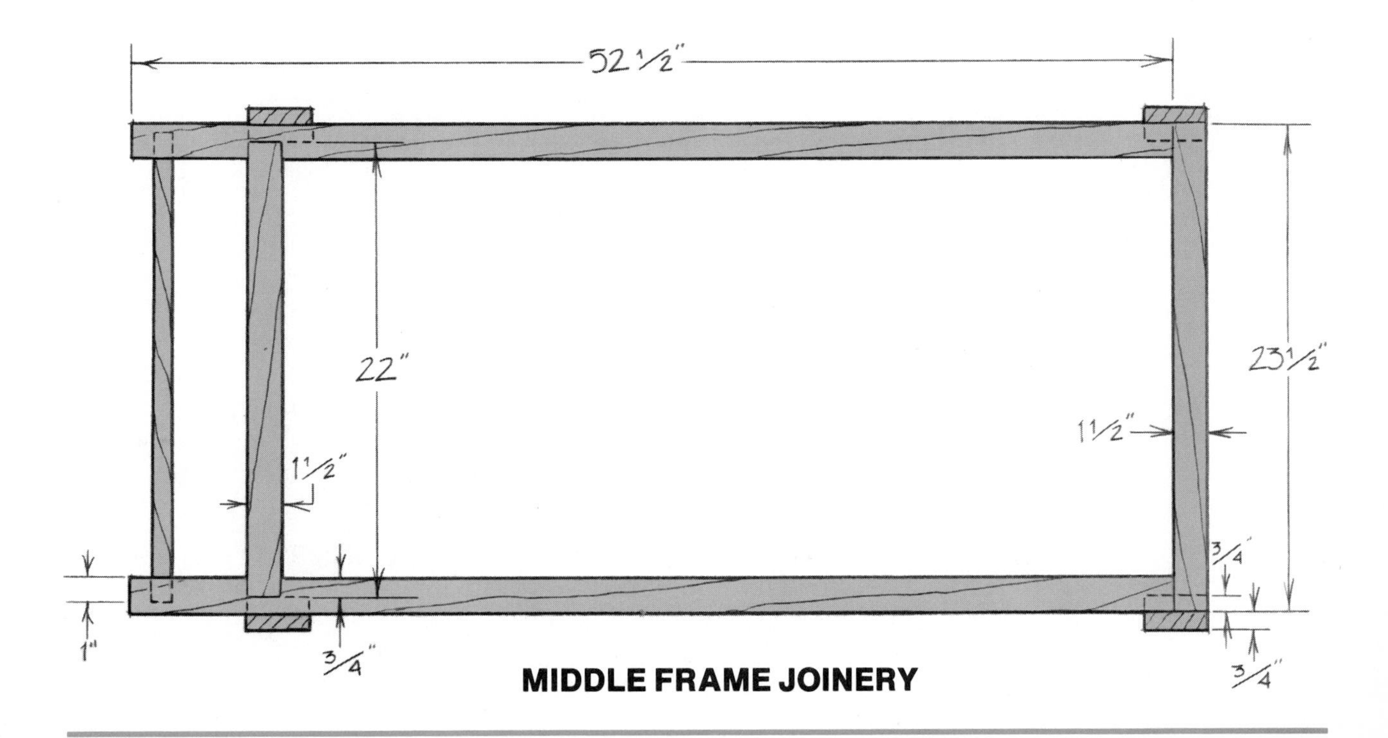

MIDDLE FRAME JOINERY

5 ***Attach the legs to the frames.*** Dry assemble the legs to the frames. Clamp them in place temporarily; *do not* screw them in place just yet. Square up the assembly, adjusting clamps as needed.

When the legs are square to the frames, remove the right long leg, and insert one long bottom rail and two end rails in their respective holes in both legs. Clamp the leg back in place. Repeat, removing the left short leg. When all the rails are in place — except for middle short rails and middle long rails — attach the legs to the frames with screws.

Note: Don't try to install the short middle rails and the long middle rails at this time. Wait until after you've nailed the slats in place.

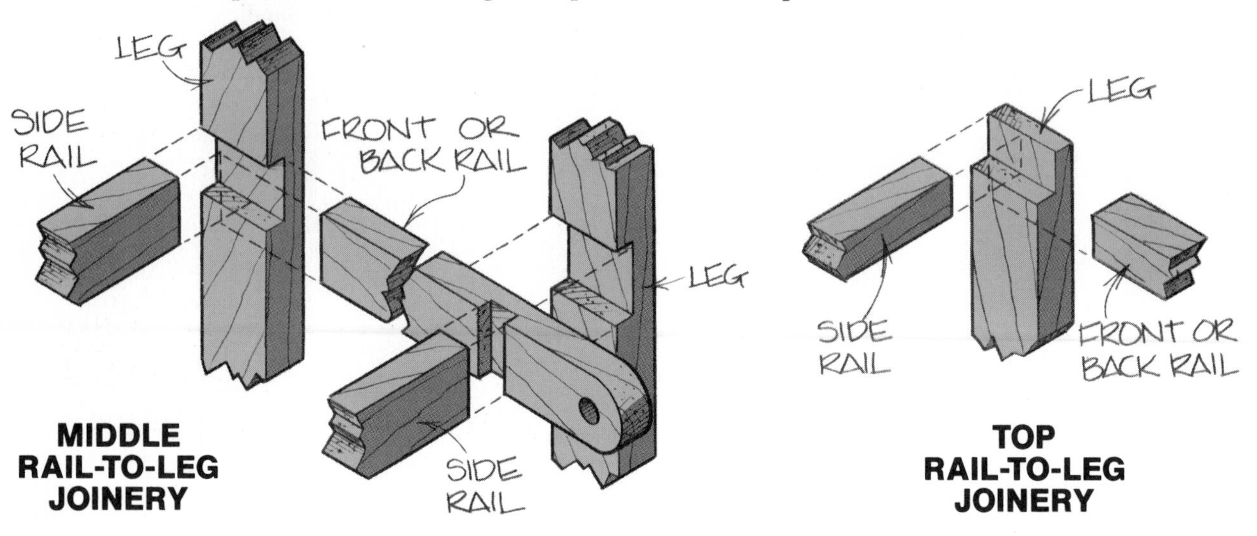

MIDDLE RAIL-TO-LEG JOINERY

TOP RAIL-TO-LEG JOINERY

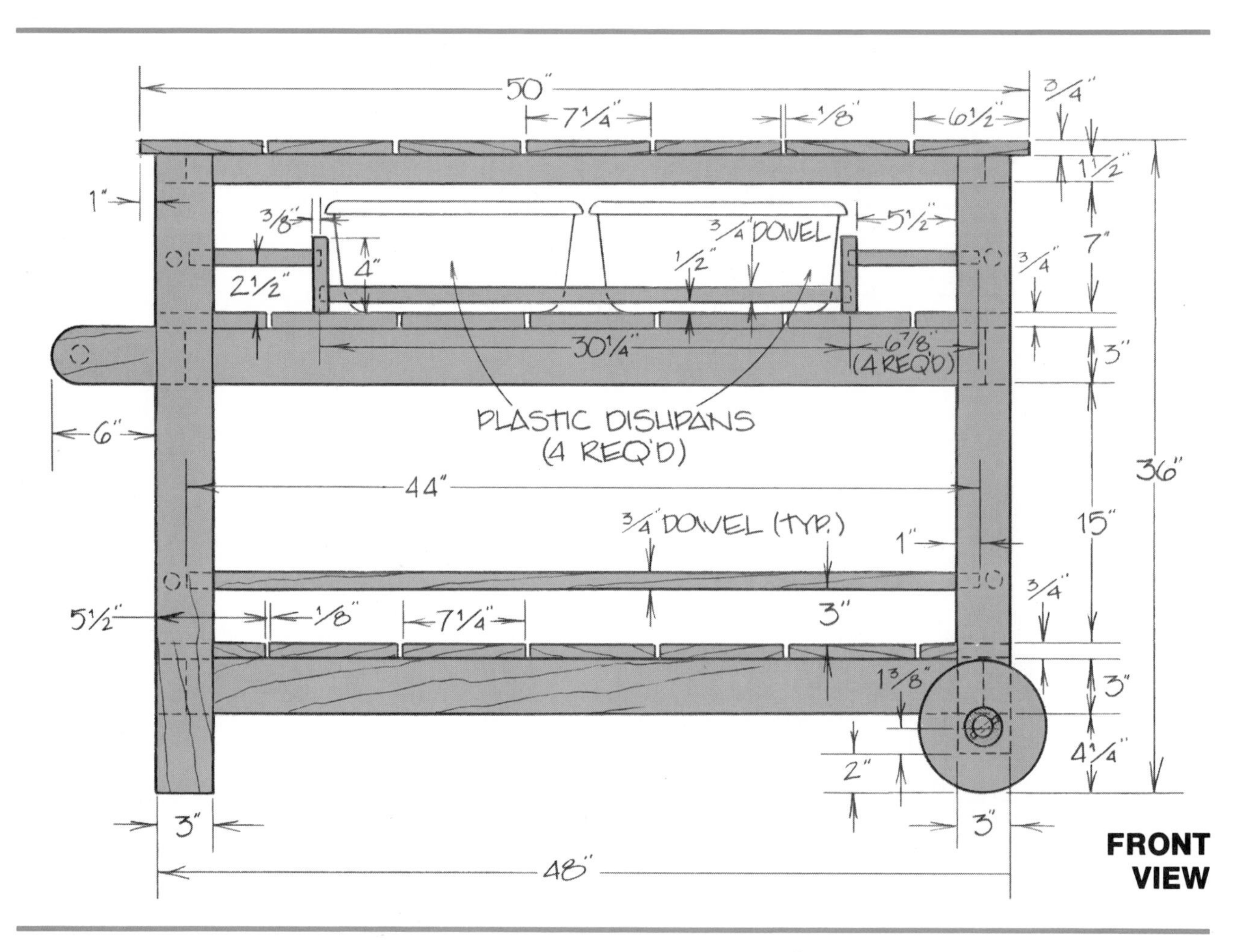

FRONT VIEW

6 Attach the slats to the frames. Lay the middle shelf slats and the middle top slats in place on the frame, carefully spacing them out as shown in the working drawings. Measure the distance spanned by the middle slats, and from that calculate the true width of the end slats.

Rip the end slats to width, and notch the end shelf slats to fit around the legs. Lay the slats in place to check their fit. When you're satisfied that they fit properly, nail all the slats in place with galvanized finishing nails.

TRY THIS! Nailing the slats toward the middle of the cart may be difficult because the long stretchers or aprons will give with each blow of the hammer. To prevent this, hold a small anvil or heavy metal "nailing block" under the frame part.

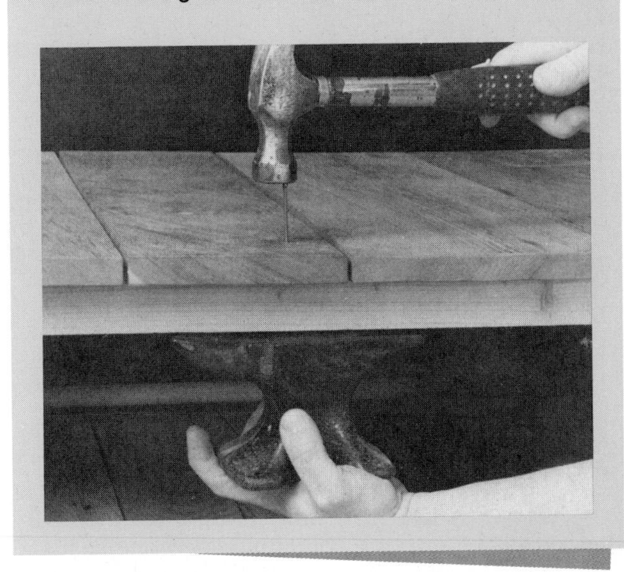

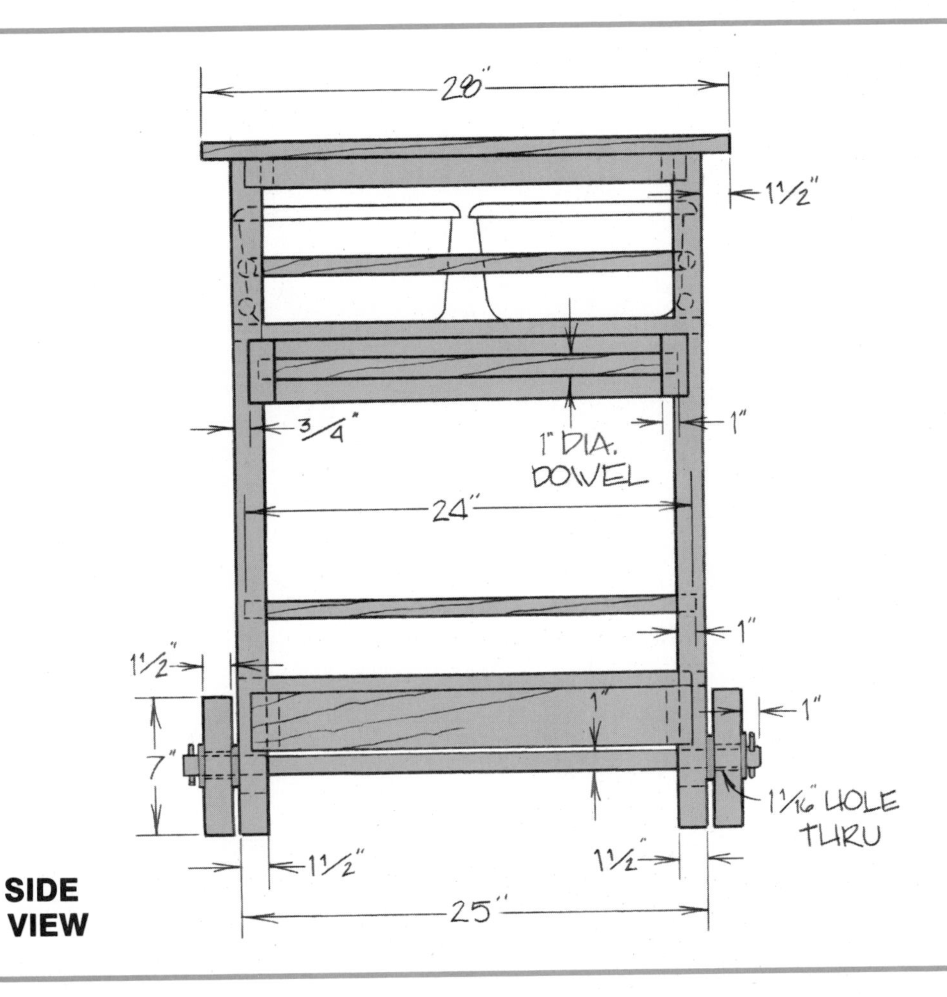

SIDE VIEW

7 *Install the dividers and remaining rails on the cart.*

Drill ¾″-diameter, ⅜″-deep stopped holes in the dividers, where shown in the drawings. Insert the short middle rails in their holes in the legs, then put the dividers in place. Cock the dividers to the right or left so that you can install the long middle rail, then straighten them up again after the rails are in place. Finally, fasten the divider-and-rail assembly in place by driving screws up through the middle shelf into the dividers. (See Figure 3.)

TRY THIS! If you have trouble installing the middle rails, enlarge the holes in the divider to 13/16″-diameter. For some reason we had trouble with one side, but not the other.

3/Secure the dividers in place with screws. Drive these screws up from underneath the shelf.

8 *Install the drawers.*

The long middle rail is closer to the shelf in order to allow you to install drawers in the patio cart. This is extremely simple: Just place standard-size plastic tubs between the dividers! The rails are low enough so that you can slip the tubs in and out easily, but high enough to prevent them from falling out when you roll the cart around.

TRY THIS! Drill ⅛″-diameter holes in the bottoms of the tubs to prevent them from filling up with rainwater.

9 *Mount the wheels on the cart.*

Cut out the wheels with a band saw or sabre saw, and drill 1″-diameter holes through their centers. Insert the uncut axle stock through the axle holes in the short legs. Place 1″ washers on either end of the axle, then the wheels, then another set of washers. (These washers prevent the wooden wheels from rubbing against the pegs and legs.)

Mark the outside edge of the outside washers, on either end of the axle. Measure 1″ out from these marks to mark the length of the axle. Disassemble the washers, wheels, and axle from the cart, and cut it to length. Drill the ends for ⅜″-diameter pegs that secure the wheels. (These peg holes should be 1/16″ beyond the marks for the outside edge of the washers. This will give the wheels a little play on the axles, but not too much.)

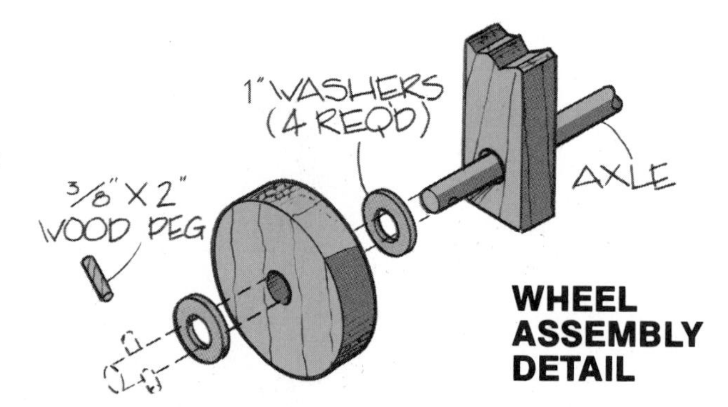

WHEEL ASSEMBLY DETAIL

Apply a little paste wax to the inside of the holes in the wheels to help them turn smoothly. Then reassemble the axle, wheels, and washers. Glue the pegs in their holes with waterproof glue to keep the wheels on the axle.

10 *Sand and finish the cart.*

Sand the completed cart, rounding any hard edges. Pay particular attention to the work surface and the handle — you want both of these to be as smooth as possible.

Finish the cart with spar varnish or a 1:1 mixture of spar varnish and tung oil. This will prevent spilt drinks and grease from discoloring the wood.

Outdoor Display Shelves

Are you looking for a way to get your small potted plants up off the deck where they won't get kicked around? Do you have some knick-knacks that you'd like to display out of doors? Do you need an attractive stand for a lamp or two when you entertain on your patio? These light-weight shelves could be just what you need.

As designed, this project has three small shelves. However, you can easily add more shelves or make them longer, if you need to. You can also adjust the spacing between the shelves to accommodate larger or smaller items. Change the plan to suit yourself; you'll find it's quite adaptable.

Materials List

FINISHED DIMENSIONS

PARTS

A.	Supports (2)	1½″ x 3½″ x 42″
B.	Legs (2)	1½″ x 3½″ x 16″
C.	Handle	¾″ x 5½″ x 16″
D.	Top shelf	¾″ x 8″ x 16″
E.	Middle shelf	¾″ x 9½″ x 16″
F.	Bottom Shelf	¾″ x 11″ x 16″

HARDWARE

#10 x 1¾″ Flathead wood screws (6)
#10 x 1¼″ Flathead wood screws (4)

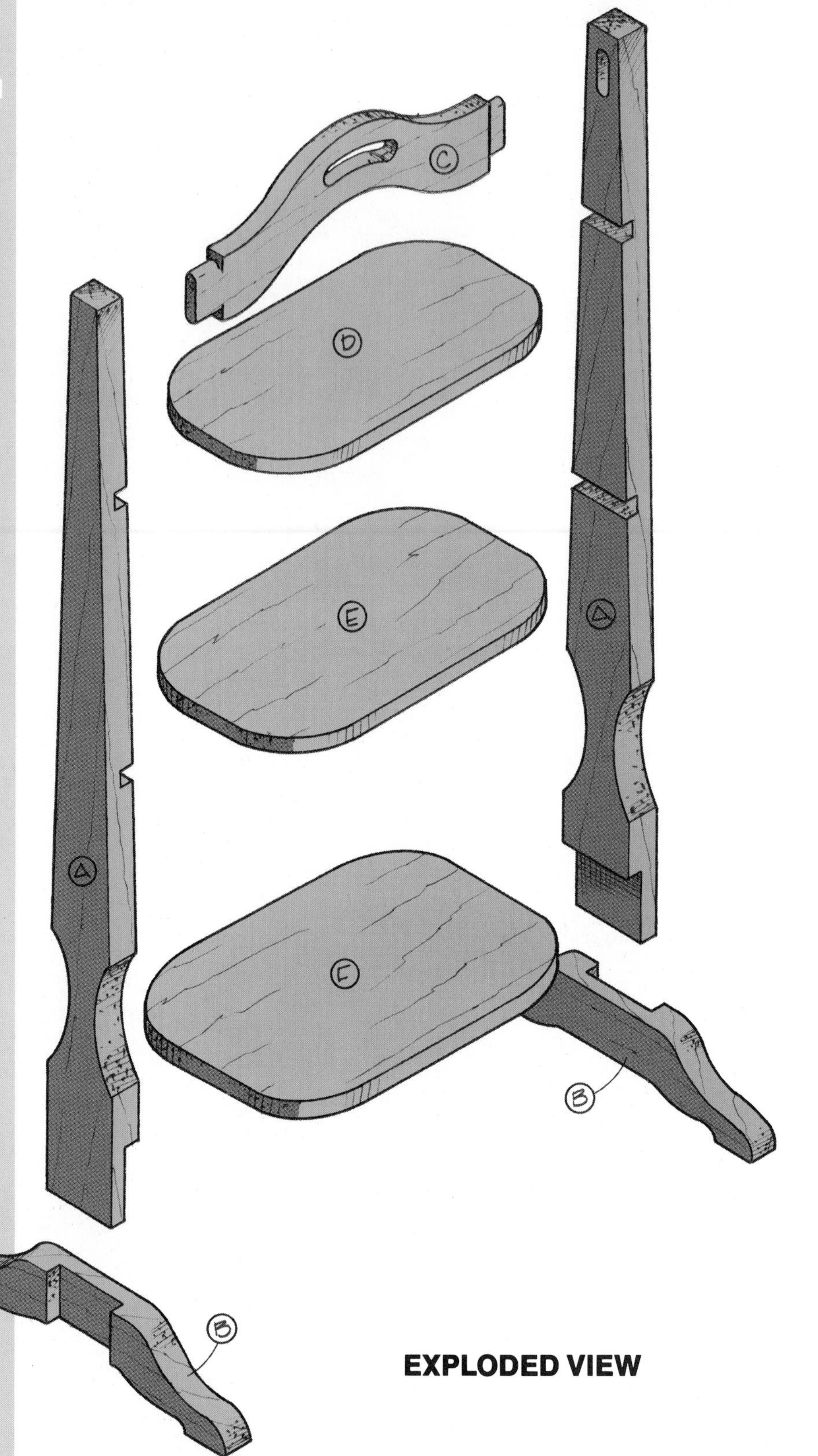

EXPLODED VIEW

1 **Cut all the parts to size.** Cut the parts to the size shown in the Materials List. The legs and supports can be cut from 2 x 4 stock, the shelves and handle from 1 x 12 lumber.

2 **Cut the joinery in the legs and supports.** Enlarge the patterns for the feet, and trace them on the stock. Lay out the supports. However, *do not* cut the shapes just yet. The joinery must be cut before you shape the parts.

Mount a dado cutter on your table saw or radial arm saw, and adjust the height to cut 3/4″ deep. Make the dadoes and the lap joints in the parts, taking care to cut both supports and both legs exactly the same. To cut the lap joints, you'll have to make several passes with the cutter.

TRY THIS! If you mount your cutter on a radial arm saw, you'll find it much easier (and safer) to cut by pushing the saw *away* from you. If you cut with the usual motion, pulling the machine towards you, the cutter will want to "climb" the board.

TRY THIS! If you don't have a drill press, you can easily cut these mortises with a hand-held router, a straight bit, and an edge guide. Mount the bit in the router, and adjust the edge guide so that the slot you cut with the bit will be centered in the face of the 2 x 4 stock. Rout each mortise in several passes, cutting 1/8″-1/4″ deeper with each pass.

Make the mortises near the top ends of the supports on your drill press. Drill a series of 3/4″-diameter holes, 3/4″ deep to "rough out" the mortises, then clean up the edges with a chisel. (See Figure 1.)

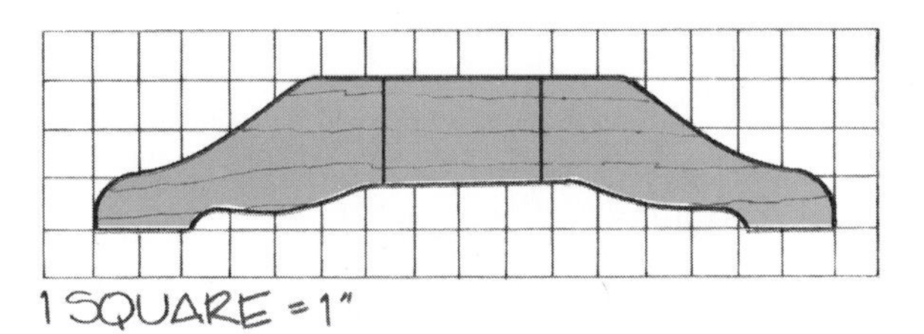

PATTERN FOR FEET

1/*To make the mortises for the handle, first drill a series of holes. Then clean up the edges with a chisel.*

3 ***Cut the shapes of the legs, supports, shelves, and handle.*** With a band saw or sabre saw, cut out the shapes of the various parts. With a chisel and a rasp, round the edges of the tenons on the handle so that they fit the mortises. (See Figure 2.) Sand the sawn edges of all the parts to remove the saw marks.

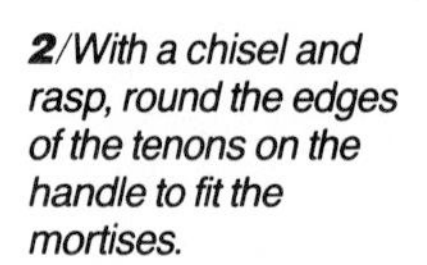
2/With a chisel and rasp, round the edges of the tenons on the handle to fit the mortises.

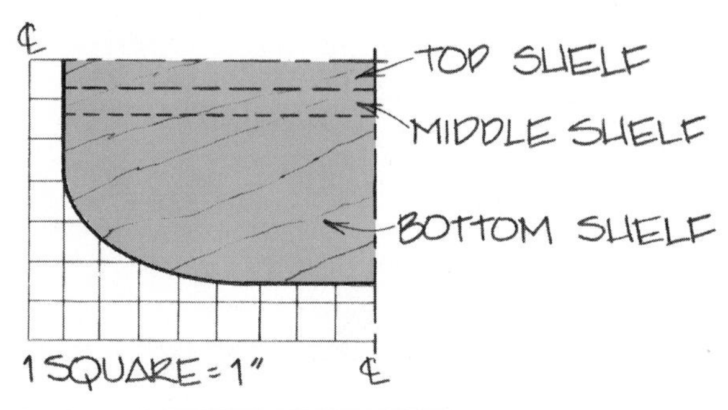

SHELF PATTERN

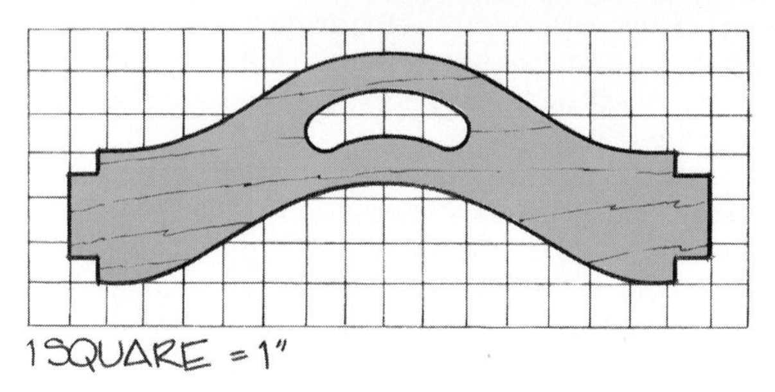

HANDLE PATTERN

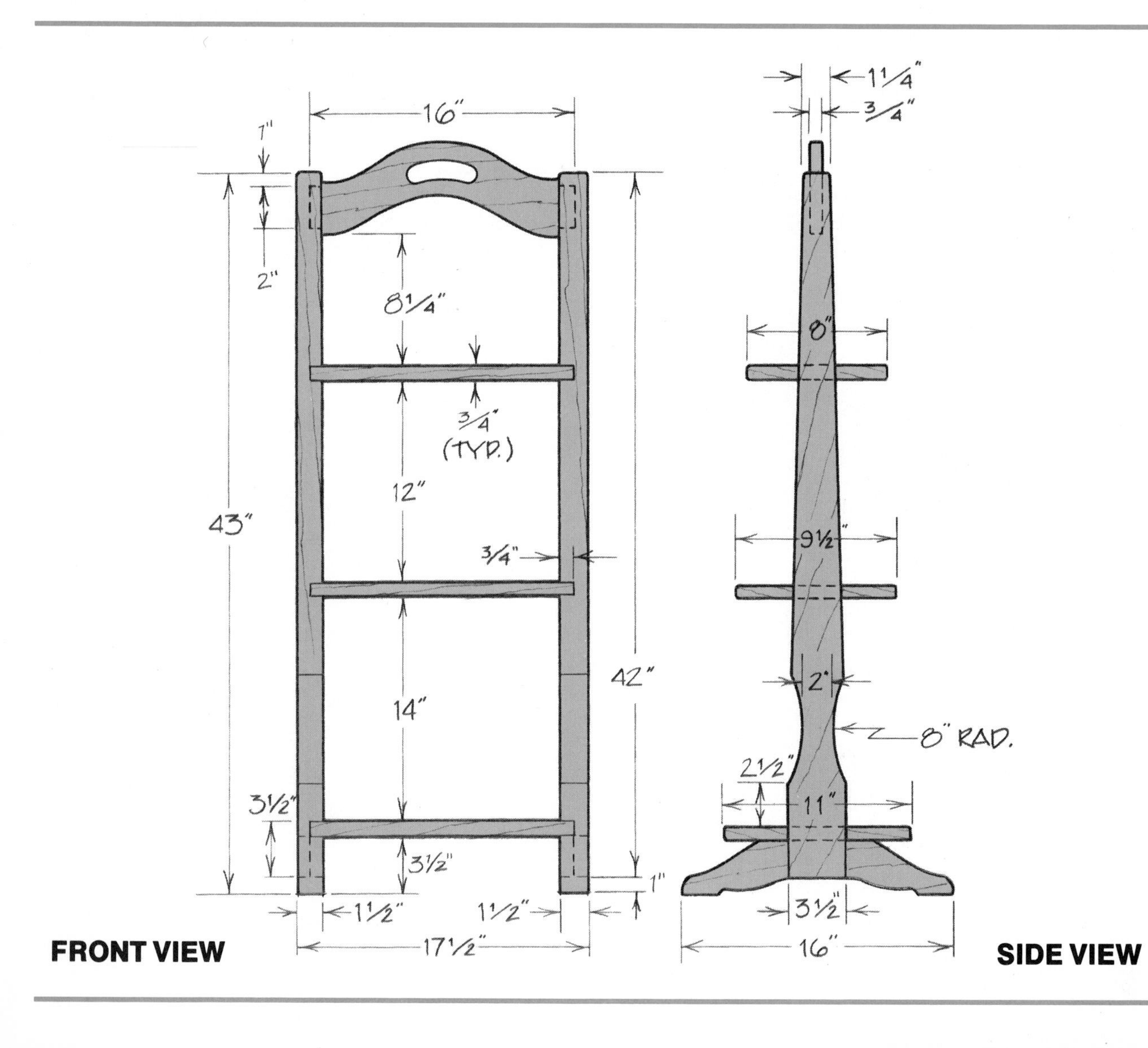

FRONT VIEW

SIDE VIEW

4 **Cut the handle opening.** Drill 1″-diameter holes at either end of the handle opening. Then cut away the waste in between the holes with a sabre saw. Round over the edges of the opening with a router or a rasp so that it fits your hand comfortably.

5 **Seal the wood inside the joints.** Paint the surfaces inside the mortises, dadoes, and lap joints with spar varnish to seal the grain and prevent any water damage. Also, seal the end grains of the handle and shelves where they will be inserted into the joints.

6 **Assemble the stand.** Insert the tenons of the handle in the support mortises; then slide the shelves in place in the dadoes. Attach the shelves to the supports with screws — one screw per joint. (There is no need to screw the handle in place; it will stay put once the shelves are attached securely.) Counterbore *and* countersink the screws, then cover the heads with wooden plugs.

Attach the legs to the supports with screws. Drive these screws from the *inside* of the legs. (See Figure 3.)

3/Screw the legs to the supports from the "inside," so the screws won't show.

7 **Sand and finish the project.** Round all the "hard" corners and edges with a rasp and sandpaper to give the piece a soft, country look. Stain the project, if you want; then apply a 1:1 mixture of tung oil and spar varnish. Give all exposed end grains a second coat to make sure they're completely sealed.

Rust-Resistant Hardware

Throughout this book, we recommend "rust-resistant" or weatherproof hardware. The Materials Lists often call for "galvanized" fasteners, but you actually have a bigger choice than that.

Galvanized — There are two types available: plated (or "coated") and "hot-dipped." Of the two, hot-dipped hardware is far superior in its ability to weather the elements.

Brass — Brass will not corrode when exposed to *fresh* water. However, it may disintegrate around salt water. Other drawbacks: It's a soft metal, and the screw heads are easily stripped. It's also expensive. Avoid "brass-plated"; this is not weatherproof.

Bronze — Bronze is a hard metal, and it will stand up to both fresh water and salt water. However, it is very expensive. Bronze hardware is available through marine supply stores. Do not purchase "bronze-plated"; this is not weatherproof.

Stainless steel — This is in the same category as bronze. Stainless steel is hard and stands up to both fresh water and salt water. It's slightly less expensive than bronze.

Zinc- or cadmium-plated — These two terms are, for most woodworkers' purposes, synonymous. Zinc/cadmium-plated hardware is rust-resistant but not really weatherproof.

Avoid hardware that has been "blued," "japanned," or "chrome-plated." These treatments make the metal resistant to corrosion, but not weatherproof.

Scissors Chair and Table

It's hard to imagine why this particular style of outdoor furniture has come to be known as "scissors" furniture. It does not fold up like a pair of scissors; there is no pivot or hingepin. Instead, the furniture pulls apart in two pieces, then one piece slides inside the other. It's more like "sword-and-scabbard" furniture.

Whatever you want to call it, the elegant table and chair you see here can be packed up in a small, easy-to-store bundle; then set up again in next to no time. They were built by Jeff and Sandra Walker, who manufacture "casual furniture" in Ravenna, Kentucky, at their business, "Oak Arts."

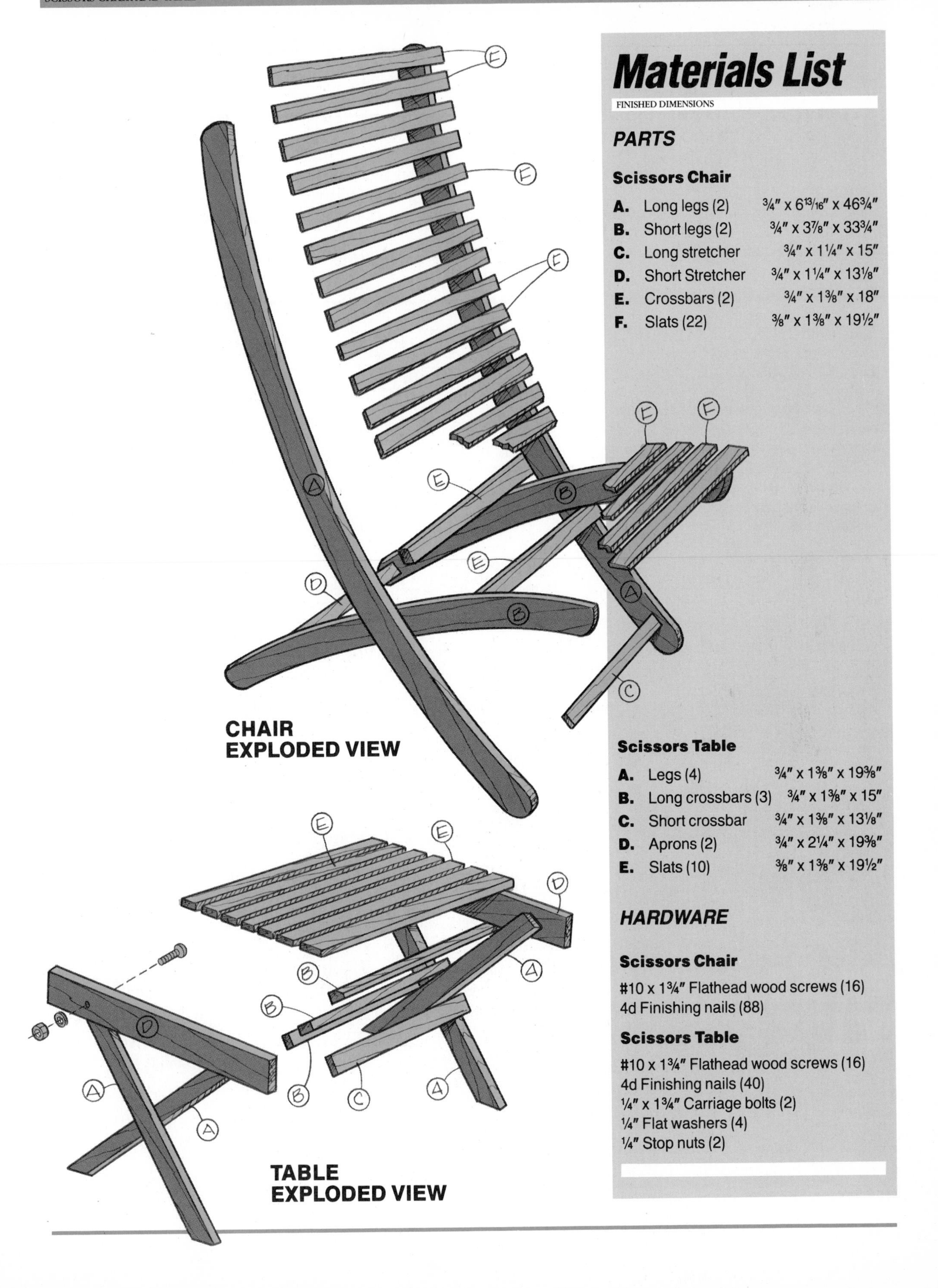

CHAIR
EXPLODED VIEW

TABLE
EXPLODED VIEW

Materials List

FINISHED DIMENSIONS

PARTS

Scissors Chair

A.	Long legs (2)	¾″ x 6 13/16″ x 46¾″
B.	Short legs (2)	¾″ x 3⅞″ x 33¾″
C.	Long stretcher	¾″ x 1¼″ x 15″
D.	Short Stretcher	¾″ x 1¼″ x 13⅛″
E.	Crossbars (2)	¾″ x 1⅜″ x 18″
F.	Slats (22)	⅜″ x 1⅜″ x 19½″

Scissors Table

A.	Legs (4)	¾″ x 1⅜″ x 19⅜″
B.	Long crossbars (3)	¾″ x 1⅜″ x 15″
C.	Short crossbar	¾″ x 1⅜″ x 13⅛″
D.	Aprons (2)	¾″ x 2¼″ x 19⅜″
E.	Slats (10)	⅜″ x 1⅜″ x 19½″

HARDWARE

Scissors Chair

#10 x 1¾″ Flathead wood screws (16)
4d Finishing nails (88)

Scissors Table

#10 x 1¾″ Flathead wood screws (16)
4d Finishing nails (40)
¼″ x 1¾″ Carriage bolts (2)
¼″ Flat washers (4)
¼″ Stop nuts (2)

Making the Chair

1 **Cut all parts to size.** Choose a clear, durable hardwood, such as oak or mahogany, to build the scissors chair. The individual parts are very slender. If you make them from softwood, they may break after a short time.

In addition, you'll need hardwood lumber of two different thicknesses — ¾″ and ⅜″. The chair requires 7-8 *square* feet of ¾″ stock, and 5-6 *square* feet of ⅜″ stock. (This estimate is approximate, and may change depending on the widths and lengths of the materials available.) If you don't have a planer to thickness the stock, have it thicknessed at the lumberyard.

Note: We've estimated the wood needed in square feet rather than the usual board feet. Depending on how your shop is equipped, you may be able to resaw and plane this stock from just 10-12 *board* feet of lumber.

After you have gathered the thicknesses of stock you need, rip and cut all the parts to the sizes shown in the Materials List for the "Scissors Chair."

2 **Cut the shapes of the chair legs.** Lay out the shapes of the long and short chair legs on ¾″ stock. Be certain that the grain of the wood is oriented parallel to the length of these parts, so that the finished legs will be as strong as possible. Cut out the shapes of the legs with a band saw or sabre saw, then sand away the saw marks.

TRY THIS! To save time when marking and cutting the legs, stack the pieces of stock on top of each other, making two "pads" — one for the short legs and one for the long legs. "Pad saw" each of these stacks, cutting two legs at once.

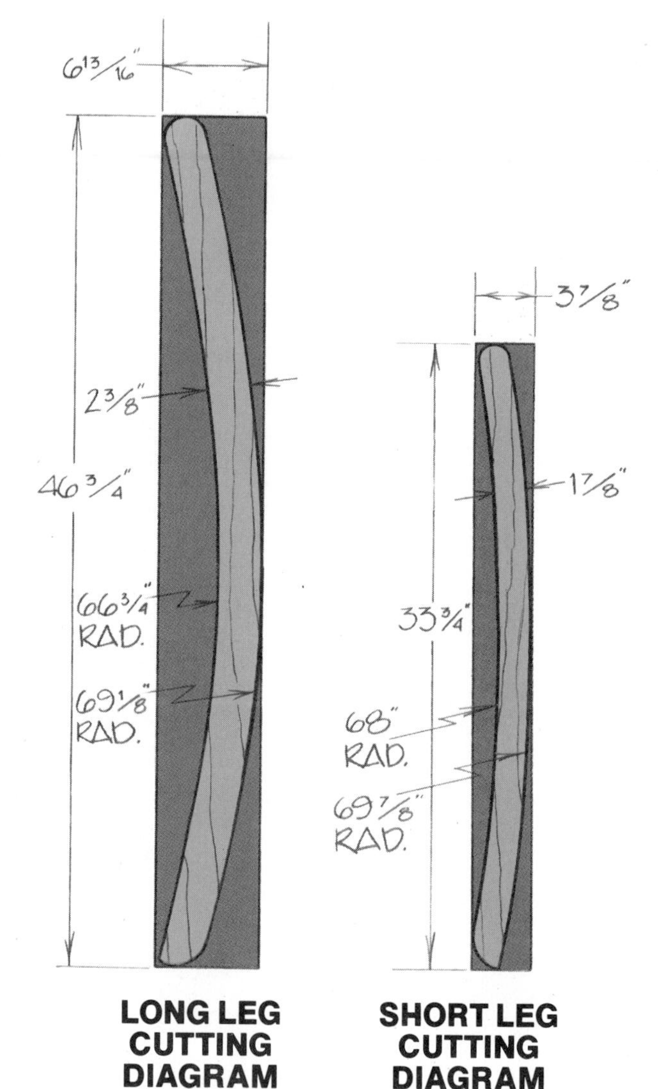

LONG LEG CUTTING DIAGRAM

SHORT LEG CUTTING DIAGRAM

3 **Sand all parts.** Sand the parts, carefully rounding hard edges and corners. This will not only make the furniture more comfortable, it will help prevent splinters.

4 ***Mark the positions of the slats.*** Carefully mark the positions of the slats on the chair legs. Do this *before* you start assembling the parts, so that you can mark both legs at the same time, and get the marks exactly the same on both parts. (See Figure 1.)

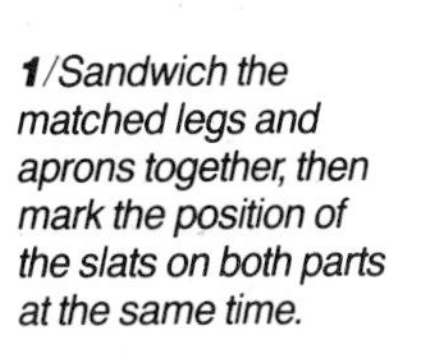

1*/Sandwich the matched legs and aprons together, then mark the position of the slats on both parts at the same time.*

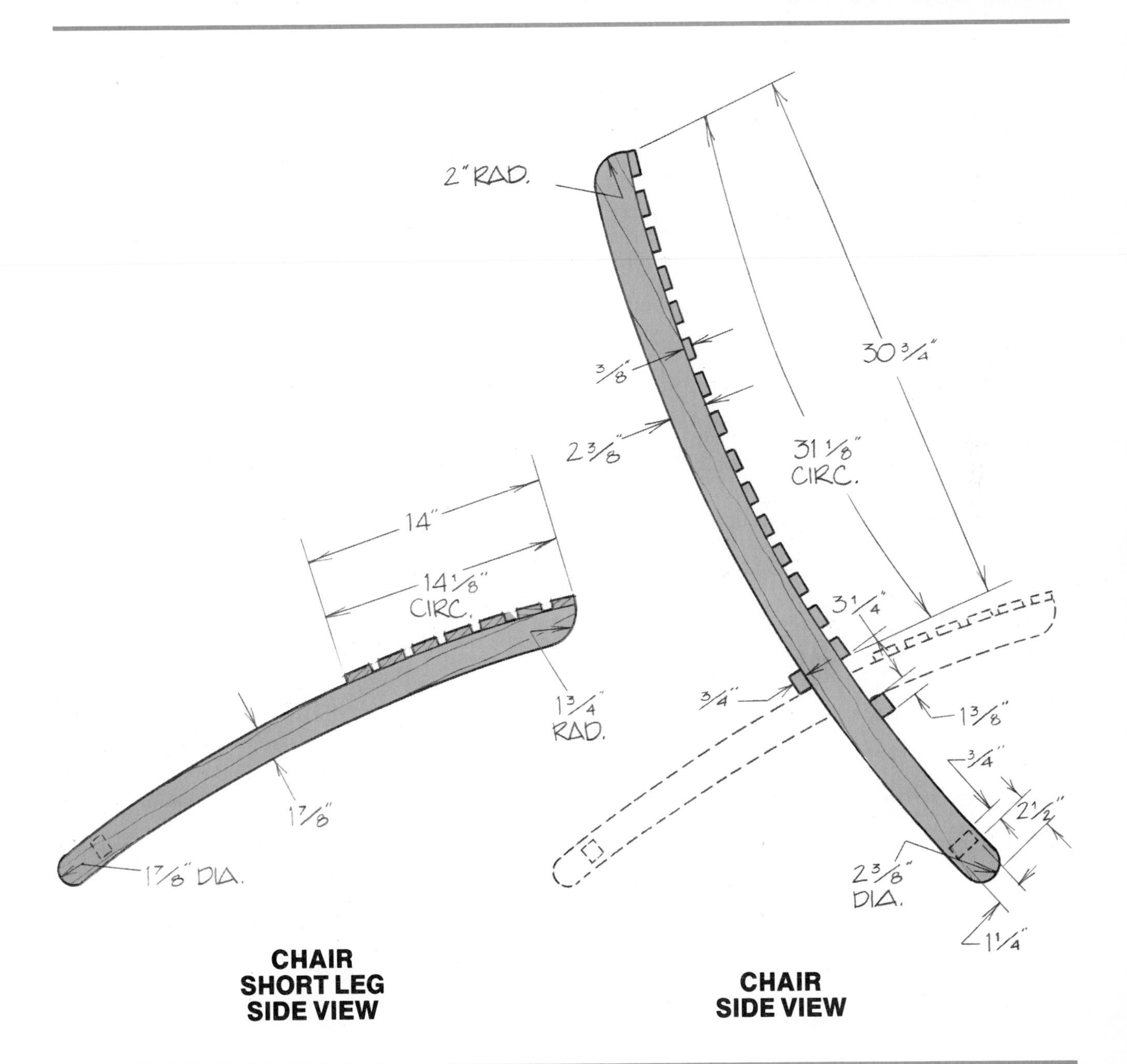

5 **Assemble the crossbars and stretchers to the legs.** Screw the crossbars to the legs, where shown in the *Crossbar Placement Detail.* Countersink the screws so that the heads are flush with the surface of the wood. If you wish, you can cover the screw heads with wooden plugs so that you don't see them at all. After you've attached the crossbars, screw the stretchers to the chair legs.

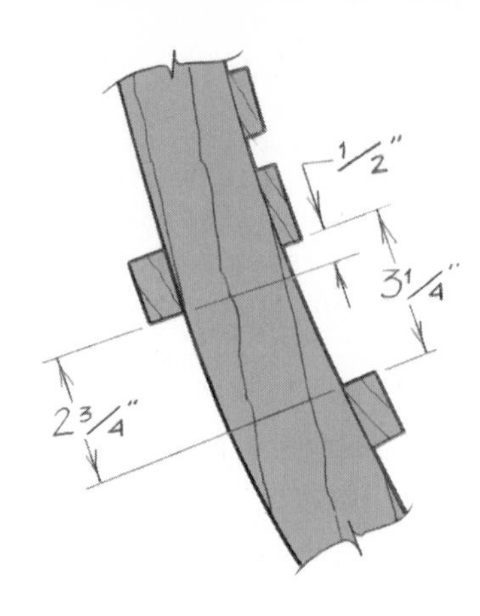

CROSSBAR PLACEMENT DETAIL

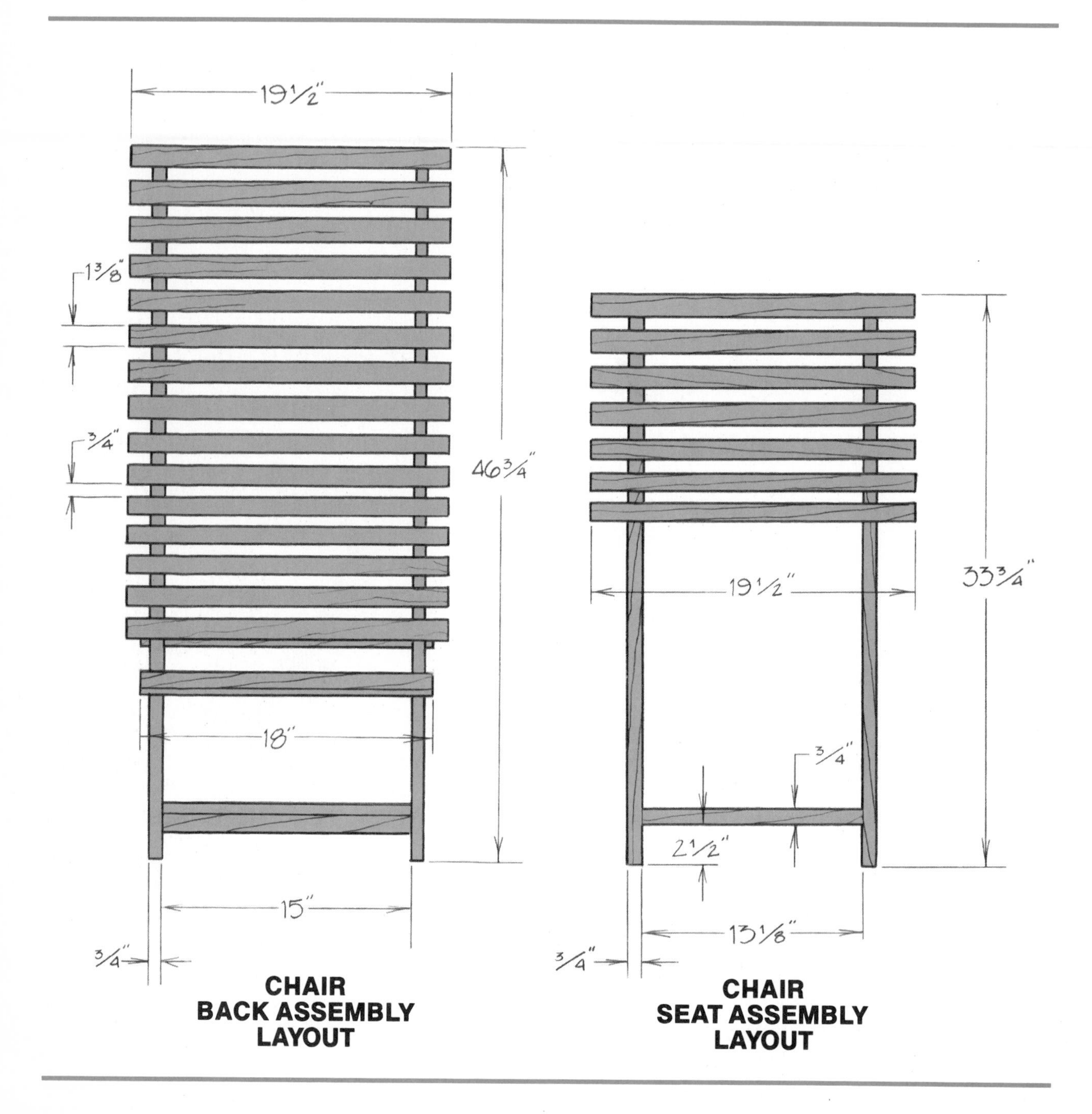

CHAIR BACK ASSEMBLY LAYOUT

CHAIR SEAT ASSEMBLY LAYOUT

6 Nail the slats in place. Nail the slats to the chair legs where you've marked them. If you can find 4d galvanized finishing nails, use them. If you can't, order special aluminum or stainless steel nails from a marine supplier.

7 Apply a finish to the completed chair. If you've built this project from a domestic hardwood, such as oak, it's particularly important that you seal the grain. These woods will decay faster out of doors than the usual "outdoor" woods, like redwood and cedar. Apply spar varnish, or a 1:1 mixture of spar varnish and tung oil.

Making the Table

1 Cut all parts to size. Select a hardwood to match the wood you used to build the chair. Make the table from 3-4 square feet of ¾" stock, and 3-4 feet of ⅜" stock. (These estimates are approximate, and may change depending on the widths and lengths of the materials available.) If you don't have a planer to thickness the stock, have it thicknessed at the lumberyard.

Note: As we said before, we've estimated the wood needed in square feet rather than the usual board feet. Depending on how your shop is equipped, you may be able to resaw and plane this stock from just 6-8 *board* feet of lumber.

Rip and cut all the parts to the sizes shown in the Materials List for the "Scissors Table." Miter the ends of the table legs at 45°; and chamfer one corner on one of the long table crossbars, as shown in the working drawings.

TRY THIS! While you're cutting the table parts, you may also wish to cut a 4" long "bite" out of one slat. Later on, use this as the *top* slat in the project. It will form a convenient "handle" with which to carry the table.

2 Drill the table legs and aprons. Drill ¼" holes in the table legs and aprons where they will be attached to each other. Counterbore the holes in the legs so that you can sink the heads of the carriage bolts flush with the surface of the wood. (See Figure 2.) These counterbores must be on the *inside* of each leg.

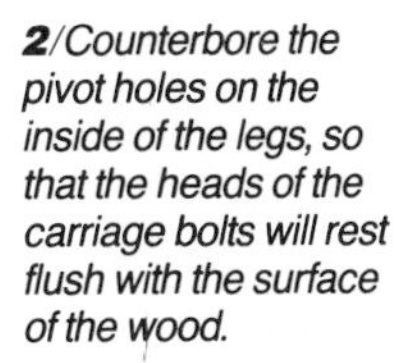

2/*Counterbore the pivot holes on the inside of the legs, so that the heads of the carriage bolts will rest flush with the surface of the wood.*

3 ***Sand all parts.*** Sand the parts, carefully rounding hard edges and corners. As we said before, this will not only make the furniture more comfortable, it will help prevent splinters.

4 ***Mark the positions of the slats.*** Carefully mark the positions of the slats on the table aprons. Do this *before* you start assembling the parts, so that you can mark both aprons at the same time, and get the marks exactly the same on both parts.

5 ***Assemble the crossbars and stretchers to the legs.*** Screw the crossbars to the legs, where shown in the *Side View*. Countersink the screws so that the heads are flush with the surface of the wood. If you wish, you can cover the screw heads with wooden plugs so that you don't see them at all.

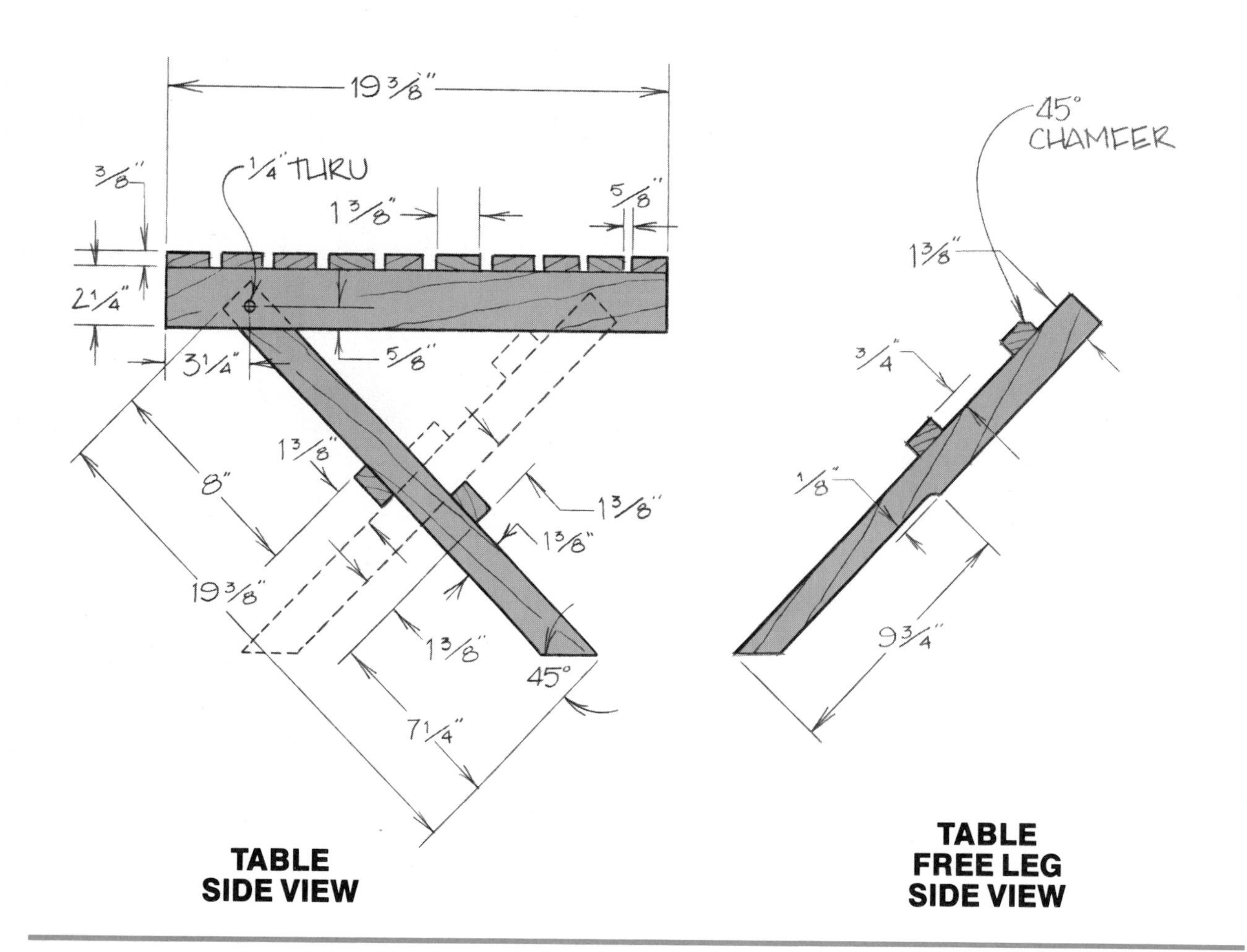

TABLE SIDE VIEW

TABLE FREE LEG SIDE VIEW

6

Bolt table legs to the aprons. Attach the folding table legs to the aprons with carriage bolts. Seat the carriage bolts with a blow of a hammer. Place a flat washer between the two wooden parts to keep them from rubbing, and secure the bolt in place with a stop nut to keep the bolt snug.

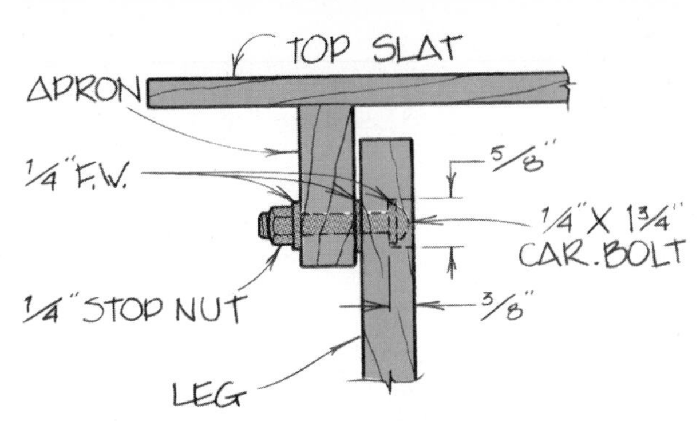

TABLE PIVOT JOINT DETAIL

7

Nail the slats in place. Nail the slats to the table aprons where you've marked them. Use 4d galvanized finishing nails, or special aluminum or stainless steel nails from a marine supplier.

8

Apply a finish to the table. Finish sand any parts that may still need sanding, then apply a finish to match the chair. Once again, if you've built this project from domestic hardwoods, be sure to seal the grain.

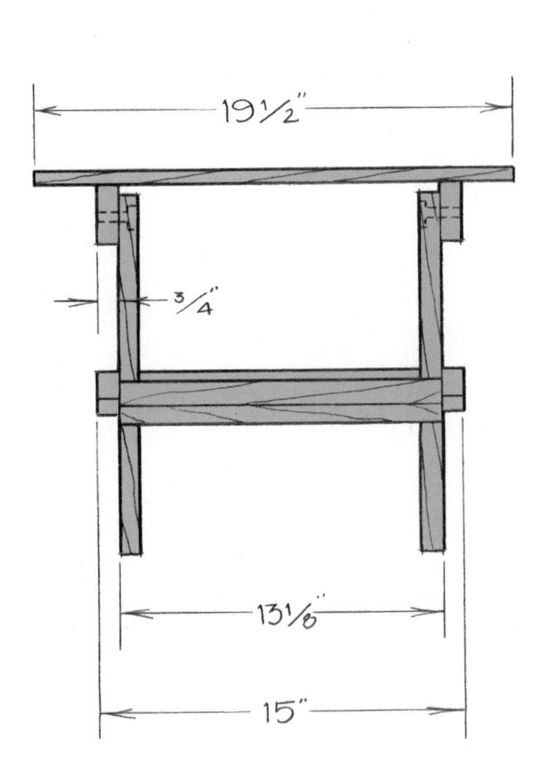

TABLE FRONT VIEW

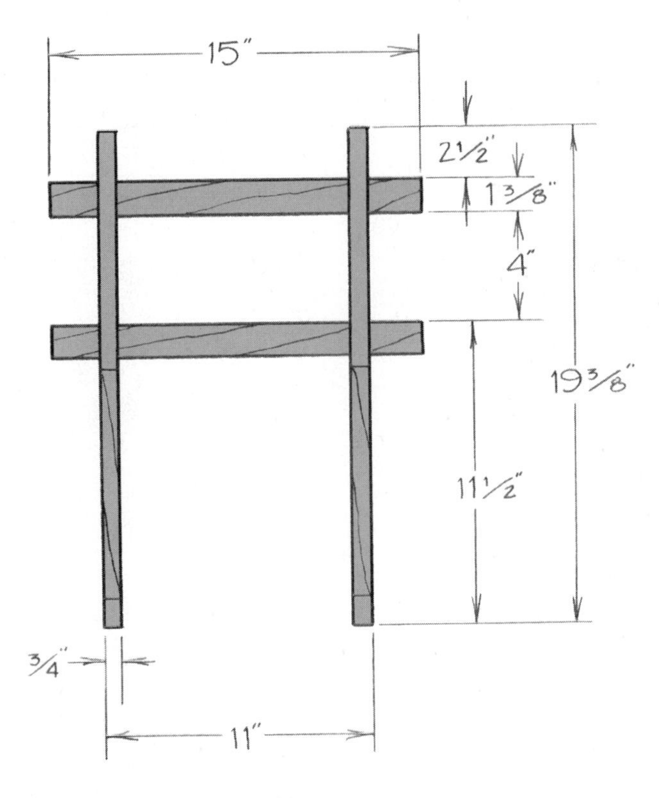

TABLE FREE LEG ASSEMBLY LAYOUT

Sling Hammock

Do you like to spend warm, sunny weekends flat on your back, napping some, reading some, and generally enjoying the good weather? Here's a simple project that will help make those lazy Saturdays and Sundays more enjoyable — and it won't take up much of your weekend snooze time to complete it.

This sling hammock is nothing more than four pieces of wood and metal held together by four bolts. You can knock this project out in two or three hours, even counting the trip to the building supply and fabric stores! Most of the time invested is in sewing the canvas "sling." And, if you're clever, you can con someone else into doing that while you're waiting for the finish to dry on the wooden parts — and taking a nap.

Materials List

FINISHED DIMENSIONS

PARTS

A.	Ends (2)	1½″ x 7¼″ x 30″
B.	Stretchers (2)	1¼″ dia. x 82″

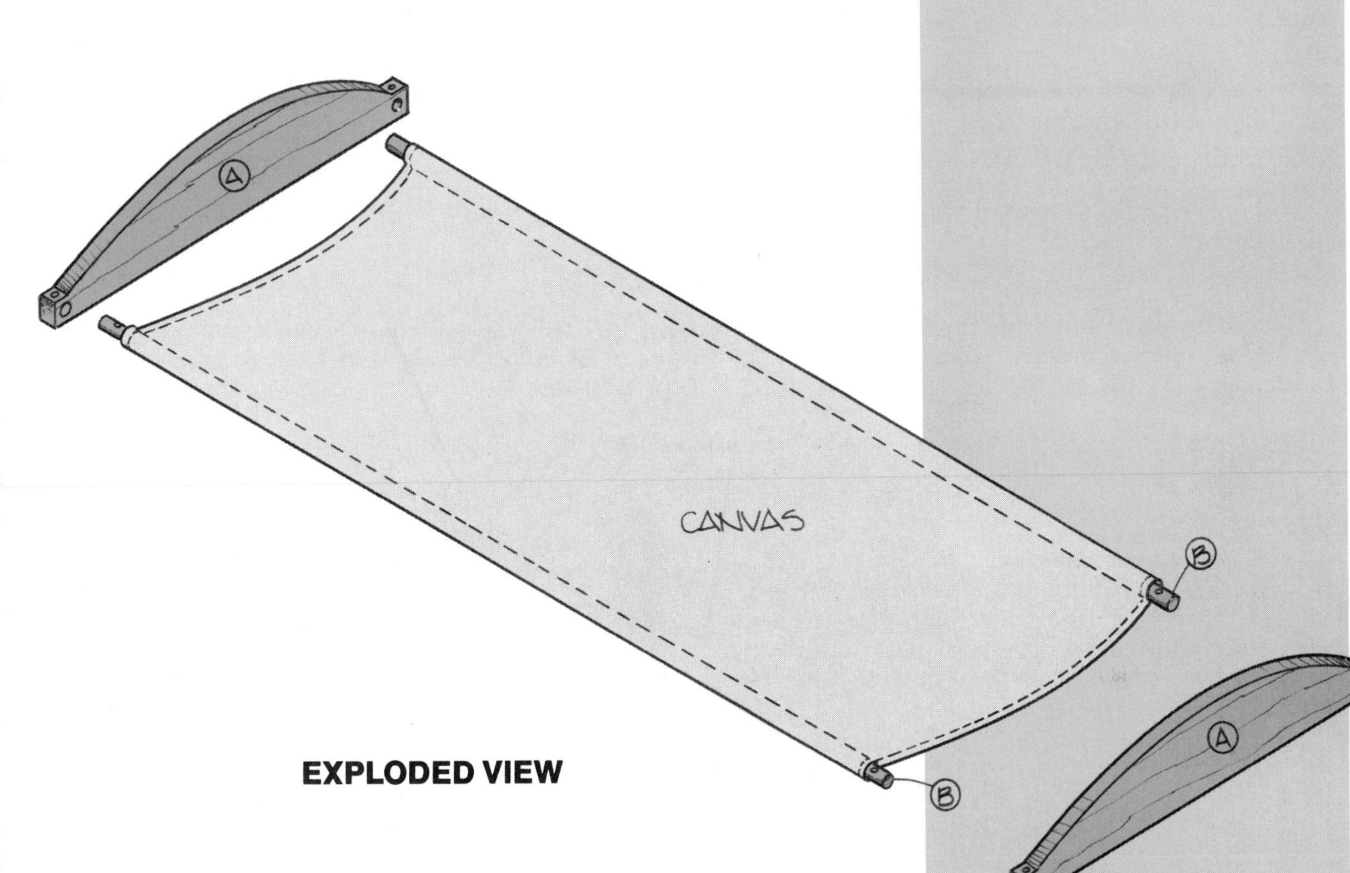

EXPLODED VIEW

HARDWARE

36″ Wide heavy canvas (2½ yards)
⅜″ x 6″ Eyebolts with 2 washers and 2 nuts each (4 sets)
2″ S-hooks (4)
Porch swing chain set, with 5′ leaders

1 *Carefully choose your materials.* Before you purchase your materials, consider carefully: Who is going to use this hammock? Who is likely to lay in it? As designed, the project uses ordinary "closet pole" for the stretchers. This is fairly strong material; if you have a large closet in your house and lots of clothes hanging in it, you know that closet poles can support a lot of weight. We don't recommend, however, that you use closet pole for the stretchers if this hammock will be used consistently by someone over 180 pounds. Instead, use 1″ I.D. steel pipe. This is available at most plumbing supply stores.

---

2 *Cut all parts to size and shape.* Cut the ends and stretchers to the sizes shown in the Materials List. Trace the pattern for the ends on the stock, and cut them out with a sabre saw or band saw. Sand off the saw marks.

---

3 *Drill holes in the ends for the stretchers.* Using a holesaw, drill 1⅜″ holes in the ends for the stretchers. Even though the closet pole is specified at 1¼″ in diameter, oftentimes it's milled slightly larger. If you're using pipe, you may want to measure the O.D. (outside diameter) of the pipe before you cut the hole.

---

4 *Sew a cloth sling.* Sew a sling for the hammock from duck canvas. The sling must have two long loops of material running the length of either side. Before you sew, temporarily pin the loops and make sure the stretcher or pipe will easily fit inside these loops. (See Figure 1.)

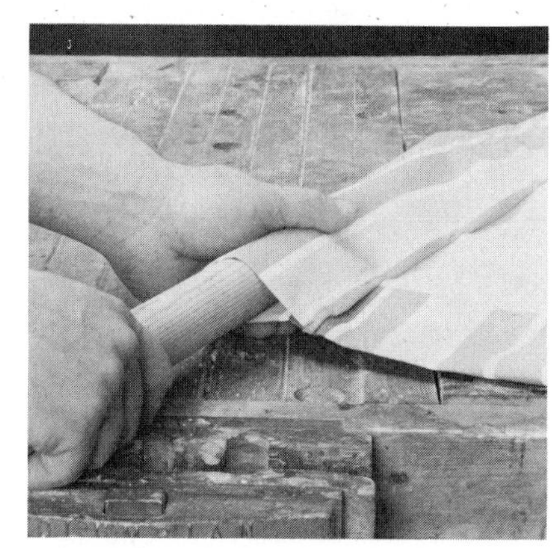

***1**/Temporarily pin the loops in the sling before you sew them, and make sure that the stretchers fit inside the loops.*

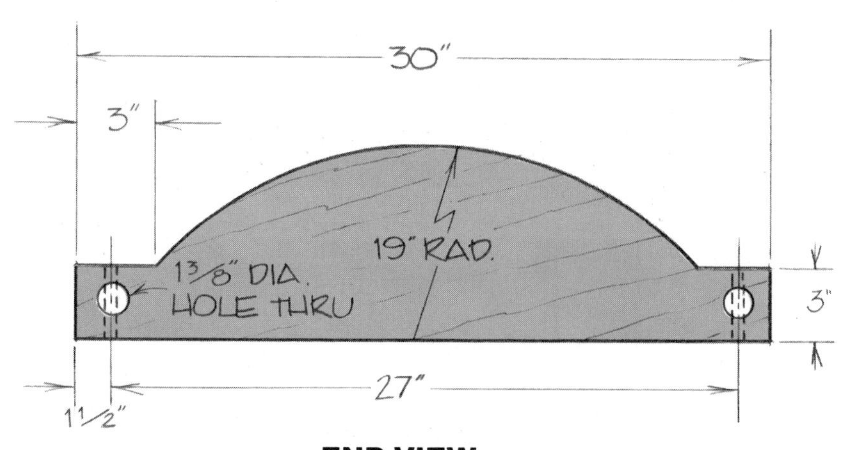

END VIEW

5 Sand and finish the parts.

Finish sand all the wooden parts. If you wish, apply a paint, varnish, or stain. Let the finish dry for at least 48 hours before assembling the hammock.

6 Assemble the hammock.

Slide the stretcher into the loops along the sides of the sling, then slide the ends of the stretchers into the holes in the ends. Drill ⅜″ holes through the ends and the stretchers, as shown in the working drawings. Insert eye bolts in these holes, and fasten them in place with washers and nuts. (There must be one nut and one washer above the wood, and one nut and washer below, on each corner of the hammock.) The eye bolts will keep the stretchers from pulling out of the ends. If ever you want to take the hammock down and store it, just remove the eye bolts.

TRY THIS! Since you have to put two nuts on each eye bolt, one above the wood and one below, look for eye bolts that are threaded all the way up the shaft. If you can't find them, you may have to cut your own threads with a die.

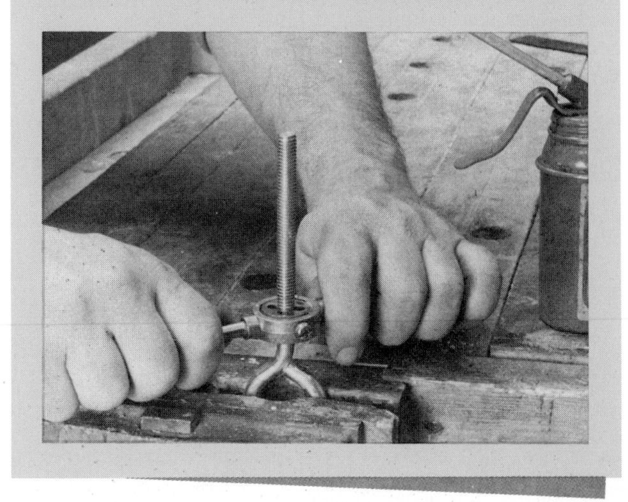

7 Hang the hammock.

Attach the leaders of the porch swing chains to the eye bolts with S-hooks. Mount screw hooks on the underside of a porch joist or tree limb, and attach the other ends of the chains to these hooks. Adjust the height of the hammock by choosing which links in the chains you'll attach to the screw hooks.

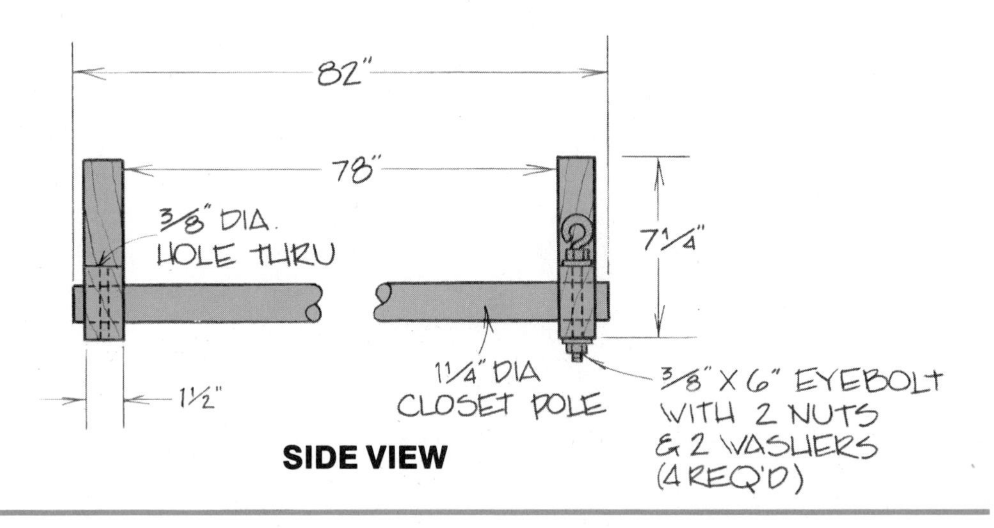

SIDE VIEW

Garden Bench

Not too long ago, sociologists studied New York City parks, to find out which ones were used the most and why. The study clearly showed that some parks were used much more than others, and the reason will surprise you. It isn't anything you'd expect, such as location, number of people nearby, or landscaping. No, the parks that were used the most were those that had the most available *seating*.

That same logic applies to your own backyard. You'll enjoy the gardens and the flower beds that you worked so hard to plant if you have someplace to *sit down* and enjoy them. To that end, here's an elegant garden bench.

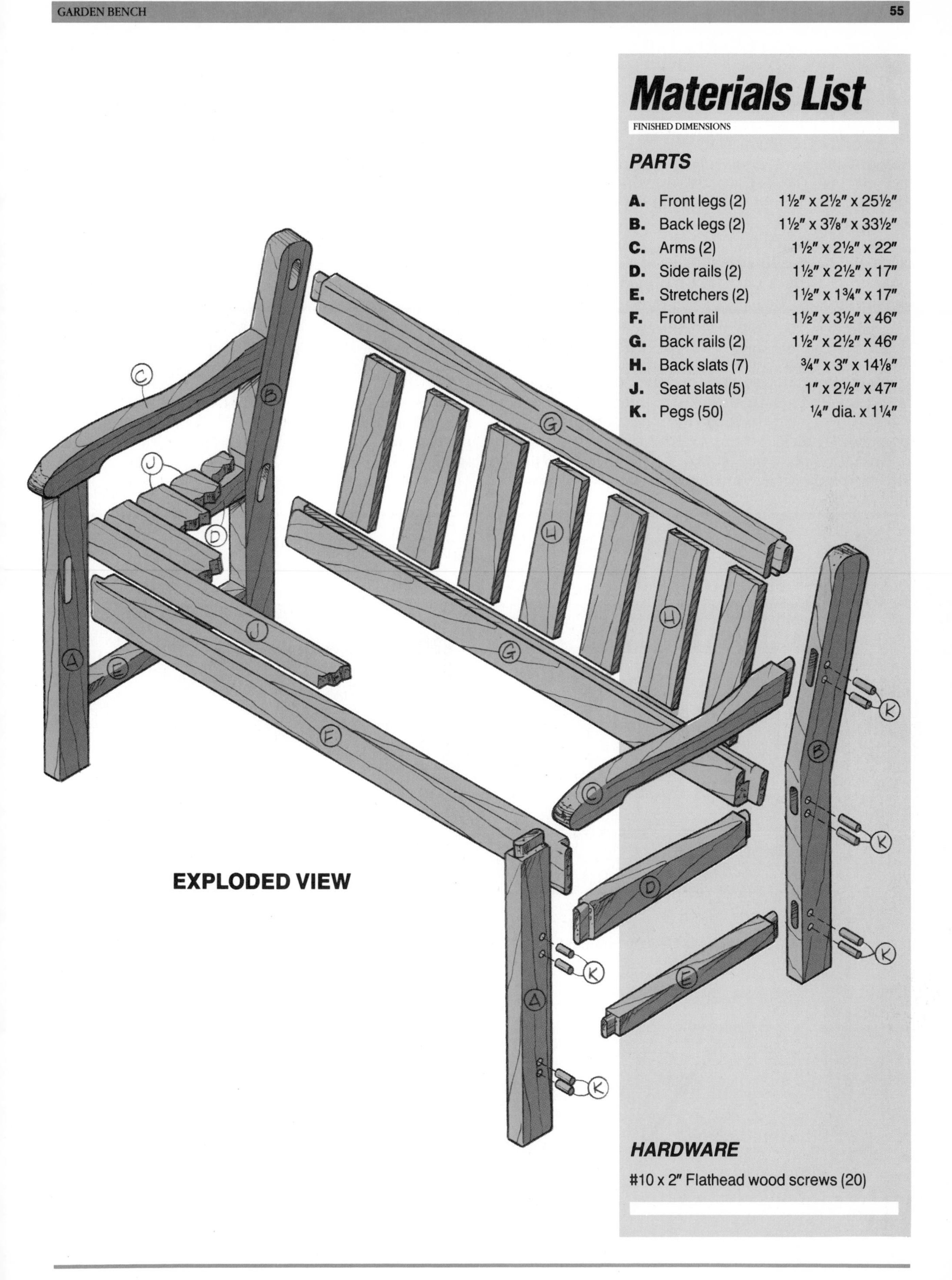

Materials List

FINISHED DIMENSIONS

PARTS

A.	Front legs (2)	1½″ x 2½″ x 25½″
B.	Back legs (2)	1½″ x 3⅞″ x 33½″
C.	Arms (2)	1½″ x 2½″ x 22″
D.	Side rails (2)	1½″ x 2½″ x 17″
E.	Stretchers (2)	1½″ x 1¾″ x 17″
F.	Front rail	1½″ x 3½″ x 46″
G.	Back rails (2)	1½″ x 2½″ x 46″
H.	Back slats (7)	¾″ x 3″ x 14⅛″
J.	Seat slats (5)	1″ x 2½″ x 47″
K.	Pegs (50)	¼″ dia. x 1¼″

HARDWARE

#10 x 2″ Flathead wood screws (20)

1 ***Cut the parts to size.*** Choose a good hard wood (not necessarily a hardwood) for this bench. The mortise-and-tenon joints will not hold up in soft wood. Mahogany is a good choice; Atlantic white cedar (juniper) is a good softwood to use, since this it is harder than most. Cedar and redwood will *not* work well; these woods are too soft.

For the legs, stretchers, and other frame parts, you'll need to purchase 18-20 board feet of wood sawn "eight-quarters" (2″ thick), and have it planed down. In some lumberyards, particularly those that do custom sawing, you may be able to get lumber cut seven-quarters thick. If you can find it, buy it. There will be less waste when the wood is planed down to 1½″.

For the seat and back slats, buy 10-12 board feet of wood sawn five-quarters. Have two-thirds of this wood planed down to 1″ thick, and the other third planed down to ¾″ thick.

Note: Don't take our estimates of board feet too literally. Most lumberyards sell their hardwoods in random lengths and widths. Depending on the wood selected, our estimates may be too little or too much. When you purchase the lumber, choose the boards yourself and give some careful thought as to what parts you will cut from each board. This way, you can cut down on the waste. ***The smart woodworker buys his lumber by the board, not the board foot.***

> TRY THIS! When you purchase your wood, take these plans with you and have the people at the yard figure your needs. Most of the better lumberyards provide this service free of charge.

When you've gathered all the materials you need, and have planed them down to the proper thicknesses, cut the parts to the sizes shown in the Materials List. Cut the stock for the back legs 1″-2″ long, so that there's plenty of room to cut out the shapes.

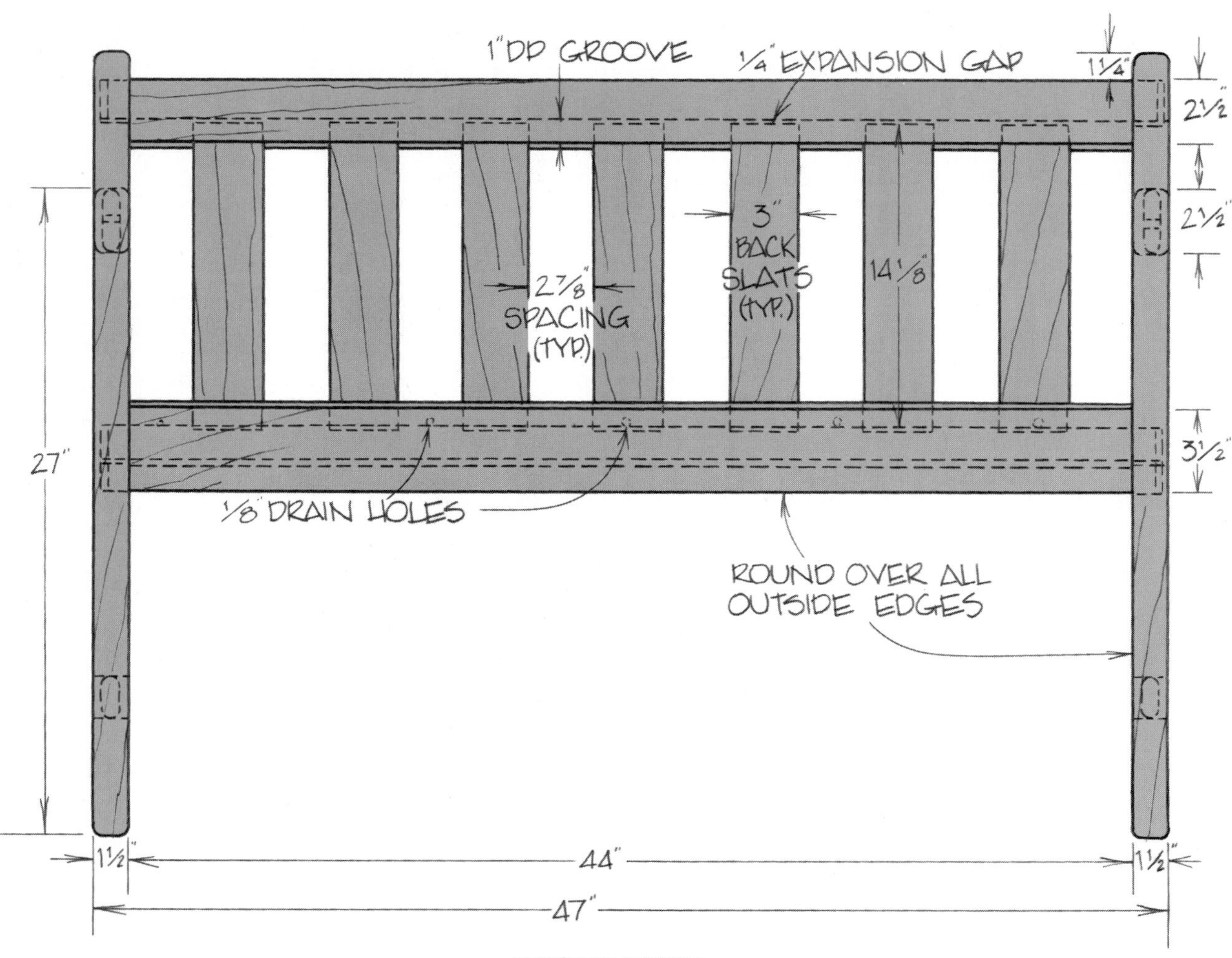

FRONT VIEW

2 Make a template for the side frame assemblies.

Draw up the *Side View* full size. You don't have to put all the measurements on it, but you will need the dotted lines. Use this full-scale plan to mark the shapes of the back legs, arms, and side rails. This can be done in one of two ways. You can photocopy the full-size plans, and use the copies to make cardboard or hardboard templates. Or you can transfer the shapes of the parts directly to the wood, using carbon paper. (See Figure 1.)

Once you've marked the shapes of the individual pieces, tape or glue the full-size plans to a piece of plywood. This will serve as a template — something for you to compare your work to as it progresses — to make sure that you get each part properly shaped and both side frame assemblies exactly the same.

Note: If you're an experienced woodworker, you may wish to omit this step. However, beginners and woodworkers who have limited experience fitting angled mortise and tenon joints, will find that a template helps to ensure accuracy.

1/Once you've made a full size drawing of the Side View, you can use carbon paper to transfer the shapes of the parts to the wood.

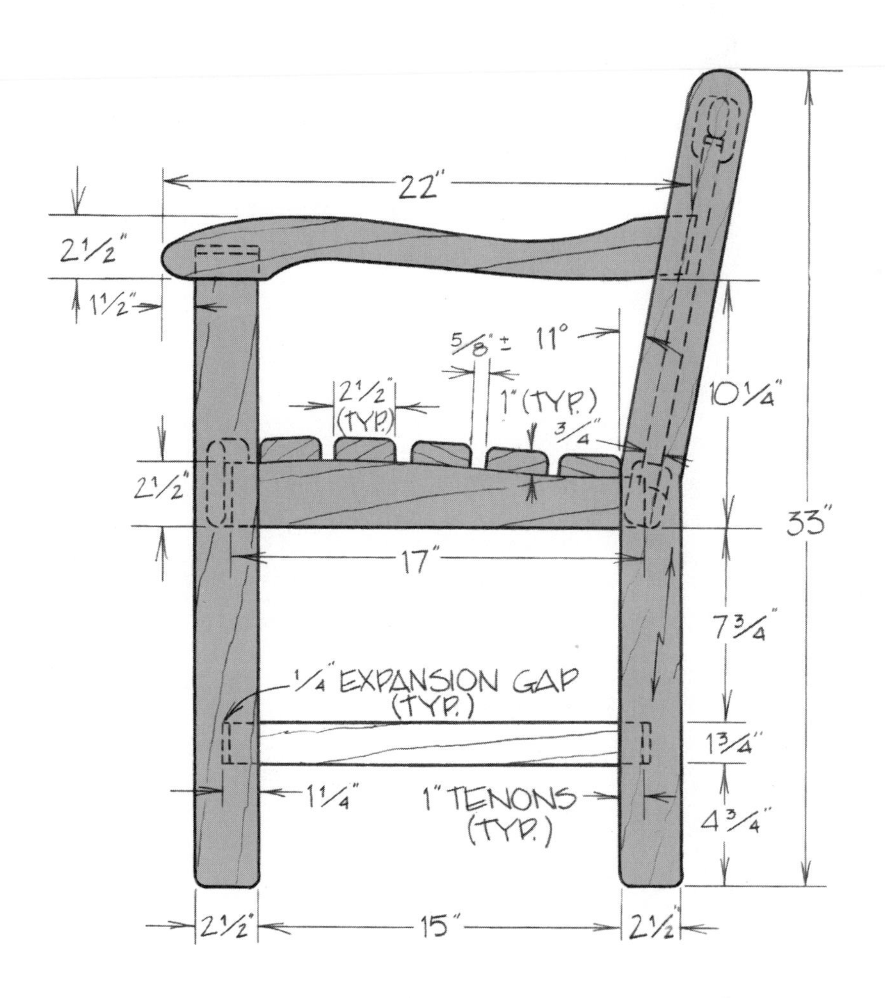

SIDE VIEW

3 ***Cut the shapes of the back legs.*** Using a band saw or sabre saw, cut out the back legs, then sand away the saw marks. *Do not* cut the shapes of the other parts at this time. Normally, it is much easier to make the joinery in a board *before* you cut an irregular shape. However, the back legs are one exception to this rule. The shapes must be cut before the joinery.

> TRY THIS! To shape the back legs precisely, cut a little wide of the marks, then sand up to them.

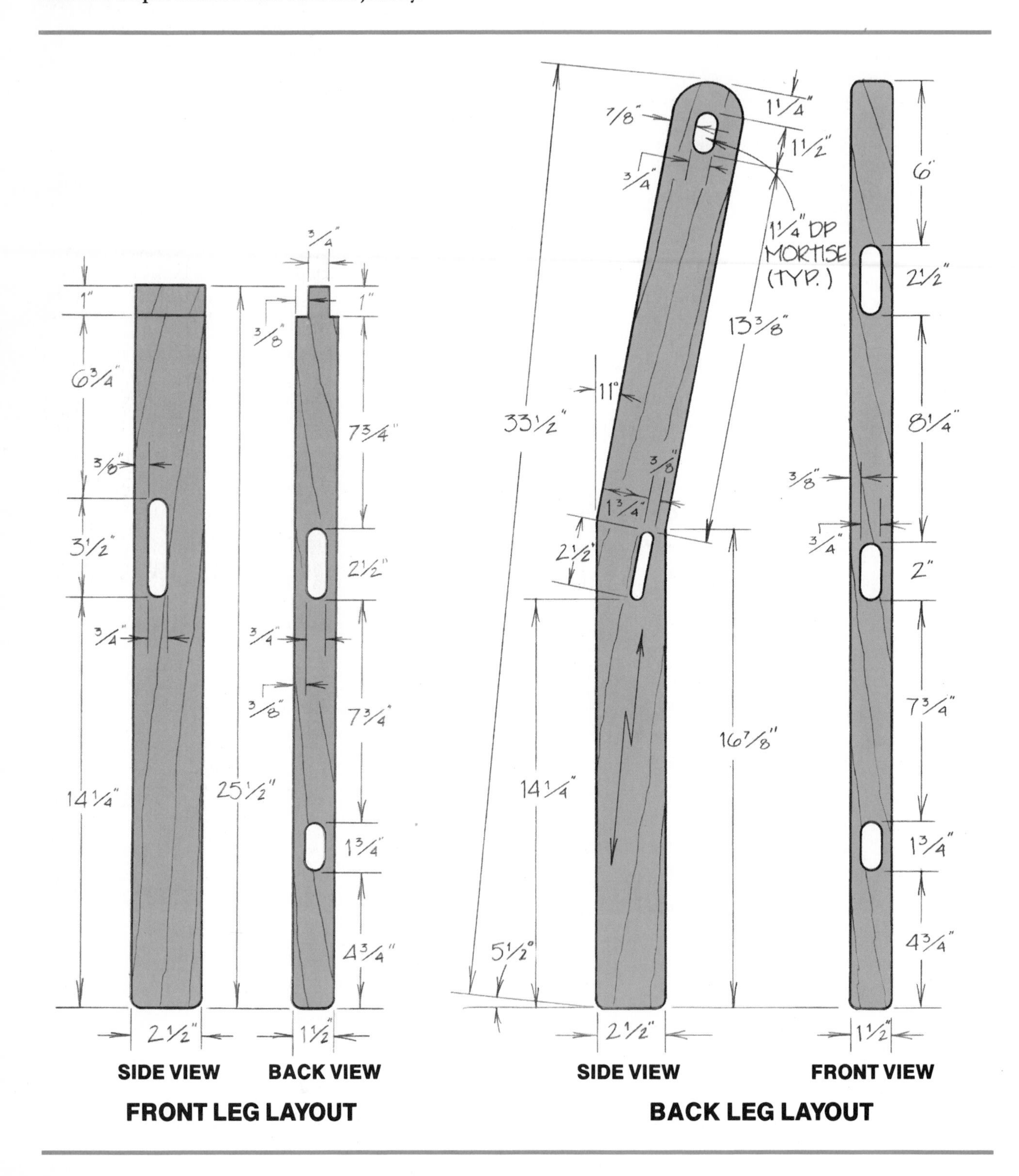

4 **Cut all the tenons.**

Using your full-size template, mark tenons on the arms, front legs, side rails, and stretchers. Also, measure and mark the tenon on the front and back rails.

You can cut out these tenons using a variety of methods. In fact, you'll probably want to use a combination of methods, since some work better on one type of tenon than another. The easiest way to cut the tenons is with a dado cutter mounted on your table saw or radial arm saw. Simply pass the wood across the cutter, flip the board, and make an identical cut on the other side. You can use stop blocks to help properly gauge the length of the tenons. (See Figure 2.) This method works best for the ordinary, square tenons at the ends of the side rails, upper back rails, stretchers, and front legs.

If you wish to use your saw blade to cut the tenons, make a single cut to mark the shoulders. Make several more cuts through the waste, to cut the waste up into small, easily removed blocks. Then remove the waste with a chisel. You'll find that the extra cuts through the waste also keep you from removing too much stock and making the tenon too thin.

For tenons that are cut at an angle, such as those at the ends of the arms, you could use either a dado cutter or a saw blade. But this requires that you change the angle of the cuts twice (11° to the left, then 11° to the right), and both those cuts must be precise. You'll find that it's much easier to get the precision you need with a hand saw and a little patience. Clamp a block to the wood to start the cuts at precisely the right points, and to help hold the saw square to the stock. (See Figure 3.) To remove the waste, cut perpendicular to the first cuts with the saw. Cut a little wide of your mark, then pare the tenon down to its finished dimensions with a chisel.

***2**/Most of the tenons in this project can be cut with a dado cutter. Use a stop block to properly gauge the length of each tenon.*

***3**/When sawing a tenon by hand, clamp a scrap block to the stock to help guide the cut and keep the blade square to the wood.*

5 **Drill the mortises.**

Carefully mark the positions of the mortises as you did the tenons. "Drill" each mortise by making a series of stopped holes, then flattening or "cleaning up" the long sides of the mortises with a chisel. (See Figure 4.)

Most of the mortises in this project are fairly straightforward to make. The only mortises that require any special consideration are those in the arm-to-back leg joints. These must be drilled at 11° off square. Tilt the table of your drill press, or build a jig to hold the wood at the proper angle.

***4**/To make a mortise, first drill a series of holes. Then clean up the long edges of the mortise with a chisel.*

6 Cut the remaining shapes and joinery.

Cut out the shapes of the arms and side rails with a band saw or sabre saw. Sand away the saw marks. With a dado cutter, make the long groove in the back rails. Don't drill the drainage holes yet; you don't need to do that until after you assemble the bench.

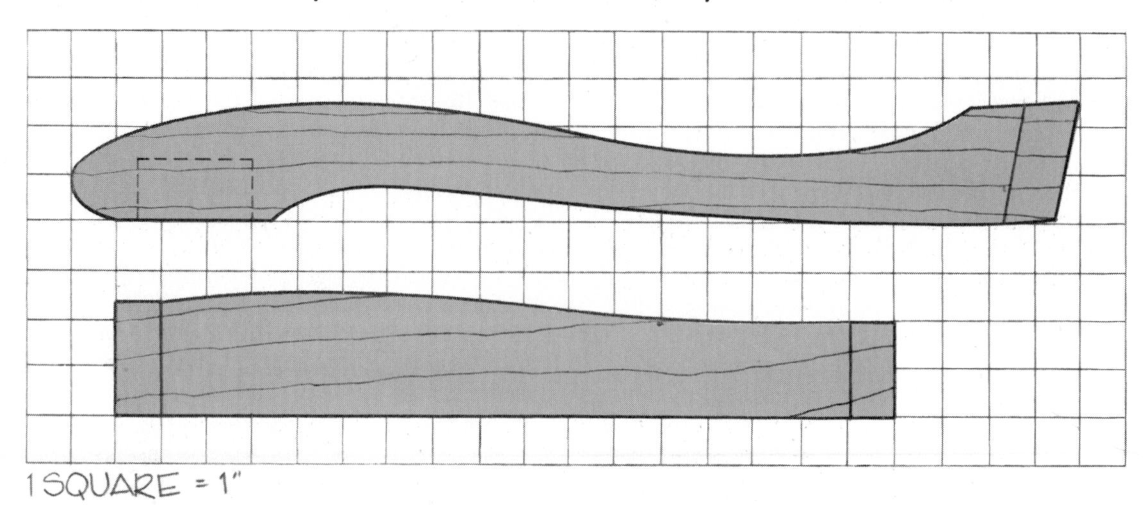

ARM AND SEAT PATTERNS

7 Fit the tenons to the mortises.

Round the corners of the tenons with a rasp and chisel to fit the mortises. (See Figure 5.) Custom fit each tenon to its mortise, and mark them carefully so that you know what part joins to another.

5/Round the tenons with a chisel and a rasp to fit the mortises.

Temporarily assemble the parts to make sure they all fit properly. There should be some slop in the joints, but not much. The entire bench frame should stand up on its own, with no need of clamps to hold it together. When you're satisfied that everything fits properly, disassemble the parts.

TRY THIS! If you wish, you could square the corners of the mortises to fit the tenons, instead of rounding the tenons to fit the mortises. Squaring the corners requires a very sharp chisel.

8 Finish sand all the parts.

Finish sand the flat surfaces of all the bench parts. Be careful not to round any corners or edges; you don't want to do that until *after* the bench is permanently assembled. If you've decided to paint or finish the bench, apply the first coat to all the disassembled parts, including the mortises and tenons.

9 Assemble the bench frame and back slats.

Reassemble the two side frame assemblies. Lay each one out on the full-size template to help square the parts to each other. When everything is properly positioned, clamp it all in place on the plywood board. Then drill peg holes — two holes per joint — and insert the pegs. Glue each peg in place with waterproof glue.

After assembling the side frames, fit the front and back rails, and back slats into place. Before you peg the joints, check that the back slats are spaced evenly. When you're satisfied that they are, peg the slats in the rails. (This requires only two pegs per slat, one at the top and one at the bottom of each board.) After the back is pegged, peg the rails at the corners. Like the joints in the side frames, the corner joints require two pegs each.

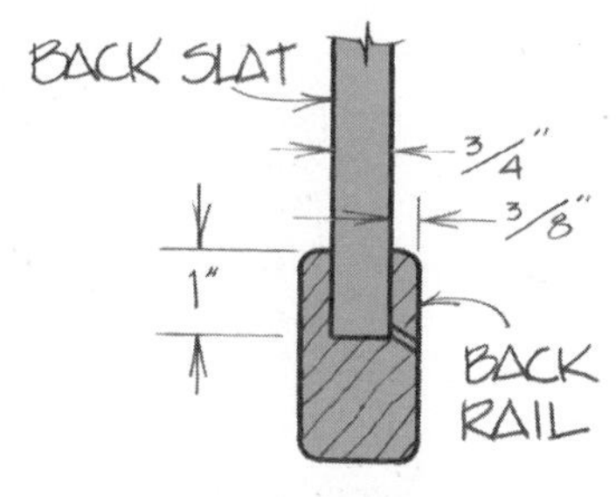

SLAT-TO-RAIL JOINERY DETAIL

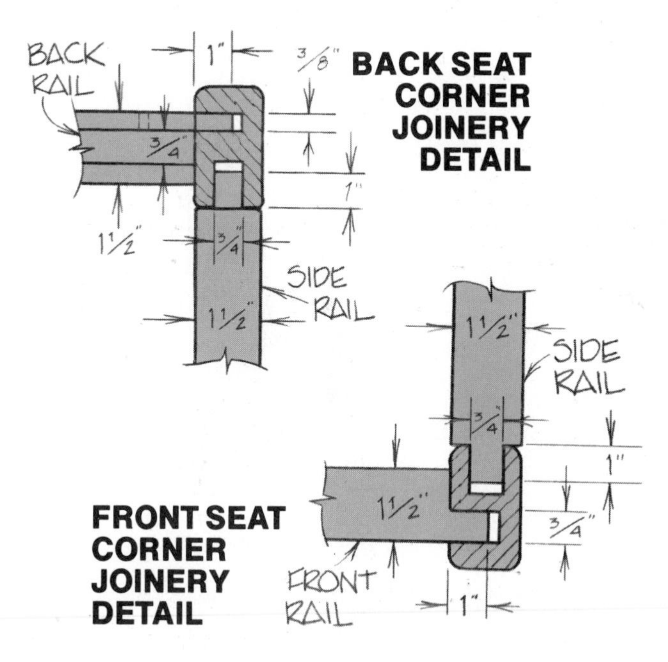

BACK SEAT CORNER JOINERY DETAIL

FRONT SEAT CORNER JOINERY DETAIL

10 Drill drainage holes in the lower back rail.

The groove in the lower back rail will tend to fill up with water unless you provide for drainage. Drill a ⅛" hole through the back side of the rail and into the groove between each slat, as shown in the *Back Rail Drain Hole Detail.* This will let the water out of the groove.

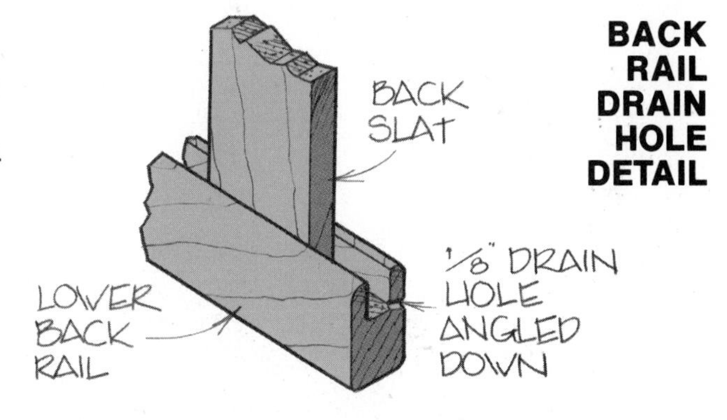

BACK RAIL DRAIN HOLE DETAIL

11 Attach the seat.

Position the seat slats, spacing them out evenly. Tack them in place temporarily with finishing nails, and check the spacing again. If you're satisfied, remove the nails one by one, and replace them with #10 x 2" flathead wood screws. Counterbore and countersink the screws, then cover the screw heads with wooden plugs. Glue these plugs in place with waterproof glue.

12 Sand and finish the assembled bench.

Sand all the pegs and screw plugs flush with the surface of the wood. Round the corners and edges of the bench, and do any necessary touch-up sanding. Then apply a finish, if you've decided you want one.

Children's Picnic Table and Benches

Indoors or outdoors, kids need their own space — a space where they can accomplish things, where the world isn't too big for them to handle, where everything is kid-size. The table and benches that you see here help to create just such a space out of doors — on your deck or in your backyard. The benches are just the right height for children from three years old on up to seven or eight. And the table provides plenty of room for kids to spread out their toys without being too big.

The construction is simple, but strong — tough enough to take the sort of punishment that kids dish out. The legs and stretchers are joined by interlocking lap joints. The seat and tabletop planks serve double-duty as diagonal braces that reinforce the frame. If you make them from good-quality woods, you'll find the table and benches are sturdy enough to last through several childhoods.

TABLE
EXPLODED VIEW

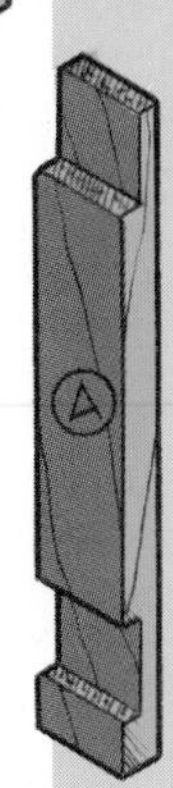

BENCH
EXPLODED VIEW

Materials List

FINISHED DIMENSIONS

PARTS

Table

	Part	Dimensions
A.	Legs (4)	1½″ x 3½″ x 21¼″
B.	Stretchers (4)	1½″ x 3½″ x 39¾″
C.	Outside slats (4)	¾″ x 3½″ x 30″
D.	Next-to-outside slats (4)	¾″ x 3½″ x 22½″
E.	Next-to-middle slats (4)	¾″ x 3½″ x 15″
F.	Middle slats (4)	¾″ x 3½″ x 7½″

Benches (2)

	Part	Dimensions
A.	Legs (8)	1½″ x 3½″ x 11¼″
B.	Stretchers (8)	1½″ x 3½″ x 16″
C.	Outside slats (8)	¾″ x 3½″ x 13″
D.	Middle slats (8)	¾″ x 2¾″ x 5½″

HARDWARE

Table

#10 x 1¼″ Flathead wood screws (16)
#12 x 2½″ Flathead wood screws (2)
6d Finishing nails (¼ lb.)

Benches (2)

#10 x 1¼″ Flathead wood screws (16)
#12 x 2½″ Flathead wood screws (2)
6d Finishing nails (¼ lb.)

1 ***Carefully choose your lumber.*** Give some careful thought to the type of lumber that you will use to build this project, particularly if it is to be used by toddlers. Avoid pressure-treated lumber, since this wood is saturated with toxic chemicals. Choose an untreated, clear softwood, free of any defects that might throw splinters.

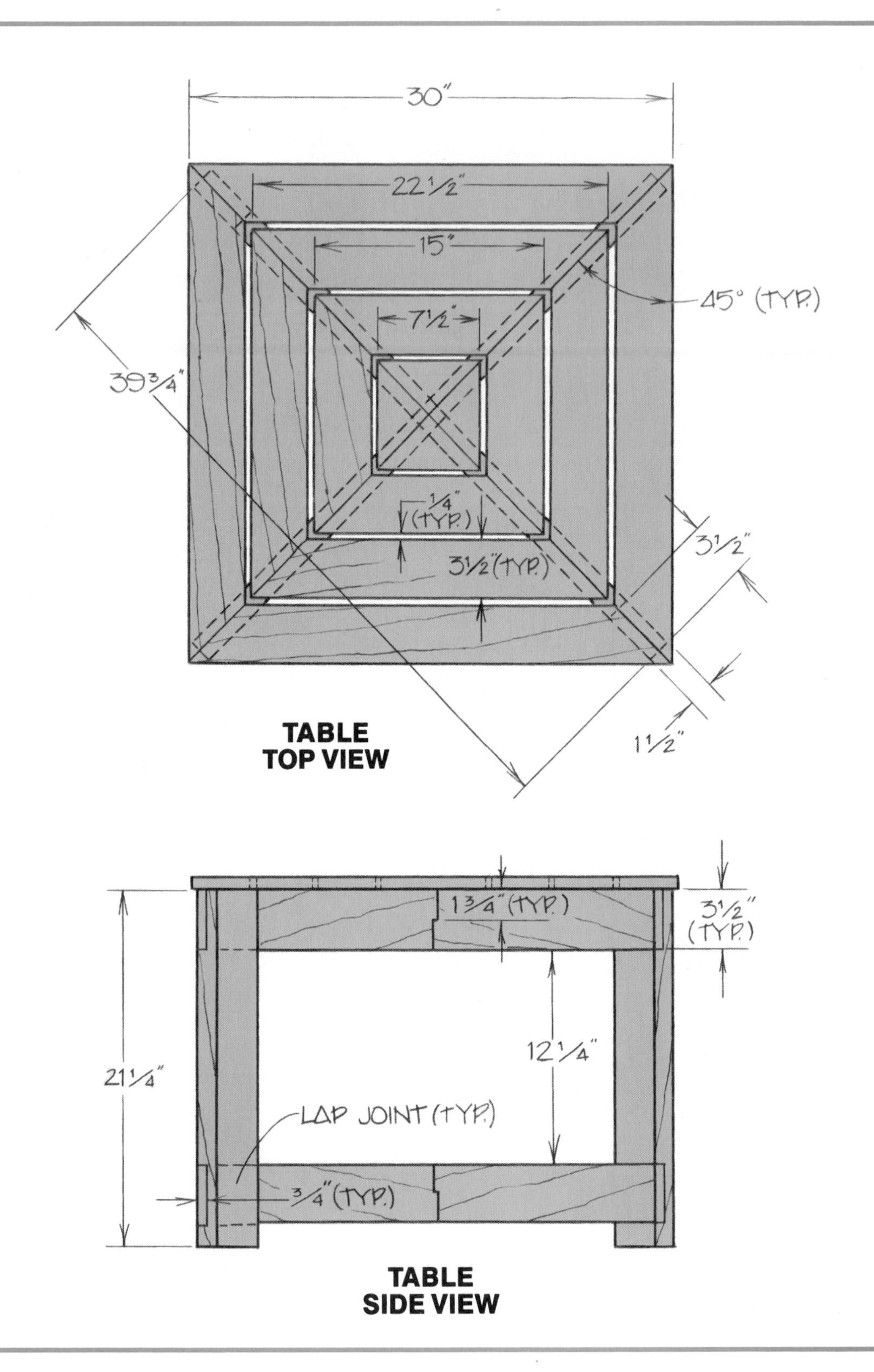

TABLE TOP VIEW

TABLE SIDE VIEW

2 ***Cut the legs and stretchers to size.*** The legs and stretchers for this project are made from 2 x 4 stock. To make one table and two benches you'll need approximately six 2 x 4s, 8′ long. Two more benches (making four altogether) require two more. Cut these parts to the sizes shown in the Materials List.

TRY THIS! To speed the cutting process, attach a stop block to the fence of your table saw or the backstop of your radial arm saw. This will help you gauge the length of identical parts, with no need to measure each one.

3 ***Cut the lap joints in the middle of the stretchers.*** Using your table saw or radial arm saw, cut the lap joints in the table and the bench stretchers. Here again, you can use stop blocks to speed the process. Since the lap joints must be centered precisely in the middle of each stretcher, you can use a stop block to position the stock for the two *outside* cuts that mark the edges of the lap.

Adjust the height of the saw blade to cut exactly halfway through the *width* of the 2 x 4 stock. Make your first cut, turn the board, and make the second. (See Figure 1.) After you have made all the outside cuts in all the stretchers, remove the stop block. Cut away the waste between the outside cuts by making repeated passes over the saw blade.

You can also use a dado cutter to make these joints. But only if the dado cutter will cut 1¾″ deep.

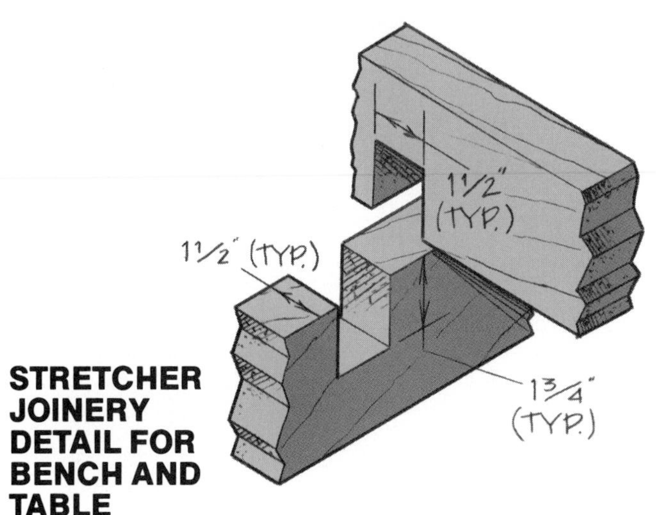

STRETCHER JOINERY DETAIL FOR BENCH AND TABLE

1/*Use a stop block to automatically position the stretchers to make the outside saw cuts on the lap joints in the middle of the stretchers.*

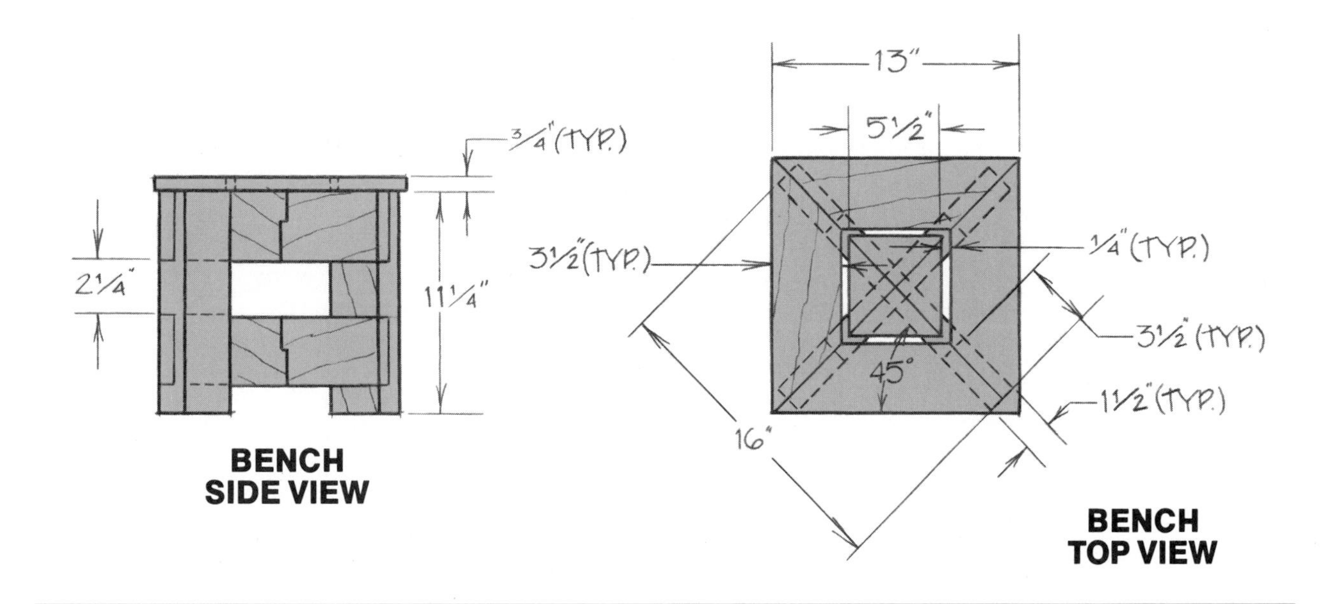

BENCH SIDE VIEW

BENCH TOP VIEW

4 *Cut the lap joints in the legs and in the ends of the stretchers.* It's easiest to cut these lap joints with a dado cutter mounted on your table saw or radial arm saw. Once again, cut the stock for both the table and the benches, and use a stop block to make the repetitive cuts all the same.

Adjust the height of the dado cutter to cut halfway through the *thickness* of a 2 x 4. To make the lower lap in the legs, position the stop block to make the first outside cuts, 2″ from the bottoms of the legs. Cut all the legs, and readjust the stop block to make the other outside cut, 5½″ from the bottoms of the legs. (See Figure 2.) Remove the stop blocks and cut away the waste in between the cuts. (See Figure 3.)

To cut the laps in the upper ends of the legs, and both ends of the stretchers, you only need to position the stop block once. Make a single outside cut, 3½″ from the ends; then saw away the waste.

2/You can also use stop blocks with a dado cutter. For the lap joints near the bottom of the legs, make the first outside cut, reposition the block, and make the second.

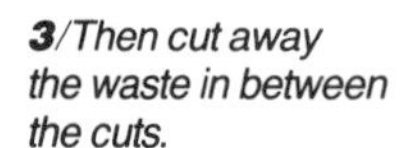

3/Then cut away the waste in between the cuts.

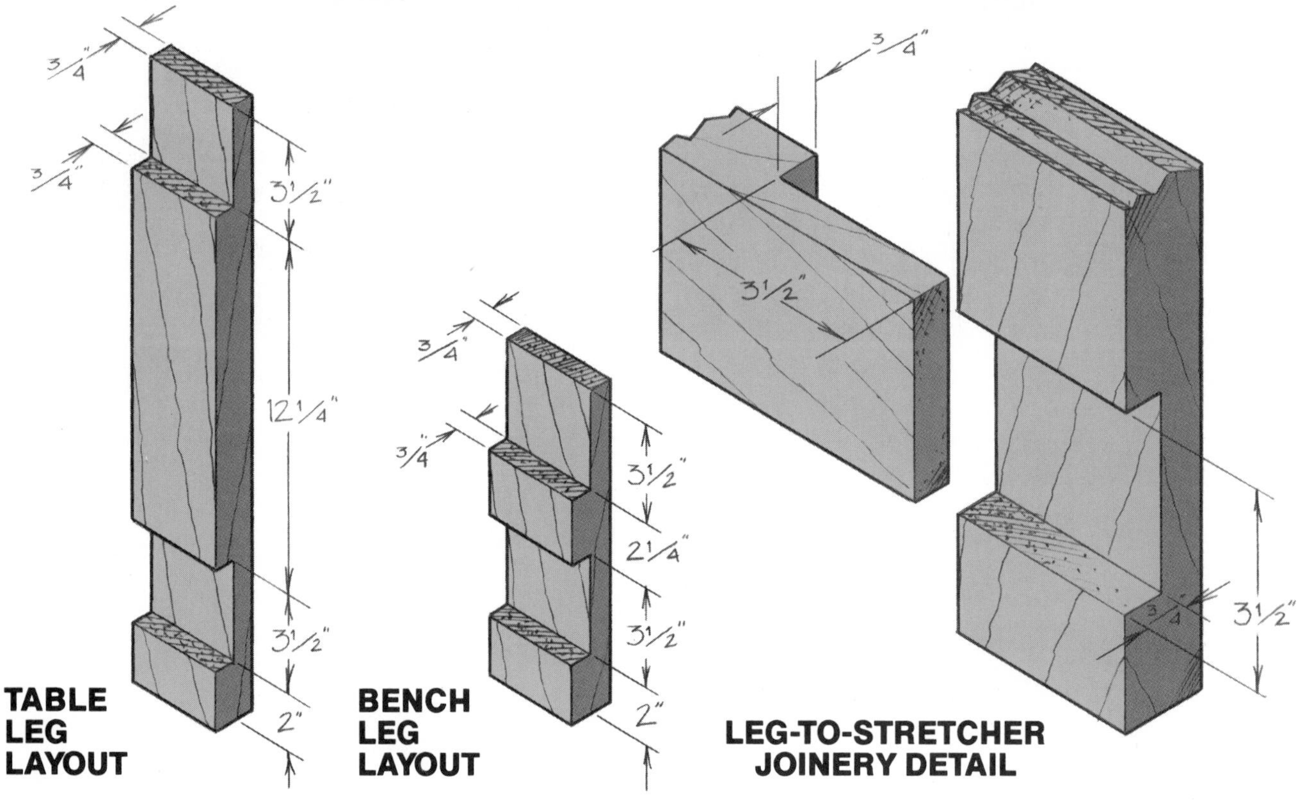

5 *Temporarily assemble the legs and stretchers.* Temporarily clamp the legs and stretchers together to check the fit of the lap joints. When you're satisfied that the joints all fit properly, leave the parts assembled while you cut and fit the table top and seats.

6 Cut the slats for the table top and the seats.

You can rip and cut all the slats for a table and two benches from a single 1 x 12, 12′ long. (To do this, you have to "alternate" on the miter cuts, to avoid wasting material.) If you're making four benches, purchase two 1 x 12s, 8′ long. Rip and join the stock to make long strips 3½″ wide.

Set up your saw for the miter cuts. After you set the saw to make 45° miters, and *before* you cut good stock, cut four pieces of scrap. Each piece of scrap must be exactly the same length and mitered on both ends. Put them together to form a square to check if the miter is true. When you adjust the saw to increase or reduce the angle of a miter, move the arm or miter gauge just ¼°-½° at a time.

4*/Stop blocks are also useful when making miter cuts. Use them to gauge the length of the slats.*

When the saw is properly adjusted, cut the slats to length, mitering the ends at 45°. Like all the parts in this project, you can use a stop block to help make repetitive cuts. (See Figure 4.) As you cut, put the parts in place on the frame assemblies to check the fit.

7 Finish sand all the parts before final assembly.

Disassemble the table and benches, and sand the unassembled parts to remove any irregularities in the wood, and to make them smooth and clean. If you plan to paint or finish the table and benches, apply the first coat before you reassemble the parts.

8 Assemble the table and bench frames.

Fasten the frames back together with flathead wood screws. Use #10 x 1¼″ screws for the lap joints in between the legs and the stretchers, and #12 x 2½″ screws for the lap joints in the middle of the stretchers. Once the table and the bench frames are assembled, sand the lap joints to make sure the ends of the stretchers are flush with the outside edges of the legs.

9 Attach the slats to the tops of the table and benches.

Make sure the stretchers in each frame are absolutely square to each other. Then position the slats on the top of each frame, and tack them in place with finishing nails. When you're satisfied that all the slats are properly positioned and spaced, drive the nails all the way home.

TRY THIS! Drill pilot holes in the slats for the nails, especially in the smaller pieces. This will help to keep them from splitting.

10 Sand and finish the completed project.

Round over all the corners and edges on both the table and benches. Inspect the completed assemblies carefully to make sure there are no rough areas, or parts that could throw splinters. If you find any, sand them down. Then apply a finish, if you've decided to use one.

TRY THIS! If this project is going to be used by toddlers, think twice before applying a finish. *All* outdoor finishes and paints are toxic, to some degree. If you think a child might decide to chew on the edge of the table, take heart that most raw softwoods have lots of fiber and trace amounts of Vitamin C.

Gardener's Kneeling Bench

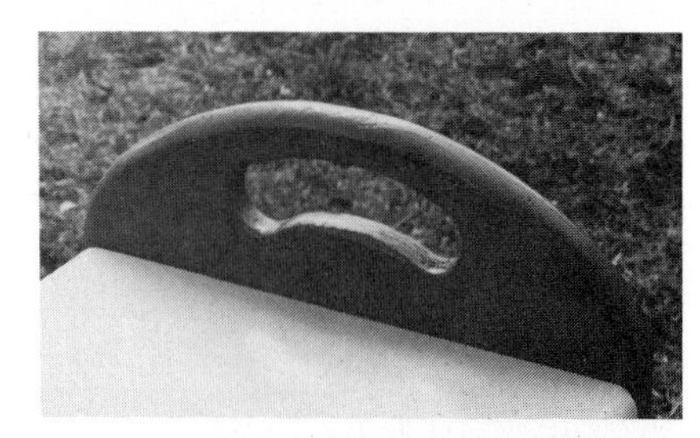

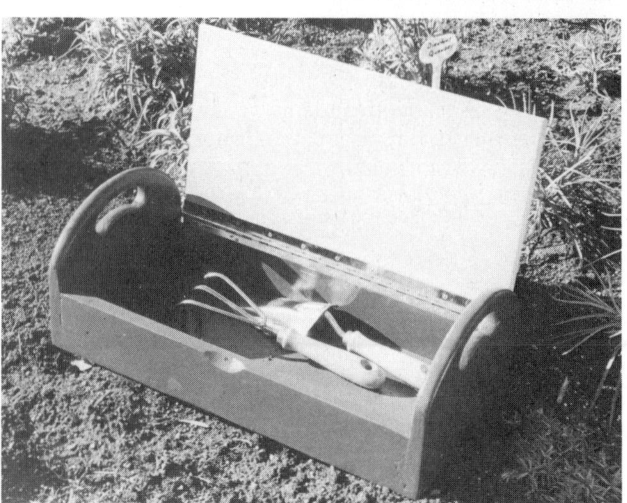

As every gardener knows, gardening is hard on the knees. It has its rewards, but in May, when your knees feel like they've been through the Inquisition, it's difficult to console yourself with flowers you'll enjoy in June or the tomatoes you'll reap in July.

Here's a quick project that will spare you some needless agony. It's a simple box that keeps your knees off the ground, and prevents the rocks from drilling holes in them. What's more, the box doubles as a tool caddy for hand tools.

EXPLODED VIEW

Materials List

FINISHED DIMENSIONS

PARTS

A.	Ends (2)	3/4" x 7" x 10"
B.	Front side	3/4" x 3 1/4" x 18 1/2"
C.	Back side	3/4" x 3 1/16" x 18 1/2"
D.	Bottom	1/4" x 9" x 19"
E.	Top	3/4" x 10" x 18 3/8"
F.	Braces (2)	3/4" x 3/4" x 8"

HARDWARE

1 1/2" x 18 3/8" Piano hinge and mounting screws

#10 x 1 1/4" Flathead wood screws (1 dozen)

1 ***Cut all the parts to size.*** Before you cut the parts, consider what tools you want to store and carry in this bench. You may have to adjust the length or the width of the sides and bottom slightly to make them fit. When you cut the sides, make the back side slightly narrower than the front side to accommodate the piano hinge. Our piano hinge was 3/16″ thick. Yours may be slightly thicker or thinner, depending on the manufacturer.

TRY THIS! You can eliminate the braces if you glue up a board for the top that's wide enough to allow you to run the grain from *side to side.* This will give you a little more room for tools.

2 ***Cut the shapes of the ends.*** Lay out the pattern for the sides on the stock, then cut the shape with a band saw or sabre saw. To make the handles, drill 1″-diameter holes at either end of the openings. Then cut away the waste in between the holes with a sabre saw. (See Figure 1.) Round over the edges of the handles with a router or a rasp so that they fit your hands comfortably.

***1**/To make a handle opening, first drill 1″ holes at either end. Then cut out the waste with a sabre saw.*

3 ***Cut the groove for the bottom.*** Make a 1/4″-wide, 1/4″-deep groove near the bottom edge of the ends and sides, to hold the bottom. You can cut this joint with a dado cutter, or make several passes with a regular saw blade.

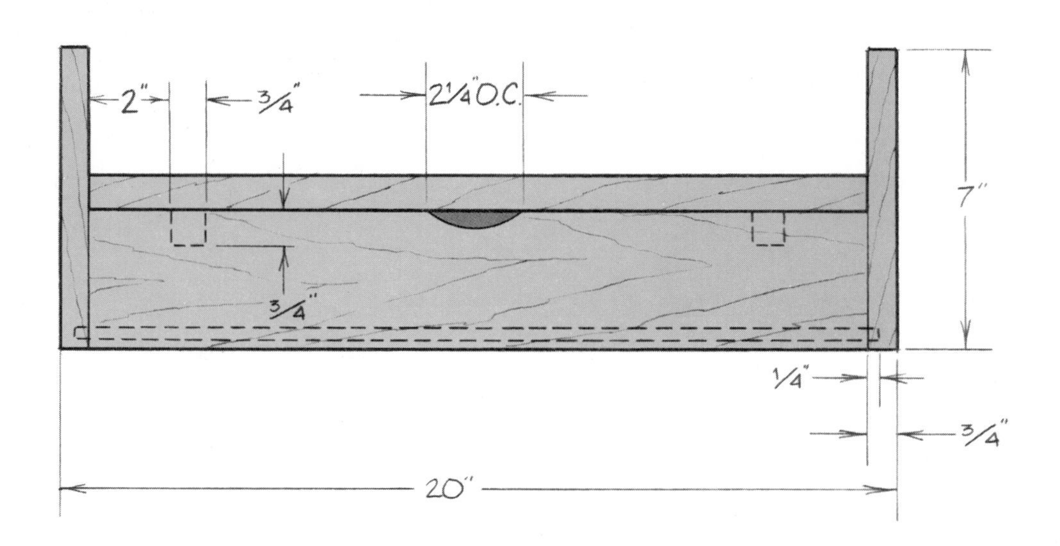

FRONT VIEW

4 Assemble the bench. With the bottom in place, attach the ends to the sides, using waterproof glue and flathead wood screws. Screw the braces to the underside of the top, centering them so that they won't rub when you open and close the top. Then hinge the top to back side of the bench. With a chisel, cut a slight indentation in the front side so that you can open the top easily. (See Figure 2.)

To finish up the garden bench, cover the screw heads with wooden plugs. Cut ¼" x ¼" x ½" wooden blocks to fill the bottom groove, where it shows on the back and the front of the project. (See Figure 3.) Fasten these plugs and blocks in place using waterproof glue. Finally, paint or stain the bench to suit yourself.

TRY THIS! For a little added comfort, glue a scrap of outdoor carpet to the top of the bench.

2/Chisel a small indentation in the top edge of the front side. This will make it easier to open the top.

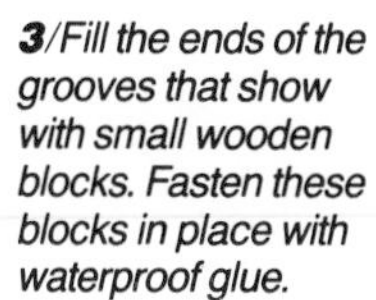

3/Fill the ends of the grooves that show with small wooden blocks. Fasten these blocks in place with waterproof glue.

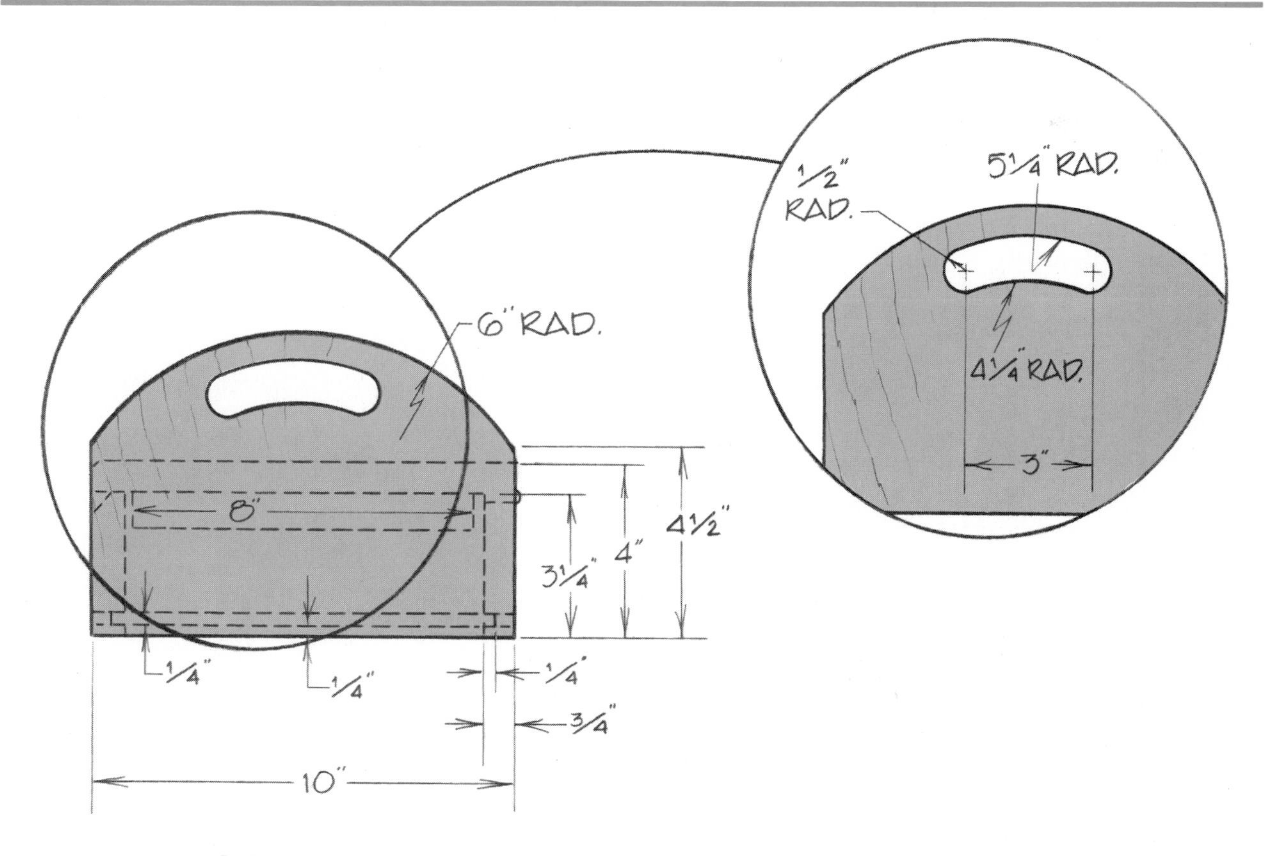

SIDE VIEW

Shrub Planter

Large planters add a refined touch to your deck or patio, creating the atmosphere of a formal garden. Properly arranged, they may be used to accent a door or gate; set apart areas of a large deck to create more intimate, private spaces; or just add shade and greenery to an otherwise barren expanse of wood or concrete.

The planter you see here is designed to hold a standard 15-gallon planting tub — large enough for shrubs and some small trees. If you wish, you can stretch the dimensions of the planter to hold larger tubs and larger plants. Or you can change the shape to fit a particular area or accommodate two tubs, side by side. The design is very versatile; you can easily alter it to suit your needs — or the needs of the shrub or tree you wish to pot.

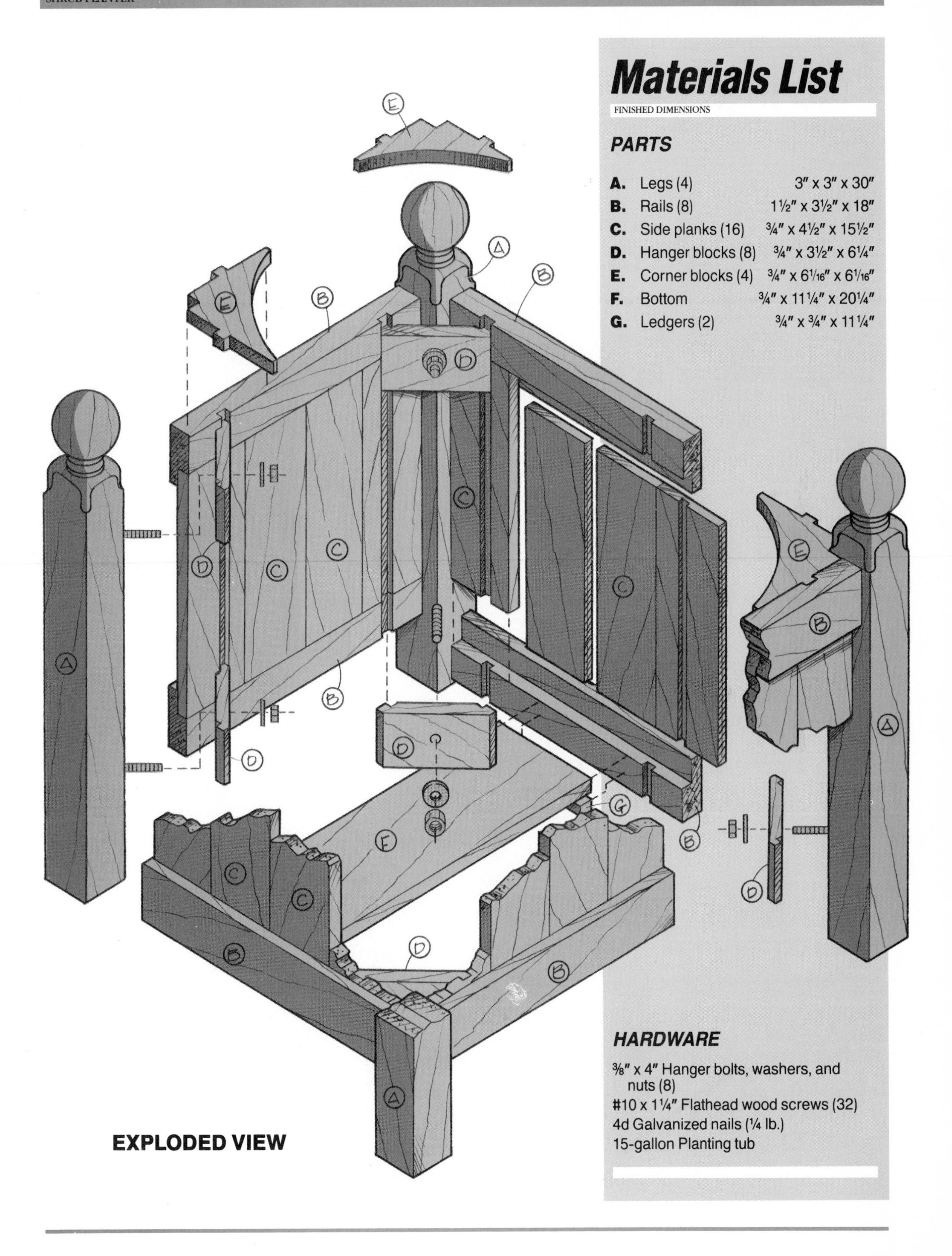

EXPLODED VIEW

Materials List

FINISHED DIMENSIONS

PARTS

A.	Legs (4)	3″ x 3″ x 30″
B.	Rails (8)	1½″ x 3½″ x 18″
C.	Side planks (16)	¾″ x 4½″ x 15½″
D.	Hanger blocks (8)	¾″ x 3½″ x 6¼″
E.	Corner blocks (4)	¾″ x 6¹⁄₁₆″ x 6¹⁄₁₆″
F.	Bottom	¾″ x 11¼″ x 20¼″
G.	Ledgers (2)	¾″ x ¾″ x 11¼″

HARDWARE

⅜″ x 4″ Hanger bolts, washers, and nuts (8)
#10 x 1¼″ Flathead wood screws (32)
4d Galvanized nails (¼ lb.)
15-gallon Planting tub

1 Cut the parts to size.

To make one of these planters, you'll need one 4 x 4, 12′ long, two 2 x 4's, 8′ long, and two 1 x 12's, 8′ long. Cut this lumber into the sizes shown in the Materials List, with the exception of the legs. Cut these 1″-2″ longer than shown. This will give you some extra stock when you turn them on the lathe.

2 Turn the tops of the legs.

Mount the legs on a lathe and turn a shape in the top 5″ of each leg. The shape shown here is just a suggestion; you can turn (or even carve) anything you want in this stock. If you do turn the ball shape that we have suggested, don't try to turn the complete shape on the lathe. Leave some waste on top of the ball. After turning all but the top of the ball, remove the stock from the lathe and cut off the waste with a band saw or coping saw. Then sand down the top of the turning to complete the ball shape. Also, sand the flat portions of the legs.

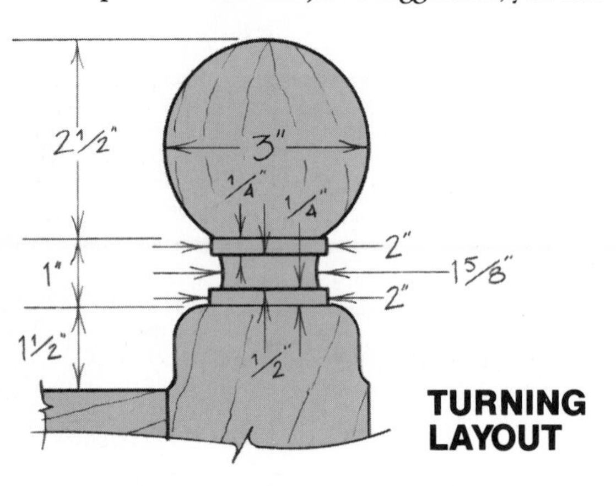

TURNING LAYOUT

> TRY THIS! If you don't have a lathe, cut a shape in the top of the legs with your band saw, using a "compound cutting" technique. Cut the design in one face; tape the waste back to the stock; turn it to an adjacent face and cut the same design again.

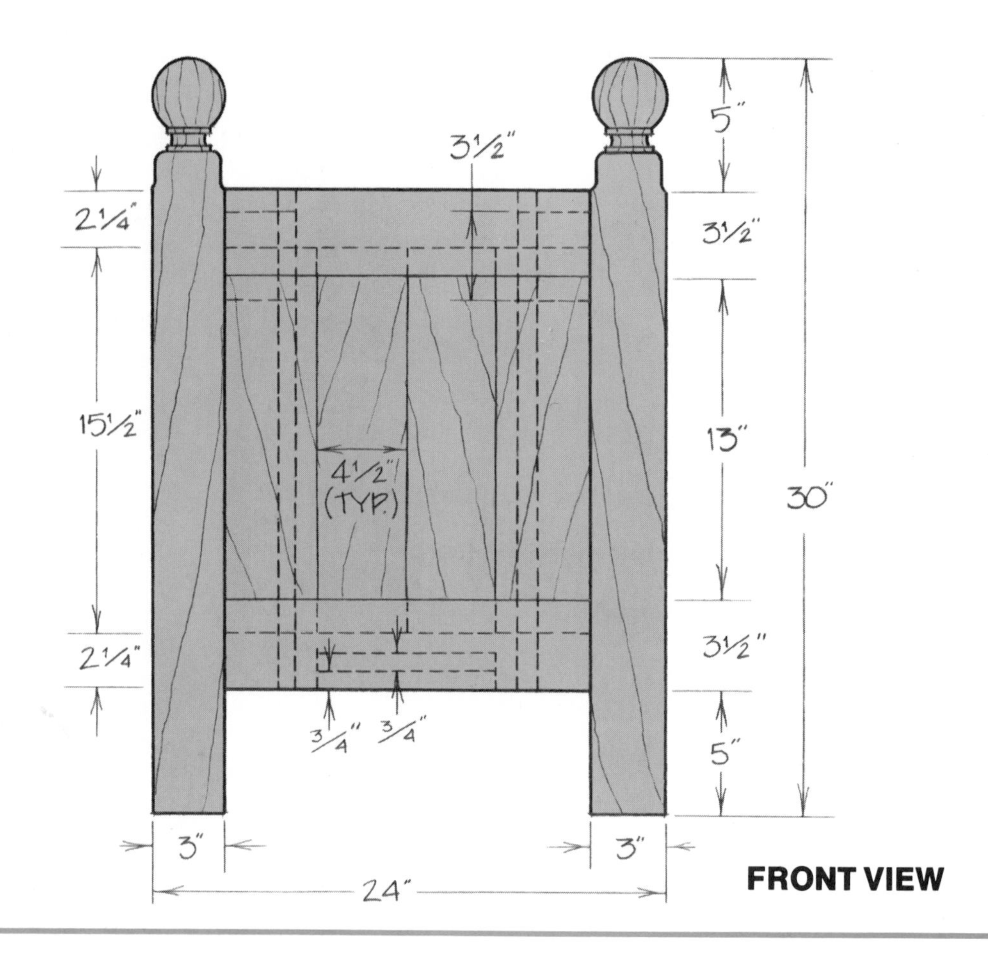

FRONT VIEW

3 ***Make the side panels.*** Cut a rabbet ¾″ deep and 1¼″ wide along one inside edge of the rails. It's easy to make large rabbets on your table saw with two passes over the blade. Adjust the blade and the rip fence to cut the depth of the rabbet, and make the first cut in the rails. (See Figure 1.) Readjust the blade and fence to cut the width, and make the second cut. (See Figure 2.)

When cutting a rabbet in this manner, be careful of two things. First of all, use push sticks and featherboards to help keep your hands clear of the saw blade. This is especially important, since you have to remove the saw guard to make these cuts. Secondly, set up your saw so that you can make the second pass without leaving the waste in between the saw and the fence. If you make this mistake, the waste will kick back with tremendous force.

After you've made the rabbets, finish sand the rails and side planks. Then attach the side planks to the rails with 4d galvanized common nails. If you can't find galvanized nails this small, you can use roofing nails instead. Be careful where you place the nails. Later on, you'll need to cut a groove down the length of the panels, and you don't want to hit a nail with the cutter.

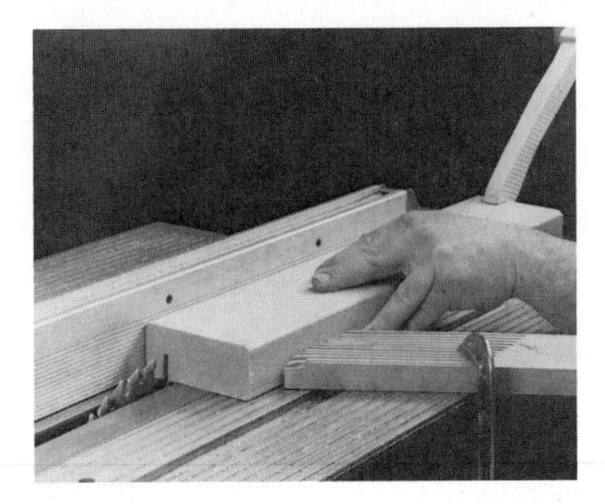

1/Make the rabbets in the rails in two cuts. First, cut the depth of the rabbets...

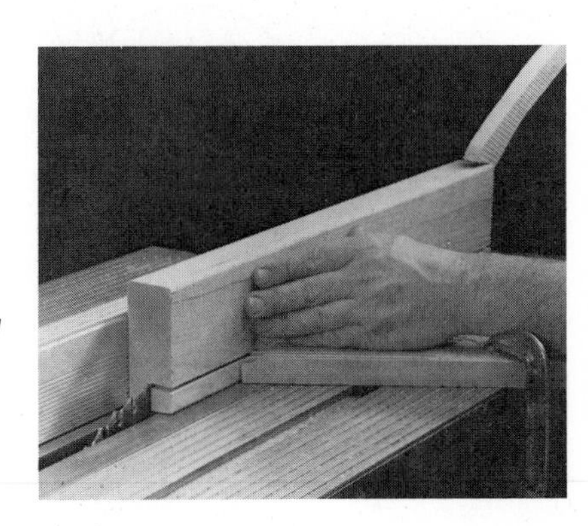

2/Then cut the width of the rabbets. On the second cut, be careful not to leave the waste in between the saw blade and the rip fence. If you do, it will kick back.

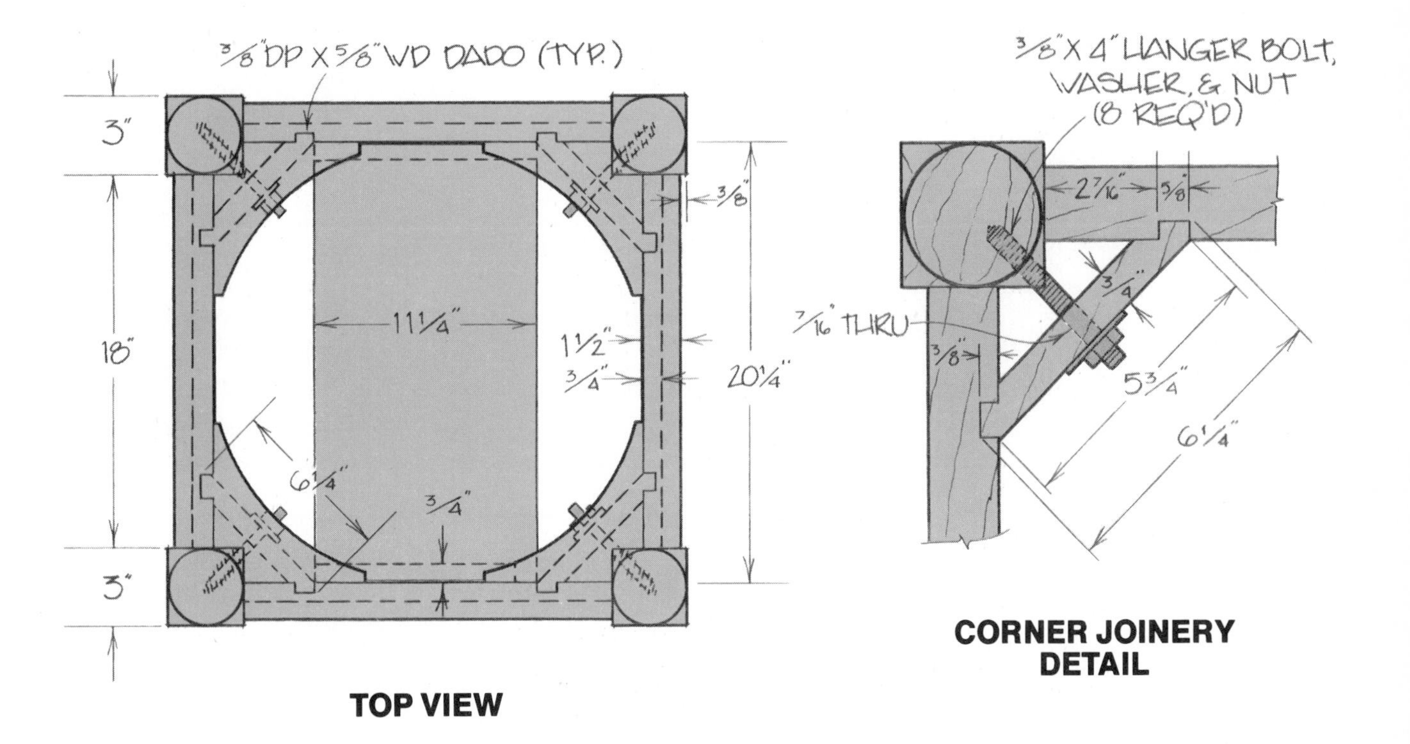

4 Make the hanger blocks.

The legs and the side panels are held together with hanger blocks. These are not only easier to make than the traditional mortise-and-tenon joints, but they give you the option of making this project into a *knock-down* planter, one that you can store away during the winter.

To make the hanger blocks, first drill 7/16″ holes through the center of the face of each block. Then make four bevel cuts across the ends of each block, all at 45°. (See Figure 3.) To make these cuts, set your table saw to cut at 45°, and position the rip fence so that you can use it as a guide. Start cutting by making one side of a V-groove near the ends of all four blocks. Make a pass, then flip each block end-for-end, and make another. Readjust the position of the fence and cut the other sides of the grooves in all the blocks. (See Figure 4.)

After you've cut the grooves, cut a narrow bevel and a wide bevel across each end. This will complete the shape of the hanger blocks. (See Figures 5 and 6.) Once again, use the rip fence as a guide, and flip the blocks end-for-end so that you make identical cuts in each end.

Important note: The rip fence must be positioned very accurately for these last two cuts. If the fence is too close to the blade on either cut, you'll shorten the block on the second-to-last pass. The last pass of the last cut will be off, making the block asymmetrical.

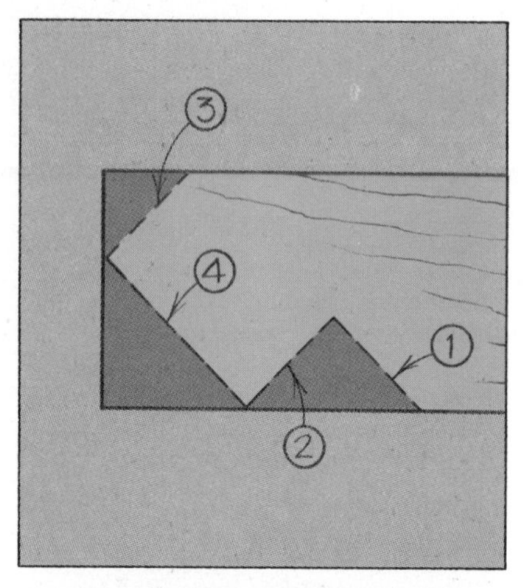

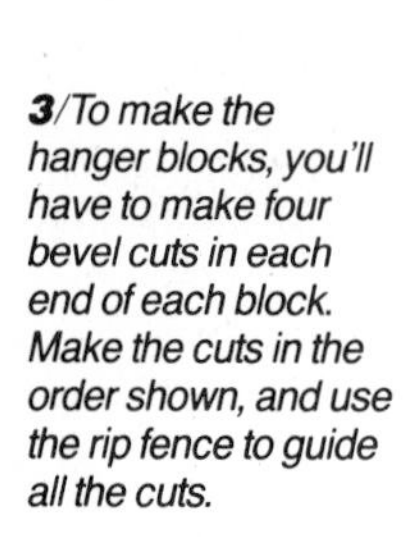
3/To make the hanger blocks, you'll have to make four bevel cuts in each end of each block. Make the cuts in the order shown, and use the rip fence to guide all the cuts.

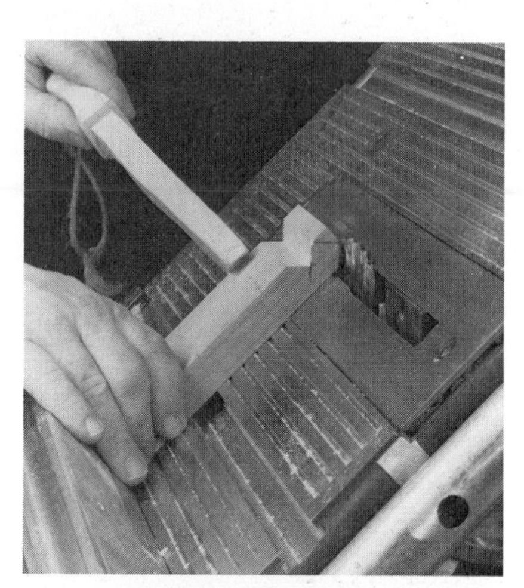
5/After cutting the V-grooves, make the narrow bevel cuts on the ends of the blocks.

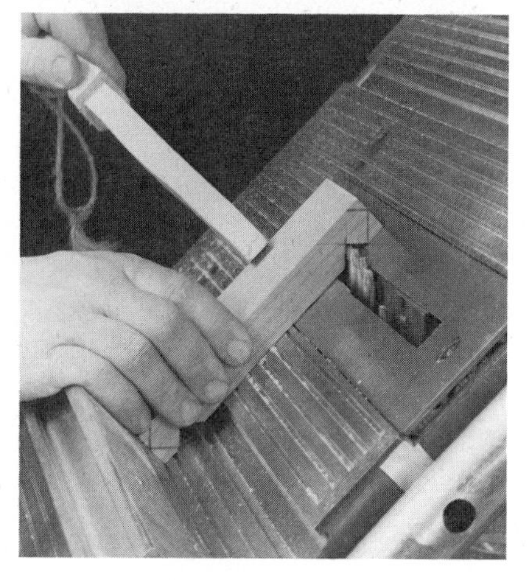
4/First, make two cuts at 45° to form V-grooves near the ends of the blocks.

6/Finish the blocks by cutting the wide bevels. The rip fence must be positioned very accurately when you make these last two miter cuts. You want a double miter on each end of each block, but you don't want to shorten the blocks when you make these cuts.

5 Cut the hanger grooves in the side panels.

With a dado cutter or a router, make two 5/8″-wide, 3/8″-deep grooves on the *inside* faces of each panel, 2 7/16″ in from each edge. Before cutting the grooves, double-check the positions of the nails. As mentioned before, you don't want to hit a nail with the cutter.

6 **Assemble the legs, side panels, and hanger blocks.** Carefully measure and mark the locations of the hanger bolts, as shown in the working drawings. Drill pilot holes for these bolts in the inside corners of the legs. To drill these holes at the proper angle (diagonally, at 45° from the two "inside" faces of the legs), tilt the worktable of your drill press or make a cradle to hold the legs. (See Figure 7.)

Turn the lag end of the bolts into the legs. The easiest way to install a hanger bolt, if you've never done it before, is to put a nut onto the threaded part of the shaft, and use this nut to turn the bolt into the leg. After the bolt is installed, remove the nut.

Now comes time to make a decision: Do you want this project to be a *knock-down* planter, or do you want to assemble it permanently? If you want to assemble it permanently, screw the hanger blocks in place in the grooves in the side panels. If not, just place them in the grooves. The tension from the hanger bolts, after you attach the legs, will hold the blocks in place.

TRY THIS! Assembling the legs, side panels, and hanger bolts *without* screwing the blocks in place is a task that will try the patience of a saint. If you don't have six extra hands, tack the blocks in place with finishing nails, then remove the nails after you attach the legs.

When the hanger blocks are properly positioned, install the legs with the hanger bolts through the holes in the hanger blocks. Put a flat washer and a nut on each bolt, and tighten the nuts. (See Figure 8.)

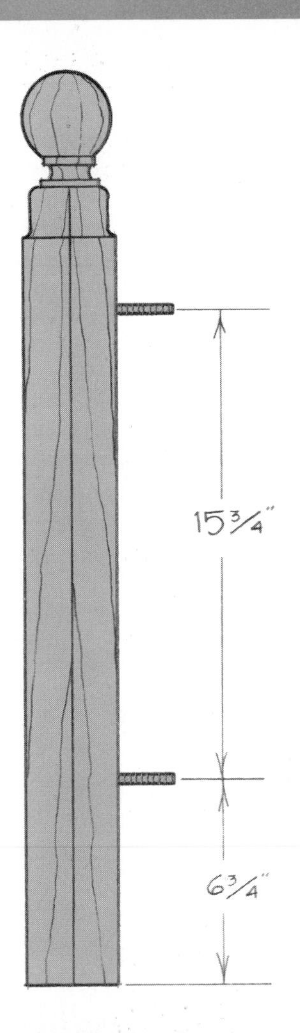

HANGER BOLT LOCATION DETAIL

7/*Drill pilot holes for the hanger bolts diagonally into the inside corners of the legs.*

8/*To attach the legs, put the hanger bolts through the holes in the hanger blocks and tighten the nuts.*

7 **Attach the bottom to the planter.** Screw the ledgers to the inside surfaces of two opposing side panels, where shown in the working drawings. Lay the bottom in place, across the ledgers. If you've opted to permanently assemble this project, you may wish to nail the bottom to the ledgers.

8 Install the corner covers. To hide the hanger bolts and to give the planter a finished look, make "corner covers." Lay out the shapes of these covers on ¾" thick stock, paying careful attention to the grain direction shown in the working drawings. Then cut out the shapes on a band saw or scroll saw. You'll probably have to do a little custom fitting to get each block to seat properly. When you've fitted the blocks, just lay them in place if you're making a knock-down planter. Nail them to the upper corner blocks if your planter is permanently assembled. (See Figure 9.)

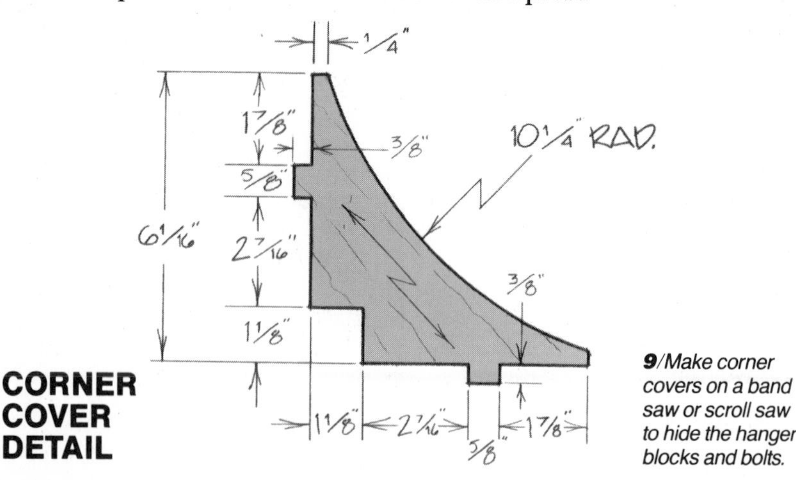

9/Make corner covers on a band saw or scroll saw to hide the hanger blocks and bolts.

Precautions for Pressure-Treated Lumber

Most pressure-treated lumber is saturated with the preservative Chromated Copper Arsenate, or CCA. As we mentioned in the introduction, this chemical poisons the lumber, preventing the growth of bacteria that would otherwise rot the wood. Unfortunately, what is poisonous to bacteria may also harm other forms of life — namely you and your family. If you use pressure-treated lumber in your outdoor furniture projects, you should take a few precautions.

CCA is an arsenic compound that chemically bonds with the wood under pressure. It gives off no fumes, and cannot be dissolved once it is bonded. Consequently, it won't "leech" out of the wood, and there is little chemical residue on the surface of a finished project to come in contact with people, pets, and plants. However, many of the craftsmen and builders who work with pressure-treated lumber regularly report rashes, watery eyes, itching, violent sneezing and other irritations. This probably comes from breathing the CCA-saturated sawdust, or cutting into the wood and being exposed to minute amounts of chemicals that haven't completely bonded.

When you work with pressure-treated lumber, wear long sleeve shirts and long pants, eye protection, and a dust mask to protect your skin, eyes, and lungs from exposure to CCA. If possible, do all sawing and sanding out of doors, where the sawdust will blow away in the wind. Wash all exposed areas of your skin before eating or drinking. If you happen to get a splinter, remove it *immediately.* Splinters from pressure-treated lumber can be much more irritating than the normal variety.

After you complete the project, carefully clean up all scraps and sawdust. Dispose of these in a local landfill or bury them yourself. *Never burn the scraps.* Pressure-treated lumber gives off poisonous gases when it's burned.

Hose down the completed outdoor furniture or let it sit through several rainstorms before you allow small children and pets to use it. This washes those fresh cuts where you may have exposed some unbonded CCA, and rinses away the chemical. *Never* let the wood come in contact with food or drinking water, no matter how many rainstorms it's been through.

Finally, avoid working with lumber that is treated with creosote or pentachlorophenol (usually called "penta"). Neither of these chemicals bond with the wood. They will leech out over time, poisoning the surrounding area. Creosote has been linked with cancer, and penta is chemically similar to the infamous "Agent Orange" used in Vietnam.

Duck Board Benches and Tables

They call them "duck boards" because water runs right off them. The individual boards in these unique assemblies are set on edge and spaced apart so that they won't trap moisture. The rain just goes right through duck board furniture. But the boards are close enough to each other to make a comfortable bench or a useful table. *You* won't fall through.

As you can see, the construction is wonderfully simple. All you need to do is rip a few boards and drill a few holes. And the design is as versatile as the construction is simple. Depending on the dimension of the bench top or table top, and its height above the ground, the duck boards can be used for long or short benches, low tables, workstations, even children's furniture.

Materials List

FINISHED DIMENSIONS

PARTS

	Part	Dimensions
A.	Duck boards (11)	¾″ x 2½″ x 48″
B.	Spacers (46)	¾″ x 2½″ x 2½″
C.	Legs (8)	¾″ x 2½″ x 16″
D.	Feet (4)	¾″ x 2½″ x 15¾″
E.	Foot blocks (4)	2½″ x 2½″ x 5¼″
F.	Seat dowels (4)	1″ dia. x 15¾″
G.	Foot dowels (2)	1″ dia. x 5¼″

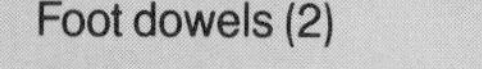

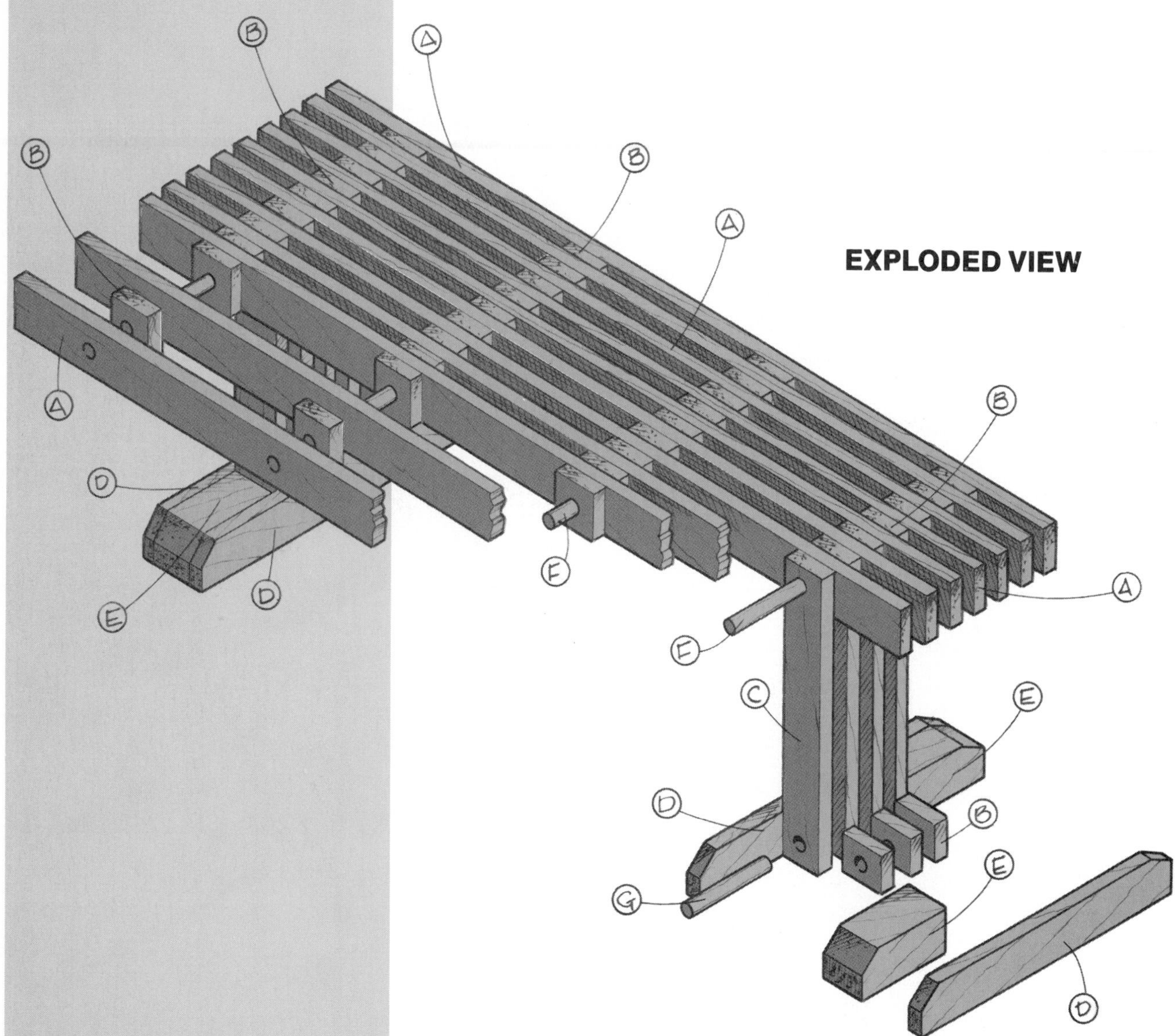

HARDWARE

8d Galvanized finishing nails (¼ lb.)

1 **Adjust the design to your own needs.** Decide what sort of outdoor furniture you'd like to make with these duck boards. Here's a chart to help show you some of the possibilities:

Length	Width	Height	Possible Uses
18"-24"	12"	10"-12"	Footrest, step-stool, seating for children
18"-60"	15"-18"	16"-18"	Seating for adults
24"-36"	18"-36"	20"-22"	Coffee table, table for children
36"-60"	30"-36"	28"-30"	Table for adults

2 **Cut the parts to size.** Cut all the *dimension lumber* to size first. Don't cut the dowels to length until you have made the other parts. The reason for this is that dimension lumber (which is what you get when you buy softwood at a lumberyard or building center) is not always precisely milled. The boards you buy may be a little thicker than ¾". On most projects, this wouldn't make any difference. But on this one, when you stack up so many layers of stock, even a little variance in the thickness can add up to a big mistake in the finished project. Cut the dowels only after you've cut the other pieces, stacked them up, and measured the stack. Then cut the dowels ¼"-½" *longer* than what you think you'll need. You can cut off the extra length later, after you assemble the project.

Since so many of these parts are identical, use a simple mass production technique when cutting them to length. Attach a stop block to the backstop of your radial arm saw or the rip fence of your table saw, and use this to gauge the length of the pieces as you cut them. That saves a lot of measuring. (See Figure 1.)

***1**/When you use a stop block on a table saw, position the block forward of the blade. You can use it to gauge the length of a cut, but it shouldn't be in actual contact with the wood when you're cutting. If it is, the wood will bind and kick back.* (Saw guard removed for clarity.)

3 **Drill holes for the dowels.** Drill 1"-diameter holes in the duck boards, spacers, and legs, for the dowel. Be very careful when you measure the positions for these holes — they *must* be placed accurately, or the project will be difficult to assemble. Use stop blocks on your drill press to help position the holes accurately. (See Figure 2.)

***2**/Clamp a fence and a stop block to your drill press to make a "jig" to help position the holes in the legs and spacers accurately.*

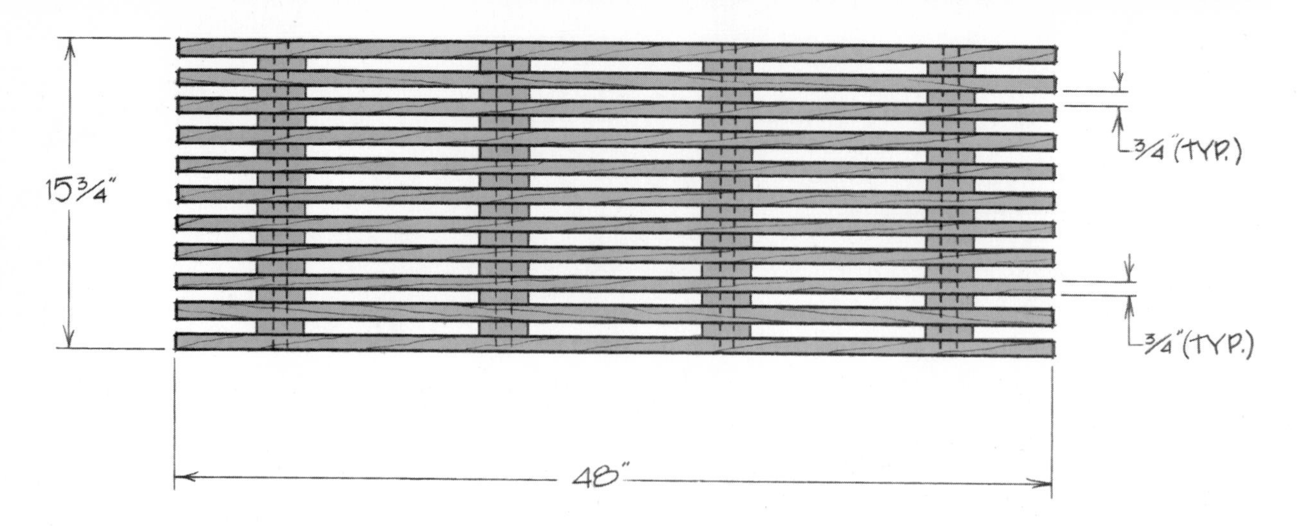

TOP VIEW

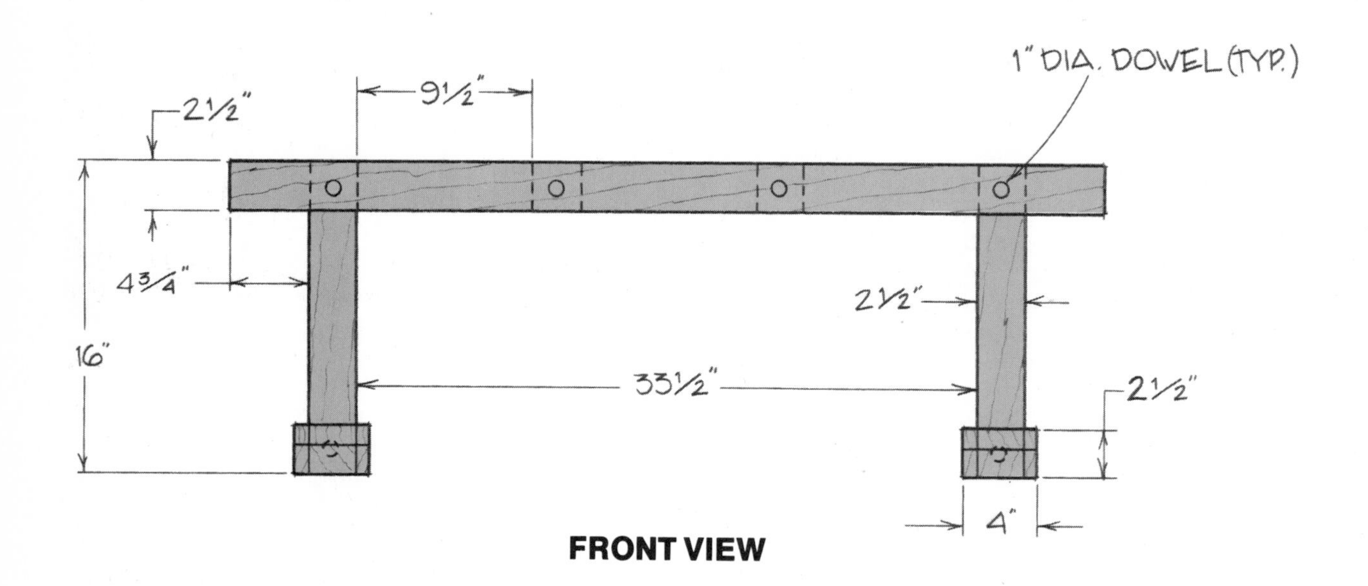

FRONT VIEW

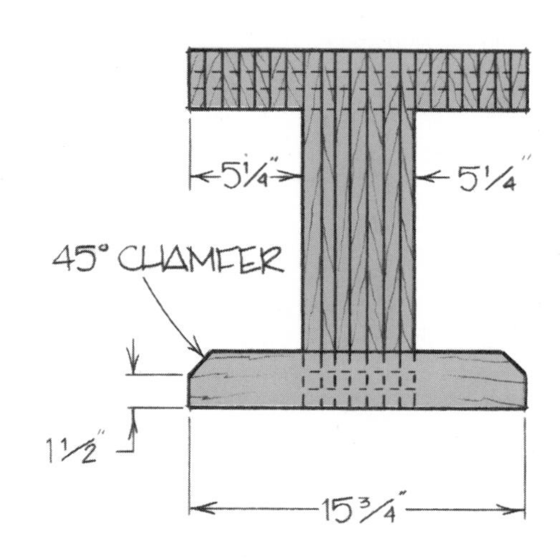

SIDE VIEW

4 Assemble the duck boards, legs, dowels, and spacers.

Begin to stack the parts, as shown in the *Exploded View.* Put a little dab of waterproof glue in between each of the parts as you stack them. This won't be enough to keep the project together, but it will prevent the spacers from turning on the dowels after the project is assembled.

When you fit the legs in place, make sure that they're square to the duck boards. Nail them to the assembly with galvanized finishing nails. (See Figure 3.) This will keep the legs from pivoting on the dowels.

When you've finished assembling these parts, clamp the duck boards together with bar clamps. Squeeze them together tightly, but not too tightly. Drive galvanized finishing nails through the edge of the outside duck boards, and into the dowels. (See Figure 4.) These nails will serve as "keepers," locking the boards together on the dowels.

TRY THIS! To hide the nails, drive them from the *underside* of the duck boards.

3/As you assemble the project, nail the legs to the duck boards. This will hold them square to the seat, and prevent them from pivoting on the dowels.

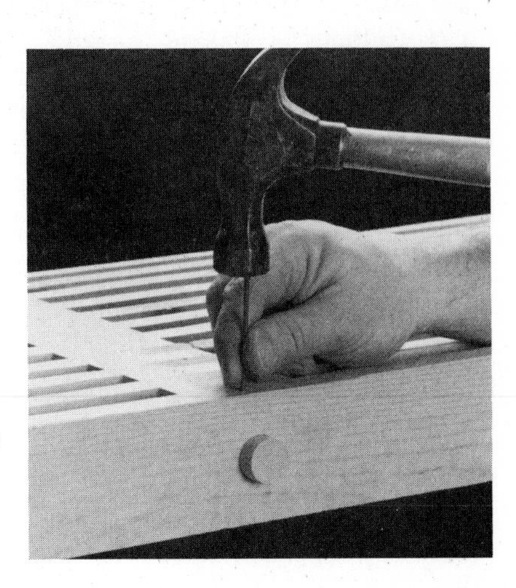

4/After assembling the seat and legs, drive nails through the outside duck boards and into the dowels. This will keep the assembly together.

5 Attach the feet and foot blocks.

Cut and sand the foot dowels flush with the legs. Test fit the feet and foot blocks to the legs, and mark them for position. If the duck board stock is thicker than ¾", the blocks may have to be shortened slightly. When you're satisfied the parts will fit properly, cut chamfers in the upper outside corners of the feet and foot blocks.

Nail the feet to the legs and spacers first. Be sure to keep the feet square to the legs, and parallel to the seat. Then nail the foot blocks in place, between the feet.

TRY THIS! As you're doing some of this nailing, you'll find that a small anvil or "nailing block" comes in handy. Hold the anvil on the opposite side of the feet from the nails, and it will prevent the boards from giving when you pound with a hammer.

6 Chamfer the edges and finish the project.

Rout or plane a small chamfer on all the outside edges and corners of the completed duck board table or bench. Sand the top of the bench perfectly flat, and finish sand any other parts that need it. If you wish to apply a finish to the bench, use a paint sprayer. You'll find it almost impossible to get a brush between the duck boards.

Rocking Sling Chair

Here's an unusual outdoor sling chair: It rocks! It doesn't rock in the same way that a rocking chair rocks, tipping back and forth. But this chair produces a very similar motion, because of the unusual way the legs are joined by the tie bars. All of the joints pivot, so that the legs — and the chair — move. These pivoting joints also make it possible for you to fold the rocking sling chair into a neat, flat package for storage.

The chair is quick and easy to build, too. The framework is nothing more than a few sticks with holes in them. These sticks are held together with machine bolts, flat washers, and stop nuts. The flat washers keep the sticks from rubbing so the chair will "rock" smoothly. The stop nuts keep the pivot joints from loosening.

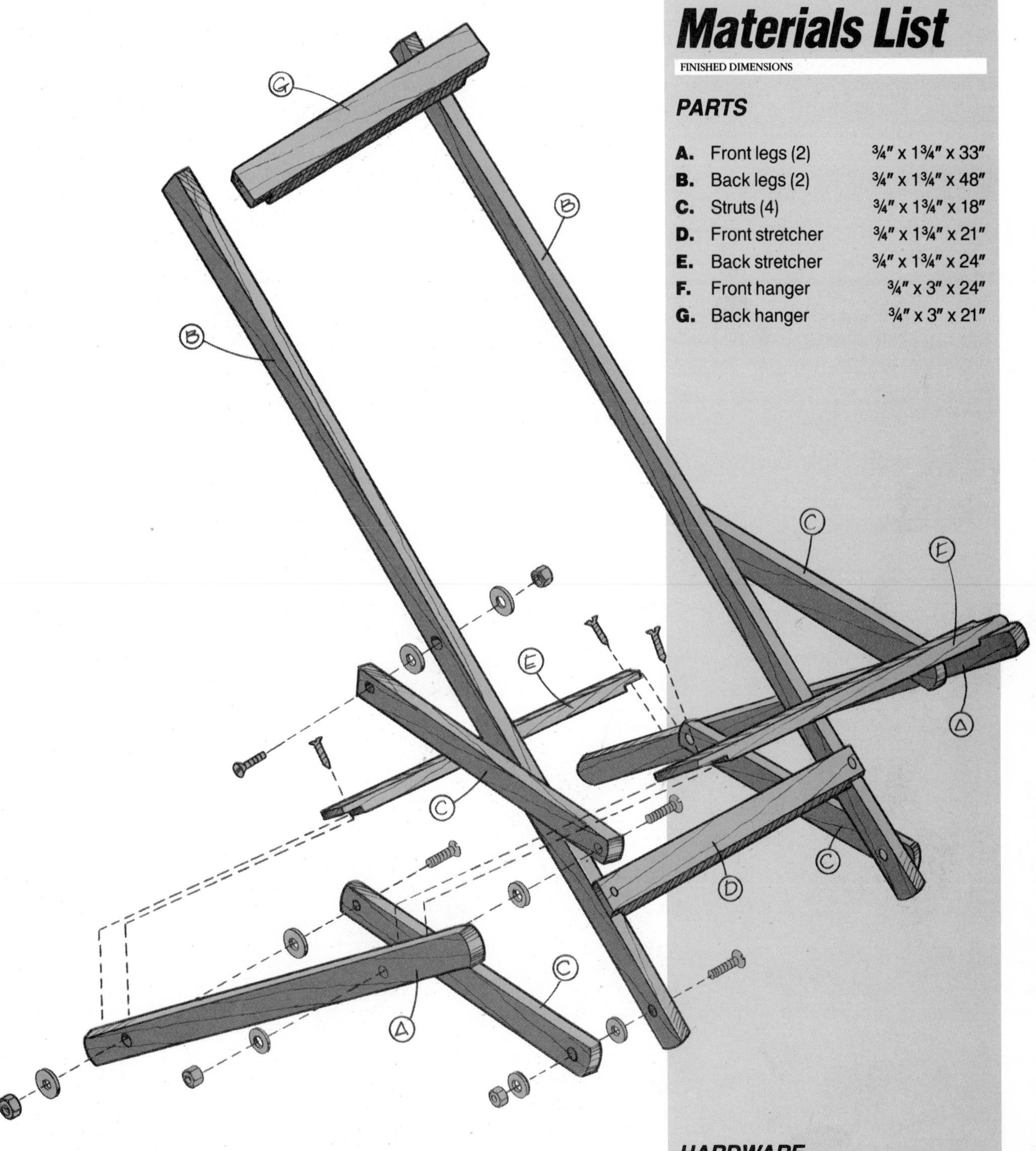

EXPLODED VIEW

Materials List

FINISHED DIMENSIONS

PARTS

A.	Front legs (2)	¾" x 1¾" x 33"
B.	Back legs (2)	¾" x 1¾" x 48"
C.	Struts (4)	¾" x 1¾" x 18"
D.	Front stretcher	¾" x 1¾" x 21"
E.	Back stretcher	¾" x 1¾" x 24"
F.	Front hanger	¾" x 3" x 24"
G.	Back hanger	¾" x 3" x 21"

HARDWARE

¼" x 2" Flathead machine bolts (8)
¼" Flat washers (16)
¼" Stop nuts (4)
#10 x 1¼" Flathead wood screws (16)
Heavy canvas (2 yards)

1 **Select the wood.** This is an easy project to make, but it must be made from *hardwood,* such as mahogany or oak. Not only that, but the hardwood must be clear and free from defects. The individual pieces of the chair are fairly narrow and thin, so the wood has got to be strong in order for the completed project to hold out.

To make this chair, you'll need 4-5 board feet of hardwood, planed to ¾" thick. Do not take this estimate too literally; the actual amount will depend on the widths and lengths available to you. It's always best to buy at least 10% *more* stock than you think you need. For a small project, like this, you may want 20% more.

2 **Cut the pieces to size.** Rip and cut the parts to the sizes shown in the Materials List. Joint the boards to remove the saw marks. **Caution:** When jointing narrow stock, always use a push stick or a push block to guide the board across the jointer. This will keep your fingers clear of the jointer knives.

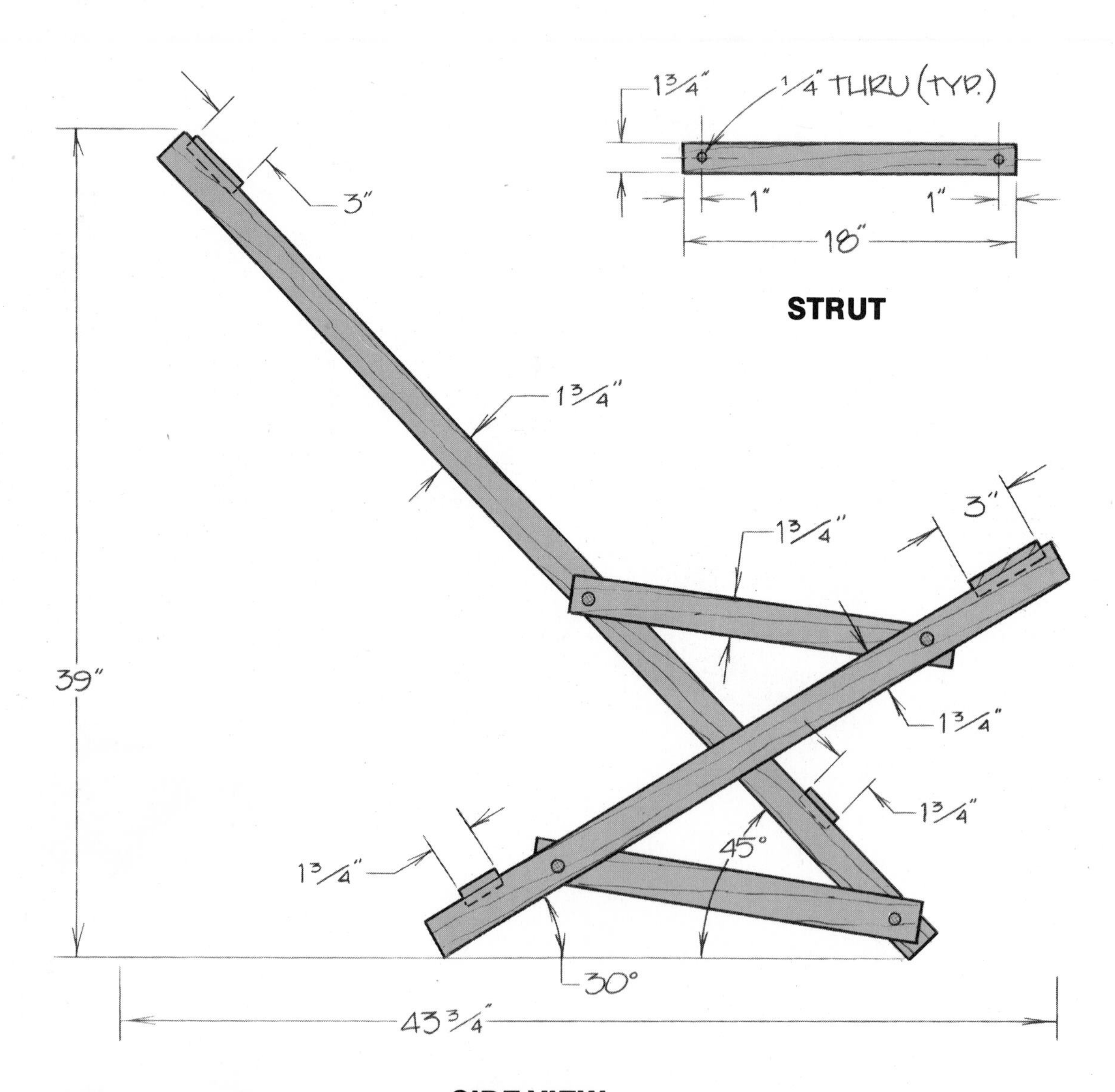

3 Drill the holes for the machine bolts.

Drill ¼″ holes in the legs and struts for the machine bolts, where shown in the drawings of the legs and struts. These parts are paired — right and left — and it's important that the pairs all be drilled precisely the same. To do this, stack the pairs up, right on top of left. Tape the stacks together so that they won't shift and "pad drill" the pairs of legs and struts. (See Figure 1.)

After you've drilled the holes, countersink them so that the heads of the machine bolts will be flush with the surface of the wood. Refer to the *Front View* to figure out which end of the holes to countersink. As you can see, with two exceptions, the heads of the bolts all face *inward*. The only bolts whose heads face outward are a pair of bolts in the back ends of the upper stretcher. It's important that the bolts be facing the right direction. If they aren't, the stop nuts will prevent the completed chair from folding.

1*/To make sure that the right and left pairs of legs and struts are drilled precisely the same, stack them up and "pad drill" them — that is, drill both parts at once. If they aren't drilled the same, the pivot joints may bind when you try to fold the chair.*

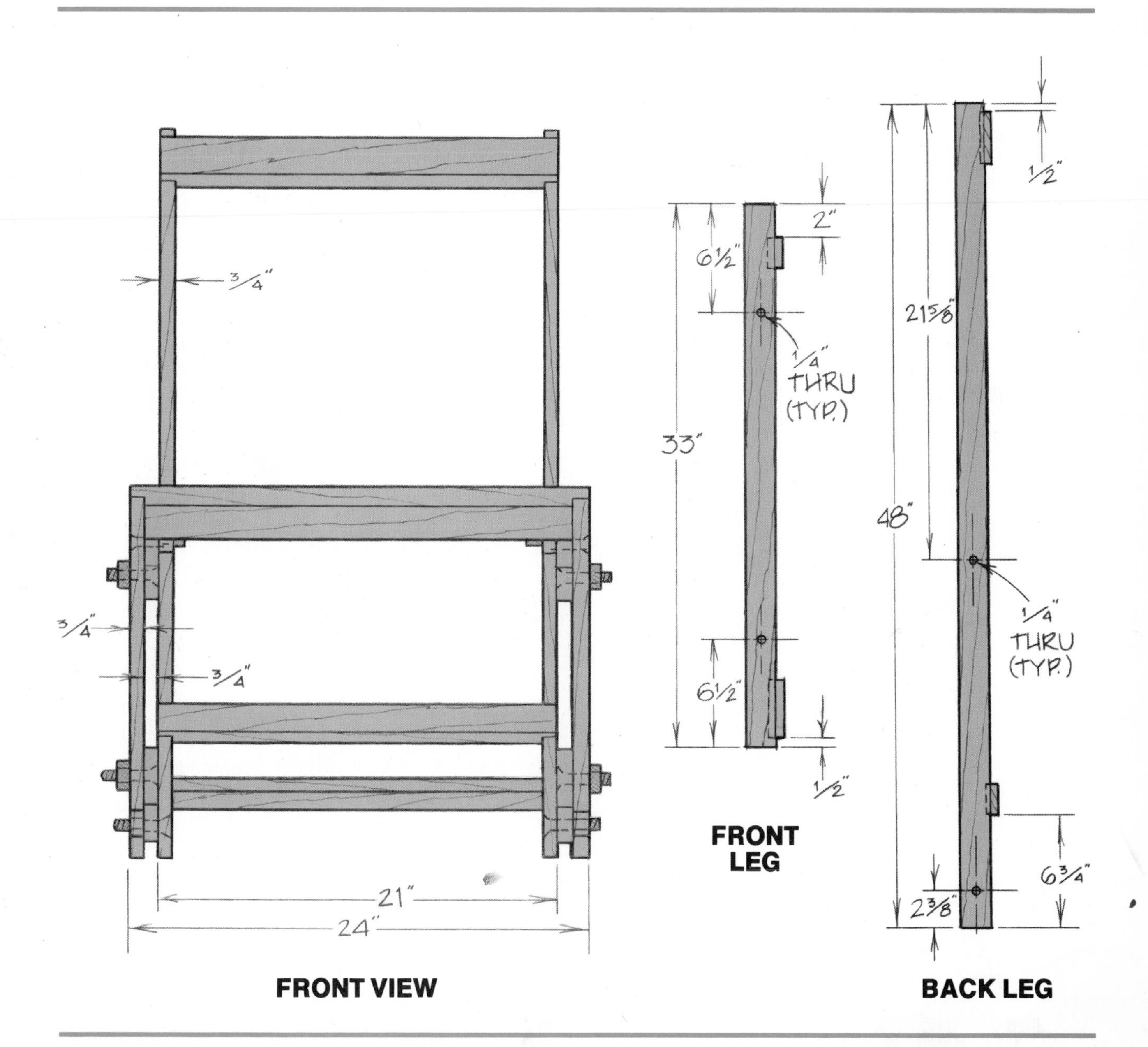

4 Cut the rabbets in the ends of the stretchers and hangers.

Mount a dado cutter in your table saw or radial arm saw, and cut ¾"-wide, ¼"-deep rabbets in both ends of the stretchers and the hangers. Use a stop block to help gauge the width of the rabbets and to make them all the same. (See Figure 2.)

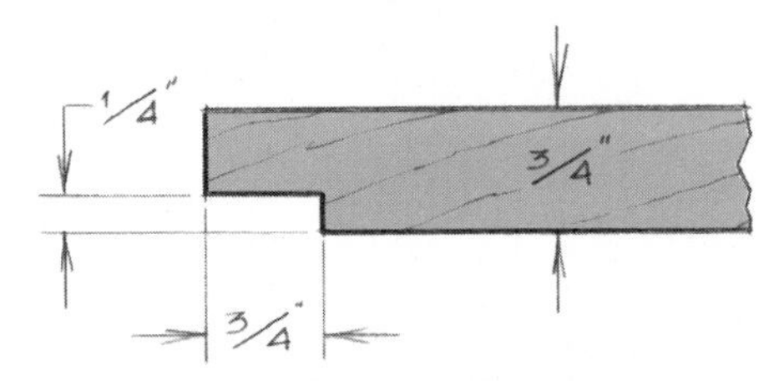

STRETCHER/HANGER JOINERY DETAIL

2/Use a stop block to cut the rabbets in the ends of the hangers and stretchers precisely the same.

5 Sand and finish the parts.

Sand the parts smooth and round all the corners and edges. If you're going to apply a finish, do it at this time. It's impossible to finish the completed chair because the cloth seat fits over some of the wooden parts.

6 Sew the sling.

Make the sling seat from heavy canvas duck. If you can't sew, have someone do it for you. The sewing required is very simple. As shown in the *Sling Seat Layout,* the seat is 45" long with 4½" long loops at both ends. The only sewing required is a single seam along both sides and a double seam at both loops.

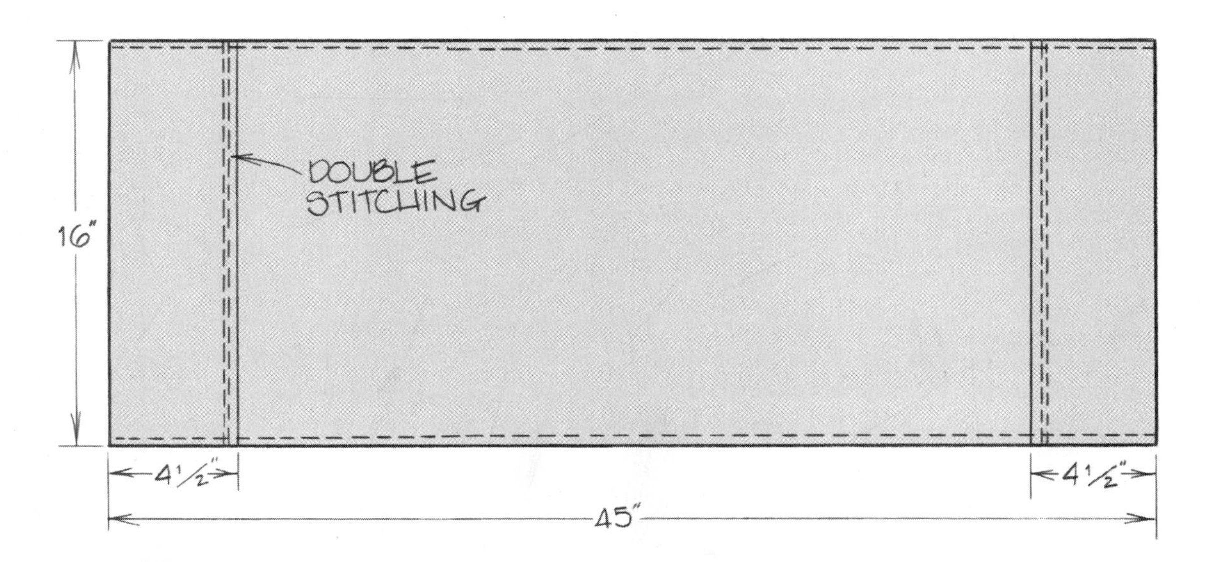

SLING SEAT LAYOUT

TRY THIS! If you don't have the skills or the inclination to make a canvas sling, you can make one out of woven wooden slats instead. Cut 28 *hardwood* slats, ⅜" x 1½" x 16". "Break" the corners of the slats with sandpaper or a block plane, slightly rounding them. With a rasp, notch the edges of the slats near the ends where cords will cross. Then "weave" the slats together with four ⅛"-diameter, 8' long cords. Use two cords on each side of the wooden-slat sling, twisting them together and winding them around the slats where you have made the notches. Leave a little extra cord (about 1') at both the top and the bottom of the sling, to tie it to the hangers.

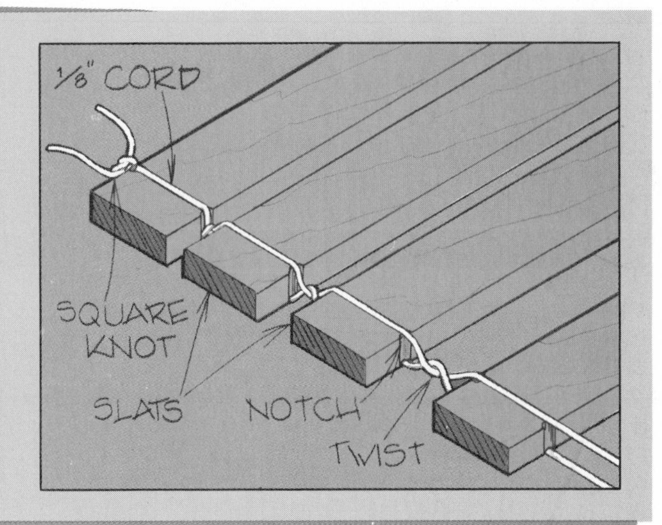

7 Assemble the chair frame.

Assemble the back leg and front leg frames, attaching the hangers and stretchers to the legs with wood screws. Check that the frames are square as you assemble them. Countersink the screws so that the heads are flush with the surface of the wood.

Attach the struts to the *inside* surfaces of the front leg frame, using machine bolts, washers, and stop nuts. At each of these pivot joints, put a flat washer in between the legs and the struts to keep them from rubbing. Turn the nuts tight enough to take any play out of the joint, but not so tight that the legs and struts bind.

Next, attach the other ends of the struts to the *outside* surfaces of the back legs. Once again, use machine bolts and put flat washers in between the struts and the legs. When you've finished, check the action of the chair frame. Resting on a flat surface, it should rock back and forth easily. If you pick it up by the hangers, it should fold up easily. (See Figure 3.)

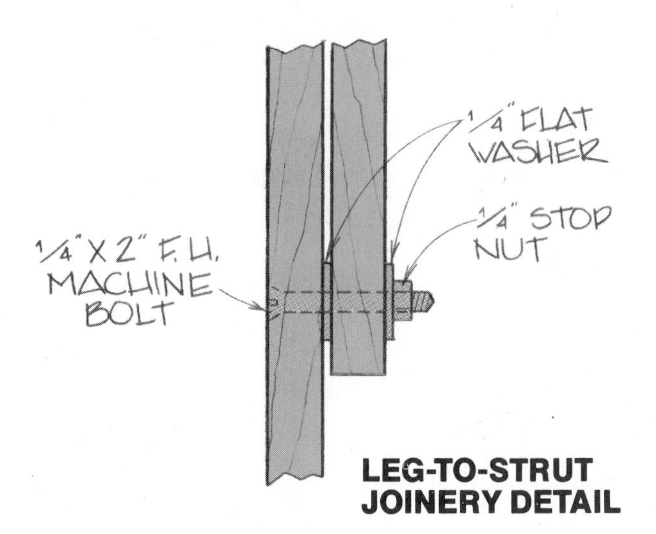

LEG-TO-STRUT JOINERY DETAIL

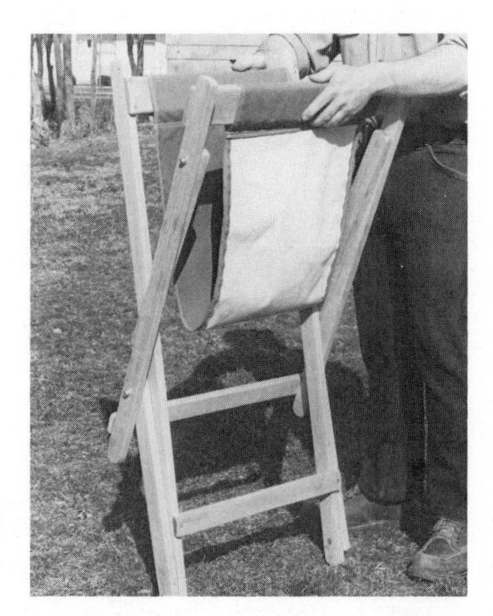

***3**/To fold up the chair frame, pick it up by the hangers and bring the hangers together.*

8 Install the sling on the frame.

Loosen one end of the back hanger and remove the screws completely. Slide the sling in place so that one of the loops is around the hanger. Replace the screws in the back hanger, and repeat this procedure for the front hanger. If you've made your sling out of canvas duck, take care that the colored side of the cloth faces up when you install the sling on the chair frame.

Tree Bench

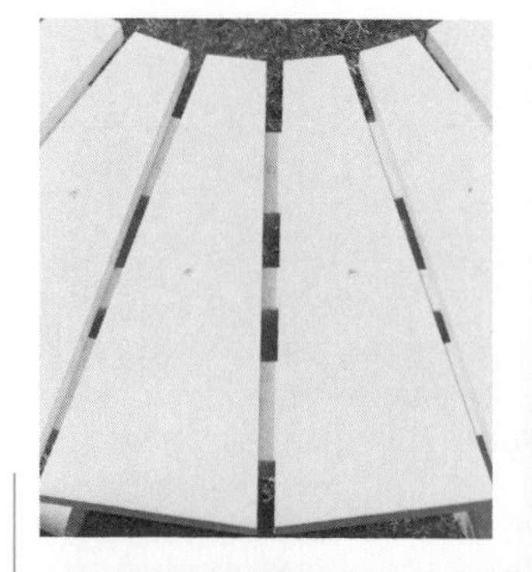

There are few pieces of outdoor furniture that are as magical as the classic "tree bench." A simple, scalloped bench girding a tree seems to turn an ordinary yard into a formal garden. It conjures up visions of ladies in long gowns and dapper gentlemen sharing the shade and each other's company. It invites you to sit a spell and just listen to the wind rustle the leaves. There is a hint of romance about a tree bench, and a promise of tranquility.

This particular tree bench is actually four separate benches. Each bench curves through 90° of a circle. The benches can be hooked together in a ring, or a variety of other configurations. Not only can you arrange the benches to circle a tree, you can make them follow the contours of a walkway or a garden.

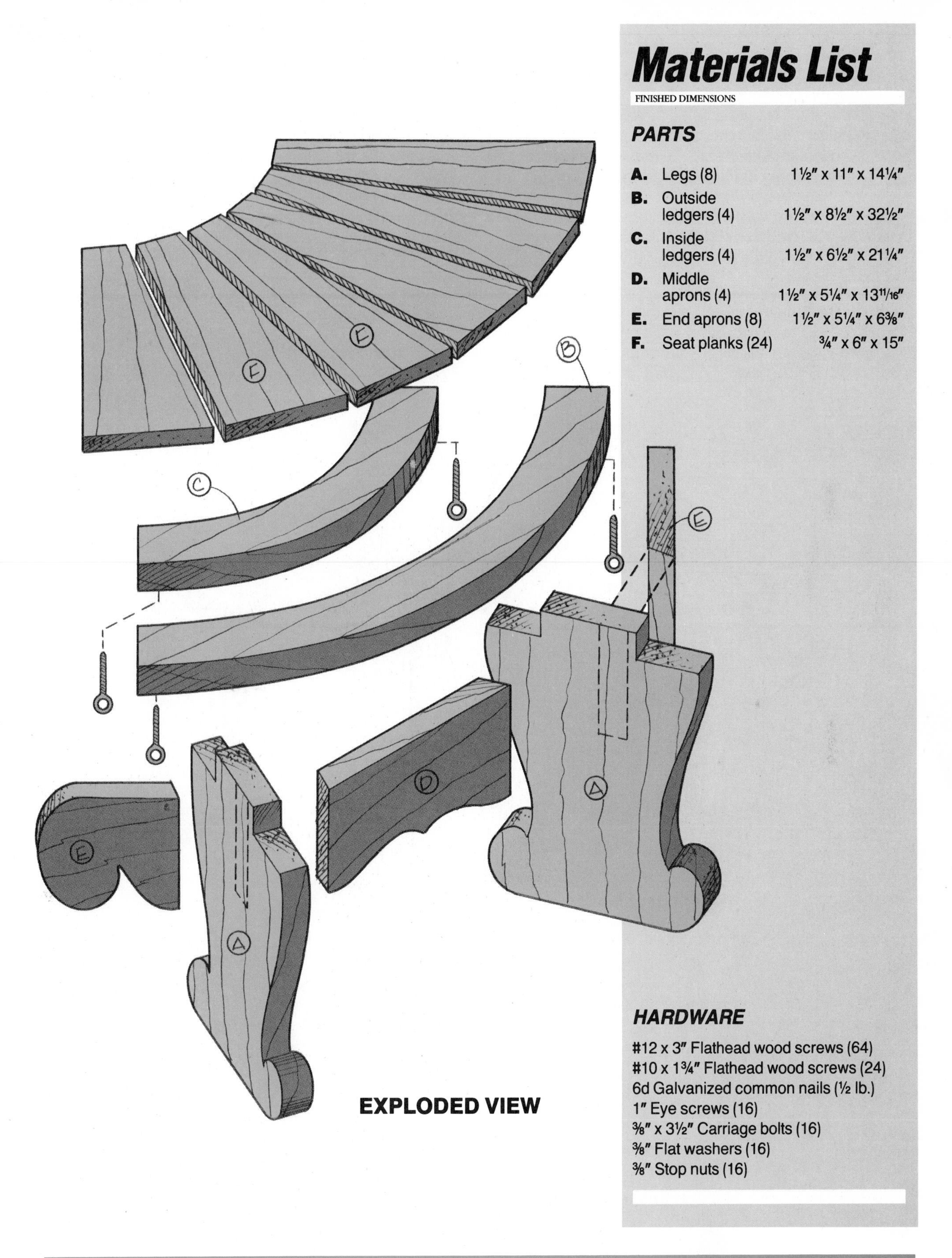

EXPLODED VIEW

Materials List

FINISHED DIMENSIONS

PARTS

	Part	Dimensions
A.	Legs (8)	1½" x 11" x 14¼"
B.	Outside ledgers (4)	1½" x 8½" x 32½"
C.	Inside ledgers (4)	1½" x 6½" x 21¼"
D.	Middle aprons (4)	1½" x 5¼" x 13 11/16"
E.	End aprons (8)	1½" x 5¼" x 6⅜"
F.	Seat planks (24)	¾" x 6" x 15"

HARDWARE

#12 x 3" Flathead wood screws (64)
#10 x 1¾" Flathead wood screws (24)
6d Galvanized common nails (½ lb.)
1" Eye screws (16)
⅜" x 3½" Carriage bolts (16)
⅜" Flat washers (16)
⅜" Stop nuts (16)

1 Cut all parts to size. As shown in our plans, this bench will encircle a small- to medium-sized tree. If your tree is larger than 12″ in diameter, you may want to enlarge the benches somewhat. To make a bigger bench, you'll need to increase the radii of the ledgers, the length of the aprons, and the width of the seat planks. To make sure that everything fits correctly *before* you cut the wood, make a new *Top View,* drawn to scale. There should be at least a 3″ gap between the bench and the tree.

Cut the various parts to the sizes you have decided upon. Miter the ends of the aprons at 22½°. All of the bench parts can be made from ordinary construction lumber, even the curved ledgers. Our outside ledgers were cut from 2 x 10s, and the inside ledgers from 2 x 8s. If you have enlarged the bench, you may want to use 2 x 12s and 2 x 10s, respectively. For very large benches, cut the ledgers from exterior grade ¾″ plywood. Sandwich two pieces together to make the 1½″ thickness required.

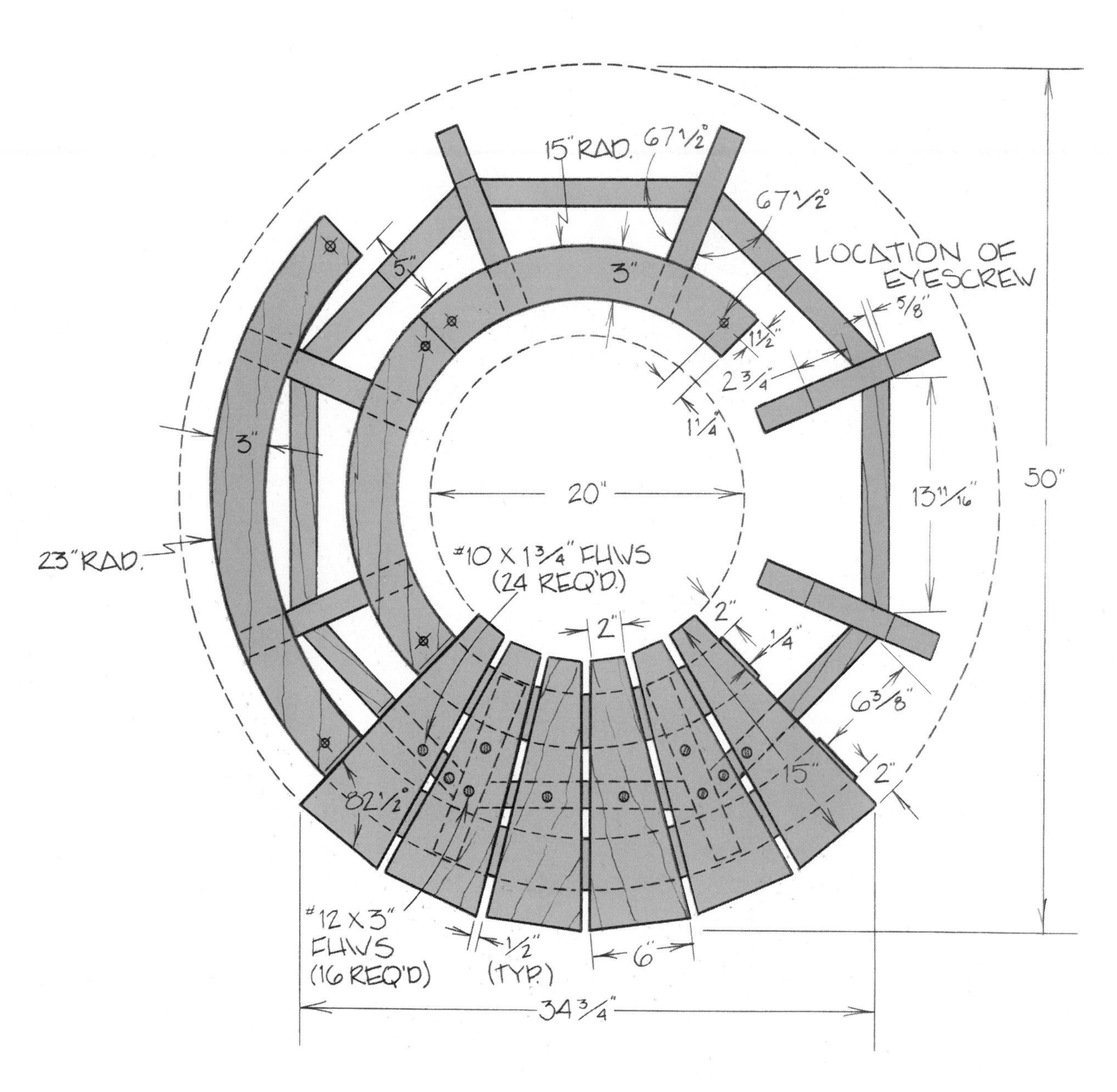

TOP VIEW

2 *Cut the shape of the frame parts.*

Enlarge the patterns for the legs and aprons, and trace them on the stock. If the tree that these benches will encircle has large, spreading roots above the ground, you may want to use the *Alternate Leg Pattern*. Unlike the ordinary legs, these legs have only one outside "foot", and they are contoured to follow the shape of a large tree trunk. The disadvantage in using the alternate legs is that the individual benches are unstable. They can't be used unless they're assembled in a circle. If the need ever arises, you wouldn't be able to use the benches in other configurations.

Trace the arcs of the ledgers with a pencil and string. Clamp the ledger stock to your workbench, and tack a nail to the bench top as shown in Figure 1. The distance from the nail to the *outside* edge of the stock should be equal to the outside radius of the ledger. Tie one end of a string to the nail, and the other end to a pencil. Wrap the string around the pencil until the distance between the nail and the pencil is the same as the outside radius. Using this arrangement as a giant compass, trace the outside arc. (See Figure 2.) Wrap some more string around the pencil, until the distance between the nail and the pencil is equal to the inside radius, and trace another arc. Mark the ends of the ledger so that its arc is a full 90.°

> TRY THIS! Lay out just one inside and one outside ledger. After you cut them out, use them for templates to lay out the other ledgers.

Cut out the shapes of the legs, aprons, and ledgers with a band saw or sabre saw. Sand the parts to remove the saw marks. A disc sander (for the convex curves) and a drum sander (for the concave curves) make short work of these sanding chores.

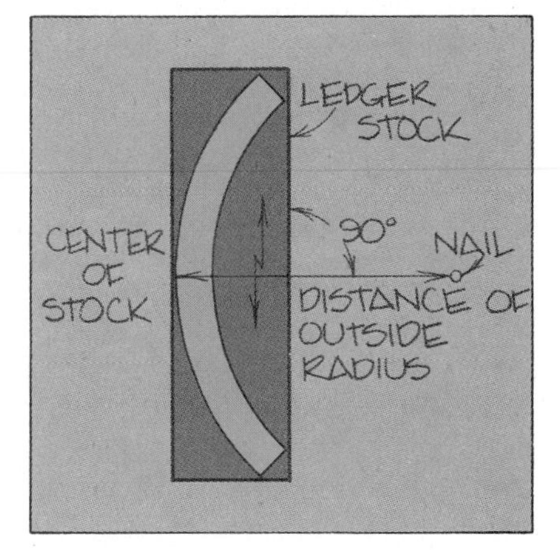

1/To lay out the ledgers, clamp the stock to your workbench and tack a nail in the bench top at the center of the arcs. The distance from the nail to the outside of the stock (measured at the center of the stock) should be equal to the outside radius of the ledger.

2/When you mark the arcs, take care to hold the pencil straight up and down.

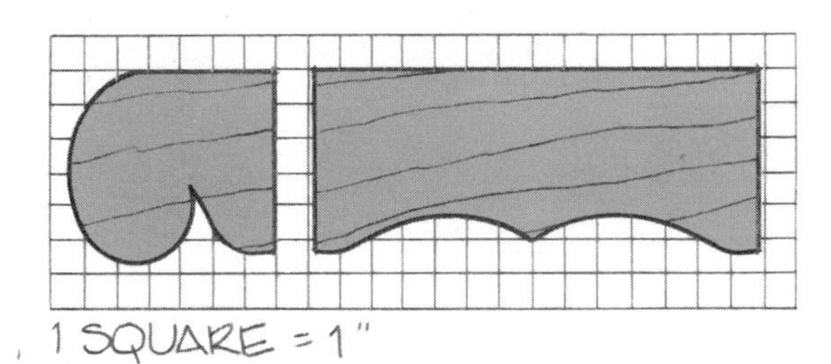

1 SQUARE = 1"

APRON PATTERNS

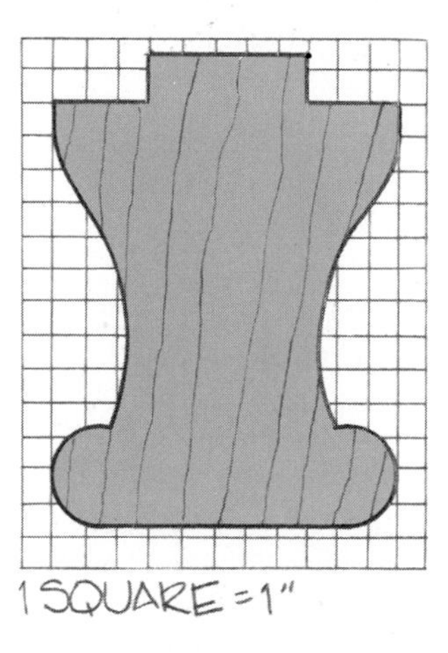

1 SQUARE = 1"

LEG PATTERN

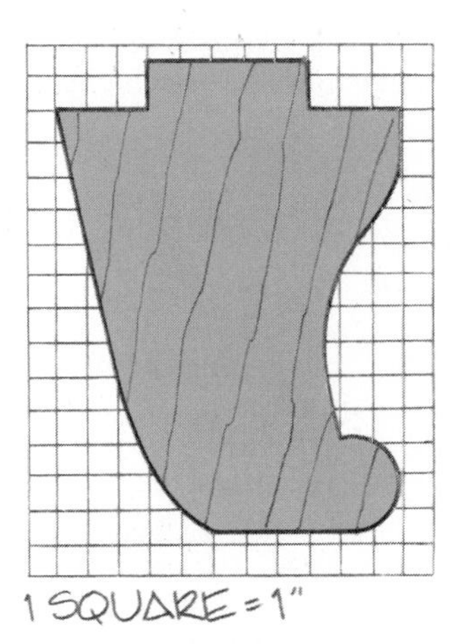

1 SQUARE = 1"

ALTERNATE LEG PATTERN

3 **Cut the seat planks.** Cut the seat planks to length from 1 x 8 stock. Each plank must be along two opposite edges. To cut this taper, make a simple tapering jig that will cock the planks at 7½° as you pass them through your table saw. Cut *one* edge of all 24 planks. (See Figure 3.) Then cut the second edge, using a piece of waste from the first series of cuts as a spacer to hold the planks at the correct angle. (See Figure 4.)

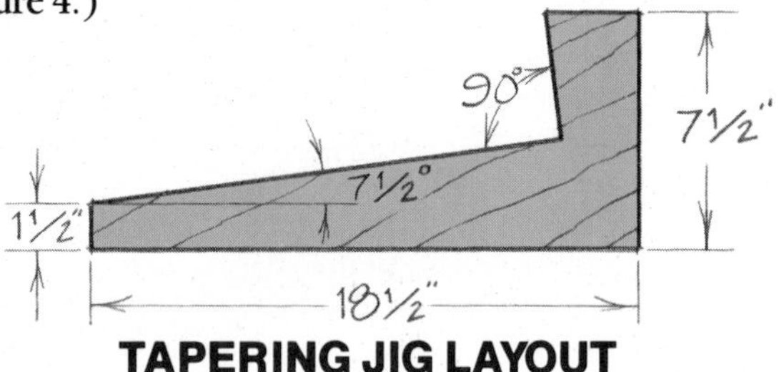

TAPERING JIG LAYOUT

3/*Use a tapering jig to taper one edge of the seat planks. Refer to the* Tapering Jig Layout *to see how to make this jig from a piece of scrap wood.*

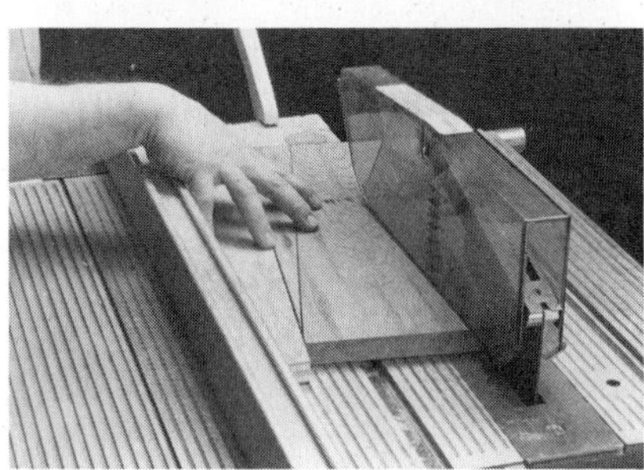

4/*When you taper the second edge, use the scrap from the first taper cut as a spacer in the jig to hold the stock at the proper angle to the blade.*

4 **Apply a primer to the parts.** It's traditional to paint a tree bench white. If you're going to paint your bench, apply a primer at this time. This will seal *all* the surfaces.

5 **Assemble the bench seats.** Carefully position one inside and one outside ledger on your workbench, spacing them 5″ apart. To help gauge and hold this spacing, cut 5″ long scraps of 1 x 1 and tack them to your workbench. (See Figure 5.) Lay out six seat planks on the ledgers, spaced as shown in the *Top View.* Mark the positions of the planks on the ledgers, then use these marked ledgers as templates to mark the plank positions on all the other ledgers. When all the ledgers have been marked, attach the planks to them with 6d nails.

5/*Tack small scraps, 5″ long, to your bench top to help space the inside and outside ledgers apart. Use additional scraps on the outside of the outside ledger and the inside of the inside ledger to keep the ledgers in place.*

6 **Attach the legs and aprons to the seats.** Turn the seat assemblies over, bottom sides up. Position the legs and aprons on them, as shown in the *Top View* and *Front View.* Screw the middle aprons to the legs first, driving #12 x 3″ screws through the legs and into the ends of the aprons. Countersink the screw heads. Then attach the end aprons, once again driving the screws through the legs and into the aprons. Counterbore *and* countersink these screws. Refer to the *Leg-to-Apron Joinery Detail* for the proper positioning of these screws.

Turn the bench over, and attach the seat to the legs by driving #12 x 3″ screws through the seat planks and into the tops of the legs. Finally attach the seat planks to the top edge of the aprons with #10 x 1¾″ screws. The positions of these screws are shown in the *Top View.*

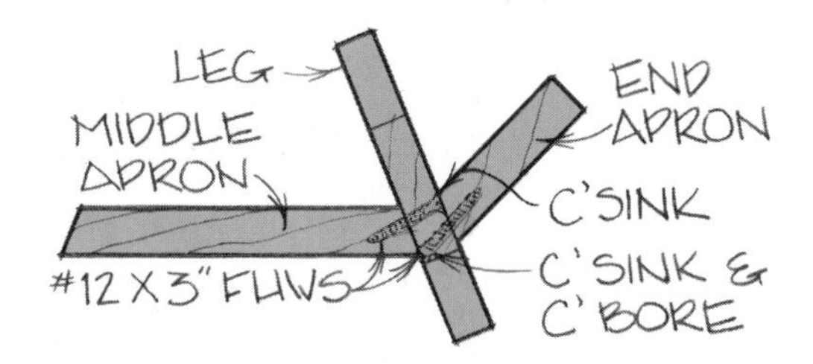

LEG-TO-APRON JOINERY DETAIL

7 Paint the benches.

Paint all the completed benches, taking care to apply paint in between all the spaces. Apply at least two coats.

TRY THIS! Because of all the spaces and irregular surfaces on these benches, it will cut your painting time in half if you use a paint sprayer.

8 Bolt the benches together.

Install eye screws in the underside of the ledgers, where shown in the *Top View* and *Bench-to-Bench Joinery Detail.* Each screw must be placed in *exactly* the same position, near each end of each ledger — 1¼″ in from the end, centered in the board.

Place the benches end-to-end in whatever configuration you want. Insert a carriage bolt through the adjoining eye screws, as shown in Figure 6. Secure each bolt in place with a stop nut. This will keep the nuts from loosening up.

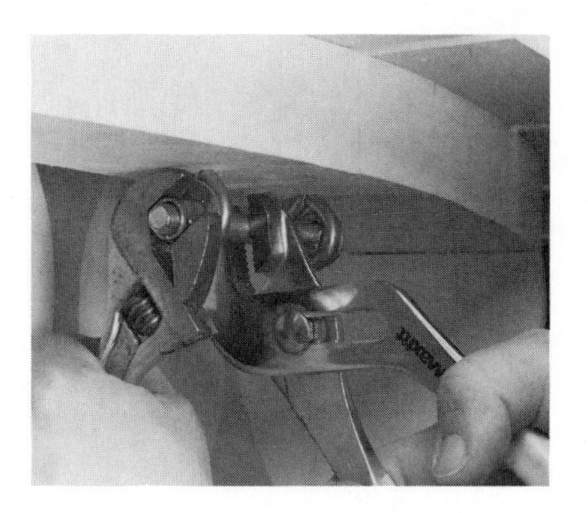

6*/Use eye screws and carriage bolts to hold the benches together, as shown. Secure the carriage bolts in place with stop nuts, so that the nuts won't loosen up over time.*

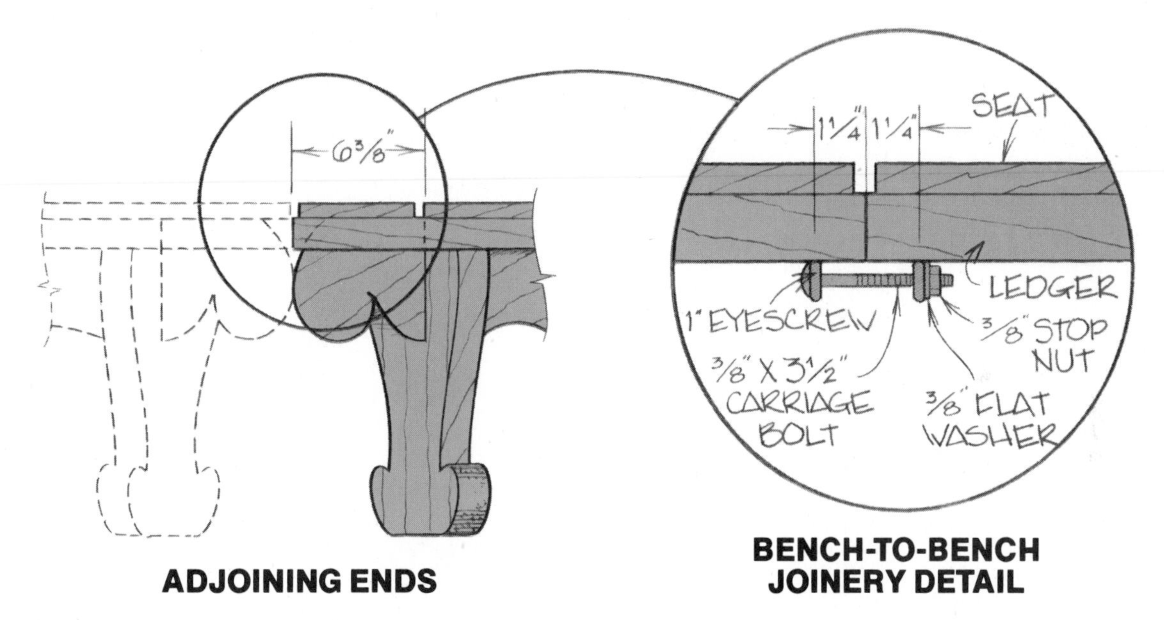

ADJOINING ENDS

BENCH-TO-BENCH JOINERY DETAIL

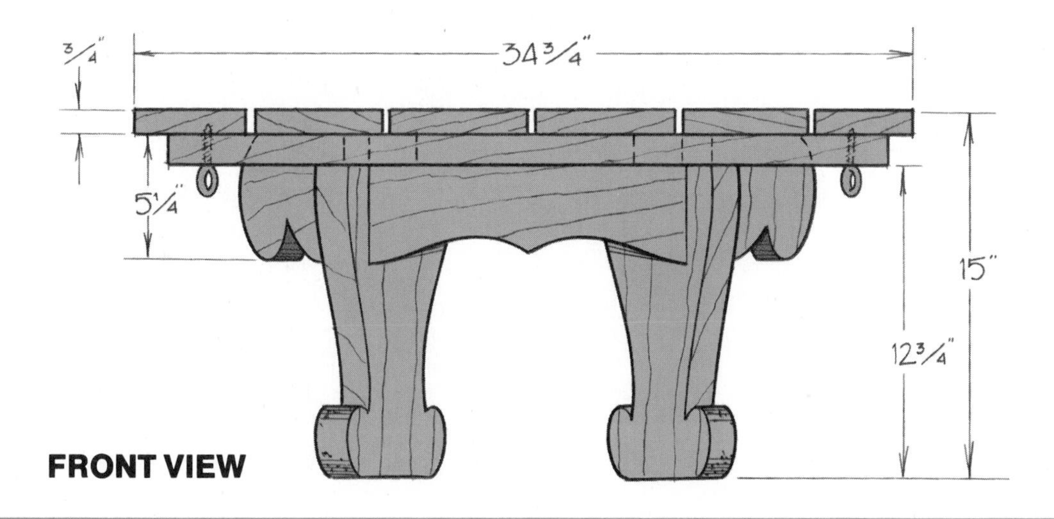

FRONT VIEW

Nesting Tables

What better place for tables to "nest" than out of doors, on your patio or deck? These three small nesting tables fit inside each other, so they won't take up much space when you don't need them all. But they come apart easily when you do.

Each of the tables can be easily built from standard 1 x 2, 1 x 4, and 2 x 2 dimension lumber. It's also quick to build; you can put together all three tables in an afternoon. To make this project as shown you'll need two 1 x 2s, six 1 x 4s, and three 2 x 2s, all 8′ long. You only have to rip and cut the parts; miter a few boards; cut tenons in the ends of a few more; and put it all together. What could be easier?

It's a versatile project, too. You can build these tables any size you need. As shown here, the tops are "coffee table" height and "side table" size. However, you can easily adjust the height or size to your own particular needs. Just change the length of the legs or aprons.

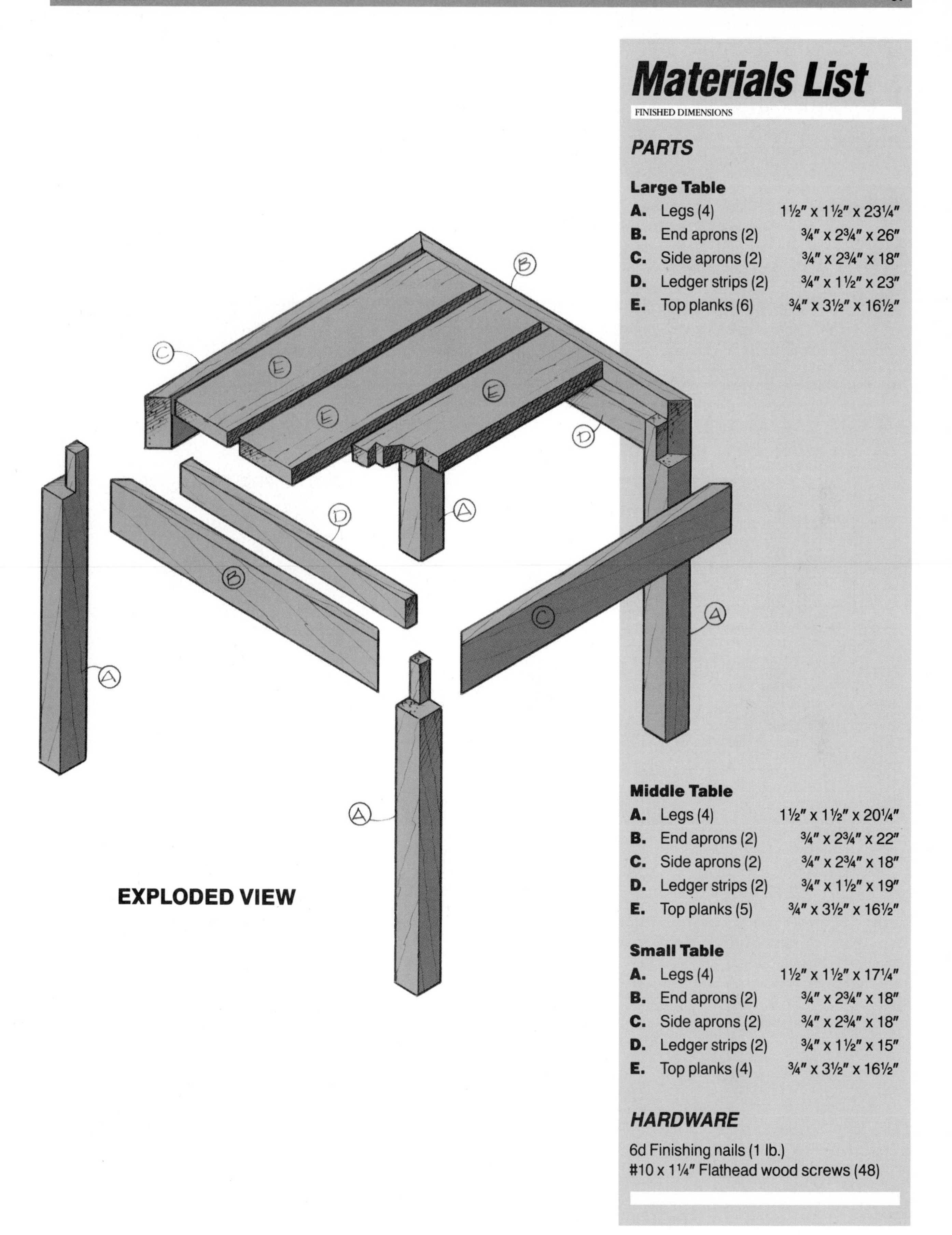

Materials List

FINISHED DIMENSIONS

PARTS

Large Table

A.	Legs (4)	1½″ x 1½″ x 23¼″
B.	End aprons (2)	¾″ x 2¾″ x 26″
C.	Side aprons (2)	¾″ x 2¾″ x 18″
D.	Ledger strips (2)	¾″ x 1½″ x 23″
E.	Top planks (6)	¾″ x 3½″ x 16½″

Middle Table

A.	Legs (4)	1½″ x 1½″ x 20¼″
B.	End aprons (2)	¾″ x 2¾″ x 22″
C.	Side aprons (2)	¾″ x 2¾″ x 18″
D.	Ledger strips (2)	¾″ x 1½″ x 19″
E.	Top planks (5)	¾″ x 3½″ x 16½″

Small Table

A.	Legs (4)	1½″ x 1½″ x 17¼″
B.	End aprons (2)	¾″ x 2¾″ x 18″
C.	Side aprons (2)	¾″ x 2¾″ x 18″
D.	Ledger strips (2)	¾″ x 1½″ x 15″
E.	Top planks (4)	¾″ x 3½″ x 16½″

HARDWARE

6d Finishing nails (1 lb.)
#10 x 1¼″ Flathead wood screws (48)

1 ***Cut all the parts to size.*** As you cut, carefully organize the parts so that you have one stack for the large table, another for the middle table, and so forth. Miter the ends of the aprons at 45°.

2 ***Cut the tenons in the legs.*** Mount a dado cutter on your table saw, and adjust the height to cut ¾" deep. Cut the tenons in the tops of the legs by making several passes over the cutter. Cut one side of the tenons first, then turn the legs 90° and cut the second side. Use a stop block to accurately gauge the length of each tenon. (See Figure 1.)

1/Make the tenons with a dado cutter, using a stop block to accurately gauge the length.

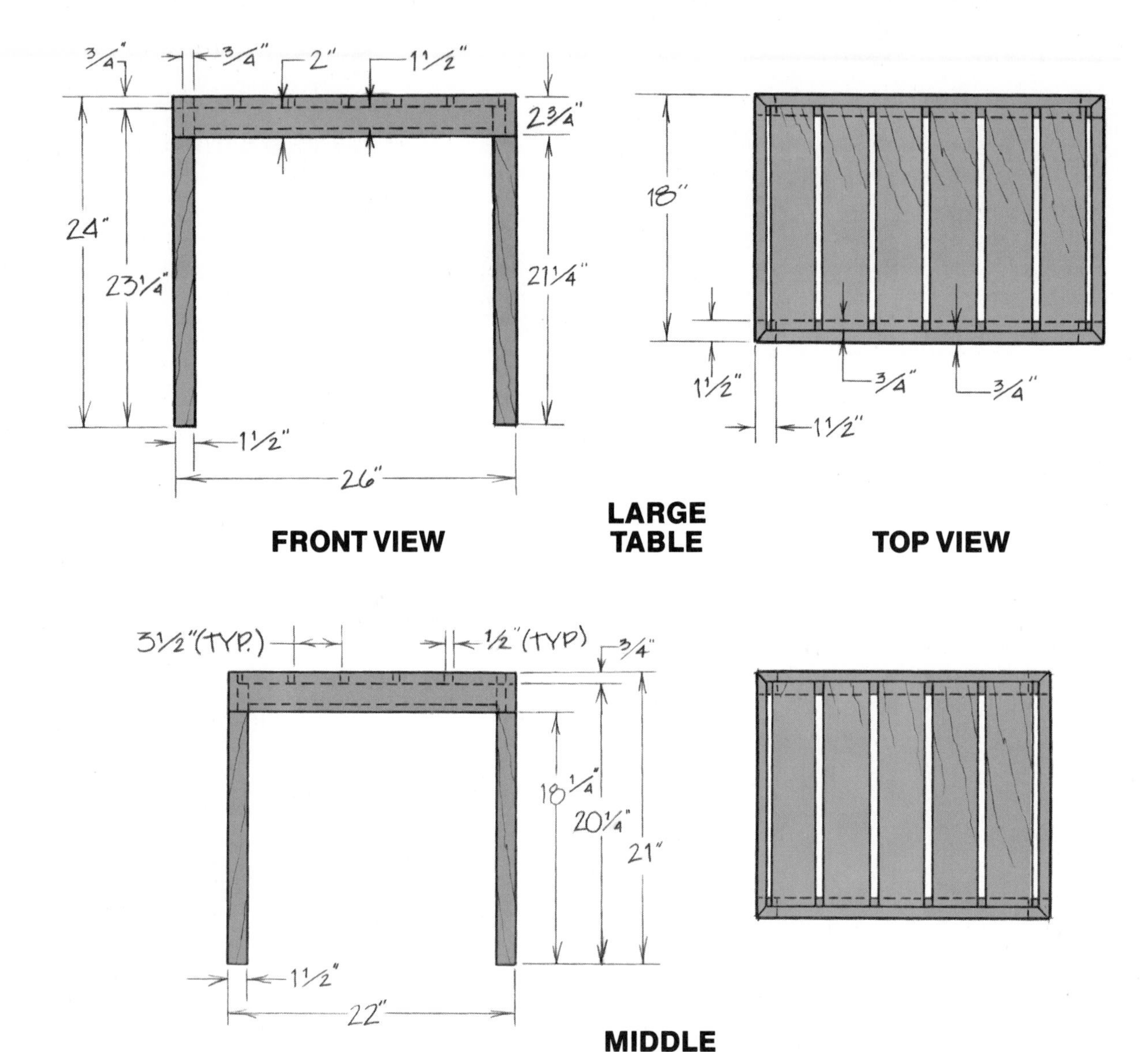

3 Assemble the legs and aprons.

The aprons are assembled like picture frames. To hold them together at the corners, drive finishing nails in from *both* sides. (See Figure 2.) Take care that the nails are positioned so they won't hit one another.

Attach the legs to the assembled aprons by driving the screws in from both sides, just as you did with the finishing nails. (See Figure 3.) This arrangement of the nails and screws will reinforce each corner joint from all possible directions.

2/*Nail the mitered aprons together from* both *directions.*

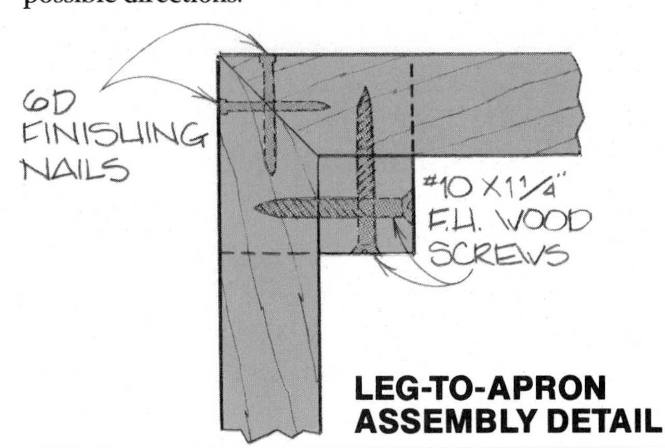

LEG-TO-APRON ASSEMBLY DETAIL

3/*Screw the tenons to the aprons from the* inside, *so the screws don't show.*

4 Attach the top planks to the tables.

Attach the ledger strips to the inside face of the side aprons with screws. Position these strips ¾" below the top edge of the aprons. When the ledger strips are in place, nail the top planks to the table assemblies.

5 Sand and finish the tables.

Even though these tables look good with crisp, hard edges and corners, it's not a good idea to leave them *too* hard — especially if you have children. With a block plane or a rasp, slightly round the edges so they have a softer look and feel. Do any necessary touch-up sanding on the tables; then apply a stain or finish.

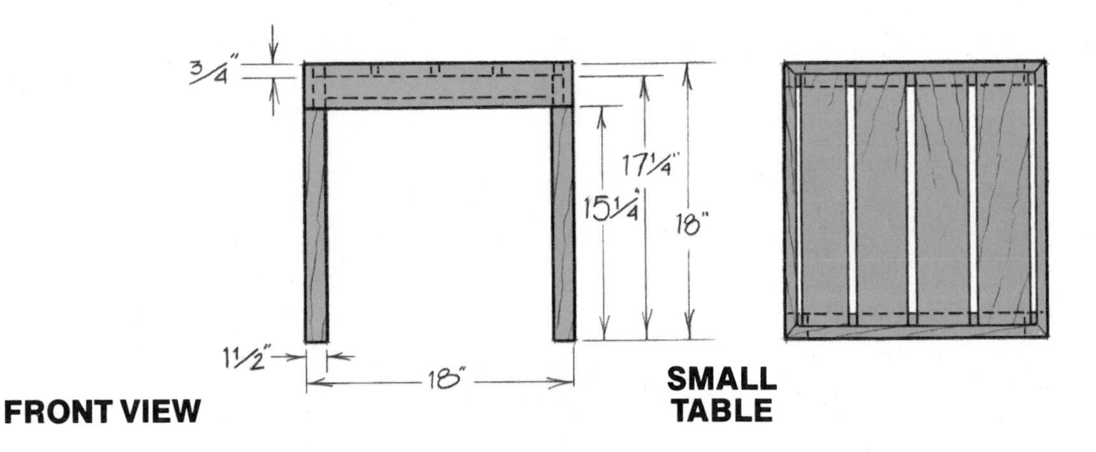

FRONT VIEW **SMALL TABLE** **TOP VIEW**

Planter/Partition

Would you like a little extra privacy from your neighbors when you're out of doors? Some extra shade? A screen from the wind? Would you like to partition one area of your deck off from another?

This "planter/partition" can provide or do all of those things. It's a simple concept, nothing more than a box with a latticework trellis attached to it. The box holds two standard 10″ clay pots. When the pots are filled with earth, they weigh the planter/partition down, and help to keep it from blowing over. The upright trellis provides privacy and shade. If you grow climbing plants in the pots, the trellis will fill up with greenery. This, in turn, will provide you with more privacy, more shade, and a more pleasant outdoor environment.

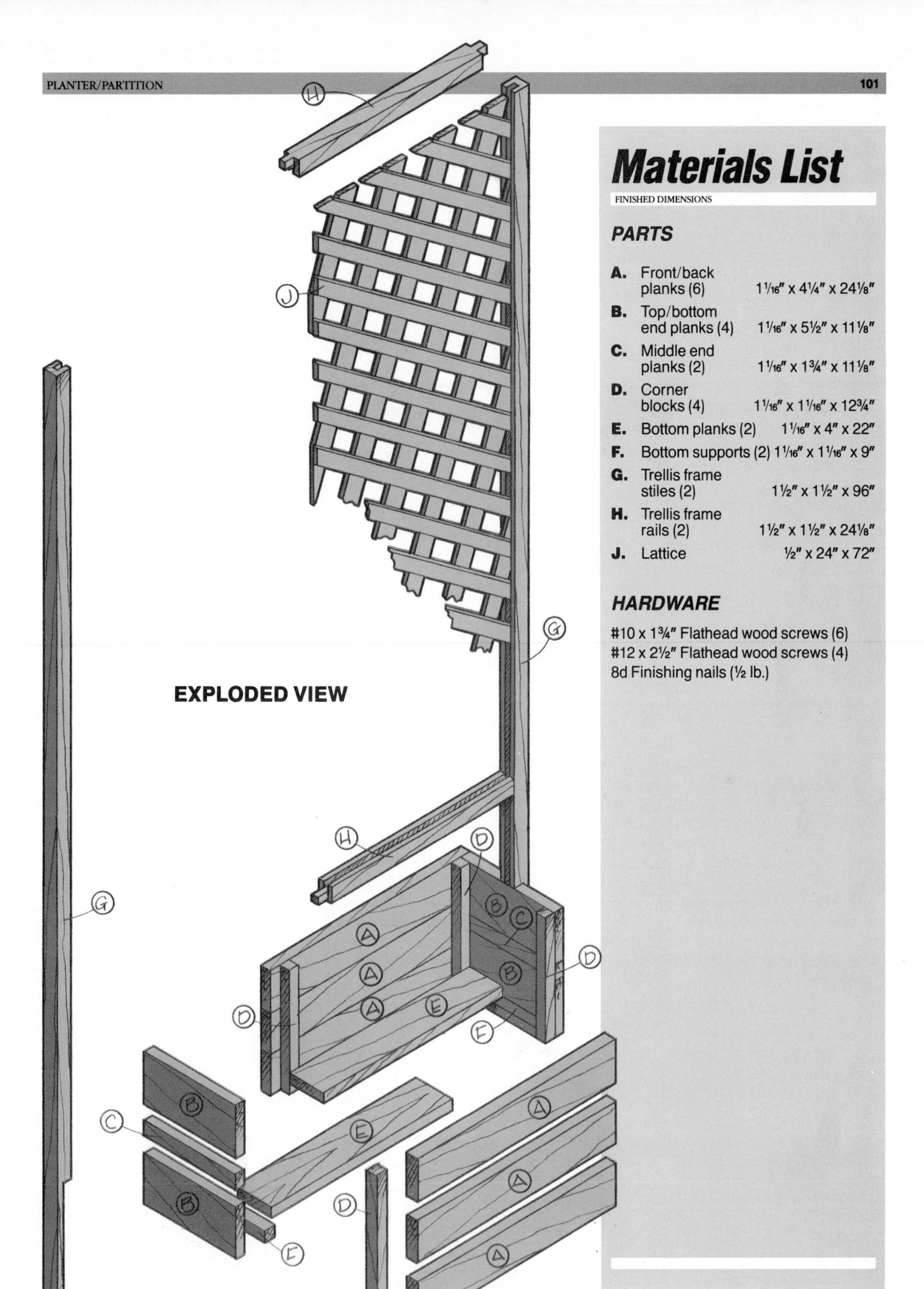

Materials List

FINISHED DIMENSIONS

PARTS

	Part	Dimensions
A.	Front/back planks (6)	1 1/16" x 4 1/4" x 24 1/8"
B.	Top/bottom end planks (4)	1 1/16" x 5 1/2" x 11 1/8"
C.	Middle end planks (2)	1 1/16" x 1 3/4" x 11 1/8"
D.	Corner blocks (4)	1 1/16" x 1 1/16" x 12 3/4"
E.	Bottom planks (2)	1 1/16" x 4" x 22"
F.	Bottom supports (2)	1 1/16" x 1 1/16" x 9"
G.	Trellis frame stiles (2)	1 1/2" x 1 1/2" x 96"
H.	Trellis frame rails (2)	1 1/2" x 1 1/2" x 24 1/8"
J.	Lattice	1/2" x 24" x 72"

HARDWARE

#10 x 1 3/4" Flathead wood screws (6)
#12 x 2 1/2" Flathead wood screws (4)
8d Finishing nails (1/2 lb.)

1 Adjust the design to suit your needs.

As we designed them, these planter/partitions are 96″ high. If you have a cover over your patio, you may not want them that high. To shorten them, simply reduce the length of the trellis frame stiles and the lattice.

You may want them shorter for another reason. At 96″ high, the lattice catches the wind. As we'll explain later in this chapter, to keep the planters from being blown over, you need to fasten them to your deck or spike them into the ground. If your area of the country is particularly windy, or if you want to use this project without having to fasten it down, then shorten the overall height to no more than 72″.

2 Cut the parts to size.

To make a single planter/partition, as we show it here, you'll need three 10′ lengths of "5/4 decking." (The actual dimensions are 1¹/₁₆″ thick x 5½″ wide.) You'll also need three 2 x 2s, 8′ long, and a 2′ x 6′ sheet of lattice. To make a set of three, as shown in the photograph, purchase eight 10′ lengths of decking, eight 2 x 2s, 8′ long, and three 2′ x 6′ sheets of lattice. You can find all of these sizes and materials wherever you buy treated lumber for decks and patio covers.

1/When cutting lattice, clamp two scrap boards together, one on either side of the lattice, near the cutline. This will help keep the material from coming apart as you cut it.

Cut the parts to the sizes shown in the Materials List. If you need to cut the lattice, you'll find this is an awful chore. The lattice bounces and wiggles and tends to come apart no matter what hand tool or power tool you try to cut it with. To make this chore somewhat easier, clamp two scrap boards together, one on either side of the lattice, near the cutline. (See Figure 1.) This will hold the stock steady as you cut it.

3 Cut joinery in the stiles and rails.

The lattice is held in place by a ½″-wide, ¾″-deep groove that runs the length of the frame stiles and rails. Using a dado cutter, make this groove in one of the faces on the 2 x 2 stock. Center the groove in the stock. (See Figure 2.)

While you still have your dado cutter set up, make the tenons in the rails. Adjust the cutter to cut ½″ deep, then cut a ¾″-wide, ½″-deep, rabbet in the end of a rail. Turn the rail over and repeat the cut in the same end, but on the opposite face. The two cuts will form a tenon in the end of the board. (See Figure 3.) Repeat this procedure for both ends of both rails.

Cut lap joints, ¾″ deep and 12¾″ long, in the lower ends of the stiles, removing the grooves in these areas. You can use a band saw, sabre saw, or an ordinary hand saw to cut these joints. When it comes time to fasten the trellis frame to the box, these laps fit over the planter box assembly.

2/With a dado cutter, make a groove down the length of the stiles and the rails.

3/Use the dado cutter to make tenons on the ends of the rails. Make two passes over the cutter to form one tenon.

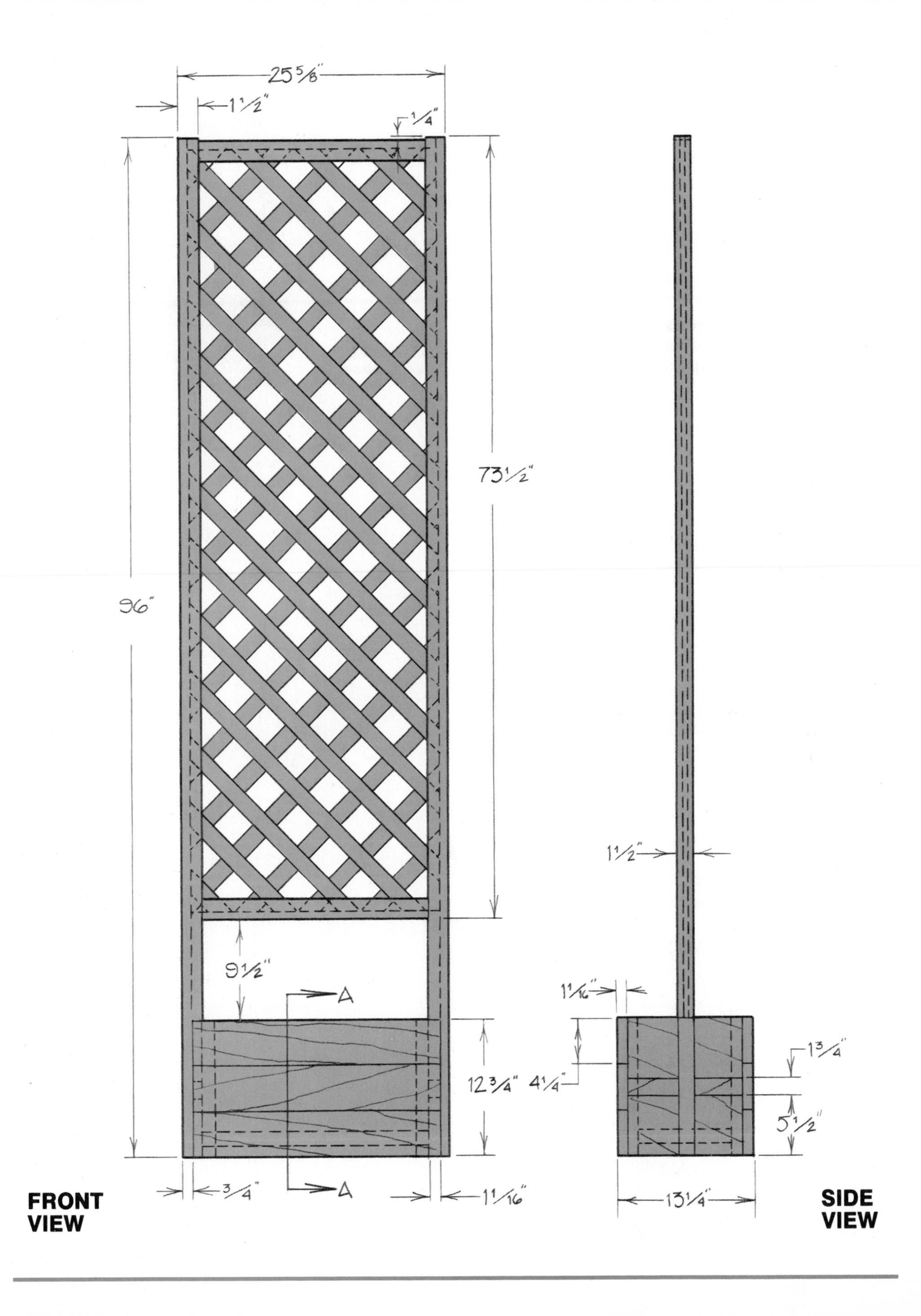
25 5/8"
1 1/2"
1/4"
96"
73 1/2"
9 1/2"
A
A
12 3/4"
4 1/4"
3/4"
1 1/16"
FRONT VIEW
1 1/2"
1 1/16"
1 3/4"
5 1/2"
13 1/4"
SIDE VIEW

4

Assemble the planter box. Nail the end planks to the corner blocks to make end panels. Then nail the bottom supports to the insides of the end panels, flush with the lower edge. Complete the box by nailing the front/back planks to the end panels. There is no need to permanently attach the bottom to the box; you can just drop it in place when it's needed.

You may be wondering why the front/back planks are different widths than the end planks. This arrangement makes the box stronger. When you nail the front/back planks to the end panels, fasten the middle front/back plank so that the nails bite into all three end planks. This will help tie all the planks together.

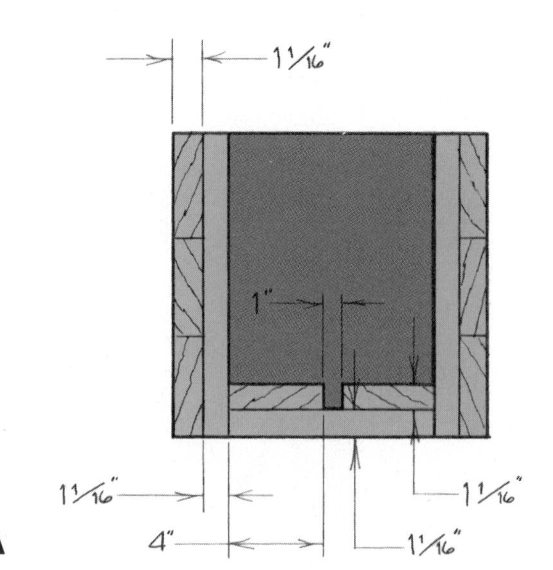

SECTION A

5

Assemble the trellis frame. Lay the stiles on a flat surface with the grooves facing each other. Put the lattice in between, and fit the lattice into the grooves in each stile.

Slide the rails in place. The tenons should fit in the grooves of the stiles, and the top and bottom edges of the lattice should fit in the grooves in the rails.

Make sure that all the parts are positioned properly, and that the rails and stiles are square to each other. Secure the trellis frame with bar clamps, drill the pilot holes, and drive 2½" long screws through the stiles and into the tenons on the rails. Then remove the clamps.

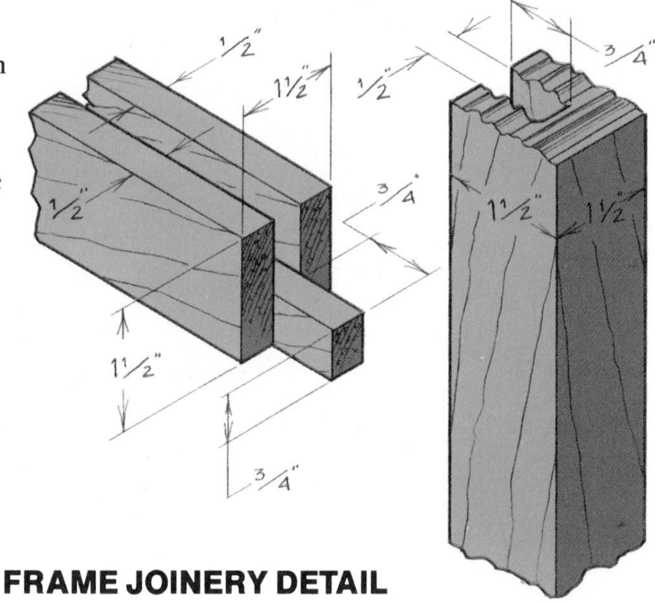

FRAME JOINERY DETAIL

6

Attach the trellis frame to the planter box. Have a helper hold the frame upright while you position the planter box under it. Make sure the frame is plumb in relation to the box, and the stiles are centered on the end panels. Then clamp the frame to the box with C-clamps or wood clamps. Fasten the trellis frame to the planter box with 1¾" long wood screws, and remove the clamps.

7 Secure the planter to the deck or the ground. As we mentioned earlier in this chapter, you may want to attach the completed planter/partition to your deck or stake it to the ground to prevent the wind from blowing it over. This does not have to impair the portability of the project; you can secure the planter/partition in such a way that you can still easily detach it from the deck or the ground and move it around.

To secure the planter to the ground, use 18″ lengths of #4 concrete reinforcing rod, or "rebar." Buy the type that has a small bend at one end, or have the building supply store put bends in them for you. Drill two ½″ holes in the bottom planks near each end. Arrange the planter where you want it in your yard, lay the bottom planks in place; then drive the rebar down through the bottom planks and into the ground. (See Figure 4.)

To secure the planter/partition to your deck, use ¼″ x 4″ carriage bolts. (In some cases, you may need longer or shorter bolts. It's best to measure the thickness of your deck before you buy them.) Drill ¼″-diameter holes through the center of two small scraps of wood. Place the planter/partitions where you want them on your deck, and lay the bottom planks in place. Drill two ¼″-diameter holes in the bottom planks, near each end of the planter box. These holes should be located over a crack between decking boards. Insert the carriage bolts in the holes in the bottom planks, and down through the deck. Under the deck, put the scraps of wood over the bolts, then secure them with flat washers and nuts. (See Figure 5.)

If you can't get under your deck, or you have a concrete patio, you'll have to try other methods. For a wooden deck that is low to the ground, attach the planter/partition to the deck boards with lag screws. For concrete, use lag screws with expandable lead shields. Both of these methods attach the planters solidly, but they are somewhat more permanent than rebar spikes or carriage bolts.

***4**/If you place the planter/partition in your yard, stake it to the ground with rebar.*

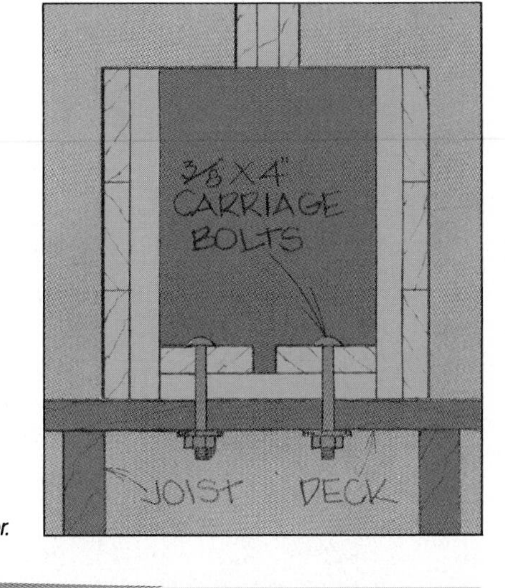

***5**/If you place the planter/partition on your deck, hold it in place with carriage bolts. Otherwise, the wind may blow it over.*

TRY THIS! There are two things you can do to make the planter/partitions more stable in a stiff breeze *without* staking or bolting them down. The first is to make the planter boxes wider, so that they hold more pots. This adds weight and surface area to the base. However, it also takes up more patio space.

To make the planter/partitions more stable *without* increasing their size, hinge the planter boxes together with 3″ strap hinges. Then arrange the planter/partitions in a zig-zag or staggered line. The hinges *and* the arrangement help to make the entire assembly harder to tip over.

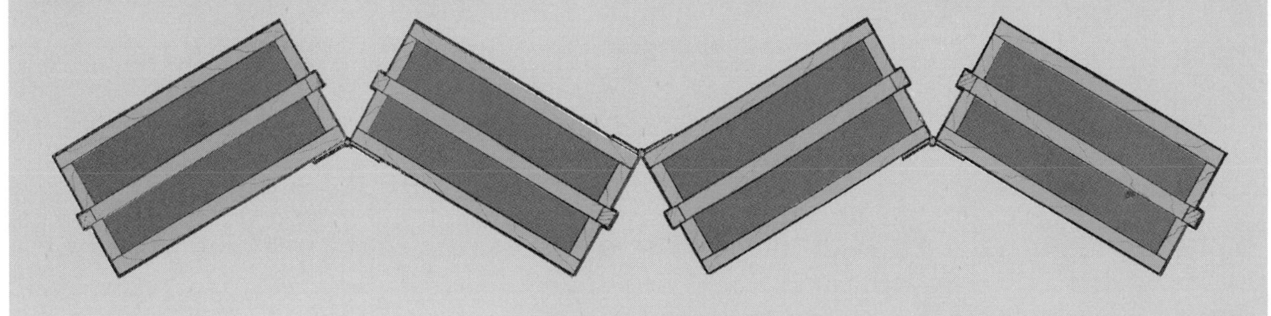

Garden Table/Bench

This unique outdoor furniture project serves two purposes: With the back tilted vertically, it's a decorative garden bench. Tilt the back horizontally, and it becomes a table with a bench seat. And if you happen to make *two* of these table/benches, you can hook them together in the table position to make a full-size picnic table.

We've designed this table/bench to be both easy and inexpensive to make. With the exception of the back/top supports, the entire project is made from 2 x 4s, and held together with decking nails and carriage bolts. The only "fancy" pieces of hardware are the eye-bolts that lock the back/top in the bench or table positions.

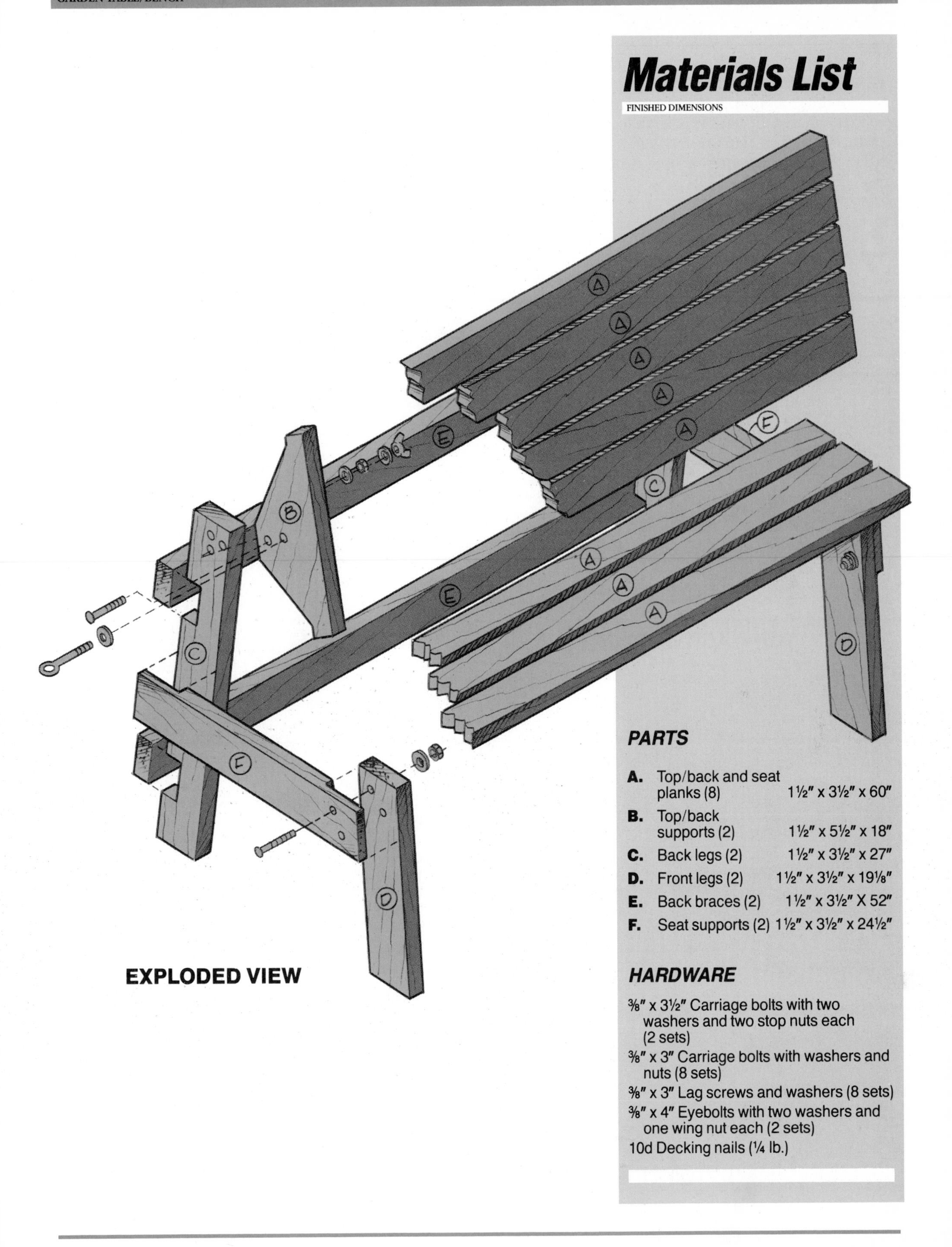

Materials List

FINISHED DIMENSIONS

PARTS

A.	Top/back and seat planks (8)	1½″ x 3½″ x 60″
B.	Top/back supports (2)	1½″ x 5½″ x 18″
C.	Back legs (2)	1½″ x 3½″ x 27″
D.	Front legs (2)	1½″ x 3½″ x 19⅛″
E.	Back braces (2)	1½″ x 3½″ X 52″
F.	Seat supports (2)	1½″ x 3½″ x 24½″

HARDWARE

⅜″ x 3½″ Carriage bolts with two washers and two stop nuts each (2 sets)

⅜″ x 3″ Carriage bolts with washers and nuts (8 sets)

⅜″ x 3″ Lag screws and washers (8 sets)

⅜″ x 4″ Eyebolts with two washers and one wing nut each (2 sets)

10d Decking nails (¼ lb.)

1 Cut all the parts to their proper size.

Cut the parts to the sizes shown in the Materials List. Miter the ends of the back legs, front legs, and seat supports at 85°, as shown in the drawings. Note that *both* ends of the front legs and the supports are mitered, while one end of the back is cut square and the other mitered. Furthermore, the mitered ends of the front legs must be cut parallel. The ends of the supports are mitered in opposite directions.

2 Shape the back legs and the back/top supports.

Cut the 1½"-deep, 3½"-long notches in the back legs using a band saw or sabre saw. Also, cut out the shapes of the back/top supports. Drill ⅜" pivot holes in the legs and the supports. *Do not*, however, drill the lock holes just yet.

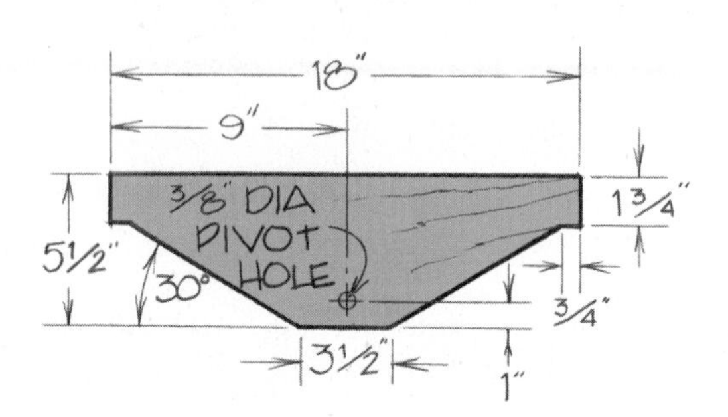

TOP/BACK SUPPORT LAYOUT

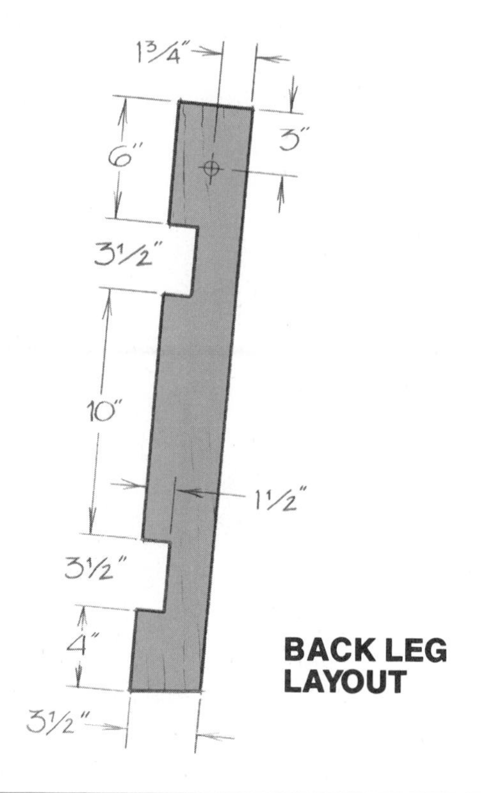

BACK LEG LAYOUT

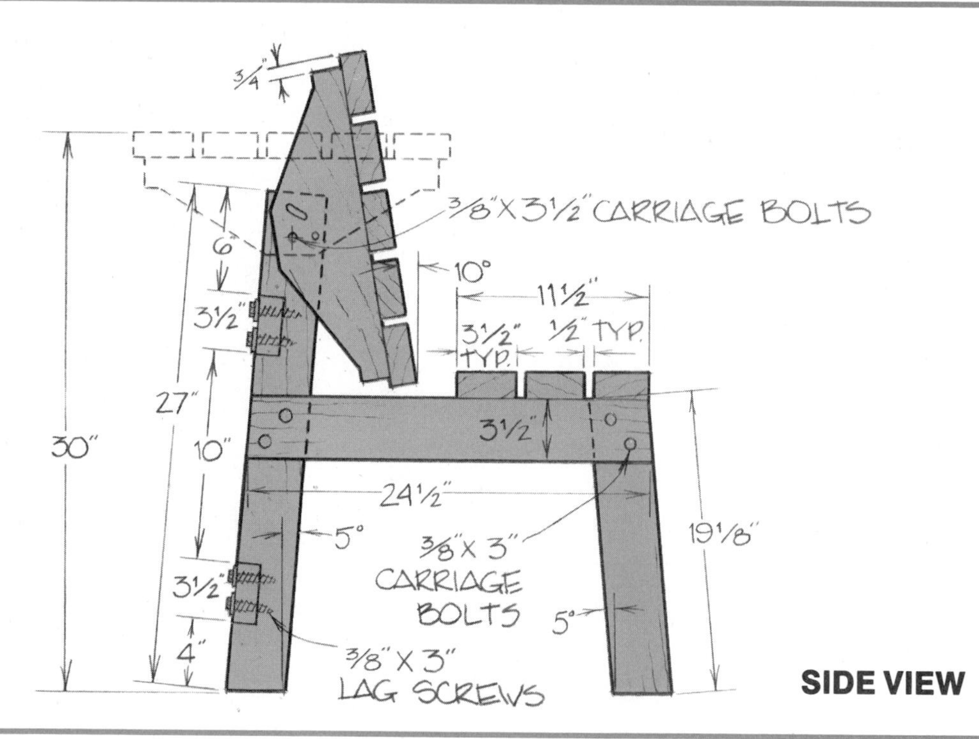

SIDE VIEW

3 Cut the rabbet joints in the seat supports.

Cut the rabbet joints in the seat supports. Using a dado cutter, cut rabbet joints in each end of the seat supports. (See Figure 1.) The rabbets must be cut parallel to the mitered ends. These joints will help to hold the front and back legs steady.

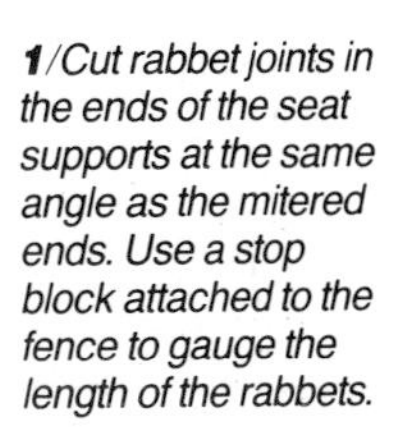

1/Cut rabbet joints in the ends of the seat supports at the same angle as the mitered ends. Use a stop block attached to the fence to gauge the length of the rabbets.

4 Assemble the frame.

Assemble the frame. Bolt the seat support to the legs with 3″-long carriage bolts. Remember, these leg/support assemblies should be mirror images of each other. Attach the back braces to the back legs with lag screws, and bolt the top/back supports to the back legs with 3½″-long carriage bolts. These supports must pivot freely, so don't tighten the nuts on the bolts too tightly. To keep the nuts on the pivot bolts from backing off, use stop nuts. (See Figure 2.)

2/Use stop nuts on the pivot bolts. These special nuts will not work loose when you change the position of the top/back.

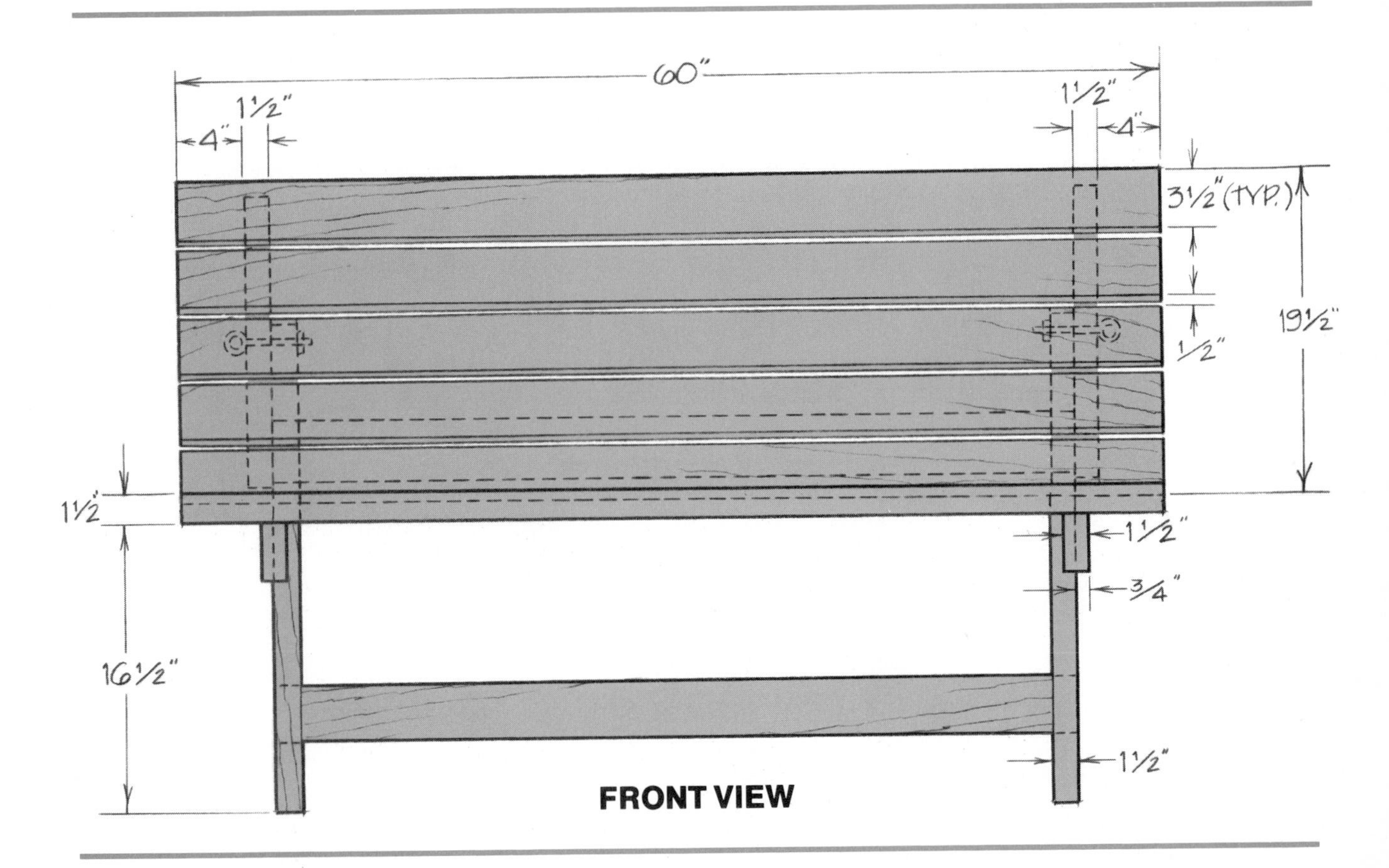

FRONT VIEW

5 Attach the top/back and the seat planks.

Clamp the top/back support in a horizontal position. Then nail the top/back and the seat planks in place. Use a spacer made from scrap wood to get the planks properly positioned. Remember, the spiral decking nails that we recommend are made to stay put. (See Figure 3.) They will be hard to remove if you make a mistake — even if you don't drive the nails all the way into the boards.

***3**/Attach the planks to the frame with 10d decking nails. These spiral nails "screw" into the wood when you hammer them in, so they stay tight.*

6 Install the "lock pins."

Place the assembled table/bench on a flat, level surface. Using a carpenter's level, adjust the position of the top/back so that it's perfectly horizontal; then clamp it in place. About 1½" above the pivot bolts, drill ⅜"-diameter holes through the back legs, then through the supports.

Loosen the clamps, and readjust the position of the top/back so that it's in the bench position, 10° off vertical. Tighten the clamps again to hold it in place. Using the lock holes in the legs as pilots, drill another set of lock holes through the supports. (See Figure 4.) Remove the clamps, and insert eyebolts as "lock pins" in the lock holes. Hold the eyebolts in place with wing nuts, so that they can be easily removed whenever you want to change the position of the top/back.

***4**/You should make two sets of lock holes in the supports, but only one set in the legs. Use the holes in the legs as "pilots" to drill the second set of holes in the supports.*

Option: As we mentioned in the beginning of this chapter, if you make *two* of these table/benches, you can put them together in the table position to make a full-size picnic table. However, you'll need to make two simple "ties" to hold them together. As shown in the working drawings, these ties fasten to the top/back supports, underneath the table tops.

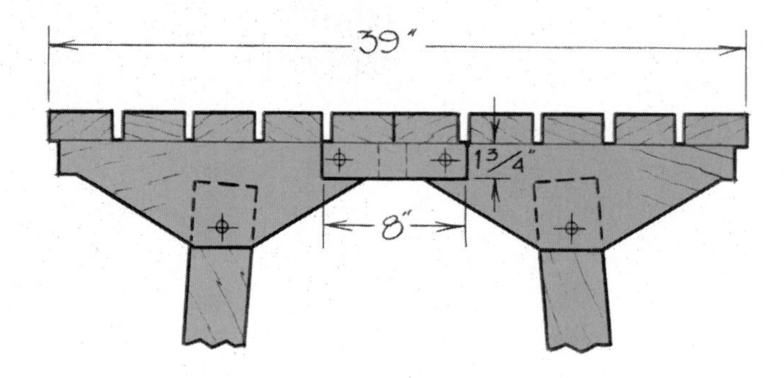

TABLE TIE DETAIL

Cedar Doormat

Make a doormat from cedar wood? Sure — what better material is there for an item that gets so much abuse? Wood is durable, attractive, and easy to clean. The corners and edges of the rough-cut boards make effective scrapers that remove the dirt from your shoes. The dirt falls between the boards where it remains out of sight until you pick up the mat and sweep it away. To clean the mat, just hose it off.

This project has other uses besides wiping your feet. Lay it under an outdoor spigot or fountain to prevent the ground from getting muddy. Make a rustic walkway by setting several mats end-to-end. You can even make a patio by arranging a number of mats on a level bed of sand and gravel.

Materials List

FINISHED DIMENSIONS

PARTS

A.	Rails (9)	¾" x 1½" x 34½"
B.	Crossmember	¾" x 1" x 22½"
C.	Diagonals (total length)	¾" x 1" x 720"*
D.	Stiles (2)	¾" x 1½" x 24"

**This includes sufficient stock for waste.*

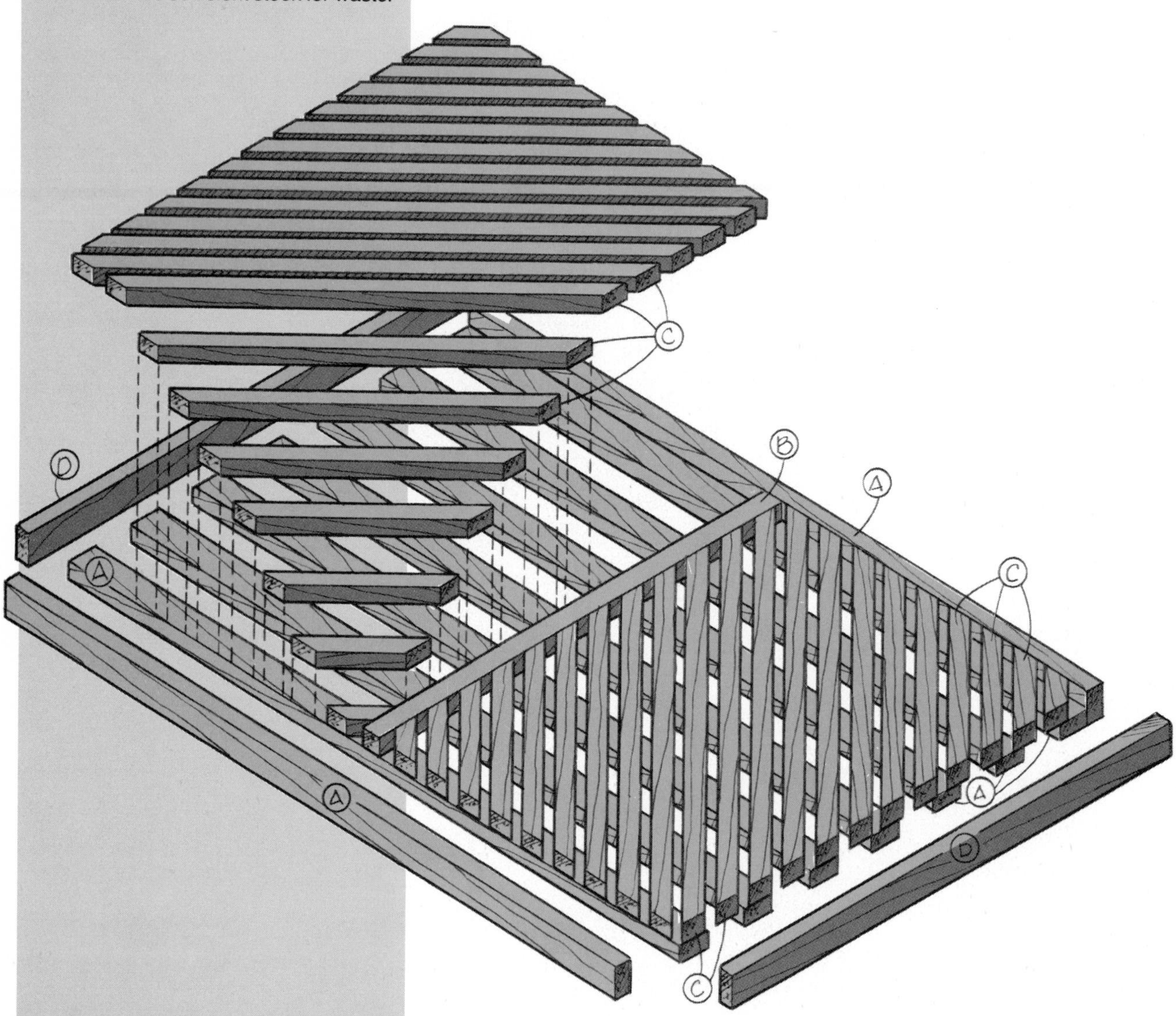

EXPLODED VIEW

HARDWARE

4d Galvanized nails (¼ lb.)
8d Galvanized nails (¼ lb.)

1 Cut the parts to size. Choose the wood you want to use for the mat. Since the parts are narrow and relatively small, you may be able to make the mat from the scraps left over from a fence or deck project. However, no matter what wood you use, make sure that at least one face of the boards is *rough-cut.* This rough surface makes a better scraper and removes the dirt from your shoes more effectively than wood that has been surfaced smooth on both faces. This is why we recommend that you use cedar — western red cedar is commonly sold with one face rough-cut.

Rip and cut the rails, stiles, and crossmember to the sizes shown in the Materials List. Rip the total length of stock you'll need to make the diagonals, but don't cut the diagonals to length just yet.

2 Assemble the base rails and crossmember. Carefully lay out the seven *base* rails on a large scrap of plywood or particle board. To keep them in place, temporarily tack both ends of each rail to the scrap. Lay the crossmember in place and fasten it to the base rails with 4d nails.

TRY THIS! If you're making more than one of these mats for a walkway or a patio, you may want to make a plywood *template.* Instead of tacking the rails to a plywood scrap, nail blocks of wood to the plywood to position the rails and keep them in place while you build each mat. This will not only save you the trouble of tacking and untacking the rails; it will ensure that all the mats you make are exactly the same size.

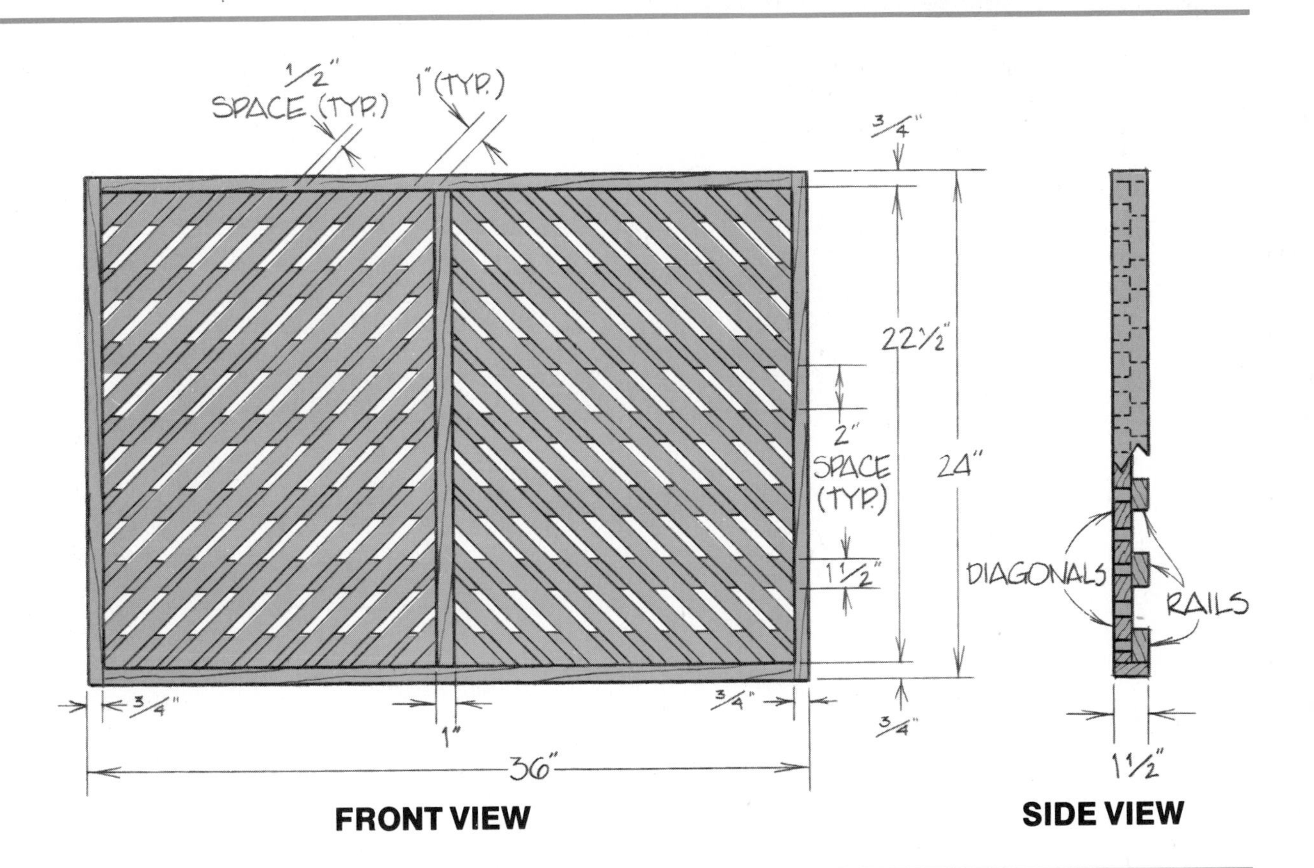

3 Attach one side rail to the rail/crossmember assembly.

Attach *one* side rail (it doesn't matter which one) to the assembly with 8d nails. The rough-cut face should be turned to the *outside.* Don't attach the other side rail until after you've cut and trimmed the diagonals.

TRY THIS! If you wish, use 8d spiral decking nails to attach the side rails and stiles. These will not pull out as easily as common nails. However, you'll have to drill pilot holes for these decking nails to prevent them from splitting out the brittle cedar stock.

4 Attach the diagonals to the rail/crossmember assembly.

Miter one end of some diagonal stock. Lay it in place on the assembly with the mitered end butting against the crossmember or side rail and the rough-cut face *up.* Mark the length, then cut the diagonal ¼"-½" *longer* than what you need, mitering the other end. Tack the diagonal you have just cut to the rails with 4d nails.

Repeat this process for all of the diagonals. (After you attach a few diagonals, you can remove the nails that tack the rails to the plywood scrap.) The ends of the diagonals should hang over the rails, as shown in the *Construction Detail.* Don't worry that the diagonals are too long or that they're uneven; they won't be after you trim them. When you've tacked all of the diagonals in place, and are sure that they are positioned properly, drive the nails home.

TRY THIS! Use a scrap of ½"-thick lumber as a gauge to help space the diagonals evenly.

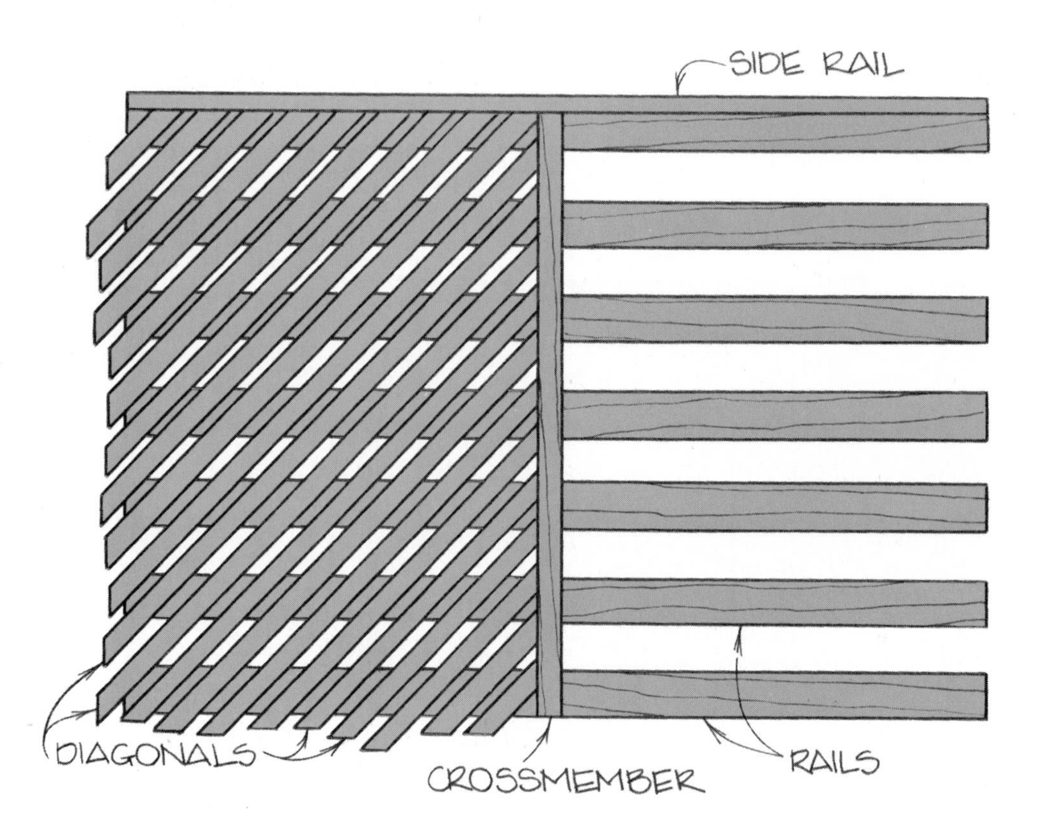

CONSTRUCTION DETAIL

5

Trim the diagonals. With a long straightedge, mark the over-long, uneven ends of the diagonals to trim them flush with the ends and edges of the rails. Cut the diagonals to their proper length with a circular saw. (See Figure 1.)

1*/Trim the diagonals after you attach them to the base rails. This way, the ends of the diagonals will all be even. A straightedge, clamped to the mat, provides a guide or a "fence" for the saw and ensures a straight cut.*

6

Attach the remaining side rail and the stiles. Attach the remaining side rail to the assembly with 8d nails. Then attach the stiles. Remember, the rough-cut faces should be turned to the *outside.*

7

Lay the mats in place (optional). If you're laying the mat directly on the ground, or if you're making a walkway or a patio from the mats, you'll need to provide drainage and a level base. Remove the sod from the area you want to cover, and dig down approximately 6″. Spread gravel 3″ deep, then 2″-3″ of sand on top of the gravel. Tamp the sand down, then level it with a trowel or the edge of a wide 2 x 4. Lay the mat or mats in place on top of the sand, and fill in around the edges with more gravel. The mats should be set in the ground, with their top surface slightly above the surface of the ground.

To keep them from shifting, drill ½″-diameter holes near the corners of the mats, through the diagonals *and* the base rails. Drive 18″ lengths of #4 "rebar" (reinforcing rod) through the holes, down through the sand and gravel, and deep into the soil. (See Figure 2.) Using a scrap of rebar as a giant nail set, "set" the upper ends of the rebar so that they are slightly below the top surface of the mats. If you hit a rock with one of the lengths of rebar, cut the rebar off flush with the mat.

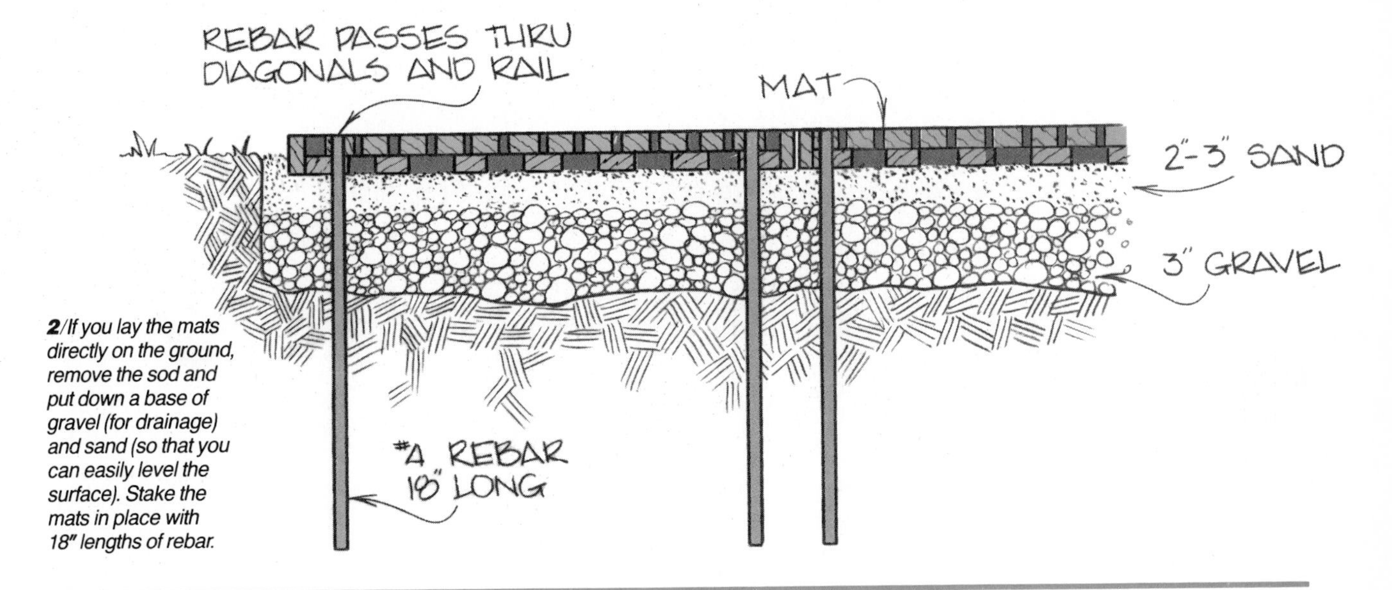

2*/If you lay the mats directly on the ground, remove the sod and put down a base of gravel (for drainage) and sand (so that you can easily level the surface). Stake the mats in place with 18″ lengths of rebar.*

Adirondack Chair

Perhaps one of the most comfortable pieces of outdoor furniture that you can build is the classic "Adirondack" chair. You're tilted back, face to the sky, almost cradled by the chair. It's hard to get up, and after a while you think: Why would you ever want to? Adirondack sitting is to ordinary sitting what a peaceful sigh is to everyday breathing.

This particular Adirondack chair has a few features that make it even more comfortable. The back is rounded and the seat is contoured to fit your body. The arms are big and wide to give you ample room to set a drink or a book within easy reach. And there is plenty of space between the arms to accommodate you and a few dozen pillows.

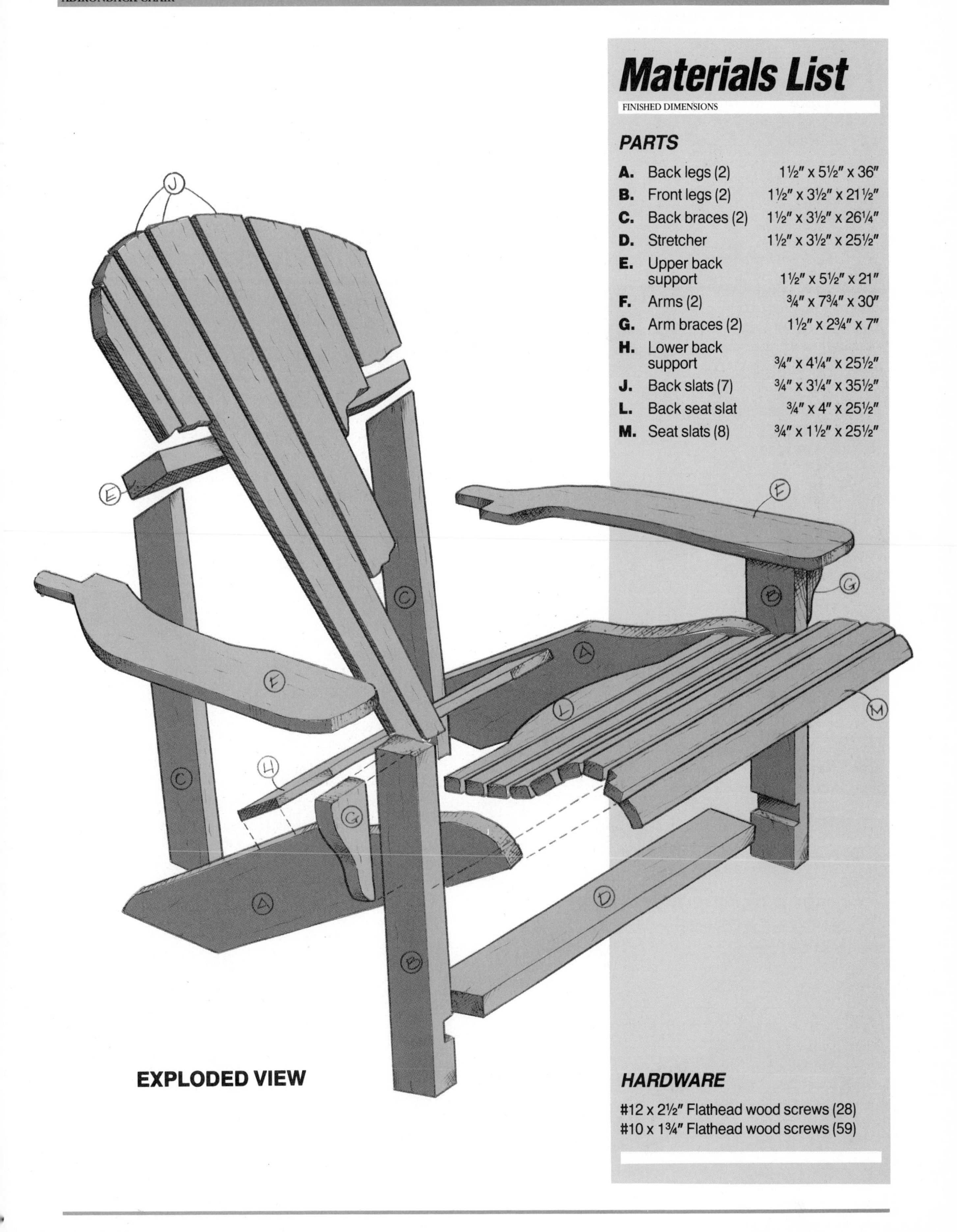

Materials List

FINISHED DIMENSIONS

PARTS

	Part	Dimensions
A.	Back legs (2)	1½″ x 5½″ x 36″
B.	Front legs (2)	1½″ x 3½″ x 21½″
C.	Back braces (2)	1½″ x 3½″ x 26¼″
D.	Stretcher	1½″ x 3½″ x 25½″
E.	Upper back support	1½″ x 5½″ x 21″
F.	Arms (2)	¾″ x 7¾″ x 30″
G.	Arm braces (2)	1½″ x 2¾″ x 7″
H.	Lower back support	¾″ x 4¼″ x 25½″
J.	Back slats (7)	¾″ x 3¼″ x 35½″
L.	Back seat slat	¾″ x 4″ x 25½″
M.	Seat slats (8)	¾″ x 1½″ x 25½″

HARDWARE

#12 x 2½″ Flathead wood screws (28)
#10 x 1¾″ Flathead wood screws (59)

1 Cut all the parts to size. This is an inexpensive project to build. To make one chair, you'll need one 2 x 4 x 12′, one 2 x 6 x 8′, and two 1 x 12 x 8's. Rip and cut the stock to the sizes shown in the Materials List, except for the back slats. Cut these parts ½″-¾″ *wider* than shown. This will give you some cutting room when it comes time to taper the slats.

2 Cut the shapes of the parts. Miter the ends of the back braces and the back legs, as shown on the working drawing. The back braces are cut at 55°, and the back legs at 30°.

Enlarge the patterns for the arms, arm supports, and back legs. Trace these patterns on the stock. Also, scribe the arcs for the upper back support, lower back support, and back seat slat.

Once you've traced and scribed all the cutlines, cut out the shapes of the parts with a band saw or sabre saw. Sand away the saw marks.

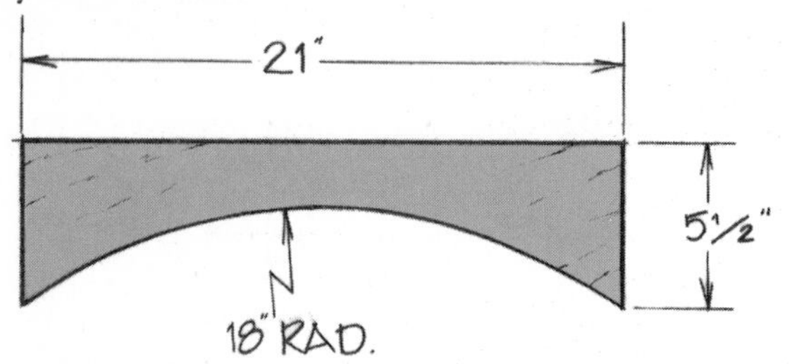

UPPER BACK SUPPORT LAYOUT

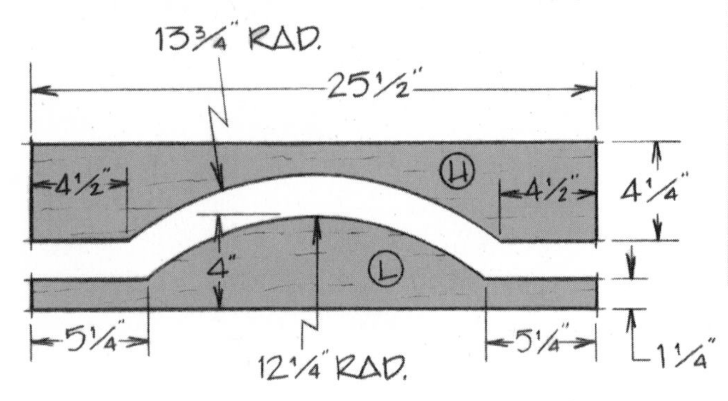

LOWER BACK SUPPORT AND BACK SEAT SLAT LAYOUTS

TRY THIS! You can scribe the arcs on the back supports and seat slat with a compass made from string, but you'll find it easier and more accurate to make yourself a "compass stick." A compass stick is nothing more than a long, thin board — a wooden yardstick is ideal. Drill small holes at ¼″ intervals along the length of the board. To use this as a compass, put a finishing nail through one of the holes in the compass stick, measure along the stick from the finishing nail to another hole, and insert the sharp end of a pencil through that second hole. Then swing the arc.

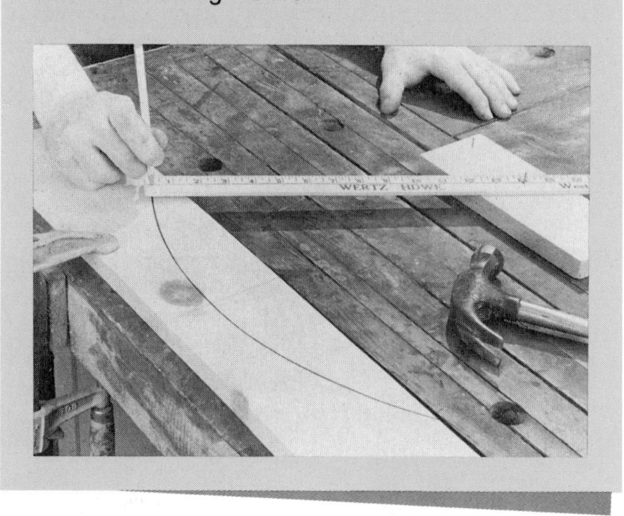

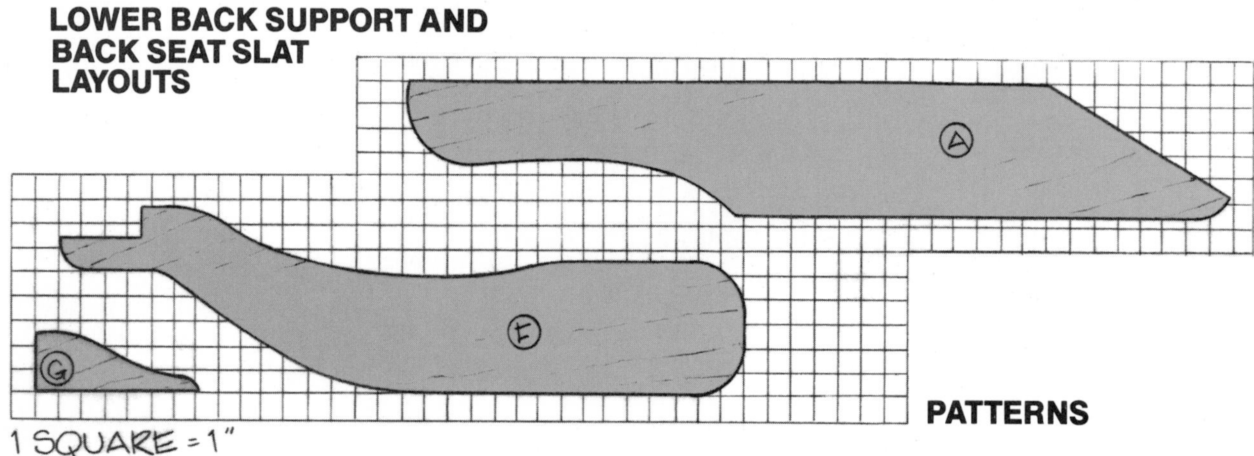

PATTERNS

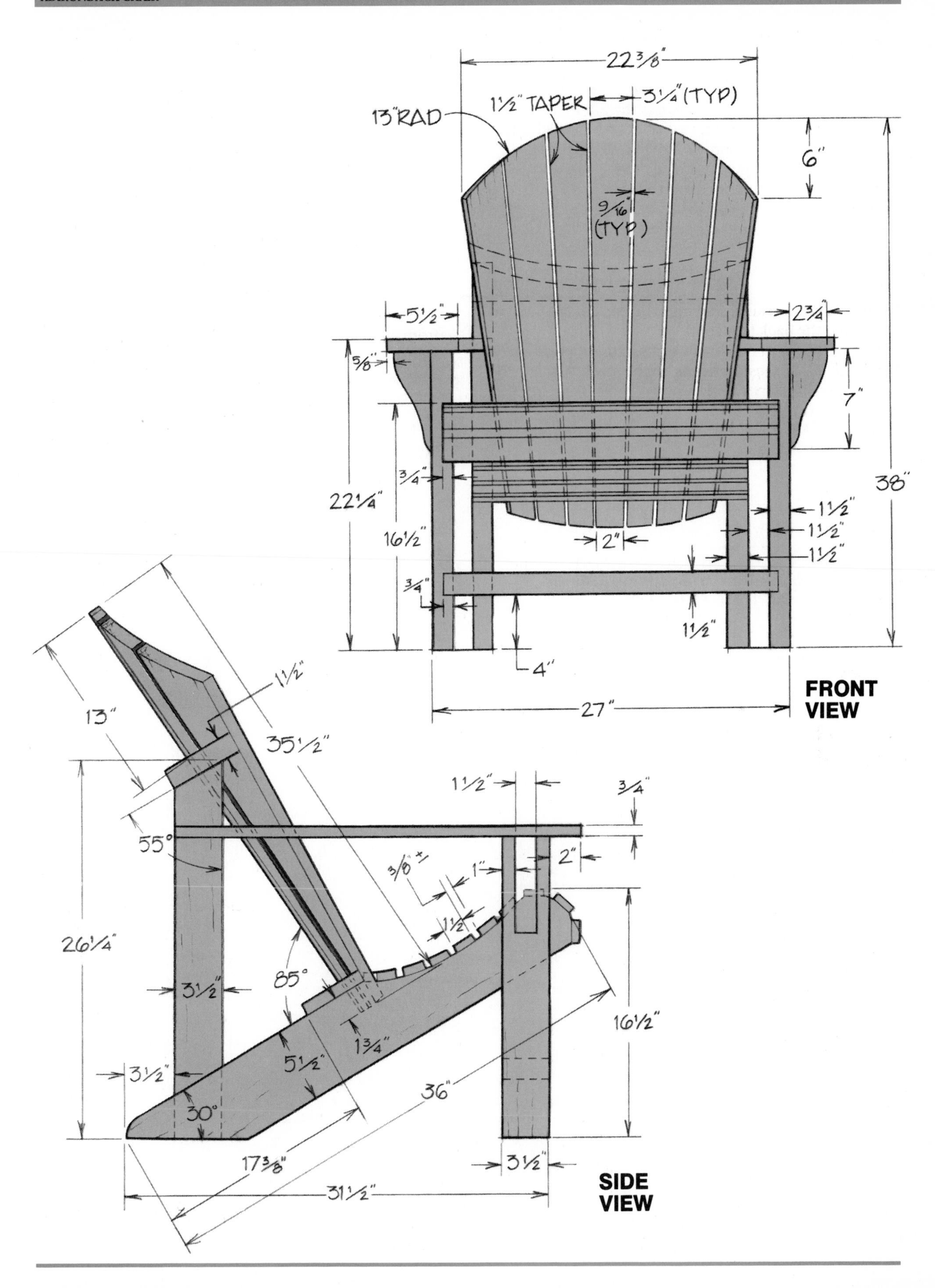
22 3/8"
1 1/2" TAPER
3 1/4" (TYP)
13" RAD
6"
9/16" (TYP)
5 1/2"
2 3/4"
5/8"
7"
38"
22 1/4"
16 1/2"
3/4"
1 1/2"
2"
4"
27"
FRONT VIEW
13"
1 1/2"
35 1/2"
55°
3/4"
2"
3/8" ±
1"
26 1/4"
85°
3 1/2"
1 3/4"
5 1/2"
36"
16 1/2"
30°
17 3/8"
31 1/2"
SIDE VIEW

3 ***Taper the back slats.*** The back slats should be tapered from 3¼″ wide at the top to 2″ wide at the bottom. This works out to a taper of 1½°. Make a tapering jig to hold the wood 1½° off parallel to the saw blade, as shown in Figure 1. Using this jig, taper one side of all seven slats. Save the scrap from one of the cuts, and use this as a spacer to hold the slats at the proper angle in the jig when you taper the other side of the slats. (See Figure 2.)

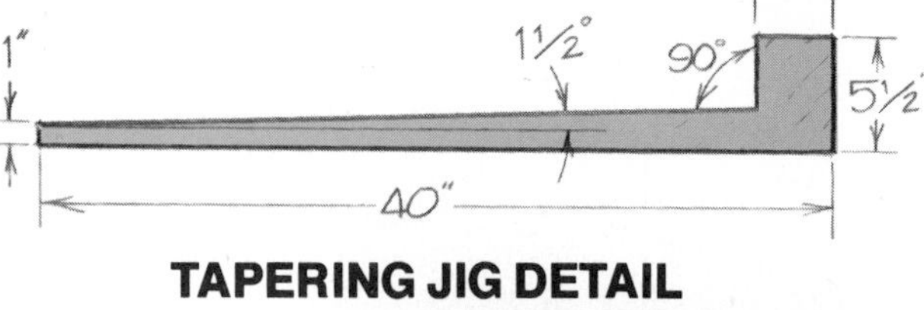

TAPERING JIG DETAIL

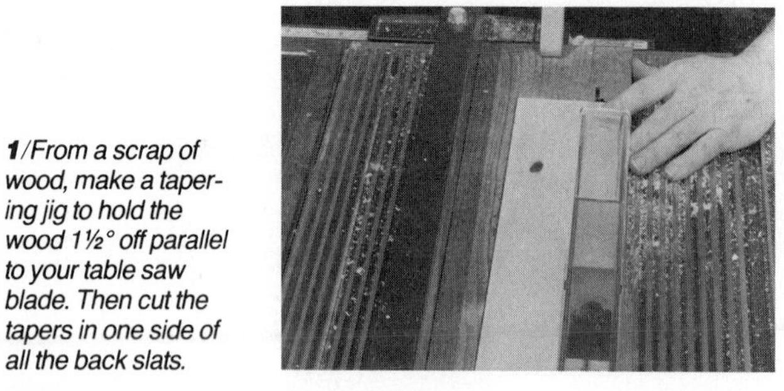

1/*From a scrap of wood, make a tapering jig to hold the wood 1½° off parallel to your table saw blade. Then cut the tapers in one side of all the back slats.*

2/*Turn the slats over, and cut the tapers in the other sides of the boards. Use a piece of waste from the first series of cuts as a spacer to hold the wood at the proper angle to the blade.*

4 ***Finish sand all the parts.*** Sand the unassembled parts of the chair to remove any irregularities in the wood, and to make it smooth and clean. If you plan to paint or finish the chair, apply the first coat before you assemble the parts.

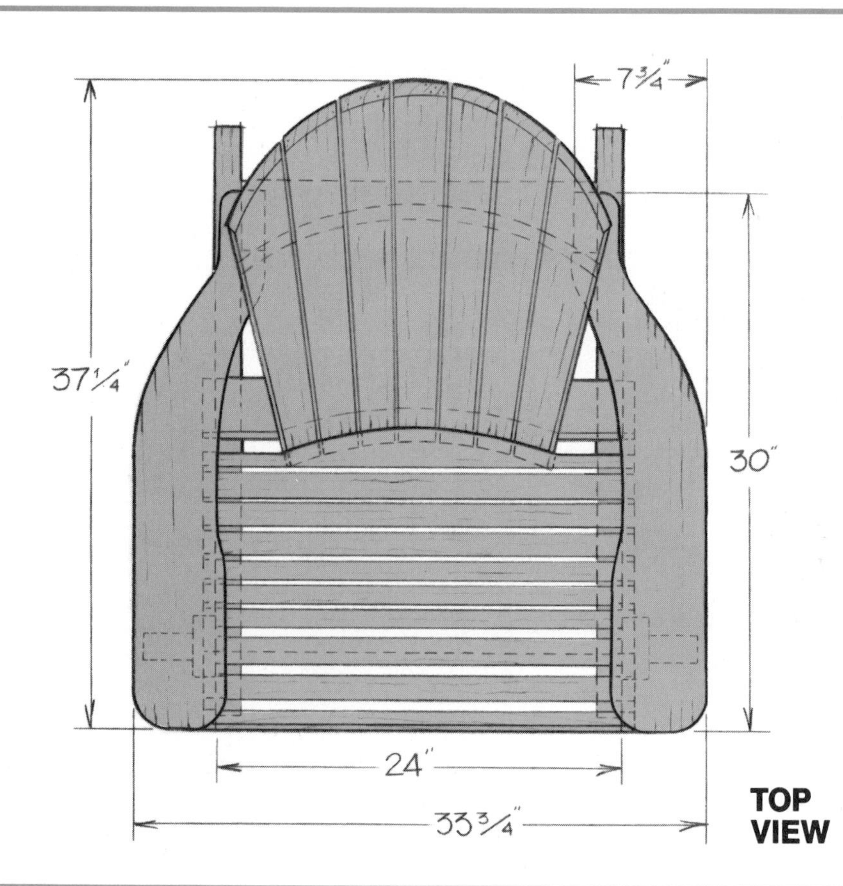

TOP VIEW

5 Assemble the chair frame.

Position the front legs and the back leg supports on the back legs. Make sure that the front legs and the supports are parallel. When you're satisfied that they are properly placed, mark their positions. Fasten them in place with #12 x 2½″ flathead wood screws. Remember that the two leg assemblies should be mirror images of each other.

Put the arms and arm braces in place, and fasten them in position, using the same type of screws. Countersink all the screws, so that the heads are flush with the surface of the wood. If you wish, you can countersink and counterbore the screws. Later, you can fill these counterbores with wooden plugs to hide the screw heads completely.

Tie the leg-and-arm assemblies together with the stretcher, upper back support, and lower back support. Use #12 x 2½″ screws to attach the upper back support and the stretcher, and #10 x 1¾″ screws to attach the lower back support.

TRY THIS! When assembled, you'll find that this is a large project, too large to fit through doors less than 30″ wide. To save yourself from a potential headache, do your assembly outside or in your garage.

6 Attach the back to the chair.

Temporarily nail the back slats to the back supports, spacing them out evenly in a fan shape. Use finishing nails (so that you make only small holes), and don't drive the nails all the way home (so that you can easily pull them out again). When all the slats are properly positioned, replace the finishing nails, one at a time, with #10 x 1¾″ wood screws.

After the slats are securely fastened to the supports, drive a small finishing nail into the middle back slat, near the bottom. Use this nail as the pivot for a string compass, and mark the curve of the back. (See Figure 3.) With a sabre saw, cut the curve. (See Figure 4.)

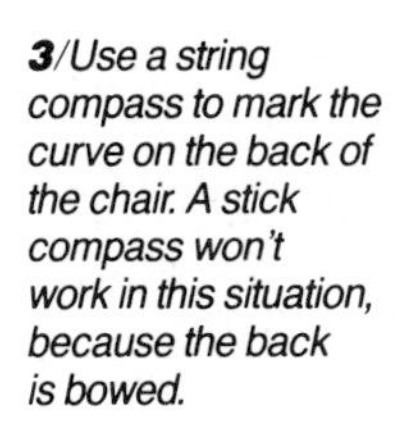
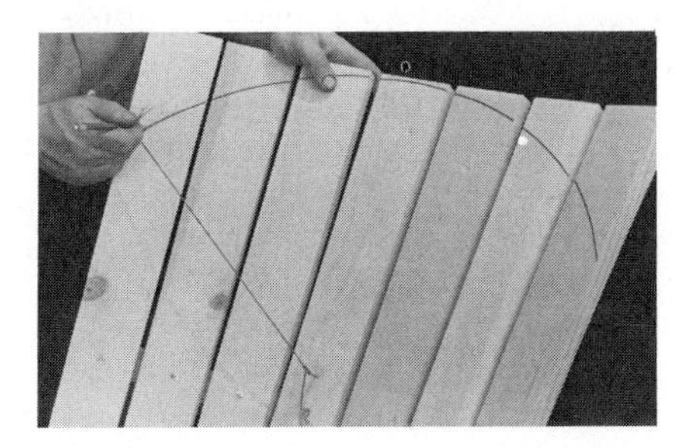

3/Use a string compass to mark the curve on the back of the chair. A stick compass won't work in this situation, because the back is bowed.

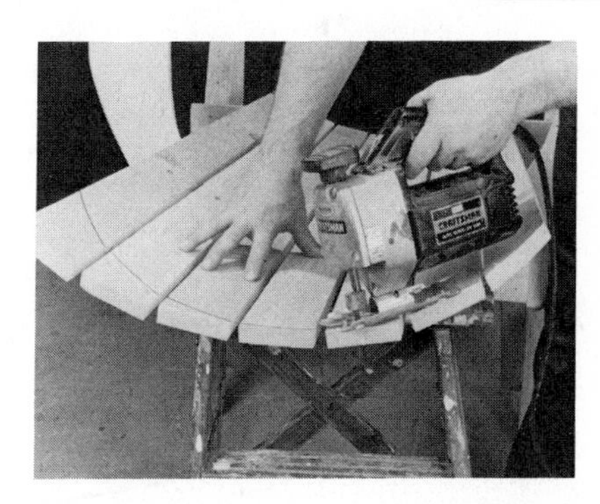

4/Cut the curve in the top of the back with a sabre saw.

7 Attach the seat to the chair.

Temporarily nail the seat slats in place, just as you did with the back slats. Tack them in place with finishing nails so that you can easily readjust their positions, if necessary. Several of the slats will either have to be shortened to 24″ long or notched to fit around the front legs. (See Figure 5.) When all the slats are in position, remove the finishing nails and replace them with screws.

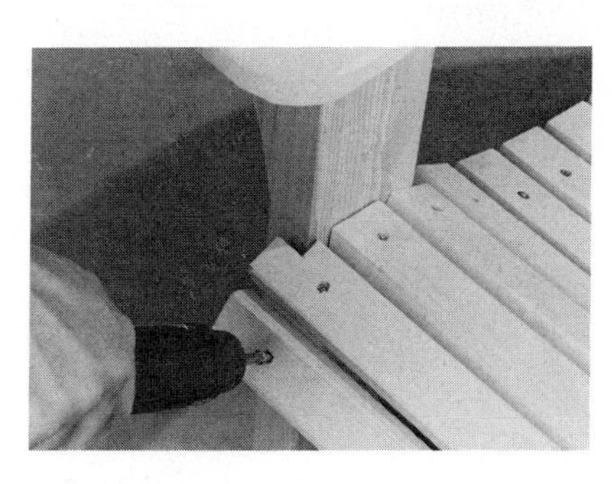

5/When positioning the bottom slats, you'll have to cut a few of them short or notch them to fit around the front legs.

8 Sand and finish the chair.

Round all the freshly cut edges, and remove the saw marks. Then apply a finish, if you've decided on using one. Because of the enormous number of crevices in this piece, you will find that using a paint sprayer will save you lots of time.

Outdoor Finishes

There is a wide variety of exterior paints, stains, and clear finishes to choose from when you finish your completed outdoor furniture project. At first glance, the sheer number of choices may seem bewildering. However, selecting the right finish is simple once you understand those few *important* differences between finishes.

How a Finish is Made

Most finishes are a mixture of two components: *pigments* and *vehicles.*

Pigments are what give a paint or a stain its color. The pigment chemicals change from finish to finish, depending on the color — or lack of it. When choosing a finish, the pigments deserve little consideration, as long as you buy a reputable brand and can be sure the colors won't fade.

Vehicles are much more important. This is what bonds the pigment to the wood — and keeps it there, through all sorts of weather. Vehicles are usually oils, resins, or emulsions. They have many characteristics, such as coverage, penetration, drying time, and so on. But the most important is the *hardness.*

Generally, the harder the vehicle dries, the better the finish will wear. Softer vehicles are easily abraded by wind and rain, and the finish becomes thin. However, a soft vehicle has its advantages. It easily expands and contracts with the wood through changes in temperature and humidity. Hard-vehicle finishes are brittle, and they may chip or "peel" when the wood breathes. The rule of thumb is to choose a soft vehicle if you live in an area where the difference in average summer and winter temperatures is more than 30°F. If the temperature is more constant, you can use finishes with harder vehicles.

Paints

Outdoor paints have enough pigments mixed into the vehicle to make the mixture opaque. When the paint dries, all you can see is the color, not the wood.

Linseed oil paint — Hardness rating: Soft. Despite the soft vehicle, many painters consider this to be the best paint for the money, especially in northern climates.

Alkyd resin paint — Hardness rating: Medium to hard. Alkyd is a soybean product that can be used in almost any environment except where there are extreme differences in temperature and humidity.

Latex emulsion paint — Hardness rating: Medium to hard. This type of paint has become very popular because it's so durable and easy to clean up. It's a good general-purpose paint, but it will peel easier than other types in a wet environment.

Epoxy resin paint — Hardness rating: Very hard. This paint is most useful in an industrial environment when you need a coating that is resistant to chemicals. Too hard to be used on wood in humid climates.

Stains

Stains are mixed just like paints, only there's less pigment and more vehicle. There's enough pigment to tint the finish, but not enough to make it opaque. After the stain dries, you can still see the wood grain through the vehicle.

Linseed oil stains — See comments under "Paints."

Alkyd resin stains — See comments under "Paints."

Latex emulsion stains — See comments under "Paints."

Varnish stains — Hardness rating: Medium. Varnish is a blend of resins from various trees: chinawood, gum, and tung. Can be used in most environments, but may not dry well in high humidity.

Polyurethane stains — Hardness rating: Hard. Polyurethane is a synthetic resin made from petroleum. Very durable, but too hard to use in environments when there are wide swings in temperature and humidity. May decay in sunlight, unless there is an ultraviolet (UV) light blocker or absorber added.

Tip: Because stains are just thin paints, many professional painters save money by mixing their own stains from paints. A good, standard recipe is one part paint, one part thinner, and one part "conditioner." Use linseed oil as a thinner for oil paints, and water for latex paints. Conditioners for both oil and latex paints are available at most paint stores.

Clear Finishes

Clear finishes are vehicles without pigments. They may slightly darken the wood but they do not change the natural color. There are two basic types: *coating* and *penetrating.* A coating finish clings to the outside of the wood, covering the surface. A penetrating finish soaks into the wood, bonds with the cells, and protects it from the inside out. There is no hardness rating for penetrating finishes, since they do not form a coat.

Varnish — See comments under "Stains."

Polyurethane — See comments under "Stains."

Tung oil — Hardness rating: None, after one coat. Soft to medium after two or more coats. Tung oil is often one of the components of varnish. Versatile — can be both a penetrating and a coating finish. First application soaks into the wood; successive applications coat the wood. Some craftsmen mix tung oil 1:1 with spar varnish to make a wipe-on "penetrating varnish." Can be used in all climates.

Wood Sealer — Hardness rating: None. This product penetrates deep into the wood, preserving it *and* sealing it against moisture. (Ordinary wood preservatives do not seal the wood.) Consists of a fungicide (usually butyl carbamate) in a blend of vehicles. Can be used in all climates. Preserves the look of raw wood.

Credits

Contributing Craftsmen and Craftswomen:

Adam Blake (Round Picnic Table and Benches, Sunlover's Chaise Lounge)

Nick Engler (Adirondack Chair, Contoured Porch Swing, Knock-Down Planter, Children's Table and Benches, Outdoor Display Shelves, Shrub Planter, Garden Table/Bench, Duck Board Benches and Tables, Gardener's Kneeling Bench, Nesting Tables, Tree Bench, Rocking Sling Chair, Patio Cart, Sling Hammock, Planter/Partition, Cedar Doormat)

Mary Jane Favorite (Adirondack Chair, Sunlover's Chaise Lounge, Contoured Porch Swing, Gardener's Kneeling Bench, Tree Bench, Outdoor Display Shelves, Knock-Down Planter, Round Picnic Table and Benches)

Phil Gehret (Garden Bench)

Jeffrey and Sandra Walker (Scissors Chair and Table)

Linda Watts (Sling Hammock, Rocking Sling Chair)

Special Thanks To:

Wertz Hardware Stores, West Milton, Ohio
Springhill Nurseries, Tipp City, Ohio
Glen and Jan Cox
Doug and Tedi Wilson
Smith & Hawken
25 Corte Madera Avenue
Mill Valley, CA 94941
telephone 415-383-4415